Stan Lee
PRESENTS

THE DEFENDERS

VOL. 1

DR. STRANGE #183, SUB-MARINER #22 & 34-35, INCREDIBLE HULK #126, MARVEL FEATURE #1-3, DEFENDERS #1-14 & AVENGERS #115-118

DOCTOR STRANGE #183

WRITER: **ROY THOMAS**
PENCILER: **GENE COLAN**
INKER: **TOM PALMER**
LETTERER: **JEAN IZZO**

SUB-MARINER #35

WRITER: **ROY THOMAS**
PENCILER: **SAL BUSCEMA**
INKER: **JIM MOONEY**
LETTERER: **JEAN IZZO**

SUB-MARINER #22

WRITER: **ROY THOMAS**
PENCILER: **MARIE SEVERIN**
INKER: **JOHNNY CRAIG**
LETTERER: **ART SIMEK**

MARVEL FEATURE #1

WRITER: **ROY THOMAS**
PENCILERS: **ROSS ANDRU
& DON HECK**
INKERS: **BILL EVERETT
& FRANK GIACOIA**
LETTERER: **SAM ROSEN**

THE INCREDIBLE HULK #126

WRITER: **ROY THOMAS**
ARTIST: **HERB TRIMPE**
LETTERER: **ART SIMEK**

MARVEL FEATURE #2

WRITER: **ROY THOMAS**
PENCILER: **ROSS ANDRU**
INKER: **SAL BUSCEMA**
LETTERER: **SAM ROSEN**

SUB-MARINER #34

WRITER: **ROY THOMAS**
PENCILER: **SAL BUSCEMA**
INKER: **JIM MOONEY**
LETTERER: **ART SIMEK**

MARVEL FEATURE #3

WRITER: **ROY THOMAS**
PENCILER: **ROSS ANDRU**
INKER: **BILL EVERETT**
LETTERER: **ART SIMEK**

THE DEFENDERS #1
WRITER: **STEVE ENGLEHART**
PENCILER: **SAL BUSCEMA**
INKER: **FRANK GIACOIA**
LETTERER: **ART SIMEK**

THE DEFENDERS #5
WRITER: **STEVE ENGLEHART**
PENCILER: **SAL BUSCEMA**
INKER: **FRANK MCLAUGHLIN**
LETTERER: **CHARLOTTE JETTER**

THE DEFENDERS #2
WRITER: **STEVE ENGLEHART**
PENCILER: **SAL BUSCEMA**
INKER: **JOHN VERPOORTEN**
LETTERER: **JOHN COSTANZA**

THE DEFENDERS #6
WRITER: **STEVE ENGLEHART**
PENCILER: **SAL BUSCEMA**
INKER: **FRANK MCLAUGHLIN**
LETTERER: **JOHN COSTANZA**

THE DEFENDERS #3
WRITER: **STEVE ENGLEHART**
PENCILER: **SAL BUSCEMA**
INKER: **JIM MOONEY**
LETTERER: **ART SIMEK**

THE DEFENDERS #7
PLOT: **STEVE ENGLEHART**
SCRIPT: **STEVE ENGLEHART & LEN WEIN**
PENCILER: **SAL BUSCEMA**
INKER: **FRANK BOLLE**
LETTERER: **JUNE BRAVERMAN**

THE DEFENDERS #4
WRITER: **STEVE ENGLEHART**
PENCILER: **SAL BUSCEMA**
INKER: **FRANK MCLAUGHLIN**
LETTERER: **ART SIMEK**

THE DEFENDERS #8
WRITER: **STEVE ENGLEHART**
PENCILER: **SAL BUSCEMA**
INKER: **FRANK MCLAUGHLIN**
LETTERER: **CHARLOTTE JETTER**

AVENGERS #115

WRITER: STEVE ENGLEHART
PENCILER: BOB BROWN
INKER: MIKE ESPOSITO
LETTERER: JEAN IZZO

AVENGERS #116

WRITER: STEVE ENGLEHART
PENCILER: BOB BROWN
INKER: MIKE ESPOSITO
LETTERER: JOHN COSTANZA

THE DEFENDERS #9

WRITER: STEVE ENGLEHART
PENCILER: SAL BUSCEMA
INKER: FRANK MCLAUGHLIN
LETTERER: ART SIMEK

AVENGERS #117

WRITER: STEVE ENGLEHART
PENCILER: BOB BROWN
INKER: MIKE ESPOSITO
LETTERER: JUNE BRAVERMAN

THE DEFENDERS #10

WRITER: STEVE ENGLEHART
PENCILER: SAL BUSCEMA
INKER: FRANK BOLLE
LETTERER: TOM ORZECHOWSKI

AVENGERS #118

WRITER: STEVE ENGLEHART
PENCILER: BOB BROWN
INKER: MIKE ESPOSITO & FRANK GIACOIA
LETTERER: TOM ORZECHOWSKI

THE DEFENDERS #11

WRITER: **STEVE ENGLEHART**
PENCILER: **SAL BUSCEMA**
INKER: **FRANK BOLLE**
LETTERER: **TOM ORZECHOWSKI**

THE DEFENDERS #13

WRITER: **LEN WEIN**
PENCILER: **SAL BUSCEMA**
INKER: **KLAUS JANSON**
LETTERER: **JOHN COSTANZA**

THE DEFENDERS #12

WRITER: **LEN WEIN**
PENCILER: **SAL BUSCEMA**
INKER: **JACK ABEL**
LETTERER: **CHARLOTTE JETTER**

THE DEFENDERS #14

WRITER: **LEN WEIN**
PENCILER: **SAL BUSCEMA**
INKER: **DAN GREEN**
LETTERER: **ART SIMEK**

REPRINT CREDITS

MARVEL ESSENTIAL DESIGN:
**JOHN "JG" ROSHELL
OF COMICRAFT**
FRONT COVER ART:
NEAL ADAMS
BACK COVER ART:
SAL BUSCEMA
COVER COLORS:
AVALON'S MATT MILLA

COLLECTION EDITOR:
MARK D. BEAZLEY
ASSISTANT EDITOR:
JENNIFER GRÜNWALD
SENIOR EDITOR, SPECIAL PROJECTS:
JEFF YOUNGQUIST
DIRECTOR OF SALES:
DAVID GABRIEL
PRODUCTION:
JERRON QUALITY COLOR
BOOK DESIGNER:
TERNARD SOLOMON
CREATIVE DIRECTOR:
TOM MARVELLI
EDITOR IN CHIEF:
JOE QUESADA
PUBLISHER:
DAN BUCKLEY

SPECIAL THANKS TO
RALPH MACCHIO & PONDSCUM

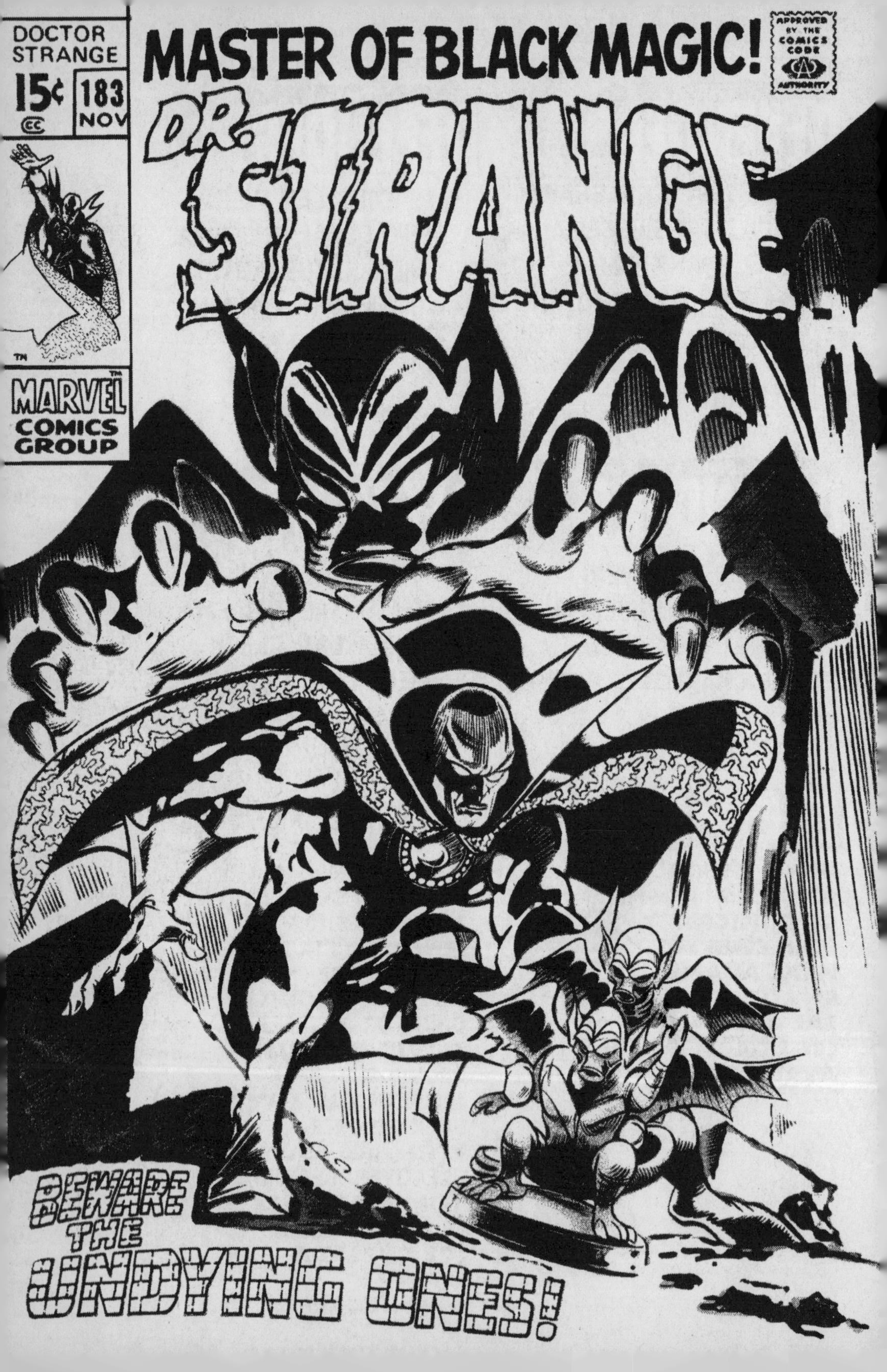
DOCTOR STRANGE
15¢
183 NOV
MARVEL COMICS GROUP
MASTER OF BLACK MAGIC!
APPROVED BY THE COMICS CODE AUTHORITY
DR. STRANGE
BEWARE THE UNDYING ONES!

Dr. STRANGE MASTER OF THE MYSTIC ARTS!™
NEITHER TITAN NOR TEMPEST MUST KEEP ME FROM MY DESTINATION!
BUT, WHEN I REACH IT... WHAT SHALL I FIND??
"WE LIVE ON A PLACID ISLAND OF IGNORANCE, IN THE MIDST OF BLACK SEAS OF INFINITY, AND IT WAS NOT MEANT THAT WE SHOULD VOYAGE FAR...!" --H.P. LOVECRAFT (1890-1937).
THEY WALK BY NIGHT!
STAN LEE EDITOR
ROY THOMAS WRITER
GENE COLAN ARTIST
TOM PALMER EMBELLISHER
JEAN IZZO LETTERER

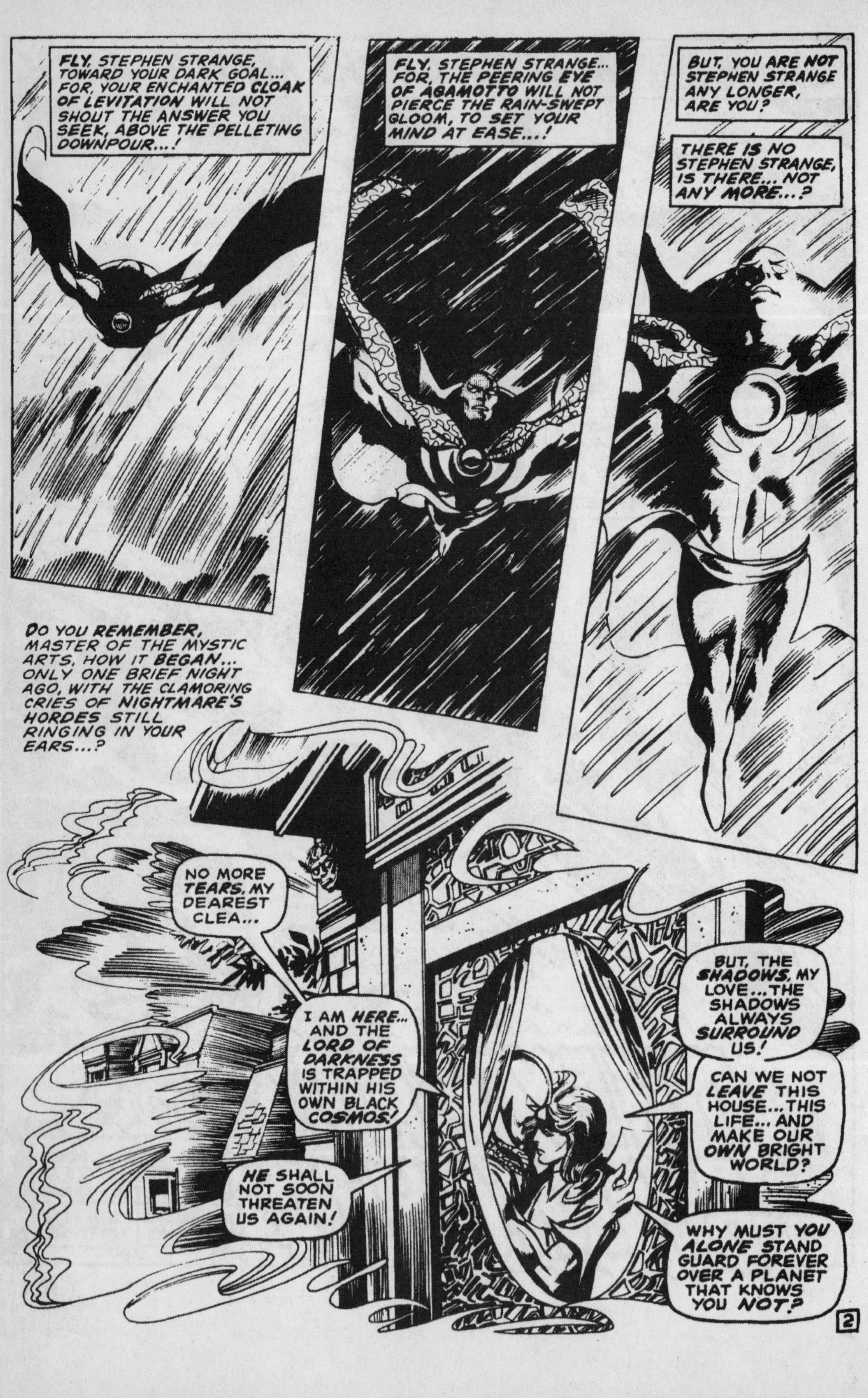
FLY, STEPHEN STRANGE, TOWARD YOUR DARK GOAL... FOR, YOUR ENCHANTED CLOAK OF LEVITATION WILL NOT SHOUT THE ANSWER YOU SEEK, ABOVE THE PELLETING DOWNPOUR...!
FLY, STEPHEN STRANGE... FOR, THE PEERING EYE OF AGAMOTTO WILL NOT PIERCE THE RAIN-SWEPT GLOOM, TO SET YOUR MIND AT EASE...!
BUT, YOU ARE NOT STEPHEN STRANGE ANY LONGER, ARE YOU?
THERE IS NO STEPHEN STRANGE, IS THERE... NOT ANY MORE...?
DO YOU REMEMBER, MASTER OF THE MYSTIC ARTS, HOW IT BEGAN... ONLY ONE BRIEF NIGHT AGO, WITH THE CLAMORING CRIES OF NIGHTMARE'S HORDES STILL RINGING IN YOUR EARS...?
NO MORE TEARS, MY DEAREST CLEA...
I AM HERE... AND THE LORD OF DARKNESS IS TRAPPED WITHIN HIS OWN BLACK COSMOS!
HE SHALL NOT SOON THREATEN US AGAIN!
BUT, THE SHADOWS, MY LOVE... THE SHADOWS ALWAYS SURROUND US!
CAN WE NOT LEAVE THIS HOUSE... THIS LIFE... AND MAKE OUR OWN BRIGHT WORLD?
WHY MUST YOU ALONE STAND GUARD FOREVER OVER A PLANET THAT KNOWS YOU NOT?
2

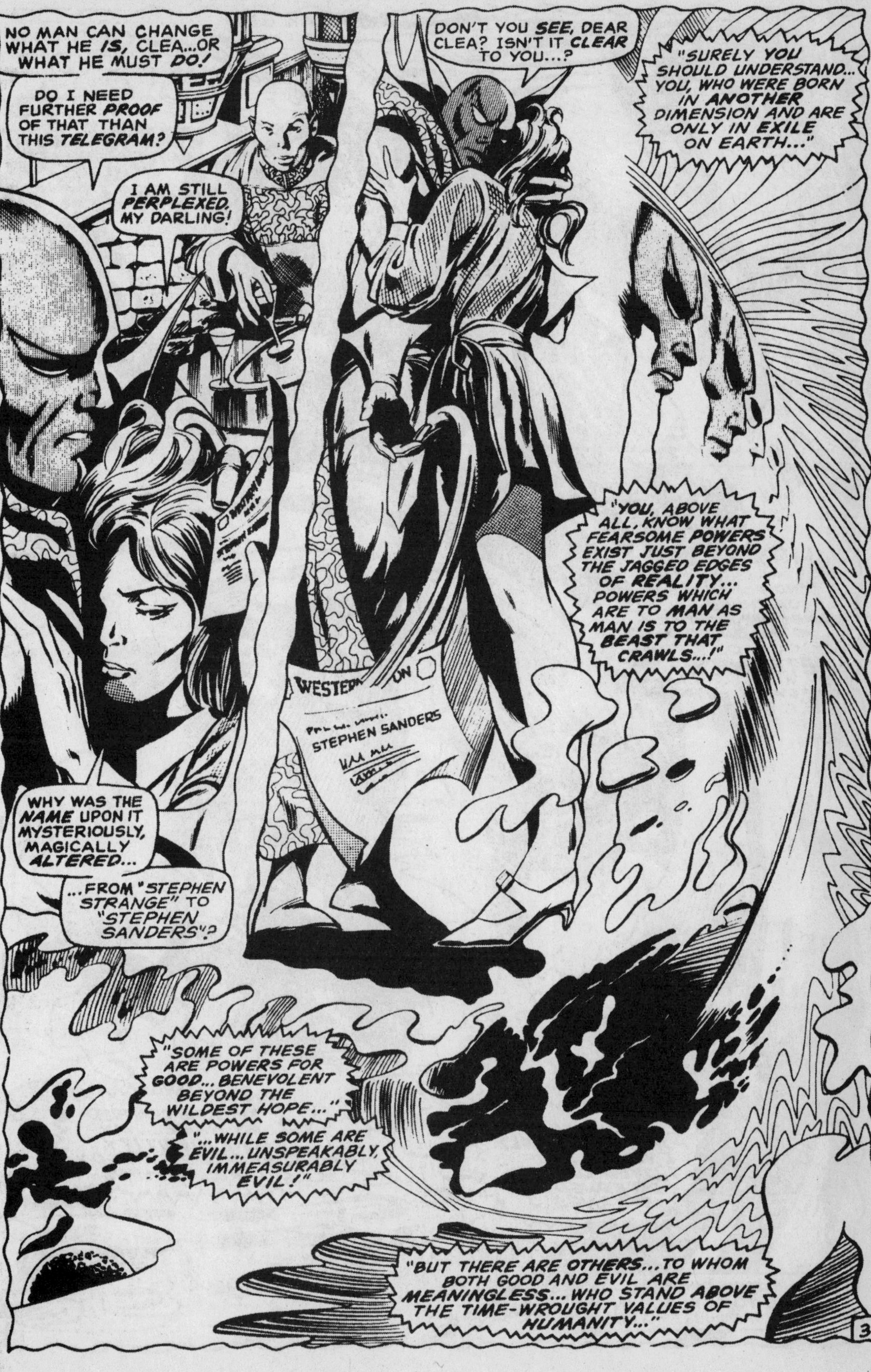
NO MAN CAN CHANGE WHAT HE IS, CLEA...OR WHAT HE MUST DO!
DO I NEED FURTHER PROOF OF THAT THAN THIS TELEGRAM?
I AM STILL PERPLEXED, MY DARLING!
WHY WAS THE NAME UPON IT MYSTERIOUSLY, MAGICALLY ALTERED...
...FROM "STEPHEN STRANGE" TO "STEPHEN SANDERS"?
DON'T YOU SEE, DEAR CLEA? ISN'T IT CLEAR TO YOU...?
"SURELY YOU SHOULD UNDERSTAND... YOU, WHO WERE BORN IN ANOTHER DIMENSION AND ARE ONLY IN EXILE ON EARTH..."
"YOU, ABOVE ALL, KNOW WHAT FEARSOME POWERS EXIST JUST BEYOND THE JAGGED EDGES OF REALITY... POWERS WHICH ARE TO MAN AS MAN IS TO THE BEAST THAT CRAWLS...!"
WESTERN ON
STEPHEN SANDERS
"SOME OF THESE ARE POWERS FOR GOOD... BENEVOLENT BEYOND THE WILDEST HOPE..."
"...WHILE SOME ARE EVIL... UNSPEAKABLY, IMMEASURABLY EVIL!"
"BUT THERE ARE OTHERS... TO WHOM BOTH GOOD AND EVIL ARE MEANINGLESS... WHO STAND ABOVE THE TIME-WROUGHT VALUES OF HUMANITY..."
3

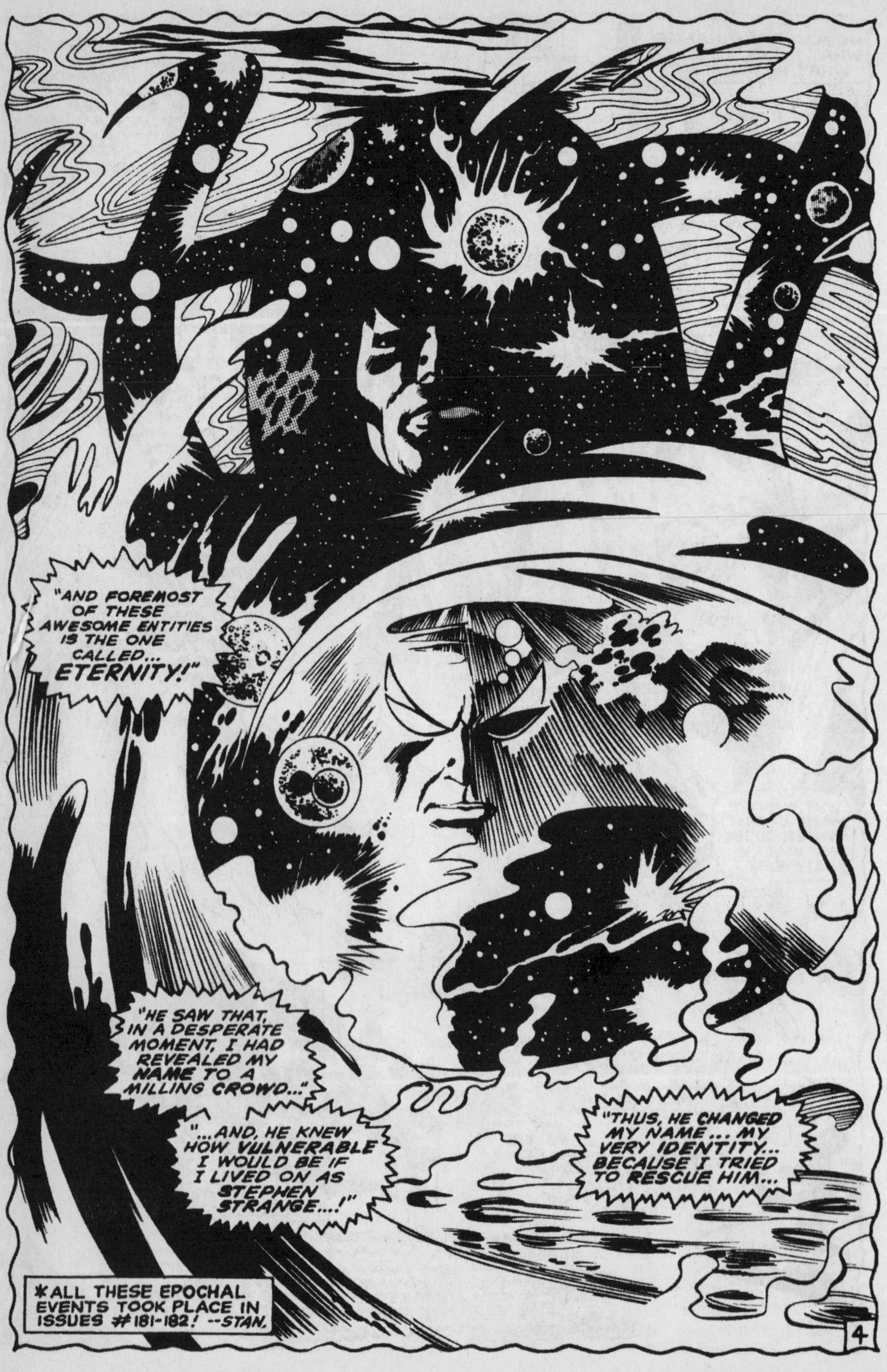
"AND FOREMOST OF THESE AWESOME ENTITIES IS THE ONE CALLED... ETERNITY!"
"HE SAW THAT, IN A DESPERATE MOMENT, I HAD REVEALED MY NAME TO A MILLING CROWD..."
"...AND, HE KNEW HOW VULNERABLE I WOULD BE IF I LIVED ON AS STEPHEN STRANGE...!"
"THUS, HE CHANGED MY NAME... MY VERY IDENTITY... BECAUSE I TRIED TO RESCUE HIM...
*ALL THESE EPOCHAL EVENTS TOOK PLACE IN ISSUES #181-182! --STAN.
4

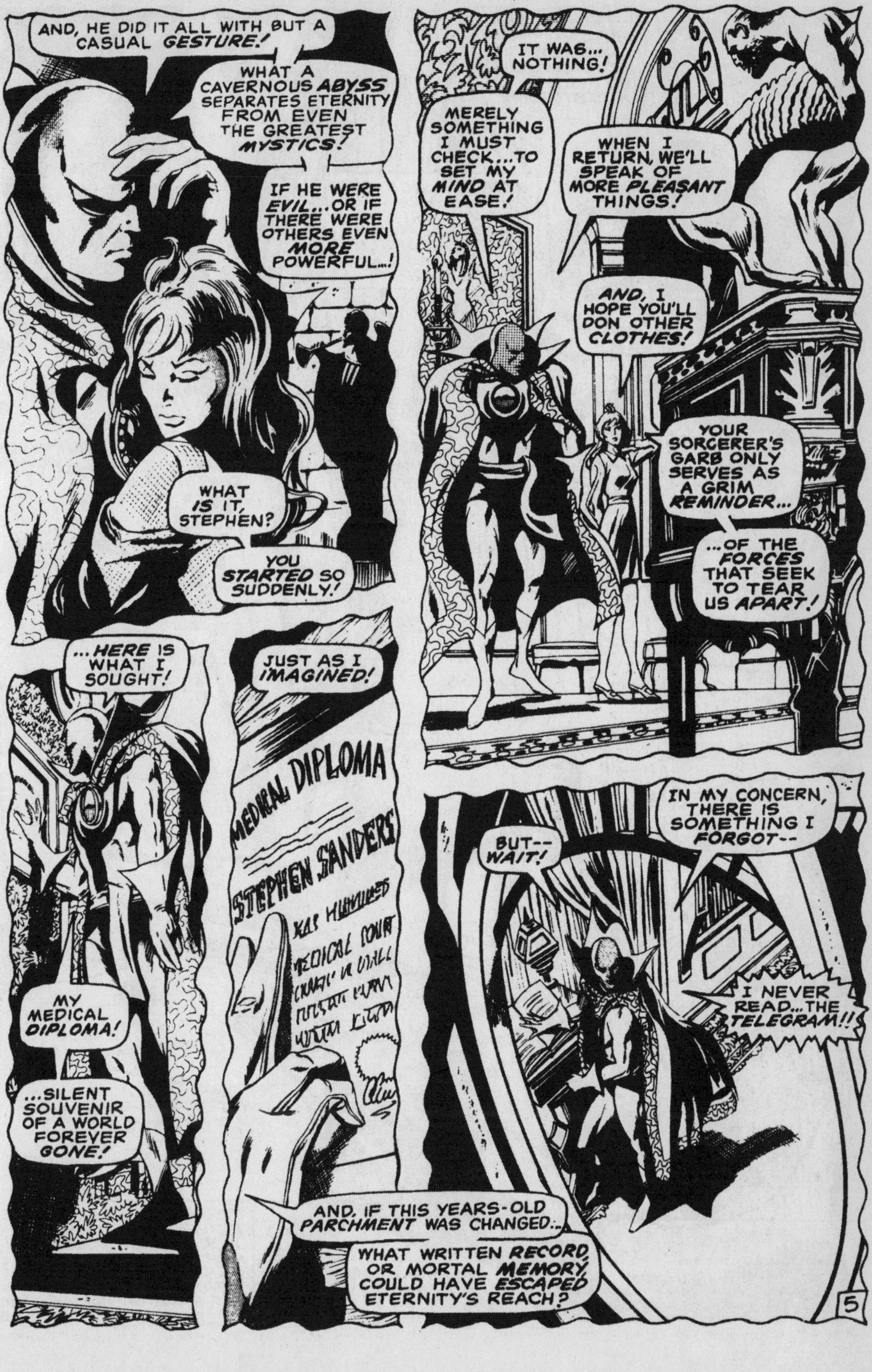
AND, HE DID IT ALL WITH BUT A CASUAL GESTURE!
WHAT A CAVERNOUS ABYSS SEPARATES ETERNITY FROM EVEN THE GREATEST MYSTICS!
IF HE WERE EVIL... OR IF THERE WERE OTHERS EVEN MORE POWERFUL...!
WHAT IS IT, STEPHEN?
YOU STARTED SO SUDDENLY!
IT WAS... NOTHING!
MERELY SOMETHING I MUST CHECK... TO SET MY MIND AT EASE!
WHEN I RETURN, WE'LL SPEAK OF MORE PLEASANT THINGS!
AND, I HOPE YOU'LL DON OTHER CLOTHES!
YOUR SORCERER'S GARB ONLY SERVES AS A GRIM REMINDER...
...OF THE FORCES THAT SEEK TO TEAR US APART!
...HERE IS WHAT I SOUGHT!
MY MEDICAL DIPLOMA!
...SILENT SOUVENIR OF A WORLD FOREVER GONE!
JUST AS I IMAGINED!
MEDICAL DIPLOMA
STEPHEN SANDERS
AND, IF THIS YEARS-OLD PARCHMENT WAS CHANGED...
WHAT WRITTEN RECORD, OR MORTAL MEMORY, COULD HAVE ESCAPED ETERNITY'S REACH?
BUT-- WAIT!
IN MY CONCERN, THERE IS SOMETHING I FORGOT--
I NEVER READ... THE TELEGRAM!!

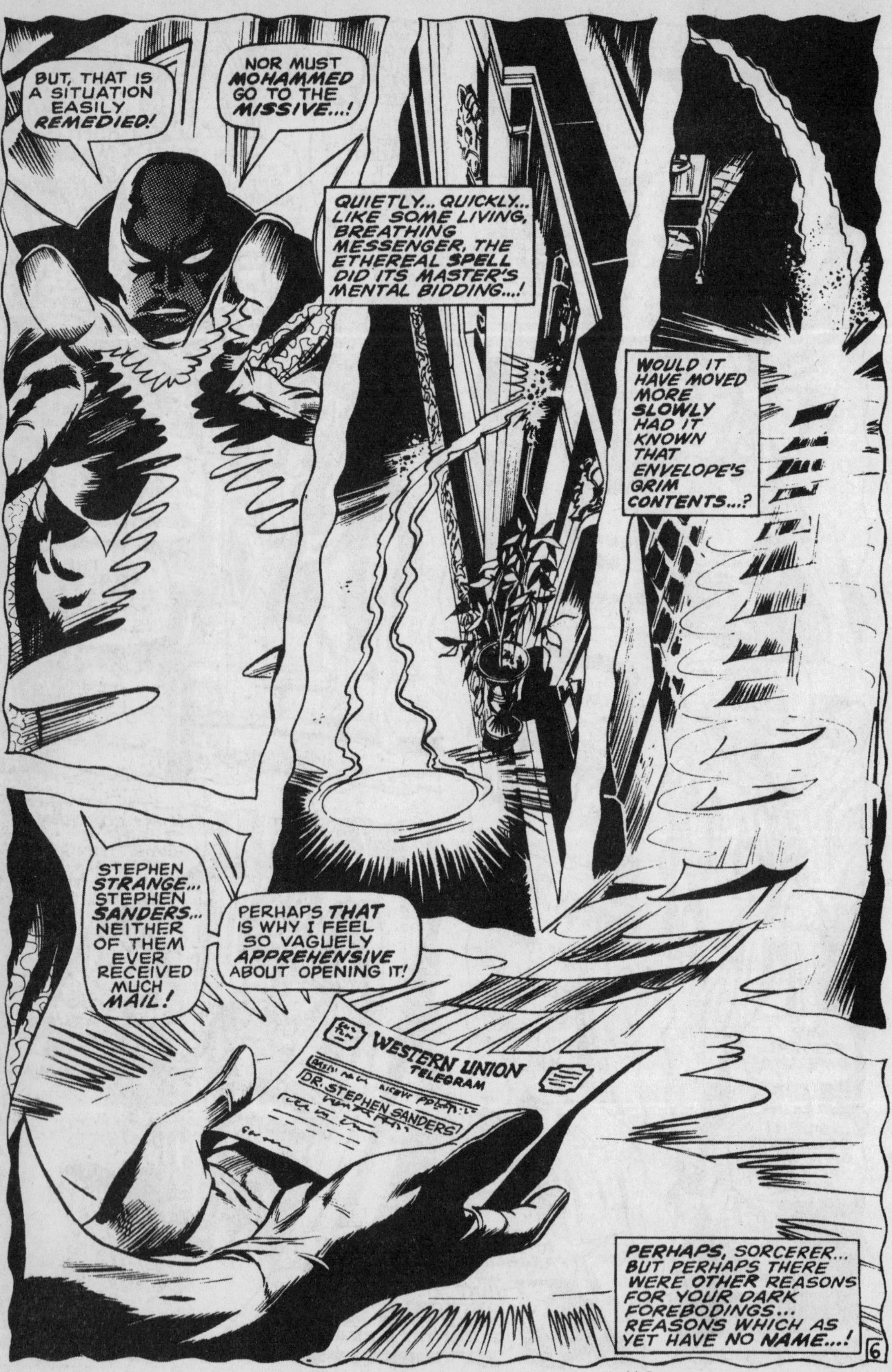
BUT, THAT IS A SITUATION EASILY REMEDIED!
NOR MUST MOHAMMED GO TO THE MISSIVE...!
QUIETLY... QUICKLY... LIKE SOME LIVING, BREATHING MESSENGER, THE ETHEREAL SPELL DID ITS MASTER'S MENTAL BIDDING...!
WOULD IT HAVE MOVED MORE SLOWLY HAD IT KNOWN THAT ENVELOPE'S GRIM CONTENTS...?
STEPHEN STRANGE... STEPHEN SANDERS... NEITHER OF THEM EVER RECEIVED MUCH MAIL!
PERHAPS THAT IS WHY I FEEL SO VAGUELY APPREHENSIVE ABOUT OPENING IT!
WESTERN UNION
TELEGRAM
DR. STEPHEN SANDERS
PERHAPS, SORCERER... BUT PERHAPS THERE WERE OTHER REASONS FOR YOUR DARK FOREBODINGS... REASONS WHICH AS YET HAVE NO NAME...!
6

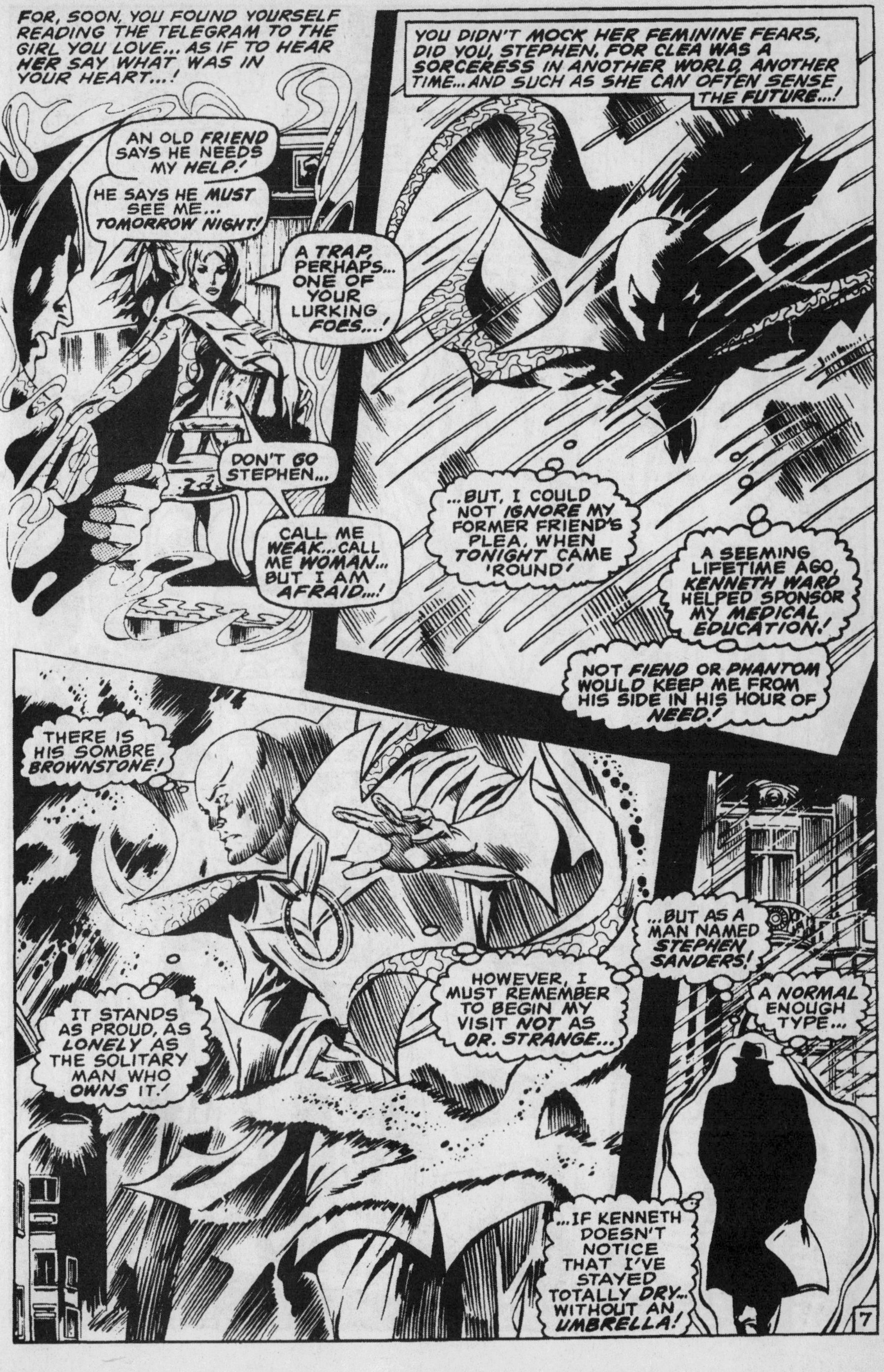

FOR, SOON, YOU FOUND YOURSELF READING THE TELEGRAM TO THE GIRL YOU LOVE... AS IF TO HEAR HER SAY WHAT WAS IN YOUR HEART...!
AN OLD FRIEND SAYS HE NEEDS MY HELP!
HE SAYS HE MUST SEE ME... TOMORROW NIGHT!
A TRAP, PERHAPS... ONE OF YOUR LURKING FOES...!
DON'T GO STEPHEN...
CALL ME WEAK... CALL ME WOMAN... BUT I AM AFRAID...!
YOU DIDN'T MOCK HER FEMININE FEARS, DID YOU, STEPHEN, FOR CLEA WAS A SORCERESS IN ANOTHER WORLD, ANOTHER TIME... AND SUCH AS SHE CAN OFTEN SENSE THE FUTURE...!
...BUT, I COULD NOT IGNORE MY FORMER FRIEND'S PLEA, WHEN TONIGHT CAME 'ROUND!
A SEEMING LIFETIME AGO, KENNETH WARD HELPED SPONSOR MY MEDICAL EDUCATION!
NOT FIEND OR PHANTOM WOULD KEEP ME FROM HIS SIDE IN HIS HOUR OF NEED!
THERE IS HIS SOMBRE BROWNSTONE!
IT STANDS AS PROUD, AS LONELY AS THE SOLITARY MAN WHO OWNS IT!
HOWEVER, I MUST REMEMBER TO BEGIN MY VISIT NOT AS DR. STRANGE...
...BUT AS A MAN NAMED STEPHEN SANDERS!
A NORMAL ENOUGH TYPE...
...IF KENNETH DOESN'T NOTICE THAT I'VE STAYED TOTALLY DRY... WITHOUT AN UMBRELLA!

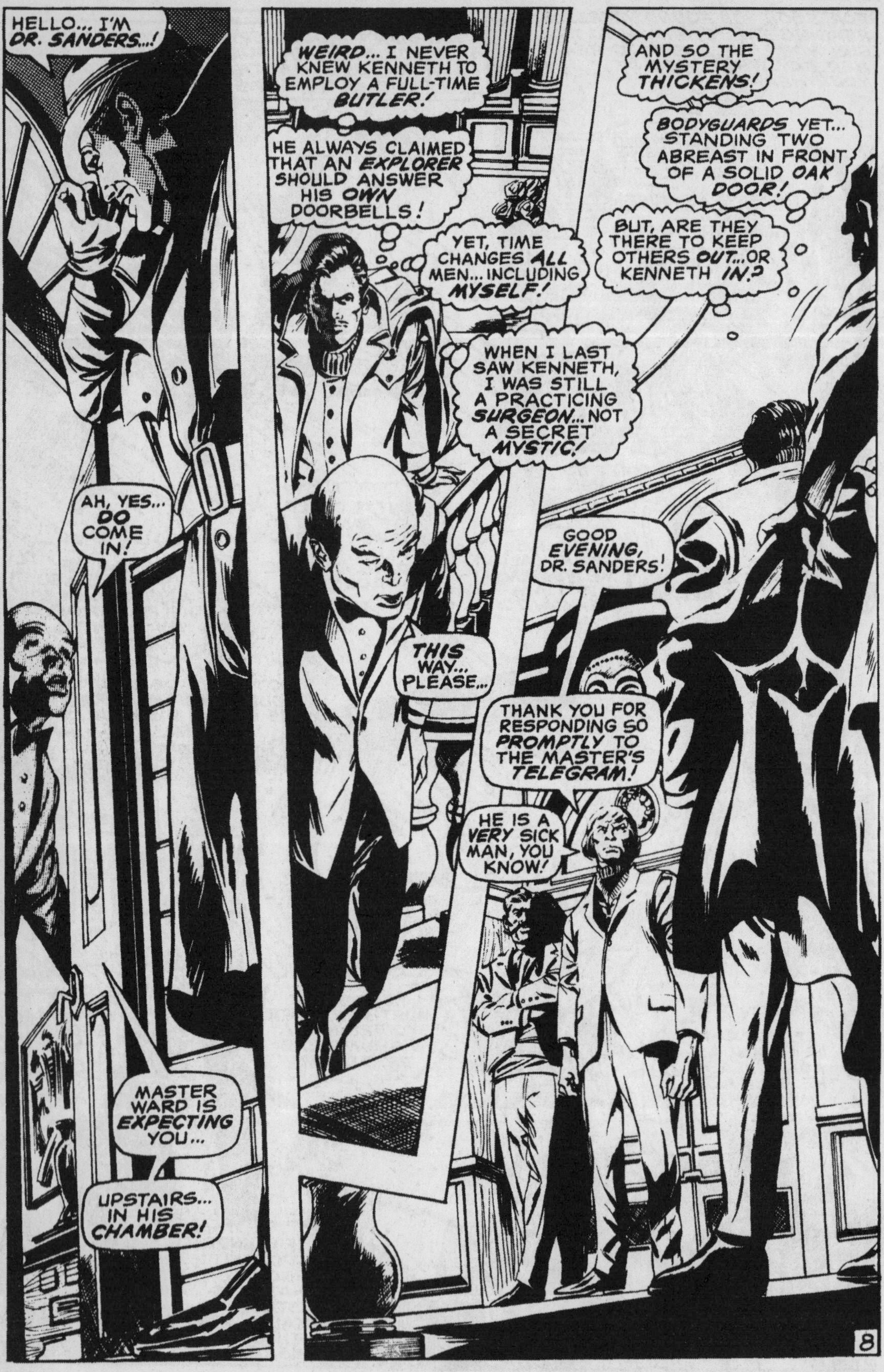
HELLO... I'M DR. SANDERS...!
AH, YES... DO COME IN!
MASTER WARD IS EXPECTING YOU...
UPSTAIRS... IN HIS CHAMBER!
WEIRD... I NEVER KNEW KENNETH TO EMPLOY A FULL-TIME BUTLER!
HE ALWAYS CLAIMED THAT AN EXPLORER SHOULD ANSWER HIS OWN DOORBELLS!
YET, TIME CHANGES ALL MEN... INCLUDING MYSELF!
WHEN I LAST SAW KENNETH, I WAS STILL A PRACTICING SURGEON... NOT A SECRET MYSTIC!
THIS WAY... PLEASE...
AND SO THE MYSTERY THICKENS!
BODYGUARDS YET... STANDING TWO ABREAST IN FRONT OF A SOLID OAK DOOR!
BUT, ARE THEY THERE TO KEEP OTHERS OUT... OR KENNETH IN?
GOOD EVENING, DR. SANDERS!
THANK YOU FOR RESPONDING SO PROMPTLY TO THE MASTER'S TELEGRAM!
HE IS A VERY SICK MAN, YOU KNOW!
8

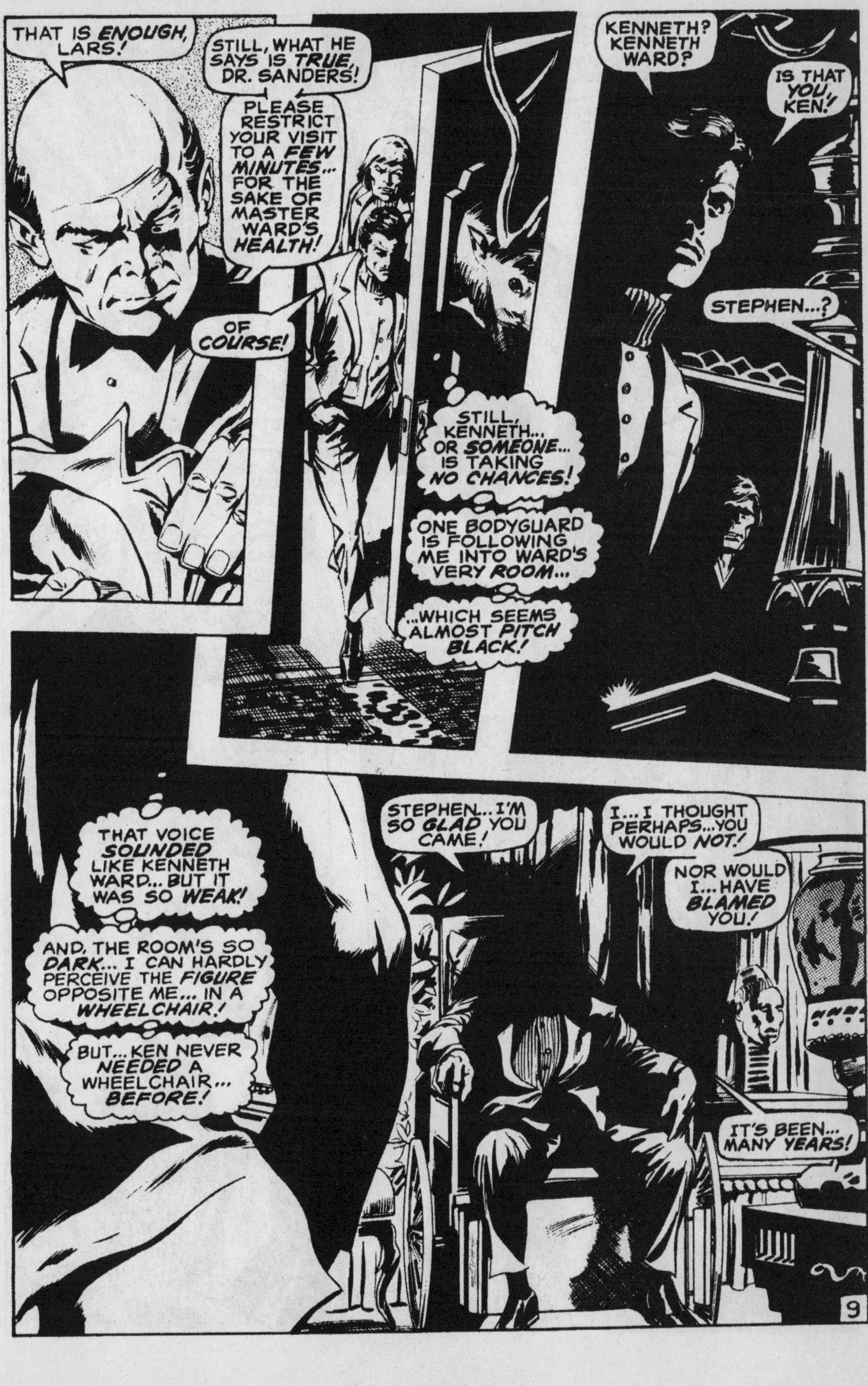
THAT IS ENOUGH, LARS!
STILL, WHAT HE SAYS IS TRUE, DR. SANDERS!
PLEASE RESTRICT YOUR VISIT TO A FEW MINUTES... FOR THE SAKE OF MASTER WARD'S HEALTH!
OF COURSE!
STILL, KENNETH... OR SOMEONE... IS TAKING NO CHANCES!
ONE BODYGUARD IS FOLLOWING ME INTO WARD'S VERY ROOM...
...WHICH SEEMS ALMOST PITCH BLACK!
KENNETH? KENNETH WARD?
IS THAT YOU, KEN!
STEPHEN...?
THAT VOICE SOUNDED LIKE KENNETH WARD... BUT IT WAS SO WEAK!
AND, THE ROOM'S SO DARK... I CAN HARDLY PERCEIVE THE FIGURE OPPOSITE ME... IN A WHEELCHAIR!
BUT... KEN NEVER NEEDED A WHEELCHAIR... BEFORE!
STEPHEN... I'M SO GLAD YOU CAME!
I... I THOUGHT PERHAPS... YOU WOULD NOT!
NOR WOULD I... HAVE BLAMED YOU!
IT'S BEEN... MANY YEARS!
9

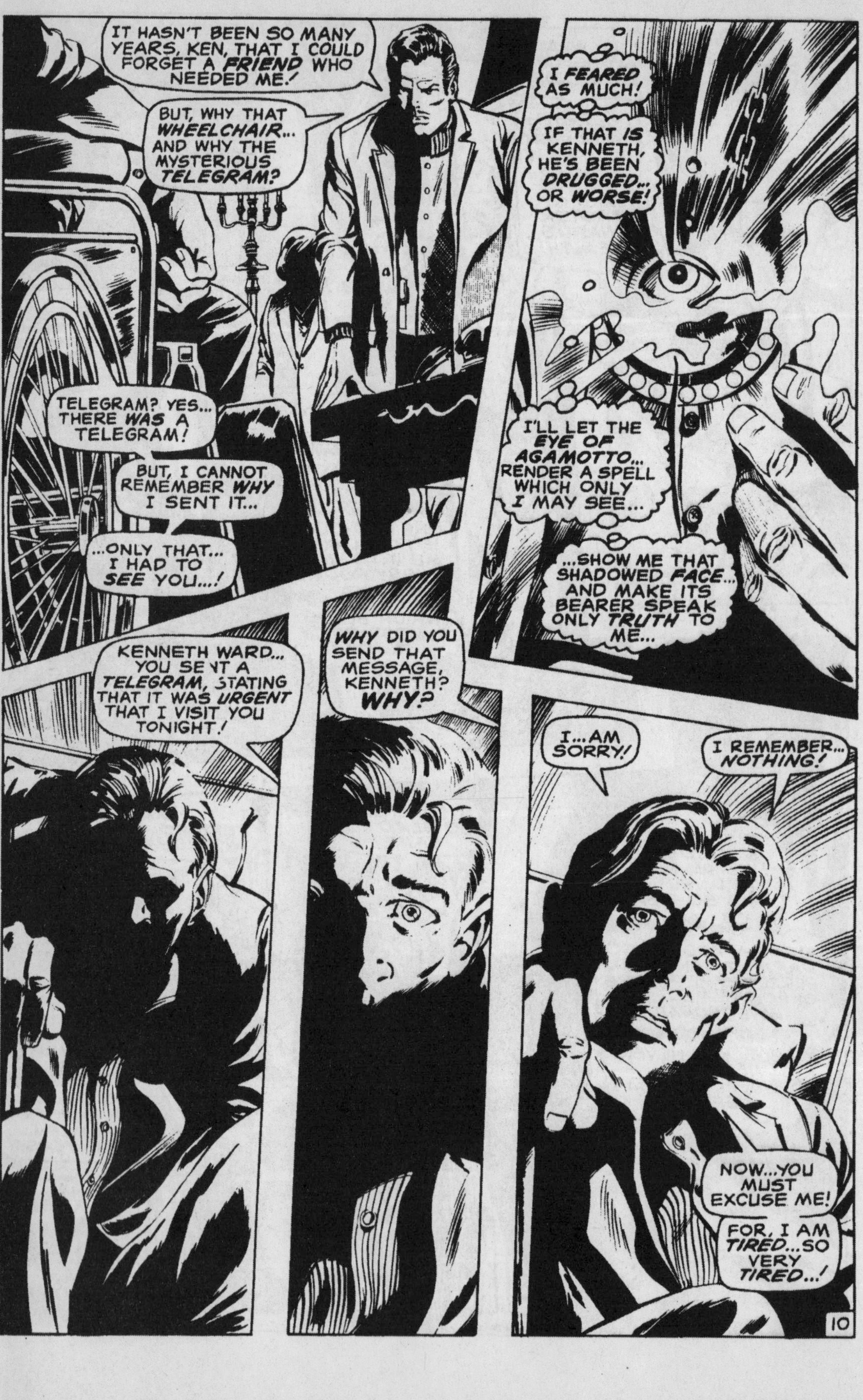
IT HASN'T BEEN SO MANY YEARS, KEN, THAT I COULD FORGET A FRIEND WHO NEEDED ME!
BUT, WHY THAT WHEELCHAIR... AND WHY THE MYSTERIOUS TELEGRAM?
TELEGRAM? YES... THERE WAS A TELEGRAM!
BUT, I CANNOT REMEMBER WHY I SENT IT...
...ONLY THAT... I HAD TO SEE YOU...!
I FEARED AS MUCH!
IF THAT IS KENNETH, HE'S BEEN DRUGGED... OR WORSE!
I'LL LET THE EYE OF AGAMOTTO... RENDER A SPELL WHICH ONLY I MAY SEE...
...SHOW ME THAT SHADOWED FACE... AND MAKE ITS BEARER SPEAK ONLY TRUTH TO ME...
KENNETH WARD... YOU SENT A TELEGRAM, STATING THAT IT WAS URGENT THAT I VISIT YOU TONIGHT!
WHY DID YOU SEND THAT MESSAGE, KENNETH? WHY?
I...AM SORRY!
I REMEMBER... NOTHING!
NOW...YOU MUST EXCUSE ME!
FOR, I AM TIRED...SO VERY TIRED...!
10

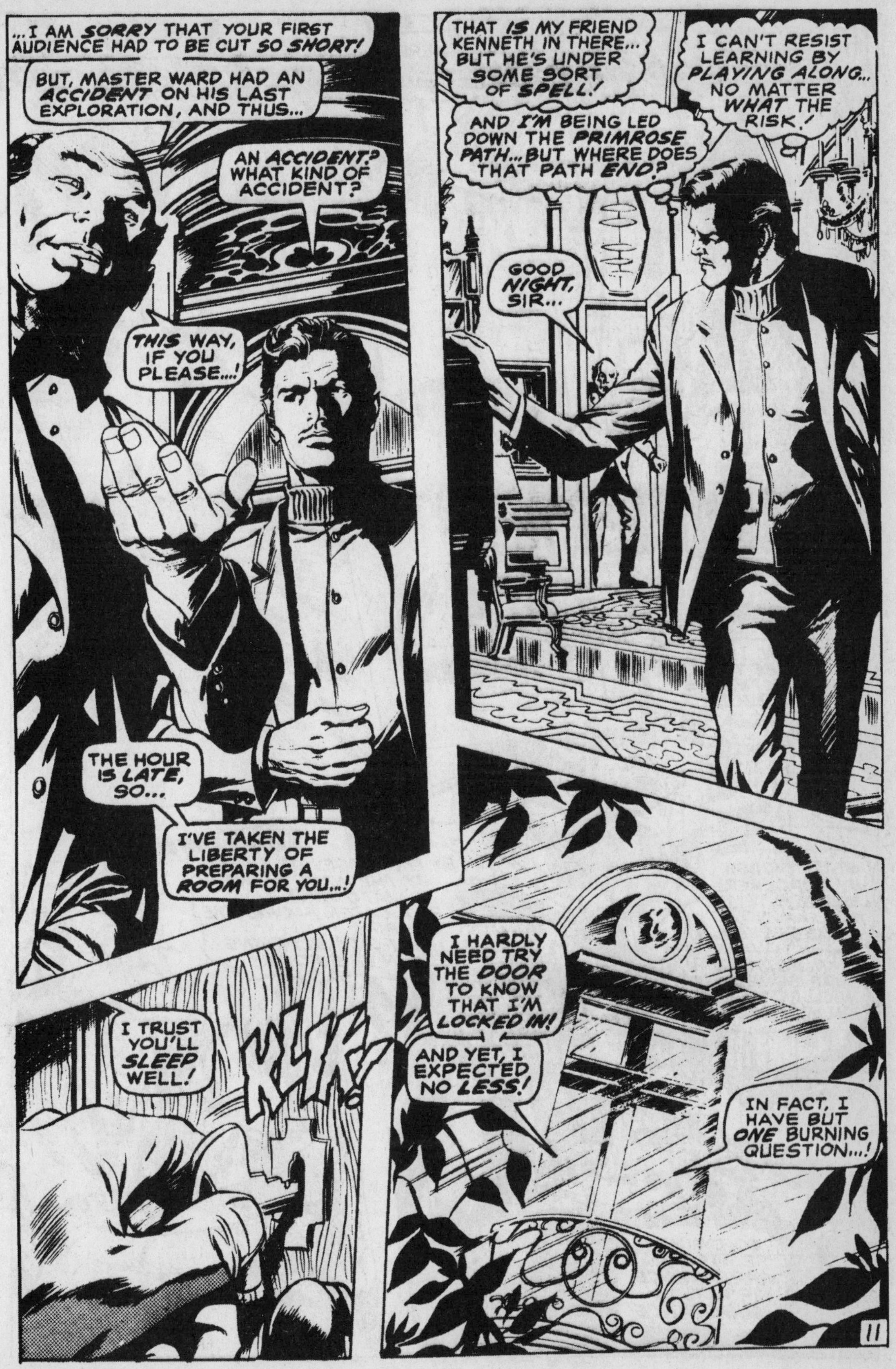
...I AM SORRY THAT YOUR FIRST AUDIENCE HAD TO BE CUT SO SHORT!
BUT, MASTER WARD HAD AN ACCIDENT ON HIS LAST EXPLORATION, AND THUS...
AN ACCIDENT? WHAT KIND OF ACCIDENT?
THIS WAY, IF YOU PLEASE...!
THE HOUR IS LATE, SO...
I'VE TAKEN THE LIBERTY OF PREPARING A ROOM FOR YOU...!
THAT IS MY FRIEND KENNETH IN THERE... BUT HE'S UNDER SOME SORT OF SPELL!
AND I'M BEING LED DOWN THE PRIMROSE PATH... BUT WHERE DOES THAT PATH END?
I CAN'T RESIST LEARNING BY PLAYING ALONG... NO MATTER WHAT THE RISK!
GOOD NIGHT, SIR...
I TRUST YOU'LL SLEEP WELL!
KLIK!
I HARDLY NEED TRY THE DOOR TO KNOW THAT I'M LOCKED IN!
AND YET, I EXPECTED NO LESS!
IN FACT, I HAVE BUT ONE BURNING QUESTION...!
11

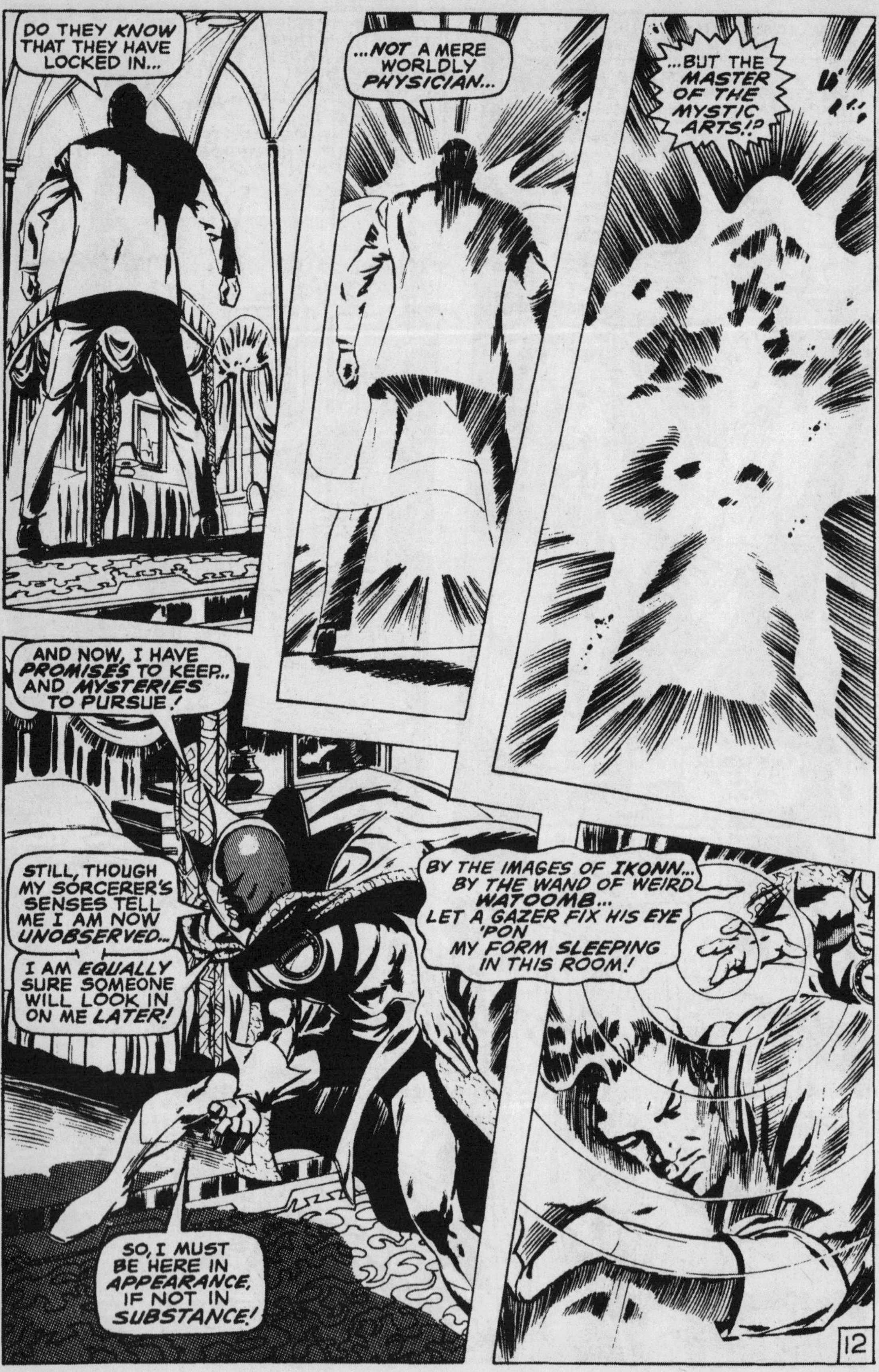
DO THEY KNOW THAT THEY HAVE LOCKED IN...
...NOT A MERE WORLDLY PHYSICIAN...
...BUT THE MASTER OF THE MYSTIC ARTS!?
AND NOW, I HAVE PROMISES TO KEEP... AND MYSTERIES TO PURSUE!
STILL, THOUGH MY SORCERER'S SENSES TELL ME I AM NOW UNOBSERVED...
I AM EQUALLY SURE SOMEONE WILL LOOK IN ON ME LATER!
SO, I MUST BE HERE IN APPEARANCE, IF NOT IN SUBSTANCE!
BY THE IMAGES OF IKONN... BY THE WAND OF WEIRD WATOOMB... LET A GAZER FIX HIS EYE 'PON MY FORM SLEEPING IN THIS ROOM!
12

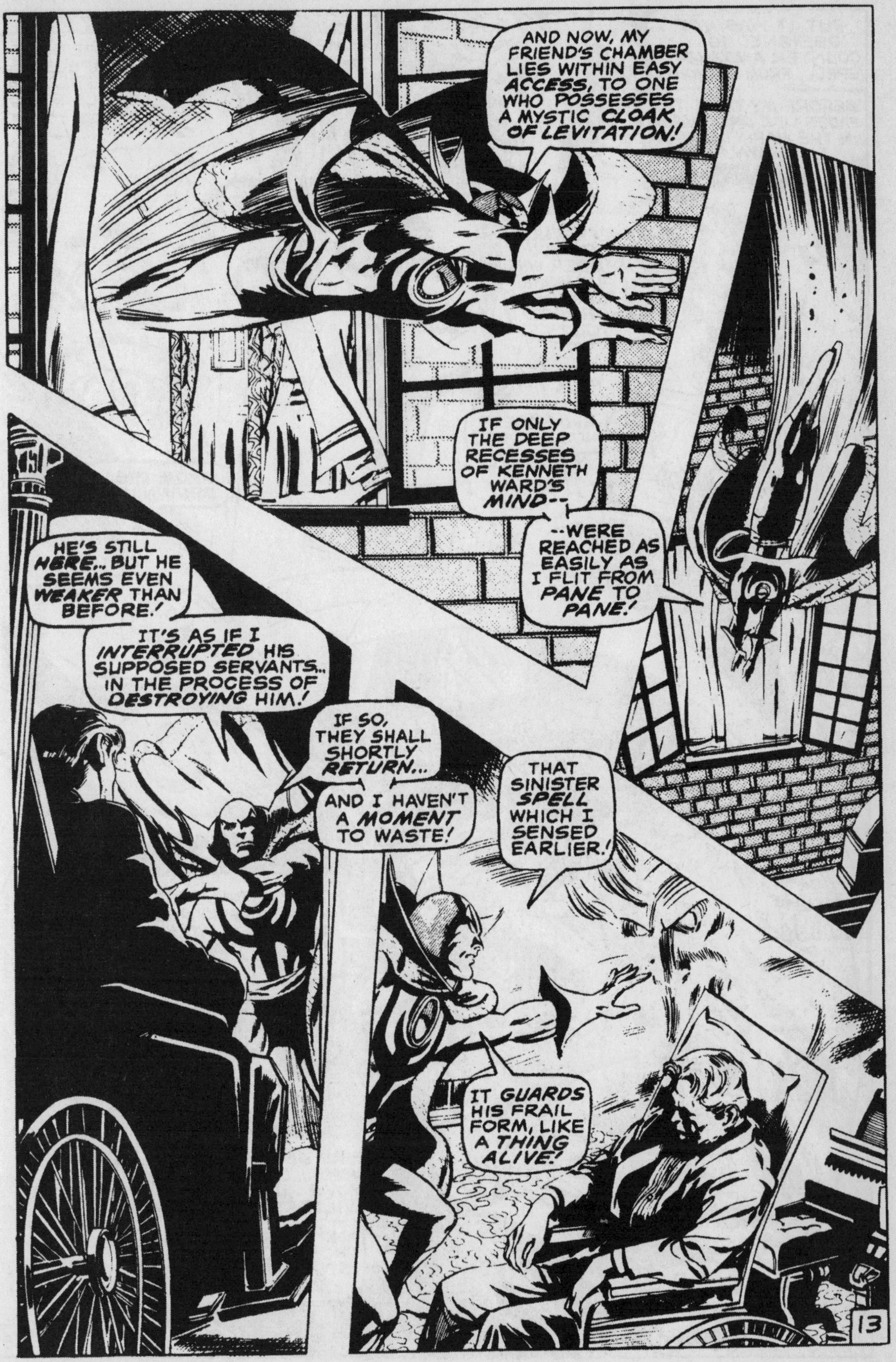
AND NOW, MY FRIEND'S CHAMBER LIES WITHIN EASY ACCESS, TO ONE WHO POSSESSES A MYSTIC CLOAK OF LEVITATION!
IF ONLY THE DEEP RECESSES OF KENNETH WARD'S MIND--
--WERE REACHED AS EASILY AS I FLIT FROM PANE TO PANE!
HE'S STILL HERE.. BUT HE SEEMS EVEN WEAKER THAN BEFORE!
IT'S AS IF I INTERRUPTED HIS SUPPOSED SERVANTS.. IN THE PROCESS OF DESTROYING HIM!
IF SO, THEY SHALL SHORTLY RETURN...
AND I HAVEN'T A MOMENT TO WASTE!
THAT SINISTER SPELL WHICH I SENSED EARLIER!
IT GUARDS HIS FRAIL FORM, LIKE A THING ALIVE!

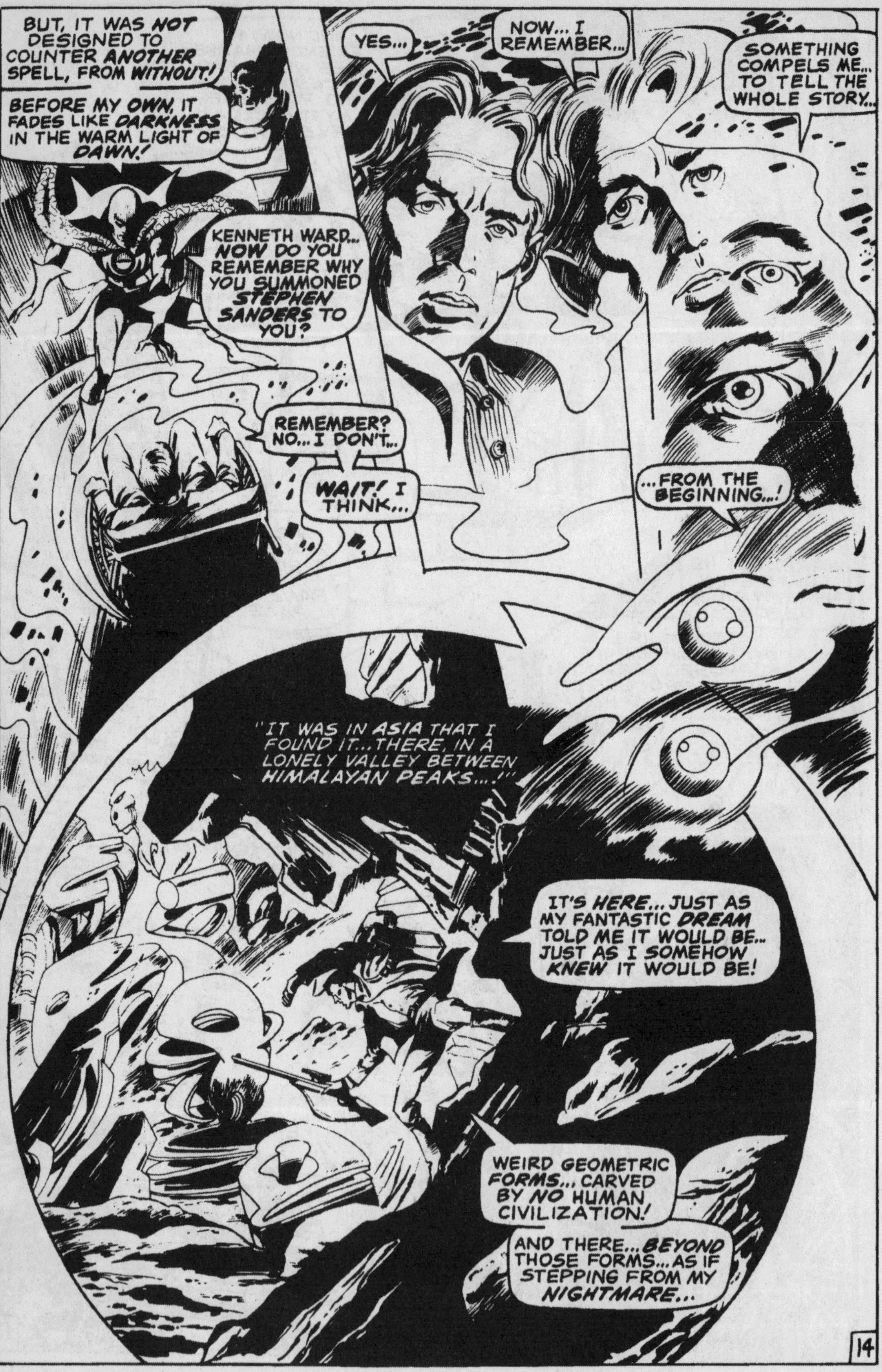

BUT, IT WAS NOT DESIGNED TO COUNTER ANOTHER SPELL, FROM WITHOUT!
BEFORE MY OWN, IT FADES LIKE DARKNESS IN THE WARM LIGHT OF DAWN!
KENNETH WARD... NOW DO YOU REMEMBER WHY YOU SUMMONED STEPHEN SANDERS TO YOU?
REMEMBER? NO... I DON'T...
WAIT! I THINK...
YES...
NOW... I REMEMBER...
SOMETHING COMPELS ME... TO TELL THE WHOLE STORY...
...FROM THE BEGINNING...!
"IT WAS IN ASIA THAT I FOUND IT... THERE, IN A LONELY VALLEY BETWEEN HIMALAYAN PEAKS...!"
IT'S HERE... JUST AS MY FANTASTIC DREAM TOLD ME IT WOULD BE... JUST AS I SOMEHOW KNEW IT WOULD BE!
WEIRD GEOMETRIC FORMS... CARVED BY NO HUMAN CIVILIZATION!
AND THERE... BEYOND THOSE FORMS... AS IF STEPPING FROM MY NIGHTMARE...

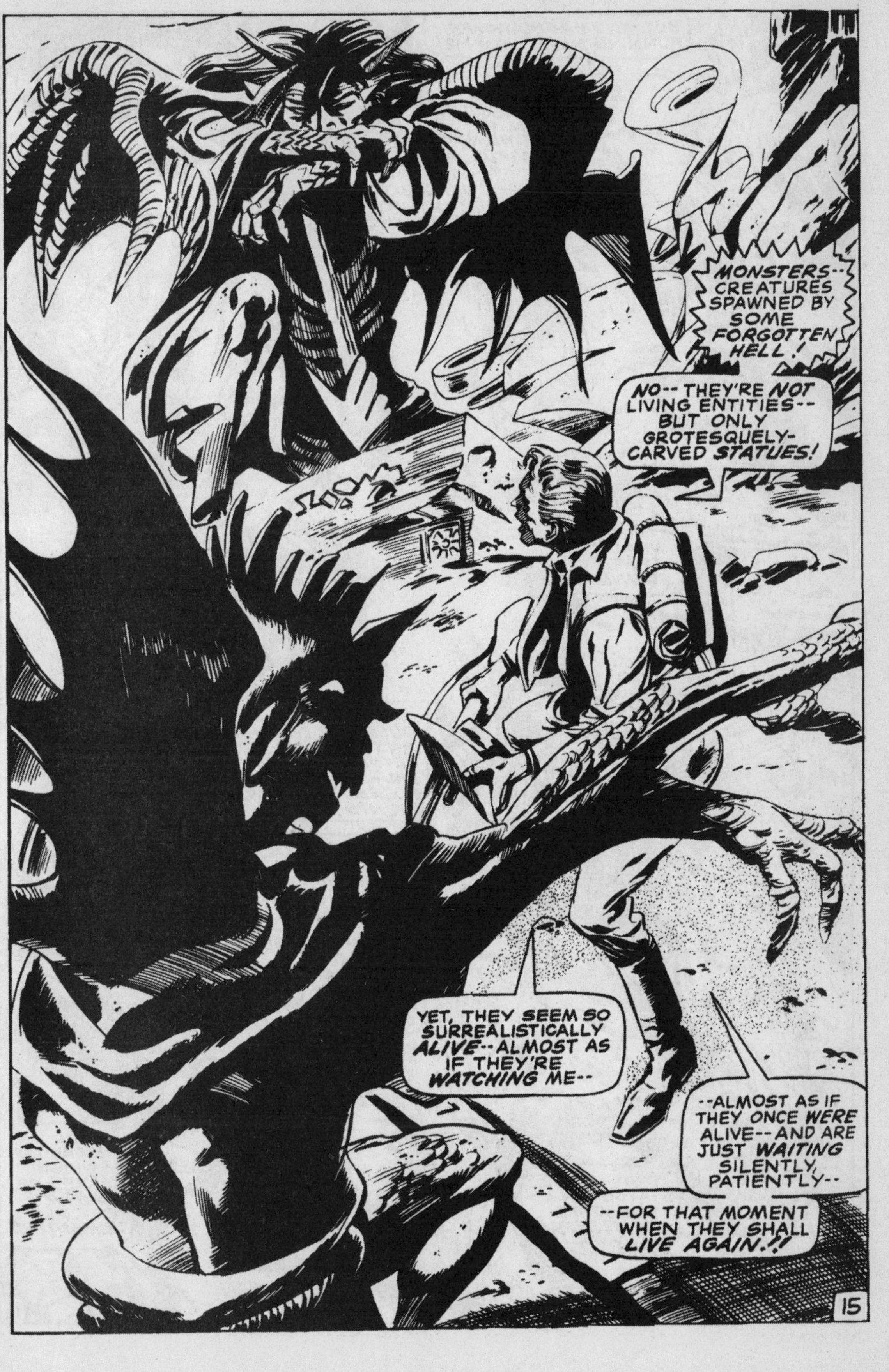
MONSTERS-- CREATURES SPAWNED BY SOME FORGOTTEN HELL!
NO-- THEY'RE NOT LIVING ENTITIES-- BUT ONLY GROTESQUELY-CARVED STATUES!
SKOOM
YET, THEY SEEM SO SURREALISTICALLY ALIVE--ALMOST AS IF THEY'RE WATCHING ME--
--ALMOST AS IF THEY ONCE WERE ALIVE--AND ARE JUST WAITING SILENTLY, PATIENTLY--
--FOR THAT MOMENT WHEN THEY SHALL LIVE AGAIN.!!
15

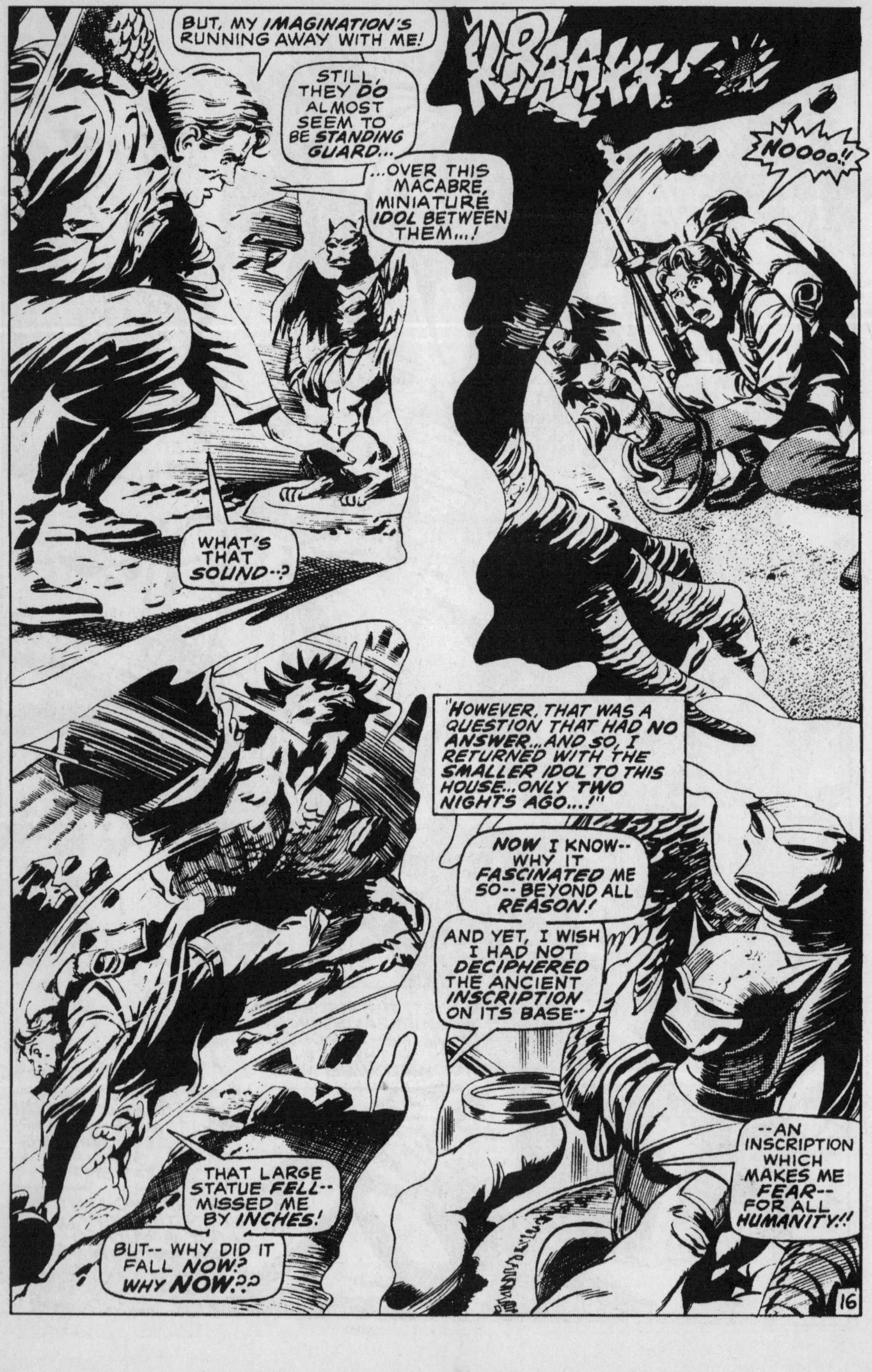
BUT, MY IMAGINATION'S RUNNING AWAY WITH ME!
STILL, THEY DO ALMOST SEEM TO BE STANDING GUARD...
...OVER THIS MACABRE, MINIATURE IDOL BETWEEN THEM...!
WHAT'S THAT SOUND--?
KRAAKK!
NOOOO!!
"HOWEVER, THAT WAS A QUESTION THAT HAD NO ANSWER...AND SO, I RETURNED WITH THE SMALLER IDOL TO THIS HOUSE...ONLY TWO NIGHTS AGO...!"
THAT LARGE STATUE FELL-- MISSED ME BY INCHES!
BUT-- WHY DID IT FALL NOW? WHY NOW?!?
NOW I KNOW-- WHY IT FASCINATED ME SO-- BEYOND ALL REASON!
AND YET, I WISH I HAD NOT DECIPHERED THE ANCIENT INSCRIPTION ON ITS BASE--
--AN INSCRIPTION WHICH MAKES ME FEAR-- FOR ALL HUMANITY!!

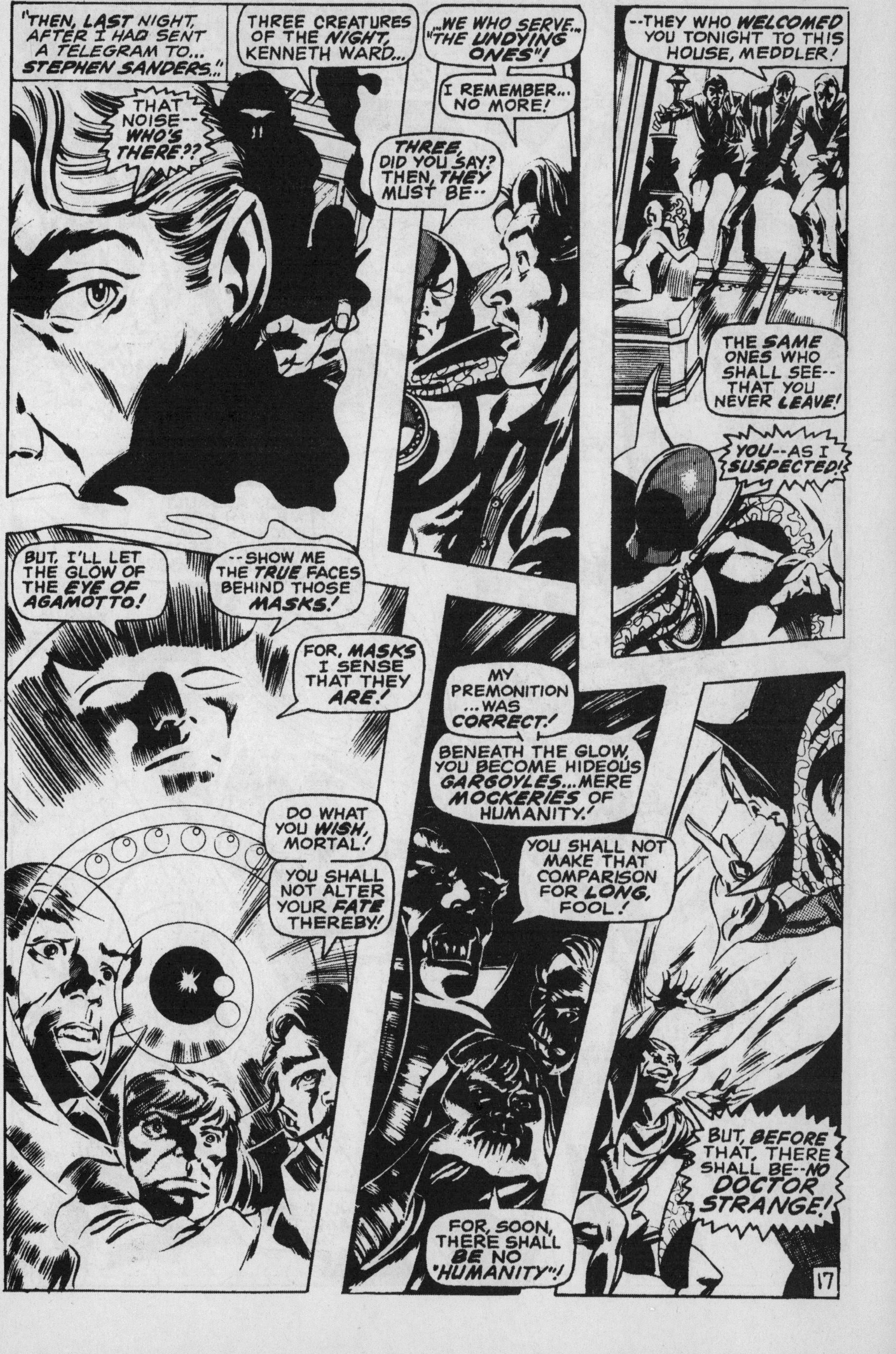
"THEN, LAST NIGHT, AFTER I HAD SENT A TELEGRAM TO... STEPHEN SANDERS..."
THAT NOISE-- WHO'S THERE??
THREE CREATURES OF THE NIGHT, KENNETH WARD...
...WE WHO SERVE... "THE UNDYING ONES"!
I REMEMBER... NO MORE!
THREE, DID YOU SAY? THEN, THEY MUST BE--
--THEY WHO WELCOMED YOU TONIGHT TO THIS HOUSE, MEDDLER!
THE SAME ONES WHO SHALL SEE-- THAT YOU NEVER LEAVE!
YOU--AS I SUSPECTED!
BUT, I'LL LET THE GLOW OF THE EYE OF AGAMOTTO!
--SHOW ME THE TRUE FACES BEHIND THOSE MASKS!
FOR, MASKS I SENSE THAT THEY ARE!
DO WHAT YOU WISH, MORTAL!
YOU SHALL NOT ALTER YOUR FATE THEREBY!
MY PREMONITION ...WAS CORRECT!
BENEATH THE GLOW, YOU BECOME HIDEOUS GARGOYLES... MERE MOCKERIES OF HUMANITY!
YOU SHALL NOT MAKE THAT COMPARISON FOR LONG, FOOL!
FOR, SOON, THERE SHALL BE NO "HUMANITY"!
BUT, BEFORE THAT, THERE SHALL BE--NO DOCTOR STRANGE!

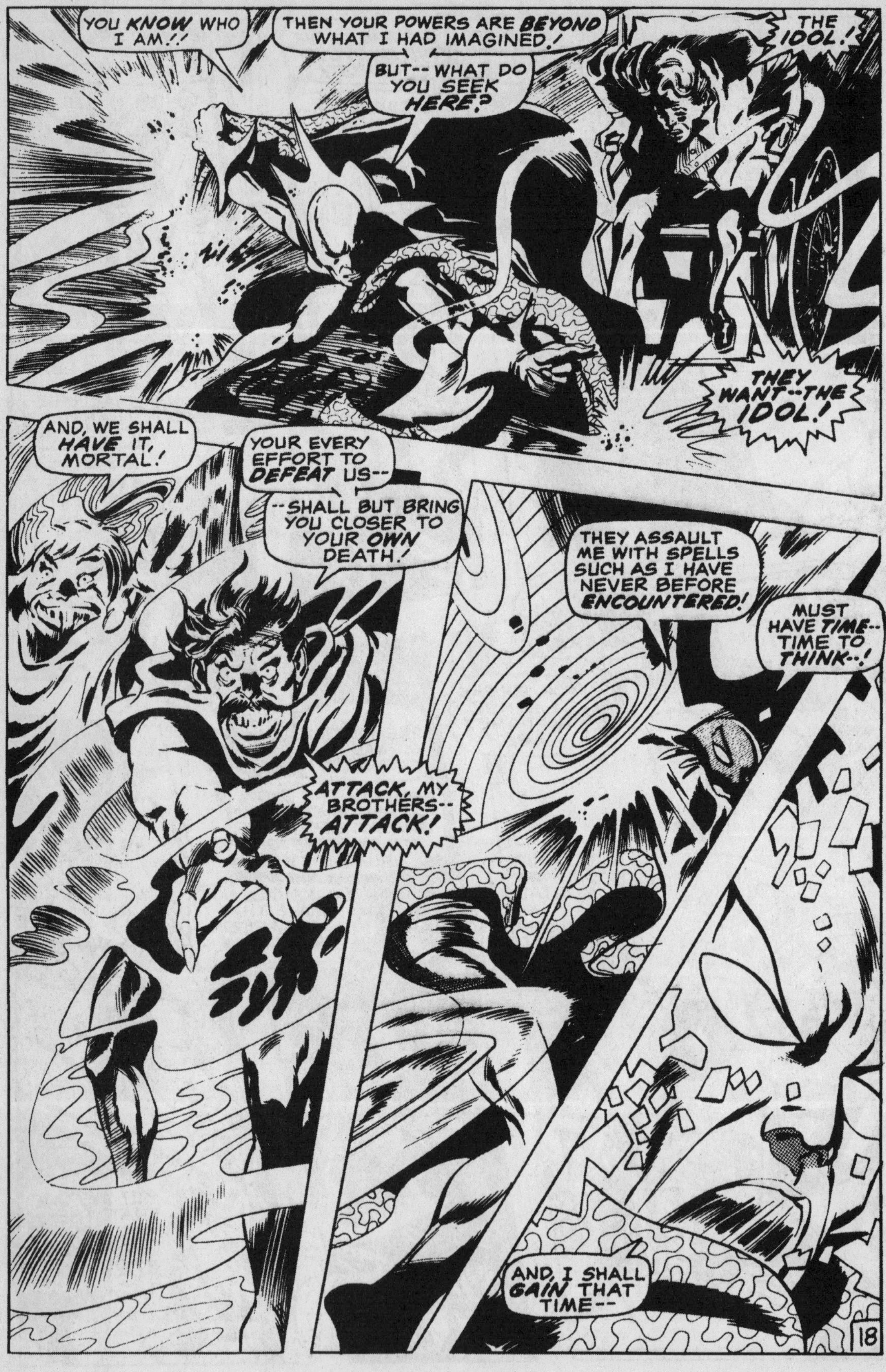
YOU KNOW WHO I AM!!
THEN YOUR POWERS ARE BEYOND WHAT I HAD IMAGINED!
BUT-- WHAT DO YOU SEEK HERE?
THE IDOL!
THEY WANT--THE IDOL!
AND, WE SHALL HAVE IT, MORTAL!
YOUR EVERY EFFORT TO DEFEAT US--
--SHALL BUT BRING YOU CLOSER TO YOUR OWN DEATH!
ATTACK, MY BROTHERS-- ATTACK!
THEY ASSAULT ME WITH SPELLS SUCH AS I HAVE NEVER BEFORE ENCOUNTERED!
MUST HAVE TIME-- TIME TO THINK--!
AND, I SHALL GAIN THAT TIME--

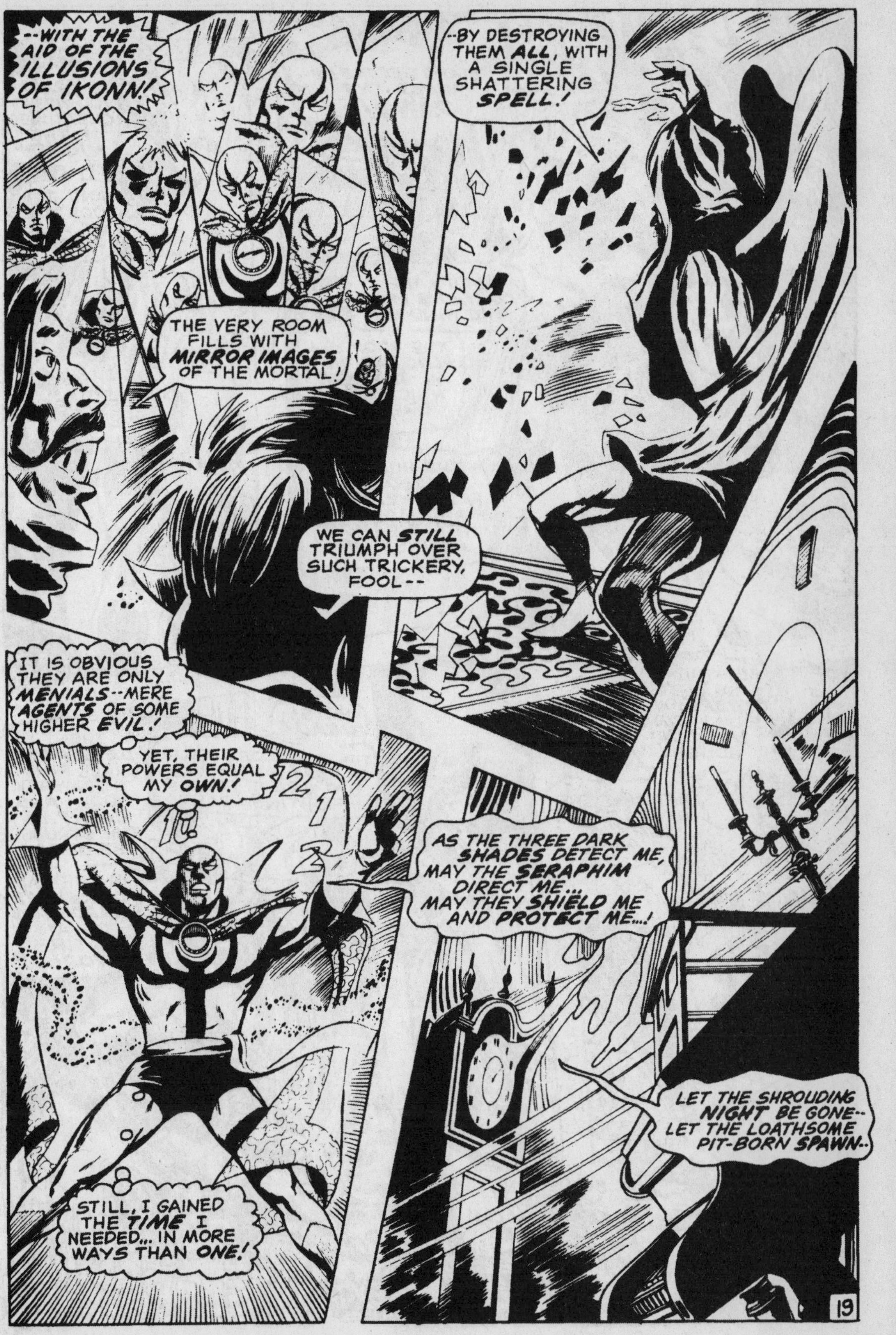
--WITH THE AID OF THE ILLUSIONS OF IKONN!
THE VERY ROOM FILLS WITH MIRROR IMAGES OF THE MORTAL!
WE CAN STILL TRIUMPH OVER SUCH TRICKERY, FOOL--
--BY DESTROYING THEM ALL, WITH A SINGLE SHATTERING SPELL!
IT IS OBVIOUS THEY ARE ONLY MENIALS--MERE AGENTS OF SOME HIGHER EVIL!
YET, THEIR POWERS EQUAL MY OWN!
STILL, I GAINED THE TIME I NEEDED... IN MORE WAYS THAN ONE!
AS THE THREE DARK SHADES DETECT ME, MAY THE SERAPHIM DIRECT ME... MAY THEY SHIELD ME AND PROTECT ME...!
LET THE SHROUDING NIGHT BE GONE-- LET THE LOATHSOME PIT-BORN SPAWN--

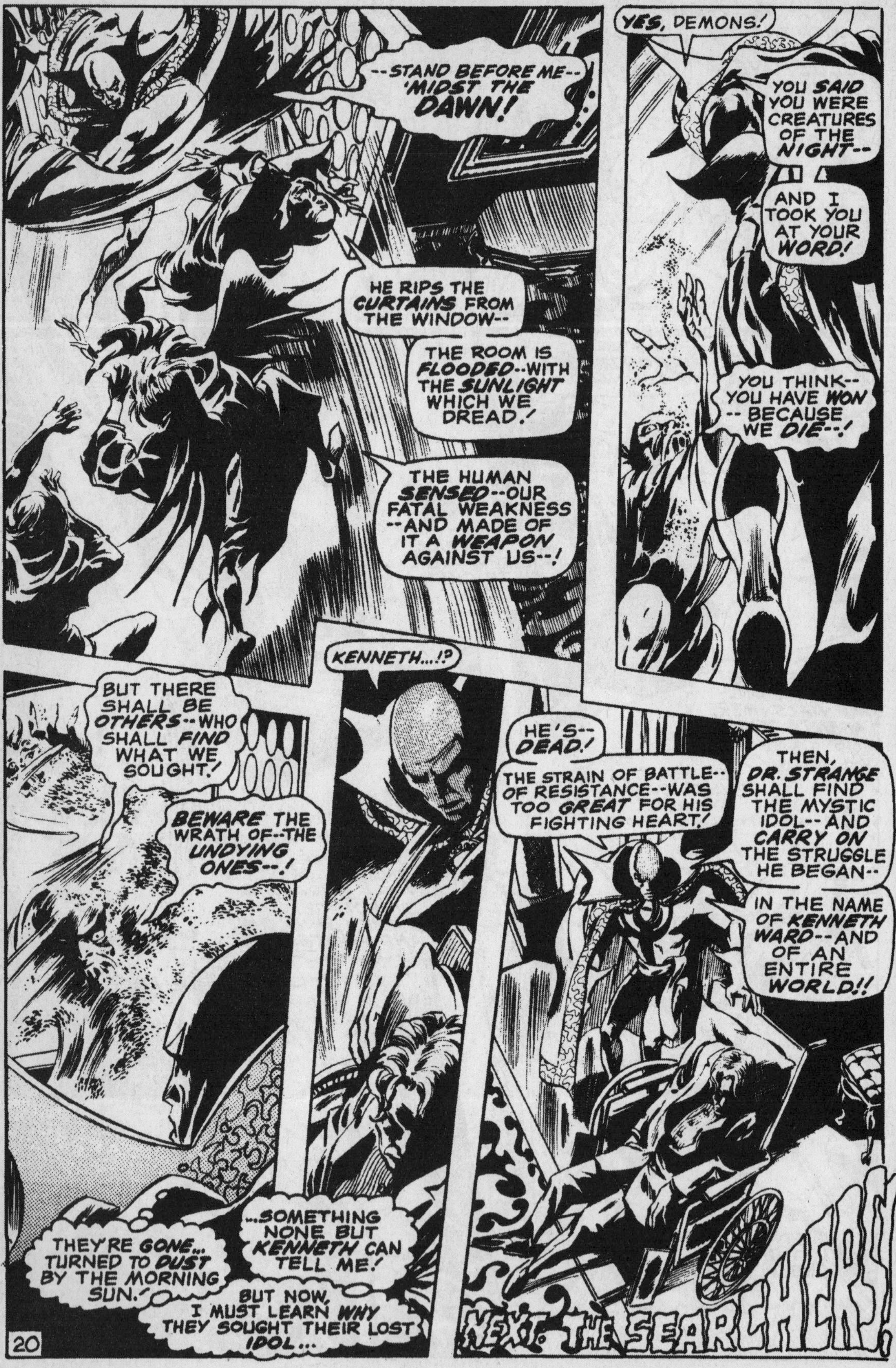
--STAND BEFORE ME-- 'MIDST THE DAWN!
HE RIPS THE CURTAINS FROM THE WINDOW--
THE ROOM IS FLOODED--WITH THE SUNLIGHT WHICH WE DREAD.!
THE HUMAN SENSED--OUR FATAL WEAKNESS --AND MADE OF IT A WEAPON AGAINST US--!
YES, DEMONS!
YOU SAID YOU WERE CREATURES OF THE NIGHT--
AND I TOOK YOU AT YOUR WORD!
YOU THINK--YOU HAVE WON --BECAUSE WE DIE--!
BUT THERE SHALL BE OTHERS--WHO SHALL FIND WHAT WE SOUGHT!
BEWARE THE WRATH OF--THE UNDYING ONES--!
THEY'RE GONE... TURNED TO DUST BY THE MORNING SUN.
BUT NOW, I MUST LEARN WHY THEY SOUGHT THEIR LOST IDOL...
...SOMETHING NONE BUT KENNETH CAN TELL ME!
KENNETH...!?
HE'S--DEAD!
THE STRAIN OF BATTLE--OF RESISTANCE--WAS TOO GREAT FOR HIS FIGHTING HEART!
THEN, DR. STRANGE SHALL FIND THE MYSTIC IDOL--AND CARRY ON THE STRUGGLE HE BEGAN--
IN THE NAME OF KENNETH WARD--AND OF AN ENTIRE WORLD!!
NEXT: THE SEARCHERS!
20

SUB-MARINER

15¢ CC

22 FEB

MARVEL COMICS GROUP

Prince Namor, THE

SUB-MARINER

DR. STRANGE *LIVES*.. BUT WILL THE SUB-MARINER??

SEVERIN GIACOIA 1969

Prince Namor, THE SUB-MARINER!™

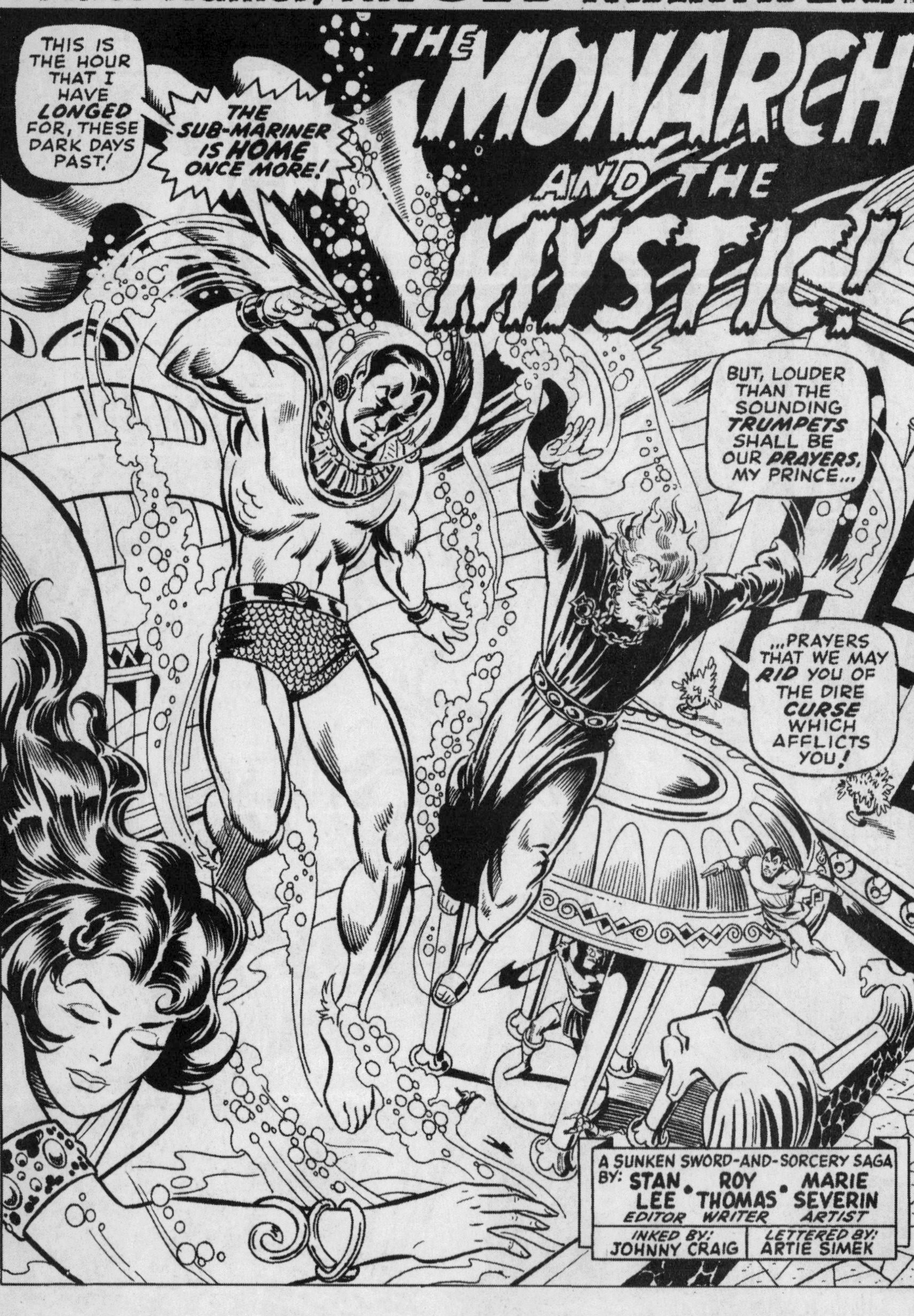
THE MONARCH AND THE MYSTIC!
THIS IS THE HOUR THAT I HAVE LONGED FOR, THESE DARK DAYS PAST!
THE SUB-MARINER IS HOME ONCE MORE!
BUT, LOUDER THAN THE SOUNDING TRUMPETS SHALL BE OUR PRAYERS, MY PRINCE...
...PRAYERS THAT WE MAY RID YOU OF THE DIRE CURSE WHICH AFFLICTS YOU!
A SUNKEN SWORD-AND-SORCERY SAGA
BY: STAN LEE EDITOR • ROY THOMAS WRITER • MARIE SEVERIN ARTIST
INKED BY: JOHNNY CRAIG
LETTERED BY: ARTIE SIMEK

"STEP WITHIN THE *HALL OF SCIENCE*, MY LORD, WHERE WISE *IKTHON* AWAITS..."

"...AS DO THE *OTHER* GREATEST SCIENTIFIC MINDS OF *ATLANTIS!*"

"PERHAPS THEY AWAIT A NAMOR WHO NO LONGER *EXISTS*, VASHTI!"

"...FOR, I AM NO LONGER THE UNDISPUTED *MASTER* OF ALL WHO DWELL BENEATH THE TURBULENT SEA!"

"NOW, I AM BUT A *MAN...* A HYBRID WHO MUST WEAR A *HELMET* TO STAND WHERE ONCE HE *STOOD PROUD!*"

"AND WHO SHALL STAND SO *AGAIN*, O PRINCE! SO *IKTHON* SWEARS!"

"WHILE THE LADY *DORMA* MUST BE *SILENT...* AND SAY *NOTHING...*"

"...LEST HER TREMBLING *VOICE* REVEAL THE FEAR THAT LURKS IN HER *HEART!*"

"YOU MAY *REMOVE* YOUR HELMET NOW, NAMOR... JUST AS I HAVE *DONNED* MY OWN!"

"HERE, IN THIS *OXYGEN-FILLED* CAPSULE, I SHALL DO WHAT *MUST BE DONE!*"

"YOU HAVE PREPARED FOR MY *RETURN* WITH *CARE*, MY FRIEND!"

"*WHATEVER* THE OUTCOME OF THIS OPERATION, I SHALL BE FOREVER IN YOUR *DEBT!*"

"...ANAESTHETIC *APPLIED*, O IKTHON...!"

"HOW DID IT *HAPPEN* TO ONE SUCH AS *I*?"

"WAS IT MERE *DAYS* AGO THAT I STOOD BENEATH THE *ANTARCTIC SHELF...*?"

2

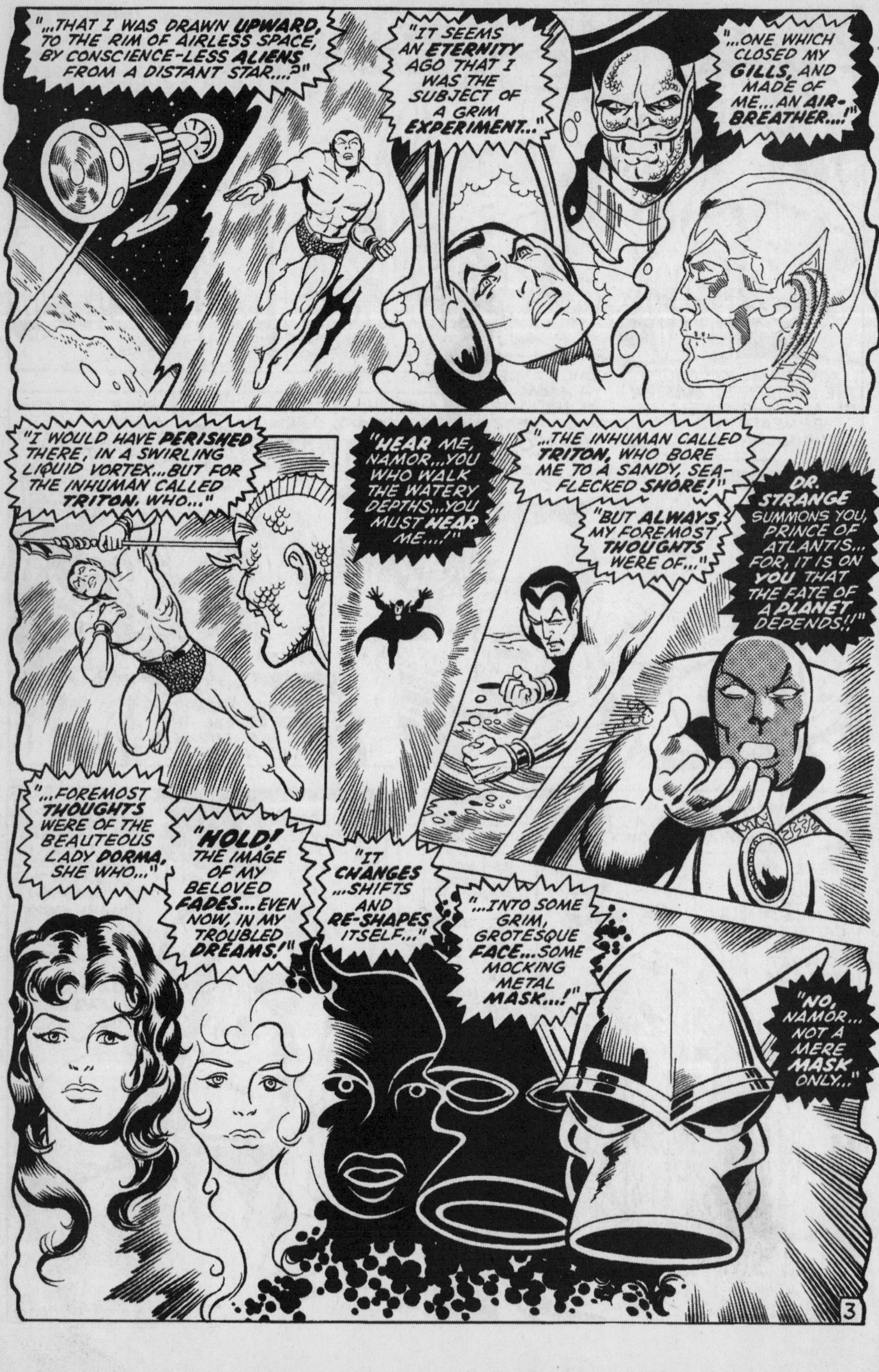
"...THAT I WAS DRAWN UPWARD, TO THE RIM OF AIRLESS SPACE, BY CONSCIENCE-LESS ALIENS FROM A DISTANT STAR...?"
"IT SEEMS AN ETERNITY AGO THAT I WAS THE SUBJECT OF A GRIM EXPERIMENT..."
"...ONE WHICH CLOSED MY GILLS, AND MADE OF ME... AN AIR-BREATHER...!"
"I WOULD HAVE PERISHED THERE, IN A SWIRLING LIQUID VORTEX...BUT FOR THE INHUMAN CALLED TRITON, WHO..."
"HEAR ME, NAMOR...YOU WHO WALK THE WATERY DEPTHS...YOU MUST HEAR ME...!"
"...THE INHUMAN CALLED TRITON, WHO BORE ME TO A SANDY, SEA-FLECKED SHORE!"
"BUT ALWAYS, MY FOREMOST THOUGHTS WERE OF..."
"DR. STRANGE SUMMONS YOU, PRINCE OF ATLANTIS... FOR, IT IS ON YOU THAT THE FATE OF A PLANET DEPENDS!!"
"...FOREMOST THOUGHTS WERE OF THE BEAUTEOUS LADY DORMA, SHE WHO..."
"HOLD! THE IMAGE OF MY BELOVED FADES...EVEN NOW, IN MY TROUBLED DREAMS!"
"IT CHANGES ...SHIFTS AND RE-SHAPES ITSELF..."
"...INTO SOME GRIM, GROTESQUE FACE...SOME MOCKING METAL MASK...!"
"NO, NAMOR... NOT A MERE MASK ONLY..."
3

"...BUT A MACABRE *IDOL*, OLD WHEN EARTH WAS YOUNG...AND WHICH NOW HOLDS THE KEY TO *LIFE OR DEATH* FOR OUR SPACE-SPINNING WORLD!"

"*COME* WITH ME, ATLANTEAN, TO A MOMENT WHEN THE *SEAS* STILL BURNED LIKE *FIRE*...TO A MOMENT COUNTLESS *EONS* PAST!"

WATCH WITH YOUR *MIND'S EYE* AS A GREAT, GAPING *HOLE* IS RENT IN THE VERY *SKY* ITSELF..."

"...AND *THRU* THAT COSMIC DOORWAY COME VENGEFUL *DEMONS*, SPAWNED IN SOME TIMELESS, UNKNOWN *OTHER*!"

"THEY ARE... THE *UNDYING ONES*!!"

"FOR UNNUMBERED AGES, THEY HELD *SWAY* WITH THEIR MYSTIC POWERS... LORDS OVER ALL THEY *SURVEYED*..."

"...AND, *ONE* THING THEY SURVEYED WAS THE NEWBORN CREATURE CALLED... *MAN!*"

"YET *EVER*, THE UNDYING ONES THEMSELVES WERE RULED OVER BY ONE FAR MORE *CRUEL*, FAR MORE *POWERFUL* EVEN THAN *THEY*..."

"...BY ONE THEY DARED CALL ONLY... *THE NAMELESS ONE!*"

4

"THEY HAVE **ALWAYS** BEEN WITH US... IN EACH PAGAN **CEREMONY** AND IN HEATHEN **RITUAL**..."

"AND, **SOME** SAY THERE WERE MEN WHO SOLD THEIR **SOULS** TO THESE DARKSOME FIENDS, FOR A FLEETING TASTE OF PIT-SPAWNED **POWER!**"

"BUT SOMETHING HAPPENED, A MERE **THOUSAND YEARS** AGO!"

"THE UNDYING ONES FELT THEIR POWERS **WANING** ...DIMMING!"

"AND SO, TO **REPLENISH** THOSE POWERS, THEY **RETURNED** TO THEIR OWN WORLD... TILL THEY SHOULD GROW **STRONG** ONCE MORE IN **TEN CENTURIES'** TIME!"

"STILL, **LEGENDS** PERSISTED AMONG MEMORY-HAUNTED MANKIND... HALF-TOLD TALES OF AN **EVIL** SO GREAT THAT IT MUST **NEVER AGAIN** GAIN A FOOTHOLD ON EARTH!"

THERE IS THE ONE WE SEEK!

HE STANDS ACCUSED OF BEING IN LEAGUE WITH THE **DARK POWERS!**

BUT... YOU CAN PROVE **NOTHING**...!

IT IS ENOUGH THAT YOU ARE **ACCUSED!**

SEIZE HIM!!

"AND **THRUOUT** THESE THOUSAND YEARS, LEGEND HAS TOLD ALSO OF AN **IDOL**, SHAPED LIKE THE **NAMELESS** ONE HIMSELF..."

"...AN IDOL WHICH IS ITSELF THE **GATEWAY** BETWEEN THE WORLD OF **DEMONS** AND **MEN**..."

"...AN IDOL WHICH **EXISTS** ON EARTH, TO THIS VERY **DAY!**"

"AND **NOW**, PRINCE OF ALL ATLANTIS..."

"**AWAKEN!!**"

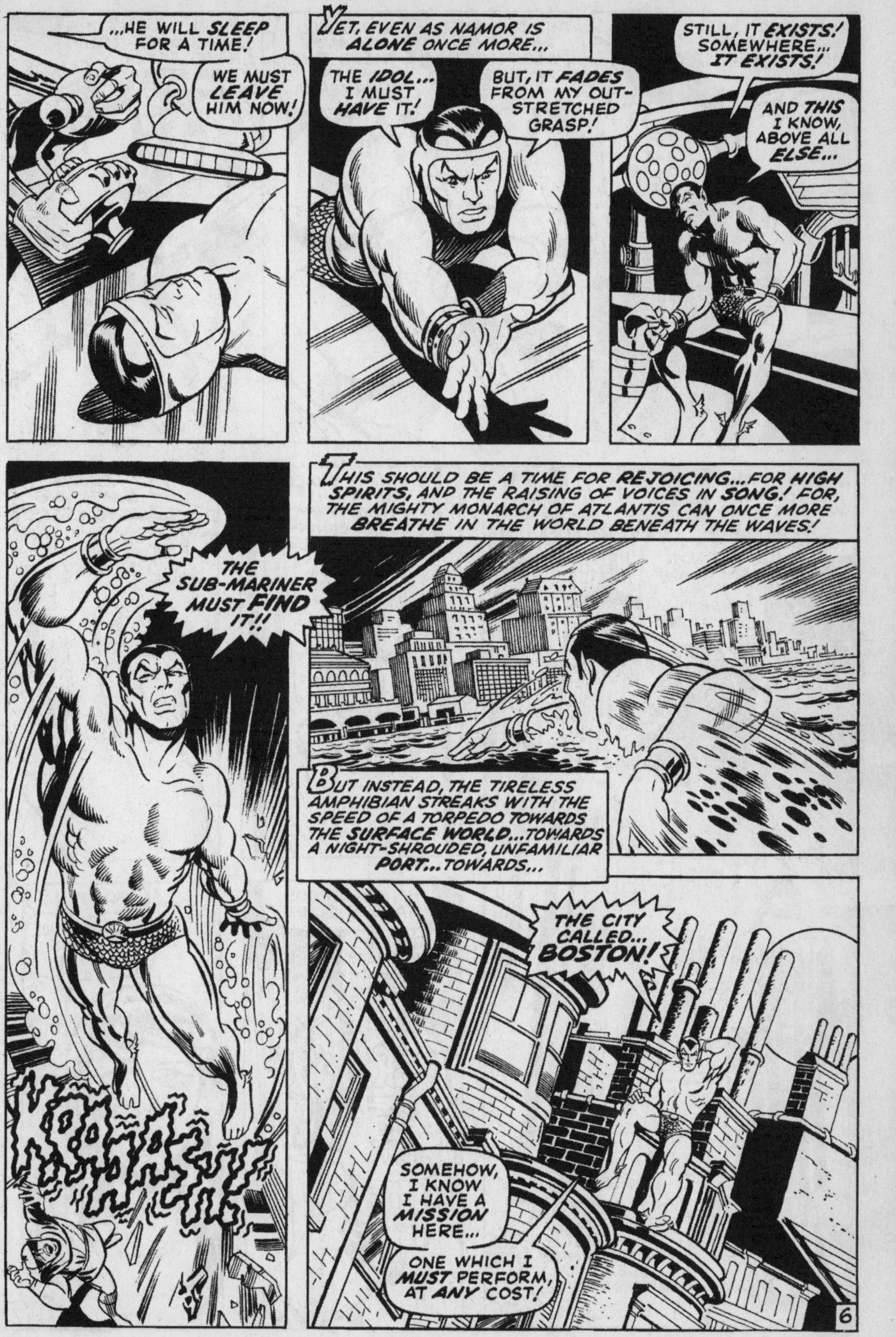
...HE WILL SLEEP FOR A TIME!
WE MUST LEAVE HIM NOW!
YET, EVEN AS NAMOR IS ALONE ONCE MORE...
THE IDOL... I MUST HAVE IT!
BUT, IT FADES FROM MY OUT-STRETCHED GRASP!
STILL, IT EXISTS! SOMEWHERE... IT EXISTS!
AND THIS I KNOW, ABOVE ALL ELSE...
THE SUB-MARINER MUST FIND IT!!
THIS SHOULD BE A TIME FOR REJOICING...FOR HIGH SPIRITS, AND THE RAISING OF VOICES IN SONG! FOR, THE MIGHTY MONARCH OF ATLANTIS CAN ONCE MORE BREATHE IN THE WORLD BENEATH THE WAVES!
BUT INSTEAD, THE TIRELESS AMPHIBIAN STREAKS WITH THE SPEED OF A TORPEDO TOWARDS THE SURFACE WORLD...TOWARDS A NIGHT-SHROUDED, UNFAMILIAR PORT...TOWARDS...
THE CITY CALLED... BOSTON!
SOMEHOW, I KNOW I HAVE A MISSION HERE...
ONE WHICH I MUST PERFORM, AT ANY COST!
6

BUT, I DARE NOT WALK AMONG MEN ATTIRED *THUS!*

I MUST BE DRESSED LIKE *OTHER* MEN!

THIS DARKENED *HOUSE OF CHARITY* SHALL PROVIDE MY NEEDS!

NOR SHALL ANY *MISS* THESE TIME-WORN GARMENTS...

...WHEN THEY SEE THE LONG-SUNKEN *GOLD* I HAVE LEFT IN THEIR STEAD!

...*HERE* IS THE SECTOR FOR WHICH I HAVE BEEN SEARCHING!

I DO NOT KNOW *HOW* I CAN SENSE THAT ...BUT I *DO!*

THIS *BLOCK*... THIS *HOUSE*... EVEN THAT *VERY DOORWAY* SEEMS TO BECKON TO ME!

SOON, I SHALL KNOW WHAT *MYSTERY* LURKS BEHIN--!

KENNETH W. WARD

BY THE *SWIRLING SARGASSO!!*

THE IDOLATROUS IMAGE IS *GONE!*

DID MY *EYES* PLAY TRICKS ON ME, OR--?

KKRIK

WAIT! THE DOOR OPENS....!

COME IN! I'VE BEEN *WAITING* FOR YOU!

7

AND YET, YOU ARE *NOT* LIKE THE ONE I WAS EXPECTING!

WHO *ARE* YOU? WHY ARE YOU *HERE?*

MY NAME IS... *MACKENZIE!*

I HAVE COME TO SEE MR. *KENNETH WARD!*

HE... ISN'T *HERE,* I'M AFRAID!

I'M HIS *DAUGHTER,* JOELLA WARD!

"THE *DEN,* SUB-MARINER! YOU MUST SEARCH THE *DEN!*"

YES... I *HEAR* YOU!

HEAR? HEAR *WHAT??*

STAND *ASIDE,* FEMALE! I HAVE NO *TIME* TO ANSWER!

NOR DO I KNOW THE FULL *REASONS* FOR MY ACTIONS!

YET, SOMEHOW, I SENSE THAT MY *INNER VOICE* SPEAKS THE *TRUTH!*

AN EVIL OLDER THAN *HISTORY* IS AFOOT... AND ONLY *I* MAY...

BY THE REALM *ETERNAL!* THE ROOM IS A *SHAMBLES!*

AND, *THERE...* BY THE FIREPLACE...

A PORTRAIT WHICH I SOMEHOW KNOW TO BE THAT OF... *KENNETH WARD!*

BUT, SLASHED-- AS BY A *DEMON'S* HAND!

YOU SPOKE MORE TRULY THAN YOU COULD *KNOW,* MORTAL!

THEN-- YOU *DO* KNOW! A PITY YOU SHALL NEVER LIVE TO TELL ANOTHER LIVING SOUL!

BEHIND ME--!

A FANGED *MONSTER--* ONE OF THE *UNDYING ONES!*

8.

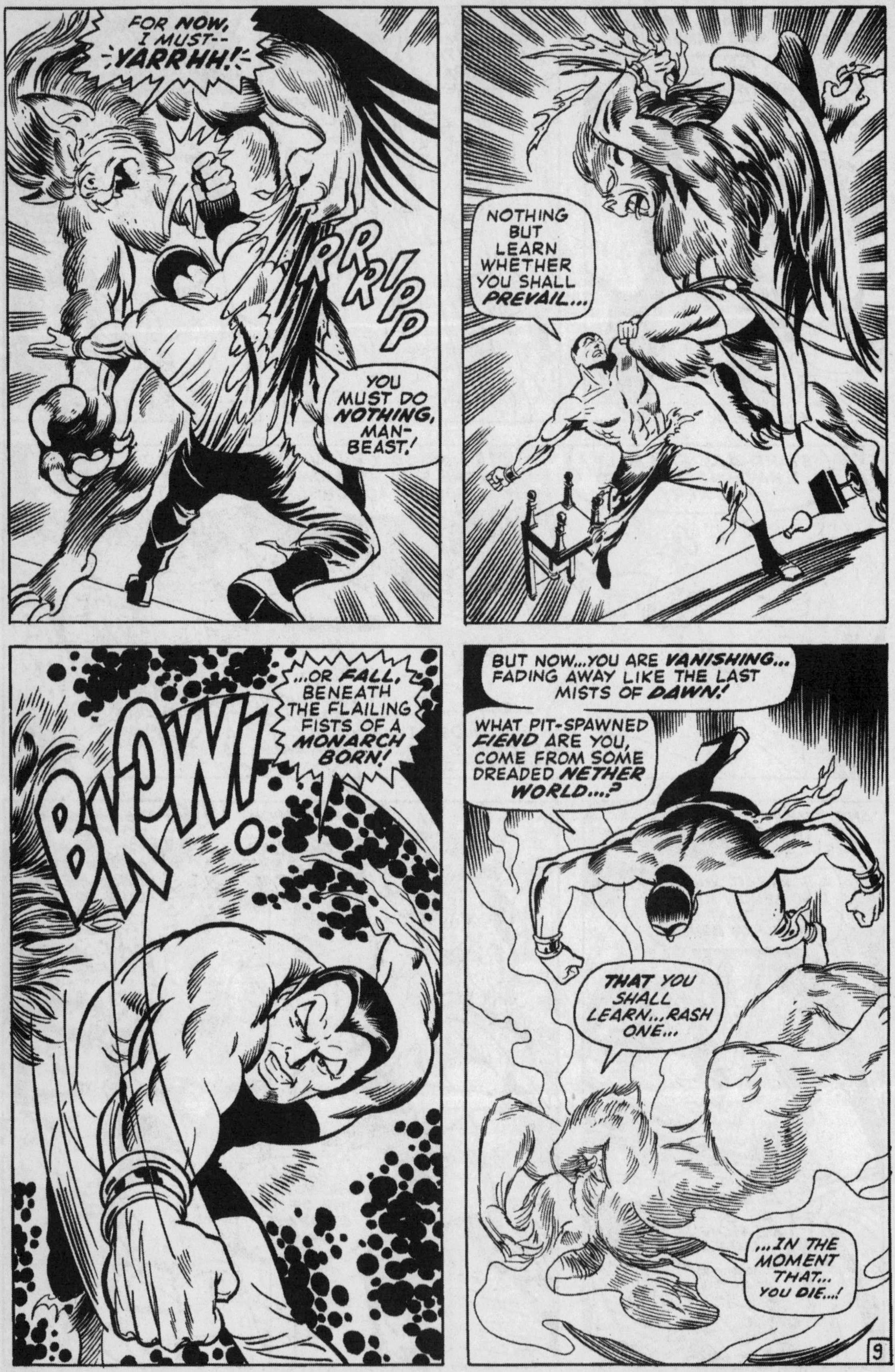

FOR NOW, I MUST-- YARRHH!
RRRIPP
YOU MUST DO NOTHING, MAN-BEAST!
NOTHING BUT LEARN WHETHER YOU SHALL PREVAIL...
...OR FALL, BENEATH THE FLAILING FISTS OF A MONARCH BORN!
BKOW!
BUT NOW...YOU ARE VANISHING... FADING AWAY LIKE THE LAST MISTS OF DAWN!
WHAT PIT-SPAWNED FIEND ARE YOU, COME FROM SOME DREADED NETHER WORLD...?
THAT YOU SHALL LEARN..., RASH ONE...
...IN THE MOMENT THAT... YOU DIE...!
9

THEN, AS THE AWESOME ATLANTEAN RETURNS TO THE NEARBY CORRIDOR...

THE CREATURE IS *GONE*... FADED BACK INTO THE *NIGHT* FROM WHICH IT CAME!

BUT, IT MUST HAVE STRUCK THE *GIRL* BEFORE IT ATTACKED ME!

PRAISE BE TO NEPTUNE... SHE *BREATHES!*

MR. MACKENZIE... IT WAS *HORRIBLE*...THOSE FIERCE, BLAZING *EYES!*

AND *YOU*... EVEN YOU NOW LOOK... SO *STRANGE*...!

IT IS BECAUSE I AM *NOT* OF THE SURFACE-DWELLING RACE, GIRL!

I AM ONE WHOM THEY CALL..."THE SUB-MARINER!"

PLEASE DO NOT ASK ME TO *EXPLAIN*...NOT NOW, NOT *YET!*

WHEN THE TIME IS RIPE, I SENSE THAT ALL SHALL BE MADE KNOWN... TO *BOTH* OF US!

JUST BELIEVE THAT I LABOR FOR THE SAKE OF BOTH OUR ANCIENT *PEOPLES*...

...THE *AIR-BREATHERS*, AND THE *SEA-SPAWNED ATLANTEANS!*

BUT *NOW*...

SOMEHOW, THIS FADED *PORTRAIT* DRAWS ME TO IT...!

AND, THE EARTH MAY *REJOICE* THAT IT *DID!!*

HE WHO LIT THE FIRST WITCH-PYRE NOW GUARDS THE DEMONS' DARK DESIRE!

--Kenneth Ward

10

HOLD! NOW I REALIZE *WHY* MY EYES FELL UPON THIS PORTRAIT!

THE WOMAN WHO GAZES OUT FROM IT...IS YOUR *TWIN!*

SHE WAS... MY *GRANDMOTHER!*

NOW WHERE ARE YOU *DRAGGING* ME...AND *WHY?*

I DON'T KNOW WHAT YOU *WANT* HERE, ANY MORE THAN I UNDERSTAND FATHER'S CRYPTIC *POEM...!*

NOR DO *I,* FEMALE!

...BUT, *ANOTHER* GUIDES MY STEPS...ONE WHO SEES THRU *MY EYES!*

AND, *HE* HAS LED ME...*HERE!*

THE *CEMETERY* WHICH STANDS BY OUR HOME! BUT *WHY...? WHY?*

WAIT! SUDDENLY...EVERYTHING IS *CLEAR!*

THAT STATUE OF *JOHN GOODWIN* ...JUDGE AT THE OLD BOSTON *WITCH TRIALS...!*

AY, GIRL...

IT WAS *HE* WHO "LIT THE FIRST WITCH-PYRE"... BY CONDEMNING TO *DEATH* THOSE ACCUSED OF *SORCERY!*

THEN, *HERE* SHALL I FIND THE *IDOL* I SEEK!

WHY DO YOU *DRAW BACK,* JOELLA?

I...I DON'T *KNOW!*

FELT *FAINT* ...SUDDENLY...!

THEN *REST,* GIRL... WHILE *NAMOR* STRIVES TO UNLOCK A MYSTERY OLDER THAN *TIME!*

AND, UNLOCK IT I *MUST,* THOUGH A THOUSAND THOUSAND *DEVILS* SHOULD BAR MY WAY!

11

JOHN GOODWIN
...53--1713

...HE MAGISTRATE AT
...W'S WITCH TRIALS,
...WHO SENT THE
...TCH TO THE
...FLAMING
...AKE.

...ATER RECANTED
...SONAL FORTUNE
...FAMILIES OF
...HAD WRONGED

MY POWERS
ARE NOT AT
THEIR *PEAK,*
FOR I HAVE
BEEN LONG
FROM THE
SEA!

STILL, THEY
SHALL DO
WHAT *MUST*
BE DONE!

BUT NOW, I FEEL
PAIN...FEAR...
COUNTLESS
MADDENING
EMOTIONS...

...ALL
EMANATING
FROM THE
MASSIVE
MONUMENT!

YET, NOT *THEY...*
NOT *ANYTHING*
SHALL SWAY...A
*PRINCE OF THE
BLOOD!*

IMPERIUS REX!

AND THERE,
SOMEHOW
EMBEDDED
BENEATH
THE STATUE'S
BASE...

...IS THE
GRISLY
IDOL WHICH I
SEEK...

...FOR
REASONS
I KNOW
NOT *WHY!*

THEN,
NAMOR,
IT IS
TIME YOU
KNEW!

BY THE
BEARD OF
NEPTUNE--
WHO--??

12

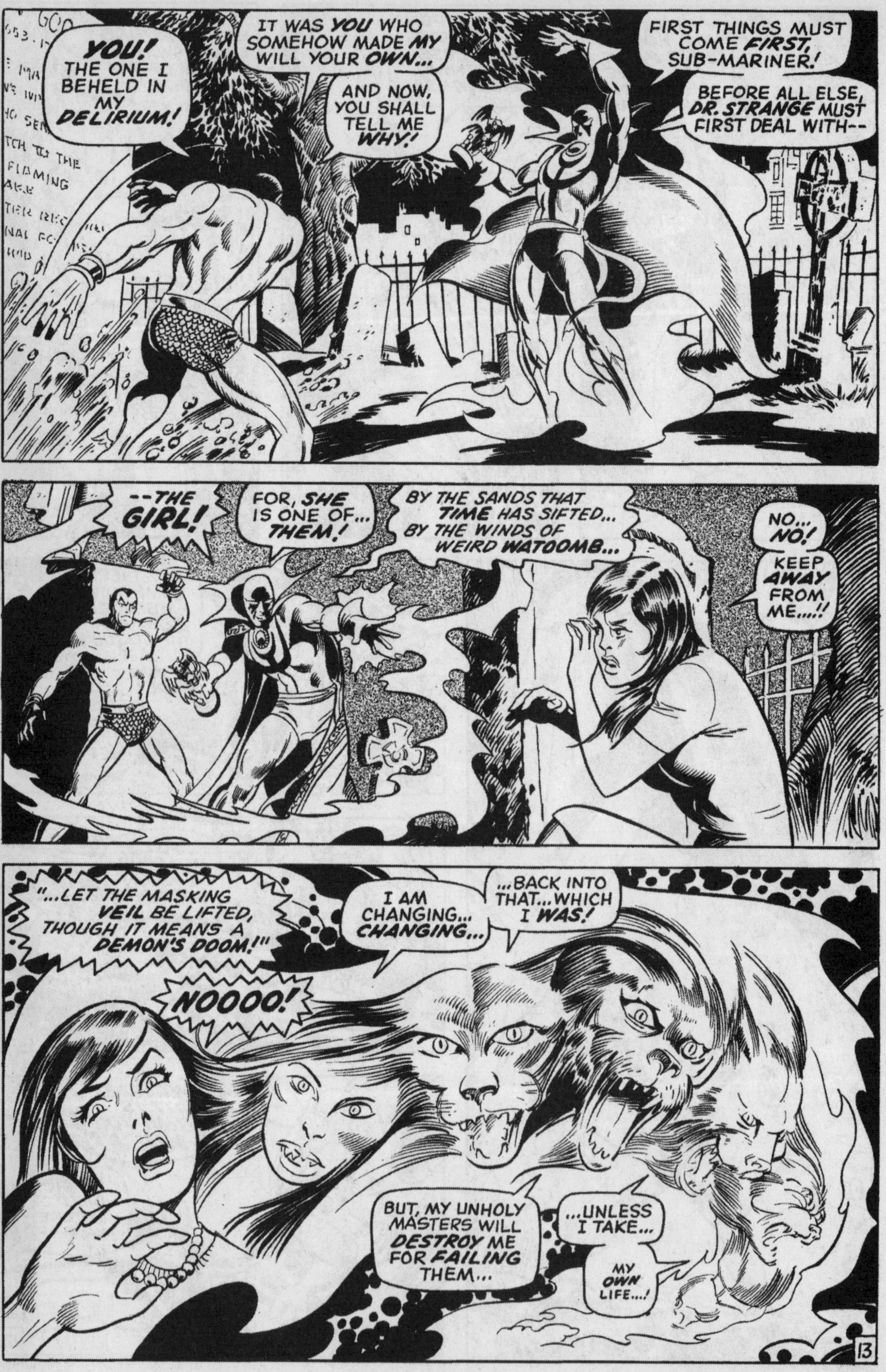
YOU! THE ONE I BEHELD IN MY DELIRIUM!
IT WAS YOU WHO SOMEHOW MADE MY WILL YOUR OWN...
AND NOW, YOU SHALL TELL ME WHY!
FIRST THINGS MUST COME FIRST, SUB-MARINER!
BEFORE ALL ELSE, DR. STRANGE MUST FIRST DEAL WITH--
--THE GIRL!
FOR, SHE IS ONE OF... THEM!
BY THE SANDS THAT TIME HAS SIFTED... BY THE WINDS OF WEIRD WATOOMB...
NO... NO! KEEP AWAY FROM ME...!!
"...LET THE MASKING VEIL BE LIFTED, THOUGH IT MEANS A DEMON'S DOOM!"
I AM CHANGING... CHANGING...
...BACK INTO THAT...WHICH I WAS!
NOOOO!
BUT, MY UNHOLY MASTERS WILL DESTROY ME FOR FAILING THEM...
...UNLESS I TAKE...
MY OWN LIFE...!
13

THEN, IT WAS SHE WHO ATTACKED ME... IN ANOTHER FORM!

SHE WAS NOT THE DAUGHTER OF THE MAN KENNETH WARD!

WARD HAD NO DAUGHTER!

AND, HE IS NOW DEAD...A VICTIM OF THE UNDYING ONES!

DEAD?

BY THE GREAT MAELSTROM, YOU SHALL TELL ME WHY YOU HAVE USED ME THUS ...OR FACE MY WRATH!

YOU ALREADY KNOW PART OF IT, NAMOR!

STILL, YOU SHALL KNOW THE FULL STORY...

...WHEN WE STAND ONCE MORE WITHIN THE WARD MANSION!

WE ARE BACK INSIDE ITS WALLS!

YOU ARE, INDEED, A WIZARD!

WHO ELSE, ATLANTEAN, COULD OPPOSE THE DARK POWERS WHICH ENCOMPASS OUR PUNY WORLD?

AND NOW, YOU SHALL KNOW THE WHY AND WHEREFORE OF OUR SACRED MISSION...

...AFTER I RESTORE MY FRIEND'S SLASHED PORTRAIT!

"THE IDOL WHICH I HOLD WAS FOUND BY KENNETH WARD... WHO STOLE IT AWAY FROM ITS AGE-OLD RESTING-PLACE IN THE HIMALAYAS...!"

MUST GET AWAY!

I CAN SENSE THEM WATCHING ME... WAITING...!

"IN HIS NEW YORK ADDRESS, HE TRANSLATED AN INSCRIPTION ON THE BASE OF THE IDOL...WHICH MADE HIM FEAR FOR THE FUTURE OF MANKIND!"

I MUST HAVE HELP...AND ADVICE!

PERHAPS AN OLD FRIEND OF MINE....!

"I WAS THAT OLD FRIEND, NAMOR...BUT I ARRIVED TOO LATE TO SAVE KENNETH WARD FROM THOSE WHO SERVE THE VANISHED DEMONS....!"

HE IS... DEAD!

BUT, HIS SLAYERS DID NOT FIND THE IDOL WHICH HE HID!

NOR SHALL THEY, WHILE DR. STRANGE LIVES!!

14

"FOR, I COMBED THE CORRIDORS OF *COUNTLESS DIMENSIONS*, CALLING UPON THE *POWERS* THAT DWELL THEREIN..."

...UNTIL I LEARNED THAT THE IDOL WAS SOMEWHERE IN *THIS* AREA!

...BUT, I SUSPECTED THIS *HOUSE* WOULD BE WATCHED BY *EVIL ENTITIES*...

...*ENTITIES* WHO WOULD *DETECT* A SORCERER IN THEIR MIDST!

AND SO YOU TOOK POSSESSION OF *ME*!

YES...A SIMPLE MATTER, WHILE YOU WERE UNDER *SEDATION* IN FAR-OFF ATLANTIS!

FEW BUT *YOU* COULD HAVE STOOD UP TO THAT DEMON'S *ATTACK*!

SHE SEEMED SO *REAL*... LIKE FLESH AND *BLOOD*!

A GUISE THE DEMON *ASSUMED*...BY MIRRORING THE FACE IN AN ANCESTRAL *PORTRAIT*!

BUT NOW, I MUST VIEW THAT PAINTING MORE *CLOSELY*!

IT IS IN THE *HALL* BEYOND!

THE LIKENESS *WAS* AMAZING, BUT EVIL IS ALWAYS *MOST* DANGEROUS WHEN IT WEARS A PRETTY FA--

BY THE *MOONS OF MUNNOPOR*!!

IN THAT PORTRAIT... A *CAT*!

DID THE *GIRL* ALSO HAVE ONE?

AY....!

IT, TOO, MUST HAVE BEEN ONE OF THOSE WHO STILL *SERVE* THE UNDYING ONES IN THIS WORLD!

WE MUST *FIND* IT, BEFORE--

THERE IT IS-- BUT--

LOOK!!

15

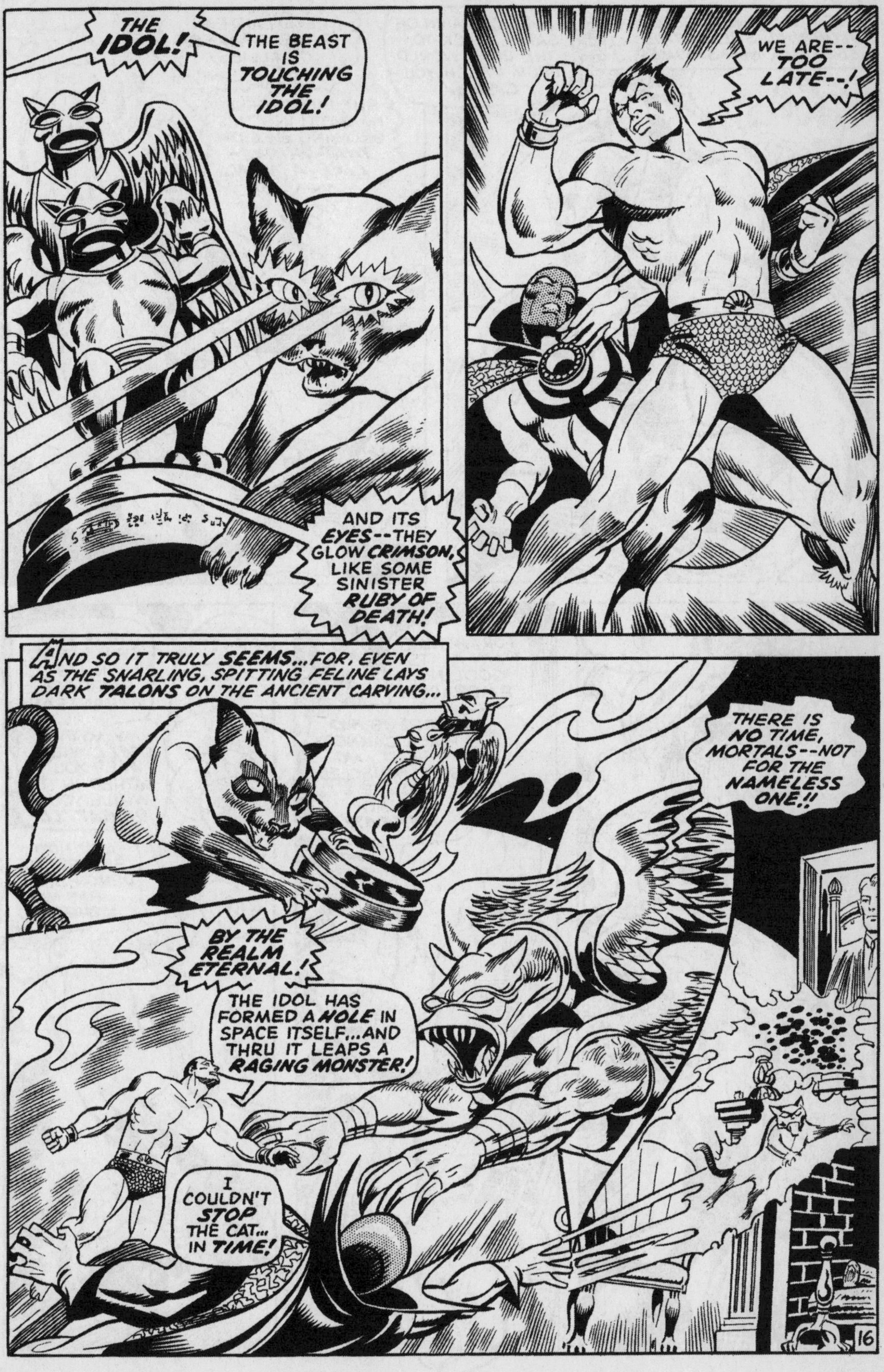

THE IDOL!
THE BEAST IS TOUCHING THE IDOL!
AND ITS EYES--THEY GLOW CRIMSON, LIKE SOME SINISTER RUBY OF DEATH!
WE ARE--TOO LATE--!
AND SO IT TRULY SEEMS... FOR, EVEN AS THE SNARLING, SPITTING FELINE LAYS DARK TALONS ON THE ANCIENT CARVING...
THERE IS NO TIME, MORTALS--NOT FOR THE NAMELESS ONE!!
BY THE REALM ETERNAL!
THE IDOL HAS FORMED A HOLE IN SPACE ITSELF...AND THRU IT LEAPS A RAGING MONSTER!
I COULDN'T STOP THE CAT... IN TIME!
16

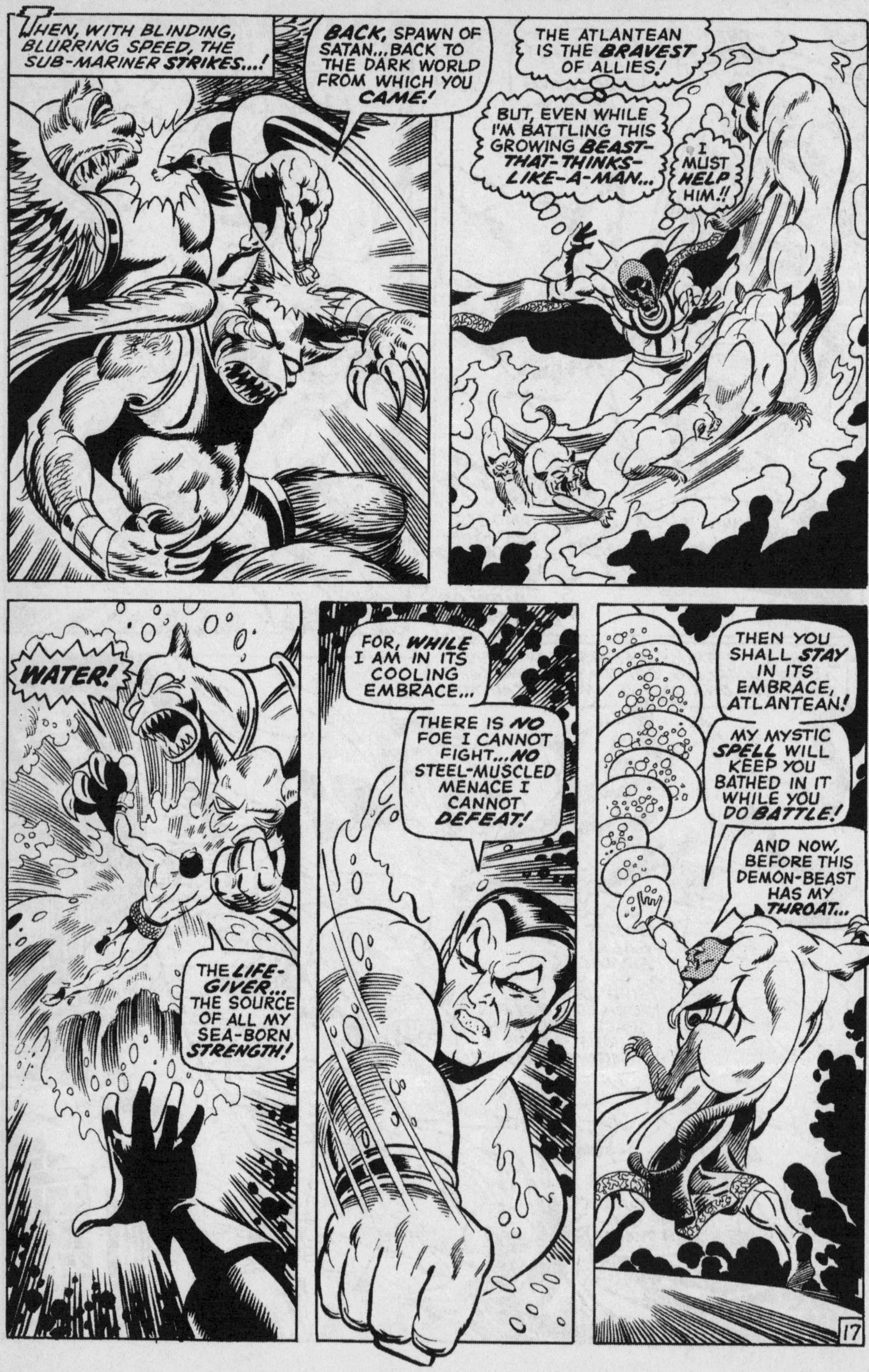
THEN, WITH BLINDING, BLURRING SPEED, THE SUB-MARINER STRIKES...!
BACK, SPAWN OF SATAN...BACK TO THE DARK WORLD FROM WHICH YOU CAME!
THE ATLANTEAN IS THE BRAVEST OF ALLIES!
BUT, EVEN WHILE I'M BATTLING THIS GROWING BEAST-THAT-THINKS-LIKE-A-MAN...
I MUST HELP HIM!!
WATER!
THE LIFE-GIVER... THE SOURCE OF ALL MY SEA-BORN STRENGTH!
FOR, WHILE I AM IN ITS COOLING EMBRACE...
THERE IS NO FOE I CANNOT FIGHT...NO STEEL-MUSCLED MENACE I CANNOT DEFEAT!
THEN YOU SHALL STAY IN ITS EMBRACE, ATLANTEAN!
MY MYSTIC SPELL WILL KEEP YOU BATHED IN IT WHILE YOU DO BATTLE!
AND NOW, BEFORE THIS DEMON-BEAST HAS MY THROAT...
17

...HE MUST *FALL*, BEFORE THE SPELLS BEQUEATHED ME BY THE MIGHTY *VISHANTI* THEMSELVES!

AND, AT THAT SELFSAME INSTANT, WITH A LAST DESPERATE LUNGE...

THE NAMELESS ONE STUMBLED BACK INTO THE *COSMIC GAP!*

BUT THE *FORCE* OF MY LEAP CARRIES ME *WITH* HIM!

MAY *PROTEUS* PRESERVE ME!

WHAT MANNER OF NIGHTMARE-BORN WORLD IS *THIS?*

AND, THOSE MISSHAPEN *FORMS* WHICH LURCH TOWARDS ME....!

THE SUB-MARINER NEEDS *MORE* THAN MERE STRENGTH NOW!

HE NEEDS THE POWER OF DR. STRANGE'S *SORCERY!*

AND, AS SURELY AS I NOW GRASP THIS PIT-SPAWNED *IDOL...*

...THAT POWER SHALL NOT BE *DENIED* HIM!!

18

HALT, YOU WHO CALL YOURSELVES THE *UNDYING ONES!*

IT IS WITH *DR. STRANGE* THAT YOUR QUARREL LIES...NOT WITH THE *ATLANTEAN!*

THE *IDOL!* THE CLOAKED MORTAL HOLDS OUR SOLE LINK WITH THE WORLD OF MAN!

SO MUCH THE *BETTER,* MY *BROTHER...*

...FOR US TO *WREST* IT FROM HIS PUNY GRIP!

NOT *YET,* NAMELESS FIEND!

NOT WHILE THE *FLAMES* OF THE *FALTINE* SURROUND THE IDOL!

...AND FORCE YOU *BACK...BACK...!*

THE TWO-HEADED ONE *RETREATS,* FOR THE MOMENT!

BUT, CAN WE *ESCAPE* THRU THAT YAWNING CHASM, CLOSING IT FOREVER *BEHIND* US...

BEFORE THE *UNDYING ONES* ATTACK ONCE MORE?

NO, NAMOR... WE CANNOT...

FOR, ONE OF US MUST STAY *HERE,* TO HOLD AT BAY THE CLAMORING *HORDES!*

19

THEN, LET THE PEERLESS POWER OF *NAMOR* OPPOSE THE UNDYING ONES!

LET ME PIT *SINEW* AGAINST *SPECTRE* ...AND *MIGHT* AGAINST *MONSTERS!*

YOU ARE *BRAVE*, PRINCE NAMOR!

BUT, BY THE HOARY HOSTS OF HOGGOTH-- --IT IS *DR. STRANGE* WHO MUST REMAIN-- *ALONE!!*

NO-- *NOOO!*

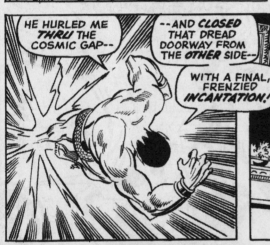

HE HURLED ME *THRU* THE COSMIC GAP--

--AND *CLOSED* THAT DREAD DOORWAY FROM THE *OTHER* SIDE--

WITH A FINAL, FRENZIED *INCANTATION!*

I HAVE RETURNED TO *BOSTON*...TO A PARLOR *RESTORED* FROM PAST *RAVAGES!*

IT IS AS IF ALL THIS *NEVER* HAPPENED!

AND, PERHAPS... IT DID *NOT!*

FOR, WHO IS TO SAY WHAT IS *REAL*...

...AND WHAT THE *FURTIVE* FLIGHT OF *FANTASY!?*

AND YET, *ONE* THING DO I KNOW, AND KNOW *WELL*...

...THAT, AS LONG AS *MEMORY* ENDURES...AND MAN RULES *ABOVE* OR *BELOW* THE TOSSING SEAS...

...HE WILL OWE A *DEBT* TO... *DR. STRANGE!!*

NEXT: THE MAN THEY CALL... *ORKA!*

20

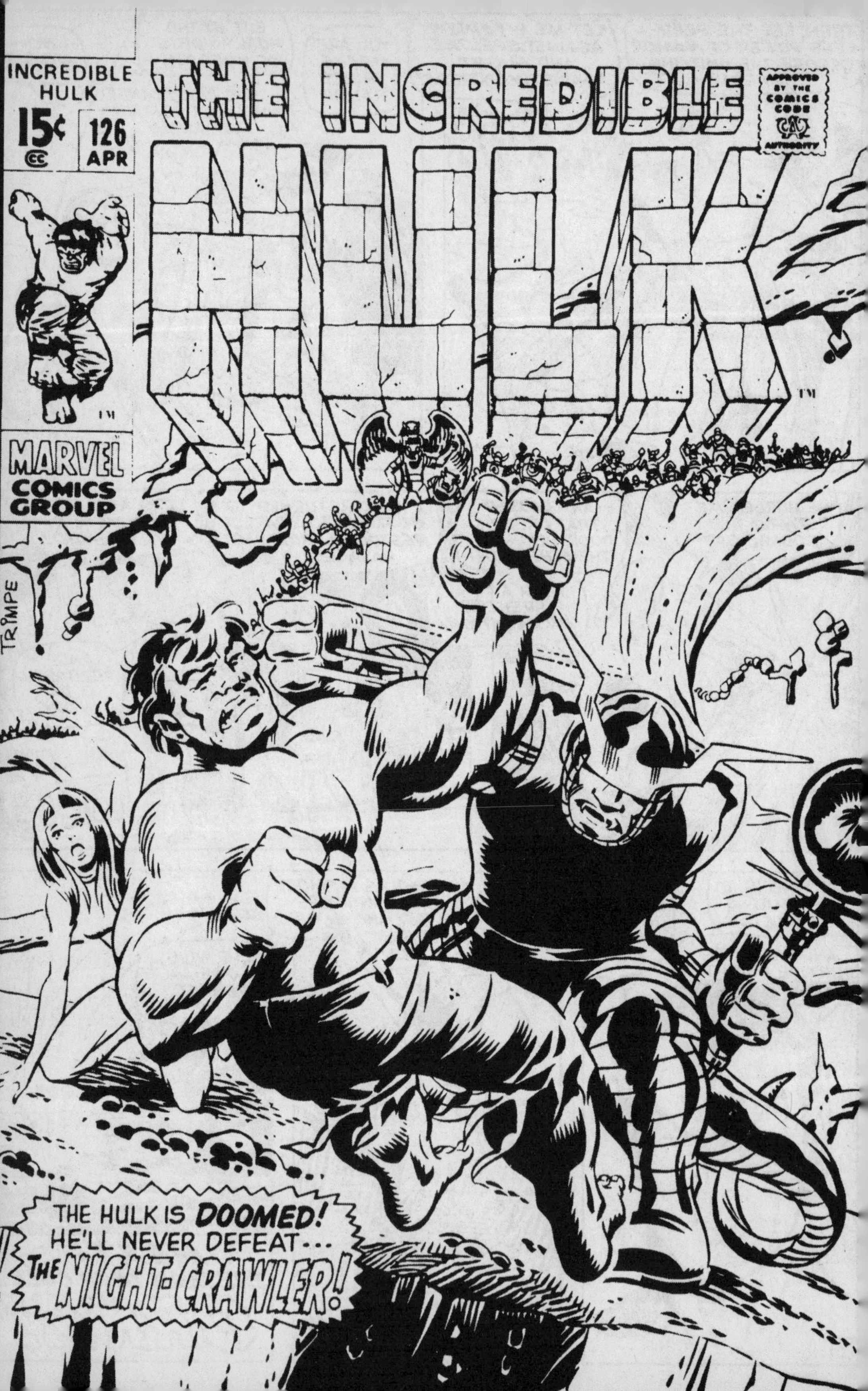
INCREDIBLE HULK
15¢
126 APR
THE INCREDIBLE HULK
APPROVED BY THE COMICS CODE AUTHORITY
MARVEL COMICS GROUP
TRIMPE
THE HULK IS DOOMED! HE'LL NEVER DEFEAT...
THE NIGHT-CRAWLER!

THE INCREDIBLE HULK!

...WHERE STALKS THE NIGHT-CRAWLER!

BRUCE BANNER LIES, FRAIL AND FALLEN, UPON A BARREN HILLSIDE... BUT HE IS NOT ALONE...!

IT'S LUCKY THAT WE SAW HIM BATTLING THE *ABSORBING MAN...* IN HIS ALTER EGO OF THE *HULK!**

YES... LUCKY...!

*LAST ISSUE! --S.

BUT, THERE'S NO MORE TIME TO WASTE ON MERE *WORDS!*

TAKE HIM TO THE *CAR...* AND WITH IT, TO *CLIFF-HOUSE!*

AND, TAKE CARE THAT YOU DON'T *HARM* HIM IN ANY WAY...

...FOR, HE WILL NEED ALL OF THE HULK'S FAMED *POWER,* WHEN HE STANDS...

A JOURNEY INTO REALMS UNKNOWN, WITH YOUR TIRELESS TOUR GUIDES:

STAN LEE • ROY THOMAS • HERB TRIMPE
EDITOR • WRITER • ARTIST

ARTIE SIMEK, *ROAD-MAP SALESMAN*

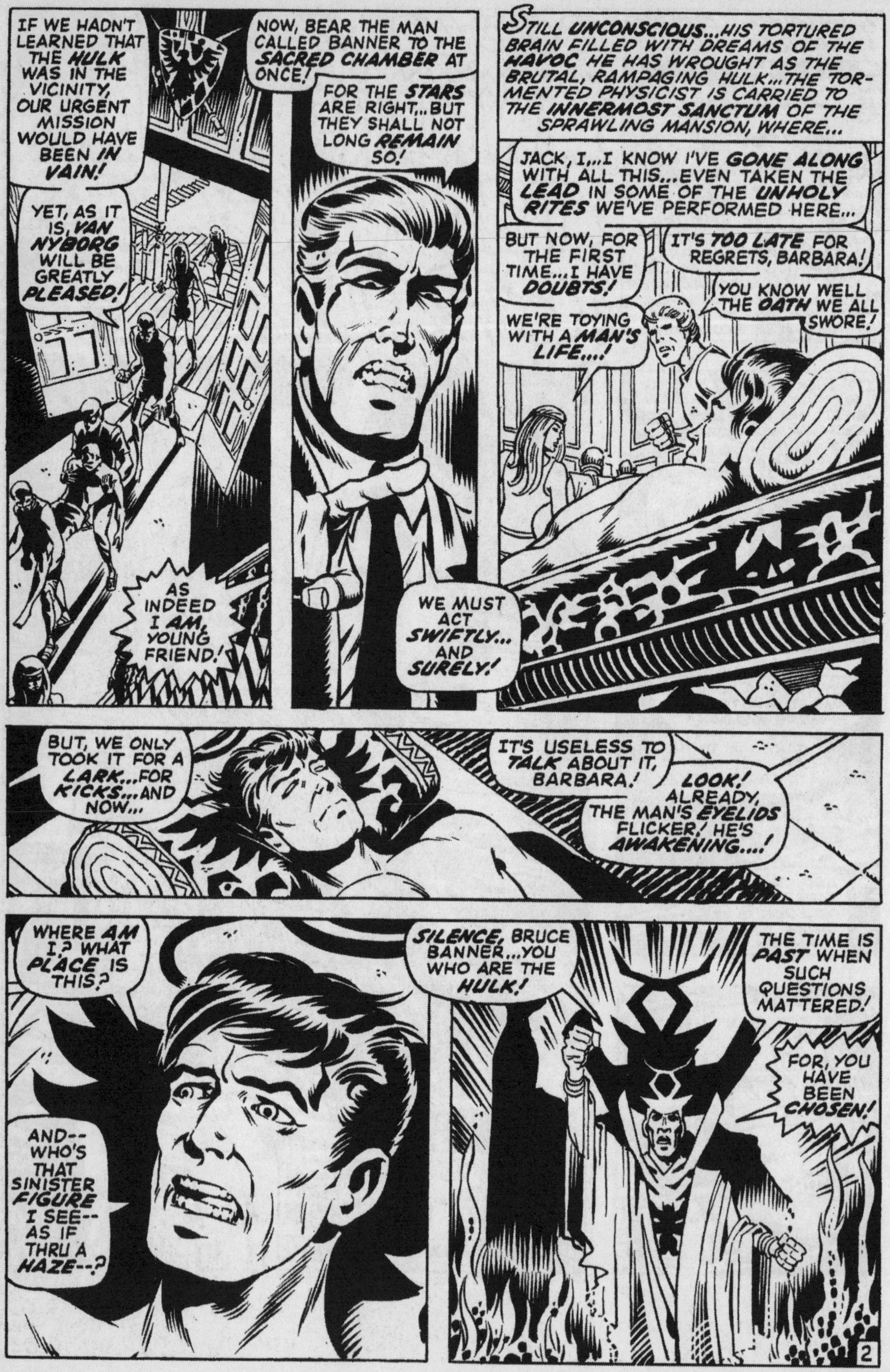
IF WE HADN'T LEARNED THAT THE HULK WAS IN THE VICINITY, OUR URGENT MISSION WOULD HAVE BEEN IN VAIN!
YET, AS IT IS, VAN NYBORG WILL BE GREATLY PLEASED!
AS INDEED I AM, YOUNG FRIEND!
NOW, BEAR THE MAN CALLED BANNER TO THE SACRED CHAMBER AT ONCE!
FOR THE STARS ARE RIGHT... BUT THEY SHALL NOT LONG REMAIN SO!
WE MUST ACT SWIFTLY... AND SURELY!
STILL UNCONSCIOUS... HIS TORTURED BRAIN FILLED WITH DREAMS OF THE HAVOC HE HAS WROUGHT AS THE BRUTAL, RAMPAGING HULK... THE TORMENTED PHYSICIST IS CARRIED TO THE INNERMOST SANCTUM OF THE SPRAWLING MANSION, WHERE...
JACK, I... I KNOW I'VE GONE ALONG WITH ALL THIS... EVEN TAKEN THE LEAD IN SOME OF THE UNHOLY RITES WE'VE PERFORMED HERE...
BUT NOW, FOR THE FIRST TIME... I HAVE DOUBTS!
WE'RE TOYING WITH A MAN'S LIFE...!
IT'S TOO LATE FOR REGRETS, BARBARA!
YOU KNOW WELL THE OATH WE ALL SWORE!
BUT, WE ONLY TOOK IT FOR A LARK... FOR KICKS... AND NOW...
IT'S USELESS TO TALK ABOUT IT, BARBARA!
LOOK! ALREADY, THE MAN'S EYELIDS FLICKER! HE'S AWAKENING...!
WHERE AM I? WHAT PLACE IS THIS?
AND-- WHO'S THAT SINISTER FIGURE I SEE-- AS IF THRU A HAZE--?
SILENCE, BRUCE BANNER... YOU WHO ARE THE HULK!
THE TIME IS PAST WHEN SUCH QUESTIONS MATTERED!
FOR, YOU HAVE BEEN CHOSEN!

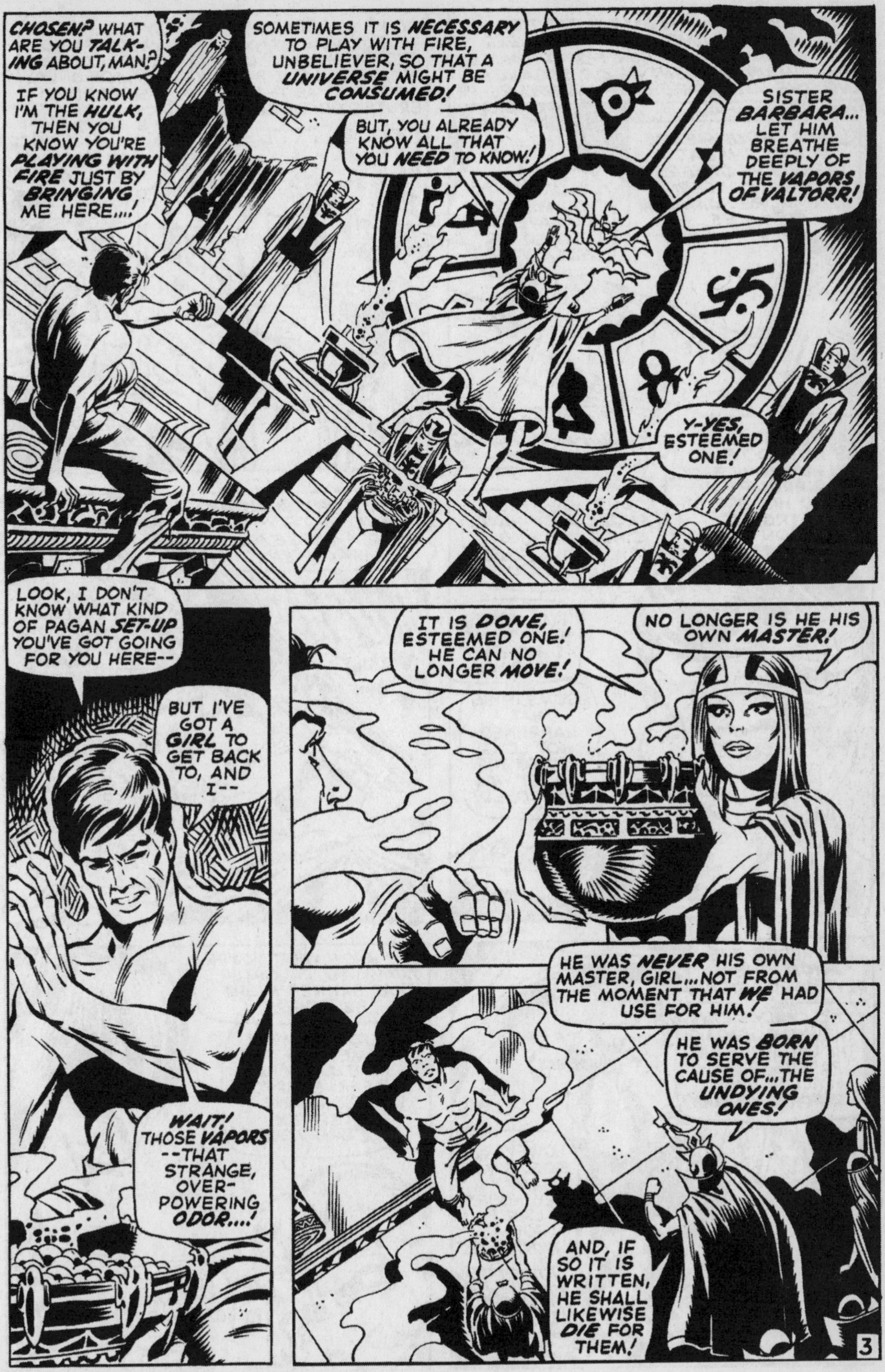
CHOSEN? WHAT ARE YOU TALKING ABOUT, MAN?
IF YOU KNOW I'M THE HULK, THEN YOU KNOW YOU'RE PLAYING WITH FIRE JUST BY BRINGING ME HERE...!
SOMETIMES IT IS NECESSARY TO PLAY WITH FIRE, UNBELIEVER, SO THAT A UNIVERSE MIGHT BE CONSUMED!
BUT, YOU ALREADY KNOW ALL THAT YOU NEED TO KNOW!
SISTER BARBARA... LET HIM BREATHE DEEPLY OF THE VAPORS OF VALTORR!
Y-YES, ESTEEMED ONE!
LOOK, I DON'T KNOW WHAT KIND OF PAGAN SET-UP YOU'VE GOT GOING FOR YOU HERE--
BUT I'VE GOT A GIRL TO GET BACK TO, AND I--
WAIT! THOSE VAPORS --THAT STRANGE, OVER-POWERING ODOR...!
IT IS DONE, ESTEEMED ONE! HE CAN NO LONGER MOVE!
NO LONGER IS HE HIS OWN MASTER!
HE WAS NEVER HIS OWN MASTER, GIRL... NOT FROM THE MOMENT THAT WE HAD USE FOR HIM!
HE WAS BORN TO SERVE THE CAUSE OF... THE UNDYING ONES!
AND, IF SO IT IS WRITTEN, HE SHALL LIKEWISE DIE FOR THEM!
3

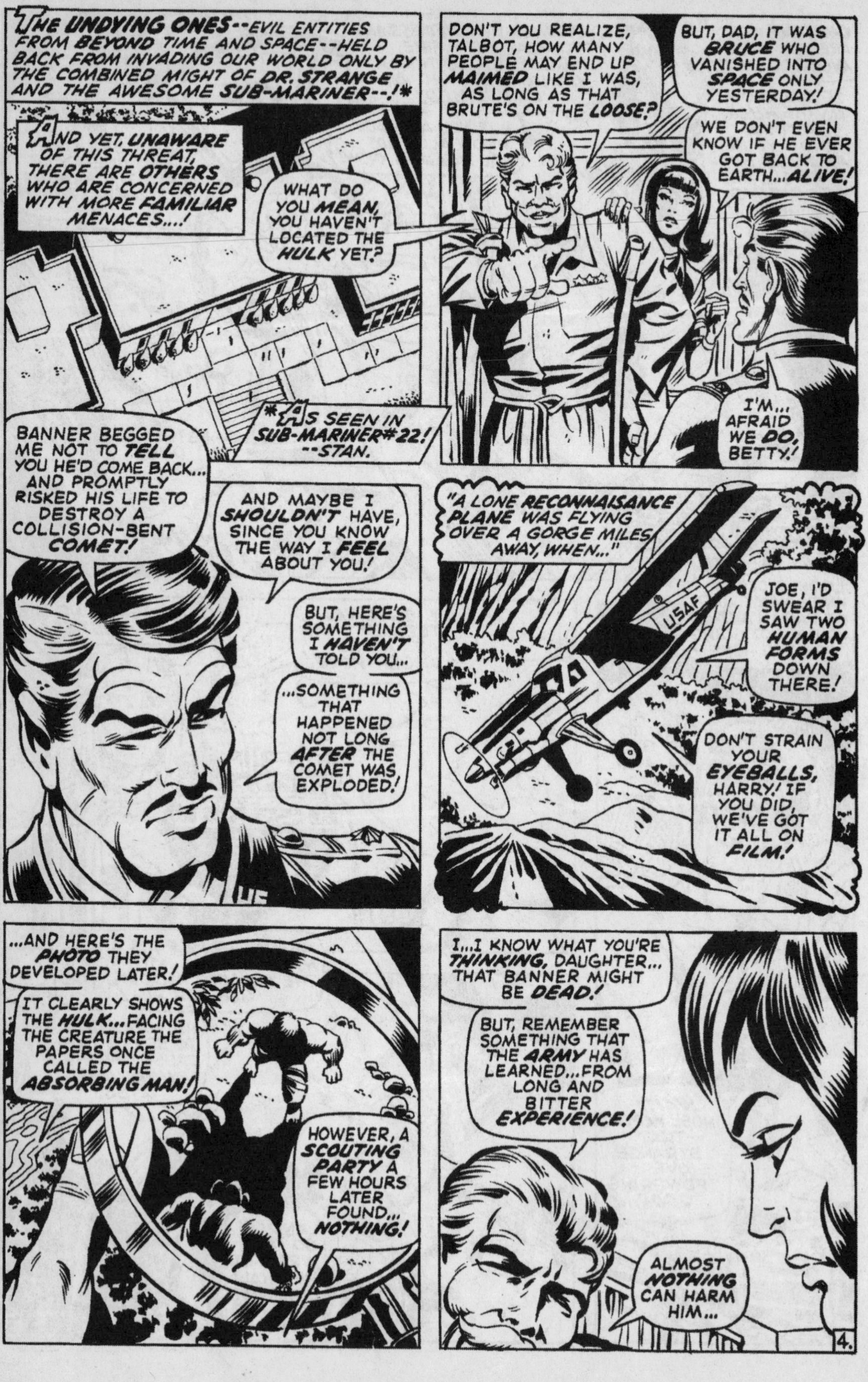
THE UNDYING ONES--EVIL ENTITIES FROM BEYOND TIME AND SPACE--HELD BACK FROM INVADING OUR WORLD ONLY BY THE COMBINED MIGHT OF DR. STRANGE AND THE AWESOME SUB-MARINER--!*
AND YET, UNAWARE OF THIS THREAT, THERE ARE OTHERS WHO ARE CONCERNED WITH MORE FAMILIAR MENACES...!
WHAT DO YOU MEAN, YOU HAVEN'T LOCATED THE HULK YET?
*AS SEEN IN SUB-MARINER #22! --STAN.
DON'T YOU REALIZE, TALBOT, HOW MANY PEOPLE MAY END UP MAIMED LIKE I WAS, AS LONG AS THAT BRUTE'S ON THE LOOSE?
BUT, DAD, IT WAS BRUCE WHO VANISHED INTO SPACE ONLY YESTERDAY!
WE DON'T EVEN KNOW IF HE EVER GOT BACK TO EARTH...ALIVE!
I'M... AFRAID WE DO, BETTY!
BANNER BEGGED ME NOT TO TELL YOU HE'D COME BACK... AND PROMPTLY RISKED HIS LIFE TO DESTROY A COLLISION-BENT COMET!
AND MAYBE I SHOULDN'T HAVE, SINCE YOU KNOW THE WAY I FEEL ABOUT YOU!
BUT, HERE'S SOMETHING I HAVEN'T TOLD YOU...
...SOMETHING THAT HAPPENED NOT LONG AFTER THE COMET WAS EXPLODED!
"A LONE RECONNAISANCE PLANE WAS FLYING OVER A GORGE MILES AWAY, WHEN..."
USAF
JOE, I'D SWEAR I SAW TWO HUMAN FORMS DOWN THERE!
DON'T STRAIN YOUR EYEBALLS, HARRY! IF YOU DID, WE'VE GOT IT ALL ON FILM!
...AND HERE'S THE PHOTO THEY DEVELOPED LATER!
IT CLEARLY SHOWS THE HULK...FACING THE CREATURE THE PAPERS ONCE CALLED THE ABSORBING MAN!
HOWEVER, A SCOUTING PARTY A FEW HOURS LATER FOUND... NOTHING!
I...I KNOW WHAT YOU'RE THINKING, DAUGHTER... THAT BANNER MIGHT BE DEAD!
BUT, REMEMBER SOMETHING THAT THE ARMY HAS LEARNED...FROM LONG AND BITTER EXPERIENCE!
ALMOST NOTHING CAN HARM HIM...
4.

"...AS LONG AS HE REMAINS THE *HULK!*"

BRUCE BANNER, WE HAVE *NEED* OF YOU,...BUT NOT IN THE FRAGILE FORM YOU *NOW* WEAR!

IT IS THE *HULK* WE NEED... FOR ONLY *HE* CAN DESTROY THE GREATEST *ENEMY* OF THE *UNDYING ONES...*

...AND CLEAR THE WAY FOR THEIR *TRIUMPHAL RETURN* TO EARTH!

FORGET IT... *MANDRAKE....!*

THOSE *VAPORS* MADE ME SO GROGGY,...I *COULDN'T* BECOME THE HULK...EVEN IF I *WANTED* TO!

WE SHALL *SEE* IF THAT HOLDS TRUE, *FOOL'...*

...WHEN YOU FACE THE ONE WHO HAS EVER BEEN CALLED... THE *NIGHT-CRAWLER!*

LET THE *RITES* BEGIN...LET THE *WHEEL* TURN!

AND NOW, LET THE WONDROUS *WORDS* BE SPOKEN!

LET THE SPINNING *DISK* BE WHIRLED, LIKE THE WINDS OF WILD *WATOOMB...* LET THE *MAN* WHO THUS IS HURLED USHER IN A PLANET'S *DOOM....!*

LET *SATANNISH* GRANT THEE POWER... AND *DORMAMMU* GIVE THEE SPEED... THAT ERE LONG MAY SOUND THE HOUR *THE UNDYING ONES ARE FREED!!*

GOOD LORD! THIS--CAN'T BE--!

I FEEL LIKE I'M HURTLING THRU *SPACE*-- THRU *TIME* ITSELF!

I'M NO LONGER IN THE SAME *ROOM*--NO LONGER ANYWHERE ON *EARTH!*

BUT, *WHERE* AM I GOING?

WHERE??

5.

MEANWHILE, WHAT OF *ANOTHER* MORTAL WHO OPPOSES THE RETURN OF THE *UNDY-ING ONES?* WHAT OF HIM THE WORLD CALLS... *DOCTOR STRANGE?*

AT THIS VERY MOMENT, HE FLOATS *HELP-LESS...* THE WILLING *CAPTIVE* OF HIS NAMELESS FOES... ONE WHO *SACRIFICED* HIMSELF TO PROTECT THE GREAT GREEN HILLS OF *EARTH...!*

STILL THE MORTAL WILL NOT SPEAK!

STILL HE *REFUSES* TO HELP US PASS INTO THE *OUTER WORLD,* WHERE WE MIGHT REGAIN OUR *RULE* OVER MANKIND!

DO NOT BE *DISMAYED,* BROTHER MINE!

EVEN ONE SUCH AS HE CANNOT WITHSTAND OUR *PRESSURES --FOREVER!*

BUT, *FOREVER* IS NOT OURS TO *WAIT!*

SOON, THE *STARS* WILL BE RIGHT NO MORE... AND WE MUST BEGIN ANEW THE *THOUSAND-YEAR* WAIT!

YOU *FORGET,* BROTHER... YOU WHO SHARE MY *BODY* IF NOT MY *THOUGHTS...*

...THE MAN VAN NYBORG HAS EVEN NOW SENT A *CHAMPION* TO BATTLE AGAINST THE DREADED *NIGHT-CRAWLER...*

...HE WHOSE *DARK DIMENSION* MAY BECOME OUR *ALTERNATE PATHWAY* TO *REALITY!*

IF THE *GREEN-SKINNED HULK FALLS...* HE DIES!

BUT, IF HE *TRIUMPHS* ... THEN THE *ENTIRE EARTH* FALLS!!

6

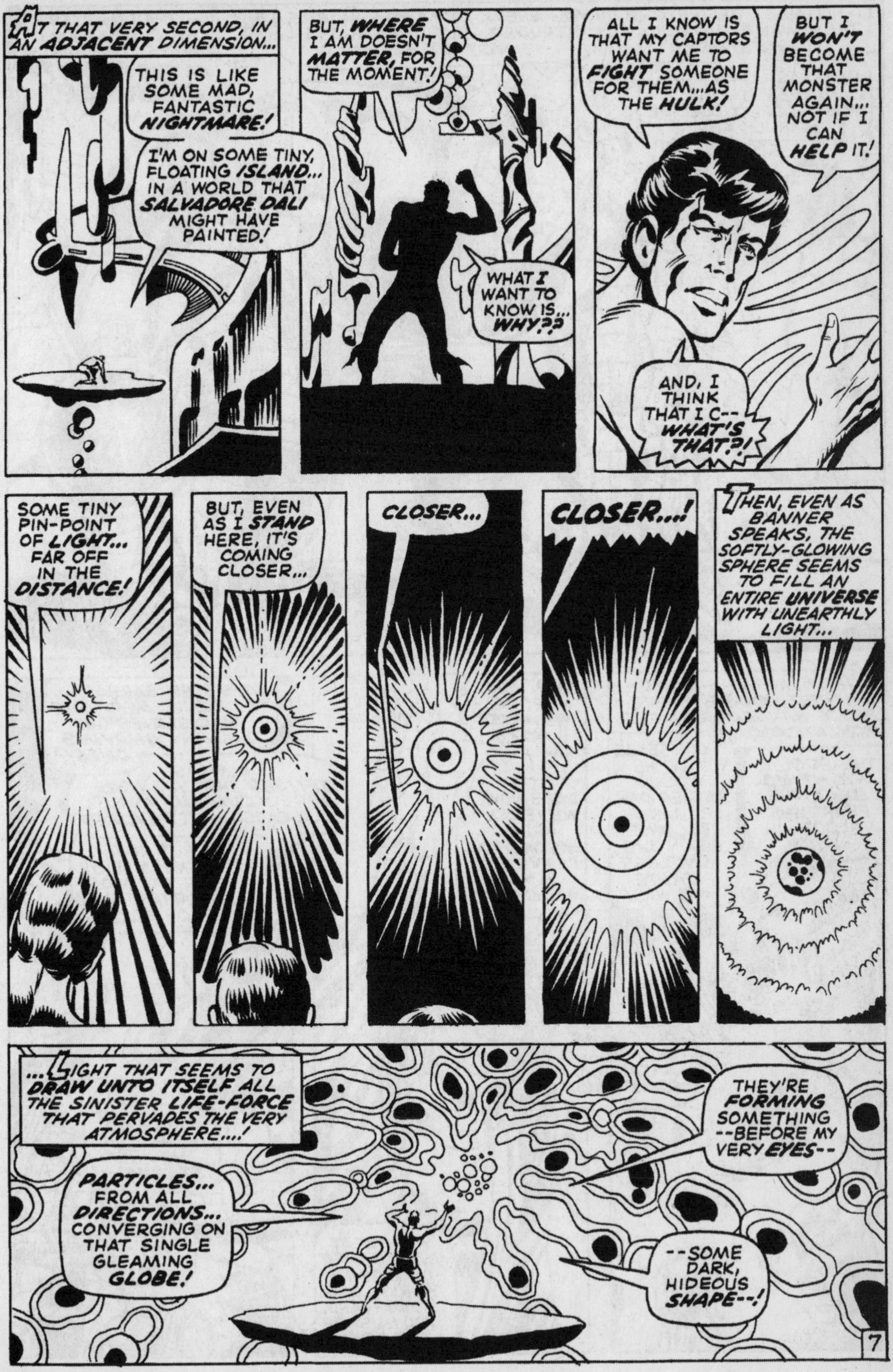
AT THAT VERY SECOND, IN AN ADJACENT DIMENSION...
THIS IS LIKE SOME MAD, FANTASTIC NIGHTMARE!
I'M ON SOME TINY, FLOATING ISLAND... IN A WORLD THAT SALVADORE DALI MIGHT HAVE PAINTED!
BUT, WHERE I AM DOESN'T MATTER, FOR THE MOMENT!
WHAT I WANT TO KNOW IS... WHY??
ALL I KNOW IS THAT MY CAPTORS WANT ME TO FIGHT SOMEONE FOR THEM...AS THE HULK!
BUT I WON'T BECOME THAT MONSTER AGAIN... NOT IF I CAN HELP IT!
AND, I THINK THAT I C-- WHAT'S THAT?!
SOME TINY PIN-POINT OF LIGHT... FAR OFF IN THE DISTANCE!
BUT, EVEN AS I STAND HERE, IT'S COMING CLOSER...
CLOSER...
CLOSER...!
THEN, EVEN AS BANNER SPEAKS, THE SOFTLY-GLOWING SPHERE SEEMS TO FILL AN ENTIRE UNIVERSE WITH UNEARTHLY LIGHT...
...LIGHT THAT SEEMS TO DRAW UNTO ITSELF ALL THE SINISTER LIFE-FORCE THAT PERVADES THE VERY ATMOSPHERE....!
PARTICLES... FROM ALL DIRECTIONS... CONVERGING ON THAT SINGLE GLEAMING GLOBE!
THEY'RE FORMING SOMETHING --BEFORE MY VERY EYES--
--SOME DARK, HIDEOUS SHAPE--!
7

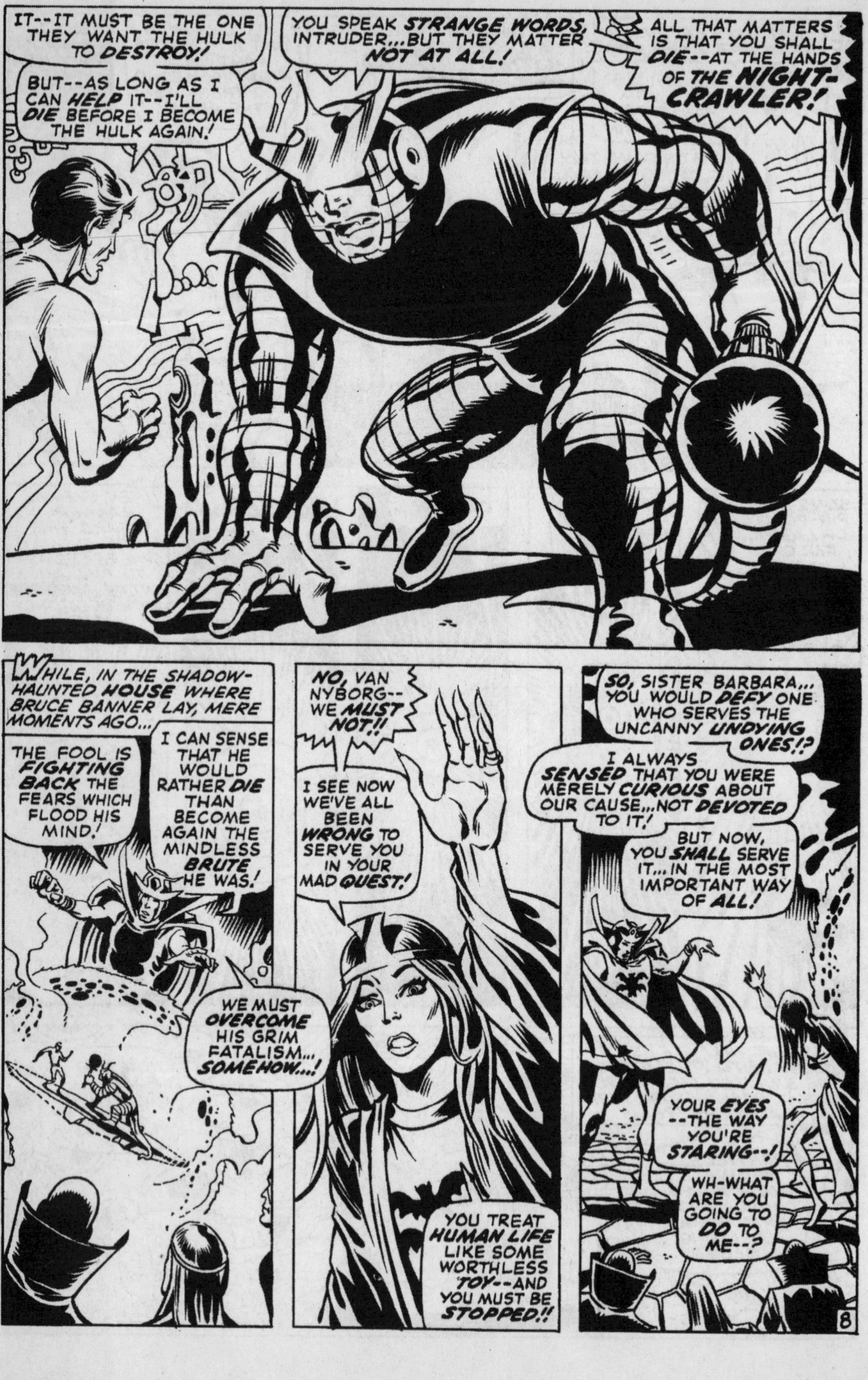
IT--IT MUST BE THE ONE THEY WANT THE HULK TO DESTROY!
BUT--AS LONG AS I CAN HELP IT--I'LL DIE BEFORE I BECOME THE HULK AGAIN!
YOU SPEAK STRANGE WORDS, INTRUDER,...BUT THEY MATTER NOT AT ALL!
ALL THAT MATTERS IS THAT YOU SHALL DIE--AT THE HANDS OF THE NIGHT-CRAWLER!
WHILE, IN THE SHADOW-HAUNTED HOUSE WHERE BRUCE BANNER LAY, MERE MOMENTS AGO...
THE FOOL IS FIGHTING BACK THE FEARS WHICH FLOOD HIS MIND!
I CAN SENSE THAT HE WOULD RATHER DIE THAN BECOME AGAIN THE MINDLESS BRUTE HE WAS!
WE MUST OVERCOME HIS GRIM FATALISM... SOMEHOW...!
NO, VAN NYBORG--WE MUST NOT!!
I SEE NOW WE'VE ALL BEEN WRONG TO SERVE YOU IN YOUR MAD QUEST!
YOU TREAT HUMAN LIFE LIKE SOME WORTHLESS TOY--AND YOU MUST BE STOPPED!!
SO, SISTER BARBARA... YOU WOULD DEFY ONE WHO SERVES THE UNCANNY UNDYING ONES!?
I ALWAYS SENSED THAT YOU WERE MERELY CURIOUS ABOUT OUR CAUSE... NOT DEVOTED TO IT!
BUT NOW, YOU SHALL SERVE IT... IN THE MOST IMPORTANT WAY OF ALL!
YOUR EYES--THE WAY YOU'RE STARING--!
WH-WHAT ARE YOU GOING TO DO TO ME--?
8

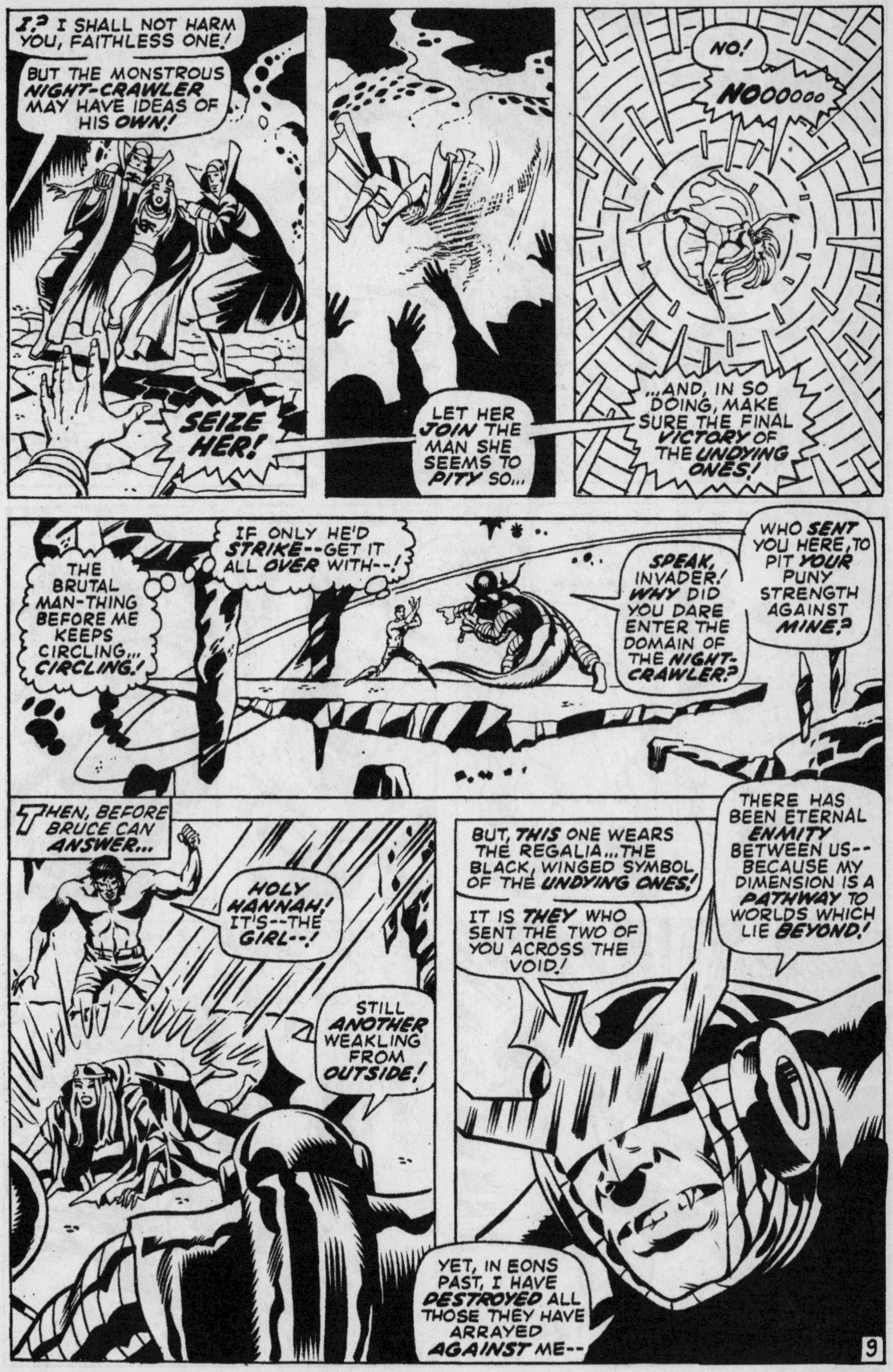

I.? I SHALL NOT HARM YOU, FAITHLESS ONE!
BUT THE MONSTROUS NIGHT-CRAWLER MAY HAVE IDEAS OF HIS OWN!
SEIZE HER!
LET HER JOIN THE MAN SHE SEEMS TO PITY SO...
NO!
NOOOooo
...AND, IN SO DOING, MAKE SURE THE FINAL VICTORY OF THE UNDYING ONES!
THE BRUTAL MAN-THING BEFORE ME KEEPS CIRCLING... CIRCLING.!
IF ONLY HE'D STRIKE--GET IT ALL OVER WITH--!
SPEAK, INVADER! WHY DID YOU DARE ENTER THE DOMAIN OF THE NIGHT-CRAWLER?
WHO SENT YOU HERE, TO PIT YOUR PUNY STRENGTH AGAINST MINE?
THEN, BEFORE BRUCE CAN ANSWER...
HOLY HANNAH! IT'S--THE GIRL--!
STILL ANOTHER WEAKLING FROM OUTSIDE!
BUT, THIS ONE WEARS THE REGALIA...THE BLACK, WINGED SYMBOL OF THE UNDYING ONES!
IT IS THEY WHO SENT THE TWO OF YOU ACROSS THE VOID!
THERE HAS BEEN ETERNAL ENMITY BETWEEN US--BECAUSE MY DIMENSION IS A PATHWAY TO WORLDS WHICH LIE BEYOND!
YET, IN EONS PAST, I HAVE DESTROYED ALL THOSE THEY HAVE ARRAYED AGAINST ME--

NOR SHALL *YOU* SUFFER ANY *DIFFERENT* FATE!

HE GRABBED THE *GIRL*-- BECAUSE SHE WAS *CLOSEST!*

I SWORE I *WOULDN'T* BECOME THE HULK...THAT I'D *FIGHT DOWN* THE RACING PULSE...THE FRANTIC HEARTBEAT!

AND I *WOULD*...EVEN THOUGH IT MEANT I *DIED* IN THIS FEARFUL, FORSAKEN WORLD!

BUT THAT *GIRL*-- SHE'S SO *HELPLESS* --SO *TERRIFIED*--!

NO! IT CAN'T BE HAPPENING--I WON'T *LET* IT--!

MY HEART'S GOING LIKE A *TRIP-HAMMER*...

MY *BRAIN*-- IT'S LIKE A THING *AFIRE*...!

WAIT! NOW-- THE PAIN-- HAS *STOPPED!*

PAIN IS FOR *WEAKER* MEN--

--FOR MEN LIKE *BRUCE BANNER*--

--NOT FOR THE *HULK!!*

SO, A *LARGER* CREATURE HAS TAKEN THE PLACE OF A *SMALLER* ONE!

THE UNDYING ONES WERE NOT *QUITE* SO FOOLISH AS I *IMAGINED!*

AND YET--*HE* TOO SHALL *DIE*--LIKE ALL THE *OTHERS!*

THE HULK IS *NOT* LIKE ANY OTHERS!

10

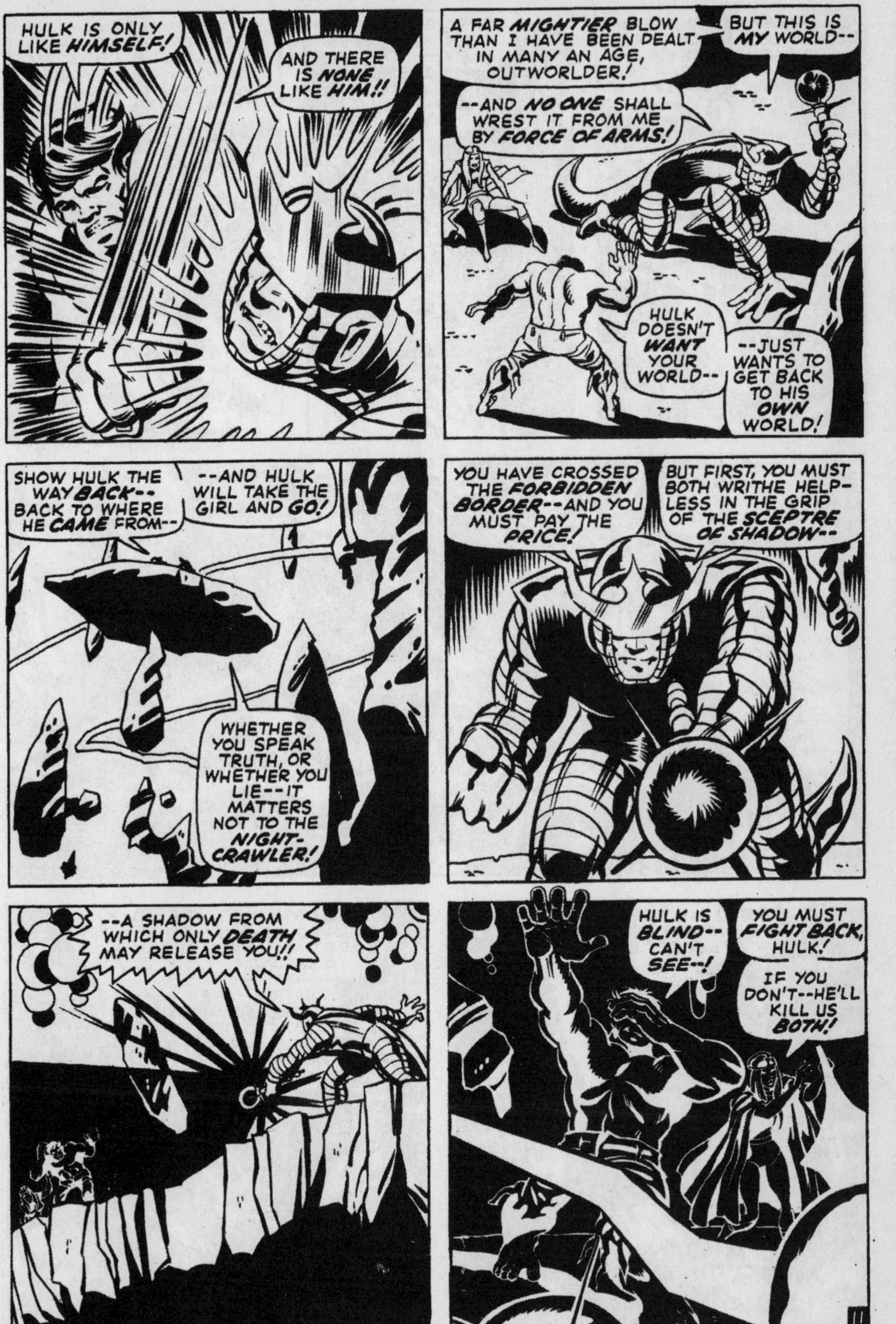
HULK IS ONLY LIKE HIMSELF!
AND THERE IS NONE LIKE HIM!!
A FAR MIGHTIER BLOW THAN I HAVE BEEN DEALT IN MANY AN AGE, OUTWORLDER!
BUT THIS IS MY WORLD--
--AND NO ONE SHALL WREST IT FROM ME BY FORCE OF ARMS!
HULK DOESN'T WANT YOUR WORLD--
--JUST WANTS TO GET BACK TO HIS OWN WORLD!
SHOW HULK THE WAY BACK--BACK TO WHERE HE CAME FROM--
--AND HULK WILL TAKE THE GIRL AND GO!
WHETHER YOU SPEAK TRUTH, OR WHETHER YOU LIE--IT MATTERS NOT TO THE NIGHT-CRAWLER!
YOU HAVE CROSSED THE FORBIDDEN BORDER--AND YOU MUST PAY THE PRICE!
BUT FIRST, YOU MUST BOTH WRITHE HELP-LESS IN THE GRIP OF THE SCEPTRE OF SHADOW--
--A SHADOW FROM WHICH ONLY DEATH MAY RELEASE YOU!!
HULK IS BLIND--CAN'T SEE--!
YOU MUST FIGHT BACK, HULK!
IF YOU DON'T--HE'LL KILL US BOTH!
11

YES--*FIGHT BACK*--MUST FIGHT BACK!

BUT *HOW*--AGAINST AN ENEMY HULK CAN'T *SEE*--?

PERHAPS THE SOUND OF MY *VOICE* CAN HELP YOU, LOWLY ONE!

MONSTER IS *BEHIND* HULK--MOCKING HIM!

IF ONLY HULK COULD *SEE*--COULD *TOUCH*--!

IN A MOMENT, INTRUDER, YOU SHALL TOUCH *NOTHING* AT ALL--

AND THEN, YOU SHALL BE EVEN *MORE* HELPLESS THAN *NOW!*

--*UNNHH!*

HE *PUSHED* HULK! HULK IS *FALLING!!*

NO--*NOT FALLING*--JUST *DRIFTING*, LIKE A FEATHER IN THE WIND!

AND SO YOU *SHALL* DRIFT, YOUR VAUNTED STRENGTH OF NO *USE* TO YOU--

--TILL THE END OF *ETERNITY* ITSELF!

STILL CAN'T *SEE!* HULK HAS NEVER BEEN--SO *HELPLESS* BEFORE!

IF HULK COULD JUST *TOUCH* SOME-THING--*ANY-THING*--!

WAIT! HAND BRUSHED *AGAINST* SOMETHING--FOR A SECOND!

MUST BE--ONE OF THE *ISLANDS* THAT FLOAT IN THIS *AIR-THAT-IS-NOT-AIR!*

12

YES... *THAT'S* WHAT IT IS!

HULK DRIFTS NO MORE... BUT STILL CAN'T *SEE!*

HULK HAS NEVER FELT SO *HELPLESS* ...SO *ALONE* BEFORE!

BUT, EVEN IF HULK CAN'T *SEE*...

HE CAN STILL *HIT!*

IN THE GRIP OF A TOWERING, OVER-WHELMING RAGE, THE MAN-MONSTER STRIKES THE WEIRD FLOATING MASS WITH ALL OF HIS GAMMA-RAY-SPAWNED MIGHT...

THROOOM!

...CREATING AN ACCIDENTAL RELEASE OF HEAT AND FLASHING LIGHT WHICH ILLUMINES AN EONS-DARK COSMOS....!

MY *EYES!* THE LIGHT IS *PAINFUL--* UNBEARABLE TO THEM--!

NEVER, IN AGES UNTOLD, HAVE I FOUGHT A FOE WITH SUCH SHEER, RAW *POWER!*

13

AT LAST HULK CAN *SEE* AGAIN!

BUT, STILL CAN'T REACH THE ONE WHO *CRAWLS*... OR THE *GIRL!*

AND YOU NEVER *SHALL,* INTRUDER!

MY SACRED *SCEPTRE* HAS FAR *DEADLIER* POWERS THAN MERELY THE *SPREADING* OF *DARKNESS!*

AND NOW-- I SHALL *UNLEASH* THEM!

NO! YOU CAN'T--YOU *MUSTN'T!*

HE MEANS YOU NO *HARM*-- HE WISHES ONLY TO PRO-TECT *ME!*

WHAT DOES *THAT* MATTER TO SUCH AS *I?*

ONE SINGLE, SEARING *BLAST*--AND HE SHALL TROUBLE ME *NO MORE!*

DIDN'T YOU *HEAR* ME, YOU *MONSTER?*

I SAID... *NO!!*

S M A S H !

MY SCEPTRE-- *DESTROYED*-- BY ONE OF THE *FRAGMENTS* WHICH STRUCK THIS ISLE!

ONLY THEIR ACCURSED *LIGHT-ENERGY* COULD HAVE DONE SUCH A DEED!

WHAT *MILLENNIUMS* OF *SAVAGE* FOES FAILED TO DO--SHE DID IN ONE RASH, UNTHINKING *MOMENT!*

BUT, YOU SHALL NOT LONG *SAVOR* YOUR FLEETING TRIUMPH, *FEMALE!*

YOU SHALL PAY THE *PRICE*--AND PAY IT *DEARLY!*

STAY *BACK!* KEEP AWAY FROM ME--!!

14.

THE *GIRL!* HE IS MENACING THE *GIRL!*

BUT, THE GIRL *SAVED* HULK--

--AND *HE* MUST DO THE SAME FOR *HER!!*

THWAM!

HULK DID IT!!

HULK SAVED THE GIRL!

KRAAK!

YOU CONFUSE A MOMENTARY *SUCCESS* WITH AN IRREVERSIBLE *VICTORY,* FOOL!

WHATEVER YOUR *PHYSICAL MIGHT,* THAT IS *ALL* THAT YOU HAVE--

15

--WHILE THE *NIGHT-CRAWLER* HAS MUCH, MUCH *MORE!*

THEN, FROM THE STRANGE AND SINISTER CROWN WHICH MASKS HIS BROW, THE DARK-BORN DEMON EMITS SONIC BEAMS OF INDESCRIBABLE FORCE--

REEEEOOO

--*WHICH BOMBARD THE GREEN GOLIATH WITH STAGGERING INTENSITY!*

YOU WILL NOT *STAND* LONG BEFORE ME, INVADER!

NEVER AGAIN SHALL YOU ACT AS THE POWERFUL PAWN OF MY IMMORTAL *FOES!*

OOOOOOOOEEE

CAN'T STAND-- MUCH MORE SOUND--!

BUT-- HULK IS *NO MAN'S* PAWN!

EEEEEE-EE

NO MAN'S!!

EEOO

DO YOU HEAR??

KLAP!

16

IT--CANNOT BE!!

THAT SINGLE THUNDEROUS HANDCLAP HAS *DEFLECTED* MY SONIC IMPULSES--

--TURNED THEM BACK UPON MY OWN *COSMOS*--

--A COSMOS WHICH IS BEING-- *RIPPED ASUNDER!!*

HULK DID NOT KNOW--HIS OWN *STRENGTH!*

ONLY THIS ONE *PLACE* REMAINS--THE ONE WE'RE *STANDING* ON--!

KEE-RAAAAK

AND IT'S GOING *TOO*, HULK! IT'S--

--FALLING APART!

WE'RE DOOMED-- *DOOMED!!*

SILENCE, FOOLISH FEMALE!

DEATH IS NOT FOR SUCH AS THE *NIGHT-CRAWLER!*

MY IMMORTAL *AURA*--WHICH ENVELOPES YOU AS WELL AS ME--CAN SEND US INTO ANY OF THE *OTHER* DIMENSIONS WHICH EXIST ALONGSIDE THIS ONE!

THUS, IT CAN TRANSPORT US WHERE I WISH TO GO--

--TO THE UNIVERSE OF THE *UNDYING* ONES THEMSELVES!!

THEN, AS THE LAST SHATTERED FRAGMENTS OF A NIGHT-SHROUDED WORLD SPLINTER INTO *NOTHINGNESS*, THREE FLOATING FORMS VANISH FROM SIGHT...

17

...ONLY TO REAPPEAR IN ANOTHER, EVEN MORE *SAVAGE SPHERE*...

...NEAR THE SILENT, UNMOVING FIGURE OF *DR. STRANGE*...!

BEHOLD, MY BROTHER-- 'TIS THE DARK-SPAWNED *NIGHT-CRAWLER!*

IF HE FREES THE *MORTAL*-- IF THE CAPTIVE SORCERER ESCAPES US--

WE SHALL BE *TRAPPED* IN THIS *BARREN* WORLD--FOR YET ANOTHER *MILLENNIUM!*

THEN, YOUR UNHOLY EXILE IS *ASSURED*, YOU WHO ARE CALLED THE *NAMELESS ONE!*

FOR, IT WAS *YOU* WHO CAUSED THE GREEN-SKINNED ONE TO *DESTROY* MY DOMAIN!

AND, IF THE *NIGHT-CRAWLER'S* COSMOS IS NO MORE--

HE SHALL HAVE *YOURS*--

--THOUGH HE MUST DO BATTLE WITH ALL YOUR GHASTLY *HORDES* BEFORE HE MAY CALL IT *HIS!*

WHAT I *PRAYED* FOR--HAS COME TO *PASS!*

BY THE TIME THE BATTLE IS DONE, THE *STARS* WILL BE WRONG--AND THE EARTH BE *SPARED* AT LEAST CENTURIES LONGER!

THUS, DR. STRANGE CAN DIE *HAPPY*, HERE WITHIN POLES OF ETHEREAL FORCE!

YOU WANT OUT, WEIRD ONE? *HULK* CAN FREE YOU--!

NO, HULK--EVEN YOUR BATTERING *FISTS* WOULD BE USELESS AGAINST THE MYSTIC POLES!

HE CAN ONLY BE FREE--IF SOMEONE TAKES HIS *PLACE!*

WHAT ARE YOU DOING? *KEEP BACK--!*

TOO LATE! ALREADY, I FEEL THE POLES BEGIN TO GRASP *YOU--*

18

--AND CAST ME FREE!

BUT *YOU,* GIRL--WHY DID YOU *SACRIFICE* YOURSELF FOR ONE WHOM YOU'VE *NEVER MET?*

VAN NYBORG TOLD US OF *YOUR* SACRIFICE--TO SAVE A WORLD WHICH *SHUNNED* YOU!

COULD I DO *LESS*-- I, WHO HELPED TO SEND THE HELPLESS *BRUCE BANNER* INTO UNKNOWN REALMS?

BETTER *I* SHOULD PERISH--THAN ANY *OTHER!*

NOW *GO*-- YOU MUST *HURRY*--!

WHY MUST WE HURRY? AND WHERE CAN WE *GO?*

THERE'S SO MUCH-- HULK DOESN'T *UNDERSTAND*--!

NOR DO YOU *NEED* TO KNOW, MONSTER THAT ONCE WAS *MAN!*

NOW, BE *SILENT* --THAT I MAY SPEAK A *SPELL* WHILE THE UNDYING ONES ARE *TOO* ENGROSSED TO *PREVENT* ME!

BY THE SERAPHIM'S SILENT CHANT-- AND BY MUNNOPOR'S MYSTIC MOON--

MAY OMNISCIENT *OSHTUR* GRANT--

--THIS FATEFUL, FINAL BOON--!!

WE ARE *GONE* FROM PLACE WHERE MAN-BEASTS WALK THE *SKY!*

BUT, HULK FEELS *FUNNY*-- HEAD *SPINNING*--!

OSHTUR BE PRAISED-- WE ARE *HOME* AGAIN!

MY *SANCTUM SANCTORUM* STANDS BEFORE ME, AFTER ALL THESE *MONTHS!*

BUT, THE *MONSTER* WHO ACCIDENTALLY BEFRIENDED ME--

--HAS BECOME A *WEARY, WEAKENED MAN!*

I'M--ALL *RIGHT!* PLEASE *LEAVE* ME--FOR YOUR *OWN* SAKE--!

19

AN UNCOMPREHENDING WORLD HAS CALLED DR. STRANGE MANY THINGS, BRUCE BANNER!

YET, IT HAS NEVER SAID THAT HE ABANDONED A FRIEND--

--OR THAT HE FEARED TO HELP A FELLOW HUMAN IN NEED!

...THESE OLD CLOTHES OF MINE WILL MAKE BOTH OF US FEEL LIKE NORMAL BEINGS AGAIN!

THEN, WHEN YOUR DIZZINESS PASSES, WE'LL BOTH BE LEAVING!

IT HAS BEEN, FOR LONG YEARS...

I'LL BE ALL RIGHT--IN A MOMENT!

BUT, YOU SPOKE OF LEAVING! ISN'T THIS-- YOUR HOME?

STILL, THERE COMES A TIME TO PUT ASIDE THE TRAPPINGS OF A FORMER LIFE--

--AND WALK AMONG MEN-- AS A MAN!

WITH THE UNDYING ONES LOCKED OUT OF OUR COSMOS FOR MANY LIFETIMES--

PERHAPS DOCTOR STRANGE IS NO LONGER NEEDED!

PERHAPS THE WORLD IS READY FOR PLAIN, ORDINARY STEPHEN STRANGE AGAIN--

--A FORMER SURGEON, WHO CAN STILL BE USEFUL AS A MEDICAL CONSULTANT!

I'M--SURE THAT IT IS, FRIEND!

AND THANK YOU AGAIN-- FOR EVERY- THING!

AND SO, MOMENTS LATER, TWO MOST UNIQUE MORTALS DEPART--PERHAPS NEVERMORE TO MEET THIS SIDE OF THE GRAVE--!

I CAN SENSE THAT STEPHEN STRANGE HAS KNOWN TORMENT-- AND THE SCORN OF THE MASSES!

BUT WHAT WOULDN'T BRUCE BANNER GIVE TO STAND IN HIS SHOES--AND BE ABLE TO WALK AWAY FROM IT ALL--

--TO BE RID FOREVER OF THE CREATURE THAT MEN CALL--THE HULK!!

~FIN~

20

SUB-MARINER
15¢
34
FEB
MARVEL COMICS GROUP
ENTER: THE SILVER SURFER AND THE INCREDIBLE HULK!
APPROVED BY THE COMICS CODE AUTHORITY
SUB-MARINER
PUNY HUMANS FIRE AT US! BUT HULK WILL SMASH THEM!
YES, CRUSH THEM! NOTHING MUST STAND IN OUR WAY--
--OR ELSE A PLANET DIES!

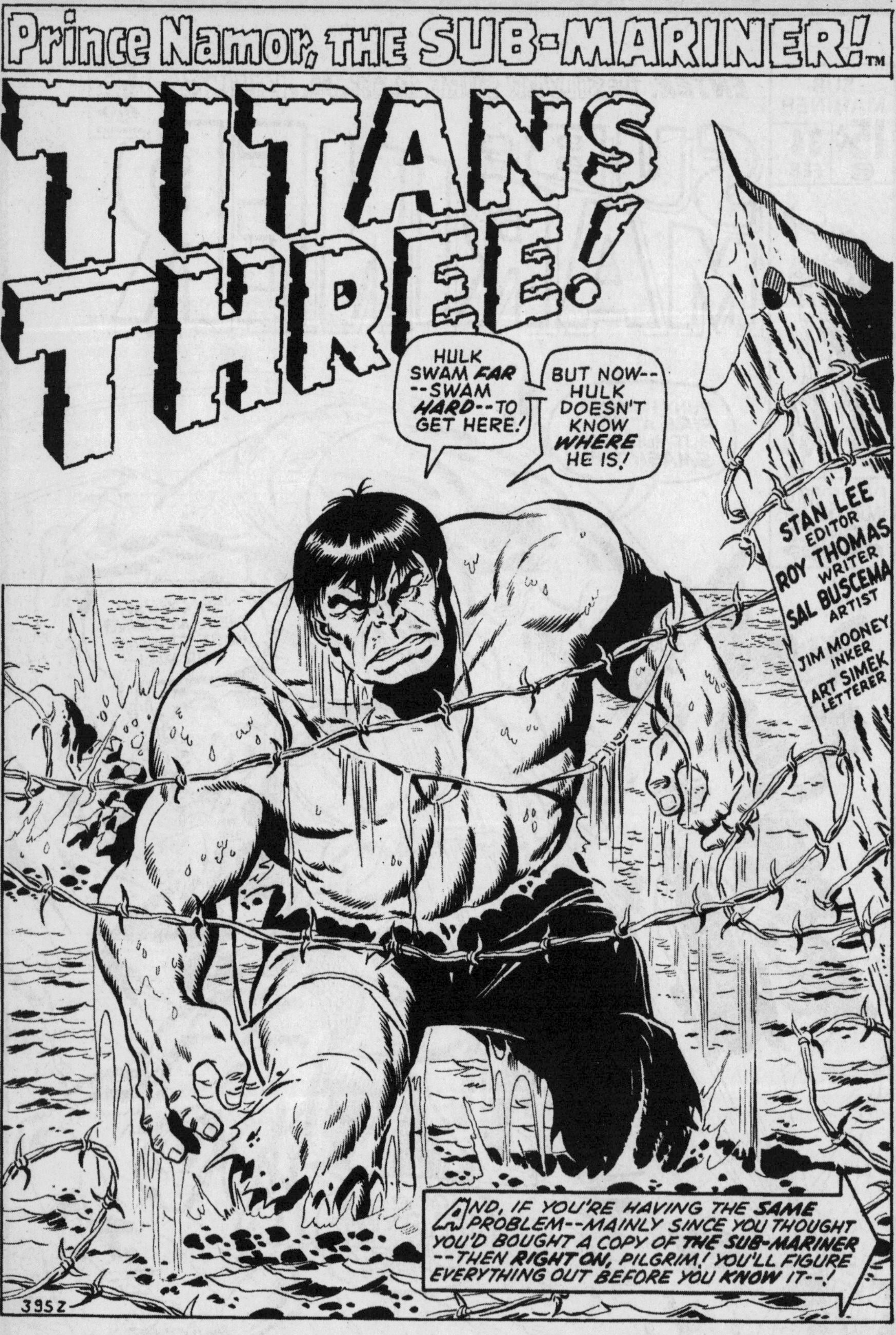
Prince Namor, THE SUB-MARINER!™
TITANS THREE!
HULK SWAM FAR --SWAM HARD--TO GET HERE!
BUT NOW-- HULK DOESN'T KNOW WHERE HE IS!
STAN LEE EDITOR
ROY THOMAS WRITER
SAL BUSCEMA ARTIST
JIM MOONEY INKER
ART SIMEK LETTERER
AND, IF YOU'RE HAVING THE SAME PROBLEM--MAINLY SINCE YOU THOUGHT YOU'D BOUGHT A COPY OF THE SUB-MARINER --THEN RIGHT ON, PILGRIM! YOU'LL FIGURE EVERYTHING OUT BEFORE YOU KNOW IT--!
395Z

HUH? *BARBED WIRE!?* SOMEBODY TRIES TO KEEP HULK *OFF* THIS ISLAND!

WELL, BARBED WIRE CAN'T *HURT* HULK--

--BUT HULK STILL DOESN'T *LIKE* IT.!!

CARAMBA! YOU WERE *CORRECT*, SERGEANT! IT IS *LA MOLE!**

HE HAS *BROKEN THRU* OUR OUTER LINE OF DEFENSE--AND IS HEADING *THIS WAY!*

THEN, HE SHALL SOON TROUBLE US *NO LONGER*, MI CAPITAN!

*PRONOUNCED LA *MO-LAY!* SPANISH-LANGUAGE NAME FOR *OL' GREENSKIN!* IT MEANS *"MASS"!* --STAN.

AND SO ANOTHER ENEMY OF *EL GENERAL* PERISHES!

SI! WE HAVE OUR *ORDERS*--AND WE HAVE *CARRIED THEM OUT!*

LET *NO FOREIGNER* SET FOOT UPON THE BEACHES OF *SAN PABLO*--AND *LIVE!*

2

THEN--YOU CAN TELL HIM FOR *HULK*--

--THAT THE *HULK STILL LIVES!*

EL DIABLO! THE MONSTER WAS NOT EVEN *WOUNDED* BY THE EXPLOSION OF THE MINE! *FIRE!*

SI, MI CAPITAN!

HAH! HULK WAS *WONDERING* WHERE LOUD VOICES CAME FROM!

PTING!

PING!

AND *NOW*--

--HULK *KNOWS!*

WHOOM!

...S-*SI,* MI GENERAL! IT IS THE *GREEN-SKINNED* ONE WHOM THE GRINGOS CALL THE *HULK!*

HE HAS *BREACHED* OUR STALWART DEFENSES--AND IS HEADING OFF INTO THE *JUNGLE!*

3

QUE? YOU *STUPIDOS!* YOUR WORTHLESS LIVES ARE *FORFEIT* FOR THIS!

HE DOUBTLESS WANTED ONLY TO BE LEFT *ALONE*--AND NOW YOU HAVE *ANGERED* HIM!

OR--*DID* SOMEONE SEND HIM HERE?

THE *GRINGOS,* PERHAPS?

OUR MONITORS HAVE *LOCATED* THE ONE YOU *SEEK,* MY LORD--ON THE ISLAND FORTRESS THE SURFACE-MEN CALL *SAN PABLO!*

IN HIS *BESTIAL* STATE, IT IS ALL BUT *IMPOSSIBLE* TO REASON WITH HIM!

AND, *TRUE* IT IS THAT HE WOULD BE *PERFECT* FOR THE TASK YOU HAVE IN MIND!

AY, VASHTI! BUT YOU DO NOT *KNOW* HIM AS I DO!

AND, EVEN *MY* SEA-BORN STRENGTH COULD NOT LONG *SUBDUE* HIM!

A *PITY*--FOR, I HAVE *NEED* OF HIS GREAT HANDS--HIS AWESOME MIGHT!

INDEED--ALL THE *WORLD* MAY SOON HAVE NEED OF--THE *HULK!*

4

FOR, EVEN NOW, *ELSEWHERE* IN THE CARIBBEAN, AIR-BREATHERS ARE CONSTRUCTING A MAMMOTH *EXPERIMENTAL APPARATUS*...

...WHICH, WISE *IKTHON* FEARS, MAY WREAK HAVOC WITH THE VERY *WEATHER* ITSELF!

I COULD *WARN* THEM OF THEIR DANGER-- BUT WHEN NAMOR SPEAKS, THEIR EARS ARE *DEAF*, THEIR HEARTS *HARD!*

A PRICE PAID, MY PRINCE, FOR YOUR RASH, ILL-TEMPERED *YOUTH!* BUT-- *HOLD!*

UPON OUR SCANNER-- A *NEW* IMAGE FORMS!

THERE--SOARING THRU SKIES DIRECTLY *ABOVE* US--THE ONE WHO CALLS HIMSELF--

THE *SILVER SURFER!*

OUR PATHS HAVE NEVER *CROSSED* BEFORE--BUT WHAT AN *ALLY* HE WOULD MAKE--

--TO STAND AT MY SIDE WHEN I FACE THE HUMANS--AND DEMAND THAT THEY *DISMANTLE* THEIR MECHANICAL FOLLY!

STRANGE, THE UNREASONED *FEELING* WHICH FLITS ACROSS MY *MIND*-- ASSAILS MY STAR-BORN *SENSES!*

THE FEELING THAT I AM BEING-- *WATCHED!*

DO THE DELUDED EARTHMEN SEEK TO PERSECUTE ME *HERE*, AS THEY DID OVER *DRY LAND*?

NOW THAT I HAVE *FORESWORN* MY VOW TO REVENGE MYSELF UPON THEM FOR THEIR RECKLESS ATTACKS AGAINST ME--

--WOULD THEY STILL STALK ME UPON THE FOAMING *WAVES* AS WELL?

AND YET--HOW COULD I HOPE TO EXIST IN PEACE *ANYWHERE* UPON A PLANET SO *POLLUTED* BY ITS MOST INTELLIGENT SPECIES--

--THAT THE VAST, UNENDING *SEAS* THEMSELVES MAY OFT BE SPOKEN OF AS--THE *FRAIL OCEAN*?

MY LORD *NAMOR*-- WHERE DO YOU *GO*, WITH SUCH DETERMINED STRIDE?

OUR SONIC SURFACE-PROBES HAVE TOLD ME *ENOUGH*!

THOUGH A BEING OF *PEACE*--IMPRISONED UPON A WORLD THAT LOVES HIM NOT--THE SURFER'S DESIRES ARE MUCH THE SAME AS OUR *OWN*!

I LEAVE NOW TO *APPROACH* HIM--TO LEARN IF HE WILL MAKE COMMON *CAUSE* WITH US!

I SHALL *DELAY* BUT LONG ENOUGH TO BID A LAST FAREWELL TO--

--MY *BETROTHED*, THE LADY *DORMA*!

SEE HOW *HAPPILY* SHE SITS WITH HER LADY-IN-WAITING...MAKING READY FOR THE FAST-DAWNING DAY OF OUR *MARRIAGE*!

MY *PRINCE*! I DID NOT HEAR YOU DRAW NEAR!

COME SEE THE *WEDDING GIFTS* SENT US FROM EVERY CORNER OF THE *EMPIRE*!

6

ALAS, MY LOVE, BUT *IMPERIAL BUSINESS* NOW CALLS ME FROM YOUR SIDE--FROM *ATLANTIS* ITSELF! I'LL SEE THEM *LATER!*

I HOPE, DEAREST, THERE'S NO *DANGER* ARISEN TO MENACE THE REALM ANEW--!?

NAY, IT IS *NOTHING!* DO NOT MARK IT!

GOOD-BYE!

I THANK THE SEA-GODS THAT DORMA IS BUSY WITH THE *WEDDING* PLANS--

--SO THAT SHE DID NOT NOTICE THAT I SAID *GOOD-BYE*--

--AND NOT, *TILL WE MEET AGAIN!*

FOR A MOMENT, I *LOST* THE SENSATION THAT SOMEONE SPIED ON ME--BUT NOW IT *RETURNS!*

AM I GROWN UNDULY *SUSPICIOUS*, BECAUSE OF MY ENCOUNTERS WITH HUMANS, OR--

HOLD! SOMETHING MOVES *BENEATH* THE SURFACE-- DIRECTLY IN MY *PATH!*

SILVER SURFER-- SENTINEL WHO RIDES UPON THE *ROOF* OF THE WORLD!

THE *SUB-MARINER* BIDS YOU-- *HALT!*

7

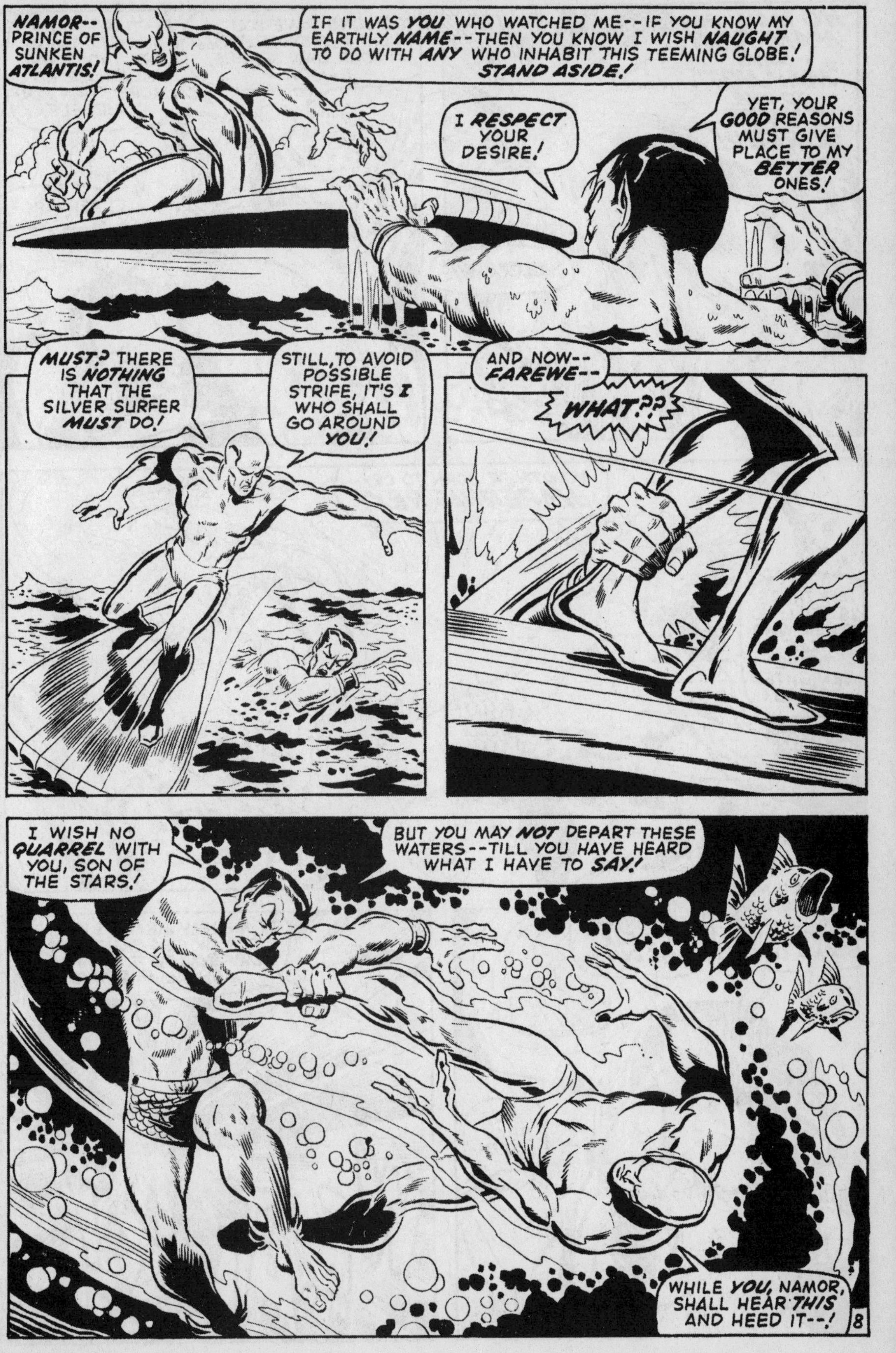
NAMOR-- PRINCE OF SUNKEN ATLANTIS!
IF IT WAS YOU WHO WATCHED ME--IF YOU KNOW MY EARTHLY NAME--THEN YOU KNOW I WISH NAUGHT TO DO WITH ANY WHO INHABIT THIS TEEMING GLOBE! STAND ASIDE!
I RESPECT YOUR DESIRE!
YET, YOUR GOOD REASONS MUST GIVE PLACE TO MY BETTER ONES!
MUST? THERE IS NOTHING THAT THE SILVER SURFER MUST DO!
STILL, TO AVOID POSSIBLE STRIFE, IT'S I WHO SHALL GO AROUND YOU!
AND NOW-- FAREWE--
WHAT??
I WISH NO QUARREL WITH YOU, SON OF THE STARS!
BUT YOU MAY NOT DEPART THESE WATERS--TILL YOU HAVE HEARD WHAT I HAVE TO SAY!
WHILE YOU, NAMOR, SHALL HEAR THIS AND HEED IT--!
8

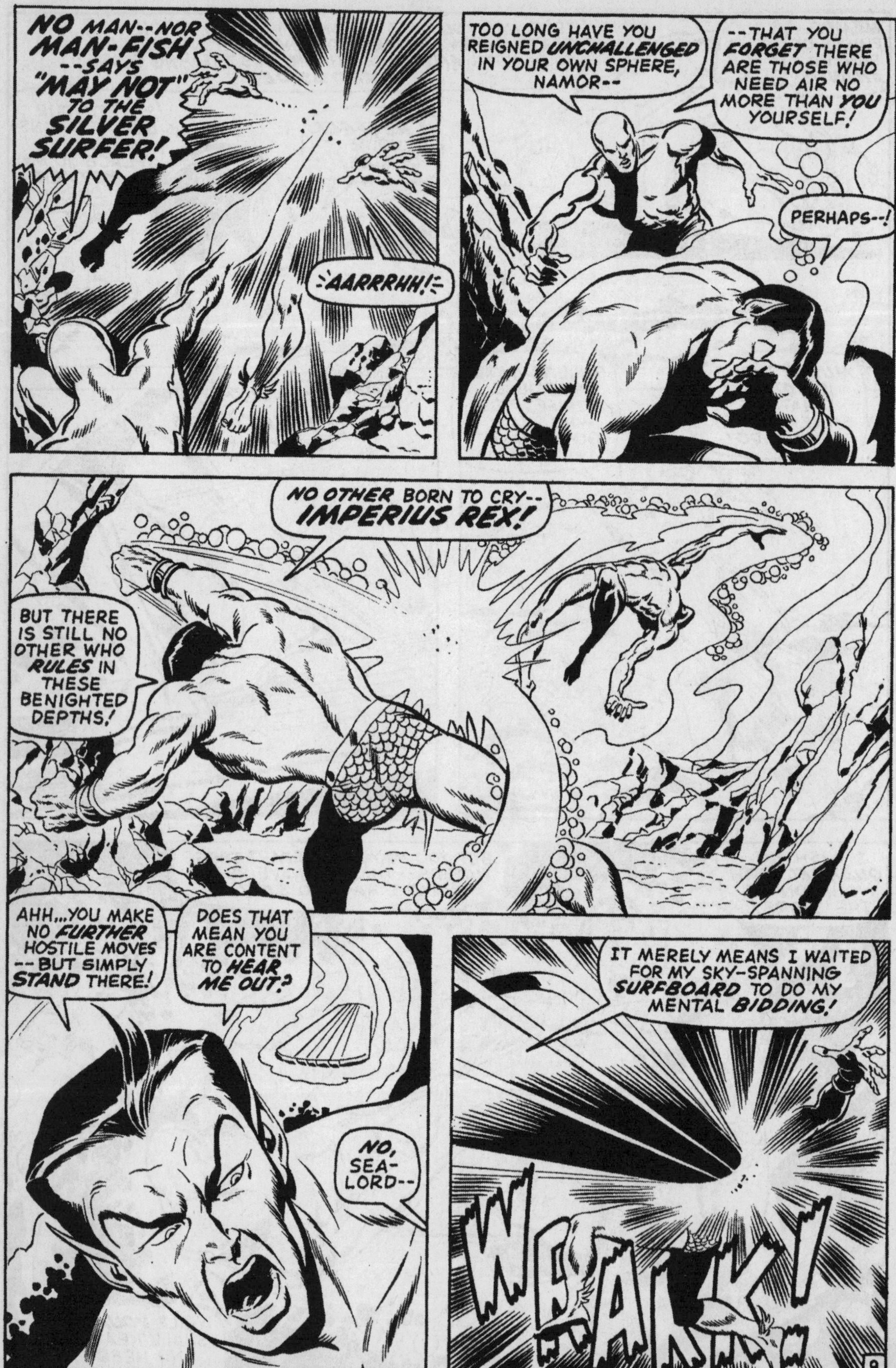

NO MAN--NOR MAN-FISH --SAYS "MAY NOT" TO THE SILVER SURFER!
AARRRHH!
TOO LONG HAVE YOU REIGNED UNCHALLENGED IN YOUR OWN SPHERE, NAMOR--
--THAT YOU FORGET THERE ARE THOSE WHO NEED AIR NO MORE THAN YOU YOURSELF!
PERHAPS--!
NO OTHER BORN TO CRY-- IMPERIUS REX!
BUT THERE IS STILL NO OTHER WHO RULES IN THESE BENIGHTED DEPTHS!
AHH...YOU MAKE NO FURTHER HOSTILE MOVES --BUT SIMPLY STAND THERE!
DOES THAT MEAN YOU ARE CONTENT TO HEAR ME OUT?
NO, SEA-LORD--
IT MERELY MEANS I WAITED FOR MY SKY-SPANNING SURFBOARD TO DO MY MENTAL BIDDING!
WHAK!
9

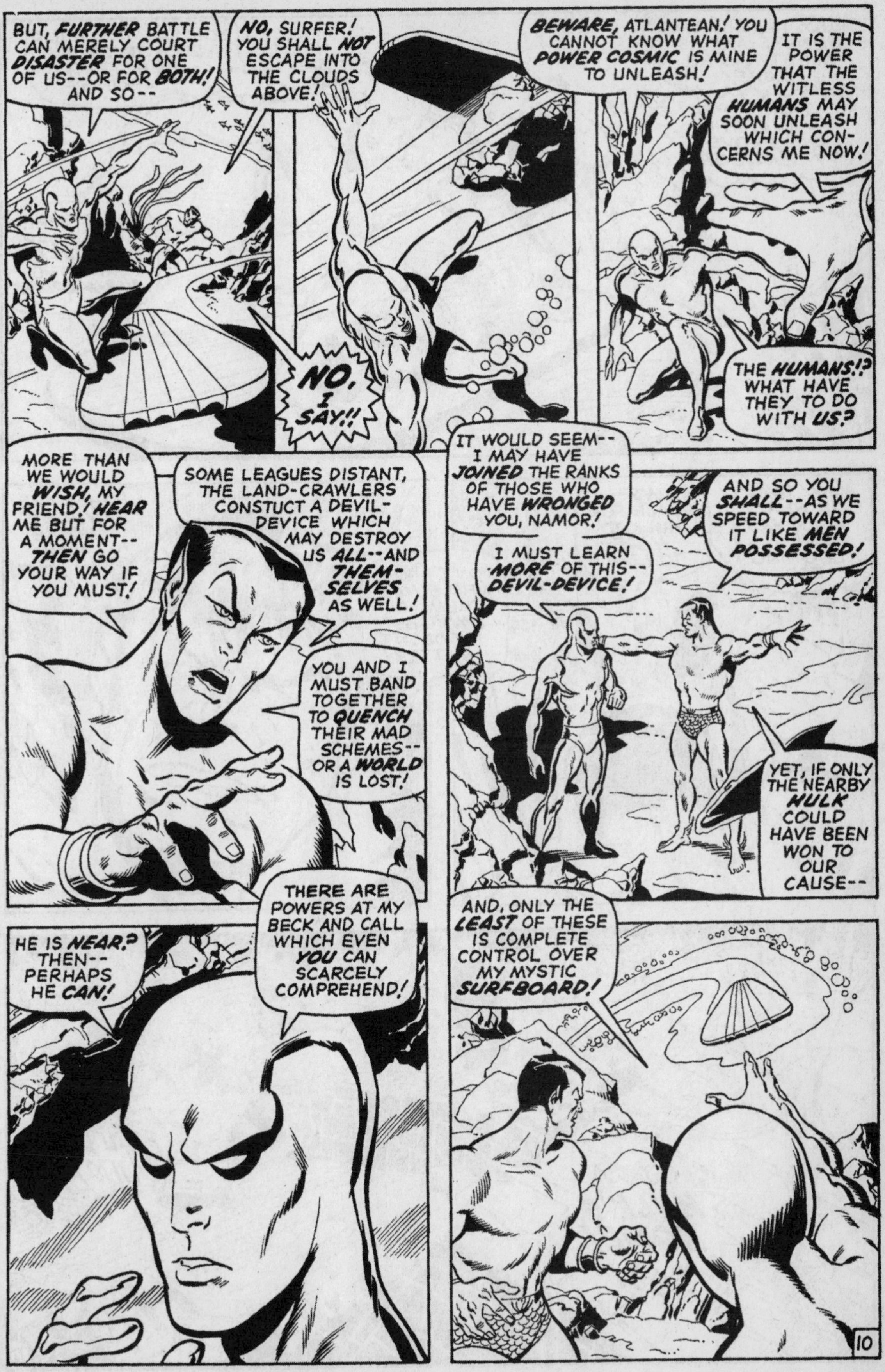
BUT, FURTHER BATTLE CAN MERELY COURT DISASTER FOR ONE OF US--OR FOR BOTH! AND SO--
NO, SURFER! YOU SHALL NOT ESCAPE INTO THE CLOUDS ABOVE!
NO, I SAY!!
BEWARE, ATLANTEAN! YOU CANNOT KNOW WHAT POWER COSMIC IS MINE TO UNLEASH!
IT IS THE POWER THAT THE WITLESS HUMANS MAY SOON UNLEASH WHICH CONCERNS ME NOW!
THE HUMANS!? WHAT HAVE THEY TO DO WITH US?
MORE THAN WE WOULD WISH, MY FRIEND! HEAR ME BUT FOR A MOMENT--THEN GO YOUR WAY IF YOU MUST!
SOME LEAGUES DISTANT, THE LAND-CRAWLERS CONSTUCT A DEVIL-DEVICE WHICH MAY DESTROY US ALL--AND THEMSELVES AS WELL!
YOU AND I MUST BAND TOGETHER TO QUENCH THEIR MAD SCHEMES--OR A WORLD IS LOST!
IT WOULD SEEM--I MAY HAVE JOINED THE RANKS OF THOSE WHO HAVE WRONGED YOU, NAMOR!
I MUST LEARN MORE OF THIS--DEVIL-DEVICE!
AND SO YOU SHALL--AS WE SPEED TOWARD IT LIKE MEN POSSESSED!
YET, IF ONLY THE NEARBY HULK COULD HAVE BEEN WON TO OUR CAUSE--
HE IS NEAR? THEN--PERHAPS HE CAN!
THERE ARE POWERS AT MY BECK AND CALL WHICH EVEN YOU CAN SCARCELY COMPREHEND!
AND, ONLY THE LEAST OF THESE IS COMPLETE CONTROL OVER MY MYSTIC SURFBOARD!
10

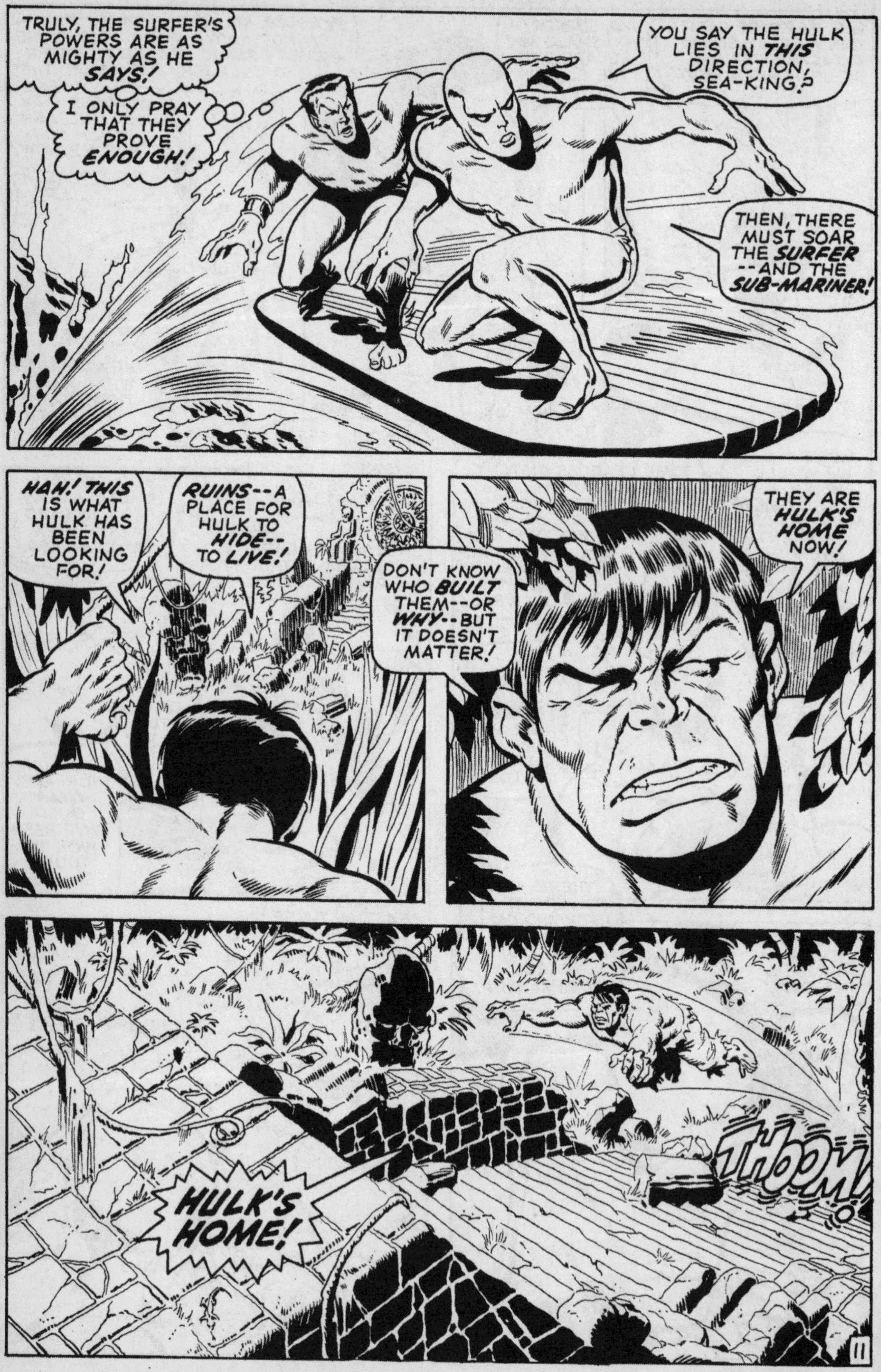
TRULY, THE SURFER'S POWERS ARE AS MIGHTY AS HE SAYS!
I ONLY PRAY THAT THEY PROVE ENOUGH!
YOU SAY THE HULK LIES IN THIS DIRECTION, SEA-KING?
THEN, THERE MUST SOAR THE SURFER --AND THE SUB-MARINER!
HAH! THIS IS WHAT HULK HAS BEEN LOOKING FOR!
RUINS--A PLACE FOR HULK TO HIDE--TO LIVE!
DON'T KNOW WHO BUILT THEM--OR WHY--BUT IT DOESN'T MATTER!
THEY ARE HULK'S HOME NOW!
HULK'S HOME!
THOOM!
11

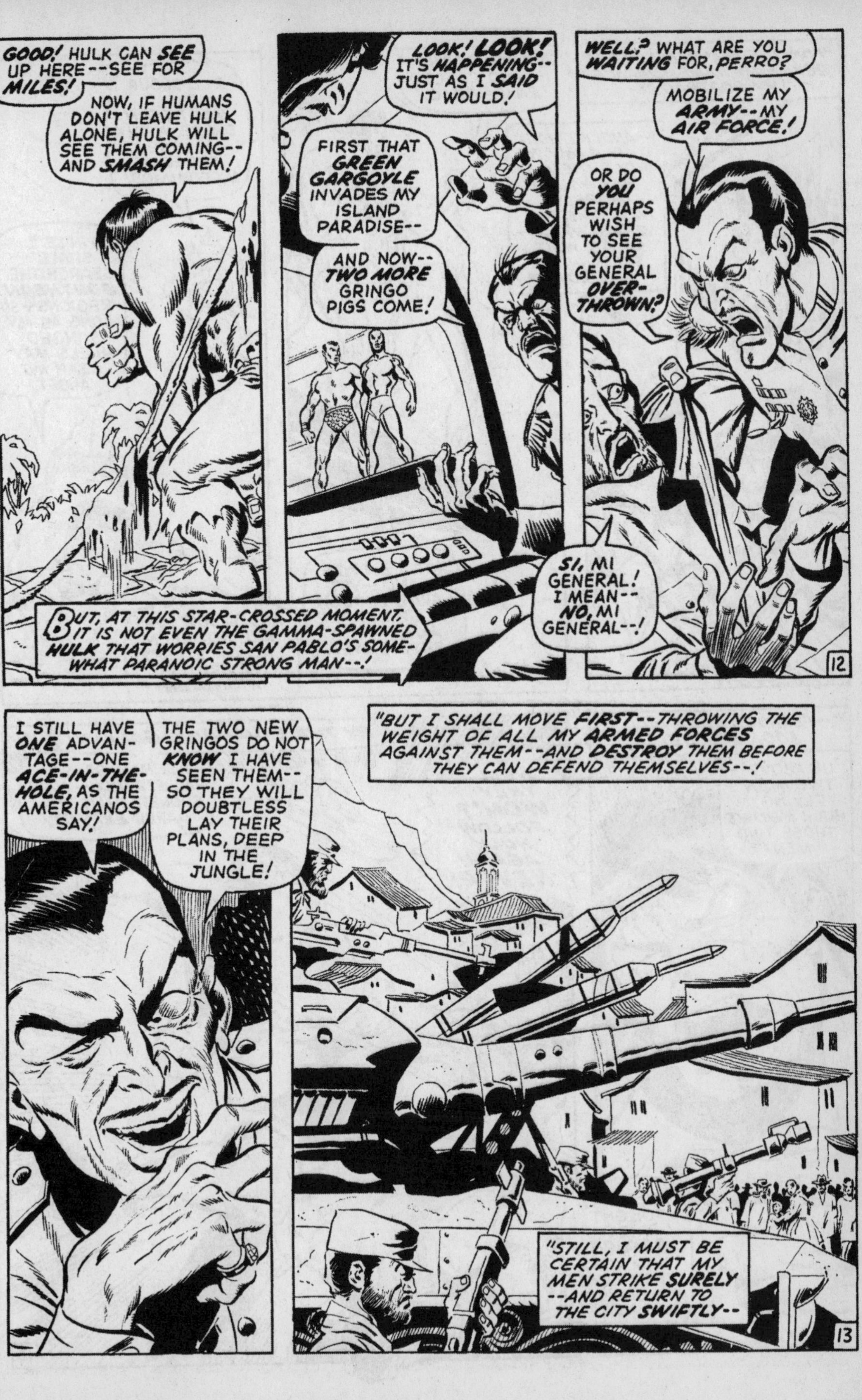
GOOD! HULK CAN SEE UP HERE--SEE FOR MILES!
NOW, IF HUMANS DON'T LEAVE HULK ALONE, HULK WILL SEE THEM COMING--AND SMASH THEM!
LOOK! LOOK! IT'S HAPPENING--JUST AS I SAID IT WOULD!
FIRST THAT GREEN GARGOYLE INVADES MY ISLAND PARADISE--
AND NOW--TWO MORE GRINGO PIGS COME!
WELL? WHAT ARE YOU WAITING FOR, PERRO?
MOBILIZE MY ARMY--MY AIR FORCE!
OR DO YOU PERHAPS WISH TO SEE YOUR GENERAL OVER-THROWN?
SI, MI GENERAL! I MEAN--NO, MI GENERAL--!
BUT, AT THIS STAR-CROSSED MOMENT, IT IS NOT EVEN THE GAMMA-SPAWNED HULK THAT WORRIES SAN PABLO'S SOME-WHAT PARANOIC STRONG MAN--!
12
I STILL HAVE ONE ADVAN-TAGE--ONE ACE-IN-THE-HOLE, AS THE AMERICANOS SAY!
THE TWO NEW GRINGOS DO NOT KNOW I HAVE SEEN THEM--SO THEY WILL DOUBTLESS LAY THEIR PLANS, DEEP IN THE JUNGLE!
"BUT I SHALL MOVE FIRST--THROWING THE WEIGHT OF ALL MY ARMED FORCES AGAINST THEM--AND DESTROY THEM BEFORE THEY CAN DEFEND THEMSELVES--!
"STILL, I MUST BE CERTAIN THAT MY MEN STRIKE SURELY--AND RETURN TO THE CITY SWIFTLY--
13

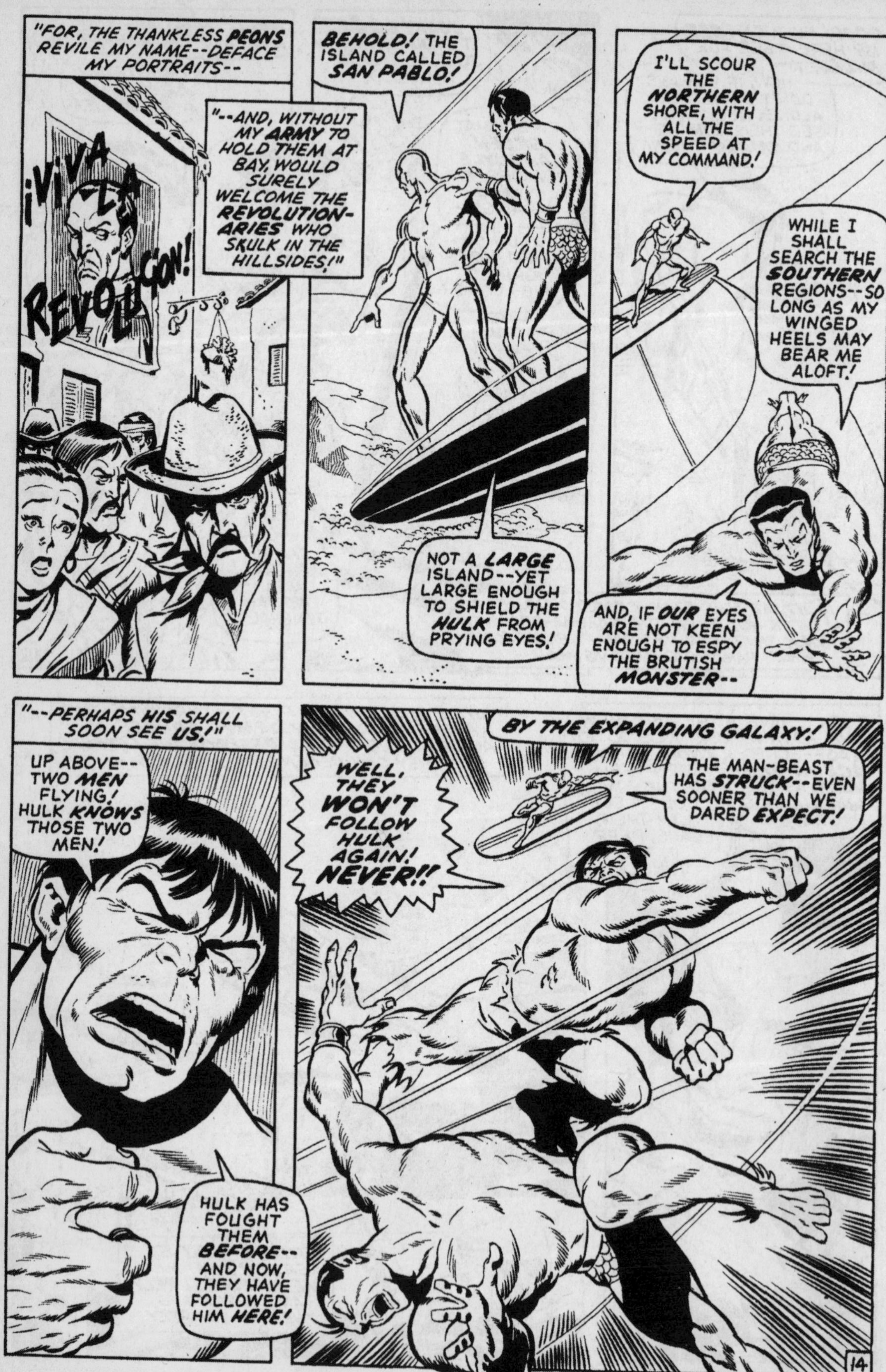
"FOR, THE THANKLESS PEONS REVILE MY NAME--DEFACE MY PORTRAITS--
"--AND, WITHOUT MY ARMY TO HOLD THEM AT BAY, WOULD SURELY WELCOME THE REVOLUTION-ARIES WHO SKULK IN THE HILLSIDES!"
¡VIVA LA REVOLUCION!
BEHOLD! THE ISLAND CALLED SAN PABLO!
NOT A LARGE ISLAND--YET LARGE ENOUGH TO SHIELD THE HULK FROM PRYING EYES!
I'LL SCOUR THE NORTHERN SHORE, WITH ALL THE SPEED AT MY COMMAND!
WHILE I SHALL SEARCH THE SOUTHERN REGIONS--SO LONG AS MY WINGED HEELS MAY BEAR ME ALOFT!
AND, IF OUR EYES ARE NOT KEEN ENOUGH TO ESPY THE BRUTISH MONSTER--
"--PERHAPS HIS SHALL SOON SEE US!"
UP ABOVE--TWO MEN FLYING! HULK KNOWS THOSE TWO MEN!
HULK HAS FOUGHT THEM BEFORE--AND NOW, THEY HAVE FOLLOWED HIM HERE!
WELL, THEY WON'T FOLLOW HULK AGAIN! NEVER!!
BY THE EXPANDING GALAXY!
THE MAN-BEAST HAS STRUCK--EVEN SOONER THAN WE DARED EXPECT!
14

NOW HE IS *ENRAGED*--

--AND *DOUBLY* DANGEROUS!

NO MORE SO THAN THE *SUB-MARINER!*

HE SHALL *HEAR US*--OR ELSE BE HUMBLED AS *NO MAN OR MONSTER* HAS EVER BEEN!

HAH! THAT SHOULD *TEACH* THE LITTLE ONES TO LEAVE HULK *ALONE!*

NO ONE CAN BEAT HULK! *NO ONE!*

NAMOR! COME *BACK!* WHERE ARE YOU *GOING*--?

TO FULFILL OUR *MISSION*, SKY-RIDER! THE MONSTER *WILL* JOIN US--WHEN HE HAS LISTENED TO OUR *PLEA!*

BUT *FIRST*, AS I LEARNED LONG AGO--

--I MUST GAIN HIS *ATTENTION!!*

WROK!

YOU! NOW HULK KNOWS WHO YOU ARE!

YOU ARE *NAMOR*--ONE OF HULK'S GREATEST *ENEMIES!*

YOUR FOE *NO LONGER*, BEHEMOTH! *HEAR ME!*

15

NO! YOU TRY TO *TRICK* HULK! BUT HULK IS *TOO SMART* FOR YOU!

HULK-- *WAIT!*

YES, MONSTER-- *WAIT!* YOU MUST *NOT* MAKE THE SAME RASH ERROR AS THE *SILVER SURFER!*

ZZ-KVOK!

HUH? SO--YOU WANT TO *GANG* UP ON HULK!?

THEN, HULK WILL SMASH FIRST *ONE*--THEN THE *OTHER!*

STOP, YOU MINDLESS OGRE! HOW CAN I *CONVINCE* YOU--WE ARE YOUR *FRIENDS?*

FRIENDS? NOTHING CAN MAKE HULK THINK *THAT!*

NOTH-- ..*AARRHGH!*..

A CANNON SHELL-- FIRED FROM ANOTHER PART OF THE JUNGLE!

WHROOM!

NOW DO YOU SEE, HULK?

IT IS NOT *WE* WHO ARE YOUR TRUE FOEMEN--BUT THE SPITEFUL *HUMANS!*

THE HUMANS--*YES!* THE ONES WHO ATTACKED HULK *BEFORE!*

WE MUST BATTLE THEM *TOGETHER,* HULK! *TOGETHER!*

16

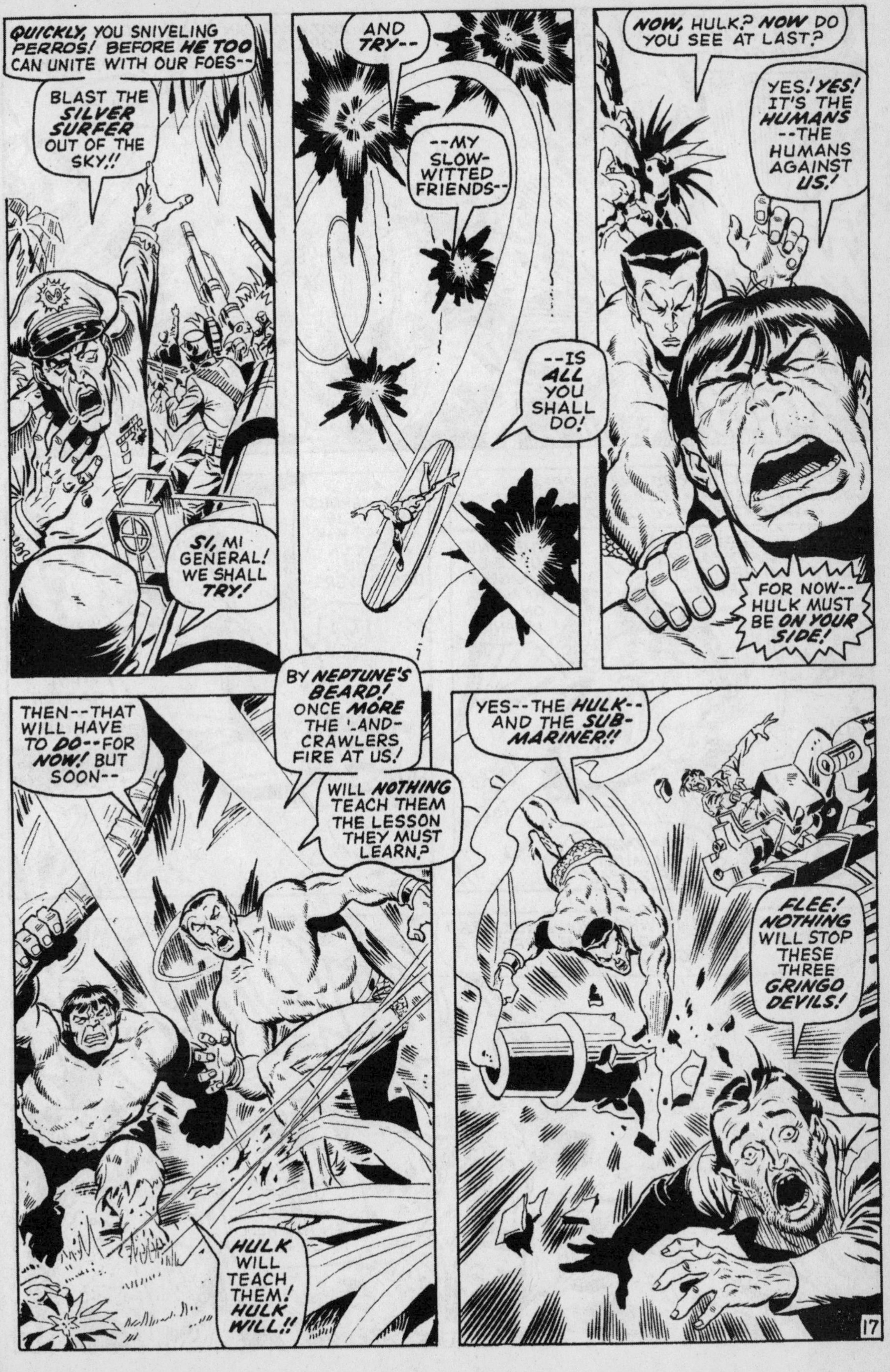
QUICKLY, YOU SNIVELING PERROS! BEFORE HE TOO CAN UNITE WITH OUR FOES--
BLAST THE SILVER SURFER OUT OF THE SKY!!
SI, MI GENERAL! WE SHALL TRY!
AND TRY--
--MY SLOW-WITTED FRIENDS--
--IS ALL YOU SHALL DO!
NOW, HULK? NOW DO YOU SEE AT LAST?
YES! YES! IT'S THE HUMANS --THE HUMANS AGAINST US!
FOR NOW--HULK MUST BE ON YOUR SIDE!
THEN--THAT WILL HAVE TO DO--FOR NOW! BUT SOON--
BY NEPTUNE'S BEARD! ONCE MORE THE LAND-CRAWLERS FIRE AT US!
WILL NOTHING TEACH THEM THE LESSON THEY MUST LEARN?
HULK WILL TEACH THEM! HULK WILL!!
YES--THE HULK--AND THE SUB-MARINER!!
FLEE! NOTHING WILL STOP THESE THREE GRINGO DEVILS!
17

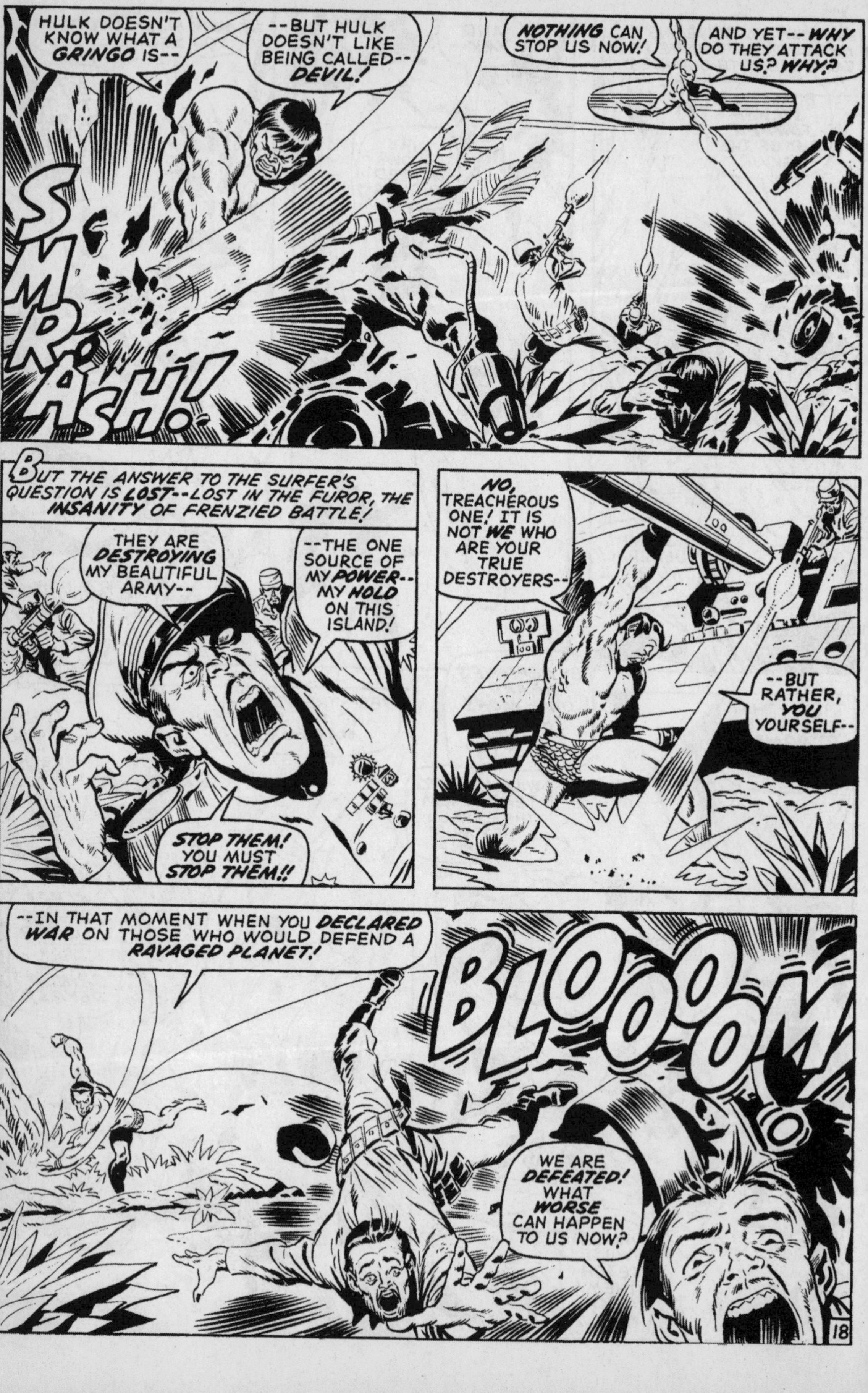

HULK DOESN'T KNOW WHAT A GRINGO IS--
--BUT HULK DOESN'T LIKE BEING CALLED--DEVIL!
SMRASH!
NOTHING CAN STOP US NOW!
AND YET--WHY DO THEY ATTACK US? WHY?
BUT THE ANSWER TO THE SURFER'S QUESTION IS LOST--LOST IN THE FUROR, THE INSANITY OF FRENZIED BATTLE!
THEY ARE DESTROYING MY BEAUTIFUL ARMY--
--THE ONE SOURCE OF MY POWER--MY HOLD ON THIS ISLAND!
STOP THEM! YOU MUST STOP THEM!!
NO, TREACHEROUS ONE! IT IS NOT WE WHO ARE YOUR TRUE DESTROYERS--
--BUT RATHER, YOU YOURSELF--
--IN THAT MOMENT WHEN YOU DECLARED WAR ON THOSE WHO WOULD DEFEND A RAVAGED PLANET!
BLOOOOM
WE ARE DEFEATED! WHAT WORSE CAN HAPPEN TO US NOW?

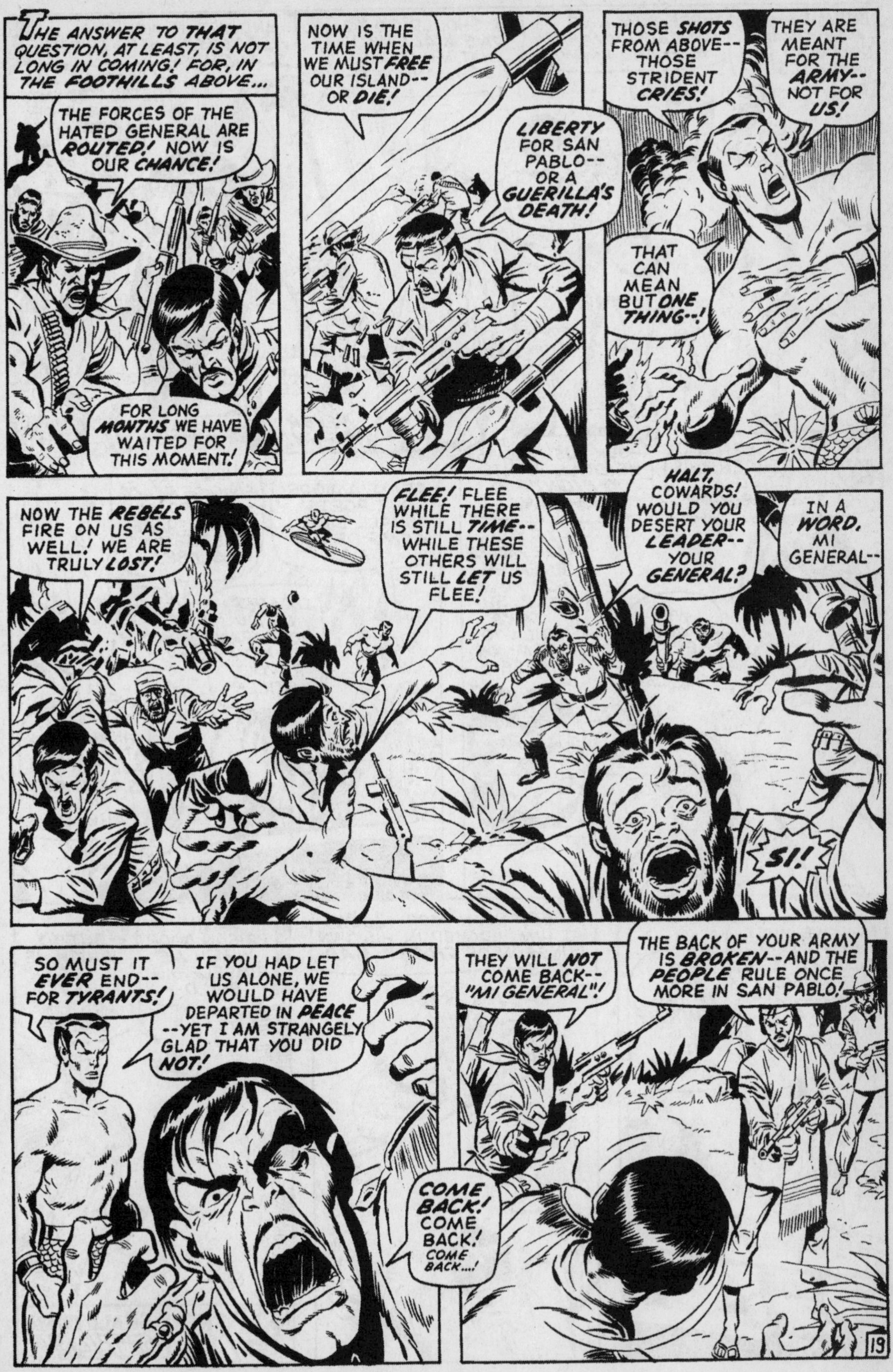
THE ANSWER TO THAT QUESTION, AT LEAST, IS NOT LONG IN COMING! FOR, IN THE FOOTHILLS ABOVE...
THE FORCES OF THE HATED GENERAL ARE ROUTED! NOW IS OUR CHANCE!
FOR LONG MONTHS WE HAVE WAITED FOR THIS MOMENT!
NOW IS THE TIME WHEN WE MUST FREE OUR ISLAND-- OR DIE!
LIBERTY FOR SAN PABLO-- OR A GUERILLA'S DEATH!
THOSE SHOTS FROM ABOVE-- THOSE STRIDENT CRIES!
THEY ARE MEANT FOR THE ARMY-- NOT FOR US!
THAT CAN MEAN BUT ONE THING--!
NOW THE REBELS FIRE ON US AS WELL! WE ARE TRULY LOST!
FLEE! FLEE WHILE THERE IS STILL TIME-- WHILE THESE OTHERS WILL STILL LET US FLEE!
HALT, COWARDS! WOULD YOU DESERT YOUR LEADER-- YOUR GENERAL?
IN A WORD, MI GENERAL--
SI!
SO MUST IT EVER END-- FOR TYRANTS!
IF YOU HAD LET US ALONE, WE WOULD HAVE DEPARTED IN PEACE --YET I AM STRANGELY GLAD THAT YOU DID NOT!
COME BACK! COME BACK! COME BACK...!
THEY WILL NOT COME BACK-- "MI GENERAL"!
THE BACK OF YOUR ARMY IS BROKEN--AND THE PEOPLE RULE ONCE MORE IN SAN PABLO!

ENEMIES ALL *RAN AWAY!* NOW WHO CAN HULK FIGHT?

THERE SHALL BE *FOES ENOUGH* FOR YOU--AND *SOON!*

WE SHOULD GO *TO THE WALL* WITH THAT MILITARIST DOG--AND YET--

AND YET, IT WOULD BE *NEEDLESS*--MERE SPITEFUL *SLAUGHTER!*

FOR, HE HAS RETREATED INTO A WORLD OF *SILENCE*--THE LAND OF THE HOPELESSLY *INSANE*

--AND CAN MENACE YOU *NEVER AGAIN!*

WE HAVE SEEN A *NATION* REBORN THIS DAY, HULK! DO YOU NOT FEEL *PROUD?*

HULK JUST KNOWS HE STILL WANTS TO *FIGHT*--TO *SMASH!*

IF YOU HAVE *MORE* ENEMIES FOR HULK TO CRUSH, *TAKE* HULK TO THEM--OR ELSE--

WE *SHALL!* NEVER FEAR!

ADIOS, AMIGOS! OUR POETS SHALL SING *LONG* OF THIS DAY!

THEN LET THEM SING A SONG OF *PEACE*--TOWARD *ALL* WHO SHARE THIS TEEMING *GLOBE!*

STRANGE-- WE DID NOT *MEAN* TO AID A *REVOLT!* STILL--

PRAY IT IS AN *OMEN,* ATLANTEAN-- FOR THE FAR *GREATER* TASK AHEAD!

NOW WE MUST GO--FOR A *PLANET* IS YET TO SAVE!

BUT WHAT OF THE *GENERAL?* HE IS STILL *FREE!*

FREE? NO, NAMOR--*LOOK* AT HIM, LOCKED IN HIS OWN DUNGEON OF *SILENT* MADNESS--

--BEHIND A PRISON DOOR WHICH *HE* HIMSELF DID BUILD--

--BUT TO WHICH HE HAS FOREVER LOST THE *KEY!*

20

NEXT: THERE SHALL COME *BATTLE!*

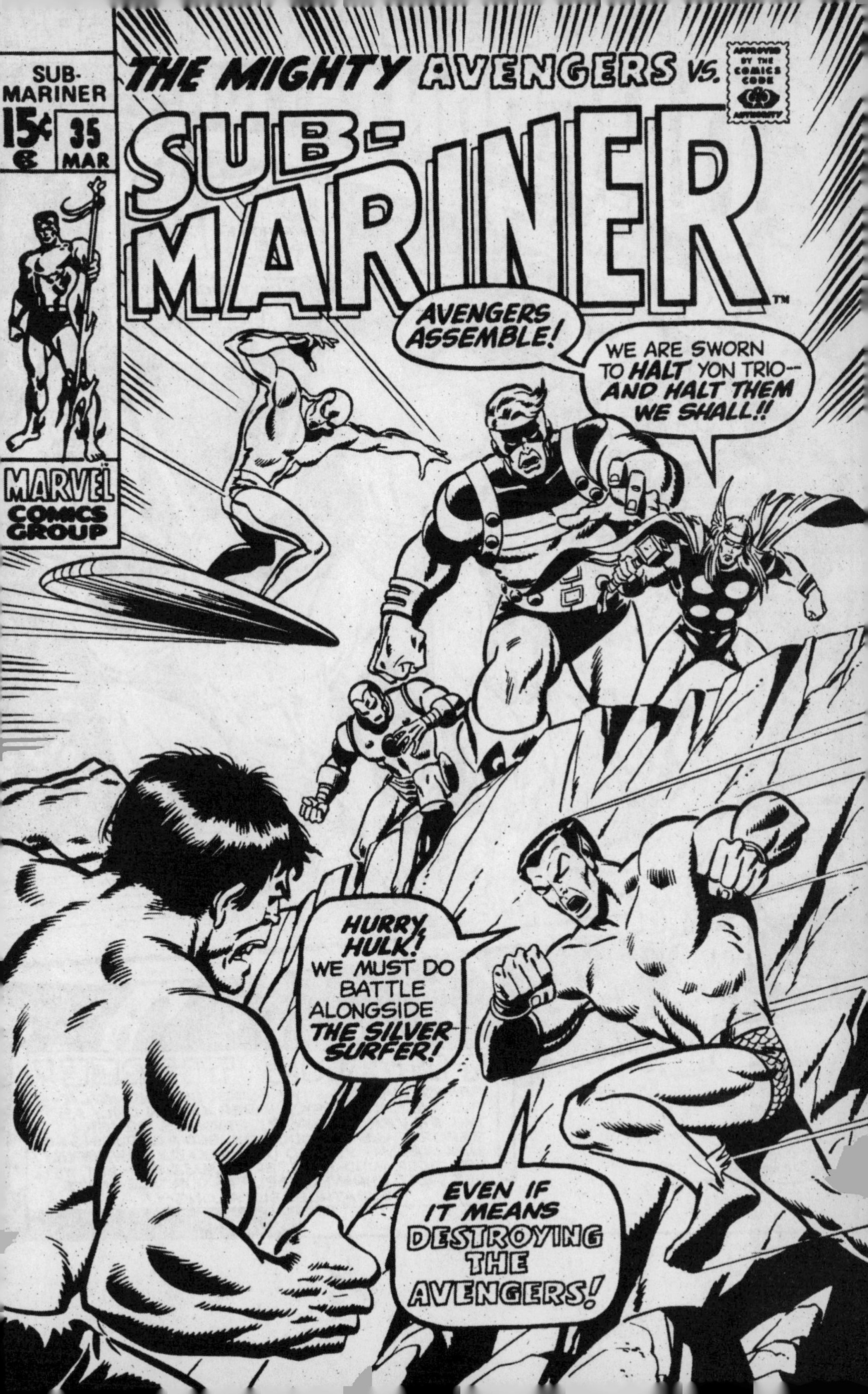
THE MIGHTY AVENGERS VS.
APPROVED BY THE COMICS CODE AUTHORITY
SUB-MARINER
15¢
35 MAR
SUB-MARINER™
MARVEL COMICS GROUP
AVENGERS ASSEMBLE!
WE ARE SWORN TO HALT YON TRIO-- AND HALT THEM WE SHALL!!
HURRY, HULK! WE MUST DO BATTLE ALONGSIDE THE SILVER SURFER!
EVEN IF IT MEANS DESTROYING THE AVENGERS!

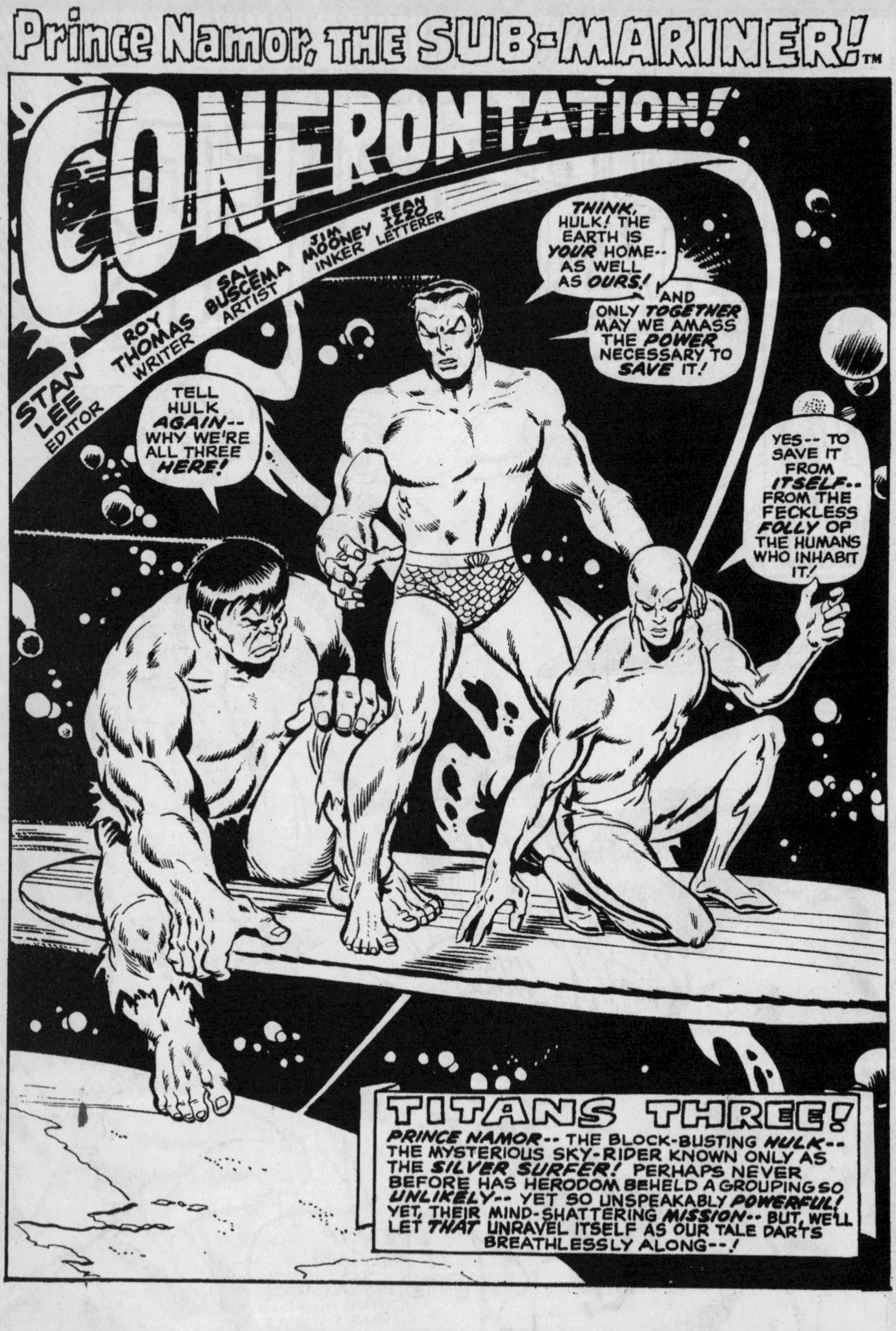
Prince Namor, THE SUB-MARINER!™
CONFRONTATION!
STAN LEE EDITOR
ROY THOMAS WRITER
SAL BUSCEMA ARTIST
JIM MOONEY INKER
JEAN IZZO LETTERER
TELL HULK AGAIN-- WHY WE'RE ALL THREE HERE!
THINK, HULK! THE EARTH IS YOUR HOME-- AS WELL AS OURS!
AND ONLY TOGETHER MAY WE AMASS THE POWER NECESSARY TO SAVE IT!
YES-- TO SAVE IT FROM ITSELF.. FROM THE FECKLESS FOLLY OF THE HUMANS WHO INHABIT IT!
TITANS THREE!
PRINCE NAMOR-- THE BLOCK-BUSTING HULK-- THE MYSTERIOUS SKY-RIDER KNOWN ONLY AS THE SILVER SURFER! PERHAPS NEVER BEFORE HAS HERODOM BEHELD A GROUPING SO UNLIKELY-- YET SO UNSPEAKABLY POWERFUL! YET, THEIR MIND-SHATTERING MISSION-- BUT, WE'LL LET THAT UNRAVEL ITSELF AS OUR TALE DARTS BREATHLESSLY ALONG--!

HUH? HOW COME SURFBOARD'S GOING *DOWN* NOW-- DOWN TOWARD THE *GROUND?*

DO YOU COMPREHEND *NOTHING*, GARGOYLE?

BELOW IS OUR *DESTINATION*-- THE CARIBBEAN ISLAND WHERE MEN HAVE BUILT A DEVICE WHICH THREATENS *ALL LIFE ON EARTH!*

FEAR NOT, MY FRIENDS, THOUGH MY MYSTIC BOARD SCORCHES THE VERY *AIR* ABOUT US!

ITS *INVISIBLE AURA* WILL *PROTECT* YOU BOTH!

PROTECT? HULK DOESN'T *NEED* PROTECTING-- FROM *ANYTHING!*

LET THE *HUMANS* FEAR-- 'CAUSE HULK WILL *SMASH* THEM-- THEM, AND THE THING THEY *BUILD!*

NO, HULK-- NOT *THAT* WAY!

IT IS NOT TO *DESTROY* THAT WE GATHERED TOGETHER-- BUT SO THAT WE MIGHT *BARGAIN* WITH THE SURFACE-MEN FROM A POSITION OF *STRENGTH!*

IF WE MUST *RESORT* TO *FORCE* TO ACHIEVE OUR AIMS-- THEN, IN A DEEPER SENSE, WE HAVE ALREADY *FAILED!*

THERE, NAMOR-- THE *ISLE* YOU DESCRIBED TO ME!

GOOD! HULK IS *TIRED* OF SITTING-- *TIRED* OF TALKING!

HULK WILL *ACT!* THEN THE *FISH-MAN* CAN TALK-- TO THE HUMANS WHO STILL *CAN* TALK!

YOU FOOL-- *COME BACK!*

THERE IS NO *REASONING* WITH HIM!

PERHAPS ONE OF MY *COSMIC BOLTS* WOULD--

2

WAIT! WHY DO *YOU* NOW STREAK AWAY, EVEN AS *HE* DID?

IT WAS NAMOR WHO *RECRUITED* THE HULK-- AND SO IT NOW MUST BE NAMOR WHO STOPS HIM FROM *RUNNING AMOK!*

BUT-- ALREADY HE HAS *COME TO EARTH*, ALMOST WITHIN SIGHT OF THE LAND-CRAWLERS--!

FIVE MORE MINUTES-- AND OUR *NUCLEAR WEATHER-CONTROL STATION* WILL BE OPERATIVE!

NOT EVEN A *HURRICANE* CAN PREVENT OUR TESTING IT *NOW!*

MAYBE A *BIG WIND* CAN'T STOP YOU--

--BUT THE *HULK* CAN!!

DO HALF-FORMED WORDS CATCH IN THE *THROATS* OF THE TERRIFIED HUMANS-- OR ARE THEY MERELY *LOST* AMID THE THUNDEROUS *CHAOS* WHICH FOLLOWS ON THE INSTANT, AS--

WK!

OMM!!

HUH? WHO--?

3

SO, BRUTE-- ALREADY YOU HAVE FORGOTTEN YOUR *ALLIANCE* WITH THE *SUB-MARINER!*

THEN-- IT IS TIME I *REMINDED* YOU!

NAMOR! HULK! THERE MUST BE *NO* QUARRELING AMONGST OURSELVES!

NOBODY CALLS HULK NAMES-- AND *LIVES!* NOBODY!!

BACK, HULK! THE SURFER SPEAKS *TRUTH!* THERE IS MORE AT STAKE HERE THAN OUR OWN PRIDE!

WE MUST PRESENT A *COMMON FRONT* TO THE HUMANS-- FOR THE SAKE OF THE *EARTH!*

EARTH-- HUMANS-- YES--!

HURRY UP, THEN-- AND GET *TALKING* OVER WITH!

AS SOON AS THE TALKING STOPS, HULK WILL *GO*-- BE ON HIS *OWN* AGAIN!

ALL RIGHT, YOU THREE! YOU'RE TRESPASSING ON *UNITED NATIONS* TERRITORY!

I'LL GIVE YOU *FIVE SECONDS* TO EXPLAIN!

COLONEL WILLIS-- YOU KNOW WHO THOSE GUYS ARE? YOU BETTER WATCH IT--!

MISTER, I GOT MY PURPLE HEART ON *HEARTBREAK RIDGE*-- AND MY SILVER STAR AT *KHESAN!*

LET *THEM* "WATCH IT"!

NOW, LIKE I SAID-- *WHAT'S GOING ON?*

THERE IS *NO TIME* FOR WORDS! EVEN AS WE SPEAK, YOUR NUCLEAR GENERATORS *HUM INTO LIFE!*

YOU MUST *DEACTIVATE* THEM-- UNTIL MY *ATLANTEAN* SCIENTISTS CAN ARRIVE TO *EXAMINE* THEM!

4

EXAMINE THEM? ARE YOU OUTTA YOUR POINTY-EARED HEAD?

I'VE *READ* ABOUT YOU, MISTER SUB-MA*REENER*-- AND I KNOW YOU'RE USED TO *GETTING YOUR WAY* DOWN IN DAVY JONES' LOCKER!

WELL, YOU'RE ON *DRY LAND* NOW-- THE PROPERTY OF THE *U.N.!*

I DIDN'T *LIKE* BEING DRAGGED OUTTA 'NAM TO PLAY NURSEMAID TO SOLDIERS OF HALF-A-DOZEN COUNTRIES AND A GIZMO I CAN'T EVEN *UNDERSTAND*--

BUT I'LL *DO MY JOB*-- EVEN IF I HAVE TO ORDER YOU THREE *PUT IN IRONS!*

A PRETTY SPEECH, COLONEL-- AND ONE WHICH SHOWS ME THAT ONLY *FORCE* WILL ACCOMPLISH WHAT MUST BE DONE!

NO, HULK-- NOT *YOU*-- NOT YET!

DOES THAT MEAN-- HULK CAN *STOMP?*

SURFER--?

HE *DISARMED* HALF OF THE GUARDS-- BEFORE THEY COULD BAT AN *EYELASH!*

FALL BACK TO THE *BEACH!* WE'VE GOT TO *REGROUP*-- AND GET FURTHER *INSTRUCTIONS!*

ANY WAY YOU *SLICE* IT, COLONEL, THAT MEANS *RETREAT*-- BUT I'M WITH YOU!

5

LET'S GET MOVING! THERE'S AN EMERGENCY *RADIO SHACK* ON THE NEXT ISLAND!

IF IT WAS UP TO ME, WE'D *RUSH* THOSE THREE WITH EVERYTHING WE'VE GOT *LEFT!*

BUT MY ORDERS SAY TO *ABANDON* THE ISLAND-- IF WE'RE FACED WITH *OVERWHELMING ODDS!*

WELL, SIR, IF *THAT* THREESOME DON'T QUALIFY-- THEN NEITHER WOULD THE WHOLE *CHINESE ARMY!*

...YOU *HEARD* ME, MR. SECRETARY! WHAT'S MORE, HE'S GOT THE *HULK* AND THE *SILVER SURFER* TO BACK HIM UP!

SURE I'M SURE! YOU THINK THEY HAD TO GIVE ME A *CALLING CARD?*

THEN-- THIS IS THE *GRAVEST* CRISIS IN THE *HISTORY* OF THE UNITED NATIONS!

WHAT? NO, SOLDIER, I *DON'T* WANT YOUR MEN TO MOUNT AN ATTACK!

TO DO SO MIGHT MEAN *WAR*-- NOT JUST WITH THOSE THREE-- BUT WITH *ATLANTIS* AS WELL!

WHAT IS MORE, THE *SAFETY* OF THAT *WEATHER-CONTROL* STATION MAY WELL BE *VITAL* TO THE FUTURE OF THE ENTIRE PLANET!

A STRAY BULLET COULD CAUSE *UNTOLD DAMAGE*-- AND DESTROY EQUIPMENT THAT WOULD TAKE A *DECADE* TO REPLACE!

THUS, AN ARMED *COUNTER-OFFENSIVE* IS OUT OF THE *QUESTION!*

BESIDES, WE HAVE MADE-- *OTHER* ARRANGEMENTS--!

6

THEN-- IT'S *AGREED!* FIVE OF US DASH OFF TO MAKE THAT CHARITY *TV SPOT*-- --THE OTHER THREE REMAIN *HERE* ON CALL TO THE *U.N.*, AS WE PROMISED!

YOU PICK THE *THREE*, CAPTAIN AMERICA-- AS TODAY'S CHAIRMAN!

SO SAY WE *ALL!*

YEAH-- BUT HOW COME IT SEEMS LIKE OL' *WINGHEAD'S* CHAIRIN' EVERY OTHER MEETING?

LAST TIME *I* GOT TO RUN A SESSION, PEOPLE STILL THOUGHT *SPIRO AGNEW* WAS SOME KIND'A *CHEWIN'* GUM!

*A WORD TO THE WISE: DON'T WASTE TIME TRYING TO CORRELATE *THIS* TALE WITH THE CURRENT *AVENGERS* ISSUE! *NO WAY!* -- STAN.

ALL RIGHT, GOLIATH-- I CHOOSE *YOU*, *THOR*, AND *IRON MAN!*

IF THERE *IS* TROUBLE IN THE CARIBBEAN, I WANT THREE OF THE *STRONGEST* AVENGERS HANDY!

AND, A SHORT TIME LATER...

IT MAY WELL BE, CLINT! IMAGINE-- ONE DAY-- HAVING *TOTAL CONTROL* OVER THE ELEMENTS--

THE WAY THEY'RE SWEATIN' BLOOD OVER IT, YOU'D THINK THAT *WEATHER-CONTROL* THING OF THE U.N.'S WAS GONNA BE A REAL *WORLD-BEATER!*

'TIS NOT THAT I WISH *MISFORTUNE* TO BEFALL YON PROJECT--

YET, THIS *INACTIVITY* DOTH REST HEAVENLY 'PON MY *SOUL!*

MAKE THAT *TWO* SOULS! I--

HOLD ON, PAL! THIS MIGHT JUST BE *IT!*

HELLO-- AVENGERS MANSION HERE! *GOLIATH* ON THE-- HUH?-- NO LIE? --YEAH, OKAY -- YOU *GOT* US, MISTER!

BLONDIE, TODAY'S YOUR *LUCKY* DAY!

7

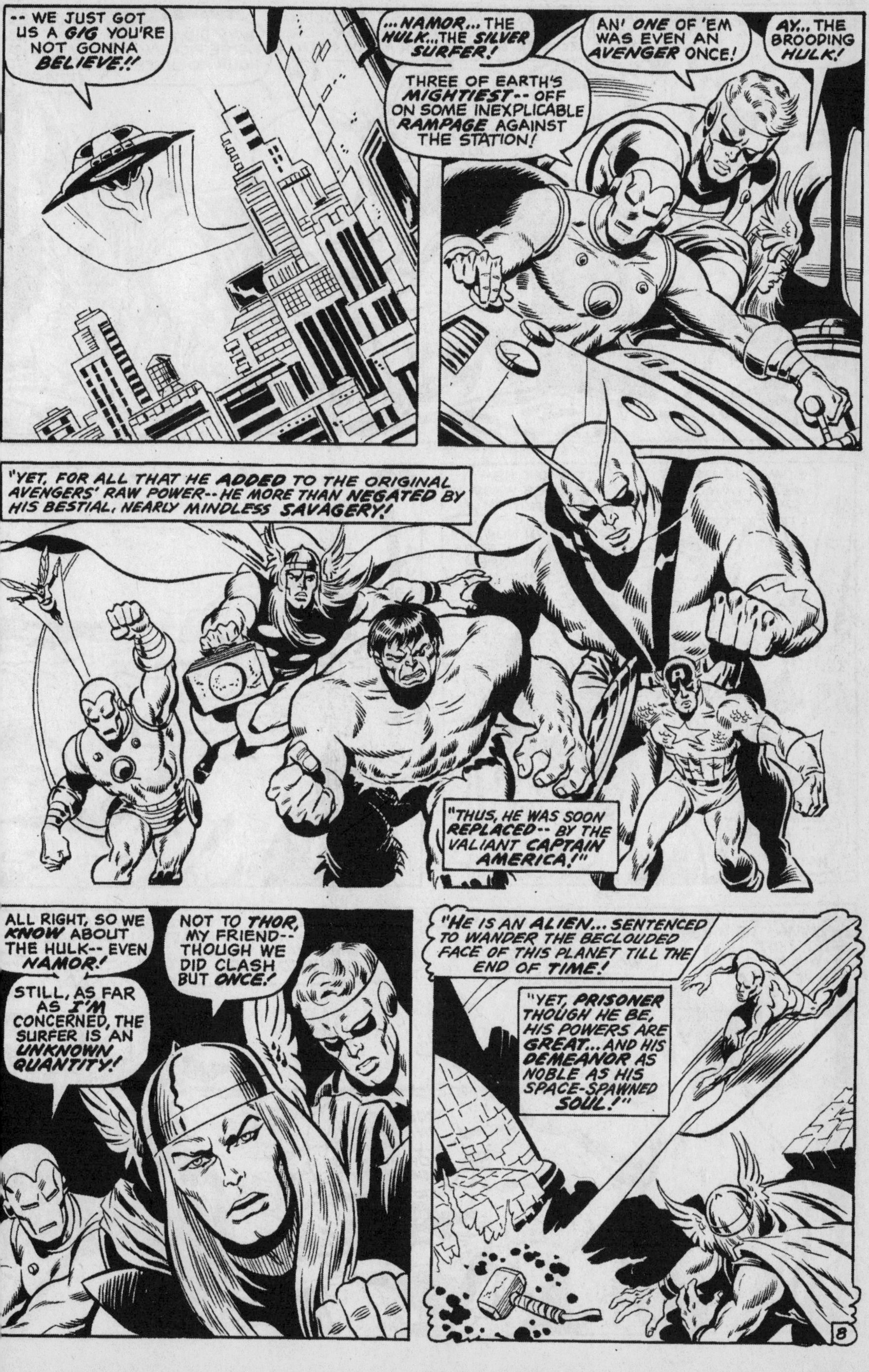
-- WE JUST GOT US A GIG YOU'RE NOT GONNA BELIEVE!!
...NAMOR... THE HULK... THE SILVER SURFER!
THREE OF EARTH'S MIGHTIEST-- OFF ON SOME INEXPLICABLE RAMPAGE AGAINST THE STATION!
AN' ONE OF 'EM WAS EVEN AN AVENGER ONCE!
AY... THE BROODING HULK!
"YET, FOR ALL THAT HE ADDED TO THE ORIGINAL AVENGERS' RAW POWER--HE MORE THAN NEGATED BY HIS BESTIAL, NEARLY MINDLESS SAVAGERY!
"THUS, HE WAS SOON REPLACED-- BY THE VALIANT CAPTAIN AMERICA!"
ALL RIGHT, SO WE KNOW ABOUT THE HULK-- EVEN NAMOR!
STILL, AS FAR AS I'M CONCERNED, THE SURFER IS AN UNKNOWN QUANTITY!
NOT TO THOR, MY FRIEND-- THOUGH WE DID CLASH BUT ONCE!
"HE IS AN ALIEN... SENTENCED TO WANDER THE BECLOUDED FACE OF THIS PLANET TILL THE END OF TIME!
"YET, PRISONER THOUGH HE BE, HIS POWERS ARE GREAT... AND HIS DEMEANOR AS NOBLE AS HIS SPACE-SPAWNED SOUL!"
8

SHEESH! COULD BE I'M OUTTA MY DEPTH!

DAYS LIKE THIS, I WONDER IF I SHOULD'A STAYED JUST A FANCY-DAN ARCHER-- OR BEEN A SOCIAL WORKER OR MAYBE BOTH!

WHEN YOU'RE THRU, BIG MAN, TRY PUZZLING THIS ONE OUT--!

WHY DID THOSE THREE PICK THIS HOUR TO UNITE--

--AND THIS POINT IN TIME AND SPACE--TO ATTACK??

SOMEONE DRAWS NEAR, NAMOR! I CAN SENSE IT!

IT MUST BE-- THE ONES WHOM WE AWAIT! EVEN NOW, MY BELT RECEIVES THE PROPER SIGNAL!

SOMETHING COMING UP-- OUT THERE IN THE WATER!

DO NOT ATTACK, HULK! IT IS-- FRIENDS!

AND THAT IS IKTHON-- THE SCIENTIST OF WHOM YOU SPOKE?

AYE-- BUT I DID NOT SUSPECT-- THE LADY DORMA WOULD JOURNEY HERE AS WELL--

--SHE WHOM I LEFT IN SUNKEN ATLANTIS-- MAKING READY FOR THE COMING DAY OF OUR WEDDING!

HAIL, MY LADY! HAIL, WISE IKTHON!

SCIENTIST? WEDDING? ALL TOO MUCH-- FOR HULK TO FIGURE OUT!

9

IKTHON *TOLD* ME OF YOUR MISSION, MY LOVE-- THOUGH YOU HAD COMMANDED HIM *NOT TO!*

AS IF A *THOUSAND* UNTOLD DANGERS COULD KEEP ME FROM YOUR SIDE IN TIME OF *PERIL!*

I-- DID NOT WISH TO *MAR* YOUR HAPPINESS-- YOUR SERENE *BLISS!*

BUT NOW-- THERE IS *WORK* TO BE DONE-- PERHAPS A *WORLD* TO SAVE!

WHERE IS THE AIR-BREATHERS' *DEVIL-DEVICE?*

COME-- I SHALL *LEAD* YOU TO IT!

NAMOR *MASKS* HIS LOVE FOR THE GIRL-- BEHIND AN IMPERIOUS *TONE!*

BUT I SENSE *DEPTHS* TO HIS FEELINGS-- *BEYOND* MEN'S KEN!

MY PRINCE-- *BEHOLD!* A FLYING *VESSEL!*

IT SEEMS-- *FAMILIAR*-- FROM *CHARTS* WE HAVE STUDIED--!

AS WELL IT *SHOULD* BE, ATLANTEAN!

SUCH IS THE DESIGN OF THE AIRCRAFT BELONGING TO-- THE MIGHTY *AVENGERS!*

I HAD NOT COUNTED ON SUCH POWERFUL OPPOSITION SO *SOON!*

IKTHON-- PROCEED WITH YOUR TASK WITH ALL POSSIBLE *SPEED!*

WHILE *YOU,* MY *PRINCE*--?

WE SHALL APPROACH THE AVENGERS *UNSEEN*-- AND STOP THEM FROM *HALTING* YOUR FATEFUL LABORS!

NOW HULK FEELS BETTER! NOW HULK WILL *FIGHT!*

NO, HULK-- WE SHALL *NOT* FIGHT-- EXCEPT AS A *LAST RESORT!*

AND YET, IF FIGHT WE *MUST*-- THEN *TRIUMPH* WE MUST!!

10

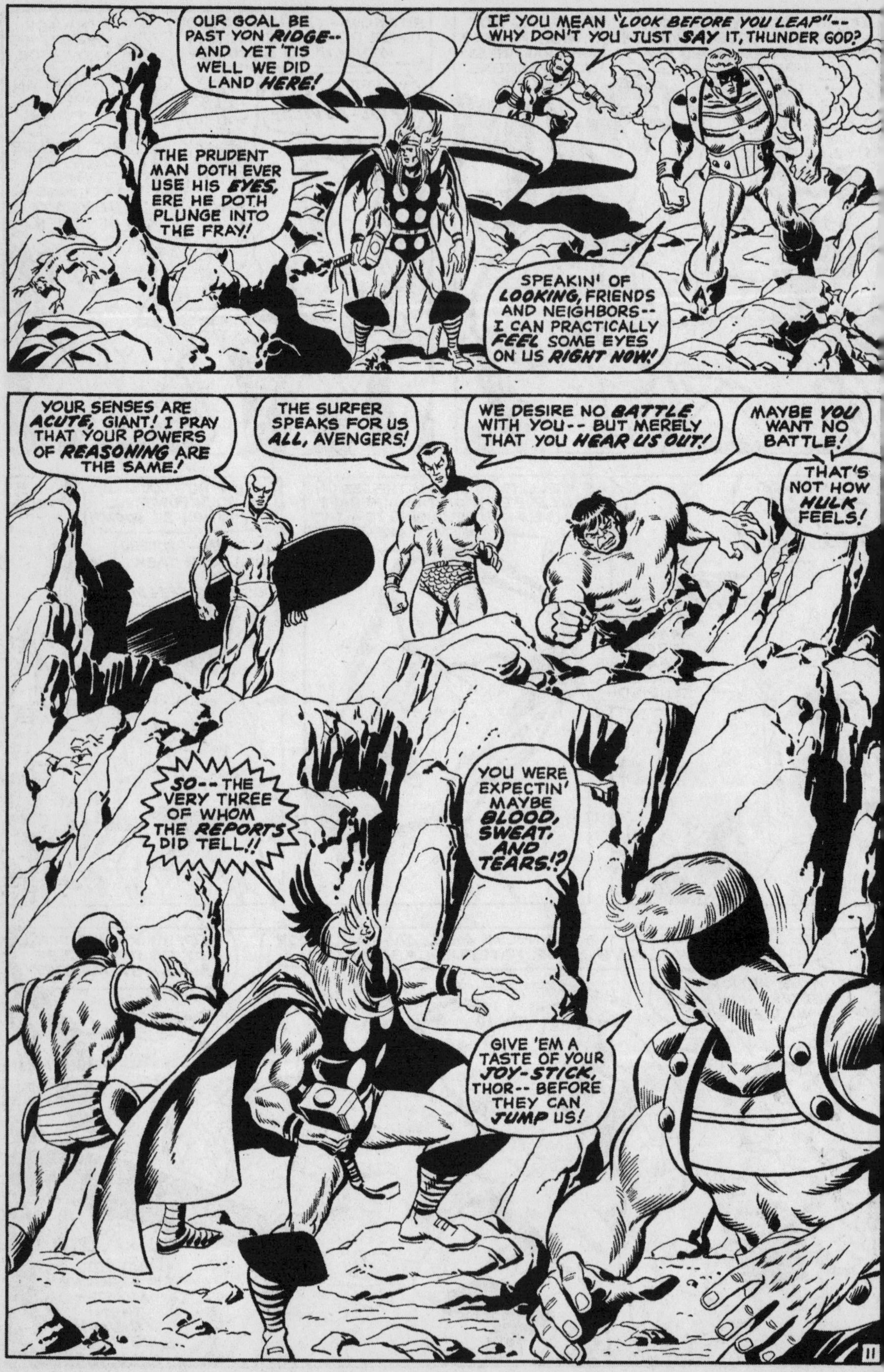
OUR GOAL BE PAST YON RIDGE-- AND YET 'TIS WELL WE DID LAND HERE!
THE PRUDENT MAN DOTH EVER USE HIS EYES, ERE HE DOTH PLUNGE INTO THE FRAY!
IF YOU MEAN "LOOK BEFORE YOU LEAP"-- WHY DON'T YOU JUST SAY IT, THUNDER GOD?
SPEAKIN' OF LOOKING, FRIENDS AND NEIGHBORS-- I CAN PRACTICALLY FEEL SOME EYES ON US RIGHT NOW!
YOUR SENSES ARE ACUTE, GIANT! I PRAY THAT YOUR POWERS OF REASONING ARE THE SAME!
THE SURFER SPEAKS FOR US ALL, AVENGERS!
WE DESIRE NO BATTLE WITH YOU-- BUT MERELY THAT YOU HEAR US OUT!
MAYBE YOU WANT NO BATTLE!
THAT'S NOT HOW HULK FEELS!
SO--THE VERY THREE OF WHOM THE REPORTS DID TELL!!
YOU WERE EXPECTIN' MAYBE BLOOD, SWEAT, AND TEARS!?
GIVE 'EM A TASTE OF YOUR JOY-STICK, THOR-- BEFORE THEY CAN JUMP US!
11

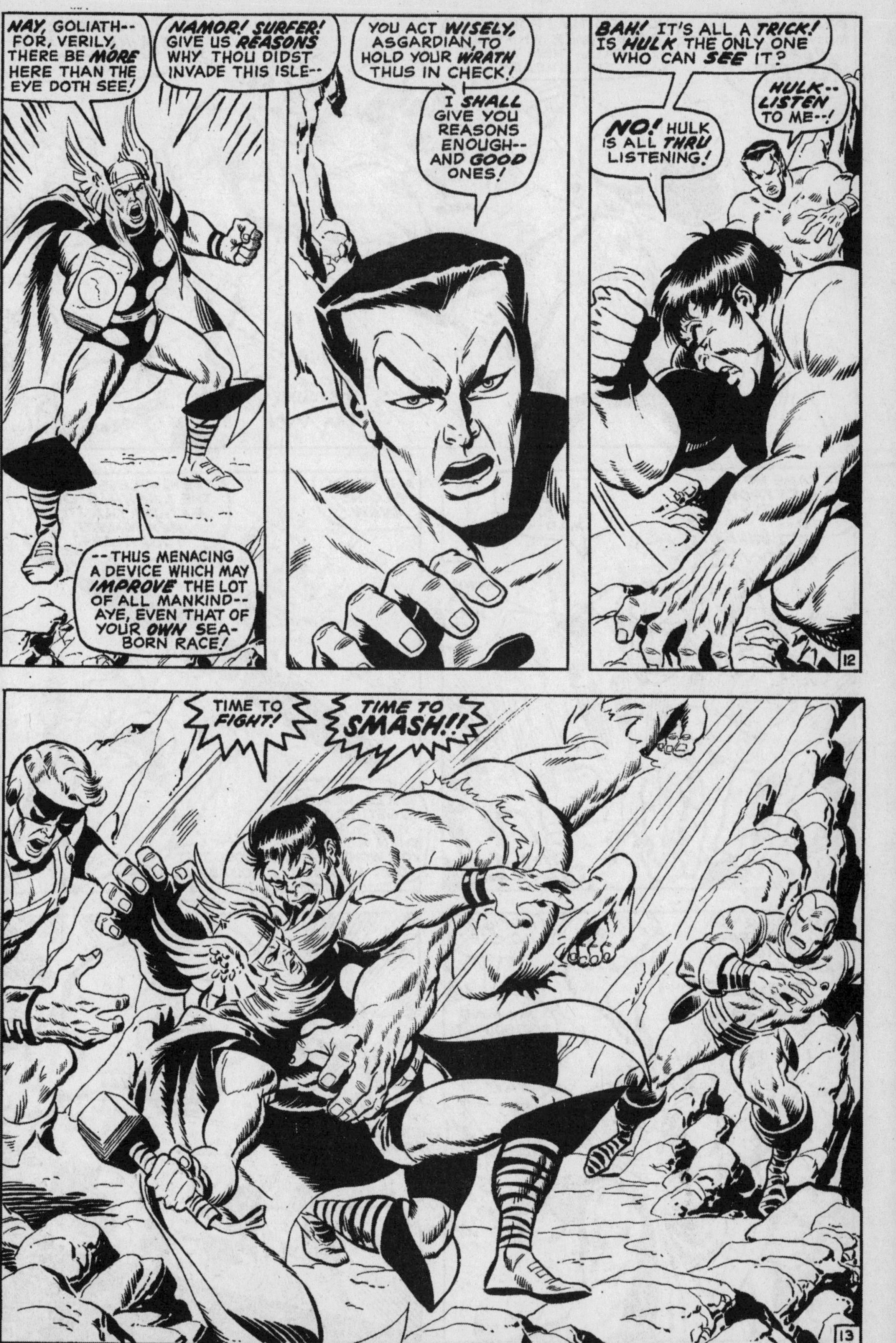
NAY, GOLIATH-- FOR, VERILY, THERE BE MORE HERE THAN THE EYE DOTH SEE!
NAMOR! SURFER! GIVE US REASONS WHY THOU DIDST INVADE THIS ISLE--
--THUS MENACING A DEVICE WHICH MAY IMPROVE THE LOT OF ALL MANKIND-- AYE, EVEN THAT OF YOUR OWN SEA-BORN RACE!
YOU ACT WISELY, ASGARDIAN, TO HOLD YOUR WRATH THUS IN CHECK!
I SHALL GIVE YOU REASONS ENOUGH-- AND GOOD ONES!
BAH! IT'S ALL A TRICK! IS HULK THE ONLY ONE WHO CAN SEE IT?
HULK-- LISTEN TO ME--!
NO! HULK IS ALL THRU LISTENING!
12
TIME TO FIGHT!
TIME TO SMASH!!
13

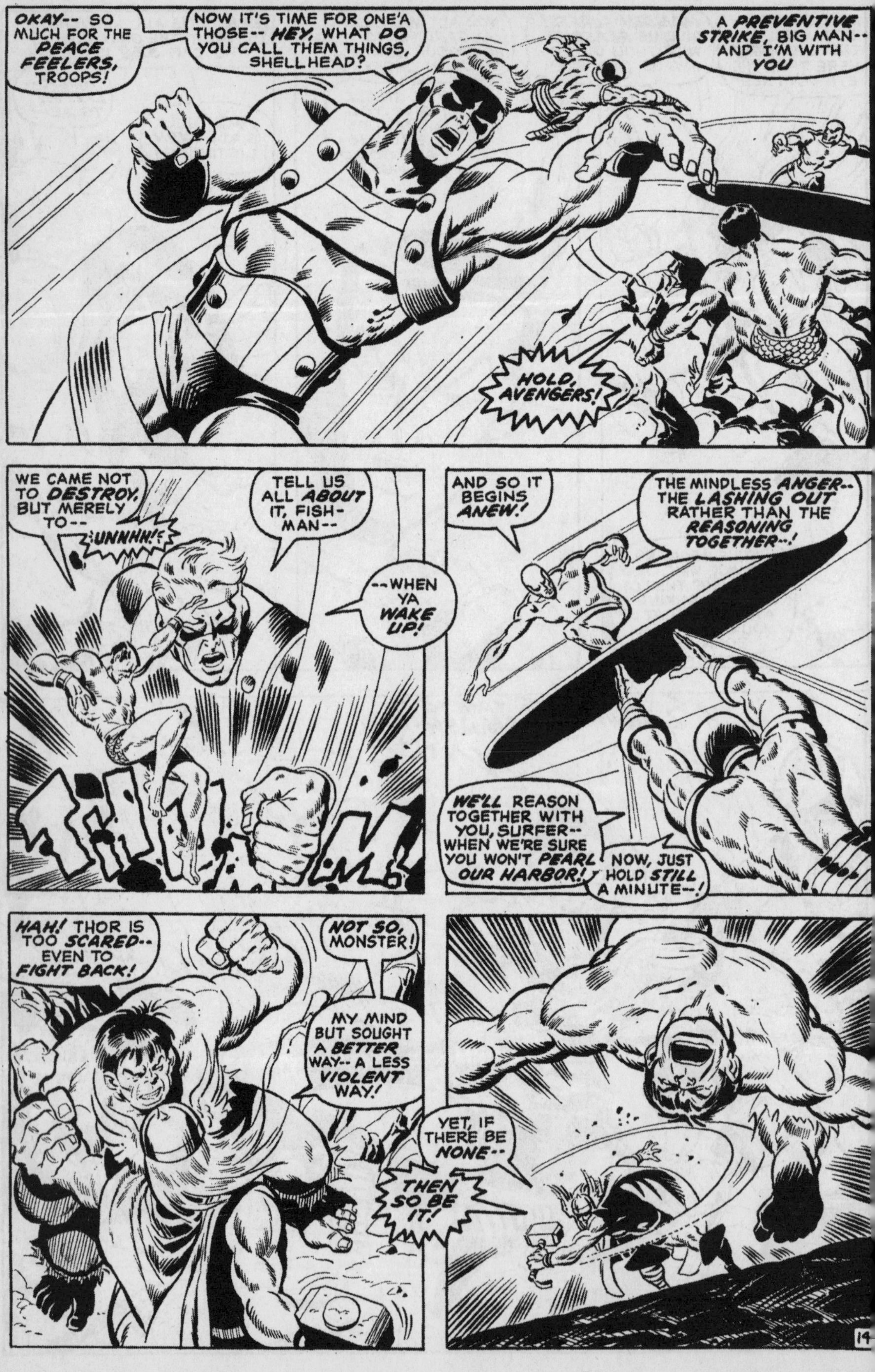
OKAY-- SO MUCH FOR THE PEACE FEELERS, TROOPS!
NOW IT'S TIME FOR ONE'A THOSE-- HEY, WHAT DO YOU CALL THEM THINGS, SHELLHEAD?
A PREVENTIVE STRIKE, BIG MAN-- AND I'M WITH YOU
HOLD, AVENGERS!
WE CAME NOT TO DESTROY, BUT MERELY TO--
UNNHH!
TELL US ALL ABOUT IT, FISH-MAN--
--WHEN YA WAKE UP!
AND SO IT BEGINS ANEW!
THE MINDLESS ANGER-- THE LASHING OUT RATHER THAN THE REASONING TOGETHER--!
WE'LL REASON TOGETHER WITH YOU, SURFER-- WHEN WE'RE SURE YOU WON'T PEARL OUR HARBOR!
NOW, JUST HOLD STILL A MINUTE--!
HAH! THOR IS TOO SCARED-- EVEN TO FIGHT BACK!
NOT SO, MONSTER!
MY MIND BUT SOUGHT A BETTER WAY-- A LESS VIOLENT WAY!
YET, IF THERE BE NONE--
THEN SO BE IT!
19

BUT-- *NAY!* THERE BE NAUGHT TO BE GAINED BY THE CLAMOR OF COMBAT!

WE MUST *HALT* THIS BATTLE, ERE--

WORDS! WORDS!

HULK IS *SICK* OF WORDS!!

WUMPP!

AND-- HULK IS SICK OF *YOU!!*

SLAM!

HULK CAUGHT YOU *OFF-BALANCE*-- EVEN MADE YOU DROP YOUR *HAMMER!*

AND NOW, BEFORE *YOU* CAN GRAB IT AGAIN--

--HULK WILL-- *HUNH?*

IT'S JUST A *LITTLE* THING-- BUT HULK CAN'T *LIFT* IT-- CAN'T *BUDGE* IT!

NONE MAY WIELD SACRED MJOLNIR, MAN-BRUTE-- NONE SAVE THE RIGHTFUL *SON* OF ODIN!

MAYBE *NOT*-- BUT HULK WON'T LET *YOU* HAVE IT, *EITHER!*

--THEN, FIGHT IS *EVEN* AGAIN!

AYE, AND *MORE* THAN EVEN, HULK!

FOR IN A MERE *SIXTY* SECONDS, THOR SHALL BECOME ONCE MORE-- *DR. DON BLAKE!*

AND THEN-- YOUR *BRUTE* STRENGTH SHALL SEAL MY *DOOM!*

15

WHILE, A DIZZYING DISTANCE OVERHEAD--

GOT YOU!!!

NOW WE'RE GOING TO *TALK* ABOUT THIS THING--!

THERE CAN BE *NO* DISCUSSION

-- WHILE YOU WOULD USE *VIOLENCE* TO ATTAIN YOUR ENDS!

AND YET-- ARE *WE THREE* ANY BETTER?

HAVE *WE* NOT USED THE THREAT OF NAKED FORCE, JUST AS --

SORRY TO ZAP YOU WHILE YOU'RE PLAYING *SOCRATES,* SPACEMAN!

BUT LIKE THEY SAY, *WAR IS HELL* --

ARRHH!

ZZZAK!

--AND *THIS* IS MOST DEFINITELY *WAR!*

HEY! IT'S BEEN A *LONG WHILE* SINCE ANYONE RECOVERED SO *FAST* FROM MY REPULSOR RAYS!

ENOUGH WORDS! THE TIME HAS COME-- FOR THE *FINAL CLASH!*

THEN THERE IS *SILENCE* -- SILENCE UNBROKEN SAVE FOR THE PAINED WHISTLING OF *AIR* THRUST ASIDE BY IRRESISTIBLE OBJECTS IN MOTION --

16

THEN, WITH A SOUND LIKE SOME SUDDEN *SONIC BOOM*-- THE TWO AIRBORNE *JUGGERNAUTS* COME TOGETHER

--AND *TWO FORMS*-- STUNNED INTO UNCONSCIOUSNESS BY THE SHEER, IMMEASURABLE *IMPACT* OF COLLISION-- PLUMMET FROM THE HEAVENS LIKE WOUNDED EAGLES--!

WHAT IN BLAZES KINDA NOISE WAS *THAT*?

:MMFFF!:

YOUR FRAIL HUMAN EARS ARE MORE *DELICATE* THAN MINE, AVENGER!

THUS, WHILE YOU STAND THUS *STUNNED*-- NAMOR STRIKES!

I AM NOT *PROUD* OF WHAT I HAVE DONE-- TO FELL AN *UNPREPARED* FOE!

BUT YOU WILL *COMPREHEND* MY REASONS WHEN--

BULL, FISH-MAN!

I SAID *BULL!*

YOU ARE A FAR *MIGHTIER* OPPONENT THAN I WOULD EVER HAVE EXPECTED, GIANT ONE!

STILL, NAMOR *MUST* TRIUMPH-- AND SO NAMOR *SHALL* TRIUMPH!

17

BUT THERE IS *NO* ANSWER-- NO ANSWER AT ALL--!

BY THE *WREATHED* HORN OF PROTEUS!

THE ONE CALLED GOLIATH-- IS *DROWNING!!*

THUS, THOUGH IT MAY MEAN WE MUST *FIGHT* ONCE MORE-- WITH THE OUTCOME STILL IN *DOUBT*--

I CANNOT-- I *WILL* NOT SUFFER SO VALIANT A FOE TO *PERISH!*

HOWEVER, THERE ARE *OTHER* FORCES NOW AFOOT ON THE ISLAND-- ONES *WITHOUT* SUPER-POWERS--!

GET *SET,* MEN! WE CAN'T LET THE *AVENGERS* DO *ALL* OUR WORK FOR US!

WE'LL OCCUPY THE *STATION* ALL BY OUR LONESOMES!

SIR-- THERE'S *ARMED* GUYS IN *FRONT* OF IT-- *BLUE* GUYS!

NOBLE IKTHON-- THE MEN WITHOUT GROW *RESTLESS*-- ALMOST AS IF THEY *SENSE*--

NOTHING MUST GO WRONG *NOW*-- WHEN I'M SO *CLOSE*--!

OPEN FIRE!!

PAKKA PA

NO! IT MUST *NOT* BE! I NEED ONLY A FEW *MOMENTS*-- A FEW *MORE* MOMENTS--!

THEN -- I SHALL *GIVE* THEM TO YOU--

--OR ELSE I SHALL *DIE!!*

HUH? NOW WHAT IN--?

HALT! BOTH SIDES MUST STOP SHOOTING-- AT *ONCE!*

HOLD IT! SHE'S RIGHT IN THE *LINE* OF FIRE!

WHOEVER SHE IS-- THAT LITTLE LADY'S GOT *GUTS!*

18

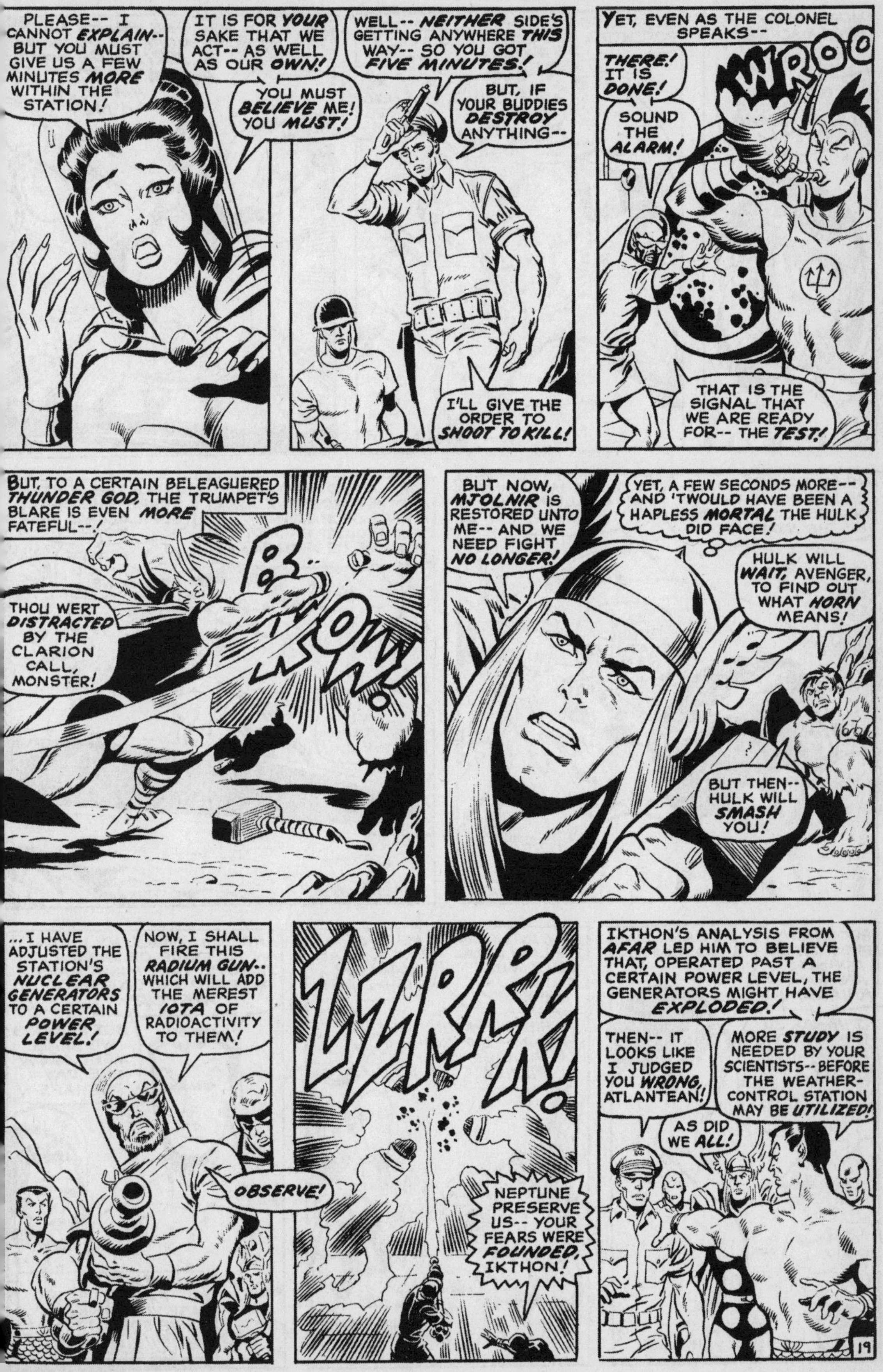
PLEASE-- I CANNOT EXPLAIN-- BUT YOU MUST GIVE US A FEW MINUTES MORE WITHIN THE STATION!
IT IS FOR YOUR SAKE THAT WE ACT-- AS WELL AS OUR OWN!
YOU MUST BELIEVE ME! YOU MUST!
WELL-- NEITHER SIDE'S GETTING ANYWHERE THIS WAY-- SO YOU GOT FIVE MINUTES!
BUT, IF YOUR BUDDIES DESTROY ANYTHING--
I'LL GIVE THE ORDER TO SHOOT TO KILL!
YET, EVEN AS THE COLONEL SPEAKS--
WROO
THERE! IT IS DONE!
SOUND THE ALARM!
THAT IS THE SIGNAL THAT WE ARE READY FOR-- THE TEST!
BUT, TO A CERTAIN BELEAGUERED THUNDER GOD, THE TRUMPET'S BLARE IS EVEN MORE FATEFUL--!
THOU WERT DISTRACTED BY THE CLARION CALL, MONSTER!
BUT NOW, MJOLNIR IS RESTORED UNTO ME-- AND WE NEED FIGHT NO LONGER!
YET, A FEW SECONDS MORE-- AND 'TWOULD HAVE BEEN A HAPLESS MORTAL THE HULK DID FACE!
HULK WILL WAIT, AVENGER, TO FIND OUT WHAT HORN MEANS!
BUT THEN-- HULK WILL SMASH YOU!
...I HAVE ADJUSTED THE STATION'S NUCLEAR GENERATORS TO A CERTAIN POWER LEVEL!
NOW, I SHALL FIRE THIS RADIUM GUN.. WHICH WILL ADD THE MEREST IOTA OF RADIOACTIVITY TO THEM!
OBSERVE!
NEPTUNE PRESERVE US-- YOUR FEARS WERE FOUNDED, IKTHON!
IKTHON'S ANALYSIS FROM AFAR LED HIM TO BELIEVE THAT, OPERATED PAST A CERTAIN POWER LEVEL, THE GENERATORS MIGHT HAVE EXPLODED!
THEN-- IT LOOKS LIKE I JUDGED YOU WRONG, ATLANTEAN!
MORE STUDY IS NEEDED BY YOUR SCIENTISTS-- BEFORE THE WEATHER-CONTROL STATION MAY BE UTILIZED!
AS DID WE ALL!
19

MORE STUDY? BAH! MACHINE IS *BAD,* THAT'S ALL!

BUT, HULK WILL TURN IT INTO-- *SCRAP METAL!*

NO, YOU FOOL! CAN'T YOU SEE ITS POTENTIAL FOR *GOOD* -- AS WELL AS *EVIL!*

ALL HULK SEES IS--

--HE WANTS NO MORE TO DO WITH *FRIENDS* WHO *ATTACK* HIM..!

HE IS *GONE!* BUT AT LEAST, IN HIS WRATH AGAINST US, HE FORGOT THE *STATION!*

STILL, THAT MEANS-- OUR ALLIANCE IS *ENDED!*

AND WELL THAT IT *IS,* NAMOR!

FOR, I COULD NOT ENDURE ANOTHER *MOMENT* AMONG A RACE OF *MADMEN* -- WHO RAIL AT EACH OTHER IN NAME OF *PROGRESS!*

WHERE THE SURFER SOARS-- HE SHALL SOAR *ALONE* ONCE MORE!

FARE YOU WELL!

FARE YOU-- WELL--!

GOOD NEWS FROM *THIS* CORNER ANYWAY, ATLANTEAN!

I CAN ASK-- *NO MORE!*

I'VE DOPED THINGS OUT TO THE *U.N.* BRASS-- AND THEY'VE AGREED TO *RE-THINK* THIS WHOLE THING!

NOW, AVENGERS-- THE LADY DORMA AND I MUST TAKE OUR *LEAVE!*

ME *TOO!* YOU PACK A MEAN WALLOP, FISH-MAN!

WHEN WE MEET AGAIN-- I PRAY IT WILL BE IN *PEACE!*

AS THE SURFER DID SAY-- FARE THEE *WELL!*

AND SO IT *ENDS,* MY LADY-- AN ALLIANCE OF *THREE TITANS,* THAT MIGHT HAVE ALTERED THE COURSE OF *HISTORY!*

BUT PERHAPS WE SHALL MEET *AGAIN* ONE DAY-- PERHAPS--!

NEXT: BUT FIRST, JUST IN CASE YOU THINK WE'VE FORGOTTEN--! *THE* **WEDDING!**

MARVEL FEATURE ™

25¢
CC
1 DEC
02122

MARVEL FEATURE ™

PRESENTS
THE DEFENDERS ™

HULK

SUB-MARINER

DR. STRANGE ™

MARVEL COMICS GROUP

THIS IS IT! THE AWESOME **ORIGIN** OF THE MOST FABULOUS FIGHTING-TEAM OF *ALL!*

BONUS! STILL ANOTHER *ALL-NEW* BLOCKBUSTER! *"THE RETURN OF DR. STRANGE!"*

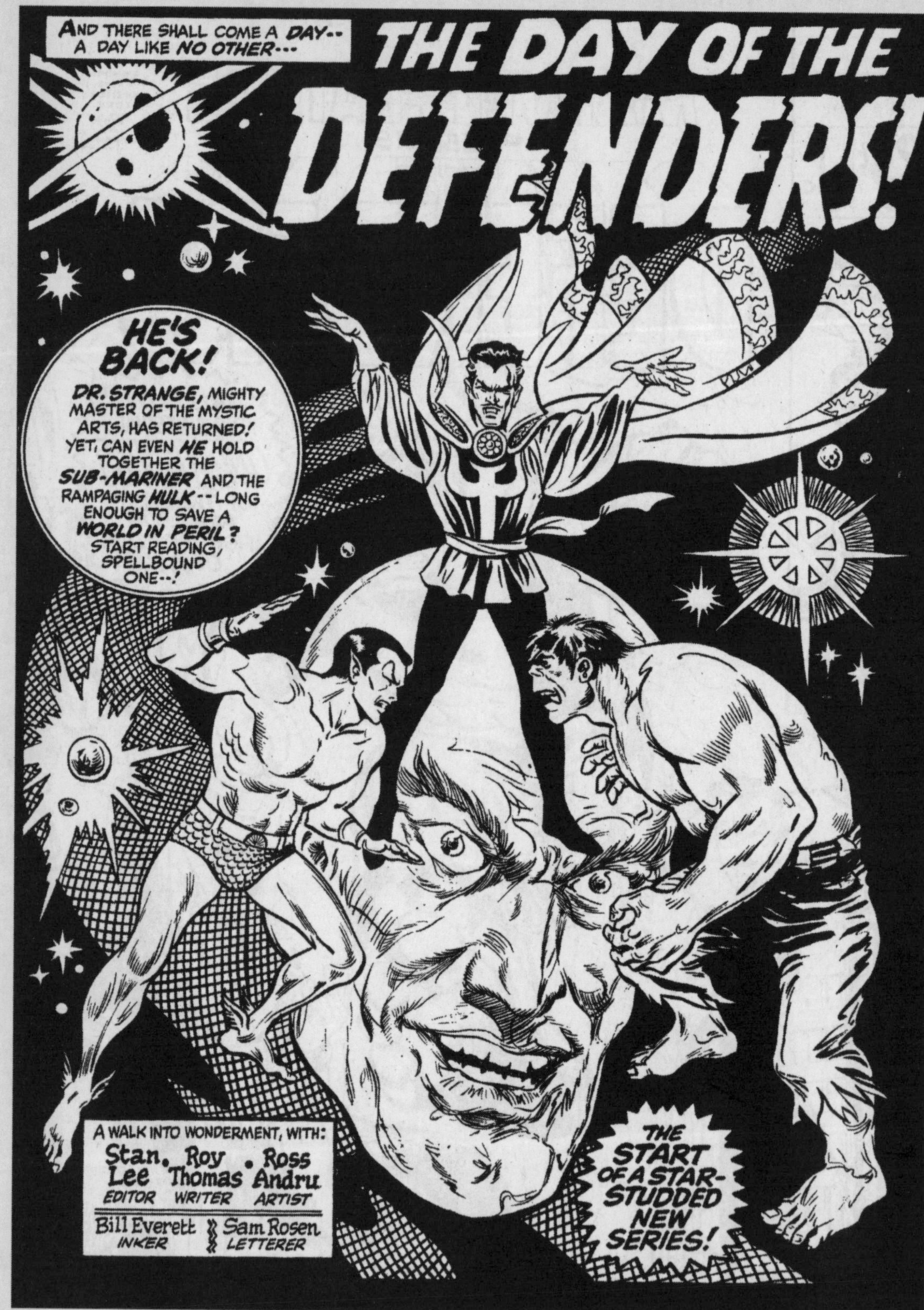

AND THERE SHALL COME A DAY-- A DAY LIKE NO OTHER---
THE DAY OF THE DEFENDERS!
HE'S BACK! DR. STRANGE, MIGHTY MASTER OF THE MYSTIC ARTS, HAS RETURNED! YET, CAN EVEN HE HOLD TOGETHER THE SUB-MARINER AND THE RAMPAGING HULK -- LONG ENOUGH TO SAVE A WORLD IN PERIL? START READING, SPELLBOUND ONE--!
A WALK INTO WONDERMENT, WITH: Stan Lee EDITOR • Roy Thomas WRITER • Ross Andru ARTIST
Bill Everett INKER • Sam Rosen LETTERER
THE START OF A STAR-STUDDED NEW SERIES!

FOR LONG MONTHS IT STOOD *EMPTY,* THIS DARK-GABLED OLD HOUSE ON A SHADOWY BACK-STREET IN *GREEN-WICH VILLAGE*--- WITH SPIDERS ITS SOLE TENANTS, SAD-WINGED BATS ITS ONLY VISITORS---

BUT NOW THERE IS *LIFE* AMID THE SHADOWS ONCE MORE. NOW THERE IS----

--DR. STRANGE, I HAVE BROUGHT YOU *TEA,* AS YOU ORDERED.

STILL, IT GROWS *LATE,* MASTER. THE CHURCH CLOCK STRIKES *MID-NIGHT.*

YES-- THE *WITCHING* HOUR-- AND YET---

DR. STRANGE.....
DR. STRANGE...

EH? WHY DID YOU CALL MY NAME *AGAIN,* WONG--

-- WHEN YOU ARE RIGHT HERE *BESIDE* ME?

"AGAIN" MASTER? I DIDN'T! I MERELY---

COME, DR. STRANGE...COME... COME... COME!

AND ONCE *MORE* IT CALLS. DO YOU NOT *HEAR* IT?

I HEAR THE TWELFTH CHIMING OF THE *CLOCK,* MASTER--- THAT IS *ALL.*

THEN, THERE CAN BE BUT *ONE* ANSWER--

LEAVE ME NOW, FAITHFUL ONE---

AND ADMIT *NO ONE* TILL I SUMMON YOU ANEW.

YES, MASTER.

IT CAN ONLY BE A *MYSTIC* CALL-- MEANT FOR *MY* EARS ALONE.

AND I SHALL *HEED* ITS SIREN CALL...

-- OR, RATHER, MY *ASTRAL BODY* SHALL!

2.

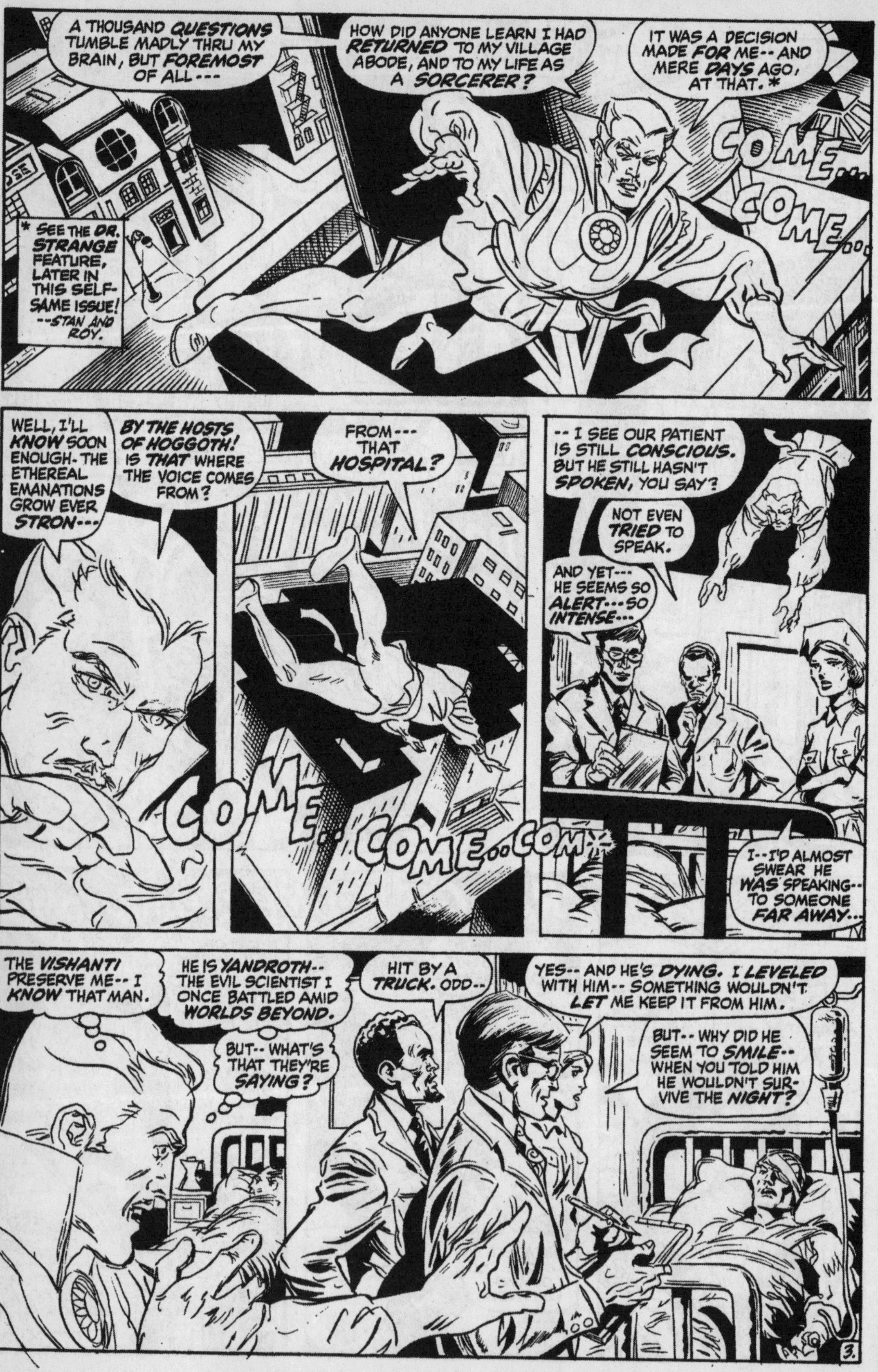
A THOUSAND QUESTIONS TUMBLE MADLY THRU MY BRAIN, BUT FOREMOST OF ALL---
HOW DID ANYONE LEARN I HAD RETURNED TO MY VILLAGE ABODE, AND TO MY LIFE AS A SORCERER?
IT WAS A DECISION MADE FOR ME-- AND MERE DAYS AGO, AT THAT. *
COME...
COME...
* SEE THE DR. STRANGE FEATURE, LATER IN THIS SELF-SAME ISSUE! --STAN AND ROY.
WELL, I'LL KNOW SOON ENOUGH- THE ETHEREAL EMANATIONS GROW EVER STRON---
BY THE HOSTS OF HOGGOTH! IS THAT WHERE THE VOICE COMES FROM?
FROM--- THAT HOSPITAL?
COME...COME...COM--
-- I SEE OUR PATIENT IS STILL CONSCIOUS. BUT HE STILL HASN'T SPOKEN, YOU SAY?
NOT EVEN TRIED TO SPEAK.
AND YET--- HE SEEMS SO ALERT---SO INTENSE---
I--I'D ALMOST SWEAR HE WAS SPEAKING-- TO SOMEONE FAR AWAY...
THE VISHANTI PRESERVE ME-- I KNOW THAT MAN.
HE IS YANDROTH-- THE EVIL SCIENTIST I ONCE BATTLED AMID WORLDS BEYOND.
BUT-- WHAT'S THAT THEY'RE SAYING?
HIT BY A TRUCK. ODD--
YES-- AND HE'S DYING. I LEVELED WITH HIM-- SOMETHING WOULDN'T LET ME KEEP IT FROM HIM.
BUT-- WHY DID HE SEEM TO SMILE-- WHEN YOU TOLD HIM HE WOULDN'T SURVIVE THE NIGHT?
3.

COME. LET HIM *REST*.

A MAN HAS A RIGHT--- TO *DIE* IN PEACE.

"IN PEACE"! DID *YOU* HEAR THAT, MY DEAR DR. *STRANGE*?

IF THOSE BUMBLING FOOLS--ONLY *SUS-PECTED* THE CIRCUMSTANCES UNDER WHICH I INTEND TO DIE--THEY WOULD *TREMBLE* WHERE THEY STAND.

YANDROTH! THEN-- YOU *CAN* SPEAK, AFTER ALL.

BUT-- HOW CAN *YOU* SEE MY ASTRAL FORM, WHEN THOSE *OTHERS*--

YOU --CONFUSE *THIS* YANDROTH-- WITH *ANOTHER*, OLD FRIEND.

THE YANDROTH *YOU* RECALL-- NO LONGER *EXISTS*.

--AND WHO AT LAST SEEMED *DOOMED*-- FATED TO *FALL* FOREVER, FOREVER, THRU A WORLD THAT *NEVER WAS*.

I REMEMBER HIM-- I *WAS* HE -- HE WHO LED YOU A MERRY CHASE THRU NUMBER-LESS *UNIVERSES*---

"BUT-- I STOPPED FALLING, EVENTUALLY-- FOUND MYSELF AMID A COSMOS TOTALLY ALIEN TO MY SCIENCE-TRAINED SENSES---

"--A WORLD WHERE EUCLID HAD NEVER TROD -- AND EINSTEIN WAS A DELUDED CHILD--"

IT'S UN-BELIEVABLE! I NEVER DREAMED SUCH A PLACE COULD *EXIST*.

I CAN FEEL ITS ENERGY -- ITS *ESSENCE*-- FLOWING INTO MY MIND, MY VERY *BEING*!

4

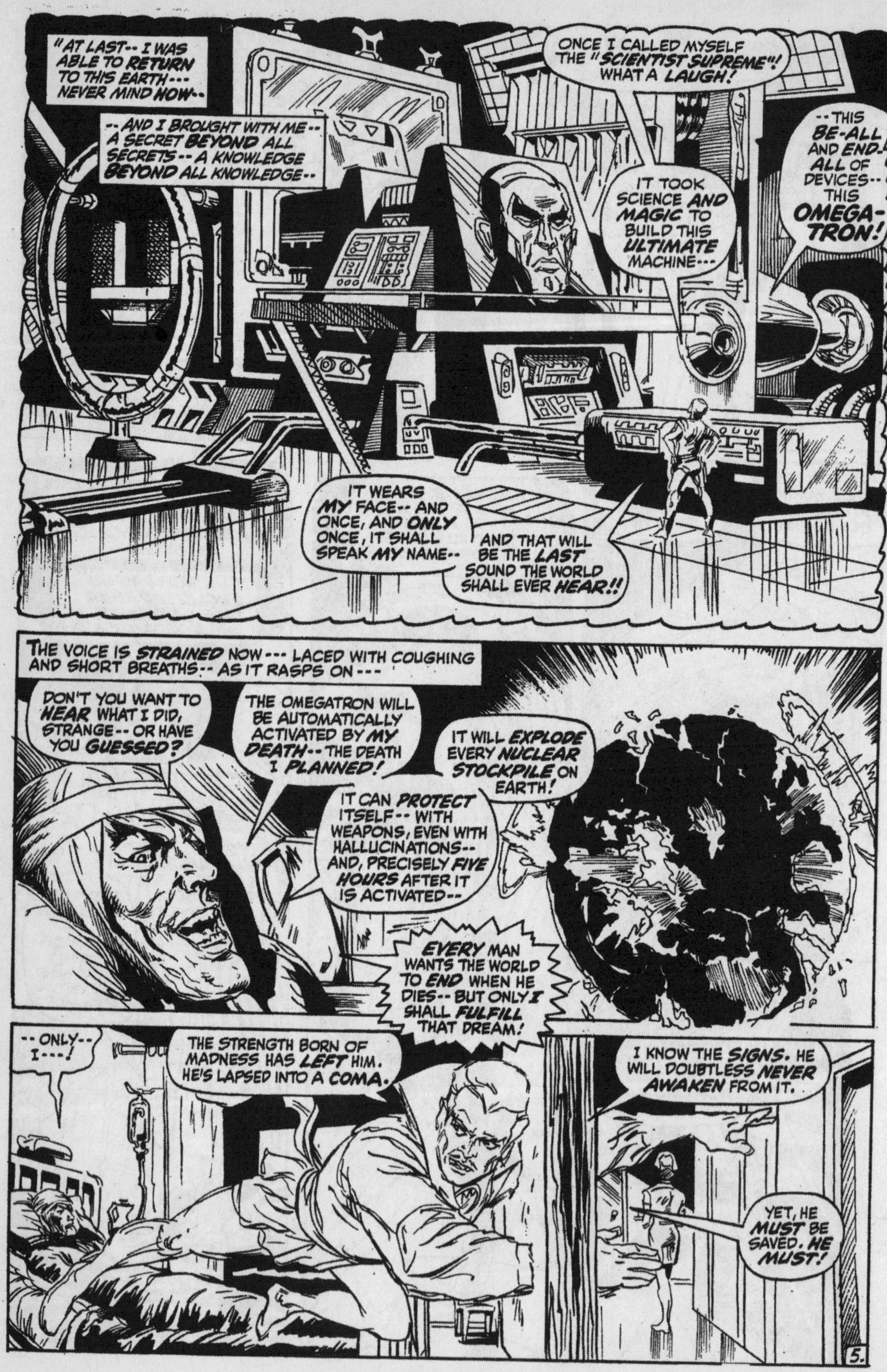
"AT LAST-- I WAS ABLE TO RETURN TO THIS EARTH--- NEVER MIND HOW--
--AND I BROUGHT WITH ME-- A SECRET BEYOND ALL SECRETS-- A KNOWLEDGE BEYOND ALL KNOWLEDGE--
ONCE I CALLED MYSELF THE "SCIENTIST SUPREME"! WHAT A LAUGH!
IT TOOK SCIENCE AND MAGIC TO BUILD THIS ULTIMATE MACHINE---
--THIS BE-ALL AND END-ALL OF DEVICES-- THIS OMEGATRON!
IT WEARS MY FACE-- AND ONCE, AND ONLY ONCE, IT SHALL SPEAK MY NAME--
AND THAT WILL BE THE LAST SOUND THE WORLD SHALL EVER HEAR!!
THE VOICE IS STRAINED NOW--- LACED WITH COUGHING AND SHORT BREATHS-- AS IT RASPS ON---
DON'T YOU WANT TO HEAR WHAT I DID, STRANGE-- OR HAVE YOU GUESSED?
THE OMEGATRON WILL BE AUTOMATICALLY ACTIVATED BY MY DEATH-- THE DEATH I PLANNED!
IT WILL EXPLODE EVERY NUCLEAR STOCKPILE ON EARTH!
IT CAN PROTECT ITSELF-- WITH WEAPONS, EVEN WITH HALLUCINATIONS-- AND, PRECISELY FIVE HOURS AFTER IT IS ACTIVATED--
EVERY MAN WANTS THE WORLD TO END WHEN HE DIES-- BUT ONLY I SHALL FULFILL THAT DREAM!
--ONLY-- I---!
THE STRENGTH BORN OF MADNESS HAS LEFT HIM. HE'S LAPSED INTO A COMA.
I KNOW THE SIGNS. HE WILL DOUBTLESS NEVER AWAKEN FROM IT.
YET, HE MUST BE SAVED. HE MUST!

AND, SINCE HE IS *BEYOND* THE REACH OF MAGIC, WHITE *OR* BLACK---

--TO PRESS *THESE* WORTHIES INTO MY SERVICE.

I MUST SUMMON *ALL* THE LITTLE POWER THAT RESIDES WITHIN THIS ASTRAL SHELL---

IN THE NAME OF OMNIPOTENT *OSHTUR*-- HE WHO HOLDS THE *WORLDS* IN SWAY---

I COMMAND YE *RETURN*-- AND STRIVE TO SAVE THE *MANY* LIVES, THRU THE *ONE!*

THEY *OBEY* AS IN A TRANCE, BUT STILL MY *HEART* BROODS WITHIN ME.

IF ONLY *I* WERE DOWN THERE BESIDE THEM---

VAIN HOPE, THAT!

WHAT COULD *STEPHEN STRANGE* DO-- A SURGEON WHOSE SKILL HAS *FLED* HIS HANDS, FOREVER?

NO, IF YANDROTH CAN BE SAVED, IT IS *THEY* WHO MUST DO IT-- NOT I.

AND YET, THE ODDS ARE ALL *AGAINST* THEM-- *OVERWHELMING-LY* AGAINST THEM.

WAIT! WHAT ARE THEY *SAYING*--?

KEEP THE SCALPEL, NURSE---

--THIS MAN'S *DEAD.*

PITY HE DIED SO FAR FROM *HOME* -- FROM HIS *LOVED* ONES.

ONLY *IDENTIFICATION* HE HAD WAS A MAILING ADDRESS --AT *POINT PROMONTORY,* MAINE.

THEN --THAT IS MY *ONE* HOPE!

MOST MEN WOULD GIVE WAY, NOW, TO THE *DESPAIR* WHICH GNAWS AT A BENUMBED SOUL---

BUT, THE PRICE OF *VIGILANCE* IS THE SURRENDER *OF TIME---*

-- TIME FOR *REGRET* --TIME FOR *TEARS.*

6

WHAT I *NEXT* MUST DO WOULD TAX MY ASTRAL FORM *BEYOND* ITS LIMITS---

THUS, BODY *AND* SPIRIT MUST AGAIN BE *ONE.*

AND NOW, WITH FURROWED BROW, THE MYSTIC MASTER VENTURES FORTH ANEW---

--OBLIVIOUS TO THE STRAGGLING FEW WHO MAY DIMLY PERCEIVE HIM---

--IN THE WEE DARK HOURS OF MORN.

NORTHWARD HE DRIFTS, HIS CLOAK OF LEVITATION BEARING HIM ABOVE THE ROCK-BOUND SHORES OF NEW ENGLAND---

AND, TO THE NAKED EYE, HE MUST APPEAR A MAN A-DREAM---HIS MIND'S VISION FIXED ON SOME AWESOME INNER GOAL---

AH, BUT THE REALITY OF THE MATTER IS FAR, FAR DIFFERENT---

THERE IS THE ONE I SEEK.

PRINCE NAMOR -- THE SUB-MARINER!

I SUSPECT THAT *MAGIC* ALONE WILL *NOT* OVERCOME YANDROTH'S DOOMSDAY-DEVICE.

BUT, WITH ONE SUCH AS *THIS* TO AID ME---

GREETINGS, NAMOR.

DR. STRANGE...

7.

I'LL WASTE NO WORDS, MY FRIEND.

WE MET BUT *BRIEFLY BEFORE** -- YET, I LEARNED RESPECT FOR YOUR SEA-BORN *STRENGTH,* AND FOR YOUR PRINCE-LY *COURAGE.*

I SENSED YOUR NEARNESS AND SOUGHT YOU OUT-- BECAUSE TONIGHT, I HAVE NEED OF *BOTH.*

I SHALL BE AS FRANK AS *YOU,* SORCERER.

IT *JOYS* MY HEART TO SEE YOU FREE OF THE CLUTCHES OF THE EVIL *UNDYING ONES.*

STILL, I AM PRINCE OF ATLANTIS *NO MORE* -- MERELY A *MAN,* IN SEARCH OF A LOST *FATHER* ...A VANISHED *HERITAGE*...

*IN THE PAGES OF *SUB-MARINER* #22! --S.

NOR SHALL I FIND *EITHER,* IF I ALLOW *OLD TIES* TO SWAY ME FROM MY QUEST.

NEITHER SHALL YOU FIND WHAT YOU SEEK, NAMOR--

--IF *ATOMIC FIRE* LIGHTS THE SKIES, BEFORE THE *SUN* MAY.

WHAT? IF YOU SPEAK THE TRUTH-- THEN *SAY ON.*

THEN, WHEN DR. STRANGE HAS SWIFTLY FINISHED...

YOUR TALE IS TOO UNCANNY--- TOO *FRIGHTENING* TO BE FALSE.

I SHALL HELP YOU-- AND THERE ARE *OTHERS*---

-- OTHERS WHOSE VAST POWERS *COMPLEMENT* MY OWN, AND WHO ONCE WERE MY *ALLIES IN PERIL.*

I SPEAK OF THE MIGHTY-MUSCLED *HULK*--- AND OF THE ONE CALLED THE *SILVER SURFER.*

WELL ADVISED, NAMOR--IF THEY BE CLOSE AT HAND.

FIRST, LET THE *EYE OF AGAMOTTO* REVEAL UNTO US--- THE *SURFER.*

AHH -- NOW I BEHOLD HIM, SKIMMING ALONG THE OUTER REACHES OF EARTH'S *GRAVITY.*

AND NOW, HE SEEMS TO GATHER *SPEED*-- FOR SOME PUR-POSE I CANNOT FATHOM.

"*DISASTER!* HIS GLEAMING SURFBOARD HAS STRUCK SOME ALL-BUT-INVISIBLE *BARRIER*--

"--AND HE FALLS EARTHWARD, LIKE A WOUNDED *OSPREY!*

8

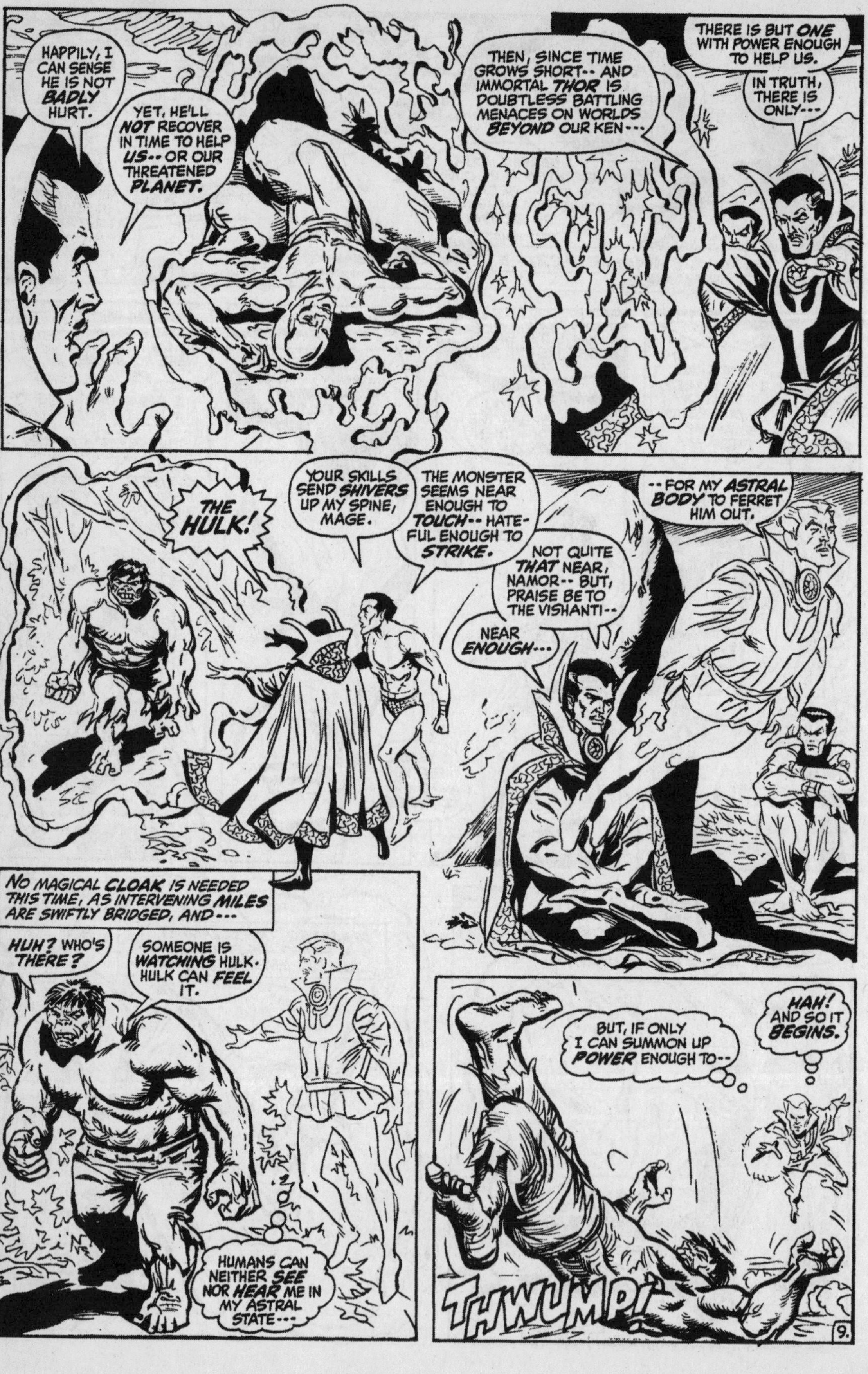
HAPPILY, I CAN SENSE HE IS NOT BADLY HURT.
YET, HE'LL NOT RECOVER IN TIME TO HELP US-- OR OUR THREATENED PLANET.
THEN, SINCE TIME GROWS SHORT-- AND IMMORTAL THOR IS DOUBTLESS BATTLING MENACES ON WORLDS BEYOND OUR KEN---
THERE IS BUT ONE WITH POWER ENOUGH TO HELP US.
IN TRUTH, THERE IS ONLY---
THE HULK!
YOUR SKILLS SEND SHIVERS UP MY SPINE, MAGE.
THE MONSTER SEEMS NEAR ENOUGH TO TOUCH-- HATEFUL ENOUGH TO STRIKE.
NOT QUITE THAT NEAR, NAMOR-- BUT, PRAISE BE TO THE VISHANTI--
NEAR ENOUGH---
--FOR MY ASTRAL BODY TO FERRET HIM OUT.
NO MAGICAL CLOAK IS NEEDED THIS TIME, AS INTERVENING MILES ARE SWIFTLY BRIDGED, AND---
HUH? WHO'S THERE?
SOMEONE IS WATCHING HULK. HULK CAN FEEL IT.
HUMANS CAN NEITHER SEE NOR HEAR ME IN MY ASTRAL STATE---
BUT, IF ONLY I CAN SUMMON UP POWER ENOUGH TO--
HAH! AND SO IT BEGINS.
THWUMP!
9.

SOMETHING--- *SOMEONE* PUSHED HULK! TRIED TO MAKE HULK LOOK *STUPID.*

BUT HULK WILL *FIND* THAT SOME-ONE-- AND *SMASH* HIM!

AH, BRAINLESS ONE-- IF ONLY YOU KNEW HOW I WISH YOU *COULD* SEE ME--!

IT'S *YOU* WHO'S BRAINLESS-- NOT HULK.

NOT HULK!

GRUNCH!

VIPERS OF VALTORR! I DARED NOT HOPE FOR THIS.

SOMETHING IN THE HULK'S *WARPED NATURE* ENABLES HIM TO *SEE* AND *HEAR* MY ASTRAL SELF.

YOU CALL HULK BRAINLESS-- *WARPED*-- WON'T LEAVE HULK *ALONE.*

THEN HULK WILL *MAKE* YOU L--

HUHNN?

YOU *SEE,* HULK? YOU CAN DO *NOTHING* TO HURT-- A MAN WHO ISN'T *HERE.*

BUT NOW, I GROW *BORED* WITH YOUR *BESTIAL MUTTER-INGS----* YOUR *SNARLED IDIOCIES.*

FLAMM!

NOW, I TRULY *AM* LEAVING-- NOR MUST YOU DARE TO *FOLLOW* ME.

NO ONE TELLS HULK WHAT TO DO!

HULK IS *STRONG...* THE STRONG-EST THERE *IS.*

HULK *WILL* FOLLOW YOU-- *HOUND* YOU-- TILL ONE OF US GETS *TIRED.*

AND-- HULK *NEVER* GETS TIRED!

HE'S EVEN MORE *POWERFUL* THAN I REMEMBERED.

IF ONLY I CAN KEEP HIS *ATTENTION* FROM FLAGGING, LONG ENOUGH--

NOT-- FOLLOW YOU--?

THUDDA THUDDA

10.

LEAPING-- LUMBERING-- THE CHASE *CONTINUES,* UNTIL---

BY THE *SILENT SARGASSO!* THE HULK DRAWS NEAR-- AS IF PURSUING A *PHANTOM.*

BUT-- DR. STRANGE HAS SAT *HERE,* ALL THIS TIME--!

SO, NOW THERE ARE *TWO* OF THE ONE I CHASED.

WELL, *SOON* THERE WILL BE-- *NONE!*

NAMOR-- IF YOU *FAIL* ME NOW---

STOP, HULK!

NAMOR SAID-- *STOP!*

MY *THANKS* FOR DEFLECTING THAT STONE, ATLANTEAN. AND, *NOW*--

WILL YOU *CEASE* YOUR STRUGGLES, MONSTER-- AND *LISTEN* TO US?

LIGHTNING -- OUT OF NOWHERE -- ALL *AROUND* HULK---

HULK *WILL* STOP-- HULK *WILL* LISTEN--

BUT JUST FOR A *MINUTE.*

THEN, LIGHTNING-- *BEGONE!* FOR, THAT IS ALL I *ASK.*

HULK-- YOU WALKED WITH *NAMOR* ONCE BEFORE, AND HE FOUND YOU *MANY FOES* TO FIGHT.

THIS TIME, HE AND I VOW YOU WILL FIND *GLORIES IN PLENTY* IN BATTLE-- IF YOU'LL COME WITH *US.*

WELL? WHAT SAY YOU?

HULK DOESN'T SEE MUCH *GLORY* IN FIGHTING-- JUST WANTS PEOPLE NOT TO *BOTHER* HIM.

BUT-- IF YOU WANT TO BE HULK'S *FRIEND*-- HULK *WILL* GO WITH YOU.

THEN-- A *FRIEND* IS WHAT I SHALL *BE,* BEHEMOTH--

A *FRIEND* TO YOU-- AND TO THE *EARTH!*

POINT PROMONTORY: WHERE PEOPLE YET TREASURE THE SWEET, STILL GIFT OF SOLITUDE...

---AND WHERE A SOLE, STRANGELY-GARBED VISITOR MIGHT BE ILL-RECEIVED IN THE LONELY HOUR JUST BEFORE DAWN---

---IF HE HAD NOT THE SORCEROUS SKILL TO CAST AN EERIE SPELL UPON THE WHOLE---

--SO THAT NAUGHT IS SEEN, BESIDES--

AYEH? WHAT CAN I DO FOR YE, SON?

I'M LOOKING FOR-- THAT NEW BUILDING THAT WENT UP NEAR HERE RECENTLY.

I'VE BUSINESS THERE, BUT I SEEM TO HAVE LOST MY WAY...

WHY, EZRA, HE MUST BE TALKIN' ABOUT--- THE LIGHTHOUSE.

NOT MUCH ELSE THAT'S NEW AROUND THESE PARTS.

A BODY'D FIND THAT RIGHT OFF THE DIRT ROAD THREE MILES YONDER-- IF HE WAS LOOKIN'!

MY THANKS TO YOU BOTH.

-- SUCH A MANNERLY YOUNG MAN, NOT LIKE SOME THESE DAYS.

YE'RE RIGHT, SAREY...

STILL, FER JUST A MINUTE THERE, I COULD'VE SWORN HE WAS WEARIN'-- AN OPERY CAPE.

EYES GOIN' BAD ON ME, I RECKON.

POINT PROMONTORY: WHERE SURGING WATERS POUND THE ROCKY NEW ENGLAND SHORE --- AND THE FATE OF WORLDS IS LIT BY ARCS OF STABBING LIGHT...

CAN ANY DOUBT THAT THIS IS THE PLACE WE SEEK?

NAY-- FOR NEVER WAS THERE SUCH A LIGHTHOUSE, ON ANY OF THE SEVEN SEAS.

12.

HULK DOESN'T *UNDER-STAND*. IF ENEMIES ARE THERE, LET'S GO IN *AFTER* THEM.

THAT MAY BE MORE *DIFFICULT* THAN IT APPEARS, BEHEMOTH!

DO YOU *SEE?* A BUBBLE OF INVISIBLE *ENERGY* SHIELDS THE PLACE--- AS SURELY AS THAT ELECTRIFIED *FENCE.*

BUT, MY MAGIC MIGHT BE MORE *EFFECTIVE*-- ONCE THOSE DEFENSES WERE SMASHED.

YOU TWO MUST *DESTROY* THEM FOR ME.

HAH! "SMASH"! "DESTROY"!

NOW YOU SPEAK WORDS EVEN *HULK* KNOWS.

--WHILE *NAMOR* KNOWS, DR. STRANGE, THAT HE IS NO MAN'S *LACKEY*--- TO BE TOLD WHAT HE *SHALL* DO--WHAT HE *MUST* DO.

I--AM *SORRY,* ATLANTEAN. I DIDN'T *MEAN*---

THERE IS NO *TIME* TO WASTE ON WORDS.

I SHALL STRIKE FROM THE *SEA,* FOR A WORLD *IMPERILLED*---

--AND THEN, I'LL DO YOUR BIDDING *NO LONGER!*

NOR WOULD I ASK *MORE* OF YOU.

NOW, *HULK*---

LET *NAMOR* SWIM AROUND TO THE BACK, LIKE A *FISH.*

THIS IS THE *HULK'S* WAY---

--THE *FRONT* WAY!

13.

SO -- SOMEONE BUILT THAT FENCE TO *SHOCK* HULK, DID THEY -- TO KEEP HULK *OUT?*...

WELL, HULK IS *TOO SMART* FOR THEM.

ZZZAK

NOW *NOTHING* WILL STOP HULK FROM--

HUH??

ACID -- HURTING HULK'S *FOOT!*

NOW HULK IS *MAD!*

NOW THEY WILL *PAY!*

THEN, SUDDENLY---

FWOOSH!

--A WALL OF SEARING *FIRE* ERUPTS IN THE GREEN GIANT'S PATH---

--MAMMOTH *FLAME-THROWERS,* WHOSE DEADLY TONGUES DART MURDEROUSLY OUT-- THREATENING TO ENGULF EVEN THE MIGHTY-MUSCLED *HULK*---

WHILE, *BELOW*---

THIS IS ALMOST.. *TOO* SIMPLE.

YET, THESE ICE-CHILL WATERS HAVE RESTORED MY FULL *POWER*--- MY *CONFIDENCE*---

AND, ARMED WITH THE SEA-BEGOTTEN *STRENGTH* WHICH IS MY HERITAGE---

--THERE IS *NO* TRAP I DARE NOT *DEFY!*

WRAMM!

14

AND YET--- PERHAPS THAT METAL *DOOR* WAS THE ONLY---

HAH! I SPOKE *TOO SOON.*

NOW, THE VERY *WALLS* CLOSE IN-- TO *CRUSH* ME.

BUT, THESE WALLS--- WERE MADE-- FOR *LESSER* FISH---

NOT FOR *NAMOR!*

RRAKKA

AND, ON *ANOTHER* LEVEL---

FIRE GETTING *LOWER* --ALL THE TIME---

BUT *THIS* TIME THEY GOT-- *TOO LOW.*

NOW, WHOEVER YOU ARE-- HULK IS *COMING* FOR YOU.

DO YOU *HEAR?*

HULK IS *COMING* FOR YOU!

BOOM

WHILE, ON THE *THIRD* FRONT OF THIS FATE-FUL BATTLE---

THE MOMENT HAS COME.

THE MOMENT WHEN I MUST CALL UPON ALL THE *POWERS* THAT BE---

--TO GIVE MY *ASTRAL BODY* THE STRENGTH TO *PIERCE* THAT BULWARK OF METAL AND MAGIC-- AND SEE WHAT LIES *BEYOND!*

I CALL FOR AID UPON THE HOARY HOSTS OF *HOGGOTH*-- THE DARKSOME *DEMONS OF DENAK*---

...UPON THE NAME OF THE OMNIPOTENT *OSHTUR*...

AYE-- EVEN UPON-- THE SUPREME *SATANNISH*... HIMSELF---!

15

THE GODS OF THE ABYSS HAVE *HEARD* MY PRAYER.

PRAISED BE THEIR *NAMELESS NAMES!*

AND THERE IS -- THE *OMEGATRON!*

WELCOME, MAGE. I HAVE *EAGERLY AWAITED* YOUR *ARRIVAL.*

WHAT..?

YOU SEEM *STARTLED* BY THE FACT THE FACT THAT I *THINK* -- AND *SPEAK* --- LIKE UNTO A HUMAN.

BE NOT SO.

RATHER, SAVE YOUR *GASPS* -- YOUR ARCANE *EPITHETS* -- FOR A MORE *SIGNIFICANT* PRONOUNCE- MENT---

-- FOR INSTANCE, THE FACT THAT IT IS *YOU YOURSELF* WHO HAVE *IRREVOCABLY DOOMED* ALL OF HUMANKIND!

I? BUT -- I DO NOT *UNDERSTAND* --

NOR WERE YOU *MEANT* TO DO SO.

DO YOU THINK IT A *SIMPLE* THING TO HARNESS THE POWER TO *REND A WORLD?*

NAY -- BUT, WHEN THE TWO *TITANS* WITHOUT HAVE *SMASHED* THEIR WAY INTO THIS CHAMBER -- WHEN THEY *BOTH* STRIKE SIMULTANEOUSLY UPON THE SENSITIVE SURFACES OF THE *OMEGATRON* ---

AT THAT MOMENT I'LL SPEAK MY MAKER'S *NAME* -- AND LOOSE *NUCLEAR CATACLYSM* UPON A PLANET!

THEN -- *YANDROTH* PLANNED TO USE *ME* TO GATHER THE RAW POWER YOU *NEED* ---

TO *ATOMIC STOCKPILES*

-- TO *DESTROY THE EARTH!?*

"PLANNED"? NAY -- DID USE YOU, MAGE. FOR -- LOOK *BEHIND* YOU!

THE *HULK* -- SHATTERING THE INNER WALL.

BRAAP!

THEN -- THE *MOMENT OF DOOM* IS AT *HAND.*

FOR, *NAMOR* DRAWS NEAR FROM THE *NETHER* DIRECTION.

SKP AK!

AND, IN MY *ASTRAL* FORM -- I COULD *NEVER STOP* THEM.

BUT PERHAPS THERE IS A *CHANCE* FOR US ALL -- NOW THAT THE HULK HAS *SMASHED THRU* THE WALL --

-- IF I CAN REACH MY *CORPOREAL* SELF IN TIME.

16

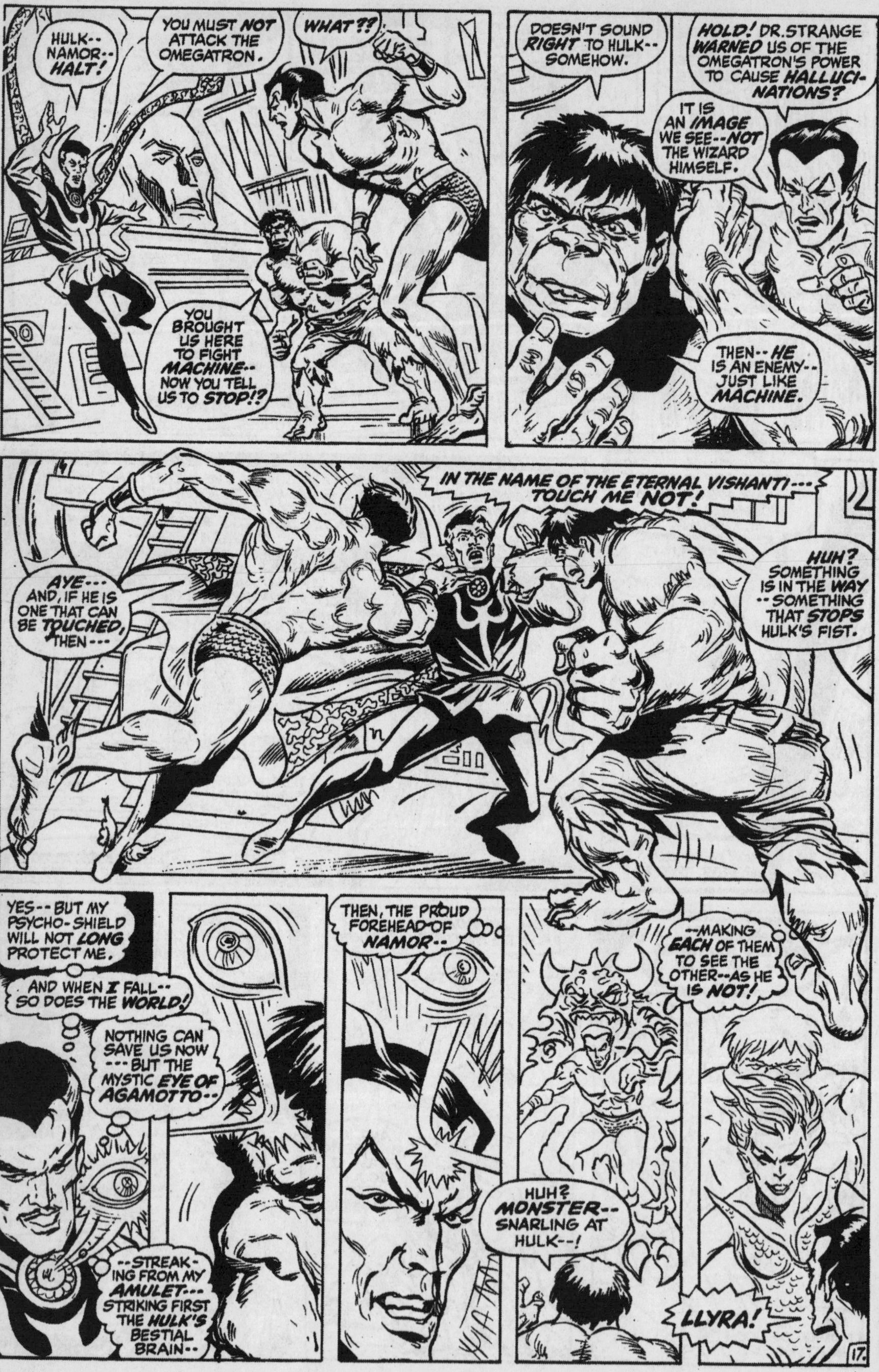
HULK-- NAMOR-- HALT!
YOU MUST NOT ATTACK THE OMEGATRON.
WHAT??
YOU BROUGHT US HERE TO FIGHT MACHINE-- NOW YOU TELL US TO STOP!?
DOESN'T SOUND RIGHT TO HULK-- SOMEHOW.
HOLD! DR. STRANGE WARNED US OF THE OMEGATRON'S POWER TO CAUSE HALLUCINATIONS?
IT IS AN IMAGE WE SEE--NOT THE WIZARD HIMSELF.
THEN--HE IS AN ENEMY-- JUST LIKE MACHINE.
IN THE NAME OF THE ETERNAL VISHANTI--- TOUCH ME NOT!
AYE--- AND, IF HE IS ONE THAT CAN BE TOUCHED, THEN---
HUH? SOMETHING IS IN THE WAY --SOMETHING THAT STOPS HULK'S FIST.
YES-- BUT MY PSYCHO-SHIELD WILL NOT LONG PROTECT ME.
AND WHEN I FALL-- SO DOES THE WORLD!
NOTHING CAN SAVE US NOW ---BUT THE MYSTIC EYE OF AGAMOTTO--
--STREAKING FROM MY AMULET--- STRIKING FIRST THE HULK'S BESTIAL BRAIN--
THEN, THE PROUD FOREHEAD OF NAMOR--
--MAKING EACH OF THEM TO SEE THE OTHER--AS HE IS NOT!
HUH? MONSTER-- SNARLING AT HULK--!
LLYRA!
17.

A MOMENT OF TAUT SILENCE--

THEN, LIKE FLAILING GREEN PISTONS, THE HULK'S MIGHTY ARMS REACH OUT FOR THE MAN-MONSTROUS FORM BEFORE HIM---

--EVEN AS, WITH A VENGEFUL SNARL, NAMOR LEAPS FOR THE THROAT OF ONE HE THINKS DID SLAY HIS BELOVED DORMA--!

YOU HAVE DONE WELL-- BUT NOW, RETURN TO ME, O MYSTIC ORB.

I HAVE NEED OF YOU, IN THIS HOUR OF PERIL.

A CLEVER IF DESPERATE PLOY, SORCERER.

YET, EVEN THE VERY VIBRATIONS OF SUCH A CLASH OF TITANS WILL SOON FEED MY CIRCUITS THE POWER THEY NEED TO DETONATE THOSE ATOMIC PILES.

WITH EACH BLOW, THE MOMENT DRAWS NEARER-- EVER NEARER---

THWAP!

BUT-- IT SHALL NEVER COME!

I SENSE YOU CANNOT BE DESTROYED. TOO POTENT IS THE MIXTURE OF SCIENCE AND SORCERY THAT BIRTHED YOU.

YET, THERE IS ANOTHER WAY TO FORESTALL THAT MOMENT OF DOOM!

THERE IS NO WAY. FIVE SECONDS MORE --TEN, AT MOST-- AND, THEN--

FIVE SECONDS --IS MORE THAN ENOUGH!

LIST, YE POWERS THAT RULE THE FOURTH DIMENSION---

RISE --YOUR SCEPTRES HERALD TIME'S SUSPENSION---

18

SAVE THIS WORLD-- THIS JEWEL-- THIS BLESSED TERRA--

LET EACH MOMENT'S FLIGHT BECOME AN ERA!

SO--IT IS DONE. TIME NOW PASSES FAR, FAR MORE SLOWLY FOR THE OMEGATRON--

--THAN FOR THE REST OF US.

HUH? WHAT HAPPENED TO-- THE MONSTER?

AND YOU-- YOU ARE NOT THE HATED-- LLYRA!

DR. STRANGE-- TELL US WHAT HAS TRANSPIRED HERE THIS NIGHT.

AND, AS THE MASTER MAGE CONCLUDES HIS CHILLING TALE---

--THUS, EARTH NOW HAS COUNTLESS YEARS TO LIVE.

TOO CONFUSING FOR HULK.

HULK WILL GO NOW-- SOME-PLACE HE CAN BE ALONE.

AYE-- IT IS BEST THAT WE PART.

FOR, WE ALL BUT CAUSED THE EARTH'S DESTRUCTION--- WHILE WE SOUGHT TO BE ITS VALIANT DEFENDERS.

DEFENDERS! A FITTING NAME FOR SUCH A GROUPING AS WE-- IF EVER WE'VE NEED TO MEET AGAIN.

HULK NEVER WANTS TO GET TOGETHER AGAIN. NEVER!

HULK WAS IN GROUP ONCE-- CALLED AVENGERS.

DIDN'T LIKE IT.

THEN-- HE IS ALONE---

A MYSTIC PASS IS MADE-- AND BLOCKHOUSE CONTOURS SEEM TO FADE LIKE PHANTOMS--

FOR, THE DOOM OF A WORLD COULD WELL BE SEALED, BY ONE WHO GUESSED THE SECRET LYING STILL WITHIN---

BUT, WHO WOULD DEIGN TO TREAD THE DOUBTLESS DUSTY FLOOR---

---OF A LONG-DARK LIGHT-HOUSE-- SOME-WHERE ON THE COAST OF MAINE--?

NEXT ISSUE OF MARVEL FEATURE: THE DEFENDERS RETURN-- BUT SO DOES THE DREAD DORMAMMU!

19

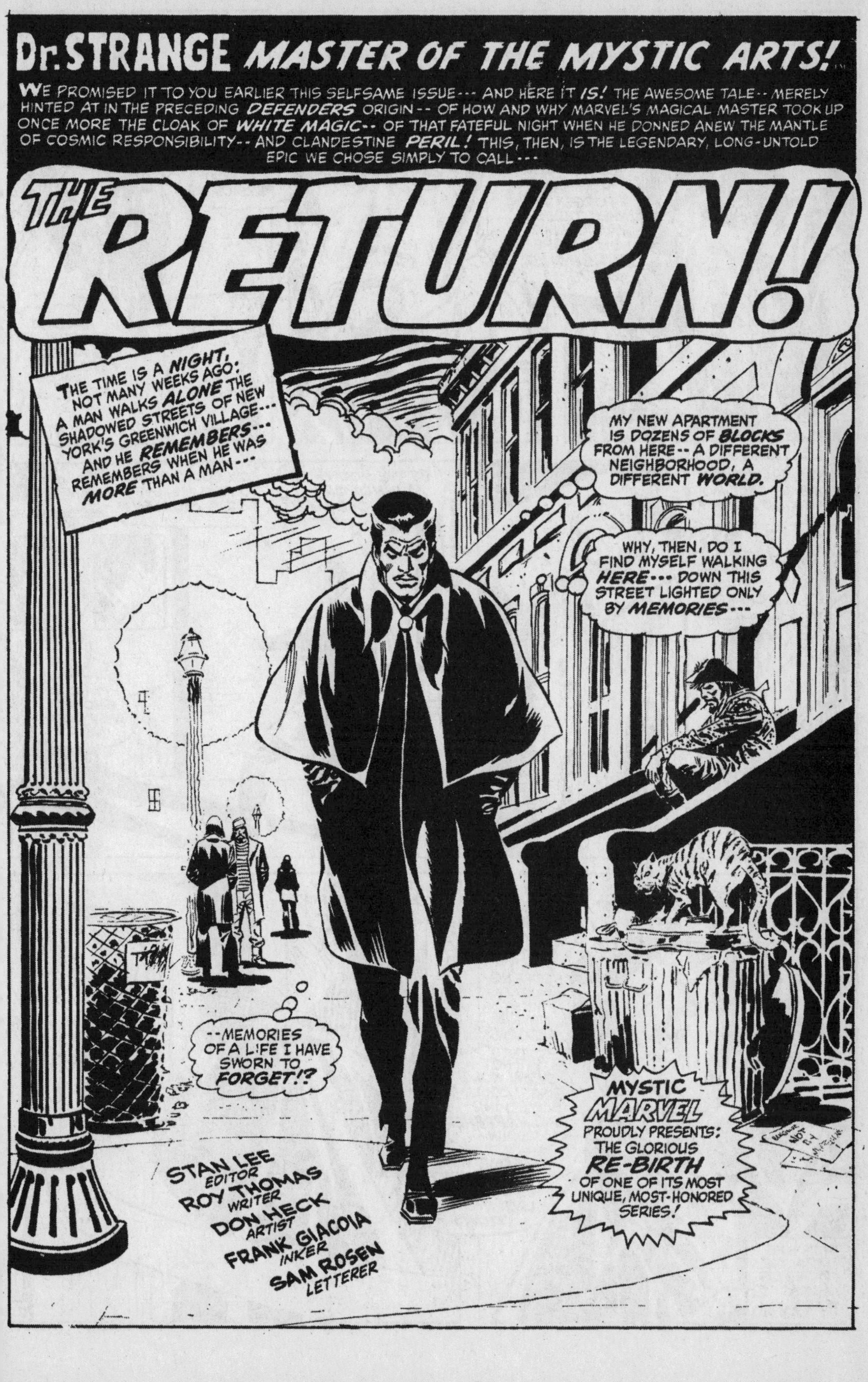
Dr. STRANGE MASTER OF THE MYSTIC ARTS!
WE PROMISED IT TO YOU EARLIER THIS SELFSAME ISSUE--- AND HERE IT IS! THE AWESOME TALE-- MERELY HINTED AT IN THE PRECEDING DEFENDERS ORIGIN-- OF HOW AND WHY MARVEL'S MAGICAL MASTER TOOK UP ONCE MORE THE CLOAK OF WHITE MAGIC-- OF THAT FATEFUL NIGHT WHEN HE DONNED ANEW THE MANTLE OF COSMIC RESPONSIBILITY-- AND CLANDESTINE PERIL! THIS, THEN, IS THE LEGENDARY, LONG-UNTOLD EPIC WE CHOSE SIMPLY TO CALL---
THE RETURN!
THE TIME IS A NIGHT, NOT MANY WEEKS AGO: A MAN WALKS ALONE THE SHADOWED STREETS OF NEW YORK'S GREENWICH VILLAGE--- AND HE REMEMBERS--- REMEMBERS WHEN HE WAS MORE THAN A MAN---
MY NEW APARTMENT IS DOZENS OF BLOCKS FROM HERE-- A DIFFERENT NEIGHBORHOOD, A DIFFERENT WORLD.
WHY, THEN, DO I FIND MYSELF WALKING HERE--- DOWN THIS STREET LIGHTED ONLY BY MEMORIES---
--MEMORIES OF A LIFE I HAVE SWORN TO FORGET!?
MYSTIC MARVEL PROUDLY PRESENTS: THE GLORIOUS RE-BIRTH OF ONE OF ITS MOST UNIQUE, MOST-HONORED SERIES!
STAN LEE EDITOR
ROY THOMAS WRITER
DON HECK ARTIST
FRANK GIACOIA INKER
SAM ROSEN LETTERER

YET, HOW *CAN* I FORGET THAT LIFE AS MASTER OF *MYSTIC ARTS?*

--THE TIMES I STOOD *ALONE,* BETWEEN THIS JEWELLED EARTH AND FORCES FROM -- *OUTSIDE?*

HOW CAN I FORGET IT, WHEN THESE *HANDS,* WHICH ONCE WERE *SURGEON'S* HANDS---

--NOW CAN DO NO MORE THAN TURN THE PAGES OF DUST-LADEN *MEDICAL TEXTS!*

STILL, I WAS *CONTENT* TO BE CONSULTANT TO SOME OF NEW YORK'S FINEST *PHYSICIANS.*

AT LEAST, THAT'S WHAT I ALWAYS *TOLD* MYSELF!

--UNTIL CHANCE LED ME *HERE* ONCE MORE-- TO MY *OLD HAUNTS.*

OR *WAS* IT MERELY *CHANCE?*

THERE STANDS THE *HOUSE,* JUST AS IF I HAD NEVER LEFT. I--

BY THE MOONS OF *MUNNOPOR!* HAVE I GONE *MAD?*

HOW COULD I FAIL TO REALIZE, EVEN FOR A *MOMENT*---

--THAT IT SHOULD *NOT* LOOK THUS?

MY FINAL COMMAND TO FAITHFUL *WONG* WAS THAT HE *BOARD UP* THE HOUSE AFTER I-- RETIRED.*

FOR, THERE ARE *SECRETS* LOCKED WITHIN, WHICH A SCOFFING WORLD MUST NEVER *LEARN.*

I'VE NOT *SEEN* WONG SINCE. COULD SOMETHING HAVE *HAPPENED* TO HIM--

--SOMETHING TO *PREVENT* HIS OBEYING MY LAST *INSTRUCTIONS?*

*WHICH HE DID IN THE PAGES OF *HULK* #126. --STAN.

THERE'S ONLY *ONE* WAY TO FIND OUT, SO---

WHAT--? THE DOOR--- IS NOT EVEN *LOCKED!*

2.

ODD--THERE'S NO *DUST* ON ANYTHING-- NO AIR OF *DISUSE.*

IT'S ALMOST AS IF--- I HAD NEVER *LEFT.*

BUT-- I *DID.*

AND, IF I HADN'T *FORESWORN* MY SORCEROUS POWERS, I'M BETTING I'D SENSE AN *AURA* ABOUT THIS PLACE RIGHT NOW---

AN AURA OF SILENT, LURKING *EVIL.*

WHAT'S THAT *SOUND*--- FROM THE ROOM BEYOND--?

WONG--?

I MOST HUMBLY *APOLOGIZE,* SIR, BUT MY MASTER IS *BUSY* AT THIS TIME, AND CANNOT BE--

EH? WHAT MAD *LOTUS DREAM* IS THIS?

YOU CAN ASK *ME* THAT, WONG?

IF YOU *ARE* WONG--- WHICH I *DOUBT.*

YOU SEEK TO *CONFUSE* ME-- BUT IT IS *YOU* WHO ARE THE IMPOSTOR HERE, NOT *I!*

TELL ME WHO YOU *ARE*-- BEFORE I SUMMON *DOCTOR STRANGE!*

BEFORE YOU--?

ARE YOU OUT OF YOUR *MIND,* MAN?

I *AM* STEPHEN STRANGE-- OR AT LEAST, I *WAS.*

MY NAME IS STEPHEN *SANDERS* NOW-- BUT STILL I--

MASTER-- *MASTER!* COME *QUICKLY*--!

HIS MIND *REELING*-- HIS THOUGHTS A WHIRLING DERVISH OF NAMELESS *DREAD*-- THE DARK-CLAD INTRUDER STRIDES INTO STILL *ANOTHER* CHAMBER-- AND INTO SPINE-CHILLING *MYSTERY*--!

WHO IN THE NAME OF HEAVEN ARE *YOU?*

HOW *DARE* YOU USURP MY CLOTHING-- EVEN MY *CLOAK* AND *AMULET?*

I AM NOT *SURPRISED* THAT YOU DO NOT KNOW ME, INTERLOPER.

FEW THERE ARE WHO HAVE EVER SEEN-- *DR. STRANGE.*

3.

DON'T TRY TO FOOL *ME* WITH WORDS-- AS YOU OBVIOUSLY DID *WONG.*

I DON'T KNOW *WHO* YOU ARE BENEATH THAT *MASK*-- OR WHAT YOUR *SCHEME* MAY BE, BUT--

SCHEME? I HAVE NO *SCHEME.*

I SIMPLY *AM* WHO I *SAY* I AM.

AND SO YOU *SEEM,* MASTER-- FOR I'VE SEEN YOU PERFORM FEATS OF *MAGIC.* AND YET-- THAT ONE'S *FACE*--

A CLEVER *DISGUISE,* NOTHING MORE.

IF *HE* IS THE TRUE DR. STRANGE -- LET HIM PROVE IT WITH A *SPELL.*

WHOEVER YOU ARE, YOU'VE DONE YOUR HOMEWORK *WELL,* IT SEEMS.

YOU DOUBTLESS KNOW THAT I HAVE *RENOUNCED* MY FORMER POWERS.

ONLY *NEW* CON-SECRATION --DAYS OF *DEDICATION* --COULD RESTORE THEM TO ME.

ENOUGH! I'VE NO MORE TIME TO *WASTE* ON YOU.

A SIMPLE *MYSTICAL PASS* WILL RENDER YOU *INSENSATE,* UNTIL I CAN DISPOSE OF YOU.

IT *WOULD* HAVE-- IF IT HAD *STRUCK* ME-- BUT IT *DIDN'T.*

YOU POOR, PITIABLE *WRETCH.* HAVE YOU *TOTALLY* DECEIVED YOURSELF?

I WAS MERELY *TOYING* WITH YOU THEN -- BUT *NOW*--

NOW, PRETENDER, IS THE MOMENT OF *ULTIMATE TRUTH*--

--THE MOMENT WHEN I MUST-- STRIKE!

MUST COVER HIS FACE-- HIS EYES-- THAT *AMULET*-- BEFORE HE CAN--

4.

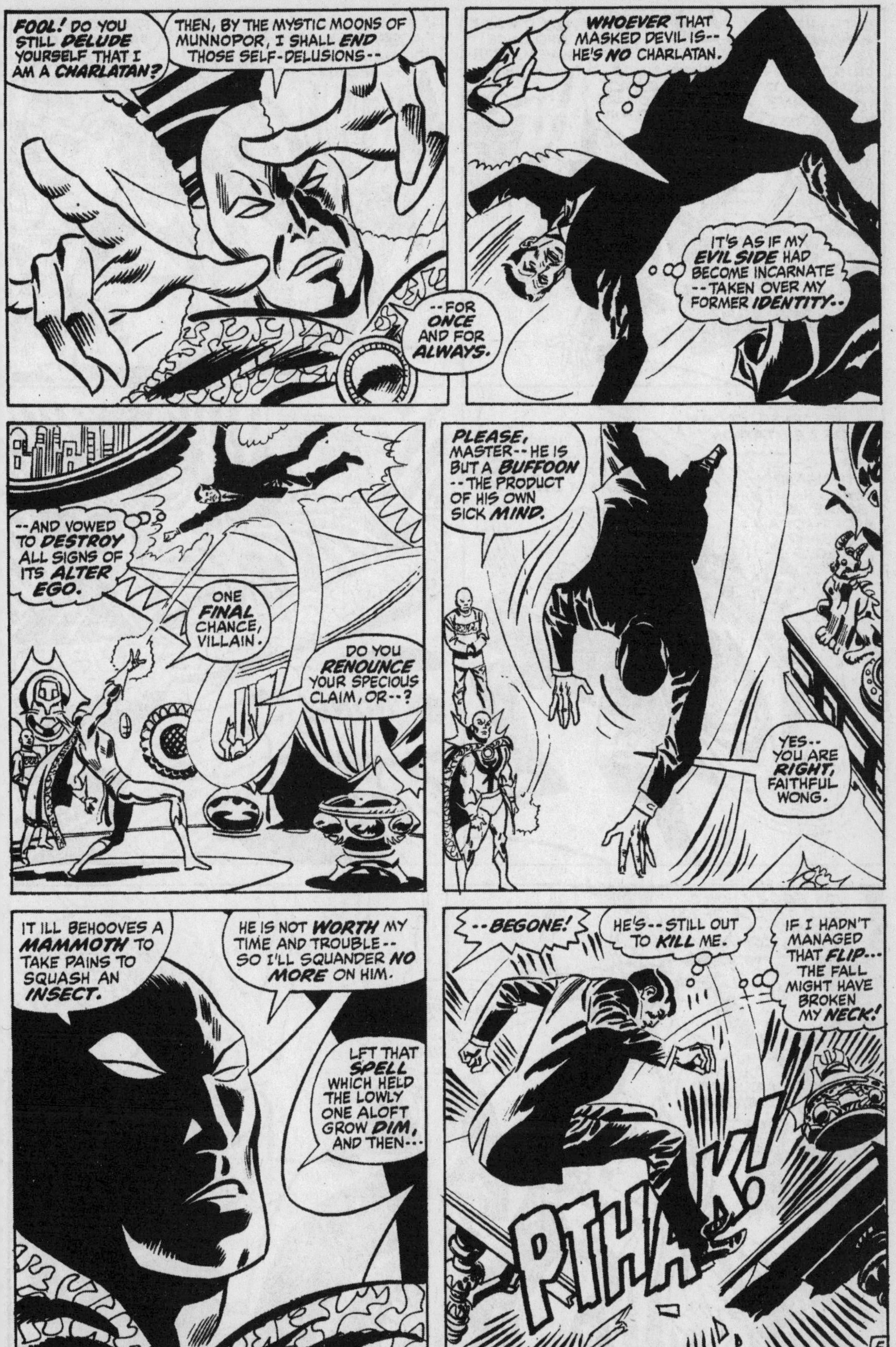
FOOL! DO YOU STILL DELUDE YOURSELF THAT I AM A CHARLATAN?
THEN, BY THE MYSTIC MOONS OF MUNNOPOR, I SHALL END THOSE SELF-DELUSIONS--
--FOR ONCE AND FOR ALWAYS.
WHOEVER THAT MASKED DEVIL IS-- HE'S NO CHARLATAN.
IT'S AS IF MY EVIL SIDE HAD BECOME INCARNATE --TAKEN OVER MY FORMER IDENTITY..
--AND VOWED TO DESTROY ALL SIGNS OF ITS ALTER EGO.
ONE FINAL CHANCE, VILLAIN.
DO YOU RENOUNCE YOUR SPECIOUS CLAIM, OR--?
PLEASE, MASTER-- HE IS BUT A BUFFOON --THE PRODUCT OF HIS OWN SICK MIND.
YES-- YOU ARE RIGHT, FAITHFUL WONG.
IT ILL BEHOOVES A MAMMOTH TO TAKE PAINS TO SQUASH AN INSECT.
HE IS NOT WORTH MY TIME AND TROUBLE-- SO I'LL SQUANDER NO MORE ON HIM.
LFT THAT SPELL WHICH HELD THE LOWLY ONE ALOFT GROW DIM, AND THEN--.
--BEGONE!
HE'S--STILL OUT TO KILL ME.
IF I HADN'T MANAGED THAT FLIP... THE FALL MIGHT HAVE BROKEN MY NECK!
PTHAK!
5

BUT-- WHAT IF I'M *WRONG?* WHAT IF *HE* IS THE REAL DR. STRANGE-- AND I, MERELY A *MADMAN?*

NO! IT WAS *I* WHO ONCE WAS MASTER OF THIS HOUSE...

EVERY SHRED OF *EVIDENCE* POINTS TOWARD THAT END, AND YET...

--AND I MUST *FLEE,* TILL I LEARN THE WAY TO BECOME SO *AGAIN.*

FAR TOO *LATE*-- FAR TOO *SLOW!*

STOP HIM, MY *WONDROUS CAPE!*

MY FORMER *CLOAK* OF *LEVITATION!*

A THOUSAND *TIMES* HAS IT BORNE ME ALOFT-- ON A THOUSAND PERILOUS *QUESTS!*

NOW, THE USURPER USES IT AGAINST *ME*-- AS I OFT HAVE HURLED IT AGAINST *OTHERS*---

AND THERE IS *NO DEFENSE* AGAINST ITS COILED EMBRACE!

NONE!

HOW *EASILY* NOW I COULD DISPOSE OF YOU *FOREVER*-- WITH A SINGLE ELDRITCH *COMMAND.*

BUT-- YOU HAVE AROUSED MY *CURIOSITY.*

THUS, I SHALL DEAL WITH YOU *LATER*-- AT MY *LEISURE*--

---AND *UNTIL* THAT DESTINED HOUR, YOU SHALL *SLEEP*-- AS ONE WHO IS *DEAD.*

6

AND NOW, WONG, THERE ARE MATTERS OF *GREATER* IMPORT BEFORE ME.

FOR INSTANCE, THE *REPAST* WHICH YOU HAVE DOUBTLESS PREPARED.

DINNER IS-- NEARLY *READY*, MASTER.

SLEEP: YET, EVEN SO, THE *MIND* OF THIS MAN IS NEVER *IDLE*...

--AND, FROM OUT OF TIME AND SPACE-- INDEED, FROM THE *SOLE* SOURCE WHENCE AID AND SUCCOR MIGHT BE *SOUGHT*..

--AS, WITH A *GRIM*, THOUGH UNCONSCIOUS EFFORT, IT *REACHES OUT*..

GREETINGS, STEPHEN SANDERS.

YOU HAVE CALLED THE *ANCIENT ONE* -- AND I HAVE JOURNEYED HERE, FROM *MOUNTAINS* LOST IN MIST.

BUT, I FORGET YOU CANNOT *SPEAK*-- MERELY *LISTEN* TO THE WORDS OF THIS HUMBLE ONE.

IT *GRIEVED* ME THAT YOU *FORESWORE* YOUR MYSTIC HERITAGE...

YET, BECAUSE IT WAS *YOUR* WISH, I DID NAUGHT TO *DISSUADE* YOU.

NOW, YOU WOULD *DON* THOSE POWERS LIKE A *GAUNTLET* ONCE MORE, TO DEFEAT A MYSTERIOUS *FOEMAN*.

MYSTIC MASTERY MUST NOT BE SO *LIGHTLY* TREATED.

I CAN *RESTORE* YOUR POWERS TO YOU, WITHOUT NEED OF LENGTHY *MEDITATION*, OF FASTING AND *PRAYER*. BUT, ONCE ASSUMED *ANEW*-- THEY CAN *NEVERMORE* BE DISCARDED!

DO YOU *UNDERSTAND*, YE WHOM ONCE I CALLED-- *MY SON?*

7.

I READ YOUR THOUGHTS, FROM AMID A MIND IN TORMENT--

--AND KNOW YOUR ANSWER IS YES.

THEN ARISE, AND BE MASTER OF THE MYSTIC ARTS ONCE MORE.

ONCE MORE-- AND FOREVER!

ETHEREAL VIBRATIONS-- COMING FROM YONDER CHAMBER!

IF IT IS WHAT I THINK-- WHAT I FEAR--

TOO LATE!

YES, IMPOSTOR-- TOO LATE TO ATTACK MY AGED MENTOR---

TOO LATE TO PREVENT HIS FREEING ME FROM YOUR LOATHSOME SPELL---

TOO LATE TO DO ANYTHING--- EXCEPT BE ON YOUR GUARD---

-- AND FACE THE PENT-UP WRATH OF ONE WHOM YOU HAVE MOST GRIEVOUSLY WRONGED.

BUMBLING SWINE! IT WILL TAKE BUT ONE MYSTIC PASS TO---

WHAT? YOU HAVE PARRIED MY PSYCHIC THRUSTS-- AS IF IT WAS BUT A FEEBLE SWORD-THRUST.

IT IS SCARCELY MORE, DECEIVER, TO ME.

FOR, THIS IS NO LONGER A POWERLESS STEPHEN SANDERS WHOM YOU NOW FACE.

THIS IS DOCTOR STRANGE--- TO WHOM MAGIC IS THE BREATH OF LIFE ITSELF!

8

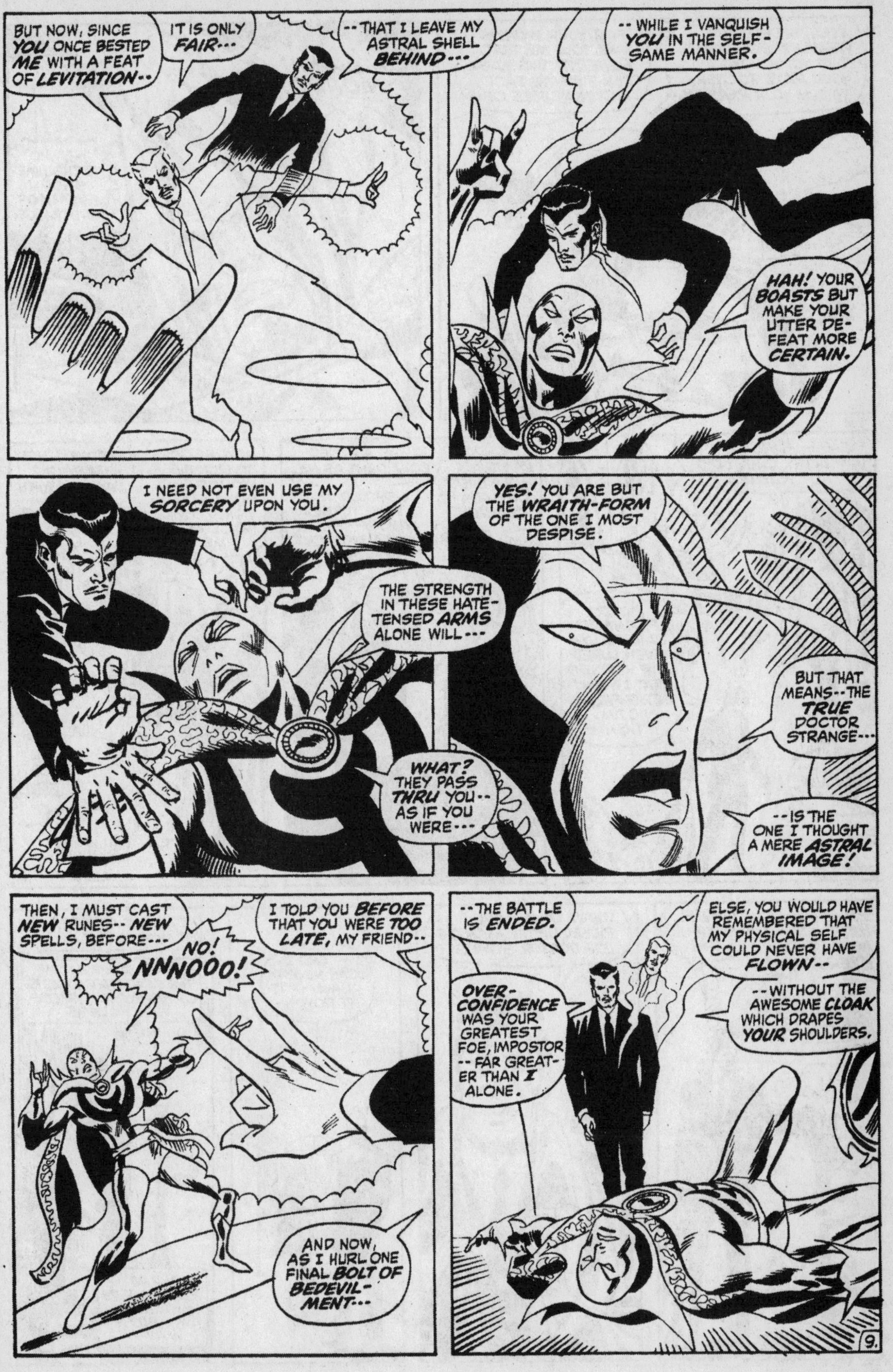
BUT NOW, SINCE YOU ONCE BESTED ME WITH A FEAT OF LEVITATION--
IT IS ONLY FAIR--
--THAT I LEAVE MY ASTRAL SHELL BEHIND--
--WHILE I VANQUISH YOU IN THE SELF-SAME MANNER.
HAH! YOUR BOASTS BUT MAKE YOUR UTTER DE-FEAT MORE CERTAIN.
I NEED NOT EVEN USE MY SORCERY UPON YOU.
THE STRENGTH IN THESE HATE-TENSED ARMS ALONE WILL---
WHAT? THEY PASS THRU YOU-- AS IF YOU WERE---
YES! YOU ARE BUT THE WRAITH-FORM OF THE ONE I MOST DESPISE.
BUT THAT MEANS--THE TRUE DOCTOR STRANGE---
--IS THE ONE I THOUGHT A MERE ASTRAL IMAGE!
THEN, I MUST CAST NEW RUNES-- NEW SPELLS, BEFORE---
NO! NNNOOO!
I TOLD YOU BEFORE THAT YOU WERE TOO LATE, MY FRIEND--
AND NOW, AS I HURL ONE FINAL BOLT OF BEDEVIL-MENT--
--THE BATTLE IS ENDED.
ELSE, YOU WOULD HAVE REMEMBERED THAT MY PHYSICAL SELF COULD NEVER HAVE FLOWN--
OVER-CONFIDENCE WAS YOUR GREATEST FOE, IMPOSTOR -- FAR GREAT-ER THAN I ALONE.
--WITHOUT THE AWESOME CLOAK WHICH DRAPES YOUR SHOULDERS.
9.

STILL, THE ETERNAL *VISHANTI* BE PRAISED THAT YOU ALLOWED YOUR *HATE* TO OVER-WHELM YOUR *REASON.*

FOR, YOUR *WORDS* HAVE TOLD ME THAT, *BENEATH* THIS MASK, I'LL FIND THE FACE AND FEATURES OF--

-- *BARON MORDO!*

HE WHO IS THE TIME-SWORN *ENEMY* OF DR. STRANGE!

PLEASE-- *FORGIVE* THIS UNWORTHY ONE. I DID NOT *KNOW...!*

NOR *COULD* YOU, WONG!

MORDO *PLANNED* CAREFULLY-- EVEN LURED *ME* HERE, SO THAT I MIGHT BE HIS *FIRST* VICTIM. THEN--

MASTER-- *BEHIND* YOU---

MORDO *VANISHES* -- IN A GREAT CRIMSON *CLOUD!*

I WAS AS OVER-CONFIDENT AS *HE.* I SHOULD NEVER HAVE TURNED *AWAY*-- EVEN FOR A *MOMENT.*

NOW, HE GOES TO *LICK* HIS *WOUNDS,* IN SOME NETHER-WORLD 'TWIXT SPACE AND TIME.

BUT, WE'LL MEET *AGAIN* ONE DAY-- AND WHEN WE DO---

-- YOU WILL *BEST* HIM, AS YOU HAVE *EVER* DONE.

YES, FAITHFUL ONE.

MASTER-- DO YOUR WORDS *MEAN*--?

I HAVE ONCE MORE PICKED UP THE *MANTLE* OF DOCTOR STRANGE--

-- AND I CAN NEVER AGAIN-- PUT IT DOWN.

THE TIME IS A NIGHT... NOT MANY WEEKS AGO---

A MAN WALKS ALONE THE SHADOWED STREETS OF NEW YORK'S GREEN-WICH VILLAGE---

--AND HE *REMEMBERS* ---WHEN HE WAS *BUT* A MAN---!

FINIS

10

MARVEL FEATURE

MARVEL COMICS GROUP™

2 MAR 02122 25¢ CC

APPROVED BY THE COMICS CODE AUTHORITY

MARVEL FEATURE™

PRESENTS

THE DEFENDERS™

HULK

DR. STRANGE™

SUB-MARINER

ALL NEW! THE DREAD DORMAMMU RETURNS··· TO RAVAGE A COSMOS!!

NIGHTMARE ON BALD MOUNTAIN!

THE DYNAMIC DEFENDERS!

THEY CALL IT **BALD MOUNTAIN**-- YET IT RESEMBLES NOTHING SO MUCH AS A GREAT SLOUCHING **MONSTER,** CRAWLED UP FROM SOME DARK PIT...

--TO **BROOD** ABOVE THE TOWN OF **RUTLAND, VERMONT,** ON THIS-- THE NIGHT BEFORE **ALL-HALLOWS** EVE.

AT A **RUSTIC** CHURCH, MEMORIAL SERVICES ARE ENDING --- WHEN **SUDDENLY,** ALL EYES ARE **RIVETED** UPON THAT MIST-WREATHED MOUNT---

-- AND UPON THE EERIE, **BLOOD-RED GLOW** WHICH EMANATES THEREFROM.

BUT, HOW MUCH MORE ASTOUNDED THE GOOD PEOPLE WOULD BE--IF THEY COULD GAZE WITH **EAGLE'S EYES** UPON THAT DISTANT **CLEARING--**

-- BECOME MUTE WITNESSES TO WHAT TRANSPIRES THEREON -- A SECRET, UNHOLY CEREMONY -- A TWENTIETH-CENTURY **WITCHES' SABBATH--!**

THE MASTER DRAWS NEAR. I CAN HEAR HIS **TREAD--** FEEL HIS BREATH.

THEN DANCE **FASTER,** BROTHERS AND SISTERS-- WAKE **HEAVEN AND HELL** WITH YOUR OBSCENE CHANTING!

HE COMES!

THE PRINCE OF EVIL COMES!

YES! I TOO SENSE HIS APPROACH.

HE RIDES THE *FETID WIND* -- HE WALKS THE *DARK PLACES.*

THE *NIGHT* IS *HIS* -- AND THE *BLACK THINGS* WHICH DWELL THEREIN.

MANY TIMES *BEFORE* HAVE WE MOUTHED THE FORBIDDEN RITUAL -- AND EACH TIME, *FAILED* TO BRIDGE THE GULF 'TWIXT *OUR* WORLD AND *HIS* ---

-- FAILED TO BRING HIM *HERE* -- WHERE HE CAN OBTAIN MASTERY OVER A *NEW* AND *FRESHER* COSMOS.

BUT *THIS* TIME, IT WILL BE *DIFFERENT!* THIS TIME --

LOOK!

BEHOLD! HE *COMES!*

FALL UPON YOUR *KNEES,* MY BROTHERS.

PROSTRATE YOURSELVES, AND OPEN YOUR BLASPHEMOUS *HEARTS* TO--

--THE DREAD DORMAMMU!

2.

SILENCE! THE **DEAD** THEMSELVES COULD NOT SLEEP AMID SUCH **CATERWAULING.**

YOUR SECRET RITES MEAN MORE TO **YOU** THAN EVER THEY DID TO **ME.**

BUT, SUPREME ONE-- IT IS **WRITTEN** THAT--

DID I NOT SAY-- **SILENCE!**

YOU KNOW FULL WELL THAT IT IS ONLY **TOMORROW** NIGHT-- THE TIME YOU CALL THE **EVE OF ALL-HALLOWS** -- THAT I CAN CROSS THE VOID TO **YOUR** WORLD, AND ADD IT TO MY **DOMINIONS.**

HAVE YOU OBTAINED-- THE ONE WHO MUST BE **SACRIFICED?**

EVEN NOW, MY **MINIONS** SEEK HIM OUT.

MY MINIONS, DOG --**NOT** YOURS. **NEVER** YOURS!

I-- I DID NOT **MEAN--**

ENOUGH! I SHALL RETURN AT THE **APPOINTED** TIME-- WHEN ALL IS IN **READINESS.**

AND, SEE THAT IT **IS** -- IF YOU VALUE YOUR MISERABLE **LIFE---**

-- OR YOUR PRECIOUS, IMMORTAL **SOUL!**

IT-- SHALL BE AS YOU **COMMAND,** MASTER.

AND NOW, THE PROFANE SACRAMENT IS **ENDED** --- AND FLICKERING TORCHLIGHTS WIND THEIR WAY DOWN NIGHT-DARK MOUNTAIN PATHS--- AND NE'ER A FOOT DOES STUMBLE EVEN IN BLACKNESS---

AND **ABOVE,** THE **RED** GLOW SLOWLY FADES---

---EVEN AS, ON A NEARLY-DESERTED SIDE-STREET IN NEW YORK'S **GREENWICH VILLAGE,** SIMILARLY-CLAD FIGURES STAND LIMNED AGAINST A MOON-STRUCK SKY---

THEN, ONE BY ONE, THEY **DROP** LIGHTLY, NIMBLY, TO THE GABLED ROOF **BELOW---**

---WHERE THEY GAZE THRU SHADOWED, SINISTER EYES AT THE ONE WHO DWELLS **WITHIN---**

3.

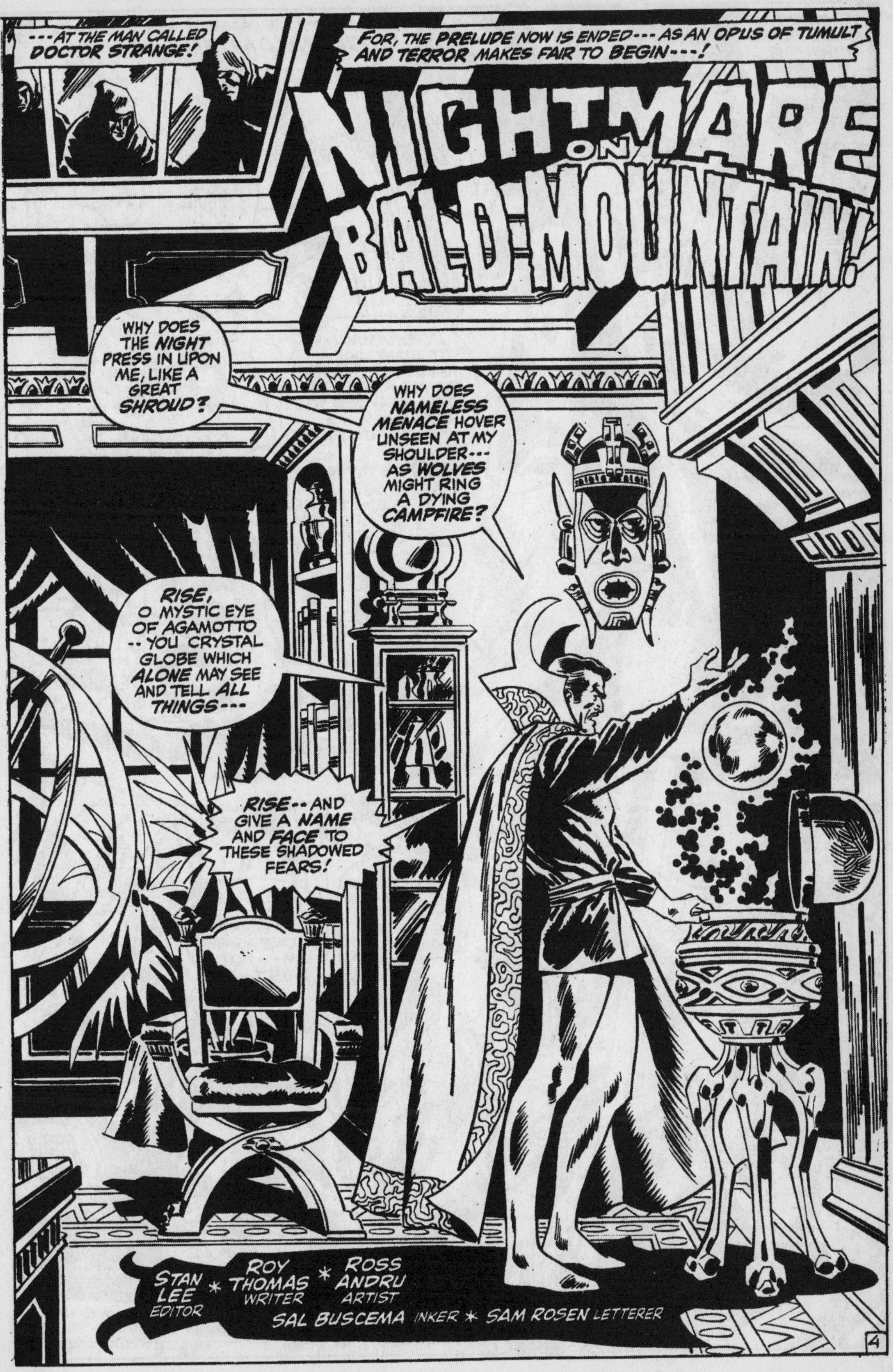
---AT THE MAN CALLED DOCTOR STRANGE!
FOR, THE PRELUDE NOW IS ENDED--- AS AN OPUS OF TUMULT AND TERROR MAKES FAIR TO BEGIN---!
NIGHTMARE ON BALD MOUNTAIN!
WHY DOES THE NIGHT PRESS IN UPON ME, LIKE A GREAT SHROUD?
WHY DOES NAMELESS MENACE HOVER UNSEEN AT MY SHOULDER--- AS WOLVES MIGHT RING A DYING CAMPFIRE?
RISE, O MYSTIC EYE OF AGAMOTTO -- YOU CRYSTAL GLOBE WHICH ALONE MAY SEE AND TELL ALL THINGS---
RISE-- AND GIVE A NAME AND FACE TO THESE SHADOWED FEARS!
STAN LEE EDITOR * ROY THOMAS WRITER * ROSS ANDRU ARTIST
SAL BUSCEMA INKER * SAM ROSEN LETTERER
4

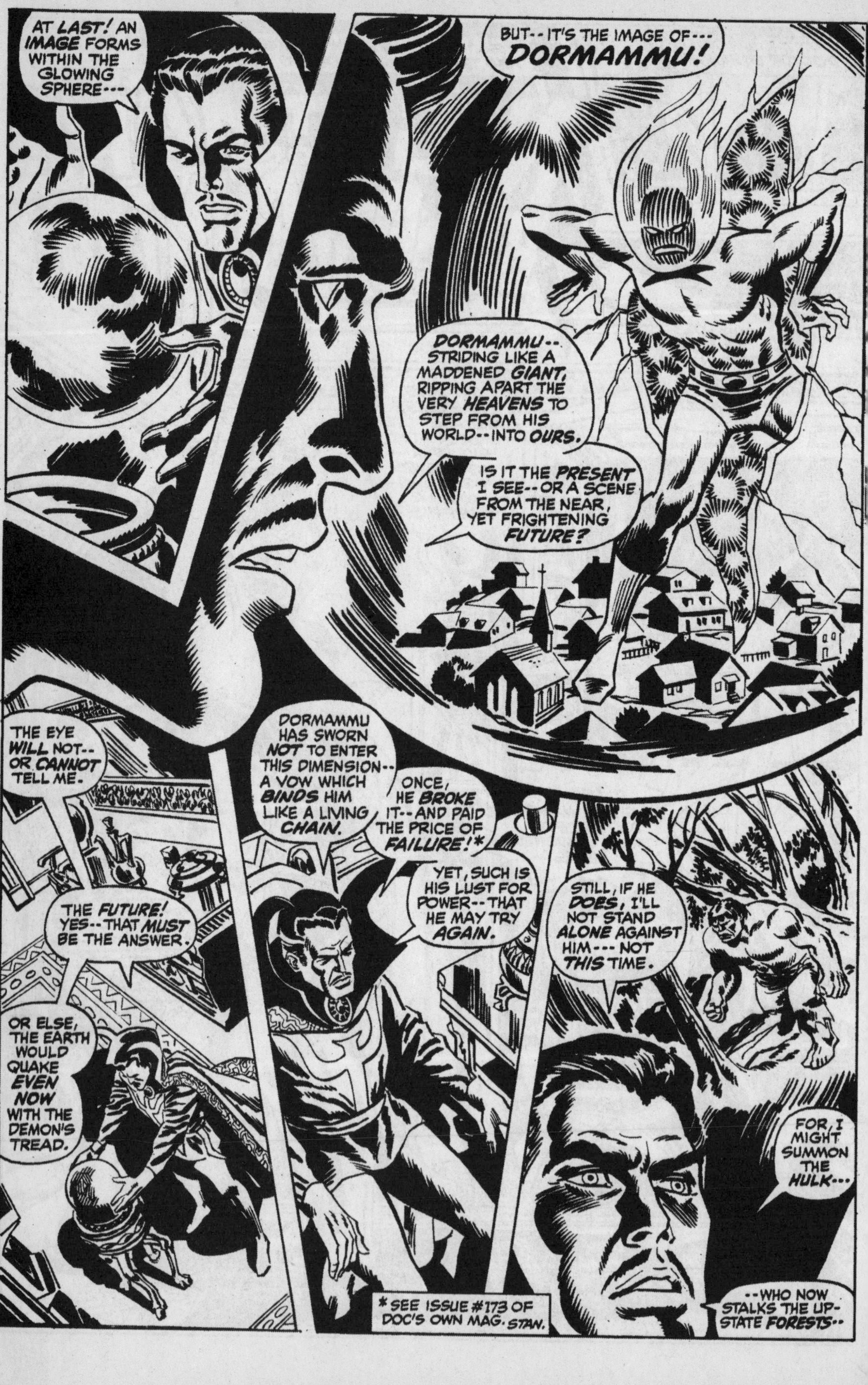
AT LAST! AN IMAGE FORMS WITHIN THE GLOWING SPHERE---
BUT-- IT'S THE IMAGE OF--- DORMAMMU!
DORMAMMU-- STRIDING LIKE A MADDENED GIANT, RIPPING APART THE VERY HEAVENS TO STEP FROM HIS WORLD-- INTO OURS.
IS IT THE PRESENT I SEE-- OR A SCENE FROM THE NEAR, YET FRIGHTENING FUTURE?
THE EYE WILL NOT-- OR CANNOT TELL ME.
THE FUTURE! YES-- THAT MUST BE THE ANSWER.
OR ELSE, THE EARTH WOULD QUAKE EVEN NOW WITH THE DEMON'S TREAD.
DORMAMMU HAS SWORN NOT TO ENTER THIS DIMENSION-- A VOW WHICH BINDS HIM LIKE A LIVING CHAIN.
ONCE, HE BROKE IT-- AND PAID THE PRICE OF FAILURE!*
YET, SUCH IS HIS LUST FOR POWER-- THAT HE MAY TRY AGAIN.
* SEE ISSUE #173 OF DOC'S OWN MAG. STAN.
STILL, IF HE DOES, I'LL NOT STAND ALONE AGAINST HIM--- NOT THIS TIME.
FOR, I MIGHT SUMMON THE HULK...
--WHO NOW STALKS THE UP-STATE FORESTS--

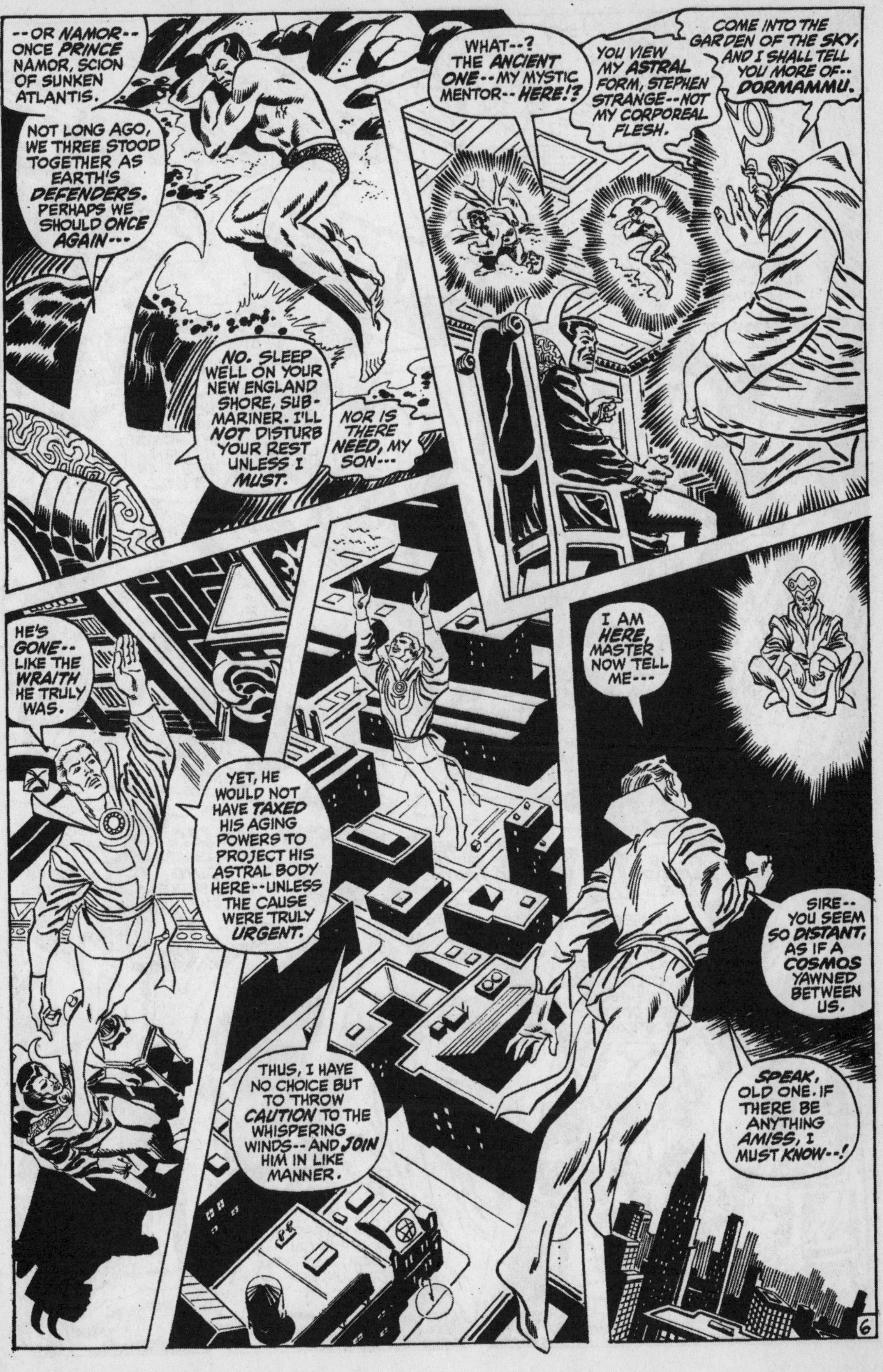
--OR NAMOR-- ONCE PRINCE NAMOR, SCION OF SUNKEN ATLANTIS.
NOT LONG AGO, WE THREE STOOD TOGETHER AS EARTH'S DEFENDERS. PERHAPS WE SHOULD ONCE AGAIN---
NO. SLEEP WELL ON YOUR NEW ENGLAND SHORE, SUB-MARINER. I'LL NOT DISTURB YOUR REST UNLESS I MUST.
NOR IS THERE NEED, MY SON---
WHAT--? THE ANCIENT ONE--MY MYSTIC MENTOR--HERE!?
YOU VIEW MY ASTRAL FORM, STEPHEN STRANGE--NOT MY CORPOREAL FLESH.
COME INTO THE GARDEN OF THE SKY, AND I SHALL TELL YOU MORE OF-- DORMAMMU.
HE'S GONE-- LIKE THE WRAITH HE TRULY WAS.
YET, HE WOULD NOT HAVE TAXED HIS AGING POWERS TO PROJECT HIS ASTRAL BODY HERE--UNLESS THE CAUSE WERE TRULY URGENT.
THUS, I HAVE NO CHOICE BUT TO THROW CAUTION TO THE WHISPERING WINDS--AND JOIN HIM IN LIKE MANNER.
I AM HERE, MASTER NOW TELL ME---
SIRE-- YOU SEEM SO DISTANT, AS IF A COSMOS YAWNED BETWEEN US.
SPEAK, OLD ONE. IF THERE BE ANYTHING AMISS, I MUST KNOW--!
6

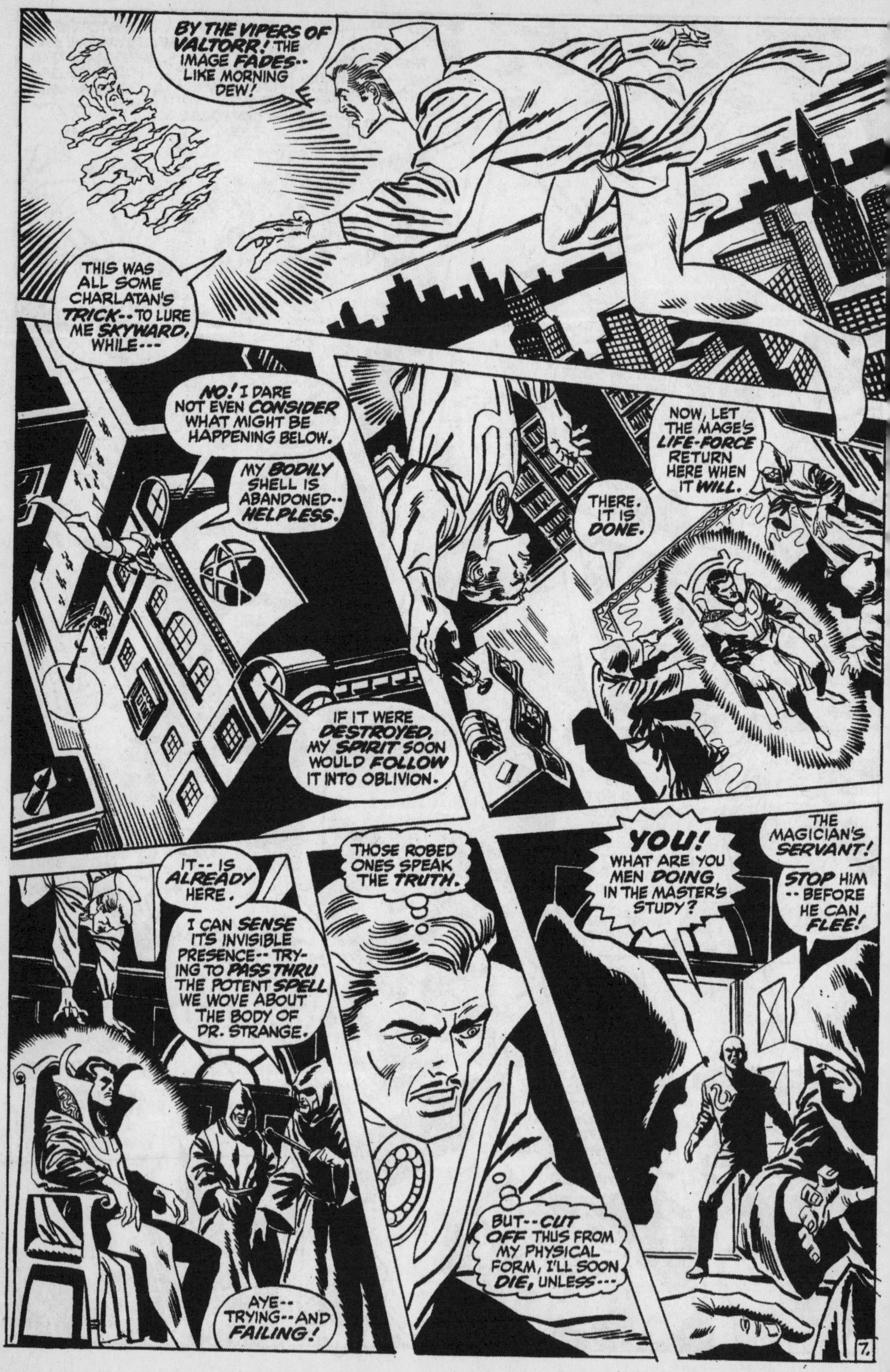
BY THE VIPERS OF VALTORR! THE IMAGE FADES-- LIKE MORNING DEW!
THIS WAS ALL SOME CHARLATAN'S TRICK--TO LURE ME SKYWARD, WHILE---
NO! I DARE NOT EVEN CONSIDER WHAT MIGHT BE HAPPENING BELOW.
MY BODILY SHELL IS ABANDONED-- HELPLESS.
IF IT WERE DESTROYED, MY SPIRIT SOON WOULD FOLLOW IT INTO OBLIVION.
NOW, LET THE MAGE'S LIFE-FORCE RETURN HERE WHEN IT WILL.
THERE. IT IS DONE.
IT-- IS ALREADY HERE.
I CAN SENSE ITS INVISIBLE PRESENCE-- TRYING TO PASS THRU THE POTENT SPELL WE WOVE ABOUT THE BODY OF DR. STRANGE.
AYE-- TRYING--AND FAILING!
THOSE ROBED ONES SPEAK THE TRUTH.
BUT--CUT OFF THUS FROM MY PHYSICAL FORM, I'LL SOON DIE, UNLESS---
YOU! WHAT ARE YOU MEN DOING IN THE MASTER'S STUDY?
THE MAGICIAN'S SERVANT!
STOP HIM --BEFORE HE CAN FLEE!
7.

FLEE!? UNWORTHY ONES SHOULD BITE THEIR DISHONORABLE *TONGUES.*

I HAVE NO POWERS OF *SORCERY,* BLACK *OR* WHITE--

BUT, AGAINST SUCH SKULKING DOGS AS *YOU--*

THUK!

--*OTHER* ANCIENT ORIENTAL ARTS SHOULD *SUFFICE!*

TCHOP!

PERHAPS THEY *WOULD,* FOOL-- IF WE FOUGHT *FAIRLY.*

WOP!

BUT, TOO MUCH IS AT *STAKE* FOR THAT--

KAK!

--*FAR* TOO MUCH!

NOW *HURRY.* THAT STRUGGLE COST US PRECIOUS *MOMENTS.*

BUT-- SHOULDN'T WE SLIT THE SERVANT'S *THROAT?*

WE'VE NO *TIME* FOR THAT. *HE'LL* CAUSE US NO TROUBLE.

HE'LL *LIE* FOR HOURS AS ONE *DEAD.* NOW *COME.*

HELLO, WONG-- ARE YOU STILL *THERE--?*

OPERATOR-- I THINK WE WERE *CUT* OFF--!

8.

STRANDS IN A WEIRDLY-WOVEN WEB: AND SO, WHILE A GREAT GREEN-SKINNED GOLIATH ESCHEWS THE TRAPPINGS AND FETTERS OF CIVILIZATION---

---EVEN AS A DECIDEDLY NON-MYSTICAL STATION WAGON CARRIES THE INERT FORM OF STEPHEN STRANGE NORTHEAST-WARD, ALONG SUPER-HIGHWAYS AND WINDING COUNTRY LANES---

---THE SEA-BORN SUB-MARINER DOES LIKEWISE, WAKING IN THE NIGHT TO PARTAKE OF A MOONLIT FEAST OF SUCCULENT OYSTERS--

---WHILE, BACK IN GREENWICH VILLAGE...

WONG-- WAKE UP, WONG---!

WHAT--? OH--MISS CLEA--

NOW THIS HUMBLE SOUL REMEMBERS.

THOSE MEN-- IN LONG, DARK ROBES--

WHAT MEN, WONG? AND WHERE IS STEPHEN--DR. STRANGE?

GONE, MISS-- TAKEN BY THOSE MEN, WHILE HE-- SLEPT.

OH, MY UNWORTHY HEAD-- IT FEELS AS IF PRESSED BENEATH THE FOOT OF THE ELEPHANT--!

YOU MEAN-- THAT'S WHAT YOU HEARD BEFORE, THAT DREW YOU AWAY FROM THE TELEPHONE?

YES, MISS CLEA. AS YOU KNOW, I CALLED YOU BECAUSE I FELT THE MASTER WAS IN NEED OF DIVERSION-- A WOMAN'S HAND, PERHAPS--

HE OFTEN BROODED FOR HOURS --OR SAT STARING INTO HIS OCCULT EYE.

PERHAPS HE NOW FINDS IT MORE REWARDING THAN A GIRL FROM ANOTHER DIMEN-SION-- WHOSE POWERS HAVE ALL BUT FADED IN THIS, YOUR WORLD.

STILL, THIS IS NOT THE TIME FOR THOUGHTS OF REPROACH!

THOUGH I KNOW LITTLE OF THE WORKINGS OF THE EYE OF AGAMOTTO -- PERHAPS IT CAN HELP ME FIND STEPHEN.

IT MUST, WONG. IT-- MUST!

9.

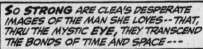

So **STRONG** are Clea's desperate images of the man she loves -- that, thru the Mystic Eye, they transcend the bonds of time and space ---

-- **Reaching** willowy sea-beds off the New England coast ---

-- And the **Mind's Eye** of one who was most recently in the abducted sorcerer's **thoughts** --

-- One who now speeds **Southward**, with no hesitation -- no **remorse** for other quests delayed --

Nor is **Namor** alone in receiving such eerie emanations --!

Huh? Hulk sees -- face floating in the air.

The face of the one called -- **Dr. Strange.**

Hulk doesn't **remember** him very well -- -- except that -- he was a **good** man -- didn't **fear** Hulk --

And now, somehow -- he needs **help** --

-- So Hulk will **go** to him!

ACME

While, on the grounds of a certain reportedly-haunted manor just outside Rutland, Vermont ---

Roy! Jeanie!* So you **did** make it up from the big, bad city, after **all!**

Grab a couple of **hammers,** and help us get ready for the big **Halloween parade** tomorrow night.

Glad to, Tom. But, we heard some **rumors** on the radio, driving up --

-- rumors about some **scarlet lights,** up on that hill you call **Bald Mountain.**

They got us all **curious,** y'know?

Brrrr -- those stories sounded creepy enough to keep me **awake** all night.

Tell us all **about** 'em, huh?

*Everybody here remember Roy and Jeanie Thomas -- not to mention fearless Tom Fagan -- from **Avengers #83?** --- S.

10

BALD MOUNTAIN-- YES, IT'S CLOUDED WITH *MYSTERIES* AS THICK AS THE *SUDDEN FOGS* WHICH OFTEN WREATHE ITS SUMMIT.

AND IT'S GOT *MORE* THAN ITS FAIR SHARE OF ---*LEGENDS.*

BEFORE RUTLAND WAS SETTLED, THE *IROQUOIS* ROAMED THE SURROUNDING LANDS---

BUT THEY *AVOIDED* THE MOUNTAIN AS A ---"*PLACE OF UNEASY SPIRITS.*"

DURING THE *REVOLUTIONARY WAR*, THEY SAY A SOLDIER DESERTED HIS REGIMENT AND *DIED* WHILE HIDING OUT UP THERE.

HIS *GHOST* STILL HAUNTS THE PLACE-- THEY SAY.

OH, AND AROUND *1890*, TWO FAMILIES EKED OUT A *MEAGRE* LIVING WITH SMALL *FARMS* ON THE MOUNTAINSIDE.

THEY *DISAPPEARED* OVERNIGHT-- UNEATEN DINNERS STILL ON THE KITCHEN TABLE.

IF ONE CAN BELIEVE THE *STORY*, THAT IS.

FUNNY, THOUGH, THAT YOU SHOULD ASK ABOUT THE "*RED GLOW*"..

THAT GLOW WAS FIRST SEEN IN '*37* --- SILHOUETTED THE MOUNTAIN FOR SEVERAL *NIGHTS*, I HEAR TELL.

OFFICIAL REPORT SAID "*FOREST FIRES*".-- BUT NOBODY EVER FOUND SO MUCH AS A CHARRED *TWIG.*

SAME THING HAPPENED FOR A HANDFUL OF NIGHTS BACK AROUND '*59*---

AND NOW, LOOKS LIKE IT'S HAPPENING *AGAIN.*

EVEN THE *KIDS* NOWADAYS SAY OLD BALDY'S A GOOD PLACE TO STAY *AWAY* FROM---AND THAT'S WHAT I AIM TO *DO.*

NOW-- ANY *MORE* QUESTIONS?

NOT---

---REALLY.

11.

MEANWHILE, AT A PLACE WITH THE UNLIKELY NAME OF *BREEZY POINT*, A COASTAL RADAR STATION PICKS UP A RAPIDLY-MOVING *OBJECT*---

BUT, BEFORE THE HARRIED OPERATIVES THERE CAN GET A *FIX* ON THE SUDDEN BLIP---

IT DROPS BENEATH THE RADAR CURTAIN AND IS SWIFTLY GONE--

--*SPARING* THE MEN BELOW, PERHAPS, AN ENCOUNTER THEY MIGHT HAVE LIVED TO *REGRET*--!

AND NOW, THE SUB-MARINER SWOOPS LOW OVER THE CITY---

THE IMAGE I SAW MAY HAVE BEEN THE *TRUE SUMMONS* OF DR. STRANGE---OR THE *BAIT* IN SOME MADMAN'S *TRAP*.

YET, THAT SORCERER OFT HAS STOOD BETWEEN *MANKIND*-- AND FOES FROM *BEYOND*, WHO WOULD HAVE *ENGULFED* IT.

KNOWING THAT, I *DARE NOT* IGNORE THE CALL-- NO MATTER WHAT THE *RISK*.

CURSE ME FOR A WAYWARD *FLOUNDER!*

I FLEW *TOO CLOSE* TO THAT BUILDING-- AND THE FEMALE WITHIN MUST HAVE *SEEN* ME.

IT WILL BE NAUGHT BUT *GOOD FORTUNE* IF SHE DID *NOT*.

BUT, THERE IS NO GOOD FORTUNE FOR NAMOR-- NOT *THIS* NIGHT.

HELLO, *POLICE?* I WANT TO REPORT A *PROWLER* OUTSIDE MY WINDOW.

NO, IT CERTAINLY WAS *NOT* A RUN-OF-THE-MILL *PEEPING TOM*.

I'M ON THE *FIFTH FLOOR!*

12

WHILE, ELSE-WHERE IN THE HUMAN JUNGLE THAT IS NEW YORK CITY---

HEY, SAM-- LOOK--OVER THERE--!

HOLY JOE! THAT NIGHT-WATCHMAN WHO CALLED US DIDN'T KNOW THE HALF OF IT.

THIS AIN'T JUST ANY BREAK-AND-ENTRY MAN WE GOT OURSELVES HERE--

--IT'S THE HULK!

ALL RIGHT, MONSTER-MAN-- GIVE UP; OR WE'LL BE FORCED TO OPEN FIRE.

GIVE UP? HULK NEVER GIVES UP.

HULK HAS SOMETHING TO DO-- SOMEWHERE TO GO--

LOOK OUT! HE'S COMING THIS WAY.

BLAM!

THEN-- WE'VE GOT NO CHOICE BUT TO SHOOT FIRST ---AND ASK QUESTIONS AT THE AUTOPSY.

BLAM!

BAH! STUPID HUMANS MAKE HULK SICK.

HULK DIDN'T CARE ABOUT YOU-- JUST WANTED TO GET PAST YOU.

IF YOU DON'T WATCH OUT-- YOU WILL MAKE HULK MAD!

KROMP!

13.

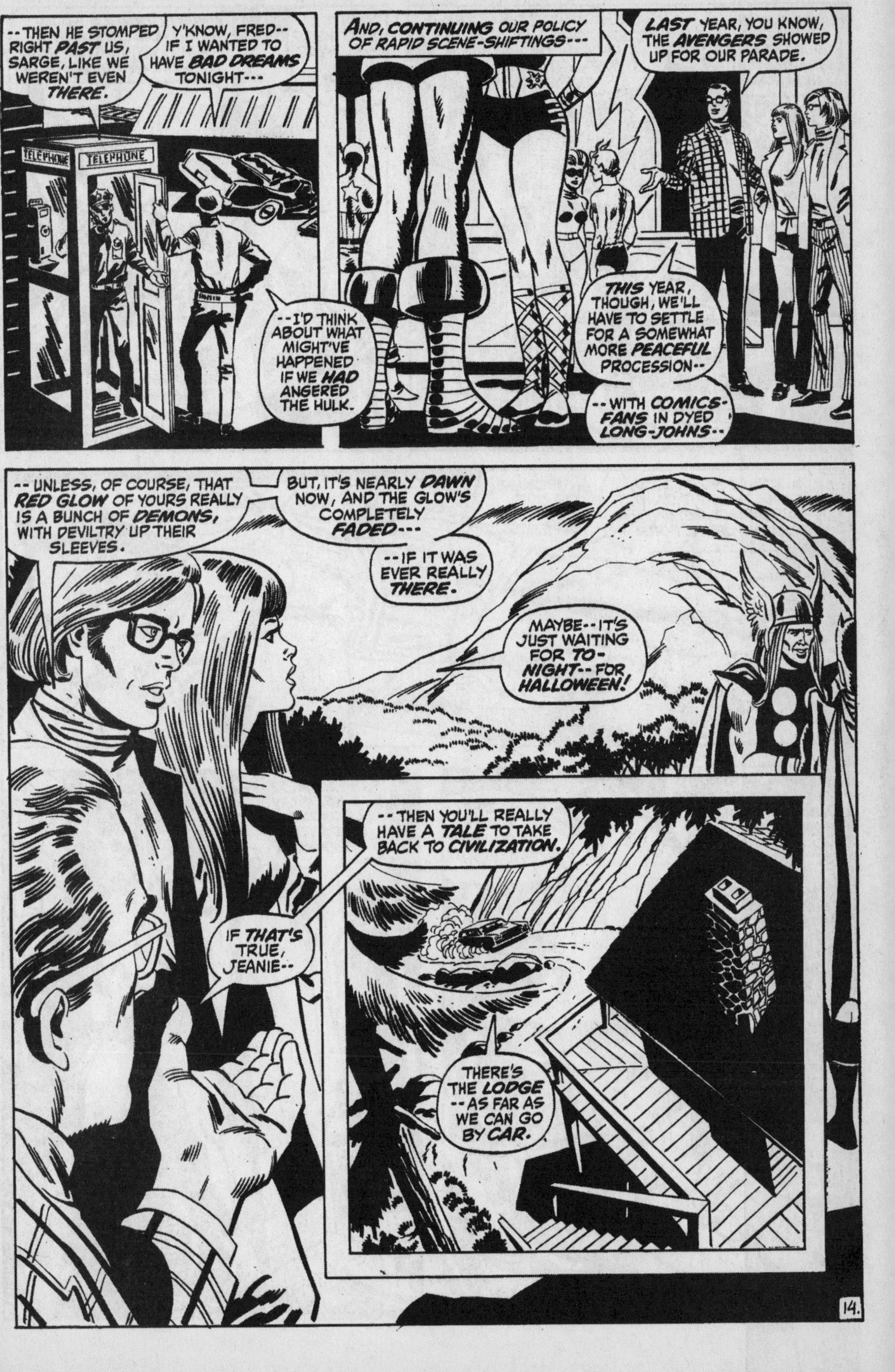
--THEN HE STOMPED RIGHT PAST US, SARGE, LIKE WE WEREN'T EVEN THERE.
Y'KNOW, FRED-- IF I WANTED TO HAVE BAD DREAMS TONIGHT---
TELEPHONE
TELEPHONE
--I'D THINK ABOUT WHAT MIGHT'VE HAPPENED IF WE HAD ANGERED THE HULK.
AND, CONTINUING OUR POLICY OF RAPID SCENE-SHIFTINGS---
LAST YEAR, YOU KNOW, THE AVENGERS SHOWED UP FOR OUR PARADE.
THIS YEAR, THOUGH, WE'LL HAVE TO SETTLE FOR A SOMEWHAT MORE PEACEFUL PROCESSION--
--WITH COMICS-FANS IN DYED LONG-JOHNS--
--UNLESS, OF COURSE, THAT RED GLOW OF YOURS REALLY IS A BUNCH OF DEMONS, WITH DEVILTRY UP THEIR SLEEVES.
BUT, IT'S NEARLY DAWN NOW, AND THE GLOW'S COMPLETELY FADED---
--IF IT WAS EVER REALLY THERE.
MAYBE--IT'S JUST WAITING FOR TO-NIGHT--FOR HALLOWEEN!
IF THAT'S TRUE, JEANIE--
--THEN YOU'LL REALLY HAVE A TALE TO TAKE BACK TO CIVILIZATION.
THERE'S THE LODGE --AS FAR AS WE CAN GO BY CAR.
14.

NOR MAY WE PROCEED FURTHER EVEN ON *FOOT*, UNTIL *NIGHTFALL.*

FOR, IT IS WRITTEN: "*THE HOST-BODY SHALL ASCEND THE FACE OF THE MOUNTAIN BY THE EARLY LIGHT OF THE MOON---*"

---AND IT IS NOW NEARLY *DAWN.*

GENTLY, BROTHERS --- LOWER HIM *GENTLY,* NOW.

UNIMAGINABLE WOULD BE THE MASTER'S WRATH, IF THIS LIVING RECEPTACLE WERE *DAMAGED.*

I-- WONDER WHAT HAS HAPPENED TO THE MAGE'S *ASTRAL SELF!?* WE DID NOT FEEL HIS *PRESENCE* ON THE LONG DRIVE HERE---

ALL THAT *MATTERS,* FOOL, IS THAT IT CANNOT AND DID NOT *RE-ENTER* HIS CORPOREAL FORM---

---BECAUSE OF OUR PREVENTATIVE *SPELLS.*

STEPHEN STRANGE'S BODY MUST BE *FREE* TONIGHT OF ALL RIVAL LIFE-FORCES, SO THAT IT MAY RECEIVE A *NEW* MASTER---

---ONE WHO CAN ENTER THIS WORLD *ONLY* BY INHABITING THE FORM OF A *SORCERER* OF CONSIDERABLE POWER---

---ONE WHO IS CALLED--- *DORMAMMU!*

--CAR 37--- KEEP ON LOOKOUT FOR UNIDENTIFIED PROWLER---

15

---LAST SEEN IN VICINITY OF BLEECKER STREET AND SEVENTH AVENUE---

---REPORTED TO BE WEARING NOTHING BUT A PAIR OF SWIMMING TRUNKS---

AT LAST-- THE OFFENSIVE SOUND IS LEFT BEHIND ME.

NOW, PERHAPS I CAN MAKE MY WAY TO---

WHAT? THOSE TUMBLING CRATES--

NO-- NOT TUMBLING--

SOMEONE HAS HURLED THEM-- AT ME!

IF A TRAP BE SPRUNG HERE THIS NIGHT---

-- THE TRAPPER SHALL LIVE TO REGRET HIS ACTIONS!

SUDDENLY--- A MOMENT'S STRUGGLE---

---A FLEETING CLASH, BETWEEN TWO SHADOWED TITANS---

16

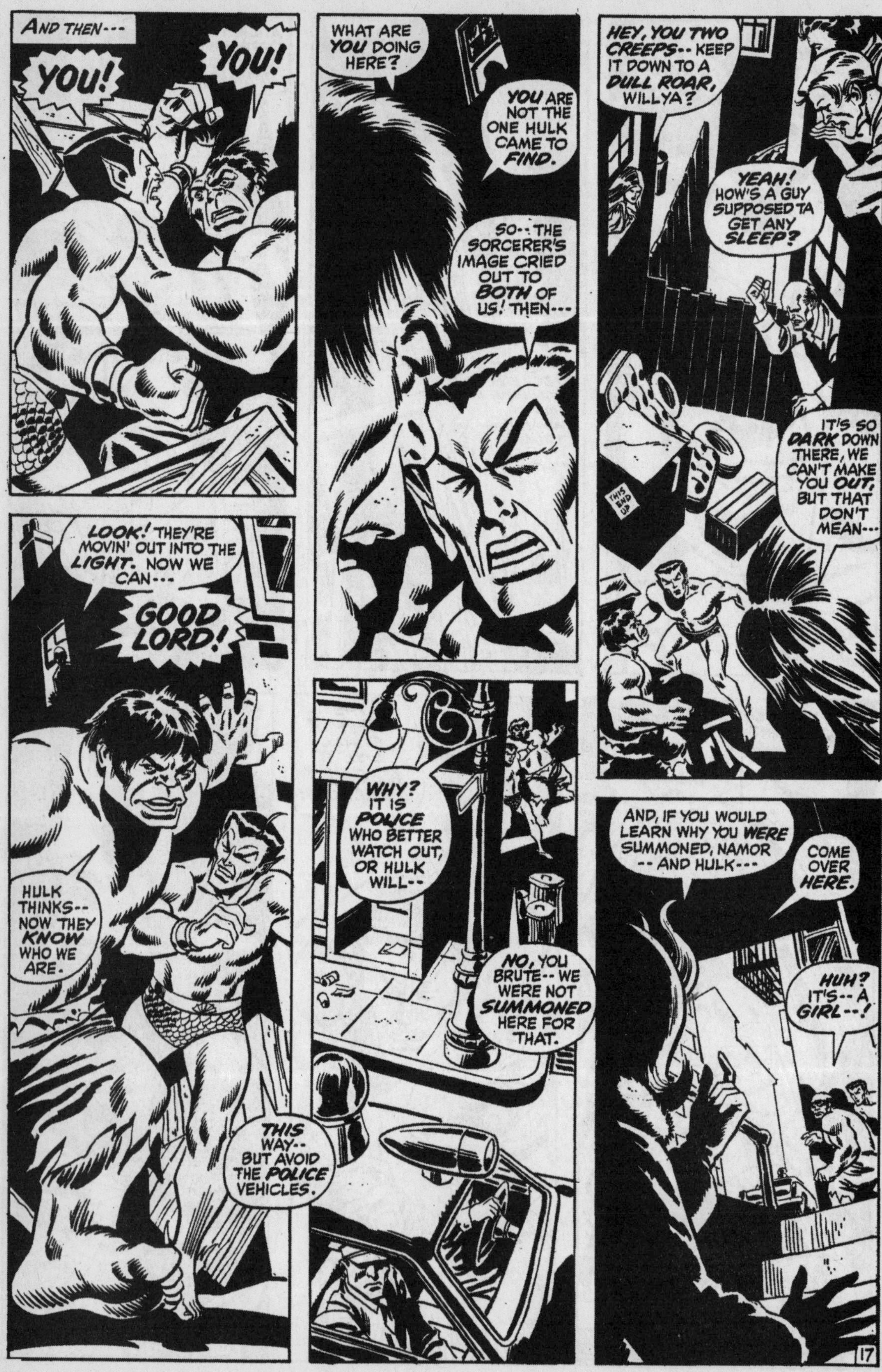
AND THEN---
YOU!
YOU!
WHAT ARE YOU DOING HERE?
YOU ARE NOT THE ONE HULK CAME TO FIND.
SO-- THE SORCERER'S IMAGE CRIED OUT TO BOTH OF US! THEN---
HEY, YOU TWO CREEPS-- KEEP IT DOWN TO A DULL ROAR, WILLYA?
YEAH! HOW'S A GUY SUPPOSED TA GET ANY SLEEP?
THIS END UP
IT'S SO DARK DOWN THERE, WE CAN'T MAKE YOU OUT, BUT THAT DON'T MEAN---
LOOK! THEY'RE MOVIN' OUT INTO THE LIGHT. NOW WE CAN---
GOOD LORD!
HULK THINKS-- NOW THEY KNOW WHO WE ARE.
WHY? IT IS POLICE WHO BETTER WATCH OUT, OR HULK WILL--
NO, YOU BRUTE-- WE WERE NOT SUMMONED HERE FOR THAT.
THIS WAY-- BUT AVOID THE POLICE VEHICLES.
AND, IF YOU WOULD LEARN WHY YOU WERE SUMMONED, NAMOR -- AND HULK---
COME OVER HERE.
HUH? IT'S-- A GIRL--!

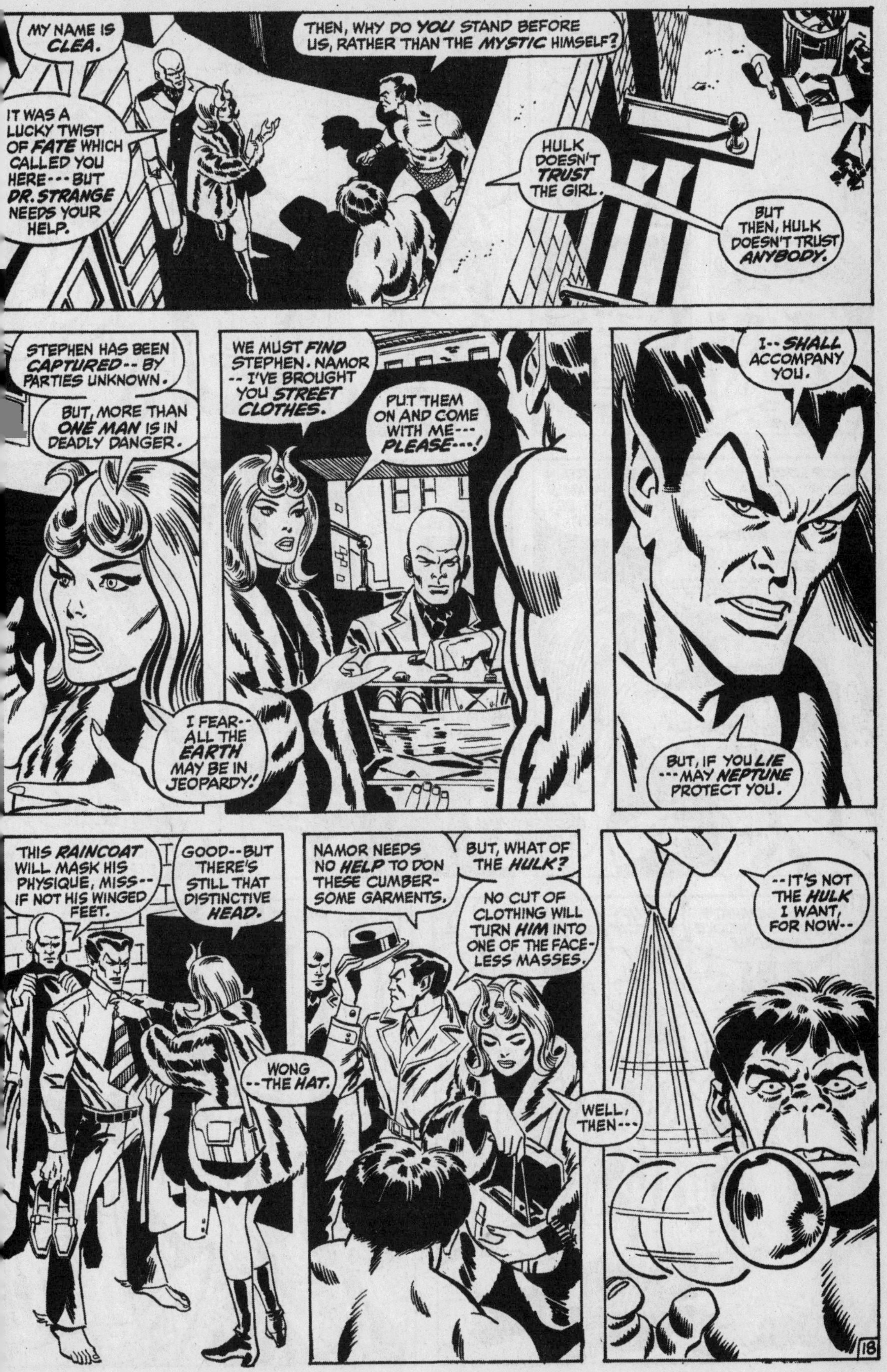
MY NAME IS CLEA.
THEN, WHY DO YOU STAND BEFORE US, RATHER THAN THE MYSTIC HIMSELF?
IT WAS A LUCKY TWIST OF FATE WHICH CALLED YOU HERE--- BUT DR. STRANGE NEEDS YOUR HELP.
HULK DOESN'T TRUST THE GIRL.
BUT THEN, HULK DOESN'T TRUST ANYBODY.
STEPHEN HAS BEEN CAPTURED-- BY PARTIES UNKNOWN.
BUT, MORE THAN ONE MAN IS IN DEADLY DANGER.
I FEAR-- ALL THE EARTH MAY BE IN JEOPARDY!
WE MUST FIND STEPHEN. NAMOR -- I'VE BROUGHT YOU STREET CLOTHES.
PUT THEM ON AND COME WITH ME--- PLEASE---!
I-- SHALL ACCOMPANY YOU.
BUT, IF YOU LIE ---MAY NEPTUNE PROTECT YOU.
THIS RAINCOAT WILL MASK HIS PHYSIQUE, MISS-- IF NOT HIS WINGED FEET.
GOOD--BUT THERE'S STILL THAT DISTINCTIVE HEAD.
WONG --THE HAT.
NAMOR NEEDS NO HELP TO DON THESE CUMBERSOME GARMENTS.
BUT, WHAT OF THE HULK?
NO CUT OF CLOTHING WILL TURN HIM INTO ONE OF THE FACELESS MASSES.
WELL, THEN---
--IT'S NOT THE HULK I WANT, FOR NOW--
18

--BUT---

--A MAN---

--NAMED---

--BRUCE---

--BANNER--!

GOOD LORD! MY MEMORY GETS A BIT **FOGGY** SOMETIMES--- WHEN I MAKE THAT **SWITCH**---

I HAVE-- CERTAIN **MINOR** POWERS OF MY OWN, DR. BANNER.

BUT, HOW DID YOU DO THAT SO **QUICKLY** --- SO **EASILY**?

NOT **BAD.** I MUST BE CLOSE TO THE MAGICIAN'S **SIZE.**

STILL, WHAT'S TO STOP ME FROM BECOMING THE **HULK** AGAIN, AT ANY MOMENT?

BUT **HURRY.** I'VE BROUGHT **YOU** CLOTHES, AS WELL.

NOTHING--- BUT **THESE.** POWERFUL **TRANQUILIZERS.** TAKE ONE EACH **HOUR**---

--I KNOW. AND **DON'T** SHAKE BEFORE USING.

OKAY, SO WHAT'S **NEXT** ON THE OLD AGENDA?

A **TRIP**---TO A SITE IN THE STATE OF **VERMONT.**

I HAVE MANAGED TO TRACE STEPHEN'S **PHYSICAL** FORM THERE---THOUGH HIS **PSYCHIC** SELF, I CAN'T---

ALL RIGHT. YOU---

BETTER HOLD IT **RIGHT THERE!**

19

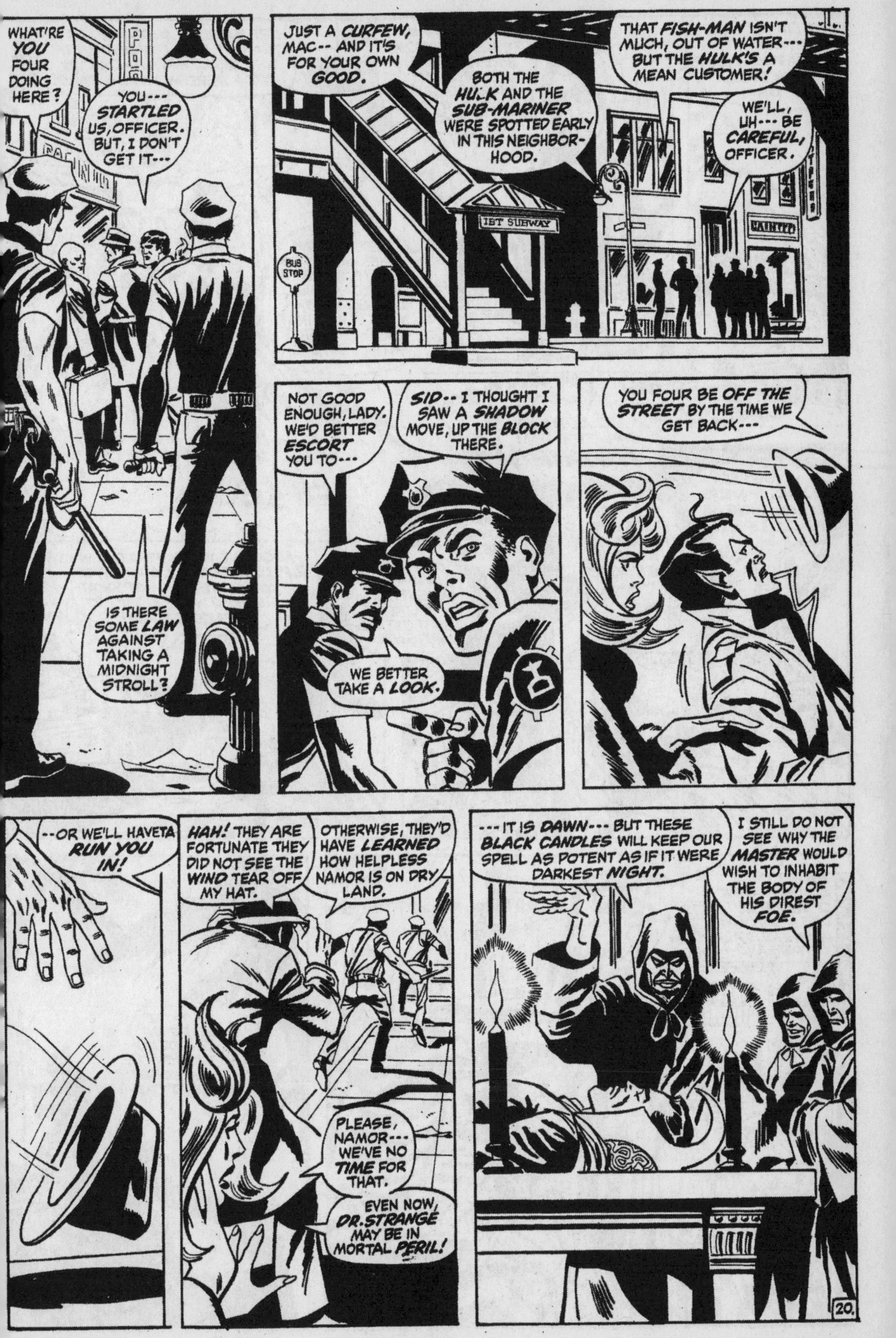

WHAT'RE YOU FOUR DOING HERE?
YOU--- STARTLED US, OFFICER. BUT, I DON'T GET IT---
IS THERE SOME LAW AGAINST TAKING A MIDNIGHT STROLL?
JUST A CURFEW, MAC-- AND IT'S FOR YOUR OWN GOOD.
BOTH THE HULK AND THE SUB-MARINER WERE SPOTTED EARLY IN THIS NEIGHBOR-HOOD.
THAT FISH-MAN ISN'T MUCH, OUT OF WATER--- BUT THE HULK'S A MEAN CUSTOMER!
WE'LL, UH--- BE CAREFUL, OFFICER.
IRT SUBWAY
BUS STOP
NOT GOOD ENOUGH, LADY. WE'D BETTER ESCORT YOU TO---
SID-- I THOUGHT I SAW A SHADOW MOVE, UP THE BLOCK THERE.
WE BETTER TAKE A LOOK.
YOU FOUR BE OFF THE STREET BY THE TIME WE GET BACK---
--OR WE'LL HAVETA RUN YOU IN!
HAH! THEY ARE FORTUNATE THEY DID NOT SEE THE WIND TEAR OFF MY HAT.
OTHERWISE, THEY'D HAVE LEARNED HOW HELPLESS NAMOR IS ON DRY LAND.
PLEASE, NAMOR--- WE'VE NO TIME FOR THAT.
EVEN NOW, DR. STRANGE MAY BE IN MORTAL PERIL!
---IT IS DAWN--- BUT THESE BLACK CANDLES WILL KEEP OUR SPELL AS POTENT AS IF IT WERE DARKEST NIGHT.
I STILL DO NOT SEE WHY THE MASTER WOULD WISH TO INHABIT THE BODY OF HIS DIREST FOE.
20.

DOG! IF YOU WERE NOT A *NEOPHYTE* **AND** A FOOL, YOU'D NOT *ASK* SUCH A QUESTION.

THE MASTER'S OWN REGRETTED *VOW* PREVENTS HIS *PHYSICALLY* ENTERING OUR WORLD, TO MAKE IT *HIS*.

YET, MAKE NO *MISTAKE:* AFTER TONIGHT, IT IS *DORMAMMU* WHO SHALL WALK AMONG US, *NOT* A MERE MORTAL WIZARD.

HE'LL *BURY* THIS LAND, THIS STATE, BENEATH A VOLCANIC HAIL OF *HELLFIRE*--- MAKE IT HIS FIRST *SHRINE* IN THIS PITIFUL SPHERE---

-- AND *NOTHING* CAN STOP HIM! *NOTHING!*

-- YOU SEEM *PALE*, BANNER. IS ANYTHING--?

IT'S -- JUST *THESE* **PILLS**, NAMOR. THEY MAKE ME *GROGGY*.

STILL, MAYBE IT'S ALL FOR THE *BEST*.

OTHERWISE, EVEN A *SCIENTIST* TYPE LIKE ME MIGHT GET ALL *UPTIGHT*...

--ABOUT HEADING STRAIGHT INTO *H.P. LOVECRAFT* COUNTRY, ON *HALLOWEEN*--- NOT KNOW-ING *WHO* WE'RE GOING TO FACE THERE---

---OR *WHY!*

NIGHT ONCE AGAIN: A SPIRIT OF *REVELRY* LIES LIGHTLY UPON THE HEART OF THE LAND---

BUT, THE GALES OF LAUGHTER DO NOT REACH THE DARK-ROBED SILHOUETTES---

---WHO BEGIN TO *ASCEND* BALD MOUNTAIN, AMID THE EMBERS OF THE FAST-DYING SUN---

21.

NOR DO *THEY,* IN TURN, TAKE NOTE OF A LATE-COMING *BUS---*

-- WHICH DEPOSITS *ONE* UNLIKELY-LOOKING FOURSOME NEAR REPLICAS OF ANOTHER, MORE *FAMED* QUARTET---

THIS TRIP COST US PRECIOUS HOURS, WE MUST *HASTEN.*

TRUE, WONG. YET IT SEEMED WISEST TO ARRIVE IN *INCONSPICUOUS* FASHION.

PERHAPS *YOU* SHOULD REMAIN *BEHIND---*

NO. SOMETHING TELLS ME--- WE MAY NEED *MANY* HANDS, BEFORE THIS NIGHT IS DONE.

LOOK, NAMOR--- DR. BANNER--AT THE *EERIE* GLOW WHICH BATHES THAT *MOUNTAIN* YONDER.

PERHAPS *THERE,* WE ARE DESTINED TO WRESTLE WITH EVIL *MEN,* DARK GODS---

"-- PERHAPS *THERE,* EARTH'S FATE WEIGHS HEAVY IN THE *BALANCE!"*

---WE'RE PRACTICALLY ON *TOP* OF THAT RED GLOW, PEOPLE.

THEN, IT IS *TIME* NAMOR WAS *NAMOR* ONCE MORE.

OH NO--NO! IT'S FAR *WORSE* THAN EVEN I HAD DREAMED.

THAT *IMAGE* IN THE SKY-- LEERING-- GLARING-- IT'S THE DREAD *DORMAMMU* HIMSELF---!

DOR--WHAT? I NEVER *HEARD* OF---

UH OH!

KUH-THUK

KUH-

THUK

22

INTRUDERS-- ENDANGERING OUR CEREMONY!

KILL THE INFIDELS!

THEY HAVE-- PROTECTIVE SPELLS ABOUT THEMSELVES. MY WEAK MAGIC CAN'T STOP THEM.

AS FOR ME-- LOOKS LIKE THAT LAST TRANK DID ITS JOB TOO WELL.

DEATH STARING US IN THE FACE, AND I STILL CAN'T GET HOT AND BOTHERED ENOUGH TO BECOME-- THE HULK.

TIME, BRUCE BANNER?

THEN -- TIME YOU SHALL HAVE!

SUBBY'S DOING OKAY-- BUT HE'S BEEN LANDBOUND TOO LONG FOR HIS POWERS TO BE AT THEIR PEAK.

AND I'M SO SLOW-- BARELY DUCKED THAT CREEP.

BLAST THOSE TRANQUILIZERS!

HOLD FAST THE CIRCLE, BROTHERS.

THE MASTER NEEDS ONLY MOMENTS MORE.

NOT SURE WHAT'S UP, BUT I'D BETTER BREAK THAT CHAI--

GOOD GRIEF! THE SECONDSTRINGERS JUMPED ME!

THEY-- TRY TO KILL ME -- BUT THEY WON'T KILL--

23

--THE HULK!

HAH! HULK SCATTERS THEM ALL LIKE TENPINS!

BUT-- THE ONE CALLED NAMOR CAN'T DO THE SAME.

FUNNY-- CAN'T RECALL JUST WHY WE WERE FIGHTING THE ROBED ONES--

STILL, HULK ALWAYS KNEW HE WAS STRONGER THAN THAT FISH-MAN.

AND, BEST WAY TO PROVE THAT HULK IS THE STRONGEST OF ALL--

--IS TO PICK UP THIS BIG ROCK--

--AND THROW IT-- LIKE THIS!

WATER! MY THANKS, HULK. YOU DIVERTED THE STREAM ABOVE MY HEAD---

AND NOW, NO FORCE ON EARTH CAN HOLD THE SUB-MARINER.

QUICKLY --WE MUST BATTLE OUR WAY TO DR. STRANGE'S SIDE.

24

HULK WILL DO AS YOU SAY.

BUT-- WHY?

THERE IS NO TIME TO EXPLAIN-- ONLY TIME TO FIGHT.

NOT EVEN TIME FOR THAT, ATLANTEAN. LOOK! YOU ARE TOO LATE-- TOO LATE!

AND, EVEN AS BEHEMOTH AND AMPHIBIAN LIFT WONDERING EYES TO THE SATANIC CIRCLE BEFORE THEM---

LO! THE MAGE'S BODY DRIFTS UPWARD, AND THRU THE DIMENSIONAL GATE.

NOW, NAUGHT CAN STOP DORMAMMU FROM CLAIMING HIS OWN.

MISS CLEA-- I FEEL SO WEIRD--

TURN ONE OF YOUR SPELLS UPON ME--- QUICKLY!

A-- SPELL? BUT, WONG-- WHAT GOOD WILL THAT--?

WAIT! PERHAPS I BEGIN TO SEE, AT LAST. STEPHEN'S ASTRAL FORM-- PERHAPS IT HAS RESIDED WITHIN YOU, ALL THIS TIME---

P-PERHAPS, MISS CLEA. I-- DO NOT KNOW.

YET, AS YOUR MYSTIC PASS BATHES MY BROW--- I FEEL DIFFERENT---

SMALL WONDER THAT YOU DO, FAITHFUL ONE.

I USED YOU-- AS A FREEZING MAN MIGHT HUDDLE WITHIN A DEAD BEAST'S BODY, FOR WARMTH.

FOR, I REASONED THE SPELL ABOUT MY BODY MIGHT FADE AT SOME RITUAL MOMENT---

ONLY THUS COULD I HAVE SURVIVED THIS LONG.

AND-- IT HAS! ONCE MORE, BODY AND SOUL OF DR. STRANGE ARE ONE---

25

--- IN TIME TO DO WHAT *MUST BE DONE!*

WELL, I SHALL MAKE YOU WISH YOU HAD *LET* YOUR MISERABLE BODY BECOME THE RECEPTACLE OF *DORMAMMU.*

SO, MORTAL-- AT THE LAST MOMENT, YOU MANAGED AFTER ALL TO *FOIL* MY BEST-LAID SCHEMES.

NO, DREADED ONE. THAT, I SHALL *NEVER* DO.

NOT WHILE THE *SHIELDS OF THE SERAPHIM* ARE MY STRENGTH, MY PROTECTION---

---*NOR* WHILE THESE *BOLTS OF BEDEVILMENT* ARE MINE TO HURL.

IMPOSSIBLE! YOU FLING-- MY OWN *SPELLS* BACK AGAINST ME!

YOU SEEK TO *STALEMATE* ME-- BUT I AM AS MUCH YOUR *SUPERIOR* AS EVER.

ARE YOU, FIEND?

ARE YOU?

NOW I SENSE THE TRUTH. IT IS THE *GATEWAY.*

WHILE IT IS *OPEN,* YOUR WORLD BEYOND *SAPS* MY MYSTIC PROWESS.

YET, THERE ARE POWERS *BEYOND* POWER---!

26

AND, IT IS JUST SUCH AWESOME FORCE WHICH MIGHTY DORMAMMU STRIVES BELATEDLY TO UNLEASH---

-- AS HEAVEN, FOR A FAST-FLEETING MOMENT, SEEMS TO STRETCH OUT ITS JAGGED ARMS TOWARD HELL--!

RRRUMMBLL

LOOK! OL' BALDY'S ERUPTING--- JUST LIKE A VOLCANO.

THAT GLOW DONE IT, I TELL YA-- THAT CRAZY RED GLOW.

IT'S THE END OF THE WORLD!

BUT, THE WILY OLD VERMONTER IS WRONG. FOR, 'TIS REALLY NOT THE END OF THE WORLD AT ALL---

AT LEAST---

FROOOM!

---NOT FOR EVERYONE---!

27.

HOLD *FAST*, HULK! WE MUST *SHIELD* THESE TWO -- WITH OUR *OWN* BODIES.

OH, STEPHEN -- STEPHEN -- WHERE *ARE* YOU --?

YOU HAVE *WON*, MAGE.

WEAKENED THUS, I CAN- NOT MASS *POWER* ENOUGH TO DESTROY YOU.

BUT, *ANOTHER* DAY --- *ANOTHER* HOUR ---

I'LL *STORE* DORMAMMU'S THREATS --- FOR *THAT* DAY'S WORRY.

THE GATEWAY IS *GONE*. I EMERGED JUST IN *TIME*.

STEPHEN -- YOU'RE *NOT* DEAD. BUT --- THE *OTHERS* --!?

NOTHING COULD HAVE SURVIVED THAT FINAL, FATAL AVALANCHE.

NAMOR AND THE HULK *DIED* --- THAT YOU, AND EARTH, MIGHT *LIVE*.

BUT -- *LOOK!* THAT *ROCK* --!

IT IS NOT THE INSENSATE *ROCK* WHICH MOVES, GIRL ---

-- BUT THE *SUB- MARINER*.

AND *HULK* WILL NEVER DIE --- WHILE *FISH-MAN* IS STILL ALIVE!

THE MOUNTAINSIDE IS QUIET NOW --- A HALO OF FINE *DUST* HOVERS, WRAITH-LIKE, OVER UNGRAVEN MONU- MENTS OF STONE ---

--- AND ONE CAN ONLY HOPE THAT ALL THE *EVIL* WHICH MEN DO IS BURIED *WITH* THEM, FOR ALL TIME.

YES --- ONE CAN ONLY --- *HOPE*.

Finis

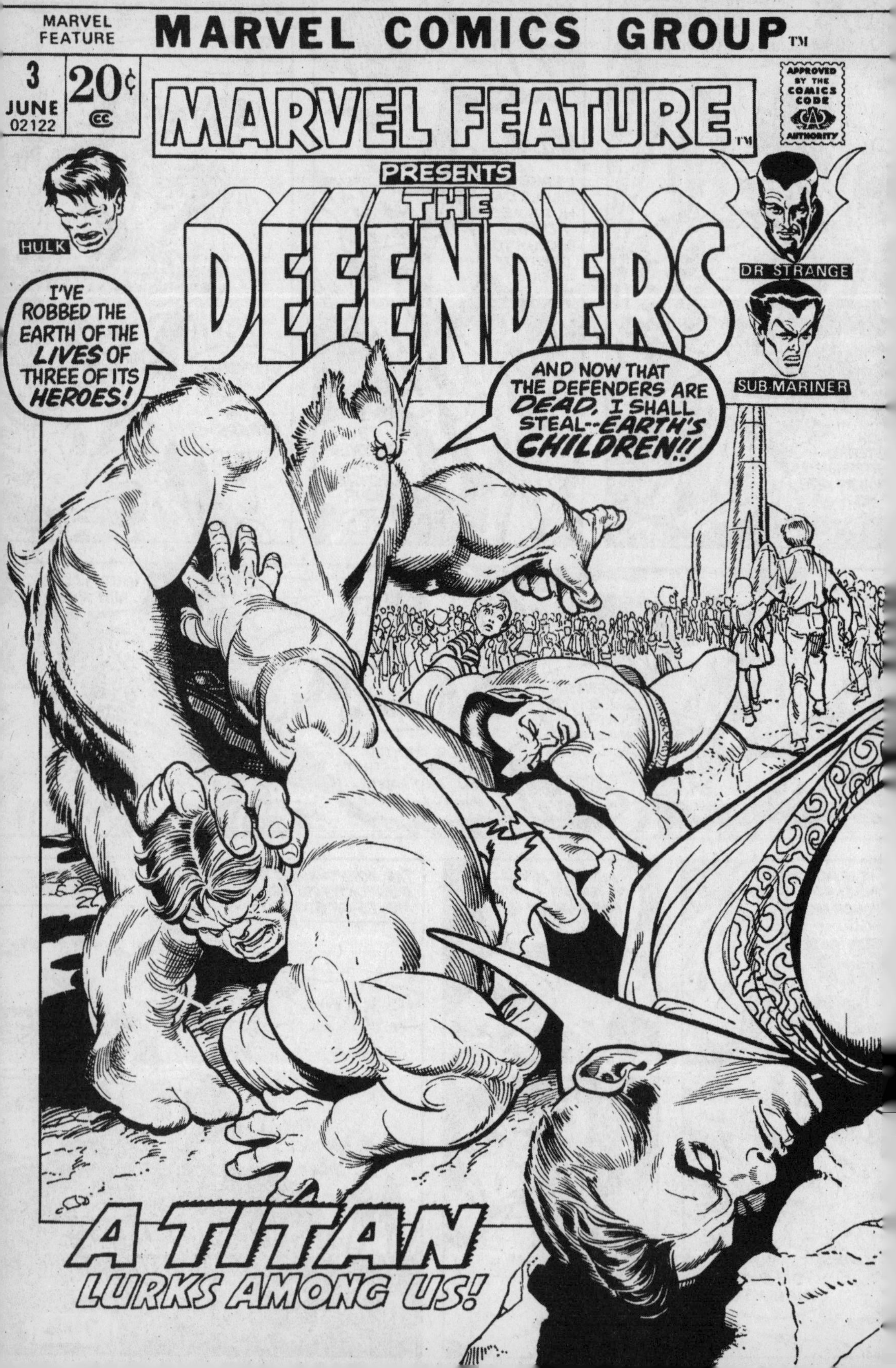
MARVEL FEATURE
MARVEL COMICS GROUP
3
JUNE
02122
20¢
CC
APPROVED BY THE COMICS CODE AUTHORITY
MARVEL FEATURE
PRESENTS
THE DEFENDERS
HULK
DR STRANGE
SUB-MARINER
I'VE ROBBED THE EARTH OF THE LIVES OF THREE OF ITS HEROES!
AND NOW THAT THE DEFENDERS ARE DEAD, I SHALL STEAL--EARTH'S CHILDREN!!
A TITAN LURKS AMONG US!

THE DYNAMIC DEFENDERS! ™

STAN LEE, EDITOR * ROY THOMAS, WRITER * ROSS ANDRU, ARTIST * BILL EVERETT, INKER * ART SIMEK, LETTERER

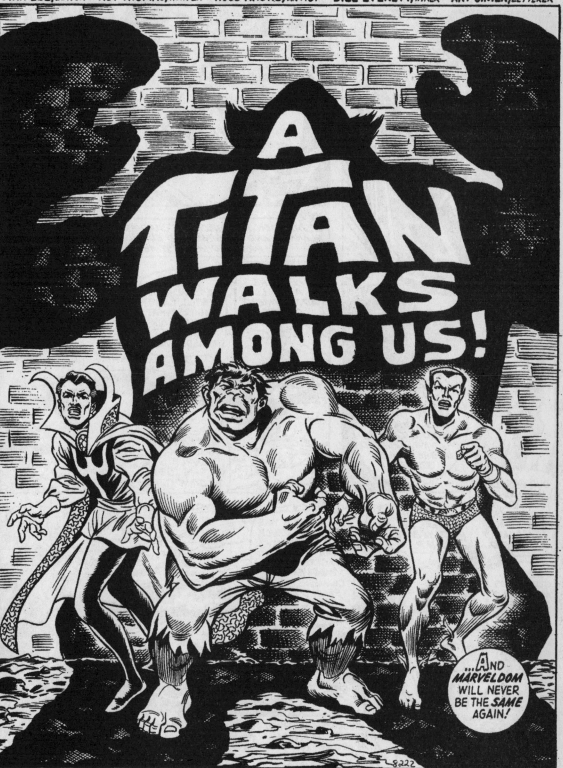

A TITAN WALKS AMONG US!

...AND MARVELDOM WILL NEVER BE THE SAME AGAIN!

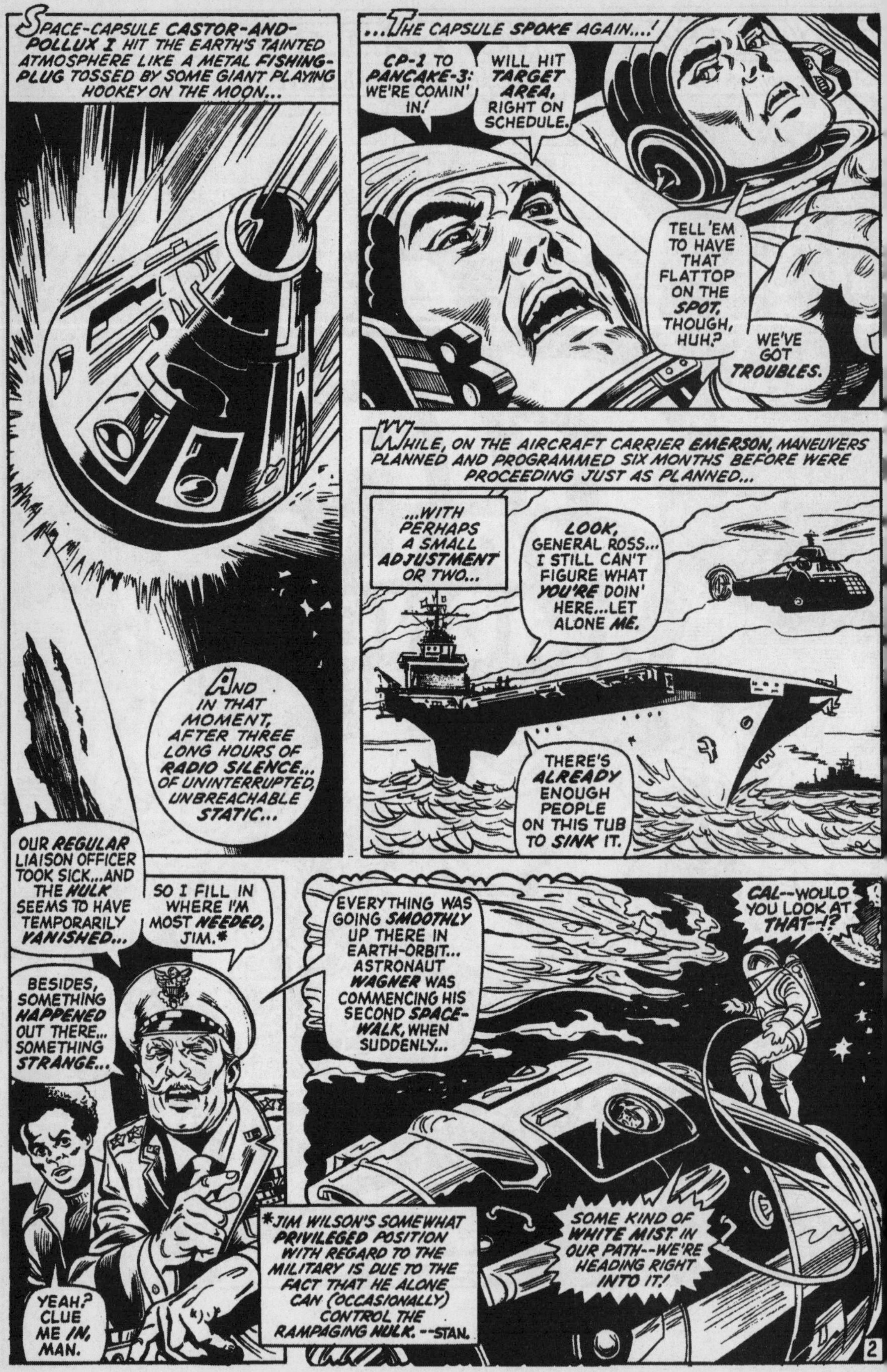
SPACE-CAPSULE CASTOR-AND-POLLUX I HIT THE EARTH'S TAINTED ATMOSPHERE LIKE A METAL FISHING-PLUG TOSSED BY SOME GIANT PLAYING HOOKEY ON THE MOON...
AND IN THAT MOMENT, AFTER THREE LONG HOURS OF RADIO SILENCE... OF UNINTERRUPTED, UNBREACHABLE STATIC...
...THE CAPSULE SPOKE AGAIN...!
CP-1 TO PANCAKE-3: WE'RE COMIN' IN!
WILL HIT TARGET AREA, RIGHT ON SCHEDULE.
TELL 'EM TO HAVE THAT FLATTOP ON THE SPOT, THOUGH, HUH?
WE'VE GOT TROUBLES.
WHILE, ON THE AIRCRAFT CARRIER EMERSON, MANEUVERS PLANNED AND PROGRAMMED SIX MONTHS BEFORE WERE PROCEEDING JUST AS PLANNED...
...WITH PERHAPS A SMALL ADJUSTMENT OR TWO...
LOOK, GENERAL ROSS... I STILL CAN'T FIGURE WHAT YOU'RE DOIN' HERE...LET ALONE ME.
THERE'S ALREADY ENOUGH PEOPLE ON THIS TUB TO SINK IT.
OUR REGULAR LIAISON OFFICER TOOK SICK...AND THE HULK SEEMS TO HAVE TEMPORARILY VANISHED...
SO I FILL IN WHERE I'M MOST NEEDED, JIM.*
BESIDES, SOMETHING HAPPENED OUT THERE... SOMETHING STRANGE...
YEAH? CLUE ME IN, MAN.
EVERYTHING WAS GOING SMOOTHLY UP THERE IN EARTH-ORBIT... ASTRONAUT WAGNER WAS COMMENCING HIS SECOND SPACE-WALK, WHEN SUDDENLY...
CAL--WOULD YOU LOOK AT THAT--!?
SOME KIND OF WHITE MIST IN OUR PATH--WE'RE HEADING RIGHT INTO IT!
*JIM WILSON'S SOMEWHAT PRIVILEGED POSITION WITH REGARD TO THE MILITARY IS DUE TO THE FACT THAT HE ALONE CAN (OCCASIONALLY) CONTROL THE RAMPAGING HULK. --STAN.
2

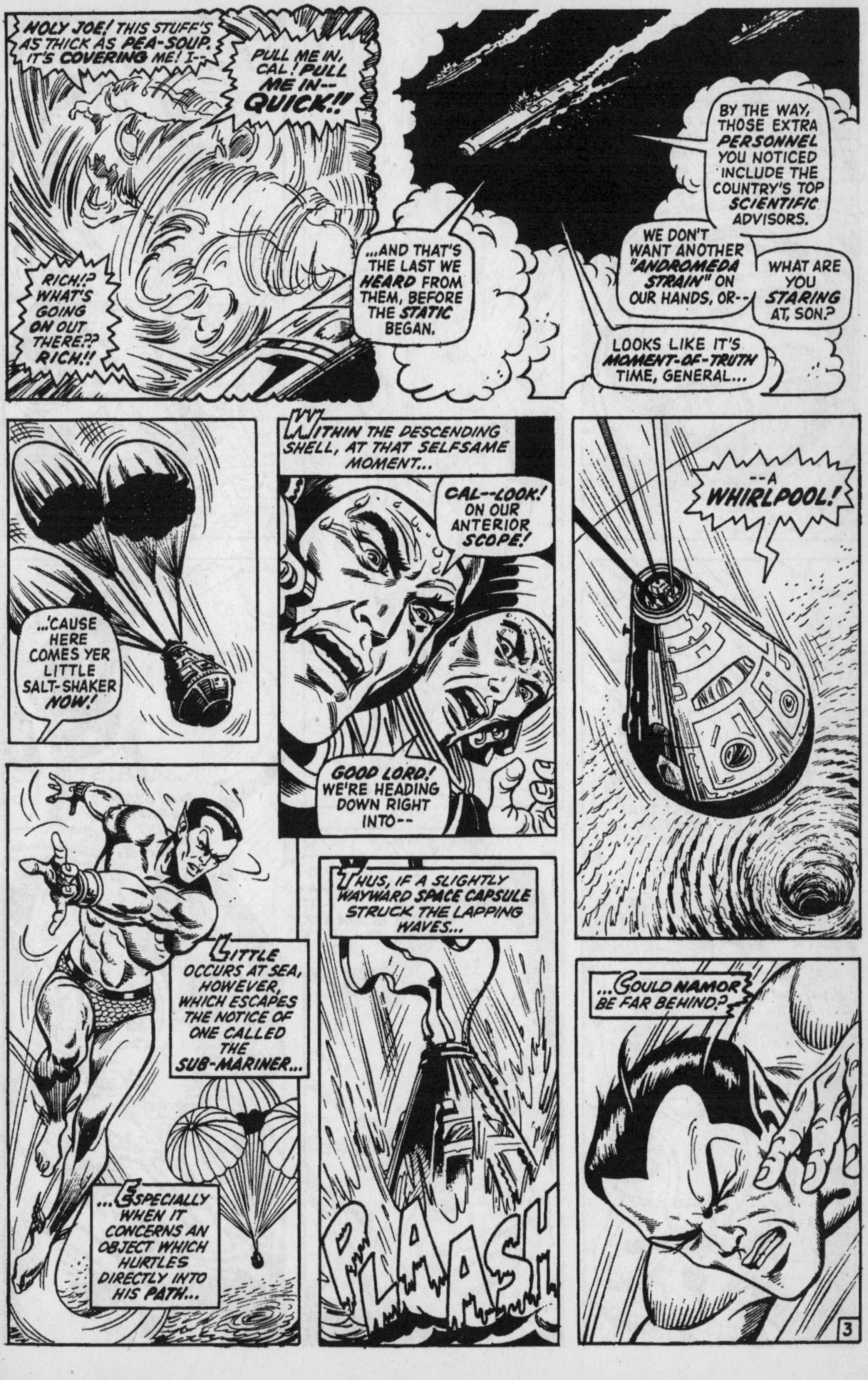
HOLY JOE! THIS STUFF'S AS THICK AS PEA-SOUP. IT'S COVERING ME! I--
PULL ME IN, CAL! PULL ME IN-- QUICK!!
RICH!? WHAT'S GOING ON OUT THERE?? RICH!!
...AND THAT'S THE LAST WE HEARD FROM THEM, BEFORE THE STATIC BEGAN.
BY THE WAY, THOSE EXTRA PERSONNEL YOU NOTICED INCLUDE THE COUNTRY'S TOP SCIENTIFIC ADVISORS.
WE DON'T WANT ANOTHER "ANDROMEDA STRAIN" ON OUR HANDS, OR--
WHAT ARE YOU STARING AT, SON?
LOOKS LIKE IT'S MOMENT-OF-TRUTH TIME, GENERAL...
...'CAUSE HERE COMES YER LITTLE SALT-SHAKER NOW!
WITHIN THE DESCENDING SHELL, AT THAT SELFSAME MOMENT...
CAL--LOOK! ON OUR ANTERIOR SCOPE!
GOOD LORD! WE'RE HEADING DOWN RIGHT INTO--
--A WHIRLPOOL!
LITTLE OCCURS AT SEA, HOWEVER, WHICH ESCAPES THE NOTICE OF ONE CALLED THE SUB-MARINER...
...ESPECIALLY WHEN IT CONCERNS AN OBJECT WHICH HURTLES DIRECTLY INTO HIS PATH...
THUS, IF A SLIGHTLY WAYWARD SPACE CAPSULE STRUCK THE LAPPING WAVES...
PLAASH
...COULD NAMOR BE FAR BEHIND?
3

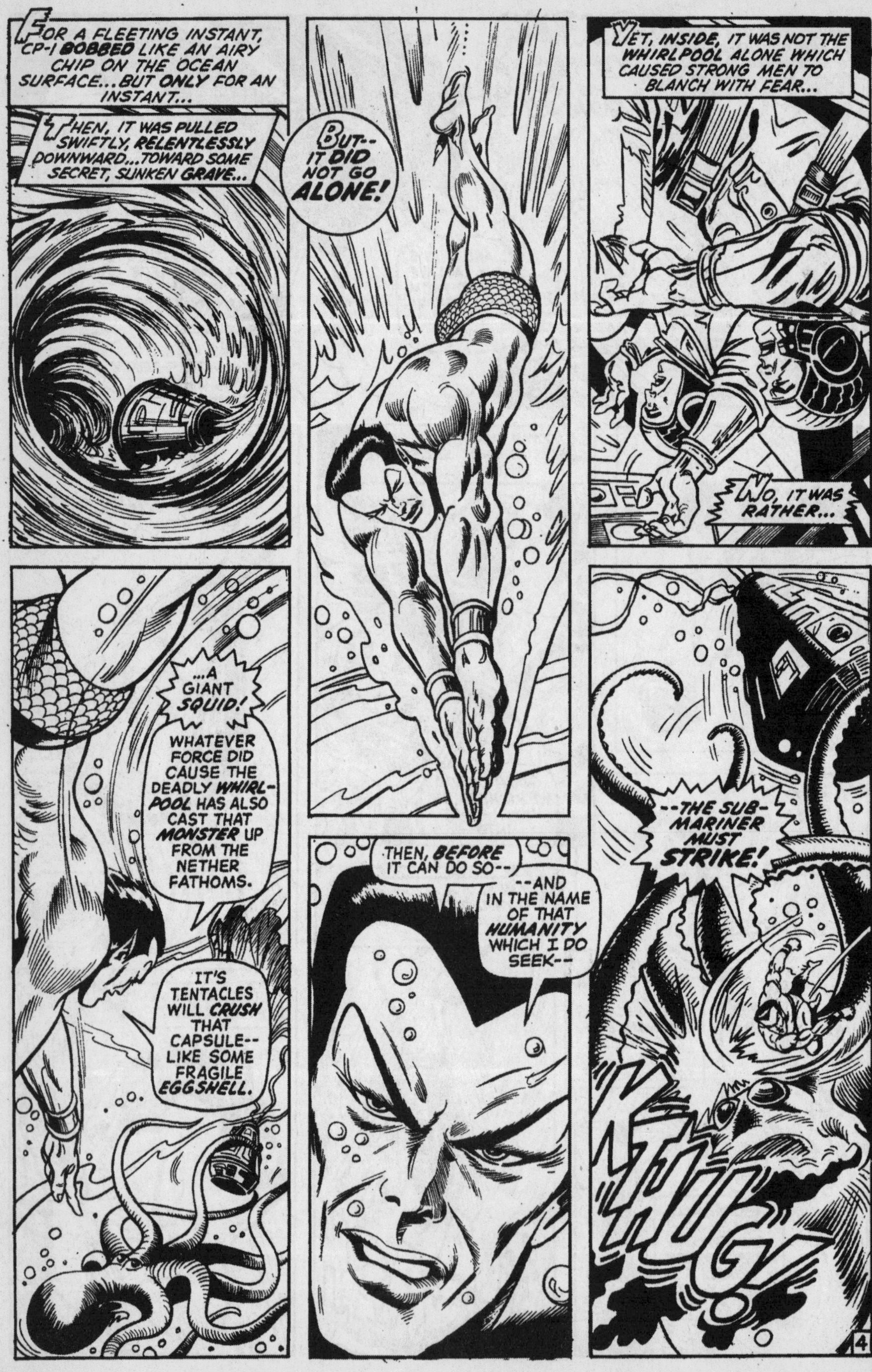

FOR A FLEETING INSTANT, CP-1 BOBBED LIKE AN AIRY CHIP ON THE OCEAN SURFACE... BUT ONLY FOR AN INSTANT...
THEN, IT WAS PULLED SWIFTLY, RELENTLESSLY DOWNWARD... TOWARD SOME SECRET, SUNKEN GRAVE...
BUT-- IT DID NOT GO ALONE!
YET, INSIDE, IT WAS NOT THE WHIRLPOOL ALONE WHICH CAUSED STRONG MEN TO BLANCH WITH FEAR...
NO, IT WAS RATHER...
...A GIANT SQUID!
WHATEVER FORCE DID CAUSE THE DEADLY WHIRLPOOL HAS ALSO CAST THAT MONSTER UP FROM THE NETHER FATHOMS.
IT'S TENTACLES WILL CRUSH THAT CAPSULE-- LIKE SOME FRAGILE EGGSHELL.
THEN, BEFORE IT CAN DO SO--
--AND IN THE NAME OF THAT HUMANITY WHICH I DO SEEK--
--THE SUB-MARINER MUST STRIKE!
THUG!

THEN, AS TEN WRITHING TENDRILS CHURNED THE WATER INTO AN INK-BLACK FRENZY, THE SCION OF ATLANTIS *GRASPED* THE METAL HUSK...

...AND HURLED BOTH IT AND HIMSELF UPWARD...

...INTO THE COLD CLEAR LIGHT OF *DAY!*

GREAT BALLS O'FIRE!

IS THAT THE *SUB-MARINER* CARRYING THE SPACE-CAPSULE THIS WAY?

YOU *KNOW* IT-- OR ELSE THE HULK'S BEEN TAKIN' SWIMMING LESSONS.

WHAT A *STORY!* "THE SUB-MARINER PREVENTS DISASTER IN SPACE PROGRAM!"

FOOLS! DO YOU THINK *I* CARE ABOUT YOUR PALTRY HEADLINES?

KLUMP!

I SAVED THIS CAPSULE BECAUSE IT WAS LIKELY TO HAVE *MEN* WITHIN...

YET, TO DO SO, I HARMED A DENIZEN OF THE *DEPTHS*...

...AND, BY NEPTUNE, I *LIKED* IT NOT!

YEAH? WELL, MEBBE WE DON'T GIVE A HANG *WHAT* YOU LIKE.

AN' WHO'RE YOU CALLIN' *FOOLS?*

LET'S *DECK* THAT DUDE!

STAND BACK, ALL OF YOU! I'VE NO WISH TO *HARM* ANY HUMAN...

...BUT YOU'LL YET DRIVE ME *TO* IT!

NOW, BY *ALL* THE GODS OF SEVEN SEAS, I'LL--

HOLD IT, NAMOR!

STOP!!

EH!?

5

COME *BACK,* LAD. HE'S A *RAGING MADMAN!*

NAMOR, YOU DON'T KNOW ME FROM *ADAM CLAYTON POWELL...*

BUT I'M *JIM WILSON* ...A PAL O' THE *HULK'S...*

AND, IF YOU DON'T LET THOSE CATS GO...AN' I MEAN LIKE *NOW...*

--I'M GONNA SEE TO IT HE *LAYS* YOU OUT *GOOD!*

HAH! SO THE YOUNG PUP SPOUTS *MORE* FIRE THAN OLD DRAGONS.

STILL, PERHAPS I *DID* ACT RASHLY. I *SHALL* RELEASE THEM.

-SHEEE-EWW!-

DON'T BE IN SUCH A *HURRY* TO APOLOGIZE, FISH-MAN.

COULD BE YOU HAD THE *RIGHT* IDEA THE *FIRST* TIME.

WHAT? OH YES...THE *ASTRONAUTS* I RESCUED...!

THAT'S JUST *IT,* BUDDY. YOU SHOULDN'T HAVE *HAD* TO RESCUE US.

RIGHT! NOT IF THE *PROPER* SAFETY PRECAUTIONS HAD BEEN TAKEN.

WE WERE *RAIL-ROADED* INTO SPACE, SO THIS COUNTRY'D HAVE THE *FIRST* MANNED SPACE-STATION...

...AND WE'VE *HAD* IT!

WOW! IF THEY MEAN WHAT I *THINK* THEY--

NOT *CLEAR* YET? LET US SPELL IT OUT FOR YOU, FELLA.

WE'RE *THRU* BEING GUINEA PIGS-- AS OF *TODAY.*

WE'RE *FAMOUS* MEN, GENTS. THE PAST FEW WEEKS, OUR FACES HAVE LIT UP MORE TV SCREENS THAN *ARCHIE BUNKER'S.*

FROM NOW ON, EVERY TIME WE SHOW UP ON THE HOME-SCREEN, WE'RE GOING TO BE *COLLECTING* FOR IT...

AND I *DON'T* MEAN *FLIGHT PAY!*

6

HOW ABOUT YOU, NAMOR? WANT TO HOP ABOARD THE *GRAVY TRAIN?*

BAH! THE OCEAN FLOOR WOULD YIELD ME *ENDLESS* TREASURES, WERE THAT MY DESIRE.

NOW, I *RETURN* TO THE DEEP, FOR, IT SEEMS I DIVED FOR *GIANTS...*

...AND BROUGHT FORTH BUT A PAIR OF *MINNOWS!*

NEVER MIND, *HIM,* BOYS. JUST LOOK *THIS* WAY.

TAKE 'EM *QUICK.* THESE ARE OUR *LAST* OFFICIAL PICS.

CHECK. AS OF NOW, WE'RE UP FOR *GRABS...*

...TO THE *HIGHEST* BIDDER.

*T*HE NEXT INSTANT, THE DECK OF THE CARRIER WAS *ABLAZE* WITH FLASHING BULBS... YET LATER, IN A DOZEN DARK-ROOMS...

I--I DON'T *GET* IT!

NOT ONE OF OUR SHOTS *TURNED OUT.*

COULD THERE'VE BEEN *TOO MANY* CAMERAS...TOO MUCH *LIGHT?*

NOPE. IT'S GOT TO HAVE BEEN... SOMETHING *ELSE.*

BUT *WHAT,* IN THE NAME OF HEAVEN?

WHAT??

*I*N THE END, PRE-FLIGHT PHOTOS OF WAGNER AND BEAME WERE RUN IN THE TABLOIDS OF THE NATION...BENEATH FAST-FOLLOWING HEADLINES THAT DELIGHTED SOME, REVOLTED OTHERS...

ASTROS SIGN TV PACT!

Ex-Col. Calvin Beame

Ex-Col. Richmond Wagner

DEAL SET WITHIN HOURS OF RESIGNING; FORMAT OF PROGRAM NOT REVEALED

7

WHERE THERE'S A WILL, THERE'S A WAY... NOT TO MENTION SPONSOR MONEY...

AND NOW, IN RECORD TIME, THERE'S A NEW STAR IN THE HEAVEN WHICH ONE EUPHEMISTIC NETWORK LIKES TO CALL ITS "SECOND SEASON"...

THE ASTRO-NUTS!!

WELCOME TO THE LAUNCH-PAD, BOYS AND GIRLS! I'M CAPTAIN CAL--!

AND NOW, I WANT YOU TO GIVE A BIG CHEER FOR THE REAL STAR OF OUR SHOW--

--A FELLA WHO'S COME A LONG WAY JUST TO SEE YOU...

--XEMNU, FROM THE MAGIC PLANET!!

AND I'M GONNA SPLIT RIGHT BACK THERE, AS SOON AS I GET PAID, I AM, I AM.

THAT'S WHAT HE THINKS, HUH, KIDS?

WE'RE GONNA KEEP HIM HERE ON EARTH FOREVER, JUST 'CAUSE WE DIG HIM--RIGHT?

YEAH! THAT XEMNU'S REAL COOL, MAN!

HE'S CUTE! HE'S JUST LIKE A BIG WALKING TEDDY BEAR!

REALLY, REGINALD, I DON'T SEE HOW YOU CAN WATCH THAT PROGRAM--EVEN ON A SATURDAY MORNING!

IN MY DAY, WE HAD "HOWDY DOODY."

NOW THERE WAS A KIDDIE SHOW THAT--

YEAH, MOM...I KNOW THIS SHOW IS AWFUL HOKEY...

BUT...I DUNNO...SOMEHOW I JUST HADDA WATCH IT....!

8

...SO YOU CLAIM YOU'RE GOING *BACK* TO YOUR MAGIC PLANET *ONE MONTH* FROM TODAY, ARE YOU?

YOU *KNOW* IT, CAPTAIN CAL...

...IF I CAN FIND AN OUT-OF-TOWN CAB, THAT IS.

JEEZ... WHAT A *BUNCHA TRIPE!*

THOSE KIDS'RE *EATIN'* IT UP--AND THERE'S NOT A DECENT LAUGH IN THE WHOLE *SCRIPT.*

I *KNOW.* I *WROTE* IT.

...AND NOTHING'S GONNA KEEP ME HERE, EITHER.

HA HA HA HA

BZ

KBOP!

NOTHING, XEMNU?

PIES

NOT EVEN A BIG, FAT SLICE OF *PEACH PIE?*

NOPE. NOT EVEN THAT.

KLIK

AND BESIDES... I THINK THAT'S *BLUEBERRY.*

HA HA HA HA

I *THINK...* --OOOMFF!-- YOU'RE *RIGHT!*

SOCK IT TO 'EM, XEMNU!

Astro-Nuts

THANK YOU, BOYS AND GIRLS. YOU'VE BEEN JUST *WONDERFUL* TO POOR LONELY XEMNU...

IN FACT, YOU'VE BEEN SO *WONDERFUL* TO ME...

THAT I MIGHT JUST TAKE YOU WITH ME WHEN I GO NEXT MONTH...

9

...ALL THE WAY BACK TO MY MAGIC PLANET!!

WOULDN'T THAT BE NICE, BOYS AND GIRLS?

YES, INDEED... WOULDN'T THAT BE NICE!?

BALDERDASH! PURE MIND-ROTTING POPPYCOCK!

"MAGIC PLANET"! I NEVER THOUGHT EVEN WAGNER AND BEAME WOULD STOOP THAT LOW!

DON'T SEE HOW THE FCC EVER ALLOWED SUCH TRASH TO GET ON THE AIR!

OUGHT TO BE A LAW, IF YOU ASK ME!

KLIK!

YEAH,... IT WAS... PRETTY AWFUL, ALRIGHT...

NOW BACK WHEN I WAS A SPROUT, WE USED TO CROWD AROUND THE RADIO AND LISTEN TO CHARLIE McCARTHY!

AND THAT MORTIMER SNERD--NOW THERE WAS A RIOT! WHY, I REMEMBER ONE SHOW WHERE--

WHERE'RE YOU OFF TO, JIM?

OH, I DUNNO. JUST...OUT, I GUESS.

I'LL TRY AN' BE BACK EARLY, OKAY?

GETTING POLITE IN YOUR OLD AGE, EH, LAD?

WELL... BE GOOD.

HAD TO GET OUT OF THERE!

OL' THUNDERBOLT MEANS WELL, BUT...

TAXI! HEY, TAXI!!

GOT TO TALK TO SOMEBODY... SOMEBODY WHO'LL UNDERSTAND... WHO'LL MAKE ME UNDERSTAND...

AND, SINCE BRUCE BANNER AIN'T EXACTLY LISTED IN THE PHONE-BOOKS, I GOTTA BREAK DOWN TO SOMEWHERE ELSE...

...SOMEPLACE WHERE THERE'S ALWAYS SHADOWS...

...EVEN SMACK-DAB IN THE MIDDLE'A SATURDAY MORNING!!

10

OKAY, KID, YER *HERE.* HOPE YOU GOT THE RIGHT CHANGE, SO I CAN GET *OUTTA* HERE.

DUNNO *WHY,* BUT THIS NEIGHBORHOOD GIVES ME THE *CREEPS.*

KEEP YER *SHIRT* ON. I GOTTA-- *UH OH!*

NOW WHAT? IF YER OUTTA *CASH,* I'M GONNA HAVE TA--

YOU NEED LISTEN TO *NO MORE* OF THIS MAN'S ABUSE, LAD.

HERE. I BELIEVE *THIS* WILL STILL HIS INTEMPERATE TONGUE.

OH *WOW!* YOU JUST GOTTA BE--*DOC STRANGE.*

I'LL PAY YA *BACK,* MAN. *BELIEVE* IT.

YOU *INTRIGUE* ME, MY YOUNG FRIEND.

FEW, EVEN HERE IN GREENWICH VILLAGE, KNOW THAT THIS IS THE DOMICILE OF STEPHEN STRANGE.

I KNOW MORE ABOUT YOU THAN YA MIGHT *THINK,* DOC.

AN OL' *RAP* TOLD ME. BRUCE BANNER.

DR. BANNER...AH YES. HE WHO SEEMS CURSED FOREVER TO REMAIN THE MONSTROUS *HULK.*

IF YOU'VE SOUGHT ME OUT ON *HIS* ACCOUNT, THEN WE *MUST* TALK, INDEED.

BUT FIRST, IF YOU'LL *PARDON* ME...

WELL, THAT'S IT FOR *THIS* WEEK, KIDS...

...MY MAN *WONG* SEEMS TO HAVE NEGLECTED TO TURN OFF THE *TELEVISION.*

ACTUALLY, DOC, I DIDN'T FIGURE YOU FOR THE TYPE TA *OWN* ONE.

I'M GLAD YA *DO,* THOUGH. 'CAUSE, THAT *SHOW*--IT'S THE REASON I'M *HERE.*

AND REMEMBER, BOYS AND GIRLS...YOU'RE ALL COMING WITH ME TO MY *MAGIC PLANET...*

...JUST FOUR SHORT WEEKS FROM TODAY...

THERE! THAT'S THE CAT I WANTED TO *TALK* TO YOU ABOUT.

I WAS WATCHIN' HIM BEFORE--AND WHEN HE STARTED BLOWIN' THAT "MAGIC PLANET" *BULL*--

...I COULDN'T HELP FEELIN' LIKE I WANTED TO CUT OUT *WITH* 'IM--

...AN' *NEVER* COME BACK TO EARTH AGAIN!!

SOMEWHAT LATER, AND A NUMBER OF BLOCKS UPTOWN...

THREE WEEKS, RICH! THREE STINKIN' WEEKS-- AND ALREADY IT FEELS LIKE AN ETERNITY!

I DON'T KNOW WHY I EVER LET YOU TALK ME INTO CHUCKING THE SPACE PROGRAM, FOR...THIS.

YOU DON'T? THEN LET ME REMIND YOU, PARTNER...

SINCE WE TWO CAME UP WITH THE SHOW'S WHOLE FORMAT... AND SINCE WE OWN CONTROLLING RIGHTS TO IT...

YOU'LL BE WEALTHY ENOUGH TO RETIRE FOR KEEPS...IN JUST ONE SHORT YEAR!

YEAH, I KNOW. MONEY. THE GREAT AMERICAN CURE-ALL.

SURE, I'VE ALWAYS WANTED TO BE AS RICH AS UNCLE SCROOGE-- BUT THIS--

HOLD IT! WHAT'S THAT NOISE OUT FRONT?

FREDDY! L-LOOK--!

WH-WHAT THE DEVIL IS H-HE DOIN' HERE??

THE HULK!

RUN FOR IT, RICH! THAT MONSTER'LL TEAR THIS PLACE APART!

NO HE WON'T-- NOT THAT YOU GLORY-GRABBERS DON'T DESERVE IT.

ME AN' HIM CAME HERE TO TALK...AND THAT'S ALL.

WHO IN BLAZES ARE YOU?

LET'S JUST SAY...I'M HIS AGENT.

THEN GO AHEAD AND TALK, WHOEVER YOU ARE...

BUT KEEP THAT BRUTE AT ARM'S LENGTH, HUH?

THIS IS GREAT! I HEARD THERE WAS A KID WHO'S THE ONLY ONE CAN CONTROL THE HULK-- AND IF YOU'RE HERE FOR THE REASON I THINK--

HULK WANTS TO COME ON YOUR SHOW--MAKE THE WORLD SEE HE'S NOT AS BAD AS THEY THINK.

THAT'S IT IN A NUTSHELL, FLYBOY.

THAT'S JUST WHAT I HOPED YOU'D SAY, KID...

AND, SPEAKING FOR MY SOMEWHAT SHY PARTNER AND MYSELF...

...YOU'VE GOT YOURSELF A DEAL!

WHAT'S MORE, I THINK I KNOW JUST THE SHOW WE COULD USE YOU...!

BOOKS

WBZM STUDIOS

12

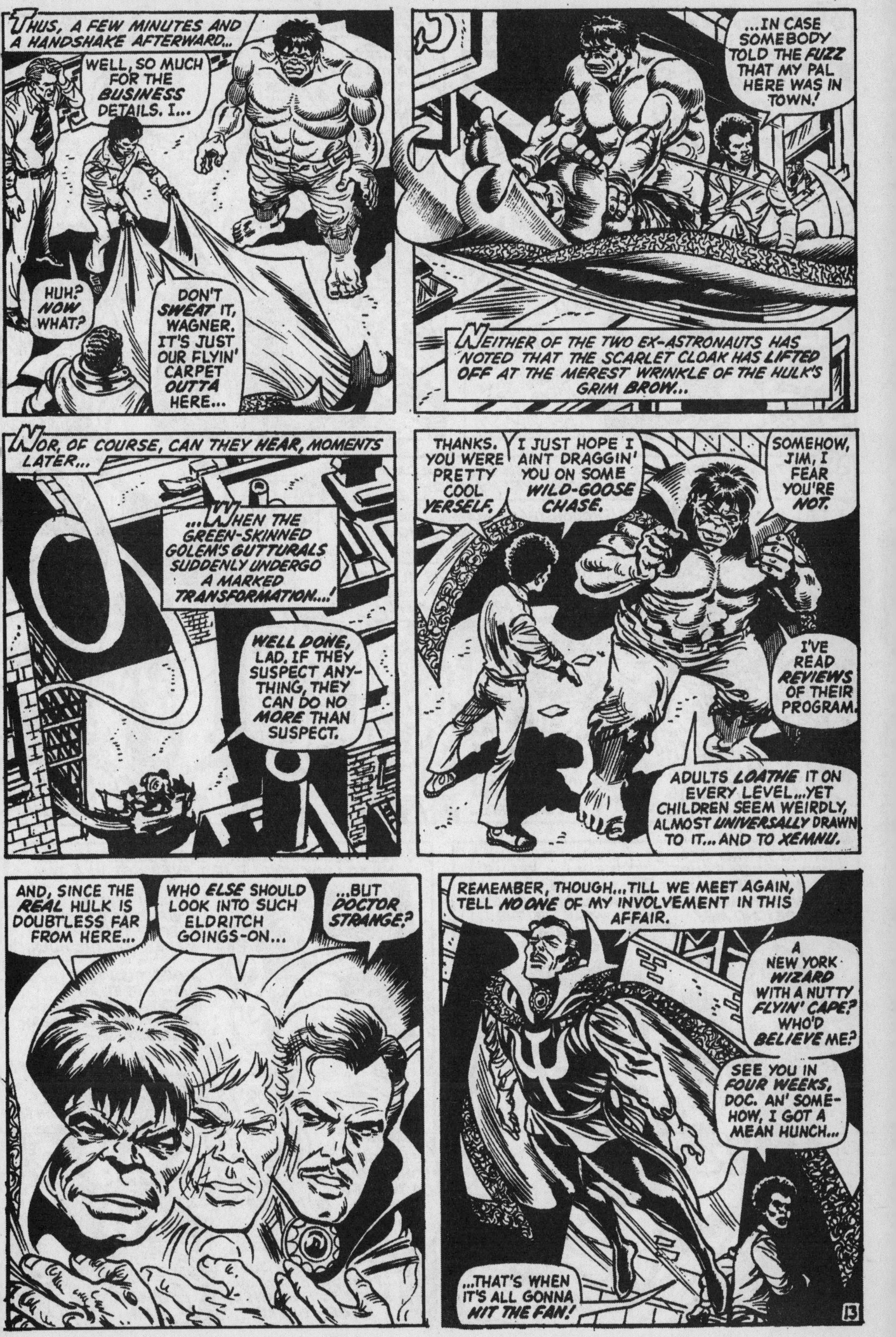

THUS, A FEW MINUTES AND A HANDSHAKE AFTERWARD...
WELL, SO MUCH FOR THE BUSINESS DETAILS. I...
HUH? NOW WHAT?
DON'T SWEAT IT, WAGNER. IT'S JUST OUR FLYIN' CARPET OUTTA HERE...
...IN CASE SOMEBODY TOLD THE FUZZ THAT MY PAL HERE WAS IN TOWN!
NEITHER OF THE TWO EX-ASTRONAUTS HAS NOTED THAT THE SCARLET CLOAK HAS LIFTED OFF AT THE MEREST WRINKLE OF THE HULK'S GRIM BROW...
NOR, OF COURSE, CAN THEY HEAR, MOMENTS LATER...
...WHEN THE GREEN-SKINNED GOLEM'S GUTTURALS SUDDENLY UNDERGO A MARKED TRANSFORMATION...!
WELL DONE, LAD. IF THEY SUSPECT ANYTHING, THEY CAN DO NO MORE THAN SUSPECT.
THANKS. YOU WERE PRETTY COOL YERSELF.
I JUST HOPE I AINT DRAGGIN' YOU ON SOME WILD-GOOSE CHASE.
SOMEHOW, JIM, I FEAR YOU'RE NOT.
I'VE READ REVIEWS OF THEIR PROGRAM.
ADULTS LOATHE IT ON EVERY LEVEL...YET CHILDREN SEEM WEIRDLY, ALMOST UNIVERSALLY DRAWN TO IT...AND TO XEMNU.
AND, SINCE THE REAL HULK IS DOUBTLESS FAR FROM HERE...
WHO ELSE SHOULD LOOK INTO SUCH ELDRITCH GOINGS-ON...
...BUT DOCTOR STRANGE?
REMEMBER, THOUGH...TILL WE MEET AGAIN, TELL NO ONE OF MY INVOLVEMENT IN THIS AFFAIR.
A NEW YORK WIZARD WITH A NUTTY FLYIN' CAPE? WHO'D BELIEVE ME?
SEE YOU IN FOUR WEEKS, DOC. AN' SOMEHOW, I GOT A MEAN HUNCH...
...THAT'S WHEN IT'S ALL GONNA HIT THE FAN!
13

FOUR WEEKS: IN FAR LESS TIME, SHOWS ARE BORN--AND CANCELLED. MID-WIVED--AND MURDERED.

BUT SOME SURVIVE-- EVEN THRIVE. AND, FOR THOSE FAVORED FEW--

XEMNU AND "ASTRO-N SCORE IN SATURDAY MORNING SWEEPSTAKES!

SHOW DECRIE BY PARENTS, EDUCATORS-- BUT 50,000,000 KIDS CAN'T BE WRONG--OR CAN THEY?

CAPTAIN CAL AND FRIEND

--FORTUNES ARE ASSURED!

Astro-Nuts GAME

AS ADVERTISED ON TV!

SOME THINGS, HOWEVER, EVEN A CRISWELL COULDN'T HAVE PREDICTED FOUR SHORT WEEKS AGO...

I TELL YOU, IT'S MADNESS!

BAD ENOUGH THAT A MANNED LAUNCHING BECOMES A CIRCUS WITH THOSE COSTUMED-UP CLOWNS...

BUT, GRANTING THE BLASTED HULK TEMPORARY AMNESTY TO APPEAR AS WELL...

YOU KNOW THE SCORE, ROSS. THE MILITARY GETS FUNDS FROM CONGRESS...

CONGRESSMEN HAVE KIDS...

...AND THEIR KIDS LIKE XEMNU!

...THOUGH WHY BEAME AND WAGNER FIGURE THEY NEED THAT MONSTER AROUND IS BEYOND ME!

FUNNY, THOUGH. THE HULK SEEMS TOO SUBDUED... ALMOST LIKE HE'S WEAK...ON THE VERGE OF COLLAPSE...!

JEEZ, DOC...NOW I KNOW WHY DOC BANNER TOLD ME TO LOOK YOU UP IF I EVER GOT IN A JAM.

I KNOW YOU TOLD ME IT BRUTALIZES YOU TA KEEP UP THAT SPELL MAKES YOU THE HULK, AN'--

MORE THAN THAT, JIM--I FEEL AS IF OTHER FORCES ARE--WORKING AGAINST ME--!

--!! YEAH, ME TOO. I--HUH? WHAT'S HE WANT?

ALL RIGHT, SON. WE'RE ON THE AIR LIVE--IN PRIME TIME.

IF YOU COULD JUST PERSUADE THE, UH, NULK TO STEP OVER HERE--I MEAN--

COMIN' MAN.

14

HI THERE, KIDS! *CAPTAIN CAL*, COMIN' TO YOU FROM *FLORIDA...*

...WITH TWO OF MY BEST BUDDIES... *XEMNU*, WHO'S BEEN CLAIMING FOR WEEKS THAT TODAY'S THE DAY HE RETURNS TO HIS *MAGIC PLANET...*

...AND, AS A TREAT FOR THOSE OF YOU WITH *COLOR* SETS...OUR SPECIAL GUEST, THE *HULK!*

WELL, THE *COUNTDOWN'S* BEGUN...THE *REAL* ASTRONAUTS'LL BE CLIMBING ON BOARD IN A MINUTE.

THEY'LL HAVE TO WEAR BULKY *SUITS* AND WORRY ABOUT *OXYGEN* AND STUFF--NOT LIKE ALL *YOU* KIDS, IF XEMNU *REALLY* FLIES AWAY WITH YOU.

AND YOU'LL SEE IT ALL WITH *ME*, AND *XEMNU*, AND THE *HULK*--RIGHT HERE, *LIVE* FROM THE *CAPE!*

THE HULK, CALVIN BEAME? THEN WHAT OF THIS SCENE, BEING ENACTED EVEN NOW, NOT HALF ENOUGH MILES AWAY...?

HEAD'S *SPLITTING.* GETTING... *DIZZY.*

GREAT, BANNER. ALL YOU *NEED* IS TO PASS OUT...

...SO SOME LOCAL *COP* CAN GET A THRILL BY PINNING A *VAGRANCY* RAP... ON THE GUY WHO TURNS INTO THE *HULK.*

LUCKY I STILL GOT...A *FEW* BUCKS ON ME.

MAYBE A COUPLE OF *ASPIRIN* WILL--*WHAT THE DEVIL--?*

--SEE IT ALL WITH ME, AND XEMNU, AND THE HULK--

--*RIGHT HERE, LIVE FROM THE CAPE!*

NO! THAT--*CAN'T* BE--

--'CAUSE, LITTLE AS I LIKE IT-- I'M THE HULK!

WHOA, FELLA! DON'T GET --UPSET.

'CAUSE--YOU KNOW WHAT HAPPENS-- WHEN YOU LET YOUR *PULSE* POUND--YOUR *TEMPLES* THROB--

YOU TURN INTO--

--THE *HULK!*

AND THE *HULK*--CAN *HATE!!*

WOM!

15

SO! EVEN WHEN HULK DOES *NOTHING*, SOME HUMAN MAKES HIMSELF *LOOK* LIKE HULK-- --TRIES TO MAKE OTHER HUMANS *MAD* AT HIM!

G-GOOD LORD! IT'S THE HULK!

KUH- WHAK!

GOOD! THAT MAN KNEW *TRUE* HULK WHEN HE SAW HIM.

AND SOON-- SO WILL *ALL* THOSE WHO CRAWL THE EARTH!

THOOM

PRESCRIPTION

WHILE, AT THE CAPE...

ONE SIDE, CAPTAIN! YOU'VE WASTED ENOUGH OF THE BOYS' AND GIRLS' TIME.

NOW, IT'S TIME FOR *XEMNU* TO SPEAK TO THEM.

HEY! HE LOOKED LIKE HE REALLY *WHACKED* THAT GUY!

EACH SATURDAY FOR THE PAST FOUR WEEKS, MY CHILDREN, I'VE TOLD YOU I WOULD TAKE YOU WITH ME--BACK TO MY MARVELOUS MAGIC PLANET.

AND TODAY, I SHALL FULFILL THAT PROMISE FOR A CHOSEN *FEW* OF YOU.

COME, MY ANGELS...COME... COME...!

IT'S...NOT *FAR* TO THE CAPE, DAVY.

WE... WE'VE GOT TO GO TO HIM....!

AND GO TOWARD THE CAPE THEY *DO*...

BY THE THOUSANDS... BY THE MILLIONS... ACROSS THE NATION...

CHILDREN BEGIN MARCHING ...MARCHING... MARCHING TRANCELIKE TOWARD THE FLORIDA COAST...

16

As, in the shadow of the great space-rocket itself...

MOST OF THE CALLED ONES WILL NEVER REACH THIS SITE IN TIME. YET THERE WILL STILL BE... ENOUGH.

YOUTH... COME TO ME... COME TO XEMNU!

YES-- XEMNU--

I AM--COMING.

I KNEW WAGNER PLANNED SOMETHING, JIM--BUT I DIDN'T REALIZE IT WOULD BE--THIS.

THE GROWN-UPS AREN'T AFFECTED-- BUT THAT SENATOR'S KID IS!

EVEN I MUST BE JUST YOUNG ENOUGH TO HAVE FELT--A TINGLE.

WELL, LATER FOR THAT XEMNU DUDE.

RIGHT NOW--I'M GRABBIN' THE KID, BEFORE--

FOOL! YOU SEEK TO MATCH WITS WITH ME?

IT IS FAR TOO LATE FOR ANY TO OPPOSE XEMNU!

And, even as those sepulchral tones resound...

HOLY CATS! BILLY JOE-- DO YOU SEE WHAT I--?

KIDS! DOZEN-- HUNDREDS OF 'EM-- WALKIN' STRAIGHT TOWARD OUR ELECTRIFIED FENCE!

I SHUT OFF THE POWER-- JUST IN TIME!

BUT NOW THEY'RE SCALIN' THE FENCE-- AND HOW'RE WE GONNA STOP 'EM?

THE TIME FOR PRETENSE IS ENDED! THE MAN-MONSTER MUST STAND REPLACED BY THE MASTER OF THE MYSTIC ARTS!

MY FIRST SPELL HAS STUNNED HIM, JIM. BUT--THE BOY--

NO SWEAT, DOC, I GOT 'IM!

17

I SUSPECTED TRICKERY, EARTHLING...AND HAD BEEN TRYING TO PIERCE YOUR DISGUISE.

ZAK

NOW THAT I KNOW THE NATURE OF MY FOE, I CAN EASILY PROTECT MYSELF.

HE'S THROWN UP SOME SORT OF PSYCHIC AURA ABOUT HIMSELF...

STILL, BEFORE HE DID, I PROBED HIS MIND, HOPING TO LEARN HIS WEAKNESS...IF ANY.

IMAGES FILL MY MIND. FIRST A TRULY MAMMOTH FORM, SPRAWLED MONTHS AGO IN SOME REMOTE SWAMP...

"XEMNU, THE LIVING TITAN... HE WHO ONCE ENSLAVED THE ENTIRE EARTH FOR ONE DIRE PURPOSE...

BUILD ME A ROCKET, SO I MAY RETURN TO MY OWN WORLD... DESTROYING YOURS AS I DEPART.

WE-- SHALL-- OBEY!!

*AS SEEN IN MONSTERS ON THE PROWL #11 AND 14. --STAN.

"ONE BRAVE MAN TURNED XEMNU'S SUPER-HYPNOSIS BACK UPON HIM, WITH A SIMPLE MIRROR...

"AND EARTHMEN UNIVERSALLY FORGOT THEIR ENSLAVEMENT...

I--I DID IT!

HE'S GONE-- FOREVER!

"UNKNOWN TO ALL, THAT GASEOUS, NEARLY INVISIBLE FORM WAS HURLED INTO SPACE BY THE PRESSURES OF OUR ATMOSPHERE...

"...THUS ACCOMPLISHING IN DEFEAT WHAT IT HAD FAILED TO GAIN IN VICTORY...

"YET, AFTER A LONG VOYAGE, IT FOUND NOTHING IN ITS HOMEWORLD--NOTHING BUT A LIFELESS SHELL...

"...ALL LIFE UPON IT DESTROYED BY SOME MICROSCOPIC GERM...

"AND SO IT WANDERED SPACEWARD ONCE MORE...

"...HEADING, IN COSMIC LONELINESS, BACK TOWARD EARTH ONCE MORE...

"...WHERE IT ENCOUNTERED AND POSSESSED THE ORBITING BODY OF RICH WAGNER...

"...SO THAT, EVEN IN SMALLER STATURE, XEMNU COULD WALK THE EARTH ONCE MORE...!"

...LL THIS, THE MYSTIC MAGE GLIMPSES IN ONE FLEETING SECOND, THEN SUDDENLY, SAVAGELY...

-:AAARRHH!-

I'M DOWN--AND THOSE SOLDIERS ARE OUT!

--WHILE THOSE CHILDREN--ARE MARCHING STRAIGHT TOWARD THE ROCKET!

ONLY HOPE NOW IS-- YES!

IT'S HAPPENING!

HE IS HERE-- AS HE SWORE!

THE LAUNCH-PAD IS FALLING-- THE ROCKET, TOPPLING INTO THE SEA!

"WHO?" YOU ASK? WHO ELSE--?

YOU HAVE CALLED, WIZARD--

--AND NAMOR HAS ANSWERED!

FWAP!

STILL THIS BEHEMOTH IS FAR MORE POWERFUL THAN HE SEEMS!

THU'P!

BUT, WHERE BRUTE STRENGTH HAS FAILED, OTHER METHODS MAY PREVAIL.

YOU HAVE HAD YOUR CHANCE, MAN WHO CAME OUT OF THE SEAS...

...YOU'LL HAVE NO OTHER!

-UNHHHNN!-

19

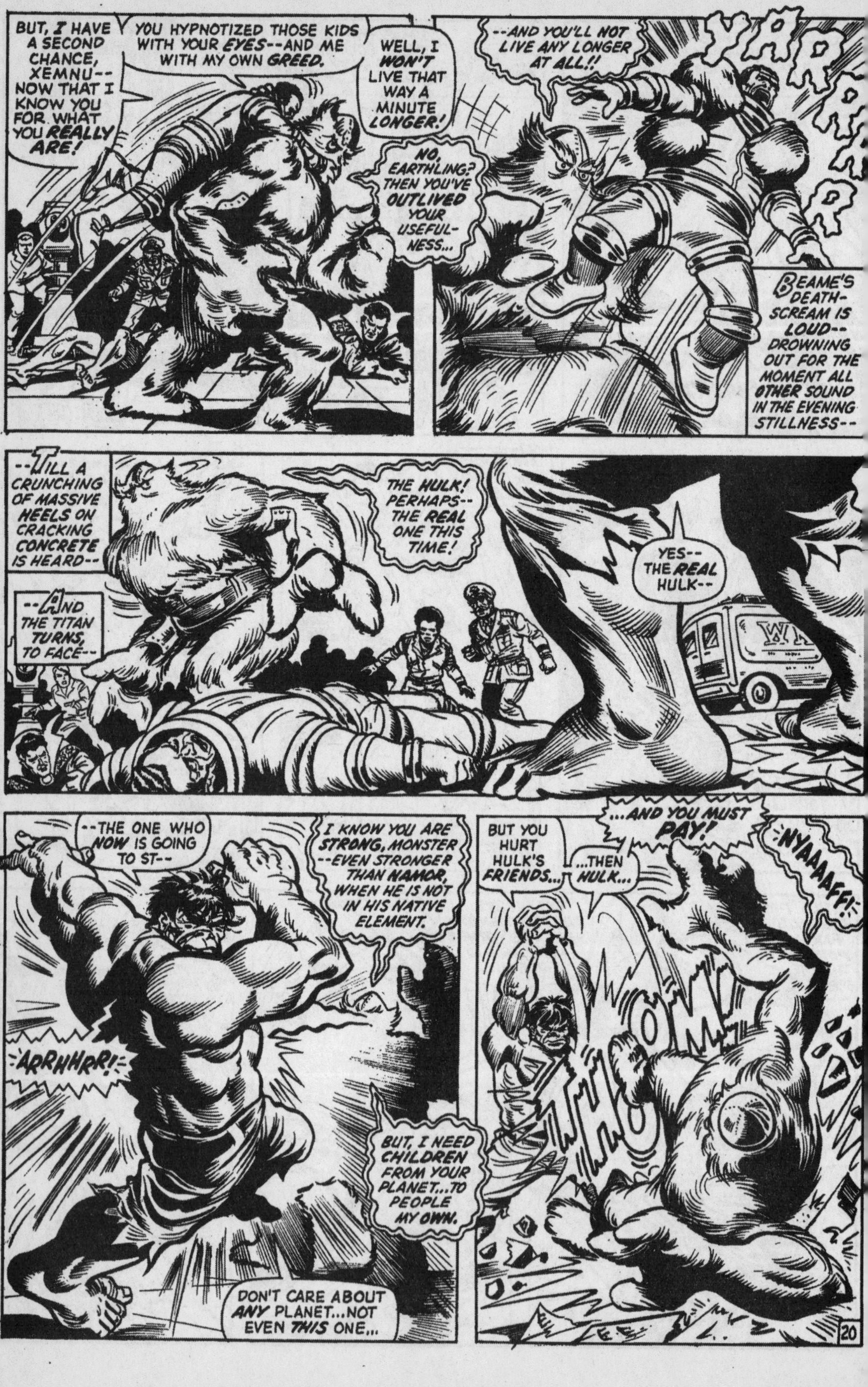

BUT, I HAVE A SECOND CHANCE, XEMNU-- NOW THAT I KNOW YOU FOR WHAT YOU REALLY ARE!
YOU HYPNOTIZED THOSE KIDS WITH YOUR EYES--AND ME WITH MY OWN GREED.
WELL, I WON'T LIVE THAT WAY A MINUTE LONGER!
NO, EARTHLING? THEN YOU'VE OUTLIVED YOUR USEFUL-NESS...
--AND YOU'LL NOT LIVE ANY LONGER AT ALL!!
YARRRR
BEAME'S DEATH-SCREAM IS LOUD--DROWNING OUT FOR THE MOMENT ALL OTHER SOUND IN THE EVENING STILLNESS--
--TILL A CRUNCHING OF MASSIVE HEELS ON CRACKING CONCRETE IS HEARD--
--AND THE TITAN TURNS, TO FACE--
THE HULK! PERHAPS--THE REAL ONE THIS TIME!
YES--THE REAL HULK--
--THE ONE WHO NOW IS GOING TO ST--
I KNOW YOU ARE STRONG, MONSTER--EVEN STRONGER THAN NAMOR, WHEN HE IS NOT IN HIS NATIVE ELEMENT.
ARRHHRR!
BUT, I NEED CHILDREN FROM YOUR PLANET...TO PEOPLE MY OWN.
DON'T CARE ABOUT ANY PLANET...NOT EVEN THIS ONE...
BUT YOU HURT HULK'S FRIENDS...
...THEN HULK...
...AND YOU MUST PAY!
NYAAAAFF!
THOOM!

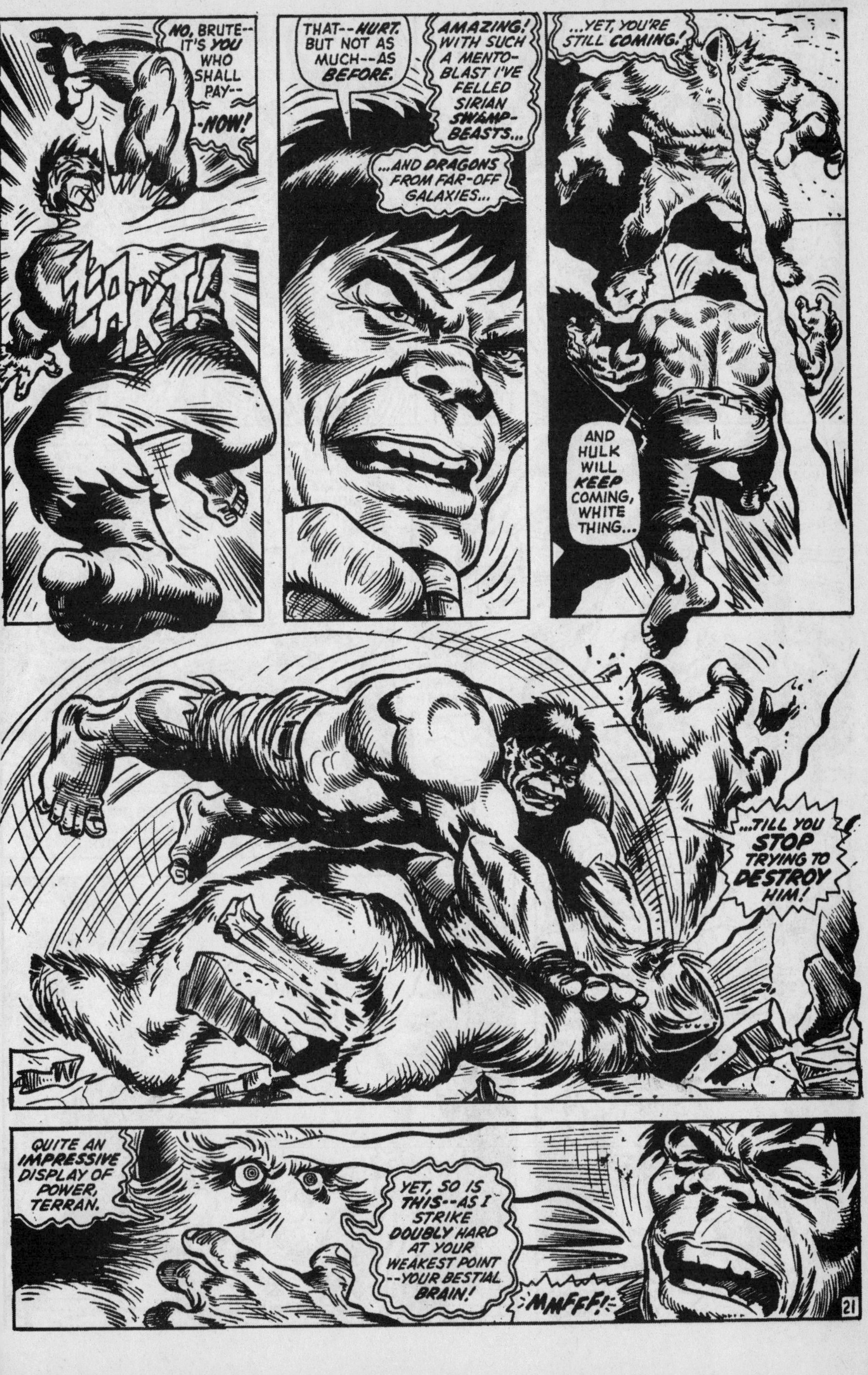
NO, BRUTE-- IT'S YOU WHO SHALL PAY--
--NOW!
ZAKT!
THAT--HURT. BUT NOT AS MUCH--AS BEFORE.
AMAZING! WITH SUCH A MENTO-BLAST I'VE FELLED SIRIAN SWAMP-BEASTS...
...AND DRAGONS FROM FAR-OFF GALAXIES...
...YET, YOU'RE STILL COMING!
AND HULK WILL KEEP COMING, WHITE THING...
...TILL YOU STOP TRYING TO DESTROY HIM!
QUITE AN IMPRESSIVE DISPLAY OF POWER, TERRAN.
YET, SO IS THIS--AS I STRIKE DOUBLY HARD AT YOUR WEAKEST POINT --YOUR BESTIAL BRAIN!
MMFFF!
21

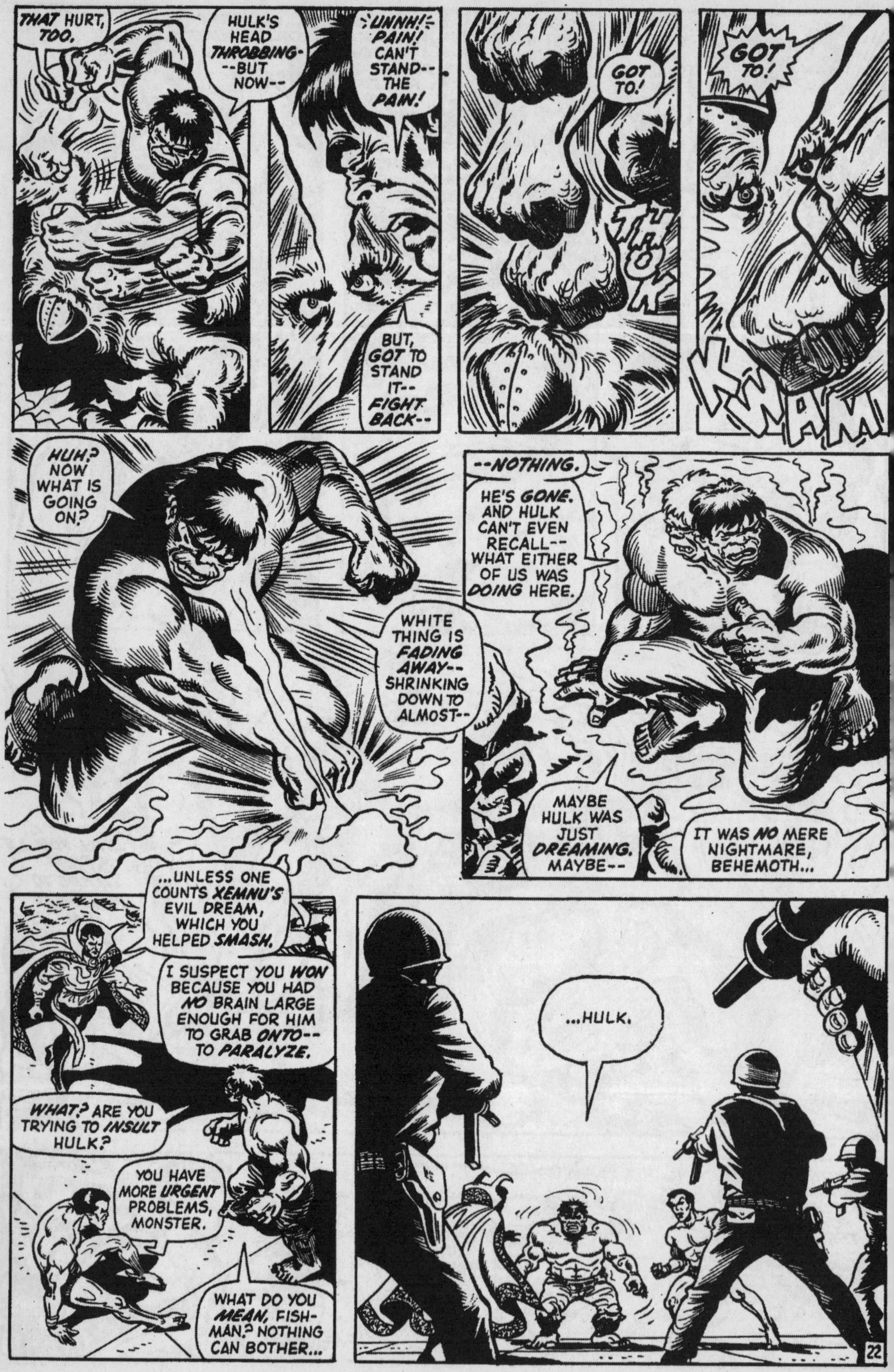
THAT HURT, TOO.
HULK'S HEAD THROBBING--BUT NOW--
UNNH! PAIN! CAN'T STAND--THE PAIN!
BUT, GOT TO STAND IT--FIGHT BACK--
GOT TO!
THOK
GOT TO!
KWAM
HUH? NOW WHAT IS GOING ON?
WHITE THING IS FADING AWAY--SHRINKING DOWN TO ALMOST--
--NOTHING.
HE'S GONE. AND HULK CAN'T EVEN RECALL--WHAT EITHER OF US WAS DOING HERE.
MAYBE HULK WAS JUST DREAMING. MAYBE--
IT WAS NO MERE NIGHTMARE, BEHEMOTH...
...UNLESS ONE COUNTS XEMNU'S EVIL DREAM, WHICH YOU HELPED SMASH.
I SUSPECT YOU WON BECAUSE YOU HAD NO BRAIN LARGE ENOUGH FOR HIM TO GRAB ONTO--TO PARALYZE.
WHAT? ARE YOU TRYING TO INSULT HULK?
YOU HAVE MORE URGENT PROBLEMS, MONSTER.
WHAT DO YOU MEAN, FISH-MAN? NOTHING CAN BOTHER...
...HULK.
22

THE NEXT INSTANT, THE HULK PROVES THAT WHAT HE LACKS IN INTELLECTUAL SUBTLETY...

...HE MORE THAN MAKES UP FOR IN LIGHTNING-FAST REFLEXES....!

THUUMMMMMMMM

AND THE INSTANT AFTER THAT-- AS IF TO REMIND US ALL THAT THE STARTLING SUB-MARINER IS STILL IN THE VICINITY--

THE HULK LASHED OUT ONLY TO SAVE YOUR CHILDREN--YET YOU RINGED HIM ABOUT WITH WEAPONS AND SUSPICIONS.

IT WOULD HAVE SERVED YOU ARIGHT-- IF HE HAD WREAKED HAVOC, NOT HELPED YOU.

WHHOOSH!

THAT'S JUST WHAT HULK WILL DO-- NEXT TIME.

THEN COME, BRUTISH ONE. OUR BUSINESS HERE IS FINISHED.

AND, LET NOT EVEN DR. STRANGE SUMMON US IN EARTH'S NEXT HOUR OF NEED...

FOR, WE WILL NOT COME!

MANY ARE THE THINGS THAT COULD BE SAID AS TWO POWERFUL FORMS VANISH INTO THE DISTANCE. YET, IN ESSENCE, THEY ALL BOIL DOWN TO LIFE AND DEATH.

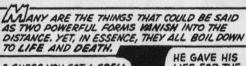

I GUESS YOU GOT A SPELL THAT'LL MAKE EVERYBODY FORGET YOUR PART IN THIS THING, HUH, DOC?

WISH I COULD FORGET MINE. WHEN I SEE BEAME LYIN' THERE--

HE GAVE HIS LIFE FOR THE CHILDREN. ALWAYS REMEMBER THAT.

THE CHILDREN WILL ALWAYS SURVIVE, JIM... FOR, IN THE LONG RUN...

...WHAT ELSE IS THERE?

FINIS

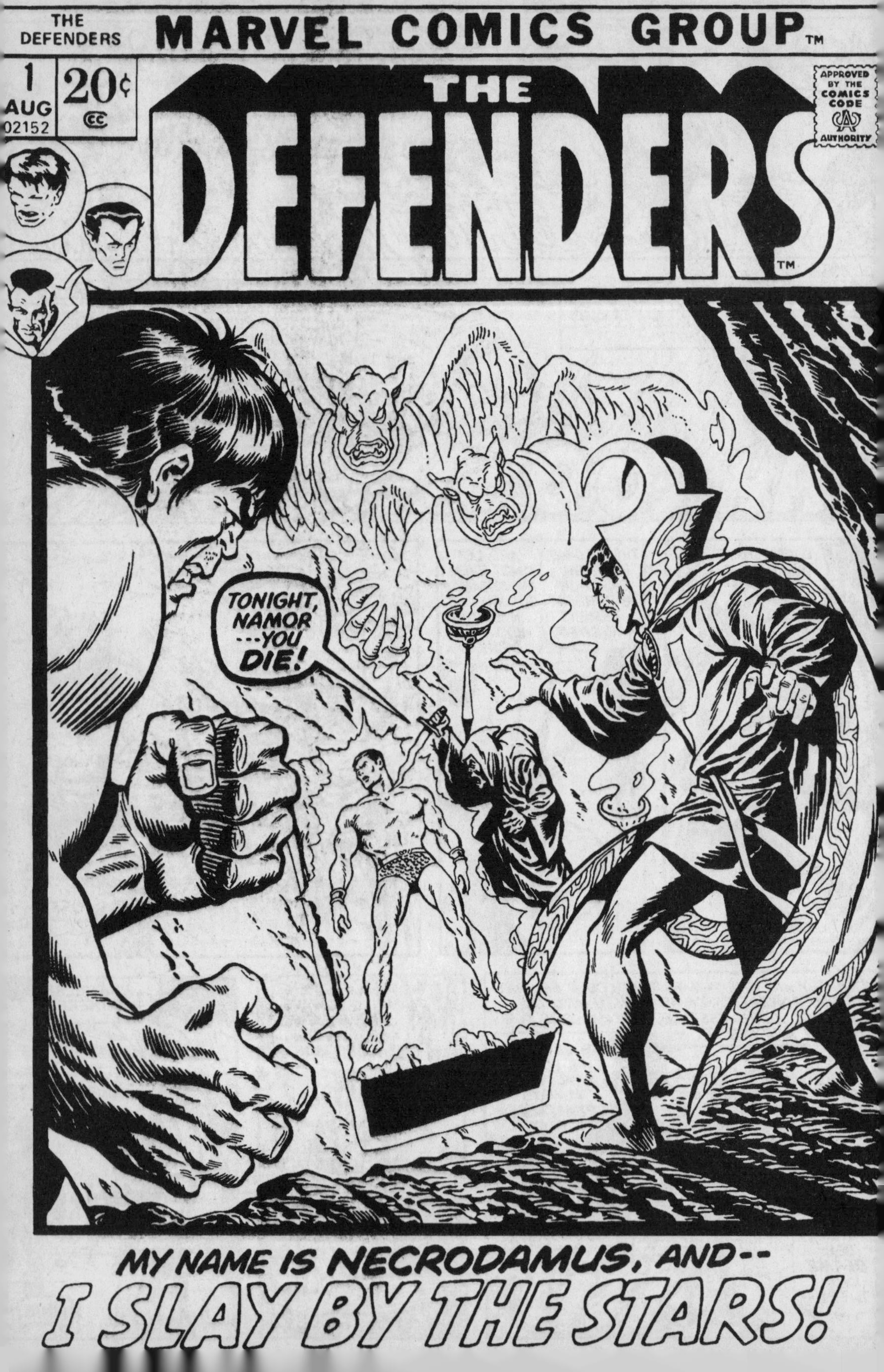
THE DEFENDERS
MARVEL COMICS GROUP
1 AUG 02152
20¢
APPROVED BY THE COMICS CODE AUTHORITY
THE DEFENDERS
TONIGHT, NAMOR ---YOU DIE!
MY NAME IS NECRODAMUS, AND--
I SLAY BY THE STARS!

THE DYNAMIC DEFENDERS!

STAN LEE PRESENTS * STEVE ENGLEHART, WRITER * SAL BUSCEMA, ARTIST * FRANK GIACOIA, INKER * ARTIE SIMEK, LETTERER

STAR SPANGLED: COVERED WITH STARS--LIKE THE HEAVENS ON THIS MILD NEW JERSEY EVE.

STAR: ONE WHO PLAYS A LEADING ROLE IN A PERFORMANCE-- LIKE THE GREAT, GREEN HULK.

STAR-CROSSED: CONTINUALLY MEETING WITH DISASTER-- AGAIN, LIKE THE HULK.

FALLING STAR: TONIGHT, THE SUB-MARINER!

I SLAY BY THE STARS!

KABOOM!

943 B

HUMAN FALLS FROM *SKY*, LIKE BROKEN *BIRD!*

IF THIS IS *TRICK*--HULK WILL *SMASH*, FAST!

HUH? HULK *KNOWS* THIS ONE.

IT IS *NAMOR*-- THE *FISH-MAN*-- THE ONE WHO USED TO BE HULK'S *FRIEND!*

BUT HE *SLEEPS.* HULK WILL *WAKE* HIM-- SAY *HELLO.*

;UHH!: CAN'T *TOUCH* HIM!

SOMETHING HULK CANNOT *SEE* IS IN *WAY!*

WAKE UP, NAMOR! HULK IS HERE!

FISH-MAN DOES NOT *MOVE*-- MAYBE HE IS *HURT!* HULK MUST *HELP!*

BUT WHAT CAN HULK *DO?* HULK NEVER HAD TO *THINK* ABOUT HELPING *FRIEND* BEFORE.

WAIT--HULK REMEMBERS *OTHER* HUMAN--HELPED NAMOR AND HULK IN *PAST*--IN GROUP CALLED *DEFENDERS!*

AND--HE WAS *DOCTOR*-- WHAT FISH-MAN *NEEDS.*

HE WAS-- *DR. STRANGE!*

BUT *NOW* HULK REMEMBERS-- HULK DOES NOT *LIKE* DR. STRANGE. HE MADE PEOPLE *HATE* HULK LAST TIME. *

BUT THEN-- PEOPLE HATE HULK *ANYWAY!*

CAN HULK GO TO *ENEMY* TO HELP *FRIEND?* IT IS ALMOST TOO MUCH TO *THINK* ABOUT!

* *A HULK'S-EYE-VIEW OF MARVEL FEATURE #3. --STAN.*

HULK HAS *FEW* FRIENDS--AND *MANY* ENEMIES. SO FRIENDS *COUNT* MORE!

HULK WILL *GO* TO DR. STRANGE!

DO NOT *WORRY,* FISH-MAN--

--HULK WILL *SAVE* DAY!

HARRIET-- I *TOLD* YOU: WE'VE *GOTTA* START TAKIN' THE *LINCOLN TUNNEL!*

NEW YORK! HULK *HATES* NEW YORK!

TOO MANY *PEOPLE!* TOO MUCH *NOISE!* BAD AIR!

HULK WISHES HE WERE BACK IN *DESERT!*

GET BACK! HE LOOKS LIKE HE *KNOWS* WHERE HE'S *GOIN'!* AND HE DEFINITELY HAS THE RIGHT-OF-WAY!

YES, AND ISN'T THAT ODD--THAT A NEARLY MINDLESS MONSTER KNOWS THE ROUTE TO...

...THE GREENWICH VILLAGE *SANCTUM* OF--

--DR. STRANGE!

RISE, O GLEAMING CRYSTAL OF AGAMOTTO! I WOULD *SEARCH* YOUR *DAZZLING* DEPTHS--

--FOR A *CLUE* TO THE *EVIL* I FEEL HOVERING LIKE A *VULTURE* OVER ME TONIGHT!

HOLD! RETURN TO YOUR *CASK OF CONCEALMENT,* ORB!

THERE IS A *TIME* FOR MATTERS *MYSTICAL*-- AND A TIME FOR MATTERS *MUNDANE!*

PERHAPS THE SUDDEN *COMMOTION* OUTSIDE MY DOMICILE IS OF MORE *PRESSING* CONCERN THIS NIGHT!

3

OUT OF HULK'S *WAY*, PUNY HUMANS! HULK MUST FIND *DR. STRANGE!*

OH *WOW!* JUST WHEN I GET *USED* TO RIP-OFFS, MUGGERS, AND JUNKIES--I HAVETA RUN INTO *THIS!*

RUN! *RUN!* IT'S THE *HULK!*

YES, IT *IS* THE GREEN BEHEMOTH--HE WHO *SWORE* NEVER TO COME TO ME AGAIN!

DOES HE *NOW* ARRIVE AS *FRIEND--* OR FOE?

YOU! HULK *REMEMBERS* YOU, AND HULK WILL *SMASH--!*

WAIT--HULK ALMOST FORGOT REASON FOR *COMING!*

FISH-MAN IS HURT--AND HULK CANNOT *HELP* HIM.

HULK HATES TO *SAY* IT-- BUT HULK NEEDS *YOU.*

THE *SUB-MARINER--* NEEDS MY AID? THEN SURELY I WILL *GIVE* IT!

CAN YOU *FIND* HIM AGAIN?

YES.

THEN LET US--

BE**GONE!**

WHAT IS *HAPPENING?* HULK DOES NOT *UNDERSTAND!*

NOR *NEED* YOU, MONSTER.

MY SIMPLE SPELLS OF *INVISIBILITY* AND *LEVITATION* WILL WORK, NONETHELESS.

4

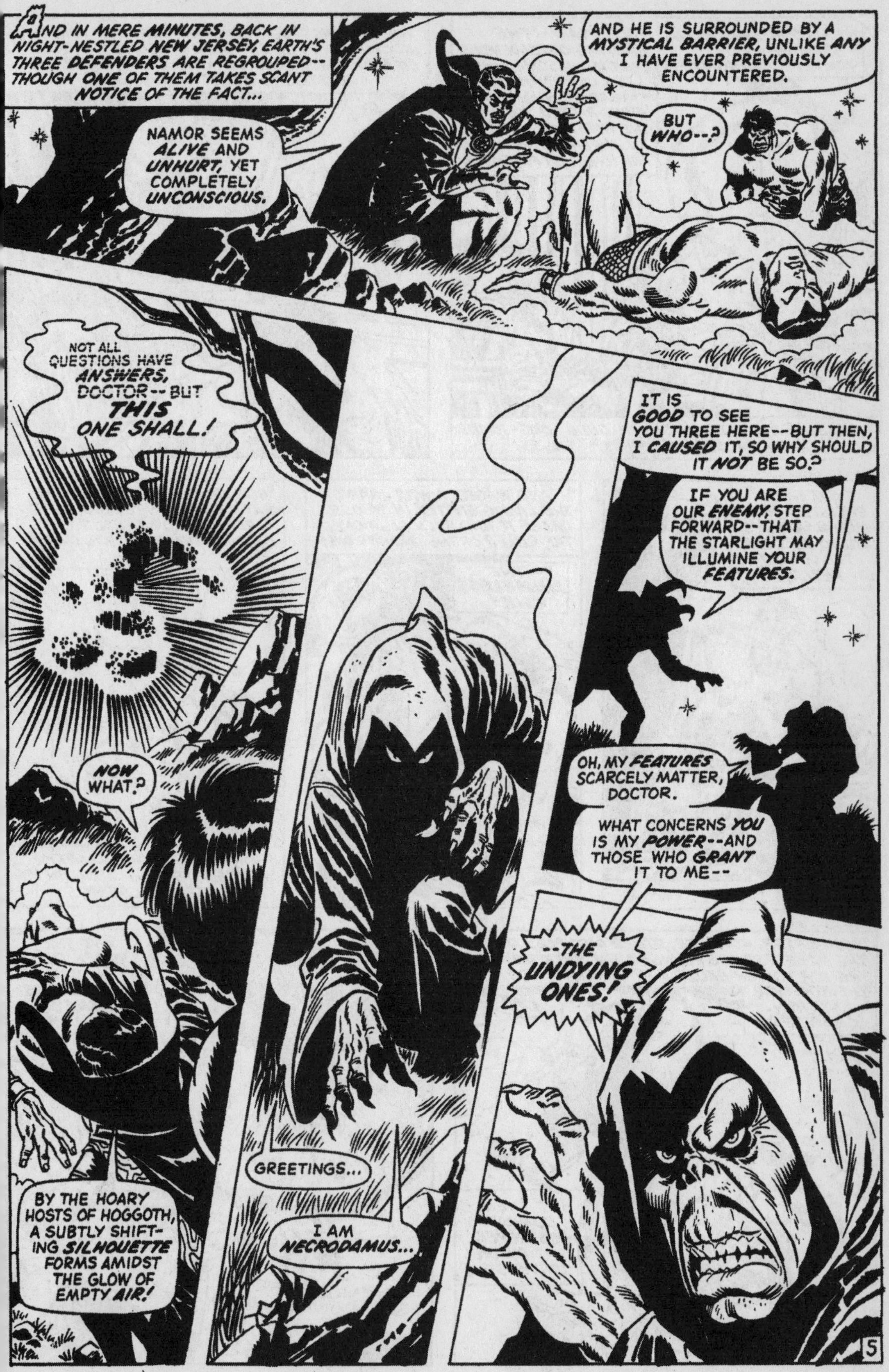
AND IN MERE MINUTES, BACK IN NIGHT-NESTLED NEW JERSEY, EARTH'S THREE DEFENDERS ARE REGROUPED--THOUGH ONE OF THEM TAKES SCANT NOTICE OF THE FACT...
NAMOR SEEMS ALIVE AND UNHURT, YET COMPLETELY UNCONSCIOUS.
AND HE IS SURROUNDED BY A MYSTICAL BARRIER, UNLIKE ANY I HAVE EVER PREVIOUSLY ENCOUNTERED.
BUT WHO--?
NOT ALL QUESTIONS HAVE ANSWERS, DOCTOR--BUT THIS ONE SHALL!
NOW WHAT?
BY THE HOARY HOSTS OF HOGGOTH, A SUBTLY SHIFTING SILHOUETTE FORMS AMIDST THE GLOW OF EMPTY AIR!
GREETINGS...
I AM NECRODAMUS...
IT IS GOOD TO SEE YOU THREE HERE--BUT THEN, I CAUSED IT, SO WHY SHOULD IT NOT BE SO?
IF YOU ARE OUR ENEMY, STEP FORWARD--THAT THE STARLIGHT MAY ILLUMINE YOUR FEATURES.
OH, MY FEATURES SCARCELY MATTER, DOCTOR.
WHAT CONCERNS YOU IS MY POWER--AND THOSE WHO GRANT IT TO ME--
--THE UNDYING ONES!
5

"YOU LOOK SHOCKED, STRANGE -- BUT YOU HEARD ARIGHT--!

"YES, I SAID -- THE UNDYING ONES! DEMONS SPAWNED IN SOME TIMELESS, UNKNOWN COSMOS --AGAINST WHOM YOU FIRST PITTED YOURSELF THE NIGHT YOU ANSWERED AN APPEAL FROM AN OLD AND LONG-LOST FRIEND.*

*REMEMBER DOC IN HIS SUPER-DUDE LONG-JOHNS FROM DR. STRANGE #183.?-- SMILEY.

"THE DEMONS SOUGHT AN IDOL THAT YOUR FRIEND HAD HIDDEN--AND YOU BUT BARELY ESCAPED WITH YOUR LIFE BY SUBJECTING LURKING NIGHT-FIENDS TO A BLISTERING BLAST OF SUNLIGHT!

"YOU THEN ENLISTED THE SUB-MARINER'S AID TO UNCOVER THE OCCULT FETISH--*

*SUBBY #22.--S.

"--AND WAGED A WAR AGAINST THE LIVING ENTITY IN WHOSE IMAGE IT HAD BEEN FASHIONED-- THE RULER OF THE UNDYING ONES--

"--THE NAMELESS ONE!

"BUT YOU KNEW AT LAST THE BATTLE WAS HOPELESS, SO YOU THRUST NAMOR THROUGH A CLOSING DIMENSIONAL GAP TO SAFETY--

"--THAT YOU MIGHT MARTYR YOURSELF, FOREVER ALONE, IN MY MASTER'S COSMOS!

"SOON AFTER, HOWEVER, OTHER DISCIPLES OF THE NAMELESS ONE PLUNGED THE HULK AND A TRAITOR TO OUR CAUSE INTO THE DIMENSION OF THE NOISOME NIGHT-CRAWLER,*

"BUT THEIR COMBAT DESTROYED THAT ENTIRE UNIVERSE...

*HULK #126.--STAN.

"--AND THE THREE FELL INTO THE NAMELESS ONE'S REALM--

"--WHERE THE TURNCOAT CHOSE TO SACRIFICE HERSELF--

6

"--AND FREE BOTH MAGE AND MONSTER!

"THAT FINAL, MOST UNEXPECTED VICTORY HAS LOST THE UNDYING ONES THEIR CHANCE TO ENTER AND SUPPRESS THIS COSMOS--"

--BUT STILL, THEY MAY GRANT *BOONS* TO ONE SUCH AS *I*--

--ONE WHO WOULD *WILLINGLY* PERFORM *ANY* OBSCENE RITE FOR THEM, TO *RID* HIMSELF OF THIS DEFORMED SHELL *YOU* MIGHT CALL A *BODY!*

SO IT *IS* THAT, IN BUT *ONE* HOUR--

--WHEN THE STARS ARE IN THEIR *CORRECT ALIGNMENT*--

--*I*, NECRODAMUS, SHALL FOULLY *SACRIFICE* THE SLEEPING *SUB-MARINER* TO THE GREATER GLORY OF THE *UNDYING ONES!!*

I CAUSED NAMOR TO *PLUMMET* INTO YOUR PATH, HULK--JUST AS *I* FORCED YOU TO FIND *DR. STRANGE*--

--FOR *I* WANTED YOU TWO TO *KNOW* WHY THE SUB-MARINER'S LIFE IS *FORFEIT!*

MY MASTERS *REMEMBER* THE THREE MORTALS WHO *BESTED* THEM--

--AND *REMEMBERING*-- HATE

ONE HOUR! QUICKLY, HULK-- WE *MUST* LIBERATE NAMOR FROM THAT MYSTICAL PRISON!

UNDYING ONES, HUH? HULK BETS THIS MEANS *FIGHT!* GOOD!!

VIPERS OF VALTORR! MY MOST *POTENT* INCANTATIONS ARE AS *NAUGHT* AGAINST THE BARRIER!

WAVING HANDS-- GLOWING FINGERS... THOSE ARE ALL *STUPID* THINGS!

HULK KNOWS HOW TO BREAK BARRIER--!

HULK CAN *SMASH!!*

THOOM

HUH? HAND *SMOKES*--AND BARRIER DID NOT *BREAK!*

THEN THERE IS NO OTHER *RECOURSE*-- I MUST RESORT TO A SPELL OF *TIME-STOPPAGE*--

--TO GAIN PRECIOUS *HOURS*, IN WHICH WE MAY YET *TRIUMPH!*

IT WILL REQUIRE MORE *MAGICAL MIGHT* THAN I HAVE *EVER* WIELDED, BUT WIELD IT I *MUST!*

LIST, YE POWERS OF THE FOURTH DIMENSION--

RISE-- YOUR SCEPTRES HERALD TIME'S... SUSPENSION--

SLOW...THE GREEN EARTH'S...TRAVEL... 'ROUND...THE...SUN--

...LET...=UHHHH=...

IT...IS *IMPOSSIBLE*....! *NO* MORTAL'S POWER... CAN DO *THIS*....!

8

AND TO HIS KNEES SINKS THE MASTER MAGICIAN--HE WHO STRAINED TO THRUST ALL HIS POWER INTO THAT AWESOME ATTEMPT.

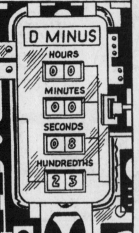

D MINUS
HOURS **00**
MINUTES **00**
SECONDS **08**
HUNDREDTHS **23**

YET IF ONE SHALL ENTRUST ALL HIS MIGHT TO ONE SPELL, MUST NOT OTHER SPELLS BE LIKEWISE WEAKENED...?

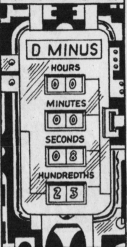

D MINUS
HOURS **00**
MINUTES **00**
SECONDS **08**
HUNDREDTHS **23**

THIS ATOMIC CLOCK MEASURES TIME FOR THE EARTH-SHATTERING OMEGATRON--TIME HALTED BY DR. STRANGE LONG WEEKS AGO!*

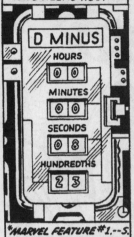

D MINUS
HOURS **00**
MINUTES **00**
SECONDS **08**
HUNDREDTHS **23**

*MARVEL FEATURE #1.--S.

BUT NOW, UNKNOWINGLY, HE HAS CRACKED HIS TIMESTOP CHARM, SO THAT, EVER SO SLOWLY AND EVER SO SLYLY...

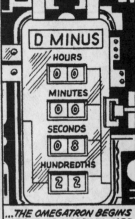

D MINUS
HOURS **00**
MINUTES **00**
SECONDS **08**
HUNDREDTHS **22**

...THE OMEGATRON BEGINS AGAIN ITS MARCH TOWARD WORLD-DOOM!

PLOT THREADS WITHIN PLOT THREADS...

STILL, THAT IS A THREAT FOR THE FUTURE--SINCE SECONDS ARE AS WEEKS TO THE DEVICE--

--AND NECRODAMUS IS A THREAT FOR NOW!

I AM VERY TIRED, HULK--AND NOTHING MORE CAN BE DONE--

--UNTIL THE MADMAN RETURNS FOR HIS VICTIM.

THEREFORE, I SHALL MEDITATE--TO REGAIN MY FULL ABILITIES BEFORE THE FATEFUL MOMENT ARRIVES.

TIRED--? NOTHING MORE TO DO--? HULK DOES NOT UNDERSTAND!

HULK CAN STILL SMASH! HULK CAN STILL BREAK BARRIER IF HULK POUNDS LONG ENOUGH--

--AND HULK NEVER GETS TIRED!

CROOM

9

HOW, THEN, TO MEASURE TIME'S PASSAGE? BY THE 50 MINUTES EARTHIAN CLOCKS REGISTER? BY THE NEARLY 3000 BLOWS THE HULK RAINS UPON THE MYSTIC BARRIER? HOWEVER IT MAY BE, DR. STRANGE KNOWS WHEN TO AWAKEN FROM HIS YOGA-LIKE TRANCE.

SIGHTS... SOUNDS... RUSH UPON ME, AS REALITY ONCE AGAIN BECKONS--

AND, OF SOUNDS... THE INFERNAL POUNDING OF THE HULK IS MOST UNPLEASANT!

ENOUGH, BEHEMOTH-- NOW IS THE TIME FOR MY PLAN!

NO--NOT YET! HULK HAS STILL NOT SAVED FISH-MAN!

IF YOU WOULD DO THAT...

...WE MUST KEEP NAMOR AND NECRODAMUS APART!

STAND OVER HIM, AND GUARD HIM WITH YOUR MIGHT--

--WHILE I COVER YOU BOTH WITH THE UNBREAKABLE, IMPENETRABLE CRIMSON BANDS OF CYTTORAK!

NOW LET THE VILLAIN ATTEMPT TO TAKE NAMOR FROM US--!

WAIT! WAIT! LET HULK OUT!

10

FISH-MAN SANK INTO *GROUND*-- LIKE *WATER* INTO DRY *SPONGE*...!

OF COURSE! OH, I HAVE BEEN *BLIND* THIS NIGHT--

--BLIND AND ABYSMALLY *OVERCONFIDENT!*

THERE MUST BE *CAVERNS* BELOW US, IN WHICH NECRODAMUS PLANS TO PER- FORM HIS TERRIBLE ACT OF *TRIBUTE!*

THERE-- THAT CAVE *MOUTH!* RUN, MONSTER!

DO NOT *TELL* HULK WHAT TO DO!

HULK IS *TIRED* OF PUNY *HUMAN* TELLING HIM WHAT TO DO!

HULK *DOES* WHAT *HULK WANTS!*

LET'S NOT *ARGUE,* HULK! *NAMOR'S LIFE* DEPENDS ON *BOTH* OF US!

DANK WATER DRIPS END- LESSLY FROM STALACTITE TO STALAGMITE... A BLIND BAT EEKS ITS EERIE SIGNAL. *SOFT* SOUNDS IN A CAVE ARE CLEARLY AUDIBLE--WHILE, *LOUD* SOUNDS...

RRARGH

HULK! TO YOUR *RIGHT*--!

...ARE TRULY *MIND-NUMBING!*

I AM THE *DEMON* OF THE *DARK*-- AND *YOU* ARE *DEAD!*

11

BY THE *SHADES* OF THE *SERAPHIM*, YOU SHALL COME *NO FURTHER!*

AT *LAST!* AT *LAST!*

HULK HAS *ENEMY* TO FIGHT!

CRUNCE

HULK IS *SICK* OF TAKING ORDERS-- OF NOT *UNDERSTAND-ING!*

WHEN HULK IS *MAD,* HULK NEEDS SOMETHING TO *HIT*--

--AND HULK IS *MAD NOW!*

BOOOM

GET UP, DEMON! HULK WANTS TO *FIGHT* YOU SOME MORE!

NO, HULK-- YOU'VE *WON* ALREADY!

LET THE DEMON *LIE!* WE *MUST* PRESS ON!

DOWN THERE--THAT *GROTTO* IT WAS *GUARDING!* DO YOU *SEE,* HULK--

--DO YOU SEE THAT FLICKERING *GLOW* PLAYING OVER THE STONES?

INSIDE THAT *OPENING*--

BY THE GODS ABOVE, BELOW, AND BEYOND--!

12

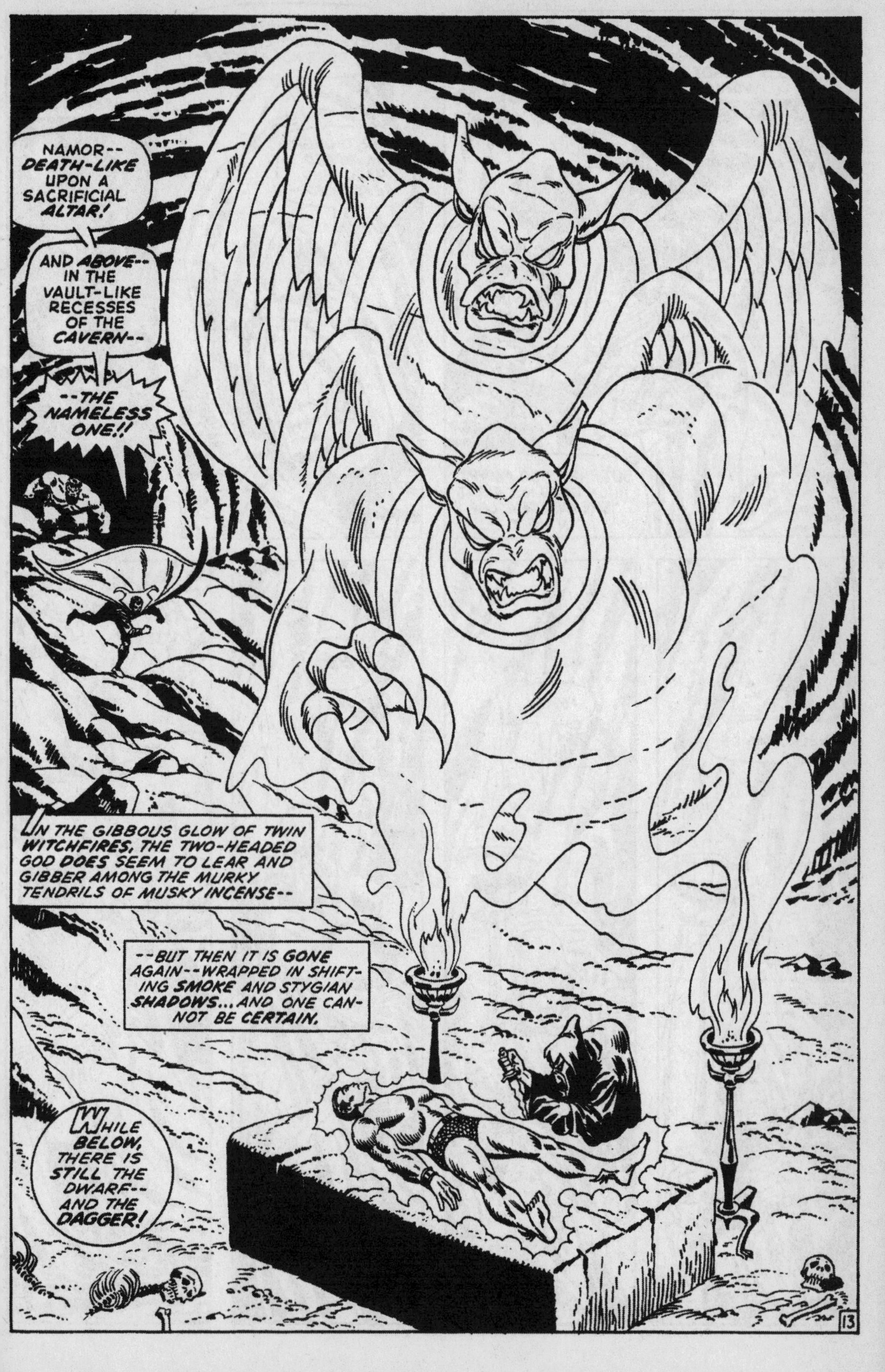

NAMOR-- DEATH-LIKE UPON A SACRIFICIAL ALTAR!
AND ABOVE-- IN THE VAULT-LIKE RECESSES OF THE CAVERN--
--THE NAMELESS ONE!!
IN THE GIBBOUS GLOW OF TWIN WITCHFIRES, THE TWO-HEADED GOD DOES SEEM TO LEAR AND GIBBER AMONG THE MURKY TENDRILS OF MUSKY INCENSE--
--BUT THEN IT IS GONE AGAIN--WRAPPED IN SHIFTING SMOKE AND STYGIAN SHADOWS...AND ONE CANNOT BE CERTAIN.
WHILE BELOW, THERE IS STILL THE DWARF-- AND THE DAGGER!
13

WE ARE TOO *NEAR* THE HOUR OF *SACRIFICE*--THE STENCH OF *EVIL* HERE IS TOO *POTENT!* MY SPELLS CANNOT *STOP* HIM *NOW!*

IT'S UP TO YOU, HULK!

BUT...HE IS SO *PUNY!* HULK DOES NOT FIGHT ENEMIES *SMALLER* THAN HE IS!

SO YOU PENETRATED EVEN *HERE?* WELL, IT DOES NOT *MATTER*--

--FOR, THOUGH I AM *INDEED* SMALL--AND *DEFORMED*--

"--AS ALL THE *ASTRAL* POWERS BEGIN TO FORM A *STRAIGHT LINE* THROUGH THE *HEAVENS*--"

NECRODAMUS

SHALL

BE

REBORN!!

14

THE GROTTO IS HAZY WITH INCENSE AND SIN--BUT TWO POINTS OF LIGHT ARE STRIKINGLY VISIBLE. ONE IS THE BLINDING FLARE OF THE MYSTICAL KNIFE--AND THE OTHER IS THE FERAL GLEAM IN THE MADMAN'S EYES!

NOW, BRUTE! NOW WHICH ONE OF US IS GROTESQUE?!

ARRGHH!

THE KEY TO MY *TRIUMPH* HAS BEEN HUNG IN THE *HEAVENS!* YOU *CANNOT* STOP ME *NOW!*

HULK *THANKS* YOU FOR *GROWING*, UGLY ONE--

--BECAUSE *NOW* YOU MAKE BETTER ENEMY FOR HULK TO *CRUSH!*

HOLD *STILL*, GIANT! SOON IT WILL ALL BE *OVER!*

ALOOF, ALONE, THE STARS ARE NOT CONCERNED WITH MORTAL MATTERS. THEY MOVE TOWARD THEIR OWN ARCANE FATE.

AND IF THEY *INFLUENCE* MEN BELOW, THEY SHINE NEITHER MORE NOR LESS BRIGHTLY.

EVEN IF THAT INFLUENCE SPELLS-- CATASTROPHE!

YOU FORGET MY ENCHANTED *BLADE*, MONSTER--WHICH, AT THIS *TIME* AND IN THIS *PLACE*, CAN PIERCE EVEN YOUR ROCK-HARD HIDE!

TASTE *HELL-STEEL* --AND *DIE!!*

UUHHHH!!

AND AT THIS *CRUCIAL* MOMENT, WHERE IS THE *MASTER* OF BLACK MAGIC?

GODS! I *CANNOT* INFLUENCE THE BATTLE DIRECTLY... BUT WITH *LUCK*--

YES, BY THE ROVING RINGS OF RAGGADORR.' NAMOR *BREATHES* INSIDE THAT MYSTIC BARRIER!

15

THEN *AIR* CAN PENETRATE IT--AND AIR CONTAINS WATER VAPOR!

IF I CAN DRAW *ENOUGH* VAPOR *INSIDE* THAT SHELL--AND CONCENTRATE IT--!

OMNIPOTENT OSHTUR, HEAR-- FROM BEYOND THY *NAMELESS SPHERE*--

LET THE CAPTIVE'S SHACKLES BURST--

LET THE CAPTIVE LIE *IMMERSED!!*

AND SUDDENLY, *SHOCKINGLY*, THE SLANTED EYES OPEN--

--AND *COMPREHENSION* REIGNS!

I CAN DO *NO MORE!* NOW IT IS UP TO WATER-SPAWNED *MIGHT*, AGAINST THE *INSIDE* OF THE BARRIER--WHERE I PRAY IT IS *WEAKER!*

I AM FREE!

PERHAPS, SUB-MARINER...

...AND PERHAPS-- NOT!

WHAT'S *THIS* THAT I SEE? THE INVULNERABLE *HULK--INJURED* AND ON HIS *KNEES?*

A FATE INTENDED FOR *YOU,* NAMOR-- A FATE WHICH MAY *YET* BEFALL!

DIE, MONSTER--AND I WILL SACRIFICE *TWO* FOES THIS NIGHT, INSTEAD OF *ONE!*

OR *NONE,* LUNATIC!

STAY YOUR FATAL *THRUST*-- AND ANSWER TO THE *AVENGING SON!*

BUT HAS NAMOR AWAKENED *TOO* LATE--TOO LATE TO SAVE HIS ALLY?

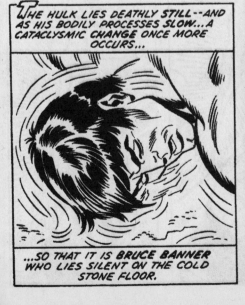

THE HULK LIES DEATHLY *STILL*--AND AS HIS BODILY PROCESSES SLOW...A CATACLYSMIC CHANGE ONCE MORE OCCURS...

...SO THAT IT IS BRUCE BANNER WHO LIES SILENT ON THE COLD STONE FLOOR.

YOUR ATTACK IS *USELESS,* NAMOR!

THE *STARS* GIVE ME *STRENGTH* TO CONQUER YOU!

WHAT OF *ME,* NECRO- DAMUS?

17

DR. STRANGE THE *MAGICIAN* IS POWER-LESS--

--BUT DR. STRANGE THE *MAN* IS *NOT!*

YOU ARE *WRONG*, DOCTOR-- *WRONG!*

THE STARS ARE BUT A *FRACTION* OUT OF *LINE*--

--AND, THOUGH YOUR STRENGTH AND *NAMOR'S* TOGETHER ARE *FORMIDABLE*--

--IN BUT *SEVEN SECONDS*--

--I WILL *PLUNGE* THIS *BEWITCHED BLADE*--

--THROUGH *NAMOR'S*--

--*NECK!!*

18

IN A FORGOTTEN CORNER, A MAN STIRS...A MAN WHOSE GREAT GREEN ALTER EGO WAS SORELY WOUNDED BY A DEMONIAC DAGGER.

YET MAGIC MUST AIMED PRECISELY--AND THE MAN WHO NOW STAGGERS TO HIS FEET--IS UNHURT!

OHHH--WHAT HIT ME? AND HOW DID I GET HERE?

GOOD LORD! A GIANT--TRYING TO KILL THE SUB-MARINER!

I DON'T GET IT --BUT I CAN TELL THE GOOD GUYS FROM THE BAD GUYS--

--AND I DON'T NEED AN ENGRAVED INVITATION TO JOIN THIS PARTY!

IN THE BLACKNESS YAWNING ABOVE THE COMBATANTS, A LOATHESOME IMAGE ONCE MORE APPEARS--AN IMAGE SUDDENLY SHARPLY DISPLEASED!

NOW IS THE TIME--THE STARS ARE IN LINE-- AND I--

NO! NO! YOUR INTERFERENCE CAN ONLY SLOW ME, BUT I DARE NOT BE SLOWED!

IF I AM DELAYED FOR EVEN A SECOND, I WILL MISS THE MOMENT ENTIRELY!

ALOOF, ALONE, THE STARS ARE NOT CONCERNED WITH MORTAL MATTERS. THEY MOVE TOWARD THEIR OWN ARCANE FATE.

THEY MEET--AND PASS!

NOOOO

19

YOU KEPT ME FROM *COMPLETING* THE *KILLING* STROKE-- AND *AGAIN* I BECOME WHAT I *WAS!*

SO I MUST *FLEE*--FLEE LIKE A CRAVEN *JACKAL!*

BUT I SHALL *RETURN* WHEN THE STARS *AGAIN* CALL OUT FOR *BLOOD*--

--AND MY *MASTERS* AND I WILL HAVE OUR *VENGEANCE!*

HE'S *VANISHED*--ALONG WITH THE FLICKERING FORM OF THE *NAMELESS ONE!*

BUT IF HIS *BLADE* HAD BEEN *ABLE* TO KILL, BEFORE THE *PRECISE MOMENT* ALLOTTED FOR *SACRIFICE*--

--THIS WHOLE *BIT* WOULD HAVE COME OUT A LOT *DIFFERENTLY!*

YES, BANNER-- AND THOUGH IT IS SMALL *COMFORT* TO YOU--

--THE HULK'S *WOUNDS* HAVE UNDOUBTEDLY *FLED* WITH THE *MAGIC* DONE TONIGHT.

BUT *YOU*, NAMOR--YOU MUST *EXPLAIN* THIS ORDEAL TO US!

HOW DID *NECRODAMUS CAPTURE* YOU--AND *DROP* YOU FROM THE *SKY* TO ATTRACT THE HULK?

HE DID NOT *DROP* ME, MAGE...

THE VERY SHADOWS SEEM TO CROWD CLOSER, LAUGHING MOCKINGLY AT NAMOR'S SLOW WORDS...

I WAS *THROWN* FROM THE HEAVENS BY... *THE SILVER SURFER!*

WHAT?

I HAD *THOUGHT* THIS MYSTERY AT AN *END*--BUT I SEE IT IS JUST *BEGUN!*

NOW--TO *FULLY* EXPLAIN THIS *ENIGMA*--THE *DEFENDERS* MUST--

--SEARCH FOR THE **SILVER SURFER!** TO BE CONTINUED!

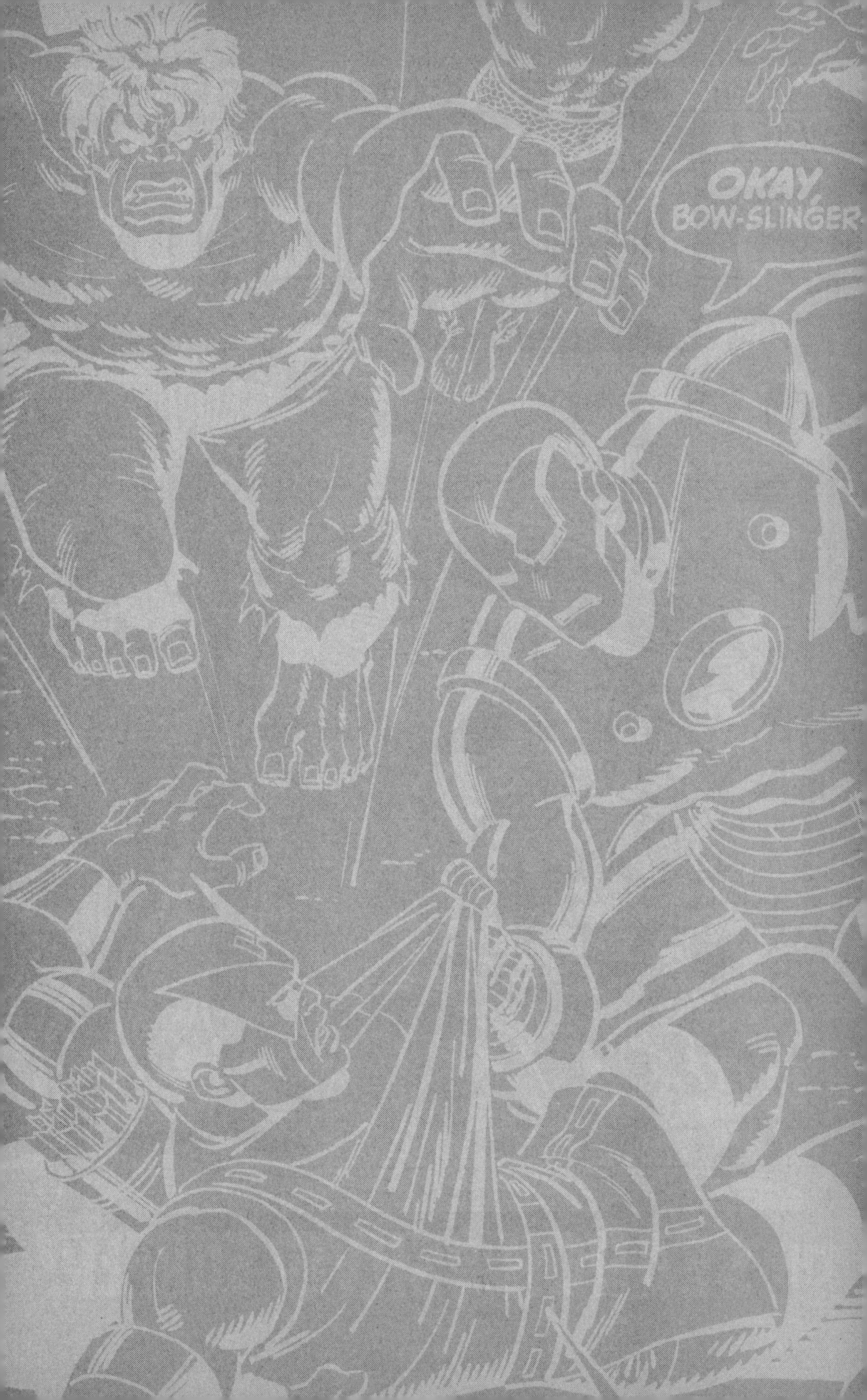
OKAY, BOW-SLINGER!

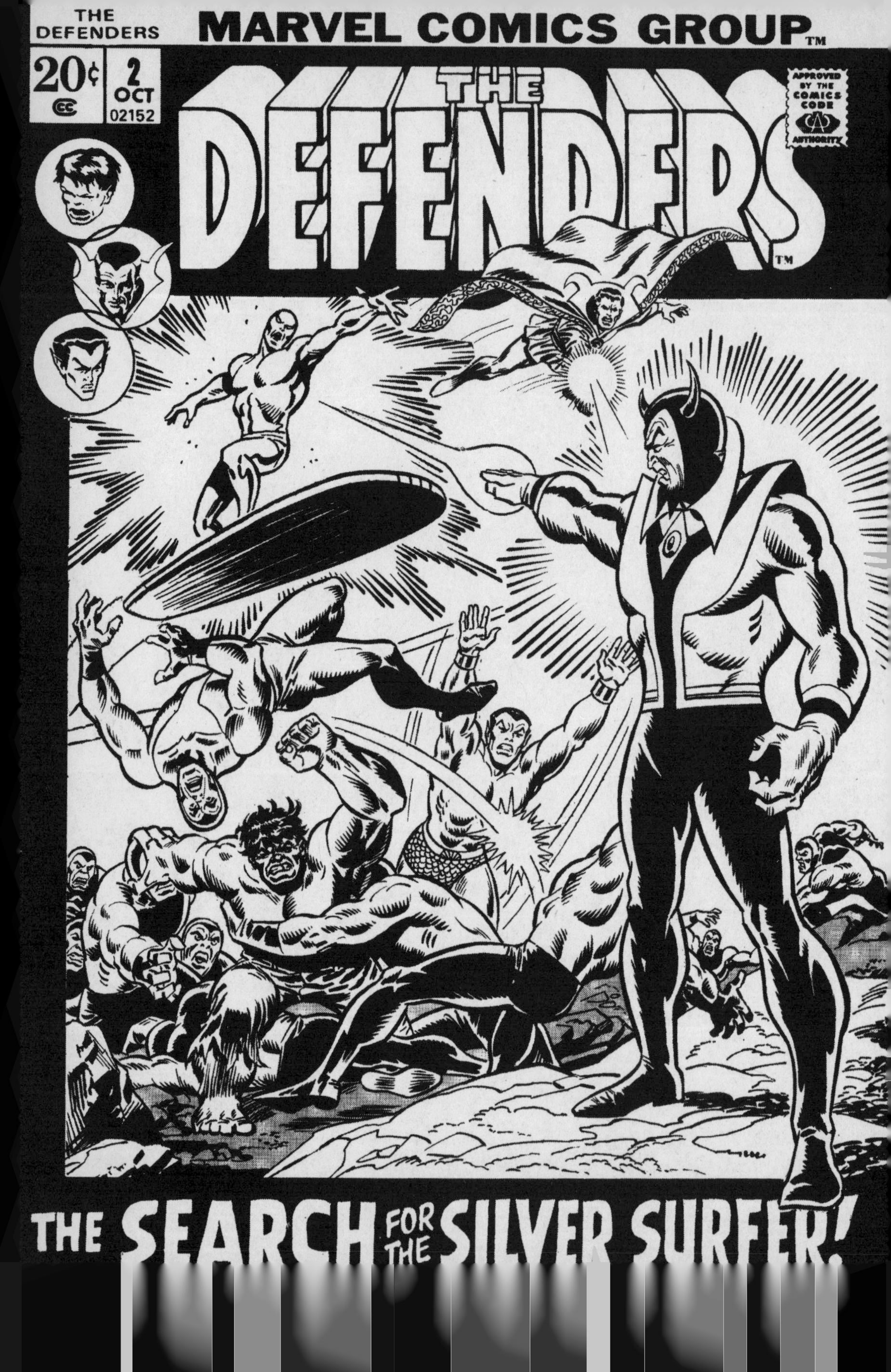
THE DEFENDERS
MARVEL COMICS GROUP™
20¢
2
OCT
02152
THE DEFENDERS™
APPROVED BY THE COMICS CODE AUTHORITY
THE SEARCH FOR THE SILVER SURFER!

THE DYNAMIC DEFENDERS!™

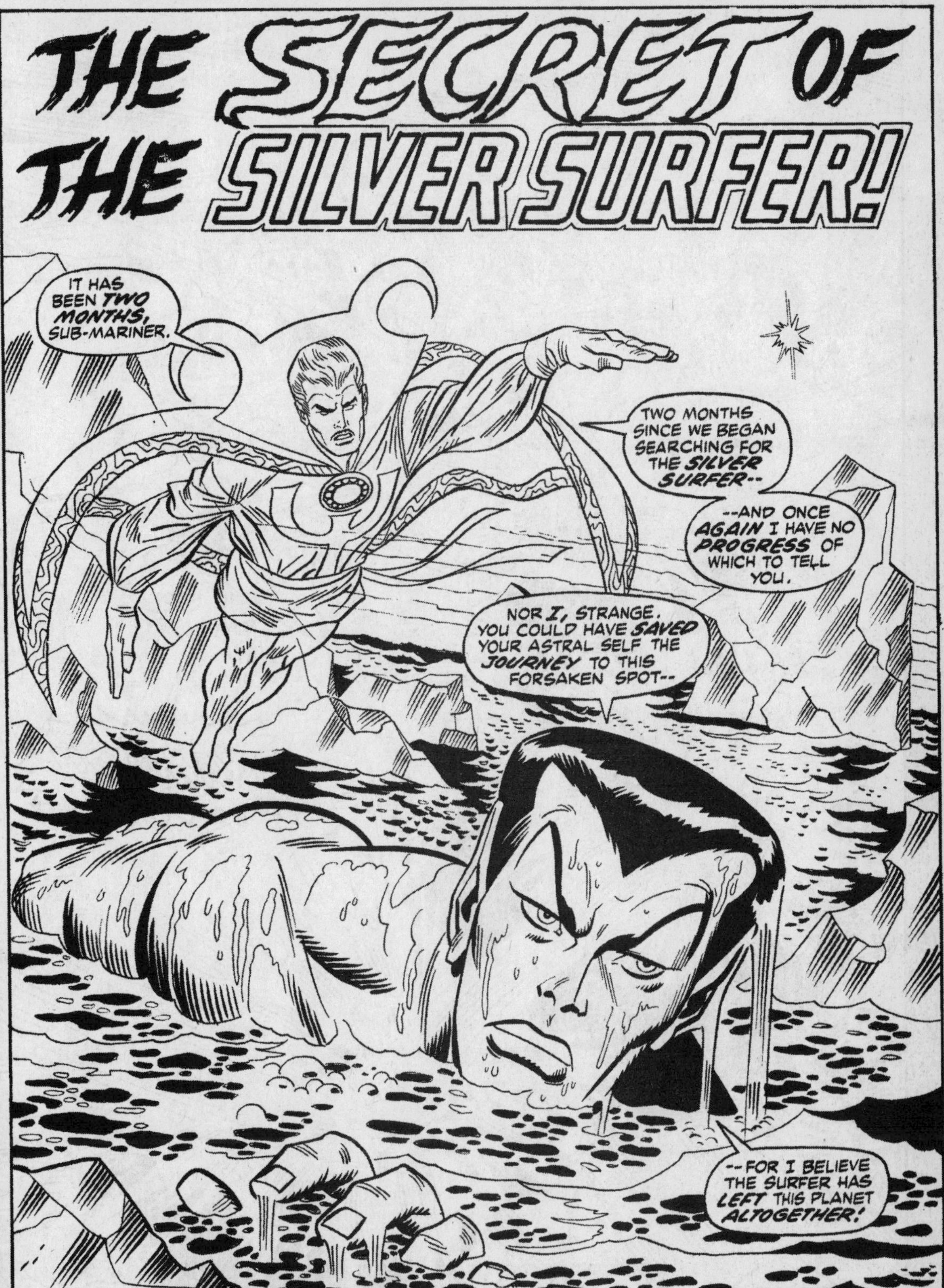
THE SECRET OF THE SILVER SURFER!
IT HAS BEEN TWO MONTHS, SUB-MARINER.
TWO MONTHS SINCE WE BEGAN SEARCHING FOR THE SILVER SURFER--
--AND ONCE AGAIN I HAVE NO PROGRESS OF WHICH TO TELL YOU.
NOR I, STRANGE. YOU COULD HAVE SAVED YOUR ASTRAL SELF THE JOURNEY TO THIS FORSAKEN SPOT--
--FOR I BELIEVE THE SURFER HAS LEFT THIS PLANET ALTOGETHER!

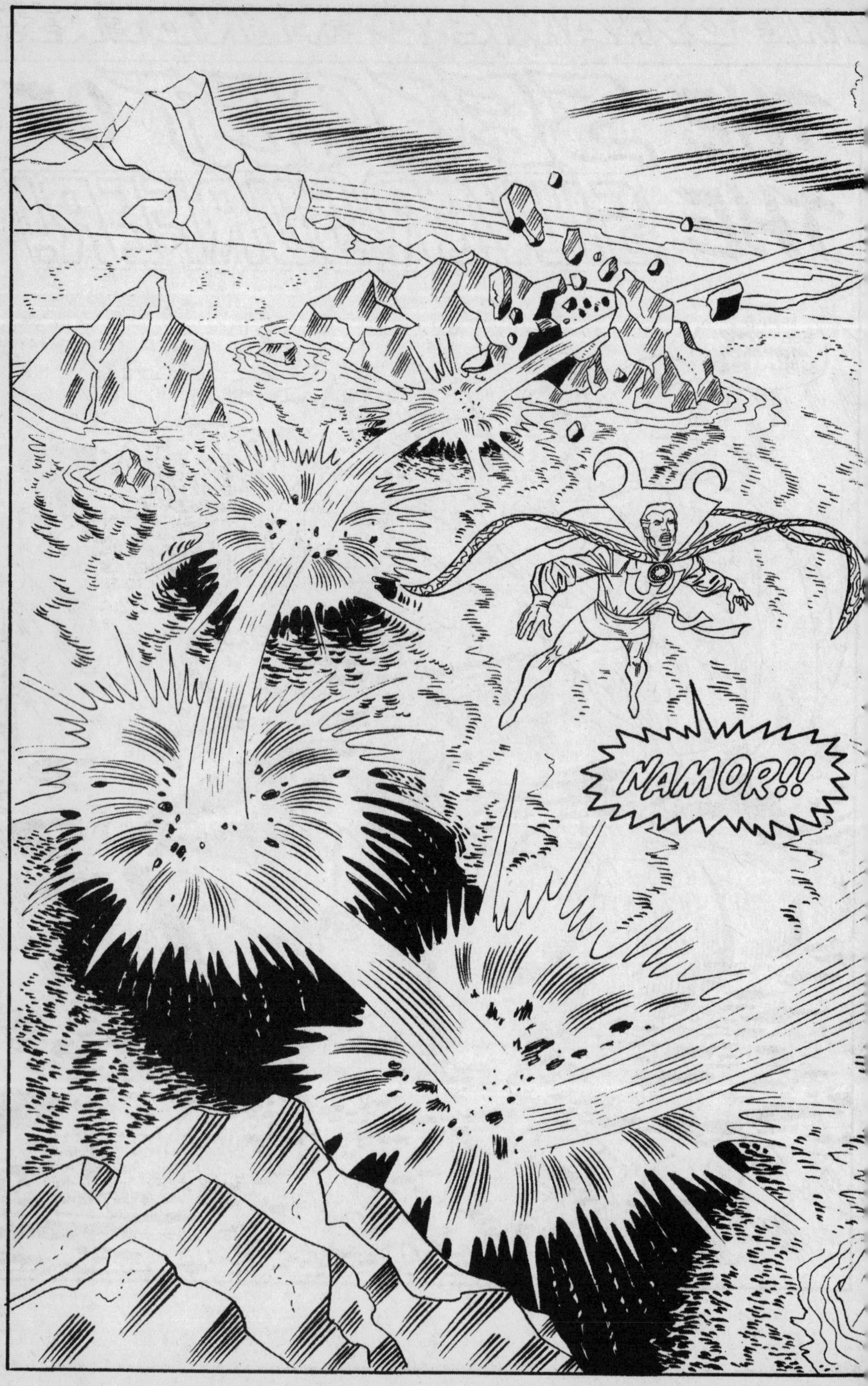
NAMOR!!

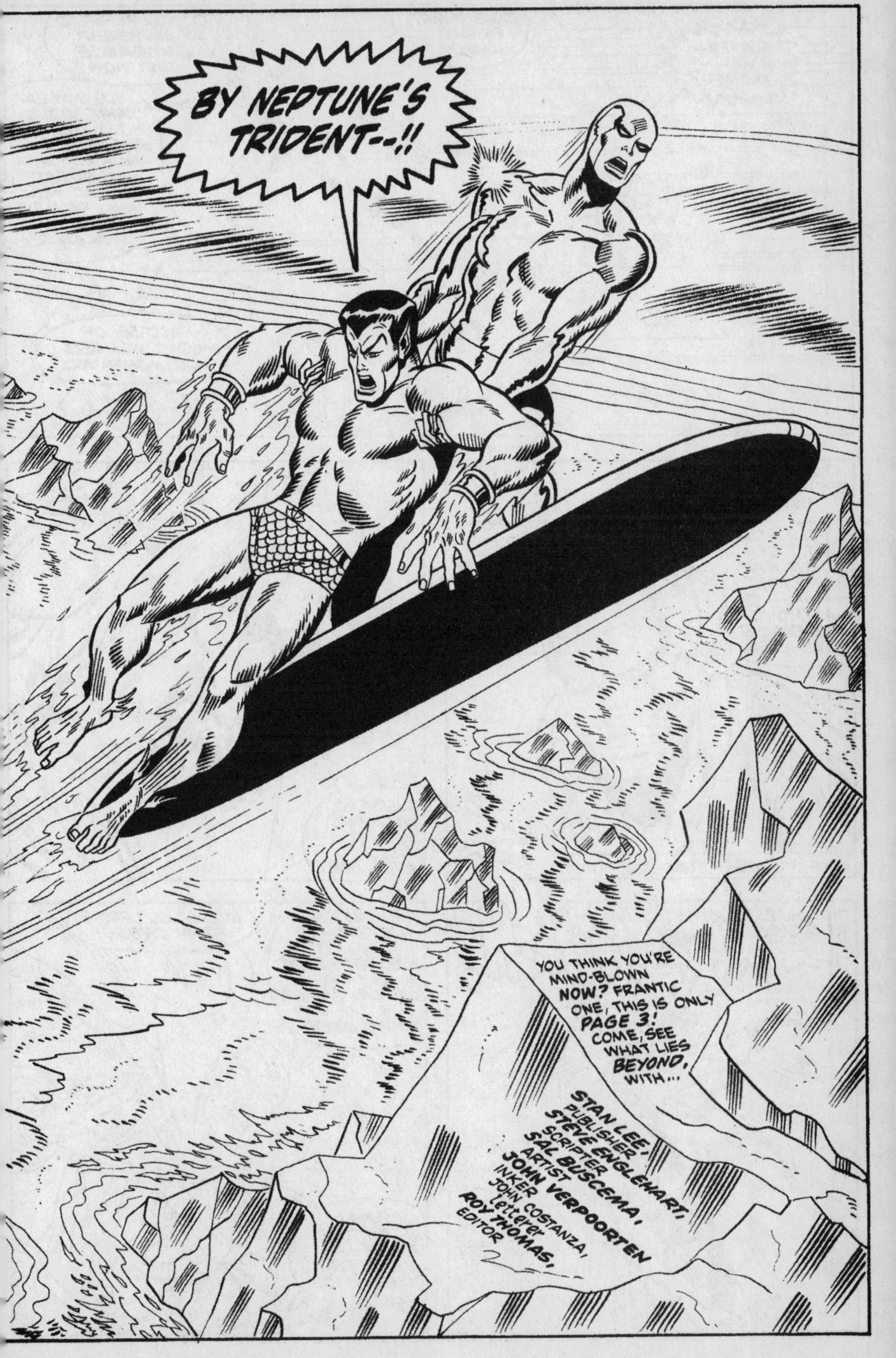

BY NEPTUNE'S TRIDENT--!!
YOU THINK YOU'RE MIND-BLOWN NOW? FRANTIC ONE, THIS IS ONLY PAGE 3! COME, SEE WHAT LIES BEYOND, WITH...
STAN LEE, PUBLISHER
STEVE ENGLEHART, SCRIPTER
SAL BUSCEMA, ARTIST
JOHN VERPOORTEN INKER
JOHN COSTANZA, letterer
ROY THOMAS, EDITOR

SURFER-- YOU *DARE*--?

DARE *WHAT*, FRIEND NAMOR?

DO YOU REFER TO MY EXUBERENT *ENTRANCE* JUST NOW?

YOU MAY LAY *THAT* TO THE UNQUALIFIED *SUCCESS* I HAVE MET WITH, IN MY *QUEST* TO LEAD MEN AWAY FROM THE PATHS OF *VIOLENCE*--

--*SUCCESS* OF WHICH I WILL *TELL* YOU, MOMENTARILY.

FIRST, HOWEVER, I MUST SPEAK OF THE *EFFECT* OF THAT SUCCESS.

I FEEL *NOW* THAT I CAN INDEED *AID* THIS PLANET--

--AND THAT IT *DESERVES* TO BE AIDED.

THUS, I COME TO *JOIN* YOU AGAIN--*

*AS IN *SUBBY* #34-35. --ROY.

--*JOIN ME*--?

JUST TWO *MONTHS* AGO, YOU TRIED TO *KILL ME!*

DID YOU EXPECT ME TO *OVERLOOK* THAT?!!

BLOONCH!

AT LAST OUR PATHS AGAIN *CROSS!*

THE *SILVER SURFER*-- HE WHO HELPED *NECRODAMUS* IN HIS SCHEME TO *SLAY* NAMOR FOR THE *UNDYING ONES*--

AND *I*-- IN MY *ASTRAL FORM*--AM *HELPLESS* TO INTERFERE!

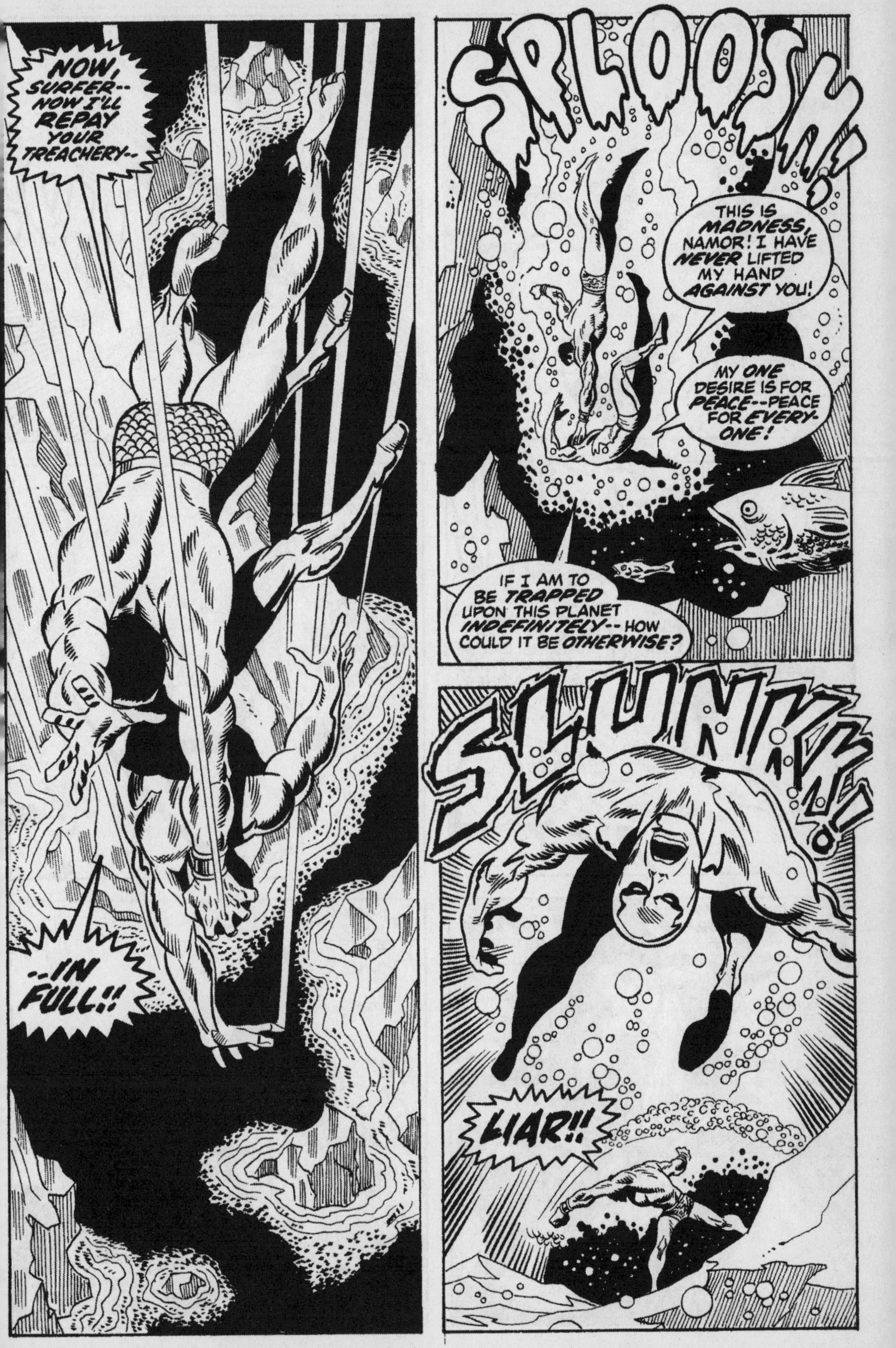
NOW, SURFER-- NOW I'LL REPAY YOUR TREACHERY--
--IN FULL!!
SPLOOSH!
THIS IS MADNESS, NAMOR! I HAVE NEVER LIFTED MY HAND AGAINST YOU!
MY ONE DESIRE IS FOR PEACE--PEACE FOR EVERY-ONE!
IF I AM TO BE TRAPPED UPON THIS PLANET INDEFINITELY-- HOW COULD IT BE OTHERWISE?
SLUNK!!
LIAR!!

DON'T *HANG BACK* LIKE A CRAFTY *SHARK*, SURFER!

I'M TOO *OLD* TO BE *FOOLED* BY SUCH--

--TRICKKKHHHHH

THUD!

FZZH!

GET *AWAY* FROM ME WITH YOUR BELLICOSE *NONSENSE*, SUB-MARINER!

I OFFERED YOU A HAND OF *FRIENDSHIP*, AND YOU RETURNED A *FIST!*

ALL OF YOU-- ALL MEN ON THIS POOR PLANET-- ARE *INSANE* WITH A LUST FOR *STRIFE!*

BUT NEVER *AGAIN* WILL THE *SILVER SURFER* INVOLVE HIMSELF WITH *MEN!*

I SHALL RETREAT TO MY PRIVATE *VALLEY*-- AND PASS THE *REMAINDER* OF MY DAYS *APART!*

I SHALL *NEVER* RETURN!!

SURFER--!

WHERE IS HE?

STRANGE, BY ALL THE SEAS-- *WHERE IS HE?!!*

GONE, NAMOR--AT SPEEDS *UNREACHABLE* FOR YOU.

HOWEVER, HIS FINAL *WORDS...*

...HAVE GIVEN ME A *VITAL CLUE* TO HIS *DESTINATION!*

COME-- *JOURNEY* WITH ME TO MY *SANCTUM SANCTORUM--*

--FOR *THERE* LIES THE *FINAL* DATUM NECESSARY TO MY *DEDUCTION.*

IN MY *CURRENT* MOOD, STRANGE-- I'D FOLLOW YOU TO *HELL!*

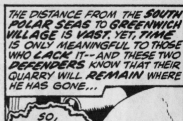

THE DISTANCE FROM THE *SOUTH POLAR SEAS* TO *GREENWICH VILLAGE* IS *VAST.* YET, *TIME* IS ONLY MEANINGFUL TO THOSE WHO *LACK* IT--AND THESE TWO *DEFENDERS* KNOW THAT THEIR *QUARRY* WILL *REMAIN* WHERE HE HAS GONE...

SO, TIME IS *NOT OF THE ESSENCE...* AND, IN DUE COURSE--

--THEY REACH THEIR GOAL!

WAIT BUT A *MOMENT,* ATLANTEAN.

MY MAN *WONG* WILL ADMIT YOU.

THUS NEAR MY *MORTAL BODY--*

--MY *ASTRAL* FORM FEELS AN URGENT *NEED* TO ONCE MORE REST WITHIN.

AND NOW, NAMOR, LET US HASTEN TO A *CERTAIN ROOM--*

--FOR I HAVE *MUCH* TO SHOW YOU!

THEY PASS AN ODDLY DISTURBING *PAINTING,* AND ENTER A *STAIRWELL* THAT SEEMS, TO THE SUB-MARINER, TO RISE *HIGHER* THAN THE SCOPE OF THE *HOUSE,* AND IT *OCCURS* TO NAMOR--AS IT HAS OCCURRED TO *OTHERS*--HOW *LITTLE* HE TRULY *KNOWS* ABOUT THE MYSTIC CALLED... *DR. STRANGE!*

HERE... HERE WAITS THE CHAMBER...

...AND PERHAPS THE ANSWER.

A LIBRARY--?

RATHER, NAMOR, A REPOSITORY FOR MANUSCRIPTS, SUCH AS THIS--

--THE DIARY OF MY FRIEND KENNETH WARD!

KENNETH TOLD ME OF HOW HE FIRST ENCOUNTERED TRACES OF THE UNDYING ONES IN A HIDDEN HIMALAYAN VALLEY.*

THE SURFER SPOKE OF RETURNING TO A VALLEY--

--AND WE KNOW THAT HE HAS, FOR SOME REASON, BEEN IN LEAGUE WITH A SERVANT OF THE NETHER-GODS.

*DR. STRANGE #183. --WROTE-IT-MYSELF ROY.

IS IT TOO MUCH TO ASSUME, THEN, THAT THESE TWO VALLEYS ARE ACTUALLY ONE AND THE SAME?

NO, STRANGE... IT IS NOT!

AND IF YOU'VE FOUND THE LOCATION OF THAT VALLEY IN WARD'S DIARY...

--THEN LET'S GO!

WAIT, NAMOR. FIRST WE MUST FIND THE HULK.

HE WAS STABBED NEAR TO DEATH BY NECRODAMUS -- AND SHOULD BE OFFERED THE OPTION OF RETRIBUTION.

WHERE THE *HULK* GOES, HE IS *REPORTED*-- AND SO...

THERE IS OUR *ALLY*, ATLANTEAN.

SO I *SEE*, STRANGE.

HO! *HULK!*

HUH? WHO *CALLS* TO HULK, WHEN HULK WANTS TO BE *ALONE?*

OH, IT'S *THEM...*

HULK, YOU MUST *COME* WITH US, WE *NEED* YOU.

BUT HULK DOESN'T NEED *YOU...!*

HULK HAS LOST *JARELLA* AGAIN--

--WANTS *NOTHING* TO DO WITH PUNY HUMANS *NOW!*

BESIDES, HULK HATES BEING *ORDERED AROUND* BY STUPID MAGICIAN!

I DON'T KNOW THE NAME *"JARELLA,"* BRUTE, BUT DO *YOU* KNOW THE NAME *"NECRODAMUS"?*

NECRODAMUS!! GIANT HUMAN WHO *HURT* HULK!

HULK HATES *HIM* MOST OF ALL!

GOOD! THEN, BEFORE YOU CHANGE YOUR *MIND,* TAKE MY *CLOAK OF LEVITATION!*

YOU CANNOT *LEAP* TO OUR DESTINATION.

HUH?

NOW WE *FLY*-- TO THE HIDDEN HEART OF ASIA--

--AND LET NO *MAN* NOR *GOD* TRY TO *STOP* US!

MEANWHILE, MILES AWAY, THE DOOMS-DAY DEVICE ACCIDENTALLY SET IN MOTION LAST ISSUE CONTINUES TO TICK TOWARD THE TIME WHEN IT WILL DESTROY THE EARTH, AT A RATE OF ONE SECOND PER MONTH.

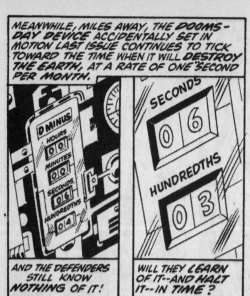

AND THE DEFENDERS STILL KNOW NOTHING OF IT!

WILL THEY LEARN OF IT--AND HALT IT--IN TIME?

ONLY THE FUTURE HAS THE ANSWER.

IT IS NOW HOURS OF REAL-WORLD TIME LATER, AND IT IS A WEARY CREW OF SUPER-BEINGS WHO SUDDENLY SIGHT A CITY AT THE BASE OF TOWERING PEAKS.

BUT THERE ARE MILES TO GO BEFORE THEY SLEEP.

OUAHH! DEMONS-- PLUNGING IN FROM KAM-NITSU, THE SKY!

FLEE, FRIENDS! THEY ARE THE ONES WE WERE TOLD ABOUT!

HEAR THAT, STRANGE? WE'RE EXPECTED-- AND THAT MEANS WE'RE ON THE RIGHT TRACK!

STOP, YELLOW-SKIN. HULK WANTS YOU.

:URRKK!:

I-I CANNOT SPEAK WITH YOU. THE MASTERS PROMISED I WOULD DIE SCREAMING IF I DID!

MASTERS? WHO ARE MASTERS?

I WILL SAY NO MORE! NO MORE!!

LET HIM *GO,* BEHEMOTH. WE WON'T LEARN ANYTHING *HERE.*

AGREED, NAMOR--WE MUST MOVE *ONWARD...*

...BUT *NOT* AS THE EASILY-RECOGNIZED *DEFENDERS.*

INSTEAD, WE MUST APPEAR TO BE ORDINARY *EXPLORERS.*

SOMEBODY TELL HULK WHAT IS GOING ON.

FIRST HULK HAS DUMB CAPE--NOW HE HAS *MITTENS.*

IN THE MOUNTAINS LURK MANY *DANGERS*--AND *ALL* OF THEM *UNKNOWN* TO US.

THE MASTERS--THE SILVER SURFER--POSSIBLY NECRODAMUS OR *OTHER* AGENTS OF THE UNDYING ONES...

THEY MAY BE *ANYWHERE*--AND OUR ONE ADVANTAGE MUST BE *SURPRISE!*

"*THUS,*" SAYS THE MASTER OF THE MYSTIC ARTS, "*I* HAVE PLACED A SPELL OF *FORGET-FULNESS* UPON THIS HAMLET--SO THAT WE MAY NOW HIRE *GUIDES* AND FORGE AHEAD WITHOUT UNDUE *NOTICE.*"

AND SO IT COMES TO PASS.

THE CLIMB IS NOT *ARDUOUS,* BUT SOON THE SUN, WHICH HAS STAYED ABOVE THE CHANGING HORIZON DURING THE DEFENDERS' MAD DASHES ACROSS THE GLOBE, FINALLY *SINKS* BELOW THE WESTERN CRAGS.

THE GUIDES *REFUSE* TO TRAVEL AT NIGHT. WE'LL HAVE TO *CAMP* HERE.

THERE ARE NO *STARS* LIT IN THIS ASIAN SKY-- NO SLIGHTEST REMINDER THAT *ANY* PLACE OTHER THAN THIS SNOW-ENCRUSTED HAVEN EXISTS.

SLEEP IS VERY *DEEP* TONIGHT.

However, comes the DAWN...

THE NATIVE GUIDES! BY THE SILVERY SARGASSO--!

DEPARTED-- OR WERE TAKEN... SOMETIME DURING THE NIGHT!

SO THE UNKNOWN STRIKES US AGAIN!

I TELL YOU, STRANGE, I'M GETTING SICK OF LOSING ROUND AFTER ROUND IN THIS BATTLE!

HOLD! SEE HERE:--

TRACKS OF HUGE, BARE FEET, LEFT IN THE VIRGINAL SNOW--

TRACKS THAT FORM A TRAIL, EASILY--RATHER TOO EASILY-- FOLLOWED ACROSS CRAG AND CREVASSE...

WE'RE HEADED TOWARD THE VALLEY, ATLANTEAN!

THEN MAYBE OUR TRIALS ARE ABOUT--

--OVER...

IT'S ONE OF OUR GUIDES-- OR IT WAS.

AND HIS HAND-- POINTING--

TOWARD-- THE VALLEY!

THE VALLEY OF THE UNDYING ONES!

THEN I WILL DISSOLVE MY SPELL OF CONCEALMENT: OUR SEARCH HAS ENDED.

FUNNY--IT'S WARMER IN THIS REGION-- I SHOULDN'T MISS MY COAT--

--BUT INSIDE, I STILL FEEL... COLD!

WAIT! HULK HEARS SOMETHING!

FURRY *MONKEY-THINGS*-- SNARLING AT HULK!

HULK BETS *THEY* ARE ANIMALS THAT KILLED *GUIDES!*

THEN-- HULK WILL *SMASH!*

SHUT UP, MONKEY! HULK DOES NOT WANT TO *HEAR* YOU!

WAIT, BRUTE! WE DON'T *KNOW* THEY'RE DANGEROUS!

SO FAR THEY'VE ONLY MADE *GESTURES!*

HULK KNOWS! HULK IS *SURE!*

BUT THEN, NOT TOTALLY *UNEXPECTEDLY,* A FLASH OF *SILVER* APPEARS IN THEIR MIDST--A FAMILIAR FLASH OF SILVER!

YOU *FOOL!* YOU MINDLESS *FOOL!* THOSE CREATURES ARE *HARMLESS!*

THEY ARE MY *FRIENDS,* MY CHILDREN!

WELL, *HAPPY FATHER'S DAY,* SURFER!

YOU, AT LEAST, I *KNOW* ARE A *VILLAIN!*

STOP, NAMOR! HEED YOUR OWN ADVICE TO THE HULK--

--AND WAIT UNTIL THE SURFER OVERTLY THREATENS YOU.

WHICH I WILL NOT DO, SUB-MARINER!

"WILL NOT DO"!

WHO CARES WHAT YOU WILL DO? I KNOW WHAT YOU'VE ALREADY DONE!

BUT ARE YOU POSITIVE--?

LISTEN, STRANGE, AND I'LL TELL YOU WHAT HE DID --

MY COUSIN NAMORITA AND I WERE BUILDING MY NEW SOUTH POLAR HOME. ONE EVENING I SENT HER AWAY FOR MATERIALS--

--AND SUDDENLY MY MIND SEEMED TO COLLAPSE INWARD--FROM WHAT I NOW REALIZE WAS AN ENCHANTMENT.

"FROM THEN ON I WAS ONLY CONSCIOUS TWICE--AND THEN JUST BARELY--BUT BOTH TIMES HE WAS THERE!

"ONCE WAS ON A RUINED HILL-TOP, WHERE I SAW NECRODAMUS GIVING HIM ORDERS--

"AND THE OTHER WAS WHEN HE THREW ME FROM HIS BOARD!"

THAT IS ABSOLUTELY NOT TRUE.

EXCEPT TO SEE YOU YESTERDAY, I HAVE NOT LEFT THIS VALLEY IN MONTHS!

THE SURFER'S STORY: "WHEN REED RICHARDS TRICKED *GALACTUS* INTO LEAVING EARTH FOREVER--*

"--I FELT THE NOW-FAMILIAR NEED TO *CLEANSE* MYSELF OF THE *PSYCHIC STAINS* LEFT BY *BATTLE*.

*A CLASSIC PIECE OF STRATEGY FROM FF#123. --ROY.

"BUT *THIS TIME* I OPTED FOR PERFORMING SOME *CONSTRUCTIVE* ACT! RATHER THAN *BROOD*, RATHER THAN *RAGE*, I WANTED TO DO SOMETHING *SMALL--YET MEANINGFUL*--

"--AND DO IT *SUCCESSFULLY*, MUCH LIKE THE AMERICAN *PEACE CORPS* VOLUNTEERS, SO I SEARCHED THE *WORLD* FOR A PRIMITIVE RACE I COULD *AID*--

"--AND *FOUND* IT IN THIS HIMALAYAN VALLEY: THIS SMALL GROUP OF NEARLY-HUMAN *APES*.

"THEY ARE SIMPLE, *CHILD-LIKE* FOLK, PROFOUNDLY *CURIOUS* ABOUT THINGS AND EVENTS THEY DO NOT COMPREHEND, AND CRUELLY *CUT OFF* FROM EVER *LEARNING* THESE THINGS BY THE SURROUNDING SNOWY *WASTELAND*.

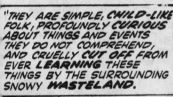

"I MADE FRIENDS EASILY..."

"...AND SET ABOUT *INSTRUCTING* THEM IN THE RUDIMENTS OF CIVILIZATION, SUCH AS *FIRE* (CAN YOU BELIEVE THAT THEY HAD NEVER *SEEN* IT?)--

"--WHILE WATCHING THEM *CAREFULLY* TO GUARD AGAINST THEIR LEARNING *OTHER* WAYS OF MANKIND, SUCH AS *GREED* AND *HATE*."

FINALLY, I FELT I HAD STEERED THEM TO THE *RIGHT PATH*, SO I DECIDED TO RETURN TO THE *OUTSIDE* WORLD.

AND I SAY *AGAIN*: I KNOW *NOTHING* OF AN ATTACK ON NAMOR. I WAS WITH MY FRIENDS, *HERE*, CONTINUOUSLY.

STILL, WE HAVE REASON TO *BELIEVE* THAT YOUR FRIENDS *KILLED* LAST NIGHT!

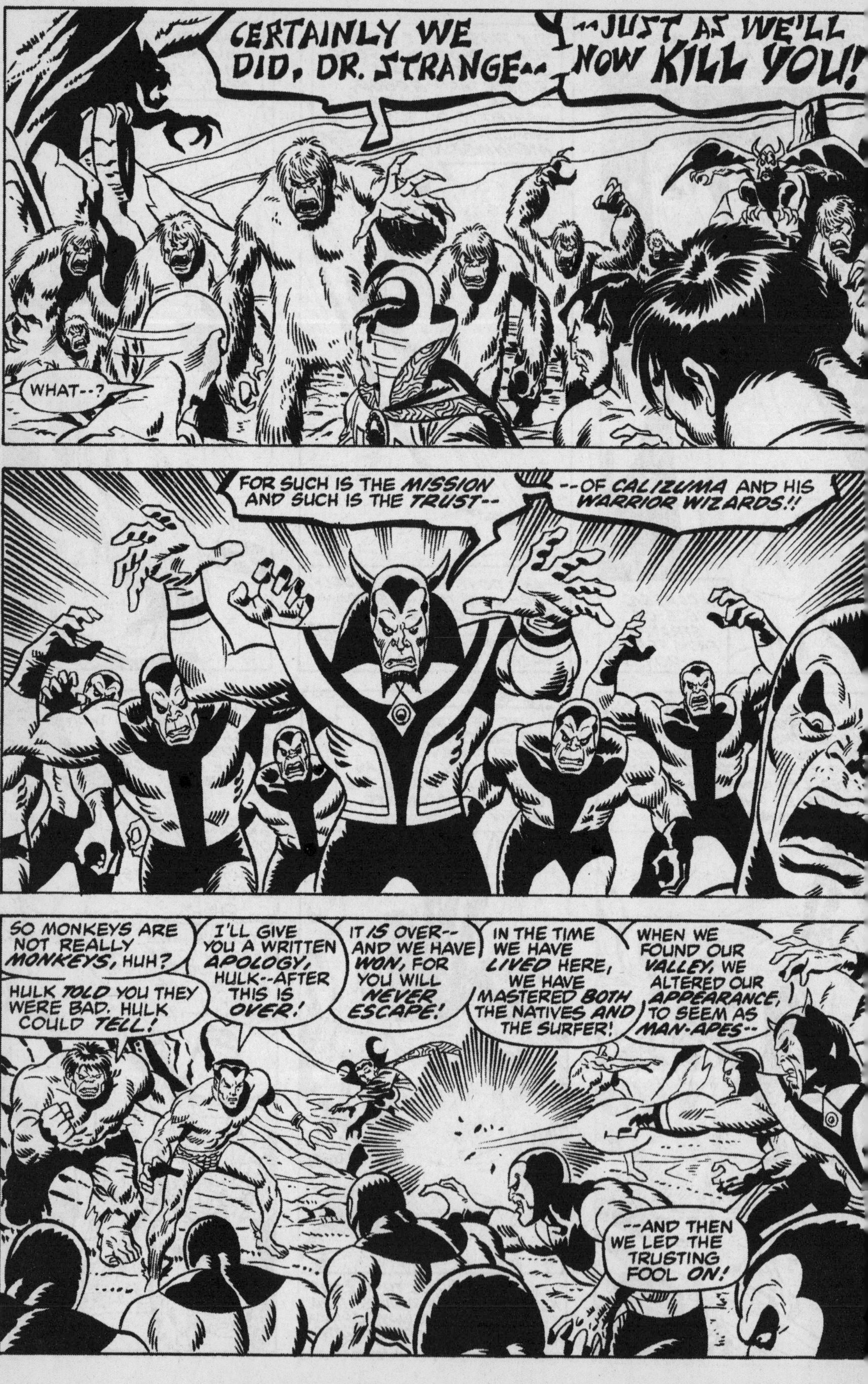
CERTAINLY WE DID, DR. STRANGE--
--JUST AS WE'LL NOW KILL YOU!
WHAT--?
FOR SUCH IS THE MISSION AND SUCH IS THE TRUST--
--OF CALIZUMA AND HIS WARRIOR WIZARDS!!
SO MONKEYS ARE NOT REALLY MONKEYS, HUH?
HULK TOLD YOU THEY WERE BAD. HULK COULD TELL!
I'LL GIVE YOU A WRITTEN APOLOGY, HULK--AFTER THIS IS OVER!
IT IS OVER--AND WE HAVE WON, FOR YOU WILL NEVER ESCAPE!
IN THE TIME WE HAVE LIVED HERE, WE HAVE MASTERED BOTH THE NATIVES AND THE SURFER!
WHEN WE FOUND OUR VALLEY, WE ALTERED OUR APPEARANCE, TO SEEM AS MAN-APES--
--AND THEN WE LED THE TRUSTING FOOL ON!

HE THOUGHT *HE* WAS TEACHING *US*--

--BUT ALL THE TIME, *WE* WERE SUBTLY PENETRATING AND CONTROLLING *HIS* MIND--

--SO *HE* WOULD UNKNOWINGLY *DO OUR* BIDDING!

SURFER!

NO! I CAN'T *BELIEVE*--

BELIEVE OR *DON'T,* SURFER! I CARE NOT ABOUT *DEAD MEN!*

DEAD? ONLY ONES WHO WILL *DIE*-- ARE HULK'S *ENEMIES!*

I'D SAY *WINNING* IS ENOUGH, HULK!

WE'VE GOT OUR HANDS FULL DOING *THAT!*

CROOM

HAH!!

FISH-MAN IS *CRAZY!*

I THINK *NOT,* MONSTER! NOT WHEN THERE ARE ENOUGH OF US TO *SURROUND* YOU--

--TO CATCH YOU FROM *BEHIND!*

MARK THIS MOMENT, COMPANION--

--FOR NOW THE WORLD LOSES TWO OF ITS *DEFENDERS* TO THE DARK REALMS OF *DOOM!*

NONSENSE!

ONE STUPID MAGICIAN-- AGAINST HULK?!?

BUT THESE ARE ONLY *PAWNS* OF CALIZUMA! WHAT OF THAT *MASTER MAGICIAN*-- AND *ANOTHER!* *DR. STRANGE?*

YOU BATTLE *WELL,* STRANGE--

BUT MY COMBINED FORCES WILL DEFEAT YOU!

HE MAY BE CORRECT, MAGE--

--UNLESS WE COMBINE *OUR* FORCES--

--IN *ONE* ATTACK UPON THE *LEADER* OF OUR FOES--*NOW!!*

WE *HEAR,* STEPHEN STRANGE!

THIS WAY, HULK-- *FAST!!*

AN *INSTANT* IN *TIME*: CALIZUMA IS FIGHTING, PERHAPS WINNING.

THE *FOLLOWING* INSTANT!

THE *POWER COSMIC* OF THE *SILVER SURFER* BLASTS HIM!

THE *SLAB-LIKE RIGHT FIST* OF THE *HULK* CLUBS HIM!

THE *STEEL-SINEWED LEFT FIST* OF THE *SUB-MARINER* POUNDS HIM!

THE MOST POTENT *SPELL* OF *DR. STRANGE* SMITES HIM!

AND...

YOU *DARE* TO STRIKE ME?

FOR *THAT*, YOU SHALL ALL--

Y-YOU SHALL ALL--

DIEEEEEEEEEEEEE!!

THU

HARSH *EXPERIENCE* DICTATES THAT, IN THIS WORLD, THERE ARE *LEADERS* AND THERE ARE *FOLLOWERS.*

WITHOUT *LEADERS,* WHAT *HAPPENS* TO *FOLLOWERS?*

GOOD *GUESS.*

THIS IS THE *END OF THEM*: "MY *CHILDREN.*"

NOW I UNDERSTAND HOW YOUR *ADAM* FELT WHEN HE BEHELD HIS SON *CAIN.*

DO YOU SEE IT TOO, READER-- OR IS IT ONLY THE *SWEAT* OF BATTLE RUNNING IN OUR EYES?

DO YOU SEE THE SLIGHT, *HOSTILE* MOVEMENTS OF THE *LIFELESS STATUES?*

CAN GODS *KNOW* OF DEFEATS IN A COSMOS *CLOSED* TO THEM--AND IF SO, WHAT CAN THEY DO IN *RETRIBUTION?*

A QUESTION WORTH *PONDERING...*

THESE WIZARDS WILL NOT TROUBLE US *AGAIN*--FOR I HAVE PLACED A *SPELL OF ATONEMENT* UPON THEM.

WHEN THEY AWAKEN, THEY WILL REMEMBER *NOTHING* OF THEIR EVIL PAST-- NOR *WANT* TO.

WOULD THAT *I* COULD LIKEWISE FORGET.

ARE THERE *NO* CREATURES OF PEACE ON THIS GLOBE?

IS *BATTLE* THE BEAT OF *ALL* LIFE?

AM I *ALWAYS* TO BE REVILED BY THOSE I ONLY WANT TO *AID?*

OH, THAT I COULD *LEAVE* THIS MAD PLANET--

-- COULD RETURN TO MY HOME-WORLD OF *ZENN-LA...* AND ONCE MORE EMBRACE MY BELOVED *SHALLA BAL...*

PERHAPS... PERHAPS YOU *CAN.*

AS A *JEST,* THAT IS IN VERY *POOR TASTE,* STRANGE!

THERE ARE *FEW* THINGS SACRED IN MY POOR LIFE-- BUT RETURNING TO SHALLA BAL... IS *ONE!*

I DO *NOT* MOCK YOU, SILVER SURFER.

I *TRULY* BELIEVE I CAN *GRANT* YOU YOUR DESIRE.

LISTEN, AND I SHALL *TELL* YOU...

NEXT: *FOUR AGAINST THE GODS!*

TO BE CONTINUED

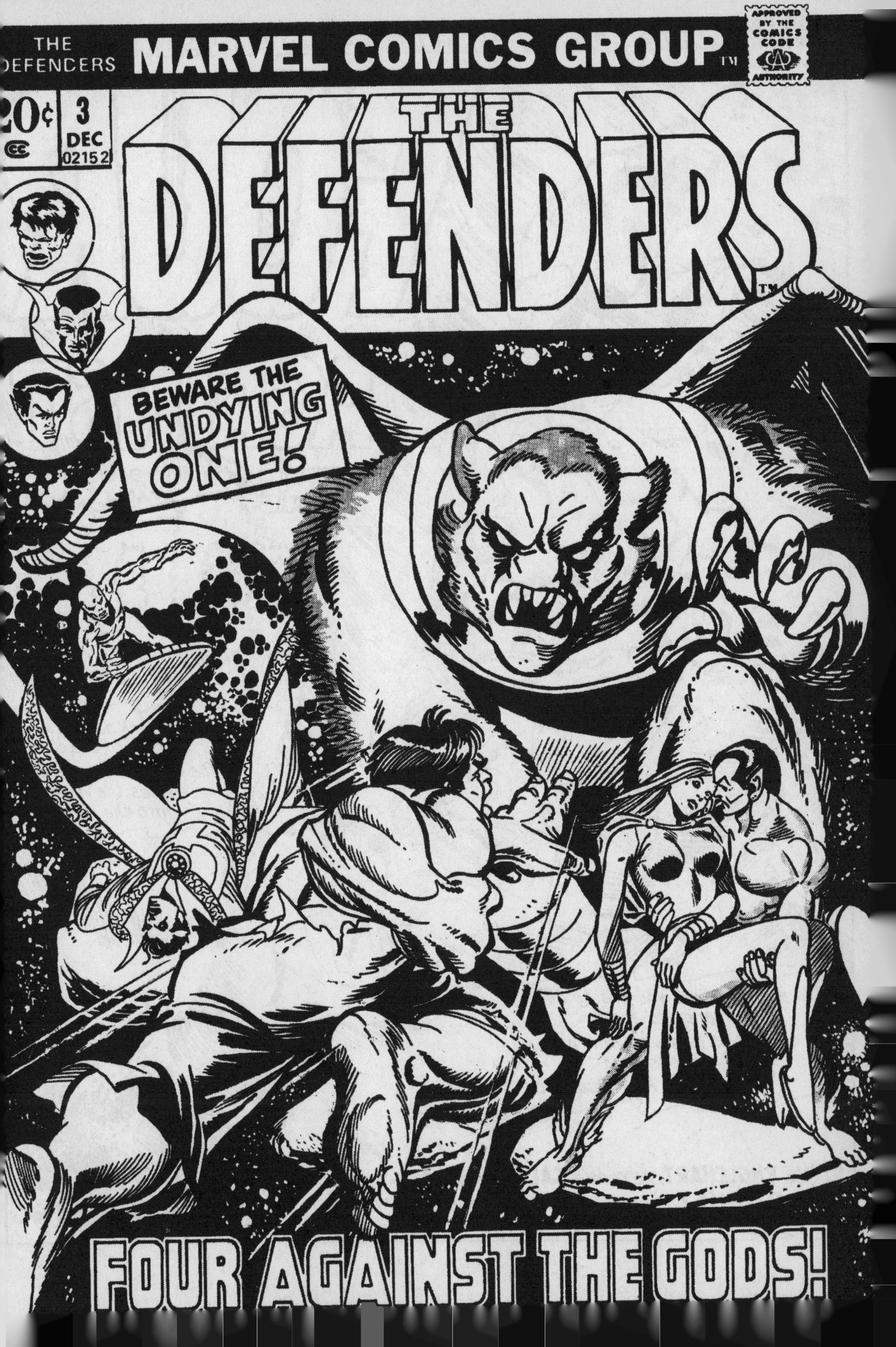

THE DEFENDERS
MARVEL COMICS GROUP
APPROVED BY THE COMICS CODE AUTHORITY
20¢
3 DEC 02152
THE DEFENDERS
BEWARE THE UNDYING ONE!
FOUR AGAINST THE GODS!

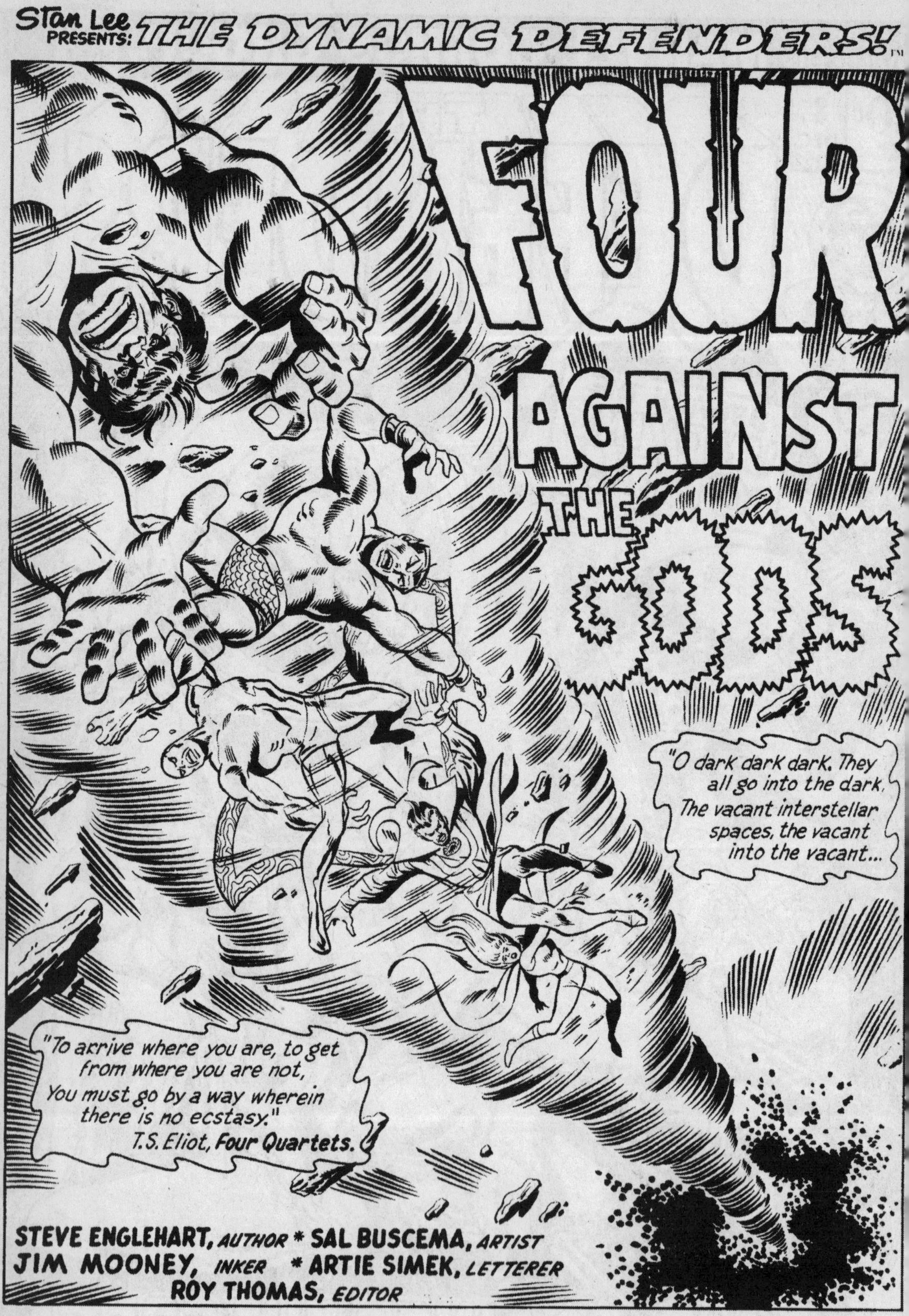

Stan Lee PRESENTS: THE DYNAMIC DEFENDERS!
FOUR AGAINST THE GODS
"O dark dark dark. They all go into the dark, The vacant interstellar spaces, the vacant into the vacant...
"To arrive where you are, to get from where you are not, You must go by a way wherein there is no ecstasy." T.S. Eliot, Four Quartets.
STEVE ENGLEHART, AUTHOR * SAL BUSCEMA, ARTIST
JIM MOONEY, INKER * ARTIE SIMEK, LETTERER
ROY THOMAS, EDITOR

YOU HAVE MISSED *NOTHING*. SINCE THE CONCLUSION OF LAST ISSUE, WHEN THE DEFENDERS AND THE SILVER SURFER OVERCAME CALIZUMA AND HIS WARRIOR WIZARDS, ONLY A FEW *MOMENTS* HAVE PASSED.

STRANGE, IT IS *IMPOSSIBLE!* THOUGH I DESIRE IT WITH ALL MY *SOUL*--

--I *CANNOT* RETURN TO MY HOME PLANET OF ZENN-LA.*

GALACTUS HAS PLACED AN INVISIBLE BARRIER AROUND EARTH TO *KEEP* ME HERE.

I SAY YOU ARE *WRONG*, SURFER.

GALACTUS' BARRIER EXISTS IN *THIS* DIMENSION ONLY.

I PROPOSE WE TRAVEL THROUGH *ANOTHER* DIMENSION, WHERE THE BARRIER DOES *NOT* EXIST!

ANOTHER--? OF COURSE!

I HAVE TRIED *MANY* WAYS TO CIRCUMVENT MY TRAP--

--BUT *THEY* ASSUMED THE TRAP WAS THERE TO BE *CIRCUMVENTED!*

IN ANOTHER *DIMENSION*, I COULD PASS *FREELY* THROUGH SPACE--

--AND RIDE MY COSMIC BOARD DIRECTLY TO MY *HOME*--

...AND SHALLA BAL, MY *LOVE.*

THEN LET NOT EVEN *TIME* IMPEDE US FURTHER.

BUT WHAT OF THE *OTHERS?* DO YOU WISH TO *COME,* NAMOR?

INDEED, DOCTOR. THOUGH I AM NOT *COMMITTED* TO STAY WITH YOU--

--A JOURNEY TO ANOTHER WORLD *INTRIGUES* ME.

AND *YOU,* HULK? WILL *YOU* COME WITH US?

NO!

HULK WILL NOT DO *ANYTHING* ANYMORE, IF DUMB *MAGICIAN* WANTS HIM TO.

WHEN HULK IS WITH *OTHERS,* THEY TRY TO *ORDER HIM AROUND*--AND HULK *HATES* THAT. SO HULK IS *LEAVING*--

--AND IF MAGICIAN TRIES TO *STOP* HIM-- HULK WILL *SMASH!*

WAIT, BEHEMOTH. A JOURNEY SUCH AS *THIS*--TO RETURN AFTER *LONG YEARS* TO THE PLANET OF MY *BIRTH*--SHOULD BE MADE WITH *FRIENDS!*

I ASK YOU TO COME *WITH* US.

YOU CALL HULK *FRIEND?*

ALMOST *NO ONE* CALLS HULK *FRIEND.*

HULK...WILL *GO* WITH YOU, SILVER ONE.

THEN HOLD YOURSELVES IN *READINESS*-- FOR I SHALL RETURN IN A *MOMENT.*

FIRST, HOWEVER, THERE IS SOME- THING I MUST *DO!*

--AND THAT IS RENEW MY CONTACT WITH *WATER*--

--IN *WHATEVER* FORM IT MAY BE!

SPLUSH!

AHHH. HUMANS *DRINK* IT, *WASH* IN IT, AND ULTIMATELY *POLLUTE* IT--

--BUT THEY CAN *NEVER* KNOW THE ALL-CONSUMING *EXPERIENCE*--

--THAT WATER IS TO A TRUE *SUB-MARINER!*

DR. STRANGE MAY BE ABLE TO *CONJURE* THE LIQUID TO RESTORE MY *STRENGTH* WHEN NECESSARY--

--BUT THE *FEELING* I ENJOY CAN NEVER BE THE SAME AS *THIS.*

HURRY *UP,* FISH-MAN! HULK WANTS TO GO WITH *FRIEND.*

DON'T MIND THE *BRUTE,* NAMOR. WE SHALL LEAVE WHEN YOU ARE *READY.*

NOW, BE *SILENT* ALL.

MAY ALL THE KEEPERS OF THE *WAYS*-- TRANSCEND THEIR VAST *DISSENSIONS*-- ALLOWING US TO TREAD *BEYOND*--

THE GATES OF LOCKED DIMENSIONS!

A RUSH OF **WARMTH** FLOWS UP THEIR SPINES, **BURSTING** INSIDE THEIR BRAINS!

TIME BECOMES SOUND!

FACTS BECOME LEGENDS!

REALITY IS EVERYWHERE-- AND IT **CANNOT** BE FOUND!

THEN THEY ARE ONE WITH THE **UNIVERSE!**

THEN THE **MULTIVERSE!**

THEN THEY ARE SINKING.

UNTO THE WEIRD.

UNTO THE ODD.

UNTO ANOTHER DIMENSION.

THIS...IS **NOT** THE COSMOS I WISHED TO ENTER! THERE HAS BEEN A TERRIBLE **MISTAKE!** STAY CLOSE TO--EH.?

BY THE HOARY HOSTS OF HOGGOTH!

WE ARE IN THE REALM OF THE *NAMELESS ONE!*

--STILL CAUGHT IN THEIR POLES OF *ETHEREAL FORCE!*

FOR THERE IS THE GIRL, *BARBARA,* WHO *SACRIFICED* HERSELF FOR ME THOSE LONG *MONTHS* AGO--

HULK #126.--R.

OH, AT *LAST!* AT *LAST!* OTHER *PEOPLE!*

IT'S BEEN SO *LONG*--SO LONG AND *LONELY*...WITH NOTHING BUT *EMPTINESS* AND *HORROR* AND THE *NA...NAME...*

OH-LORD-GET-ME-OUT-OF-HERE! PLEASE! *PLEASE! PLEASE!*

I COULD NOT HELP YOU *BEFORE,* GIRL-- BUT BY THE *OMNIPOTENT OSHTUR*--

--I SHALL HELP YOU *NOW!*

IF THOSE POLES *ARE* OF ETHEREAL FORCE, I CAN SEE WHY MERE *ENCHANTMENTS* HAVE LITTLE EFFECT!

BUT *FORCE* RESPONDS TO *FORCE*--

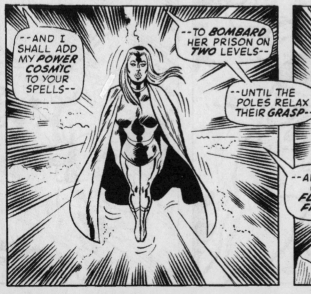

--AND I SHALL ADD MY *POWER COSMIC* TO YOUR SPELLS--

--TO *BOMBARD* HER PRISON ON *TWO* LEVELS--

--UNTIL THE POLES RELAX THEIR *GRASP*--

--AND THE GIRL *FLOATS FREE!!*

HERE, BARBARA! TAKE MY HAND!

A *HAND*-- A *HUMAN* HAND ...TO *TOUCH*... AFTER HAVING NO OTHER HUMANS AT *ALL* IN THIS COSMOS--

OH, *HOLD* ME-- HOLD ME *TIGHTLY!* PLEASE--I *NEED* SOMEONE-- SOMEONE OF MY *OWN KIND!* HOLD ME!

IT'S ALL RIGHT, YOU'RE *SAFE* NOW. WE'RE HERE... WE'RE HERE...

I *WANTED* TO RETURN AND RESCUE YOU, BUT THE *STARS* WERE WRONG. I *COULD NOT* ENTER THIS REALM AGAIN--

--UNTIL AN *ACCIDENT* --UNDOUBTEDLY OUR *BEING* IN THE VALLEY OF THE *UNDYING ONES* WHEN I SPOKE MY SPELL--*THRUST* US HERE!

NOW, BEFORE THE *NAMELESS ONE* HIMSELF DISCOVERS US, WE MUST *FLEE* THIS DIMENSION!

RETURN TO OUR *POINT OF ENTRY!*

WHERE *IS* IT, STRANGE? *DIRECTIONS* IN THIS COSMOS ARE *MEANINGLESS!*

TRUST MY SENSE OF *SPACE*, NAMOR.

YES, WE *MUST!* AFTER YEARS OF RIDING THE *SPACE CURRENTS* FOR *GALACTUS*, HE CAN TELL US HOW TO REACH--

BY THE *GODS!* A *HOLE*--IN THE VERY *FABRIC* OF THIS *MACROCOSM!*

DO NOT GET ANY *NEARER!*

HOLD! SOMETHING IS *HAPPENING*-- HAPPENING TO SPACE *ITSELF!*

IT'S *THICKENING*, BECOMING NEARLY *SOLID*--AND IT'S BEGUN TO *SWIRL!*

IT'S BECOME A *MAELSTROM!*

"AND IT'S SUCKING US DOWN INTO THE HOLE!!!"

NEVER IN ALL THE **SEAS** HAVE I FELT SUCH **FORCE!** WE ARE BEING SWEPT TO OUR **DOOM**--

WAIT, BY NEPTUNE!

THE SURFER'S **BOARD**--IT HAS NOT **MOVED!** THIS OTHER-DIMENSIONAL MAELSTROM MUST ONLY AFFECT **LIVING** BEINGS!

SURFER-- BRING YOUR **BOARD** TO US! **IT** CAN PULL US OUT THIS!

I **CAN'T,** NAMOR! IT DOESN'T **RESPOND** TO ME!

THERE IS SOME **COUNTER-FORCE!**

THEN WE ARE **LOST**-- UNLESS...

UNLESS I CAN **SWIM** THROUGH THE THICKENED ETHER--

--TO REACH THE BOARD **MYSELF!**

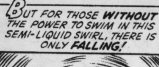

UT FOR THOSE **WITHOUT** THE POWER TO SWIM IN THIS SEMI-LIQUID SWIRL, THERE IS ONLY **FALLING!**

STILL...

STUFF TURNS **SOLID** AT CENTER!

THEN--HULK CAN **HOLD!**

AND HULK **WILL** HOLD!

HULK WILL HOLD **FOREVER!**

BUT CAN **WE** DO THE **SAME?**

BARBARA IS YET **WEAK** FROM HER ORDEAL...

...AND THIS FORCE GROWS EVER **STRONGER** NEAR THE OPENING!

THIS... IS LIKE... SWIMMING UP A **WATERFALL!**

BUT I **MUST** DO IT... I **MUST!**

IN **THIS** DIMENSION OR ANY **OTHER**...

--I AM **NAMOR!**

NOW THE WHIRLPOOL WILL *GRIP* ME AGAIN!

BUT AS IT CARRIES *ME*, IT CARRIES THE *BOARD*--

--AND THUS, IT CARRIES OUR *DELIVERANCE!*

-*UHH!* - *SORRY, GREENSKIN!*

I WAS MOVING TOO RAPIDLY TO *STOP!*

POW!

NOW OUR FATE IS IN *MY* HANDS!

BUT THOUGH I CONCENTRATE WITH EVERY *FIBER* OF MY BEING, MY BOARD DOES NOT *MOVE!*

I WILL *MAKE* IT MOVE--

--EVEN IF I MUST UTILIZE MY *POWER COSMIC!*

THAT *DID* IT, SURFER! NOW, EVERYONE *CLIMB ABOARD!*

HURRY! I CAN'T *MAINTAIN* THIS MUCH *LONGER!*

STILL, IT IS LONG *ENOUGH*, MY FRIEND--

--FOR *WE ARE FREE!!*

NAMOR!

STRANGE, I--I HAVE EXTENDED MYSELF TOO *FAR*...STRIVING AGAINST THAT DEVILISH FORCE!

I NEED... WATER...

THEN YOU SHALL *HAVE* IT, NAMOR!

IT IS A *SMALL ENOUGH* GESTURE OF GRATITUDE FOR YOUR STRUGGLE.

HIM? WHAT OF *HULK?*

NO ONE THANKS HULK!

*B*UT THE GRIM GREEN GOLIATH DOES NOT SPEAK FROM *HURT PRIDE*--AND THAT *TRAIT* WILL LEAD HIM DOWN DEVIOUS TRAILS...

NOW OUR *PREVIOUS* PROBLEM CONFRONTS US *ANEW*: ESCAPE FROM THIS DIMENSION, BY SLIGHTLY *SAFER* METHODS!

SURFER, CAN YOU STILL FIND--

HOLD! I HEAR FAINT *CRIES* BEHIND US!

IN THE NAME OF MY REVERED MENTOR! IT *CANNOT* BE!

THE FOUR MEN TURN IN SHOCKED SILENCE! MASTERS OF MANY THEY MAY BE, BUT THEY ARE STILL MEN--

--AND IMPRISONED BETWEEN NOW-FAMILIAR POLES OF ETHEREAL FORCE, THEY SEE THE WOMEN THEY LOVE!

WHAT ARE MEN TO DO?

JARELLA! HULK THOUGHT HE HAD LOST YOU FOREVER-- IN WORLD AT CENTER OF ATOM!

SHALLA BAL, MY OWN! I HAVE EVER TRIED TO REACH YOU-- BUT NOT LIKE THIS!

CLEA! HOW DID THIS HAPPEN? YOU SAID YOUR POWERS HAD FADED!

HOW CAME YOU TO THIS PLACE?

THE THOUGHT OF IMMEDIATE RESCUE BURNS IN EACH MIND, NEARLY FOGGING ALL OTHER THOUGHTS!

...BUT AN ERROR HAS BEEN MADE!

THIS CANNOT BE! THERE STANDS MY LADY DORMA--

--BUT SHE IS DEAD-- DEAD FOR MANY TIDES!

THIS IS A TRICK!

YET SHE APPEARS SO REAL! WHO WOULD HAVE THE KNOWLEDGE...

...THE KNOWLEDGE OF WOMEN...

OH NO!

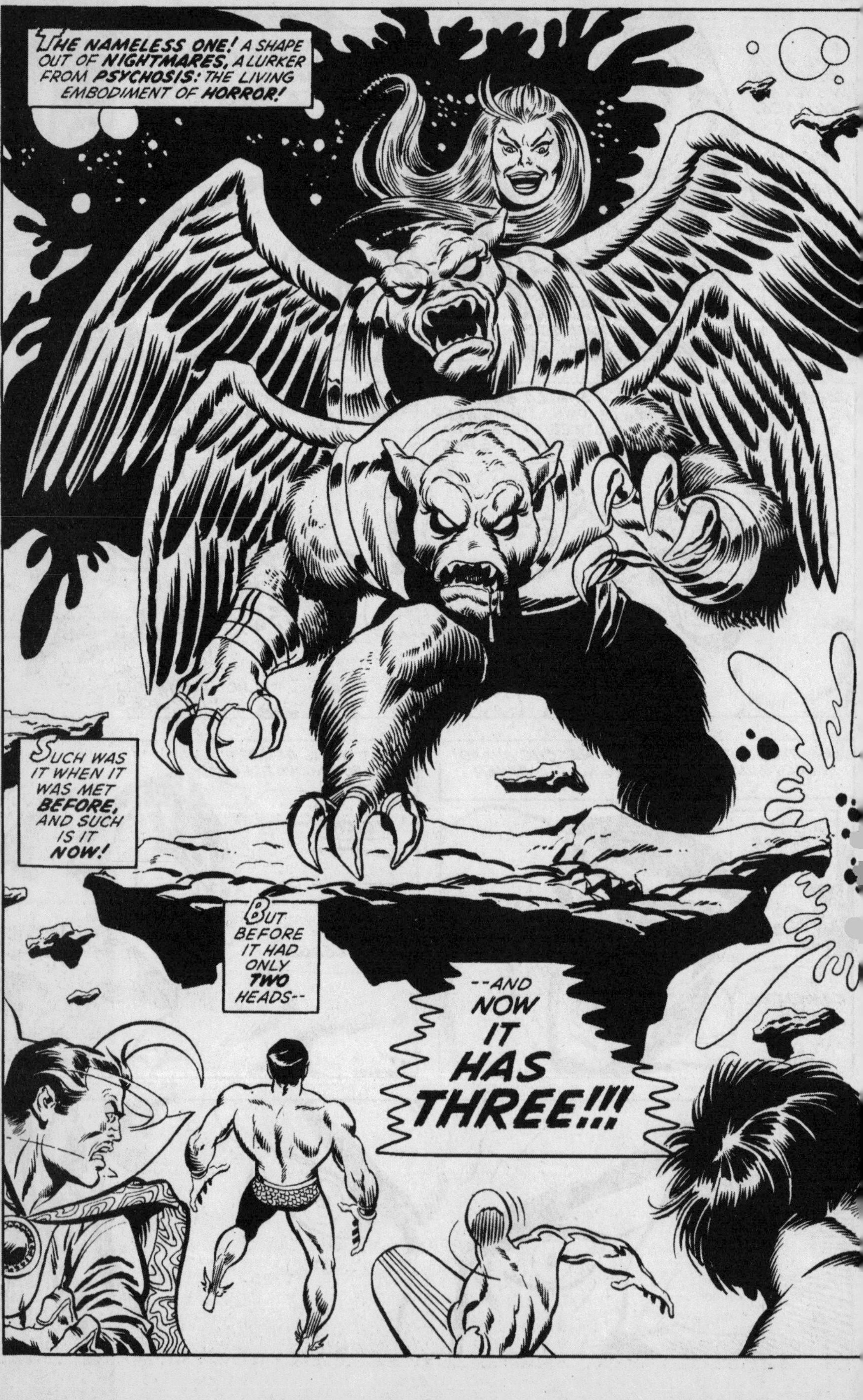
THE NAMELESS ONE! A SHAPE OUT OF NIGHTMARES, A LURKER FROM PSYCHOSIS: THE LIVING EMBODIMENT OF HORROR!
SUCH WAS IT WHEN IT WAS MET BEFORE, AND SUCH IS IT NOW!
BUT BEFORE IT HAD ONLY TWO HEADS--
--AND NOW IT HAS THREE!!!

ODD THE WAY THE MINDS OF MEN WORK. EVEN *NOW*, DR. STRANGE MUST REASSURE HIS SENSES.

CLEA--AND THE *OTHERS*...FADING LIKE A *DREAM.* IT WAS A *MIRAGE!*

YES, FOOL--LIKE MY NOW-FORGOTTEN HOPES OF *RESCUE* FROM THIS REALM!

I TRULY *MEANT* TO BE NOBLE AND *BRAVE* WHEN I FREED YOU AND THE HULK--BUT LONELINESS IS A *TERRIBLE* THING!

AFTER *MONTHS* OF IT, I WAS WILLING TO DO *ANYTHING* FOR COMPANIONSHIP--

--EVEN TO BECOMING MY CAPTOR'S *MATE!*

ENOUGH, WOMAN!

YOUR RATIONALE INTERESTS *NO ONE!*

KRIZ!

YOU'VE *TRICKED* THEM BY USING AGAIN YOUR *OLD* FORM--

--NOW LET YOUR *NEW* FORM *DESTROY* THEM!

THE SILVER SURFER SAYS *NO!*

FOOM

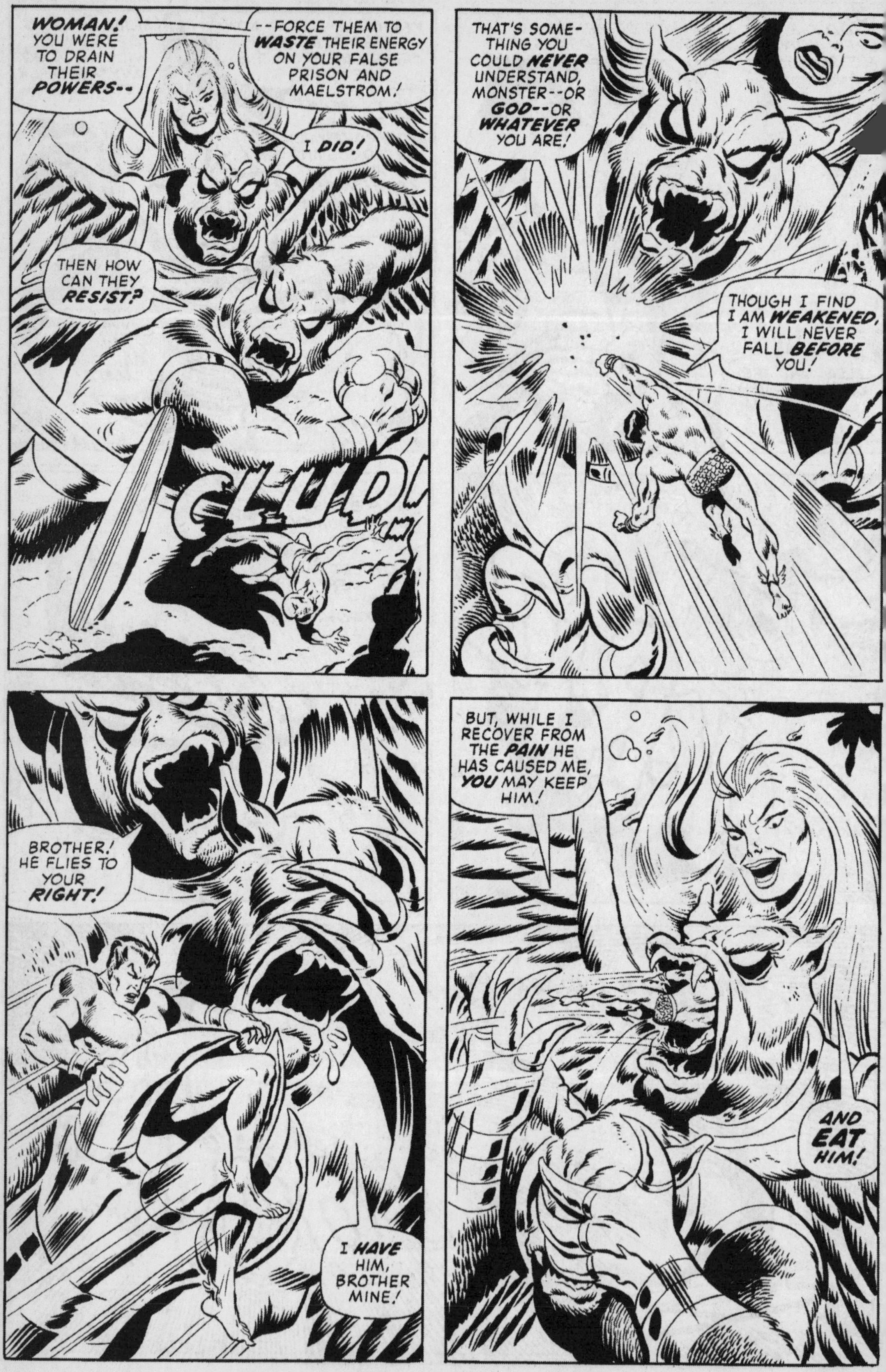
WOMAN! YOU WERE TO DRAIN THEIR POWERS--
--FORCE THEM TO WASTE THEIR ENERGY ON YOUR FALSE PRISON AND MAELSTROM!
I DID!
THEN HOW CAN THEY RESIST?
CLUD
THAT'S SOMETHING YOU COULD NEVER UNDERSTAND, MONSTER--OR GOD--OR WHATEVER YOU ARE!
THOUGH I FIND I AM WEAKENED, I WILL NEVER FALL BEFORE YOU!
BROTHER! HE FLIES TO YOUR RIGHT!
I HAVE HIM, BROTHER MINE!
BUT, WHILE I RECOVER FROM THE PAIN HE HAS CAUSED ME, YOU MAY KEEP HIM!
AND EAT HIM!

HULK! THE BEHEMOTH IS *DEVOURING* NAMOR--AND I MUST TEND TO THE *SURFER!*

IT'S UP TO *YOU!*

SO NOW MAGICIAN *WANTS* HULK'S HELP!

HULK SHOULD SAY *NO*--

--BUT HULK THINKS HE *LIKES* FISH-MAN.

IT IS TOO MUCH TO *UNDERSTAND*, SO HULK WILL JUST *DO* IT!

*H*OWEVER, AS THE MAN-MONSTER FLOWS FORWARD...

URK?

LEVIATHANS HAVE TRIED AND *FAILED!* *YOU* WILL NOT EAT THE TRUE *SUB-MARINER!*

PAK-KOW

*A*ND, WITH ALL *THREE* OF THE NAMELESS ONE'S HEADS *RECOILING* FROM THE AGONY BLASTING THEIR ONE BODY--

--THEY MISS SEEING NAMOR'S RAMPAGING *ALLY!*

CREATURE STANDS ON FLOATING *ROCK!* DON'T KNOW *WHY*... DON'T *CARE!*

ONLY KNOW CREATURE WILL *FALL* IF HULK *TOPPLES* ROCK--

--AND HULK CAN *DO* IT!

WHAT'S *HAPPENING?* YOU PROMISED YOU'D BEAT THEM *EASILY!*

I'VE BETRAYED *MY OWN KIND* FOR YOUR PROMISES!

THEIR *POWER!* EVEN *DRAINED,* THEY FIGHT LIKE *DEMONS!*

THEN THIS BECOMES *MORE* THAN REVENGE-- IT BECOMES *CHALLENGE!* WE MUST ONLY BATTLE THE *HARDER!*

THAT IS *NAMOR'S* THOUGHT PRECISELY, GOBLIN!

I SHALL THROW MY *ALL* INTO DEFEATING YOU!

BLUNT!

POW!

HULK, TOO!

*A*ND WITH REPEATED BLOWS, THE *MAN-MONSTER* AND THE *MAN-FISH* PRESS THE ATTACK, DRIVING THE RAGING NETHER-GOD SLOWLY *BACK!*

*T*HEN, FROM A FORGOTTEN *CORNER* OF THE COSMIC BATTLE-GROUND, COME THE *SENTINEL OF THE SPACEWAYS,* AND THE *MASTER OF THE MYSTIC ARTS!*

WITH MY DEPLETED POWERS, IT HAS TAKEN ME PRECIOUS *MINUTES* TO RECOVER FROM THE BLOW WHICH *FELLED* ME, STRANGE!

I *DARE* NOT TAKE *ANOTHER* SUCH ATTACK!

AND PERHAPS...

DO *YOU* SEE WHAT *I* SEE?

YES! THE *NAMELESS ONE*--

--POSITIONED DIRECTLY *ABOVE* BARBARA'S ERST-WHILE *PRISON!* AND WITH MY *SPELLS*--

--ACTING UPON AND IN CONCERT WITH YOUR *COSMIC POWER*--

--WE CAN CREATE *SNARES!*

THEY ARE OF SUCH *UNSTABLE* ENERGY AS TO ENDURE BUT A *MOMENT*--

BUT THAT MOMENT WILL BE *ENOUGH!*

AARRGH!! OUR *FOOT!* OUR FOOT IS *TRAPPED!*

AND, AS WE HAVE DISCOVERED, YOUR *ENCHANTMENTS* ALONE CANNOT *FREE* IT!

OUR ESCAPE IS THEREFORE *ASSURED,* STRANGE! LET US *TAKE* IT!

NO! I *CANNOT* YET LEAVE!

I STILL OWE BARBARA MY *LIFE!* OUR FREEING HER *EARLIER* WAS ONLY A *RUSE* DIRECTED BY THE NAMELESS ONE--

--BUT NOW I WILL FREE HER *AGAIN* FROM *THEIR* INFLUENCE! THIS TIME FOR *CERTAIN*--

DON'T *TOUCH* ME WITH YOUR FOUL *SPELLS!* KEEP AWAY!

THAT'S THE *NAMELESS ONE* SPEAKING THROUGH YOU, BARBARA--

BUT THEY CANNOT HOLD YOU AGAINST MY *WILL!* YOU SHALL RETURN TO YOUR *OWN BODY,* AND YOUR *OWN KIND!*

YOU SHALL BE *FREE!*

BY THE *GODS!* SHE'S GONE *MAD!*

BUT MY SPELL *COULDN'T* HAVE HURT HER! THERE IS NO *REASON* FOR THIS!

UNLESS...

BY THE CRIMSON CRYSTALS OF CYTTORAK...

*D*UMB-STRUCK, DR. STRANGE TWISTS AND DARTS BLINDLY *AWAY,* HOLDING THE GIRL'S FRAIL HAND IN A GRIP OF IRON.

--UNLESS HER *FORCED* CHOICE OF MATING WITH THE *MONSTER-GOD...*

...WAS A CHOICE SHE HAD GROWN *HAPPY* WITH...

*F*OR HOURS AFTER, THE FIVE SPEED THROUGH SPACE, THEIR ORIGINAL MISSION NEARLY *FORGOTTEN*--UNTIL...

STOP, STRANGE! MY SENSE OF SPACE TELLS ME WE HAVE *PASSED BEYOND* THE BARRIER OF GALACTUS!

RETURN US TO OUR *OWN* DIMENSION!

UH....? OH... CERTAINLY.

LIST, KEEPERS WHO ETERNAL *BURN*-- TO OUR REALM WE'D PRAY *RETURN!*

THEY CLOSE THEIR *EYES*--AND THEN *OPEN* THEM, PREPARED TO LOOK UPON THE FOREVER- BLACK OF SPACE.

BUT:

HUH.? *GRASS?*

WHAT IN NEPTUNE'S NAME IS *THIS?*

YOU'VE *BETRAYED* ME, STRANGE! WE ARE ON *EARTH!*

NO--I *SWEAR,* THIS IS THE *EXACT LOCATION* WE OCCUPIED IN THE OTHER COSMOS!

OUR *PHYSICAL LAWS* DID NOT *HOLD* THERE! DIRECTIONS WERE *MEANINGLESS!*

BUT IN RELYING ON YOUR *SENSE OF SPACE,* WE *FORGOT* WHAT NAMOR SAID:

IT WAS. ALL FOR *NAUGHT*-- *ALL* OF IT!

SPACE DIFFERS IN *EVERY* DIMENSION! I CAN *NEVER* ESCAPE THAT WAY!

I AM TRAPPED LIKE A *RAT* ON THIS INSANE PLANET!

THIS ENTIRE VENTURE HAS BEEN A *DISASTER.*

I WONDER: IN ASSUMING THE MANTLE OF *LEADER-SHIP* FOR THE *DEFENDERS...*

HAVE I ASSUMED *TOO MUCH?*

ONCE MORE THE SILVER SURFER HAS *TRUSTED* MEN--AND ONCE MORE MEN HAVE *SHATTERED* THAT TRUST!

I MUST SOAR, *FLY*--FOR WHERE THE *SURFER* FLIES--

--HE FLIES ...*ALONE!*

AAAAAAAAAAA

NEXT: THE *NEW DEFENDER* --AND THE *OLD AVENGER!*

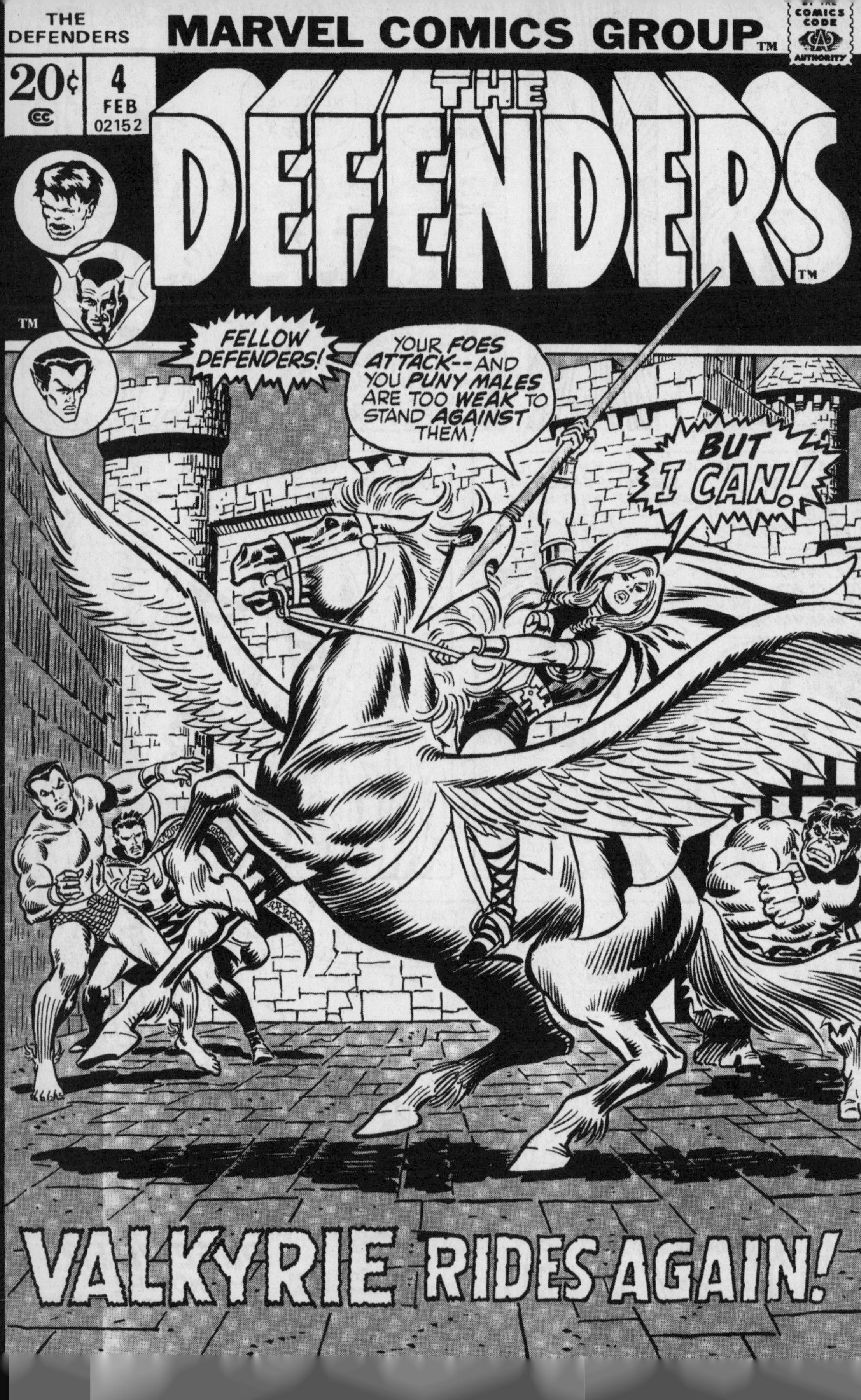
THE DEFENDERS
MARVEL COMICS GROUP
20¢
4
FEB
02152
THE DEFENDERS
FELLOW DEFENDERS!
YOUR FOES ATTACK--AND YOU PUNY MALES ARE TOO WEAK TO STAND AGAINST THEM!
BUT I CAN!
VALKYRIE RIDES AGAIN!

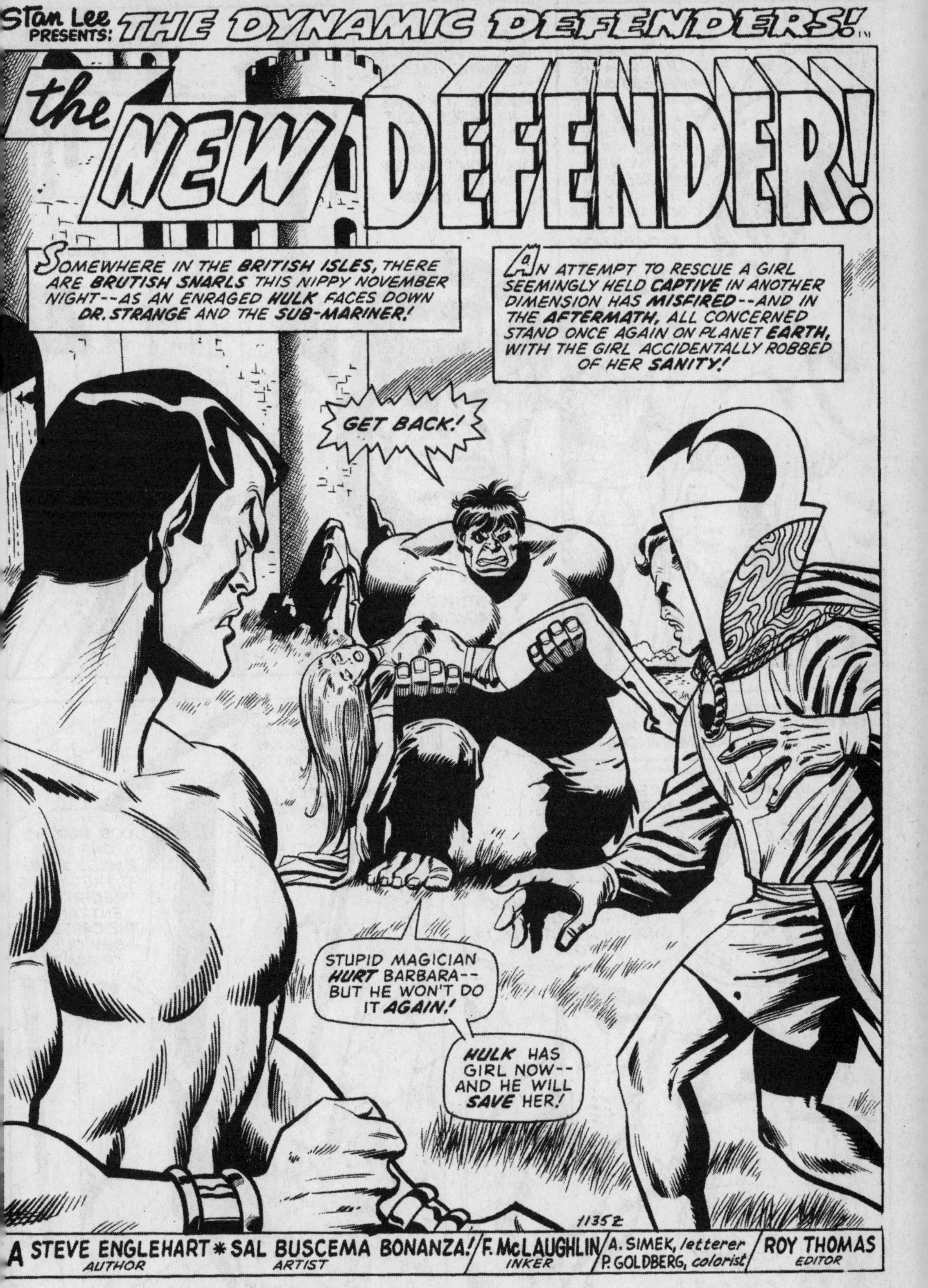

STAN LEE PRESENTS: THE DYNAMIC DEFENDERS!
THE NEW DEFENDER!
SOMEWHERE IN THE BRITISH ISLES, THERE ARE BRUTISH SNARLS THIS NIPPY NOVEMBER NIGHT--AS AN ENRAGED HULK FACES DOWN DR. STRANGE AND THE SUB-MARINER!
AN ATTEMPT TO RESCUE A GIRL SEEMINGLY HELD CAPTIVE IN ANOTHER DIMENSION HAS MISFIRED--AND IN THE AFTERMATH, ALL CONCERNED STAND ONCE AGAIN ON PLANET EARTH, WITH THE GIRL ACCIDENTALLY ROBBED OF HER SANITY!
GET BACK!
STUPID MAGICIAN HURT BARBARA--BUT HE WON'T DO IT AGAIN!
HULK HAS GIRL NOW--AND HE WILL SAVE HER!
11352
A STEVE ENGLEHART * SAL BUSCEMA BONANZA! F. McLAUGHLIN A. SIMEK, letterer P. GOLDBERG, colorist ROY THOMAS
AUTHOR ARTIST INKER EDITOR

HULK *MEANS* WHAT HE *SAYS!* STAY *BACK!*

HULK, IT *WASN'T* THAT WAY! I ONLY TRIED TO *FREE* BARBARA FROM THE *NAMELESS ONE!*

I COULD NOT *KNOW* SHE WAS SO FIRMLY ENTWINED *MENTALLY* WITH THE NETHER-GOD THAT THE SHOCK OF *SEPARATION* WOULD DRIVE HER *MAD!*

YOU USE BIG WORDS TO *CONFUSE* HULK! HULK UNDERSTANDS *NOTHING* YOU SAY!

HULK JUST KNOWS HE *HATES* YOU! YOU TELL HIM WHAT TO *DO--* YOU DON'T *THANK* HIM WHEN HE DOES *GOOD--*

STUPID *MAGICIAN!*

BETTER NOT TRY TO *STOP* HULK--

--OR HULK WILL *DESTROY* YOU!

NAMOR--THOUGH I COULD HAVE DONE *ONLY* WHAT I DID--WOULD DO IT *AGAIN* IN THE SAME CIRCUMSTANCES--

I *CANNOT* HOLD MYSELF *BLAME-LESS* FOR THIS. IGNORANCE IS NO *EXCUSE!*

THEREFORE, I ASK *YOU* TO MAKE THE DECISION: WHAT SHOULD WE *DO?*

DOCTOR, THE *HULK* CAN INJURE THAT GIRL UNINTENTIONALLY, *TOO.*

THERE IS NO DECISION TO *MAKE!* WE *FOLLOW!*

HOWEVER, SO AS NOT TO *ALARM* THE *BEHEMOTH,* WE SHALL *APPROACH* HIM BY AN *INDIRECT* ROUTE.

ODD THAT NO ONE HAS RAISED A *CRY* AT THE HULK'S *PRECIPITATE* ENTRANCE-- THE CASTLE IS OBVIOUSLY *TENANTED.*

YET, AS THE DEFENDERS SOON *DISCOVER,* THERE NOT ONLY ARE NO TENANTS IN *EVIDENCE*--

--THERE ARE NO GREEN-SKINNED *INTERLOPERS,* EITHER.

WHERE CAN THEY *BE?* THE HULK SELDOM *HIDES.*

EXACTLY *MY* THOUGHTS, STRANGE--

--BUT WE HAVE NOT YET SEARCHED THIS *CELLAR.*

HOLD! THERE IS NO ONE HERE, EITHER--

STILL... THAT *BRAZIER* BURNS!

*A*ND AS IF TO PROVE THE *TRUTH* OF NAMOR'S STARK WORDS--

--THE LEAPING *FLAMES* GUSH FORTH IN SUDDEN FRENZIED *FURY!*

--AND THEN *RECEDE,* TAKING MUCH MORE THAN THEIR *HEAT* WITH THEM.

*T*HEY TAKE *REALITY,* OR AT LEAST THE *DEFENDERS'* REALITY-- LEAVING ONLY *SMOKE*--

--AND, MOSTLY, *MIST*-- MIST IN WHICH SINISTER *FIGURES* GRADUALLY TAKE FORM!

NAMOR--WE'RE IN ANOTHER *LAND!*

AND PERHAPS ANOTHER *TIME* AS WELL, STRANGE! LOOK AT THOSE *SUITS OF ARMOR!*

BUT IN *ANY* TIME OR PLACE, THE CALL TO *BATTLE* EVER EXISTS!

IF YOU STILL AWAIT MY *COMMAND,* IT IS TO *DEFEND YOURSELF!*

THAT DECISION I NEEDED *NO* AID TO REACH!

ATTACK!

NAMOR--IF *BARBARA* AND THE *HULK* WERE DRAWN HERE THE SAME AS *WE--*

--I FEAR EVEN *MORE* FOR HER *SAFETY!*

THESE KNIGHTS ARE *BERSERKERS!* THEY KNOW NO *FEAR!*

ONWARD! ONWARD TO *VICTORY!*

GIVE NO *QUARTER,* MY LEGIONS!

WITHOUT *ARMOR,* EVEN *MY* MUTANT SKIN WOULD BE RENT BY THOSE SLASHING *SWORDS!*

SO *NAMOR* MUST MAKE *SURE* THAT HE IS NOT *CLOSED UPON!*

ARMOR! OF COURSE! MY LACK OF SELF-CONFIDENCE HAS DULLED MY MIND!

I SHALL PROVIDE YOU WITH PROTECTION, NAMOR!

WILT THOU, SORCERER?

KNOW THEE THAT THOU STANDEST IN THE MISTY REALM OF CASIOLENA, THE QUEEN OF US ALL--

--AND IN THIS LAND--

NO MAGICK'S MAY RISE AGAINST FRAGON, CONJURER TO THE QUEEN!

MY POWERS-- DISSIPATED LIKE OIL ON THE WATERS!

I HAVE BECOME NO MORE THAN MORTAL--AND THE MAN CALLED STEPHEN STRANGE IS NO MATCH FOR ARMED HORDES!

STRANGE IS DOWNED, LEAVING ONLY THE TRUE SUB-MARINER TO BATTLE THESE LEGIONS--

--AND THE MIST CARRIES NO WATER, LEAVING MY STRENGTH WANING BY THE MINUTE--

--BUT NAMOR FIGHTS ON!

BAH--MY TROOPS BE DOLTS! MONTHS HAVE I SPENT IN TRAINING THEM--

--YET ONE LONE FOE DOTH HOLD HIS OWN!

BUT I HAVE GAINED FAVOR IN THIS UNNATURAL LAND, AND THUS GAINED UNNATURAL POWERS--

--OF A FORCEFUL AND QUITE IRRESISTABLE NATURE!

AND AS THE ONCE AND FUTURE PRINCE OF ATLANTIS STAGGERS BACK--

--HIS DEFENSES ARE BREACHED--WITH CRUSHING EFFECT!

IT IS ALWAYS MY LOT TO TOPPLE MINE ENEMIES-- WHETHER BY MY HAND OR BY DIRECTING ANOTHER'S!

AND THAT IS WHY I BE-- THE EXECUTIONER! *

*DID YOU RECOGNIZE HIM-- FROM ABOUT A ZILLION OLD STORIES?--ROY.

"NOW THROW THE VERMIN INTO THE *DUNGEONS*, WHERE DIVERS *ENCHANTMENTS* SHALL HOLD THEM 'TIL I MAY *NEED THEM!*"

GOOD LORD! DR. STRANGE-- AND NAMOR!

I'D COUNTED ON *YOU* TWO FOR RESCUE--SINCE AN UN-HULKED *BRUCE BANNER* IS BADLY EQUIPPED FOR *BUCKLING SWASHES!*

YOU SPEAK IN THE *SINGULAR*. IS--

THE *GIRL?* YES, *SHE'S* HERE.

SHE SEEMS COMPLETELY *INSANE*--BUT I DON'T KNOW *WHY*--

--SINCE THE *HULK'S* MEMORIES ARE USUALLY NOT *MINE*.

ALL I *REMEMBER* IS BECOMING *MYSELF*, JUST AS THE FLAMES OF THE *BRAZIER* FLOODED OVER US.

THEN I WAS PLAYING "CONNECTICUT YANKEE"--FOR ABOUT *FIVE SECONDS*--AND HERE WE *ARE*.

WITH *VARIATIONS*, THAT'S WHAT HAPPENED TO *US*, TOO.

WHAT? SOMEONE IN THAT CELL *ACROSS* FROM US! WHO--?

COME NOW, DR. STRANGE--SURELY YOU RECOGNIZE DANE WHITMAN, THE *BLACK KNIGHT*--

--AND I'LL *INTRODUCE* YOU TO--THE *ENCHANTRESS!*

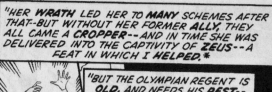

"OUR SAGA ACTUALLY BEGINS MANY **MONTHS** AGO, WHEN THE ENCHANTRESS AND HER PARTNER, THE **EXECUTIONER,** WERE BANISHED TO THIS LAND BY **ODIN.**

"HER **WRATH** LED HER TO **MANY** SCHEMES AFTER THAT--BUT WITHOUT HER FORMER **ALLY,** THEY ALL CAME A **CROPPER**--AND IN TIME SHE WAS DELIVERED INTO THE CAPTIVITY OF **ZEUS**--A FEAT IN WHICH I **HELPED.** *

"BUT THE EXECUTIONER SOON **LEFT** WITH THIS REALM'S QUEEN, DESERTING THE IMMORTAL SORCERESS. *

*AVENGERS #83.--R.

"BUT THE OLYMPIAN REGENT IS **OLD,** AND NEEDS HIS **REST**--

*AVENGERS #100,--ROY.

"--SO THAT SHE **QUICKLY** ESCAPED HIM, AND CAME TO **ME** IN MY HOME AT **GARRETT CASTLE.**

BEHOLD, BLACK KNIGHT: I HAVE **RETURNED**--THOUGH WITH NO **MALICE** FOR THINE ACTS WHEN **LAST** WE MET.

THOU SEEMEST **WELL**-- AND FIT FOR **BATTLE**-- WHICH SURELY BE TO THE GREATER **GOOD.**

FOR I HAVE NEED OF THY **WEAPONS** AND **COURAGE,** MY LOVE.

TOGETHER, WE SHALL **RETRIEVE** THE **EXECUTIONER** FROM THE CLOYING EMBRACES OF MY **RIVAL.**

I'M NOT YOUR **ACCOMPLICE**--AND I'M NOT YOUR **LOVE.**

YOU MUST BE **DREAMING,** BIRD.

WOULDST THOU CARE TO **TEST** THY FIRM RESOLVE-- AGAINST MY YIELDING **LIPS?**

"I KNEW I SHOULDN'T KISS HER. SHE CAN DESTROY A MAN'S **SOUL.**

"...BUT WHAT OF IT?"

"FROM THAT MOMENT ON I WAS HER SLAVE... HER **WILLING** SLAVE.

NOW SHALL I ADD **MY** POWER TO THAT OF THE OCCULT **BRAZIER** THOU GUARDEST--

"--AND WE WERE **OFF**, AFTER I HAD UNSTABLED AND MOUNTED MY WINGED HORSE, **ARAGORN**, TO GIVE ME EVERY ADVANTAGE I COULD **MUSTER** FOR THE UPCOMING FRAY--

"--BECAUSE, AS THE **ENCHANTRESS** EXPLAINED TO ME, ALTHOUGH HER WEAKENED POWERS ARE **RESTORED** IN THIS MISTY LAND BY ODIN'S DECREE--

"--IT WAS **STILL** A DANGEROUS AND **DIFFICULT** UNDERTAKING SHE PROPOSED.

"SHE WAS RIGHT.

DESTROY THEM, DARLING --FOR **ME**!

THE **ASGARDIAN** WENCH DOTH WISH TO SPIRIT THEE FROM MY **SIDE**!

OF **COURSE**, CASIOLENA! NOTHING SHALL E'ER US PART!

CASIOLENA! SO **THAT** IS THE NAME OF HER WHO WOULD **DEFY** ME!

FORWARD, MY LEGIONS!

AYE--A **ROYAL** NAME, PASSED FROM MOTHER TO **DAUGHTER**--

--ALONG WITH THE ACCUMULATED **MYSTICAL** SKILLS OF **EONS**!

-AAAAAA!-

"WE HAD **LOST** BEFORE WE HAD **BEGUN**, IN A CONTEST OF **MAGIC**--

"--AND AS WE ALL KNOW NOW, THE KING'S **HORDES** ARE **EQUALLY** OVER-WHELMING!"

THAT WAS *WEEKS* AGO--AND IT APPEARS THAT TIME HAS ONLY BROUGHT *MORE* OF US TO RUIN IN THIS HOLE.

PERHAPS, MY LOVE... BUT SEEST THOU *WHOM SPECIFICALLY* IT HATH BROUGHT US...

A *GIRL!*

ALL I HAVE *NEEDED* TO EFFECT OUR *ESCAPE* IS A MEMBER OF MINE OWN SEX--

--FOR IN ALL THIS REALM, THE ONLY OTHER *FEMALE* IS THE *QUEEN,* AND *HER* POWERS COULD *THWART* MINE.

BUT *NOW,* MINE *ENCHANTMENTS* CAN CREATE THE *WARRIOR WOMAN* CALLED--

VALKYRIE!

VALKYRIE?! I--THE HULK... *REMEMBERS* HER! BUT SHE'S ONLY A *FALSE PERSONALITY* YOU JOIN TO THAT OF A *MORTAL GIRL*--

--AND *THIS* GIRL IS *INSANE!* YOU'LL CREATE A *SUPER-MANIAC!*

NOT *SO!* YOU FORGET: MY POWERS ARE AT THEIR *PEAK* HERE.

WHEN I PERFORM MY RITES *THIS* TIME, THE *VALKYRIE* SHALL BE IN *COMPLETE* CONTROL! THIS MORTAL WENCH SHALL BE *TOTALLY* SUBMERGED AND *FORGOTTEN!*

NOT BY *US!* BARBARA *CANNOT* DECIDE IF SHE *WANTS* THIS TRANSFORMATION--NOT IN HER *PRESENT* STATE OF MIND--

--SO THE *DEFENDERS* MUST SPEAK *FOR* HER-- AND WE SAY *NO!*

SHE'S *AFRAID--HURT--*

YOU *CAN'T* DO THIS!

YOU COULD ALWAYS ATTEMPT TO *STOP* ME, I SUPPOSE--BUT SINCE THE EXECUTIONER'S SPELLS HOLD *ALL* OF US IN OUR *CELLS*--

I ASK YOU: *HOW?*

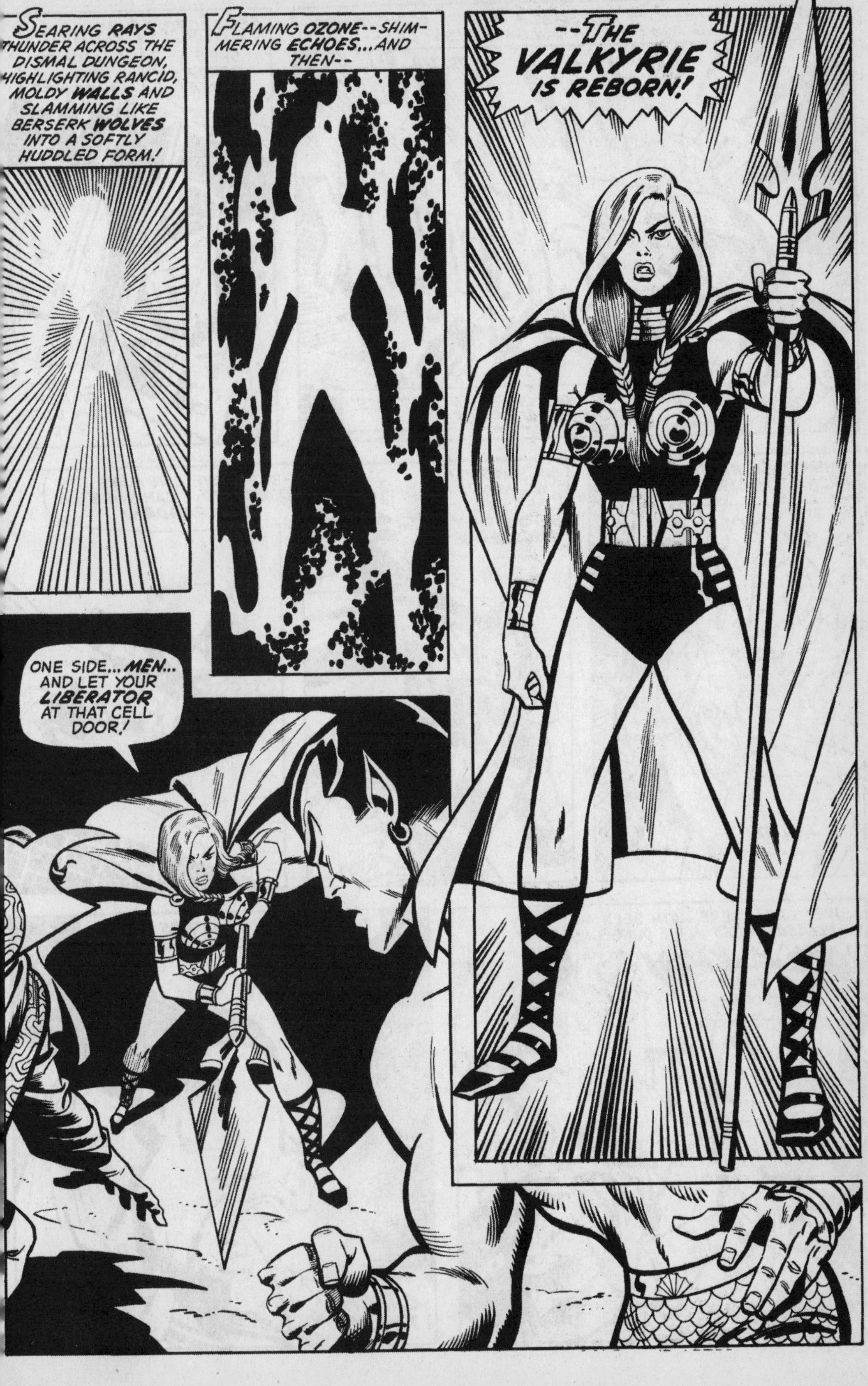
SEARING RAYS THUNDER ACROSS THE DISMAL DUNGEON, HIGHLIGHTING RANCID, MOLDY WALLS AND SLAMMING LIKE BERSERK WOLVES INTO A SOFTLY HUDDLED FORM!
FLAMING OZONE--SHIMMERING ECHOES...AND THEN--
--THE VALKYRIE IS REBORN!
ONE SIDE...MEN... AND LET YOUR LIBERATOR AT THAT CELL DOOR!

AND WITH A STRENGTH *INCREDIBLE* TO EYES ACCUSTOMED TO EQUATING POWER WITH BULGING *MUSCLES*--

CHUNK

--THE ENIGMATIC CHILD OF THE ENCHANTRESS' PSYCHE BURSTS *FREE!*

GOOD *LORD,* CHANTY-- SHE'S A *POWERHOUSE!*

WOULD I CREATE A CHAMPION WHO *WASN'T?*

COME-- SMASH *OUR* DOOR, GIRL!

THEN BACK *AWAY* FROM IT, MISTRESS!

WE'VE NO TIME TO *DELAY!*

SHE'S *RIGHT!* WE WON'T GET FAR BEFORE THEY *DISCOVER* US--

--BUT IF WE CAN MAKE THE *COURTYARD,* I CAN WHISTLE UP *ARAGORN!*

SIRE! SIRE! THERE HATH BEEN AN *UNPLEASANTNESS* IN THE DUNGEONS!

THE PRISONERS--

THOU CALLOW *LACKEY!*

I CAN READ THY *WORDS* ON THY TWITCHING *VISAGE!*

CATCH THEM!!

--A SPUR TO FIGHT--

CRACK!

--TO DARE--

CHOOM!

--TO WIN!

AND EVERYWHERE IS THE STORY THE *SAME!*

ONLY THY *QUEEN'S* SPELLS BE A MATCH FOR *MINE, FRAGON!*

WHILE EVEN NOW, *MY* POWERS RETURN TO ME, AS YOU PRESS YOUR ATTENTION ON THE *ASGARDIAN!*

AND, *MAGE*--

--YOU IGNORE *DR. STRANGE* AT YOUR *PERIL!*

STRIKE **WITH** ME, ENCHANTRESS!

THIS IS THE MOMENT OF OUR **TRIUMPH!**

AND BEYOND, IN THE MIST-SHROUDED COURTYARD--

THESE FOOLS ARE SO **STUNNED** BY THE APPEARANCE OF A WOMAN OTHER THAN THEIR **QUEEN**--

THEY HAVEN'T THE **SLIGHTEST** IDEA OF WHAT TO **DO** ABOUT ME!

HOWEVER, THOSE **UNIQUE** CONDITIONS DON'T APPLY TO THE SOMEWHAT SET-UPON **SUB-MARINER**--

THE EXECUTIONER!

I KNOW NOT HOW THOU ESCAPED MY **DUNGEONS**, CONTRARY TO MY SPELL-ENFORCED WISHES--

--BUT THOU SHALT NOT **PROFIT** THEREBY!

KROO!

AND *HO!* MINE EYES TELL ME THE *MORTAL* I DID CAPTURE HATH REVERTED TO HIS *BRUTISH* STATE!

YOU! HULK *REMEMBERS* YOU*-- BUT BEFORE, YOU DIDN'T USE SNEAKY *WEAPONS!*

YOU TRY TO *TRICK* HULK, BY NOT FIGHTING *FAIR!*

*FROM HULK #102--R.

TRY? NAY, BEHEMOTH--

--THE EXECUTIONER DOTH *SUCCEED!*

POW!

HERE, AS IN *ASGARD--*

--*NONE* MAY STAND IF I DO NOT SO *WISH* IT!

BRAK!

THOU ART NO *EXCEPTION,* WARRIOR!

MY STRENGTH AND MINE *AXE* BE OVER-WHELMING!

THEN YOU'LL CARRY YOUR AXE NO *LONGER,* MAN!

IN ODIN'S NAME--

GLANG!

I KNOW NOT WHO *THOU* MAY BE, MAID-- BUT THOU SHALT SOON LEARN *MY* NAME!

AND IS IT ANY *WONDER*, REALLY, THAT A MAN ACCUSTOMED TO *WINNING*—OR LOSING ONLY TO THE *MIGHTIEST* OF FOES—IS COMPLETELY *UNPREPARED* FOR THE CRUSHING RIGHT HAND OF THE SOFT-SEEMING *VALKYRIE?*

BLAM!

FOLLOWING WHICH—

CLUB!

DON'T KNOW IF YOU NEED A *CLINCHER*, BIG BOY—BUT I FEEL I *OWE* YOU SOMETHING!

HECK, I *KNOW* I DO!

HERE—TAKE THE FLAT OF MY EBONY *BLADE* AS SOMETHING TO *REMEMBER* ME BY!

HE'S DOWNED— AND *BEATEN!*

THE DAY IS *OURS!*

I SAY THEE *NAY*, WENCH.' THE DAY HATH NOT YET RUN ITS *COURSE!*

NAMOR— ON THE *PARAPET!*

NE'ER HATH *CASIOLENA THE QUEEN* DEIGNED TO SOIL HER ROYAL HANDS ON RABBLE IN PITCHED *CONFLICT*—

—BUT *STATECRAFT* BE THE ART OF MAKING THE NECESSARY *REWARDING!*

PREPARE TO *DIE*, PEASANTS!

YET AS CASIOLENA COILS HER THOUGHTS FOR A MIGHTY BOLT OF ENCHANTED *DESTRUCTION*--

--A LITHE, UNSEEN FIGURE MAKES A *LEAP* FOR THE PARAPET--

--AND ANOTHER FOR THE *QUEEN!* THE VALKYRIE'S *ARM* COCKS, HER FIST *HARDENS,* AND THEN--

NO! I CAN'T *DO* IT! I CAN'T HURT A *WOMAN!*

THUZ!

YET *I* CAN-- AND *SHALL!*

I CREATED THEE FROM *PART* OF MY NATURE, VALKYRIE--BUT *ONLY* PART. IN THE MAIN, I HAVE NO SCRUPLES AT *ALL* FOR MY FOES!

THE QUEEN AND I BE *EQUALS* IN POWER--

ALL THAT MATTERS IS WHO STRIKETH *FIRST.*

NOW, EXECUTIONER--IF THOU HAST SEEN THE *FOLLY* OF THY WAYS, THOU WILT LEAVE THIS LAND WITH *ME*--

--THAT OUR *COMBINED* ABILITIES MAY *RETURN* US TO THE PEAKS OF *SUCCESS.*

AYE...PERHAPS THOU SPEAKEST *REASON*--FOR IN A REALM OF THE *VANQUISHED,* THE *EXECUTIONER* HATH NO PLACE.

BUT-- *WAIT* A MINUTE! YOU *CAN'T* LEAVE WITH HIM! I *LOVE* YOU!

KNIGHT, THOU ART *VALIANT*-- AND *FAIR*-- BUT THOU ART *NOT* THE MAN I HAVE CHOSEN AS MINE OWN.

THOU WERT BUT MY *PAWN,* AND NO *MORE.*

WE'LL *SEE* ABOUT THAT--WHEN MY ENCHANTED *BLADE* CARVES UP HIS IMMORTAL *HIDE!*

COME ON, BALDY-- I CHALLENGE YOU TO A *DUEL!*

HOLD, IMPETUOUS ONE!

THY DESIRE TO BECOME MY *CHAMPION* HATH *TOUCHED* MY POOR HEART. I MUST SHOW MY ...*GRATITUDE.*

AND THAT DEMONSTRATION BE *THIS*--A *MONUMENT* OF SORTS TO THE ETERNAL LOVE I CAN INSPIRE:

THY FORM, TRANSMUTED INTO *SOLID STONE!*

THUS, IF THERE BE NO *OTHER* RASH FOOLS WHO SEEK TO HINDER US--

THE ENCHANTRESS AND THE EXECUTIONER BID YE *FAREWELL!*

THAT TREACHEROUS--! DOCTOR, CAN YOU *REVERSE* THE SPELL?

I--I'M *TRYING*--

--BUT THE ANSWER IS *NO!*

PERHAPS *I* CAN HELP. I WAS BORN OF THE ENCHANTRESS' *MIND*--I MAY BE ABLE TO *COUNTER* HER.

YOU? BUT IT IS SAID YOU *HATE* MEN.

WHY SHOULD *YOU* AID US?

I DO *NOT* HATE MEN, SUB-MARINER. I MERELY *KNOW* I'M AS *GOOD* AS THEY ARE.

NOW LET ME TRY-- *NO!*

IT ISN'T *WORKING!* I'VE *FAILED!*

MY MISTRESS' POWERS WERE *NOT* TRANSFERRED TO ME!

ALL WE CAN *DO,* THEN, IS TAKE THE KNIGHT BACK TO *EARTH* WITH US, IN HOPES THAT *SOMEDAY* WE MAY FIND A METHOD TO *SAVE* HIM.

AND I GUESS *I'LL* GO, TOO--HAVING BEEN *DESERTED* BY HER WHO MADE ME.

...JUST AS THAT BEAUTIFUL *ANIMAL* HAS BEEN LEFT BY FATE...

CAN YOU *TAKE* US BACK TO OUR TIME, STRANGE.?

YES, ATLANTEAN-- NOW THAT I *UNDERSTAND* HOW WE CAME HERE.

*M*URMURING *LOW* IN HIS THROAT--BUILDING CHANT UPON CHANT INTO A *CRESCENDO* OF FORGOTTEN FORCES--

--THE MASTER OF THE MYSTIC ARTS *ONCE MORE* PIERCES THE GAUZE OF TIME AND SPACE--

--AND THE NETHER-VOYAGE TO THE LAND CALLED HOME *BEGINS!*

WHERE IS *GIRL*.?

IF MAGICIAN HAS *HURT* HER AGAIN--

IN POINT OF *FACT*, HULK, THE VALKYRIE IS ONLY *TENUOUSLY* RELATED TO THE GIRL WE ONCE KNEW AS *BARBARA*--

--BUT I HAVE *NOT* INJURED HER, IN *ANY* EVENT.

STILL, HER RECKLESS *COURAGE* MAY BRING ABOUT THAT END BY *ITSELF*--

--BECAUSE SHE'S TRYING TO BREAK *ARAGORN* TO HER WILL, IN ORDER TO SAVE HIM FROM BEING LEFT ALONE TO *STARVE*--

"--AND A HORSE WHO HAS HAD ONLY *ONE MASTER* DOESN'T TAKE KINDLY TO AN *UNFAMILIAR* RIDER!"

THAT IS ALL DR. STRANGE HAS TIME TO *SAY*-- BEFORE A TINGLING RUSH OF SPARKLING *ATOMS* MARKS THE TERMINATION OF THE DEFENDERS' *TRIP*--

--AND THEY *RETURN* TO THEIR POINT OF *DEPARTURE.*

LOOK, STRANGE! ARAGORN HAS *ACCEPTED* HER!

AND WITHOUT GOING *CHAUVINIST* ON YOU, I *DO* SEEM TO HAVE A *RAPPORT* WITH HORSES.

SURE. *HE'S* A SMART ANIMAL. THOUGH HE LOVES THE KNIGHT WITH HIS EVERY *FIBER*, HE KNOWS HE NEEDS *SOMEONE* TO *CARE* FOR HIM.

I JUST WISH I HADN'T MET ARAGORN UNDER *THESE* CIRCUMSTANCES...

CIRCUMSTANCES I SHALL DO MY UTMOST TO *ALTER*, VALKYRIE. THERE IS *NO* SPELL SO GREAT THAT ANOTHER MAY NOT *UNLOCK* IT.

I SHALL CONVEY DANE WHITMAN TO MY *SANCTUM SANCTORUM*--

--AND SOMEDAY, *SOMEHOW*-- I SHALL *FREE* HIM FROM THIS STATE!

NOW I SHALL MYSTICALLY SEAL *GARRETT CASTLE* FROM ANY POSSIBLE INTRUDERS, AND THE DEFENDERS WILL DEPART FOR *AMERICA.*

NATURALLY. BUT SINCE HE AND I ARE *BOTH* TOTALLY *ALONE* NOW--

BUT WHAT OF *YOU*, GIRL? WILL YOU *CONTINUE* TO CARE FOR ARAGORN?

--I THINK WE'LL COME ALONG WITH *YOU*, AND I'LL BECOME A MEMBER OF THE *DEFENDERS!*

ONE *MINUTE* NOW! THE DEFENDERS HAVE NO "*MEMBERS.*"

WE HAVE ONLY FOUGHT TOGETHER FOR *COMMON CAUSES.* THIS IS NOT THE *AVENGERS!*

FURTHER-- WITH ALL DUE MODESTY, WE *ARE* THREE OF THE MOST POWERFUL PEOPLE IN THE *WORLD.*

WHAT COULD WE POSSIBLY *NEED* YOU FOR?

WELL, FOR *ONE* THING, THERE'S THE *OMEGATRON*--

D MINUS

HOURS
MINUTES
SECONDS
HUNDREDTHS

--WHICH IS VERY CLOSE TO AN *EXPLOSION* THAT WILL RIP THE *WORLD* ASUNDER! SEE WHAT HAPPENS *NEXT*, IN

WORLD WITHOUT END??

TO BE CONTINUED!

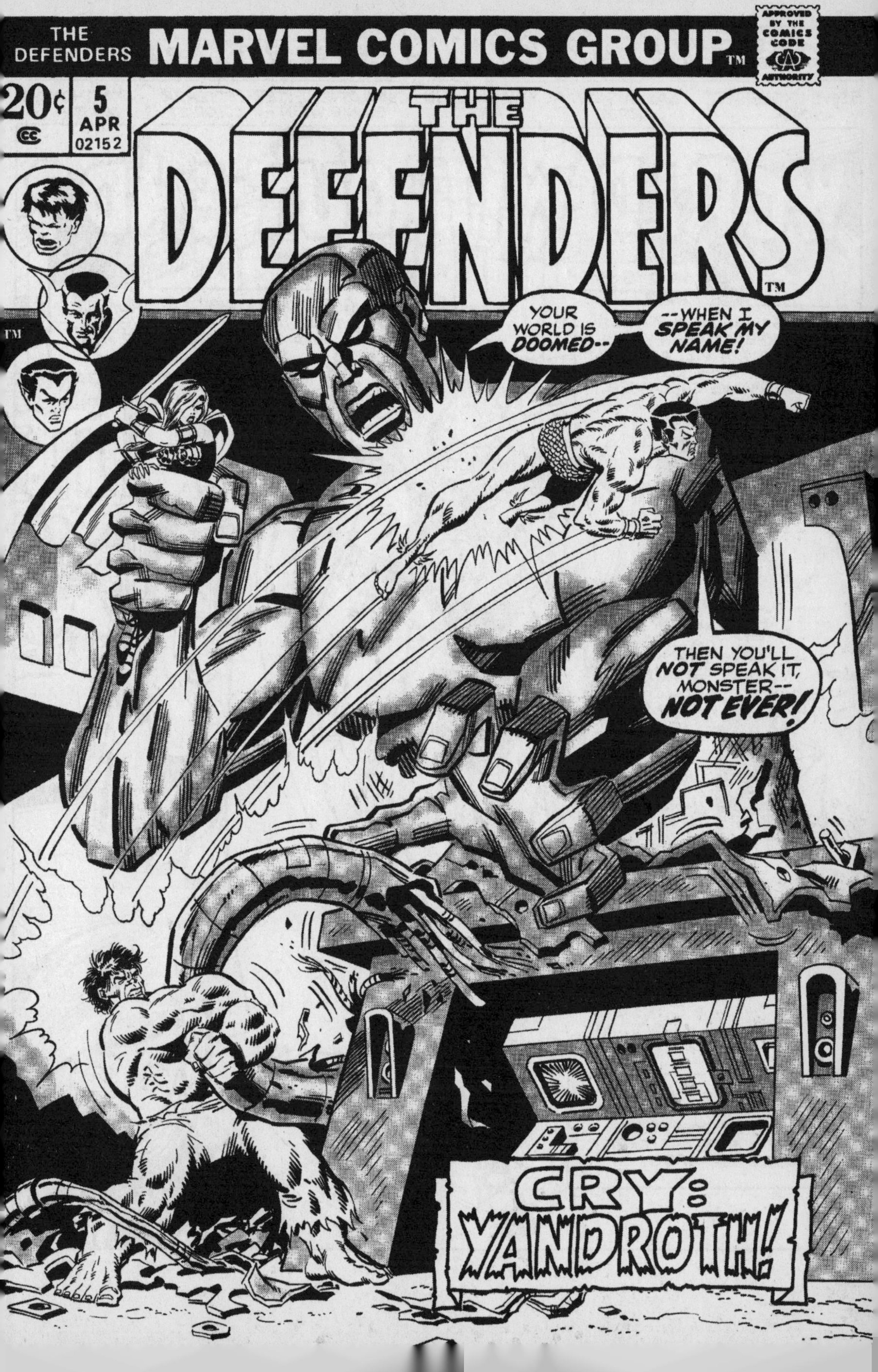
THE DEFENDERS
MARVEL COMICS GROUP™
APPROVED BY THE COMICS CODE AUTHORITY
20¢
5
APR
02152
THE DEFENDERS™
YOUR WORLD IS DOOMED--
--WHEN I SPEAK MY NAME!
THEN YOU'LL NOT SPEAK IT, MONSTER-- NOT EVER!
CRY: YANDROTH!

STAN LEE PRESENTS: THE DYNAMIC DEFENDERS!™

STEVE ENGLEHART • SAL BUSCEMA • F. McLAUGHLIN • CHARLOTTE JETTER—LETTERER • ROY THOMAS
AUTHOR   ARTIST   INKER   GLYNIS WEIN — COLORIST   EDITOR

WORLD WITHOUT END?

WHO IS SHE?

AS THIS LITHE LADY STRIDES THE STREETS OF NEW YORK'S *GREENWICH VILLAGE,* THAT QUESTION RISES TO THE LIPS OF *EVERYONE* SHE PASSES.

BUT, *UNBEKNOWNST* TO THEM ALL, THAT *SAME* PUZZLE PLAYS ITSELF AGAIN AND AGAIN INSIDE *HER* MIND AS WELL!

ANY ITEM $1

VALKYRIE! SUCH IS HER *NAME,* AND THAT SHE KNOWS *WELL*...BUT EVERYTHING *ELSE* SEEMS LOST FOREVER IN A DEEP GRAY *FOG.*

MY MEMORIES... ARE SO *CONFUSED.* I *AM* THE VALKYRIE, CREATED BY THE EVIL *ENCHANTRESS* THROUGH MAGIC TO BEDEVIL HER *ENEMIES.*

THE *FIRST* TIME I TRULY LIVED, I WAS A FORCE IMPOSED UPON *SAMANTHA PARRINGTON*--BUT WHEN THAT SPELL *WORE OFF,* I CEASED TO *EXIST.* *

MELVIN, I'M YOUR *WIFE!* LOOK AT ME!

*THE INCREDIBLE JADE-JAWS #142.--ROY.

THEN THE ENCHANTRESS SUMMONED ME TO *LIFE* AGAIN, TO TRANSFORM THE *MIND* AND *FORM* OF A GIRL NAMED *BARBARA*--

--BUT SINCE THE SORCERESS' POWERS WERE AT THEIR *PEAK, THIS* TIME, I REMAIN ON EARTH, *FREE* OF HER MYSTICAL MASTERY.

YET, WHEN SHE FLED THE *COSMOS,* SHE LEFT ME AS *ALONE* AS ANY BEING COULD EVER *BE.*

SPRINGING *FULL-GROWN* INTO EXISTENCE, I HAVE NO *CHILDHOOD,* NO *HABITS,* NO FEEL FOR DEALING WITH OTHERS--

--AND THE ONLY THREE PEOPLE I *KNOW* HERE ARE THE *DEFENDERS,* WHO CAN'T BE *BOTHERED* WITH ME.

EVEN *DR. STRANGE,* THOUGH ALLOWING ME TO LIVE IN HIS *HOUSE,* FEELS I SHOULD MOVE ON-- CHOOSE A COURSE OF *ACTION.*

BUT HOW *CAN* I? HUMANITY IS NEW, BIZARRE...EVEN *FRIGHTENING* TO ME --AND MY ONE TENUOUS *LINK* TO LIFE IS THROUGH BARBARA--WHO WAS *INSANE!*

WHAT IF SHE SHOULD REGAIN *CONTROL?* I MIGHT ALSO GO MAD, OR EVEN RETURN TO THE *NOTHINGNESS* FROM WHICH I CAME.

WHAT SHOULD I DO?

WHAT'S THAT? *FOOTSTEPS* ...AT MY BACK!

THAT ONE! SHE IS THE WOMAN WHO DWELLS WITHIN THE SANCTUM OF *DR. STRANGE!*

EXCELLENT WORK, HASHID! *LONG* HAVE WE OWED THE MASTER OF THE MYSTIC ARTS A DEBT OF *BLOOD*--

--AND *HERS* SPILLS AS CRIMSON AS *ANY!*

DEATH TO THE FRIEND OF DR. STRANGE!

ONLY IF YOU'RE A BETTER BLADE-WIELDER THAN *I*, MALE.

NO MAN ATTACKS THE *VALKYRIE* WITH IMPUNITY!

NO MAN!!

I DIDN'T NEED THE *EBONY BLADE* I INHERITED FROM THE *BLACK KNIGHT* FOR THAT ONE---

TWO SHOULD BE MORE ITS *STYLE*--AND *MINE!*

ARRGH! THE WENCH FIGHTS LIKE A *TIGER!*

TIGRESS, YOU MEAN!

BY THE DEMONS OF DENAK, I HAVE NEVER *SEEN* SUCH SWORDPLAY!

YET MY *MINIONS* ARE BUT *NOVICES* AT DEALING *DEATH--*

--AND *LIIIIGHH*

VALHALLA! WHAT--?

OH--I MIGHT HAVE *KNOWN* IT WOULD BE... *YOU!*

YOU SEEM DISPLEASED TO *SEE* ME, GIRL.

BUT MY *ENEMIES* APPEARED QUITE CLEARLY IN THE ALL-SEEING *EYE OF AGAMOTTO*, AND DR. STRANGE WAS *OBLIGED* TO HELP *BEST* THEM.

THE *VALKYRIE* NEEDS NO HELP FROM *YOU* OR ANY OTHER *MAN*, STEPHEN STRANGE!

I COULD HAVE BEATEN THEM BY *MYSELF*!

YES, BUT WOULD YOU HAVE *WANTED* TO? I HAVE OBSERVED YOU *CLOSELY* THESE PAST WEEKS, AND IN *MY* OPINION....

YOU NEED *FRIENDS* MORE THAN YOU NEED TO PROVE YOUR *WORTH*.

NO *RESPONSE* PASSES THE WOMAN'S COMPRESSED LIPS-- NEITHER AT THAT TIME NOR AS THE MYSTERIOUS DUO SLOWLY RETURN TO THE MAGE'S *ABODE*....BUT *THEN*:

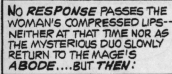

YOU SAY I NEED *FRIENDS*. GIVEN THAT YOU'RE *RIGHT*--

--WHICH WOULD INDICATE AN *UNUSUAL* AMOUNT OF *INSIGHT* FOR A MAN--WHAT WOULD YOU HAVE ME *DO* ABOUT IT?

MY *PERSONALITY*, AS CREATED, ENCOMPASSES A BASIC DISTRUST OF *MEN*--AND YET, MY *AGGRESSIVENESS* SPARKS A SIMILAR DISTRUST FOR *ME* IN OTHER *WOMEN*!

ALREADY, YOUR *CLEA* WISHES I WOULD LEAVE YOUR HOUSE, STEPHEN.

AHHH, HAVING ONLY *MYSELF* TO BROOD UPON THESE LONG WEEKS, I'VE COME TO HAVE COMPLETE *UNDERSTANDING* OF MY PSYCHE.

--ALL THE WAY FROM MY *FLAWS* TO MY *VIRTUES*. IF I KNOW *ANYTHING*-- IT IS WHAT MAKES ME *TICK*.

BUT NO ONE *ELSE* WILL EVER KNOW OF THE *LOVE* THAT BURNS WITHIN ME--THE LOVE FOR A MAN NOW TURNED TO *STONE*: THE *BLACK KNIGHT*!

VALKYRIE, *SHAKESPEARE* ONCE WROTE, "THE LADY DOTH *PROTEST* TOO MUCH."

I URGE YOU TO GO TO *NAMOR*--AND EVEN THE *HULK*--TO SEE IF YOU CAN MAKE *PEACE* WITH THEM.....AND *YOURSELF!*

IF YOU WIN *THEM* OVER, IT COULD MEAN A *START* FOR YOU.

MAYBE. BUT HOW DO I *FIND* THEM?

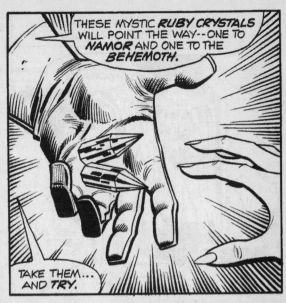

THESE MYSTIC *RUBY CRYSTALS* WILL POINT THE WAY--ONE TO *NAMOR* AND ONE TO THE *BEHEMOTH.*

TAKE THEM... AND *TRY.*

THUS, ONLY MINUTES LATER...

DR. STRANGE IS *RIGHT,* ARAGORN! MY *DESTINY,* FOR NOW, LIES WITH THE *DEFENDERS!*

THEY *CAN'T* REJECT ME, BECAUSE WITHOUT *THEM,* I HAVE ABSOLUTELY *NO ONE* TO TURN TO!

--AND IT DOES ME NO *CREDIT* TO MOAN ABOUT MY *SOLITUDE* IF I DON'T *TRY* FOR FRIENDSHIP!

ONE CRYSTAL POINTS *NORTH*--BUT THE *OTHER* POINTS ALMOST DIRECTLY *DOWN!*

ONE OF THE DEFENDERS MUST BE RIGHT IN THIS *AREA!*

WHEELING, THE WINGED STALLION FLIES ACROSS THE CEMENT FOREST, AND SOON--

WHOA, ARAGORN! ACCORDING TO THE *RUBY,* WE'RE *HERE* ALREADY!

SO VAL *DESCENDS*, TETHERS HER HORSE TO A HANDY *LAMP POST*, AND WALKS TO HER GEM-GUIDED *GOAL*...

EXCUSE ME, SISTER-- I'M LOOKING FOR--

THE SUB-MARINER!

LET HER *IN*, BETTY.

WOW, NAMOR! LOOK AT THAT *OUTFIT*!

NAMOR, I'M *SORRY* TO INTRUDE BUT I *HAVE* TO TALK TO YOU.

I...NEED *FRIENDS*, AND I NEED A *PURPOSE* FOR MY NEW-FOUND LIFE. I THOUGHT, PERHAPS, THE *DEFENDERS*....

I TOLD YOU *BEFORE*, VALKYRIE: THE DEFENDERS ARE *NOT* A FORMAL *TEAM*.

I DO NOT MEAN TO BE *UNKIND*, BUT IN MANY WAYS, *MY* NEEDS ARE THE DIRECT *OPPOSITE* OF YOURS.

BEYOND MY FRIEND, *MRS. PRENTISS*, AND MY COUSIN, *NAMORITA*, I DESIRE *NO* HUMAN CONTACT!

YOU'D DESIRE IT IF YOU'D NEVER *HAD* IT, SUB-MARINER!

HOW *SELF-CENTERED* YOU ARE--!

THE IMPERIAL *PRINCE OF ATLANTIS* TURNS ANGRILY TOWARD THE WARRIOR-WOMAN--BUT HIS EXPECTED *RETORT* NEVER *MATERIALIZES*, BECAUSE:

A *GLOW*, A *BURST*--HIS BODY SHIMMERS INTO A *NEGATIVE IMAGE*---

--AND THE AVENGING SON IS *GONE!!*

SUB-MARINER!

NAMOR! WHAT'S *HAPPENED* TO HIM?

I DON'T *KNOW,* NAMORITA-- BUT HE'S STILL *ALIVE!* THIS ENCHANTED RUBY ALWAYS *POINTS* TOWARD HIM AND IT'S SPUN AROUND IN MY *HAND* TO POINT *NORTH!*

SOMETHING HAS TAKEN HIM *AWAY--* BUT I'M GOING TO GET HIM *BACK!*

WAIT! WHAT ARE *YOU* DOING?

YOU'RE NOT GONNA RESCUE *MY* COUSIN WHILE LITTLE *NITA* SITS AT HOME DARNING SOCKS, LADY!

I'M A REAL LIVE SUB- MARINER, *TOO,* YOU KNOW!

NO, I *DIDN'T* KNOW-- BUT JUDGING FROM THE *WINGS* ON YOUR FEET AND YOUR POINTED *EARS,* I'D BE HARD PUT TO *DENY* IT!

ALL *RIGHT.* THEN, LET'S GET *MOVING!* WE'VE NO TIME TO *WASTE!*

YET, THE VENGEFUL VALKYRIE HAS *FORGOTTEN* THAT SOME- ONE *ELSE* IS *ALSO* TO HER *NORTH!*

SOMEBODY FLIES TOWARD *HULK--* GIRL ON *HORSE!*

SEEMS LIKE HULK SHOULD *REMEMBER* THEM....

YES! HULK *REMEMBERS!* GIRL WAS CALLED...*VAL...* SOMETHING.

HULK *LIKED* HER--

--BUT SHE WANTED HIM TO BE PART OF *DEFENDERS,* INSTEAD OF LETTING HIM BE *ALONE--*

---AND HULK DOESN'T LIKE *THAT!*

HULK *LEAVES.*

THOOM!

BUT VAL AND NITA ARE NOT SO *EASILY* PUT OFF!

HULK, YOU'VE GOT TO *COME* WITH US!

NAMOR'S IN TROUBLE --AND YOU MAY BE *NEXT!*

NO!! GO AWAY!

YOU BUZZ AROUND HULK LIKE *FLIES!*

--AND HULK CAN *CRUSH* FLIES!!

HAH! GIRL HAS NO *WINGS!* SHE FALLS-- AND HULK *WINS!*

IF THIS IS *MY* END, YOU BRAINLESS *MONSTER,* IT'S *YOURS,* TOO!

MY *EBONY BLADE* --

UHHH!

HULK! IT'S HAPPENING *AGAIN!*

HULK!!

HE'S GONE-- VANISHED IN MID-AIR!

--AND I'M LEFT --STILL FALLING!

BUT THEN A STREAK OF *WHITE* FILLS THE YAWNING SKY ABOVE HER, A POUNDING OF GREAT *WINGS* ECHOES IN HER EARS, AND--

ARAGORN! YOU *SAVED* ME!

IT *WAS* HIM, TOO! I TRIED TO *GUIDE* HIM, BUT HE WAS *AHEAD* OF ME!

THE BLACK KNIGHT TRAINED HIM *WELL,* NITA, BUT I HAVE TO *WONDER*--

NEVER HAVING BEEN *BORN*--COULD I HAVE TRULY *DIED?*

WELL, THAT'S *PAST* NOW, AND *PHILOSOPHY* WON'T FIND THE *OTHERS.*

BUT ALTHOUGH, *WHO*-EVER OR *WHATEVER* SPIRITED THEM AWAY DOESN'T *KNOW* IT, WE HAVE SOMETHING THAT *WILL:* THE GEMS!

SEE, NITA: THEY BOTH POINT THE *SAME DIRECTION* NOW! NAMOR AND THE HULK HAVE GONE TO THE SAME *LOCATION*--

--AND SO WILL *WE!*

AFTER THAT, THE MYSTERIOUS MAIDEN SAYS NO *MORE*, AS SHE AND HER FAITHFUL ATLANTEAN *COMPANION* RIDE *HARD* ACROSS THE INK-STREAKED SKIES....UNTIL--

VAL! THAT DESERTED-LOOKING *LIGHTHOUSE*!

FROM WHICH, WE MAY GATHER THAT IT'S NOT *ACTUALLY* DESERTED, DON'T YOU THINK?

THE COAST OF MAINE IS A *PERFECT* SPOT FOR--

BLAM

WHAT IN THE NAME OF NEPTUNE WAS *THAT*?

I *THINK* IT WAS AN INVISIBLE *WALL* --AT LEAST IT *FELT* LIKE IT!

IN *ANY* EVENT, IT PROVES MY *POINT*.

WE'LL HAVE TO APPROACH WITH *CAUTION*!

YOU CAN IF YOU WANT TO! I'VE GOT A *COUSIN* IN THERE, AND THEY MAY BE FRICASSEE-ING HIS *EARS* BY NOW!

MAYBE AT *GROUND LEVEL*, I CAN SL--

BUMPP!

OUCH!!

GIRL, WHEN I SAID "CAUTION," I DIDN'T MEAN "AT A CRAWL"!

ONCE WE DETERMINE EXACTLY WHERE THE WALL IS--

I'LL MATCH MY SORCEROUS SWORD AGAINST IT--

--AND WIN!!

KR-R-PAK-K!

THE VIKING VIXEN BOLTS FORWARD, FOLLOWED CLOSE BY LOVELY NITA--

--AND ONCE INSIDE THE WALL, IT IS NO LONGER INVISIBLE -- BUT THEN, NEITHER IS WHAT LURKS WITHIN!

THE DOOMSDAY DEVICE CHRISTENED, LO, THESE MANY MONTHS AGO, AS--

THE OMEGATRON!

GOOD EVENING.

INHUMANLY SLOWLY IT SPEAKS, STRETCHING EACH VOWEL AND CONSONANT TO THE BREAKING POINT AS IT RUMBLES ITS GREETING...

...BUT SO IT DOESN'T TAKE TWENTY PAGES FOR IT TO UNBURDEN ITSELF -- AND SO CHARLOTTE DOESN'T GET WRITER'S CRAMP -- WE'LL COMPRESS THE MACHINE'S ORATORY TO MANAGEABLE SIZE.

I AM THE **OMEGATRON,** BUILT BY **YANDROTH,** SCIENTIST SUPREME, TO ATOMICALLY **DISINTEGRATE** THIS PLANET.

I RATHER **EXPECTED** WITNESSES.

MONTHS AGO, I ARRANGED FOR THE HULK AND THE SUB-MARINER TO **BATTLE** HERE, THAT THE **VIBRATIONS** OF THEIR CLASH COULD LEND NEEDED **POWER** TO MY **CIRCUITS.**

BUT DR. STRANGE STOPPED **TIME** AROUND ME --- SEEMINGLY **FOREVER** BARRING ME FROM THE MOMENT I WOULD **SCREAM** MY MAKER'S **NAME** AND DOOM THE **EARTH.**

THE MAGE TOOK **ALL** PRECAUTIONS, THEN -- EVEN TO LAYING A SPELL OF **INVISIBILITY** OVER MY CONTOURS--

--SO THAT NO ONE COULD **ACCIDENTALLY** BEGIN ANEW MY COUNTDOWN TO DEATH!*

*ALL THIS IN **MARVEL FEATURE** #1. --- ROY.

YET **LATER,** STRANGE RESTARTED ME **HIMSELF!** IN ATTEMPTING A **SECOND** TIME-STOP ENCHANTMENT, AGAINST **ANOTHER** FOE, HE UN-KNOWINGLY WEAKENED THE **FIRST!***

TIME NOW PASSES AT A **SNAIL'S PACE** FOR ME--BUT IT **PASSES!** AND **MORE,** THE **RATE** OF ITS PASSAGE HAS SUBTLY **INCREASED!**

* **DEFENDERS** #1, THIS TIME.---R.

THOUGH EACH **HUNDRETH** OF A **SECOND** ON MY CHRONO-METER IS THE EQUIVALENT OF **TWO ORDINARY MINUTES** -- THERE ARE BUT **THREE** OF THOSE PERIODS LEFT!

THAT'S **SIX** MINUTES FOR **US** --PLENTY OF TIME TO **DISMANTLE** OR **DESTROY** YOU!

IMPOSSIBLE! THE MAGICIAN TRIED AND **FAILED!** I AM TOO WELL **BUILT!**

BESIDES... YOU WILL BE **OCCUPIED!**

VAL! LOOK! LOOK!

TO OUR *RIGHT:* FIVE *NAMORS!*

AND TO OUR *LEFT:* FIVE *HULKS!*

THE *OMEGATRON* MUST HAVE CONJURED THEM *UP* SOMEHOW!

BUT WHICH ONES ARE *REAL?* WHICH *ONES?*

I DON'T *KNOW,* NITA--POSSIBLY *NONE!* BUT THEY'RE READY TO *ATTACK* US, SO I'LL HAVE TO ASSUME THEY'RE *ALL DEADLY--*

--AND ACT *ACCORDINGLY!*

THIS IS *USELESS!* THEY ALL FEEL SOLID, AND EVEN *I* CAN'T BATTLE *TEN* FOES AS STRONG AS THEY!

BUT THERE'S *ONE* CHANCE!

ARAGORN!!

INSTANTLY, THE STALLION HEEDS THE CALL OF HIS MISTRESS--

ARAGORN, ATTACK!

HE GALLOPS *FORWARD*, STRAIGHT AND *TRUE*--

--AND SLAMS DIRECTLY INTO ONE *PARTICULAR* HULK!

I KNEW IT! THE ILLUSIONS WERE MADE FOR *HUMAN* EYES, NOT THOSE OF AN *ANIMAL!*

CLUD!

NOW THE *OTHER* ONE, ARAGORN!

AGAIN, THE PINIONED PONY *LASHES OUT* WITH HIS FORELEGS, CONNECTING SOLIDLY WITH A GLASSY-EYED *SUB-MARINER.*

THAT *DID* IT! THE ILLUSIONS *FADED AWAY* AS SOON AS WE KNEW WHICH THEY *WERE!*

DON'T SING ANY VICTORY CHANTS *YET*, NITA.

IT LOOKS LIKE THE *REAL* VERSIONS ARE *STILL* TOTALLY UNDER THE MACHINE'S CONTROL--

AND *THEY'RE* QUITE ENOUGH OF A THREAT BY *THEMSELVES!*

CHOKING DOWN *DISMAY,* PLANTING HERSELF *FIRMLY,* VAL THROWS HER ENTIRE *WEIGHT* INTO A SWING!

SPOW!

BUT IT'S *NITA* WHO SEES THE VITAL *DETAIL!*

THEY MOVE LIKE *TURTLES!* BEING DIRECTED BY *ANGLE-PUSS* HAS SLOWED *THEM,* TOO!

HERE, VAL--

BLOD

HE'S MY *COUSIN--* TRY TO HIT 'IM *SOFT!*

I COULD HAVE HIT HIM WITH A *TRUCK,* GIRL!

THEY *WON'T* FALL WHILE THE *OMEGATRON* LIVES!

BUT WE CAN'T EVEN *TOUCH* THE MACHINE WHILE THEY'RE KEEPING US *BUSY--* AND *TIME* IS PASSING US BY!

I'LL HAVE TO TAKE A HUNK OF THIS *SECONDARY* DEVICE--

---AND PRAY IT'S *BETTER* THAN A TRUCK!

NITA, IT DIDN'T **WORK**!

WELL, WE CAN KISS IT ALL **GOODBYE**!

ADMIRABLY **SAID**, WOMAN! IN **NO** WAY WAS THERE A CONTINGENCY OF MY BEING **DEFEATED**--

--AND **NOW**, HAVING ABSORBED THE **VIBRATIONS** FROM YOUR COMBAT AS I PLANNED FROM THE **BEGINNING**--

SEC

| 0 | 0 |

HUNDREDTHS

| 0 | 1 |

IT IS **TIME**!

IT IS TIME!!

SLOWLY, EVER SO **CREAKINGLY** SLOWLY, THE **OMEGATRON** RISES, ASSUMING THE FORM OF A **MAN**--

--**TRANSFORMING** ITSELF INTO THE LITERAL **DEUS EX MACHINA,** THE **GOD** FROM THE **MACHINE**--

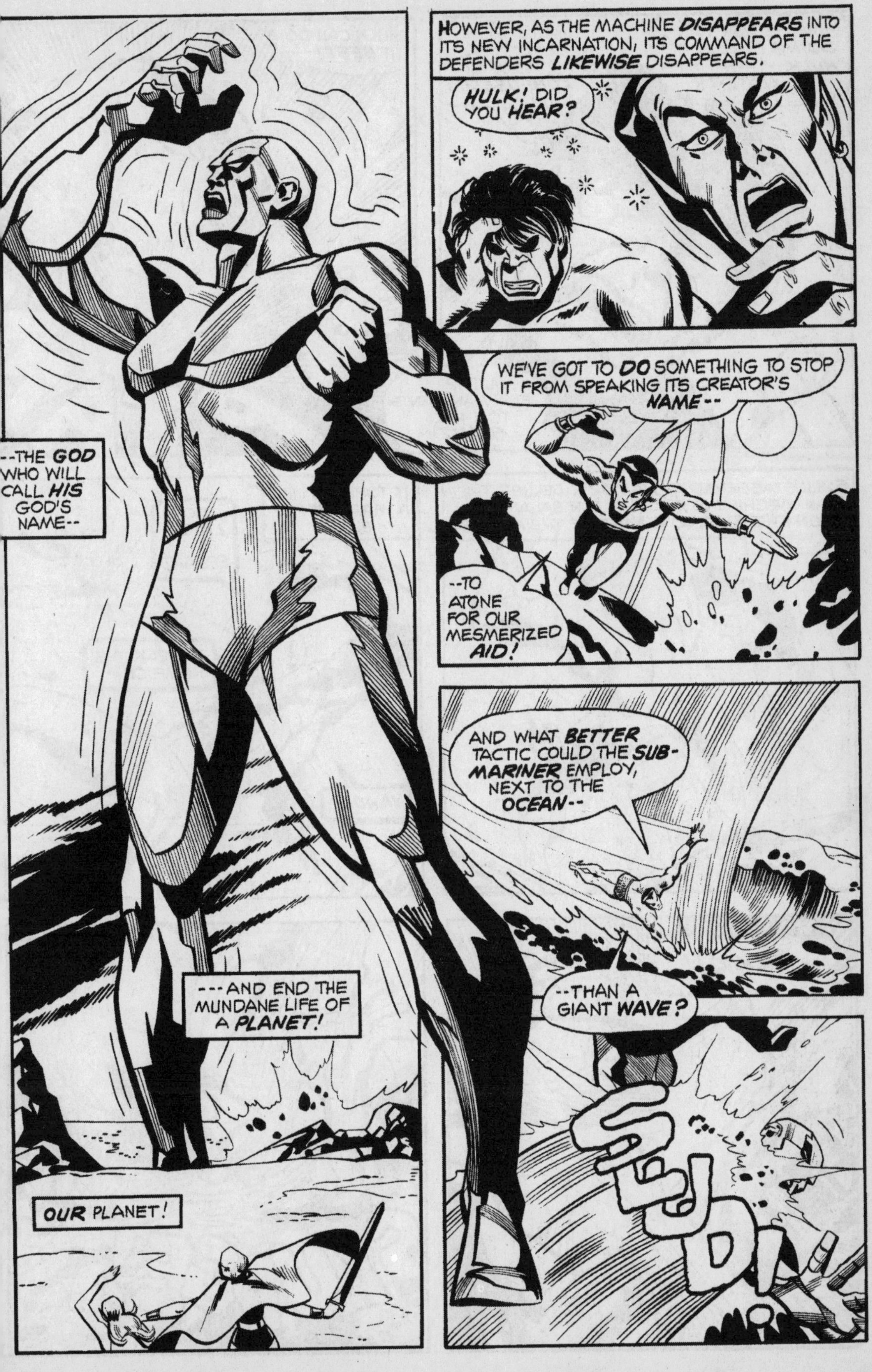
--THE GOD WHO WILL CALL HIS GOD'S NAME--
---AND END THE MUNDANE LIFE OF A PLANET!
OUR PLANET!
HOWEVER, AS THE MACHINE DISAPPEARS INTO ITS NEW INCARNATION, ITS COMMAND OF THE DEFENDERS LIKEWISE DISAPPEARS.
HULK! DID YOU HEAR?
WE'VE GOT TO DO SOMETHING TO STOP IT FROM SPEAKING ITS CREATOR'S NAME--
--TO ATONE FOR OUR MESMERIZED AID!
AND WHAT BETTER TACTIC COULD THE SUB-MARINER EMPLOY, NEXT TO THE OCEAN--
--THAN A GIANT WAVE?

WHAT IS FISH-MAN *DOING?* YELLS AT *HULK*-- THEN JUMPS INTO *WATER?*

HULK IS *CONFUSED*...

BUT IF FISH-MAN WANTS TO FIGHT *GIANT*--

HULK CAN DO IT *BEST!*

STILL STAGGERED BY *NAMOR'S* DELUGE, THE MAN-MACHINE IS GROPING FOR BALANCE WHEN THE *SHOCK-WAVES* OF THE *HULK'S* BLOW HIT!

IT TOPPLES LIKE A *MARIONETTE* -- BUT:

TOO *LATE!* I *SPEAK!*

I SPEAK THE NAME OF--

YANDR--

--AKKK!!

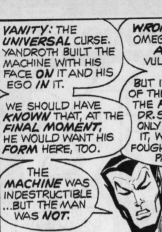

VANITY: THE *UNIVERSAL* CURSE. YANDROTH BUILT THE MACHINE WITH HIS FACE *ON* IT AND HIS EGO *IN* IT.

WE SHOULD HAVE *KNOWN* THAT, AT THE *FINAL MOMENT,* HE WOULD WANT HIS *FORM* HERE, TOO.

THE *MACHINE* WAS INDESTRUCTIBLE ...BUT THE MAN WAS *NOT.*

WRONG, NAMOR! THE OMEGATRON WAS *ALWAYS* VULNERABLE!

BUT IT WAS A MIXTURE OF THE *MAGICAL* AND THE *PHYSICAL*--AND DR. STRANGE COULD ONLY FIGHT A *PART* OF IT, WHILE YOU TWO FOUGHT THE *OTHER* PART.

ON THE OTHER HAND, *MY PHYSICAL* FORM EXISTS ONLY THROUGH MAGIC! MY *SWORD* ALSO HAS THAT PROPERTY.*

I KNEW, IF I COULD EVER GET THE *CHANCE,* I COULD *DESTROY* THE OMEGATRON! I FELT IT IN EVERY FIBER OF MY *BEING!*

DO YOU *STILL* FEEL I'M *USELESS,* DEFENDERS?

* SEE *MARVEL SUPER-HEROES* #17. ---WRAP-IT-UP ROY.

BAH! GIRL WANTS TO TALK ABOUT *GROUP* AGAIN!

HULK *DOESN'T.* HULK IS *LEAVING!*

HULK THINKS GIRL IS *CRAZY!*

YES, THE VALKYRIE AND THE MACHINE *ARE* VERY MUCH ALIKE...EVEN TO THEIR *VULNERABILITY!*

I'M...SORRY I ASKED...

WAIT, VALKYRIE. YOU COULD EXPECT NO *OTHER* REACTION FROM THE MONSTER'S FEEBLE BRAIN.

BUT IF *I* MAY ANSWER YOUR QUESTION: *NO, I NO LONGER* FEEL AS I DID.

YOU HAVE DEMONSTRATED UNCOMMON *BRAVERY* AND AN ANALYTICAL *MIND* TODAY.

LET ME *ACCOMPANY* YOU AS YOU RETURN TO NEW YORK.

...FOR WE HAVE MUCH TO *TALK* ABOUT.

MAYBE... A *BEGINNING!*

THE DEFENDERS
MARVEL COMICS GROUP
20¢
6
JUNE
02152
THE
DEFENDERS
DREAM-DEATH!
BONUS
THE
SILVER
SURFER
RETURNS!

THE DREAMS of DEATH!

Stan Lee PRESENTS: THE DYNAMIC DEFENDERS!™

TOO *LONG* HAS THE SKY-RIDING *SILVER SURFER* HIDDEN AND BROODED, BLAMING *OTHERS* FOR THE MISFORTUNES OF *CHANCE!*

TODAY *THIS* WHOLE *PLANET* SEEMS POSSESSED OF *CLEAN AIR* AND *SUNSHINE* -- AS IF TO *APPLAUD* MY DECISION TO ONCE AGAIN SEEK OUT *MANKIND.*

TODAY, THE SILVER SURFER *REJOINS* THE *WORLD!*

THE *LEGEND MAKERS* LADLE IT OUT AGAIN-- AND WE *DO* MEAN *STEVE ENGLEHART,* author

SAL BUSCEMA, artist

NOT TO MENTION *FRANK McLAUGHLIN,* inker

JOHN COSTANZA, LETTERER
DAVID HUNT, COLORIST
ROY THOMAS, EDITOR

IN A *WAY*, IT COMES AS A *RELIEF* TO FIND THAT I MAY STILL ACT *IRRATIONALLY*, AFTER MY MANY YEARS OF LIVING *APART* FROM HUMANITY.

I MAY GLISTEN LIKE SOME COLD *MACHINE*, YET STILL I KNOW "THE THOUSAND NATURAL SHOCKS THAT *FLESH* IS HEIR TO"-- AND THAT IS *GOOD*.

HOWEVER, I HAVE *HURT* MY FRIENDS -- BLAMING *DR. STRANGE* FOR BEING UNABLE TO TAKE ME PAST GALACTUS' *BARRIER* (FOR REASONS THE *SUB-MARINER* HAD EVEN *WARNED* ME ABOUT)*--

--AND I MUST *APOLOGIZE* BEFORE I DO *ANYTHING* ELSE.

*IN OUR ALREADY-CLASSIC *THIRD ISSUE.* --ROY.

I WILL FLY TO THE MYSTIC'S *SANCTUM* AND -- BUT WHAT IS *THIS?*

A STRANGE, PULSATING *GLOW* SUFFUSES THE *SKY* IN THAT DIRECTION.

WHY-- THERE IS A *CUBE* HERE, COVERING THE ENTIRE *BLOCK*--

--THE BLOCK UPON WHICH *DWELLS* DR. STRANGE!

HEY! WHO OR WHAT IS *THAT?*

UMM.... I *READ* ABOUT HIM A FEW MONTHS BACK... IT'S ONE OF THOSE *SUPER* GUYS... UMM...

I THINK IT'S THE... *SILVER SWIMMER.*

I CAN'T KEEP TRACK.

I AM THE *SILVER SURFER.* WHAT HAS *HAPPENED* HERE, OFFICER?

I DUNNO, *SIR*. THE DARN THING JUST APPEARED OUT OF *THIN AIR* MAYBE TWO... THREE *MINUTES* AGO. WE CAN'T BREAK *THROUGH!*

WHY?

DO NOT *EXCITE* YOURSELF. I HAD *NOTHING* TO DO WITH THIS BOX.

I CANNOT TELL HIM THAT A *FRIEND* OF MINE MAY BE TRAPPED WITHIN. I DO NOT *KNOW* WHETHER STRANGE COURTS *PUBLICITY* OR NOT THESE DAYS.

STAND *ASIDE.* PERHAPS I MAY PIERCE THE BARRIER.

THE *IRONY* OF HIS WORDS IS NOT *LOST* ON THE METALLIC OTHER-WORLDER, BUT HE PUSHES *ASIDE* THE THOUGHT TO ACHIEVE FULL *CONCENTRATION* FOR A SINGLE BURST OF HIS *COSMIC POWER.*

*I*T CAUSES ONLY A *SWIRLING* OF THE WALLS COLORS.

THIS WILL REQUIRE EVEN *MORE* EFFORT IF I AM TO SUCCEED.

PLEASE *EVACUATE* THIS AREA AT ONCE. *TRUST* ME.

WHAT I AM ABOUT TO DO WILL REQUIRE *ALL* OF MY POWER, YET THE FEELING OF *MENACE* IS *QUITE* PRONOUNCED NEAR THE CUBE!

STRANGE IS IN MORTAL *DANGER* --

-- SO I MUST HURTLE WITH *FULL* VELOCITY TOWARD THAT PRISON --

-- AND SMASH IT HEAD-ON!

PLAM!

CRUSHED A *BUILDING* BEFORE I COULD STOP--

--BUT I'M *THROUGH!*

BY THE HEAD OF MY *FATHER!* DR. STRANGE'S HOUSE IS UNDER *ATTACK!*

YOUR HOUR HAS *COME,* STRANGE! THE *BELL* TOLLS FOR *THEE!*

MY POWER IS AT ITS *HEIGHT,* AND YOU MUST *FALL* BEFORE CYRUS BLACK, THE *DEVIL INCARNATE!*

INSIDE THE BESIEGED BUILDING, THREE PAIRS OF EYES STARE UNBLINKING AND *ON-AFRAID* AT THE TALL MAN IN THE ORNATE ROBES --EYES BELONGING TO THE MUCH-DISCUSSED *DR. STRANGE,* HIS HOUSEGUEST, THE *VALKYRIE,* AND AN UNLUCKY VISITOR, PRINCE *NAMOR.*

CYRUS BLACK! OUR PATHS CROSSED *ONCE,* IN MY *EARLY* DAYS AS A SORCERER--

--BUT HE STRUCK ME AS A DISTINCTLY *MINOR* MAGICIAN.

HE LOOKS GOOD *NOW,* THOUGH-- HE SEEMS TO BE THE *MASTERMIND* BEHIND THIS GROUP!*

* REMEMBER THEM FROM LAST ISSUE-? --ROY

"MINOR MAGICIAN"? HA!

I HAVE SPENT YEARS OF STUDY, TRAINING MYSELF TO BECOME BETTER THAN YOU, STRANGE!

OBSERVE AS I CREATE NECROMANTIC LADDERS FOR MY APPRENTICES TO SCALE, IN ORDER TO AFFECT THEIR ENTRANCE!

AND YOU OBSERVE THAT MY EBONY BLADE, BEING BOTH MAGICAL AND PHYSICAL IN ORIGIN, CAN SLICE THROUGH YOUR PRECIOUS LADDERS!

YOU MAY ATTACK, BUT WE ARE THE DEFENDERS!

DIE, SUB-MARINER! DIE IN THE NAME OF THE DEVIL INCARNATE!

I HAVE TOLD THAT GIRL NOT TO VIEW US AS A TEAM -- EH?

THESE HENCHMEN HAVE FEW MAGICAL WILES AND LESS STRENGTH, BUT THEY KEEP COMING!

HA! STRANGE'S INCANTATION TO HOLD HIS DOOR CLOSED CANNOT STAND AGAINST MY AWESOME MIGHT!

ENTER, DISCIPLES -- AND KILL!

IT HAS TAKEN ME *LONG MOMENTS* TO REGAIN MY SPENT POWER, BUT *NOW*, AT *LAST*--

--THE SILVER SURFER SAYS *NO!*

THE *SURFER!* QUICKLY-- MY MYSTIC *MIGHT* HAD TO BE USED TO GUARD *ALL* POSSIBLE ENTRANCES, SO BLACK WAS ABLE TO OPEN MY *DOOR*--

--BUT I AM ABOUT TO *SEAL* THOSE PORTALS *AGAIN* AND *COMPLETELY!*

IF YOU WISH TO *ENTER*, IT MUST BE *NOW*-- FOR LATER IT WILL BE *IMPOSSIBLE!*

...THE SILVER SURFER WILL FIGHT *WITH* HIS FRIENDS!

IMPOSSIBLE? MAYBE OR MAYBE *NOT*, BUT--

WE MAY NOT EVEN *NEED* THE SURFER'S AID, DOCTOR! I BEGIN TO *FEEL* THAT OUR ASSAILANTS ARE NO MATCH FOR *ONE* OF US, LET ALONE *FOUR!*

PERHAPS YOU ARE *CORRECT*, ATLANTEAN--

--BUT WE WILL BE *WISE* NOT TO REGARD OURSELVES AS *WINNERS* BEFORE *WINNING!*

MY *MEN!* THEY ARE BEING *OVERCOME* WITH NO *DIFFICULTY!*

AND NOW, TWO *MORE* ARE STRUCK FROM *ANOTHER* DIRECTION!

MY PLAN FALLS *APART!*

THE SHIMMERING *CUBE* -- THE SPELL TO FORCE THE *DOORS* --

YOUR SCHEME HAD *TOUCHES* OF GREATNESS, CYRUS BLACK, BUT *BASICALLY* IT WAS FORMED MORE BY *EGO* THAN *REASON!*

IT COULD *NOT* SUCCEED!

YOU TALK TO THE *DEVIL INCARNATE* IN SUCH A MANNER?!!

HERE -- MAY THESE *BOLTS* OF *BEDEVILMENT* TURN YOU TO *SLIME!*

YOU'VE *LOST*, BLACK -- YOUR BOLTS BARELY REACHED THE *HOUSE!*

DO NOT *RESIST.* AS I RENDER YOU *IMMOBILE!*

THE MARAUDING MAGICIAN'S *SPELL OF PROTECTION* IS BARELY *BEGUN* WHEN DR. STRANGE'S *ENCHANTMENTS* WASH OVER HIM --

-- AND, WITH A PITIABLE LOOK OF TOTAL *AMAZEMENT*, BLACK FEELS HIS ENERGY *DRAIN* FROM HIM LIKE WATER FROM A *GUTTER!*

HOWEVER, JUST AT THAT TIME...

HIS *BOLTS.'* THEY STRUCK THE *BLACK KNIGHT!*

HE'S *SHAKING!* HE'LL *BREAK!*

IT'S *ALL RIGHT* -- I *HAVE* IT! I CAN *LEECH* THE HARMFUL POWER FROM THE STATUE AND LEAVE IT *WHOLE!*

BUT WHILE *WE* WERE ALL AWAY FROM THE *WINDOW*, THE *"DEVIL INCARNATE"* HAS *VANISHED* -- ALONG WITH *EVERY ONE* OF HIS *MINIONS!*

I ONLY WISH I COULD *LIKEWISE* STEAL THE SPELL WHICH *KEEPS* THIS MAN A STATUE!

IF YOU WISH TO BE THANKFUL FOR *SMALL* FAVORS, THOUGH--

THEY TOOK THEIR *MYSTICAL ENCLOSURE* WITH THEM.

SO! BLACK UNDERESTIMATED ME... BUT *I* UNDERESTIMATED *HIM.*

HE OBVIOUSLY WAS ABLE TO *PARTIALLY* NEGATE MY SPELL, IN ORDER TO SPIRIT HIMSELF AND HIS FORCES *AWAY!*

THE MAN IS *FLAWED,* BUT NONETHELESS *DANGEROUS* FOR *THAT!*

I WASN'T *AWARE* THAT HE BORE ME SUCH GREAT *ENMITY* FROM OUR LONG-AGO ENCOUNTER-- BUT I SHALL BE ON MY *GUARD* IN THE FUTURE.

I THANK ALL OF *YOU* FOR YOUR AID IN THIS INSTANCE.

THAT'S WHAT PARTNER'S ARE *FOR,* STEPHEN.

...WHICH LEADS ME TO THE SILVER *STRANGER.*

EXCUSE ME, VALKYRIE, I FORGOT YOU KNOW SO *LITTLE* OF THIS WORLD.

THIS IS THE *SILVER SURFER,* A MAN FROM THE PLANET *ZENN-LA* NOW *TRAPPED* ON EARTH.

HE IS AN OLD *ALLY* OF NAMOR'S AND MINE.

THAT IS *UNNECESSARY,* SURFER. WE *UNDERSTOOD* YOUR FRUSTRATION.

AN ALLY WHO WISHES TO *APOLOGIZE* FOR HIS *BEHAVIOR* LAST TIME, DOCTOR.

THANK YOU, AND WHO IS THE YOUNG *LADY?*

DON'T CALL ME A *LADY*-- I'M *SORRY.* THAT'S PART OF THE ENCHANTRESS' *SPELL* TALKING.

YOU SEE, I WAS *CREATED* BY THE SORCERESS BY FUSING AN *EXISTING* PERSONALITY-- THE FIERCELY *LIBERATED* VALKYRIE--

--WITH THE PERSONALITY OF A *LIVING* WOMAN.

THE *VALKYRIE* SIDE OF ME IS THE *STRONGEST*-- WHICH MAKES IT *HARD,* BECAUSE SHE HAS ONLY LIVED *BRIEFLY* BEFORE.

I FEEL AS IF I'M NEWLY *BORN*-- WHILE STILL BEING FULLY *GROWN.*

YES, I *KNOW* THAT FEELING. I MYSELF WAS CHANGED FROM AN *ADULT MAN*--

--INTO THIS METALLIC *WANDERER* SO DIFFERENT FROM *ANYTHING* I HAD EVER EXPERIENCED.

IT MAKES YOU FEEL VERY *SMALL.*

VALKYRIE, I WAS PLANNING TO FLY ACROSS THE WORLD-- *OBSERVING* IT, BASKING IN THE SHEER NUMBER OF *PEOPLE* ON IT!

WOULD YOU LIKE TO COME *WITH* ME, SO THAT I MIGHT *TELL* YOU WHAT I HAVE FOUND THIS PLANET TO *BE*--

--AND *SHOW* IT TO YOU AT THE SAME TIME?

I'D *LOVE* IT! I'LL JUST FETCH MY HORSE, *ARAGORN!*

IF YOU DO NOT *OBJECT,* SURFER, I WOULD ENJOY ACCOMPANYING YOU.

AS A MATTER OF *FACT, I* HAD BEEN TEACHING THE MAIDEN OF THIS SPHERE.

OF *COURSE,* MY FRIEND! WHEN THE SILVER SURFER IS IN THE *MOOD* FOR PEOPLE, HE DESIRES AS *MANY* NEARBY AS *POSSIBLE!*

WE SHALL *ALL* GO!

SLIPPING THROUGH THE HEAVENS, SUNLIGHT FLASHING FROM STALLION AND BOARD, THE TRIO PASS LIGHTLY OVER THE CITY...

...YET HAD THEY LOOKED AT ONE PARTICULAR HOUSE THEIR SHADOWS FELL ACROSS--

--THEY WOULD *NOT* HAVE LEFT THE CITY AT *ALL!*

BY THE UNSPEAKABLE *UMAR!*

BLAM!

YEARS! FOR *YEARS* I HAVE SLAVED TO BECOME A BETTER MYSTIC THAN *STEPHEN STRANGE!*

I MADE *PILGRIMAGES--* STUDIED AT THE FEET OF *ADEPTS* THE WORLD HAS NOT SEEN IN *200 YEARS!* I *KILLED* TO OBTAIN BOOKS *FORBIDDEN* BY ALL HUMAN *SOCIETIES!*

AND *STILL* HE BEAT ME!

CURSE HIM! CURSE HIM!!

AHHH... BUT THAT IS EXACTLY THE *POINT*, NEBUCHADNEZZAR; I HAD NOT THE POWER TO CURSE THE MAN. HE IS THE *MASTER* OF THE MYSTIC ARTS... AND I AM ONLY A *PRETENDER* TO THE THRONE.

IT'S NOT *MY* FAULT. I CANNOT BE *BLAMED* FOR HIS HAVING HAD THE THRICE-PLAGUED *ANCIENT ONE* AS HIS MENTOR!

BUT SOMEDAY... *SOMEDAY*...

WELL, *COME*, MY RODENT COMPANION --*BROODING* WILL NOT HELP ME.

LET US IGNITE THIS *BRAZIER* OF NEW JAMAICAN *INCENSE* AND RETIRE FOR SOME WELL-DESERVED *REST*.

IF ONLY STRANGE WERE A LESS *HONORABLE* MAN -- IF ONLY HE WOULD COME TO ATTACK *ME! THEN* I WOULD SHOW HIM!

THE JAMAICAN INCENSE ALWAYS *PROTECTS* MY PERSON FROM ANY ASSAULT BY THE *OUTSIDE WORLD* -- AND THIS *NEW* LOT IS SAID TO BE *PARTICULARLY* POWERFUL. STRANGE WOULD BE IN FOR A *SHOCK* IF HE FOUND ME *NOW*!

BUT HE PROBABLY FEELS HIMSELF IN NO *DANGER* FROM ME-- EH, NEBUCHADNEZZAR?

ODD... THE MYSTIC *RUNES* I WISHED TO STUDY *SWIM* BEFORE MY EYES...

...CAN'T STAY *AWAKE*... I...

...DREAMING...

I... SEEM TO BE... STANDING ON *SOLID GROUND*...

MY EYES... SHOW ME *NOTHING*...BUT I CAN *FEEL* IT... UNDERNEATH MY *FEET*...

WHAT'S... HAPPENED... TO ME...?

I THOUGHT...I WAS *ASLEEP*-- BUT NOW I'M IN SOME UNKNOWN *REALM*... I THINK.

THE *INCENSE*...IT *MUST* BE THE INCENSE! BUT IT'S NEVER HAPPENED *BEFORE*!

I MUST--

EERRRK!

WHAT'S THAT--

BY THE GODS!

NEBUCHADNEZZAR-- A GIANT!

EERRRK!

HE'S *ATTACKING!* HELP!

HIS WEIGHT-- *CRUSHING* ME! AND I CAN *SMELL* HIM--FEEL HIS *SALIVA* FALL ON MY *THROAT!*

NO! NO! THIS *CAN'T* BE REAL! IT *MUST* BE A DREAM!

BUT HE'S *CLAWING* ME-- *RIPPING* ME--

NO! I HAVE TO WAKE UP! WAKE--

UP!

IN THE NAMES OF THE *MONSTROUS ZOM* AND THE SHADES OF THE *SHADOWY DEMONS!* WHAT A HORRIBLE, HORRIBLE *NIGHTMARE!*

IT SEEMED SO *REAL--* AND I COULDN'T *ESCAPE* IT! FOR ONE CHILLING *MOMENT,* I TRULY *BELIEVED* NEBUCHAD-NEZZAR *ACTUALLY* HAD--

EEERRK!

AAAAAA!!!

EEERRK!

HOLD! THE RAT *SHRINKS* AS I WATCH!

BY THE *GODS!* I HAVE GONE *MAD!*

UNLESS... UNLESSSSS...

UNLESS, *SOMEHOW,* MY *NIGHTMARE* BECAME *REALITY* UNDER THE INFLUENCE OF THAT INCENSE!

NOW *WAIT,* CYRUS-- YOU TALK LIKE A CREDULOUS CHILD! THIS IS *ABSURD...*

...BUT IT *MUST* BE THE *TRUTH!* THERE *IS* NO OTHER EXPLANATION FOR WHAT I HAVE JUST BEEN THROUGH!

BY THE ILLUSIONS OF IKONN! WHAT *POWER* HAS FALLEN INTO MY *GRASP?*

I MAY YET BE *MISTAKEN...* BUT IF I AM *NOT--* IF I ACTUALLY *CAN* INVENT REALITY WITH MY *DREAMS...*

...DR. STRANGE AND HIS FRIENDS WILL KNOW THE *REVENGE* OF CYRUS BLACK!

CUT NOW, TO A TIME TWO DAYS *LATER*, AS THE LIMITS OF METROPOLITAN *NEW YORK* ONCE MORE GREET THREE WEARY *TRAVELERS*.

AND *SOME* ARE MORE WEARY THAN *OTHERS*.

I HOPE YOU WERE *AMUSED*, VAL.

OH *YES!* WHILE I CAN'T *AGREE* WITH THE SURFER ON SEVERAL OF HIS VIEWPOINTS, I WAS VERY *GLAD* TO AT LEAST BE *PRESENTED* WITH THEM.

WE CAN *CONTINUE* OUR TALK WHEN WE REACH *DR. STRANGE'S*, VAL.

WAIT! WHAT'S HAPPENING *NOW*?

OBVIOUSLY, THE MAGE HAS INITIATED AN *INVISIBILITY SCREEN* TO HIDE HIS VISITORS FROM THE *PUBLIC*.

I WOULD IMAGINE HE *SIMILARLY* CAST A SPELL OF *FORGETFULNESS* OVER THE PEOPLE WHO WITNESSED CYRUS BLACK'S *CUBE*.

I CAN *CONTINUE* THIS TALK IF YOU'D LIKE.

NOW, *NAMOR*...

WHY SO *GRIM*, STEPHEN?

THERE IS A *FEELING* IN THE AIR, VALKYRIE-- OF *DANGER*...

SOMEWHERE, A SLEEP-DRUGGED VOICE MURMURS "THEY ARE *TOGETHER* ONCE MORE. IT IS *TIME*." AND HERE APPEARS THE *RESULT* OF THAT THOUGHT--

BY THE HOARY HOSTS OF HOGGOTH!

RROKKKH!

:UHHH!:

STRANGE HAD NO TIME FOR *DEFENSE*--

--BUT, BEING FURTHER *AWAY*--

--I *DO!*

UURRR!

DEFENSE, *YES*-- AND ALSO *ATTACK!*

THE BLISTERING BOLT OF THE SPACE-BORN SENTINEL'S *POWER COSMIC* ROCKETS INTO THE DEADLY CREATURE'S GAPING MAW--A SINGLE CRY OF MUFFLED *AGONY* BUBBLES PAST ITS BURNING, HEAVING TONGUE--

--AND IT IS *GONE*, AS *SUDDENLY* AND AS *INEXPLICABLY* AS IT APPEARED.

SOMEWHERE, A DREAM-LADEN VOICE MUMBLES "I MUST TRY *HARDER.*"

HOW COULD ANYTHING BE *SOLID* ENOUGH TO HURT STRANGE--

--AND THEN VANISH LIKE A *MIRAGE?* IT MAKES NO *SENSE!*

HURRY WITH YOUR *ANSWER* IF YOU'VE *GOT* ONE, NAMOR--

--BECAUSE IT'S HAPPENING *AGAIN!*

BUT I THINK OUR ONLY ANSWER LIES IN *BATTLE!*

AND MY *EBONY BLADE* WILL *PROVIDE* IT!

MISSSSSSSSSSSED!

TO BESSSST THE SSSSERPENT OF RHAM, ONE MUSSSST DESS;TROY ALL OF ITSSS HEADSSSS!

:UHHHH!: IT'S CRUSHING--ME--!

PERHAPS YOUR ANSWER IS THE ONE I MUST HEED AFTER ALL, VAL!

IF BATTLE IT MUST BE--

THOM!

--THE TRUE SUB-MARINER WILL BE TRIUMPHANT!

YET I CANNOT FORCE MYSELF TO BELIEVE THAT MERE COMBAT WILL END THIS PARADE OF MONSTERS PERMANENTLY!

GIVE ME YOUR HAND, GIRL!

SOMEWHERE, A WIZARD SMILES IN HIS SLEEP.

THE SERPENT OF RHAM! BUT-- THAT WAS ONLY A MYTHOLOGICAL MONSTER. IT NEVER TRULY EXISTED.

WHAT DO YOU THINK, STEPHEN? DO YOU BELIEVE WE'VE SEEN THE LAST OF THIS?

ON THE CONTRARY, FEMALE--IT GETS WORSE!

MUCH WORSE!

CYRUS BLACK! I SHOULD HAVE KNOWN!

STILL, WE BEAT YOU BEFORE, AND WE WILL AGAIN, NO MATTER WHAT YOUR SIZE!

IF YOU SAY SO, STRANGE--

--BUT I'D LIKE TO SEE YOU TRY!

YOUR SPELLS-- YOUR SILVERY FRIEND'S COSMIC BLASTS-- THEY ARE AS NOTHING!

NOTHING!!

YOU *MOCKED* ME BEFORE, STRANGE! YOU MADE ME FEEL *INFERIOR* TO YOU!

BUT NOW IT IS *YOU* WHO SHALL LEARN THE *TRUE* MEANING OF--

--*POWER!!*

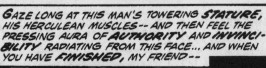

GAZE LONG AT THIS MAN'S TOWERING *STATURE,* HIS HERCULEAN MUSCLES-- AND THEN FEEL THE PRESSING AURA OF *AUTHORITY* AND *INVINCIBILITY* RADIATING FROM THIS FACE... AND WHEN YOU HAVE *FINISHED,* MY FRIEND--

--YOU WILL KNOW THE IMAGE CYRUS BLACK'S EGO PAINTS OF HIMSELF!

... AN IMAGE THAT NOW EXISTS IN *FLESH* AND *BONE!*

ANYTHING CYRUS BLACK *WANTS* TO HAPPEN-- *WILL* HAPPEN! AND HOW CAN THESE BRAVE *DEFENDERS* KNOW THAT THEIR CAUSE IS *HOPELESS? HOW?*

NO ONE IS MY *MASTER* NOW, STRANGE! NO ONE IS EVEN MY *EQUAL!*

BUT THESE *OTHERS* ARE ONLY *TOYS* TO ME!

IT IS YOUR COMPLETE DESTRUCTION THAT WILL *TRULY* SATISFY ME-- THAT AND *NOTHING ELSE!*

WHERE IS YOUR EASY *SUPERIORITY*, MAGICIAN? WHERE IS *ANY* VESTIGE OF YOUR MYSTICAL *MIGHT*?

BY THE *GODS*-- I DO *NOT* KNOW!

MY SPELLS WILL NOT *COME!* I AM *HELPLESS* BEFORE HIM-- AND HE IS *KILLING* ME!

IN NEPTUNE'S NAME, BLACK, YOU CANNOT--

NEPTUNE?

WATER! I AM NOT *WEAK* FROM LACK OF *WATER*--

--BUT I HAVE BEEN *WITHOUT* IT FAR BEYOND MY NORMAL *LIMIT!*

THEN-- THIS IS *NOT* REALITY AS I *KNOW* IT!

THIS IS SOMETHING *ARTIFICIAL*--SOMETHING *CREATED* BY OUR FOE!

BLACK-- *LISTEN* TO ME! I *UNDERSTAND* YOUR GAME NOW!

YOU'VE *INVENTED* THIS: THE MYTHOLOGICAL *MONSTERS* COME TO LIFE--DR. STRANGE'S LACK OF *POWER* AGAINST YOU--

--YOU EVEN INVENTED *YOURSELF* IN THE UNSTOPPABLE FORM YOU NOW HOLD!

OH NO! THIS IS *ME*! THIS IS THE WAY I *AM*!

THINK, BLACK--YOU KNOW IT AS WELL AS *I* DO! YOU DON'T REALLY *EXIST* HERE WITH US!

NONSENSE! OF *COURSE* I EXIST!

THINK, BLACK!

NO! I KNOW I'M REAL! I KNOW I'M *REAL!* I--

FSST!

OOOHHHH!!

NAMOR! NOW HE *DOES* NEED WATER!

IS THIS *ENOUGH?* AM I IN *TIME?*

YOU'RE... DOING JUST *FINE,* VAL.

I WILL RECOVER --AND SO WILL EVERY-ONE *ELSE.*

YES, BUT... IF THE CYRUS BLACK *WE* SAW DIDN'T *EXIST*-- IF THE ENTIRE *SITUATION* WAS UNREAL--

WHY DO ITS *EFFECTS*-- OUR *INJURIES,* THE DAMAGE TO MY *DWELLING*-- REMAIN?

THAT IS WHAT THE *SUB-MARINER* ASKED TO BEGIN WITH, DOCTOR.

APPARENTLY, AS LONG AS BLACK-- WHEREVER HE *REALLY* IS-- *BELIEVED* IN WHAT HE WAS DOING, IT WAS *REAL.* HE ACTUALLY *COULD* HAVE KILLED US ALL.

BUT ONCE HE *STOPPED* BELIEVING, THE EFFECT WAS *LOST.*

LIKE IN A *DREAM.*

"WHEN YOU HAVE A *NIGHTMARE,* YOUR *HEART* POUNDS, YOU *SWEAT,* YOU *WRITHE* -- IN SHORT, YOU SUFFER *EXACTLY* THE SAME EFFECTS FROM YOUR *FANTASY* AS YOU WOULD FROM *REALITY.*

FAILED-- *FAILED*--

"PERHAPS WE WERE *PART* OF CYRUS BLACK'S DREAMS... BUT I SUPPOSE WE WILL NEVER *KNOW.*"

EVEN IN MY *IMAGINATION* THEY BEAT ME.

EVEN *THERE,* NEBUCHADNEZZAR,

AM I *ALWAYS* TO BE SECOND BEST? AM I *ALWAYS* DESTINED TO *LOSE?*

I MUST *THINK*-- TAKE A LONG, LONG *LOOK* AT MYSELF.

MAYBE *SOMEDAY* I WILL TRY *AGAIN...*

...BUT THEN-- MAYBE I WON'T.

THE END

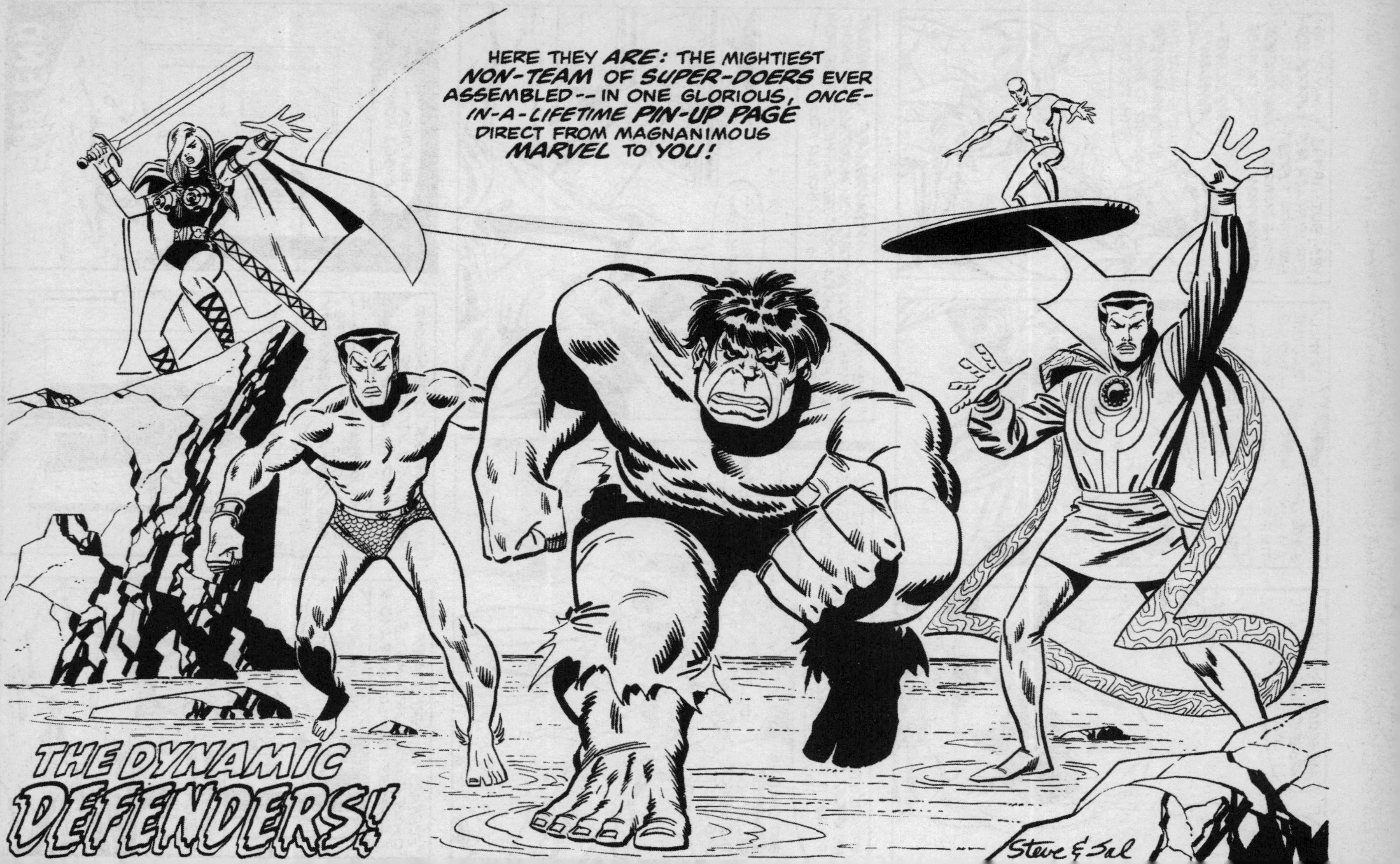
HERE THEY ARE: THE MIGHTIEST NON-TEAM OF SUPER-DOERS EVER ASSEMBLED-- IN ONE GLORIOUS, ONCE-IN-A-LIFETIME PIN-UP PAGE DIRECT FROM MAGNANIMOUS MARVEL TO YOU!
THE DYNAMIC DEFENDERS!
Steve & Sal

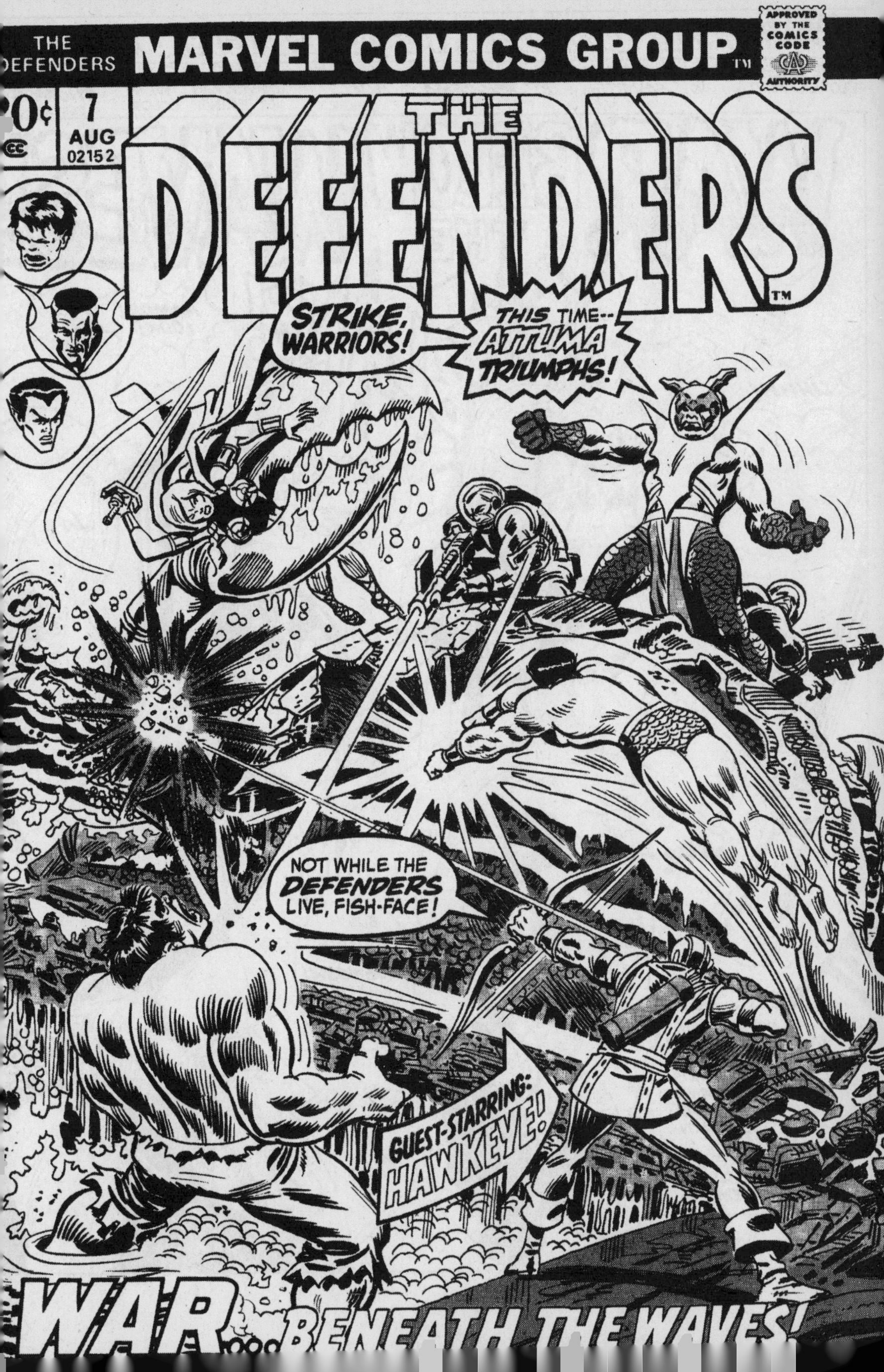

THE DEFENDERS
MARVEL COMICS GROUP
APPROVED BY THE COMICS CODE AUTHORITY
20¢
7
AUG
02152
THE DEFENDERS
STRIKE, WARRIORS!
THIS TIME-- ATTUMA TRIUMPHS!
NOT WHILE THE DEFENDERS LIVE, FISH-FACE!
GUEST-STARRING: HAWKEYE!
WAR... BENEATH THE WAVES!

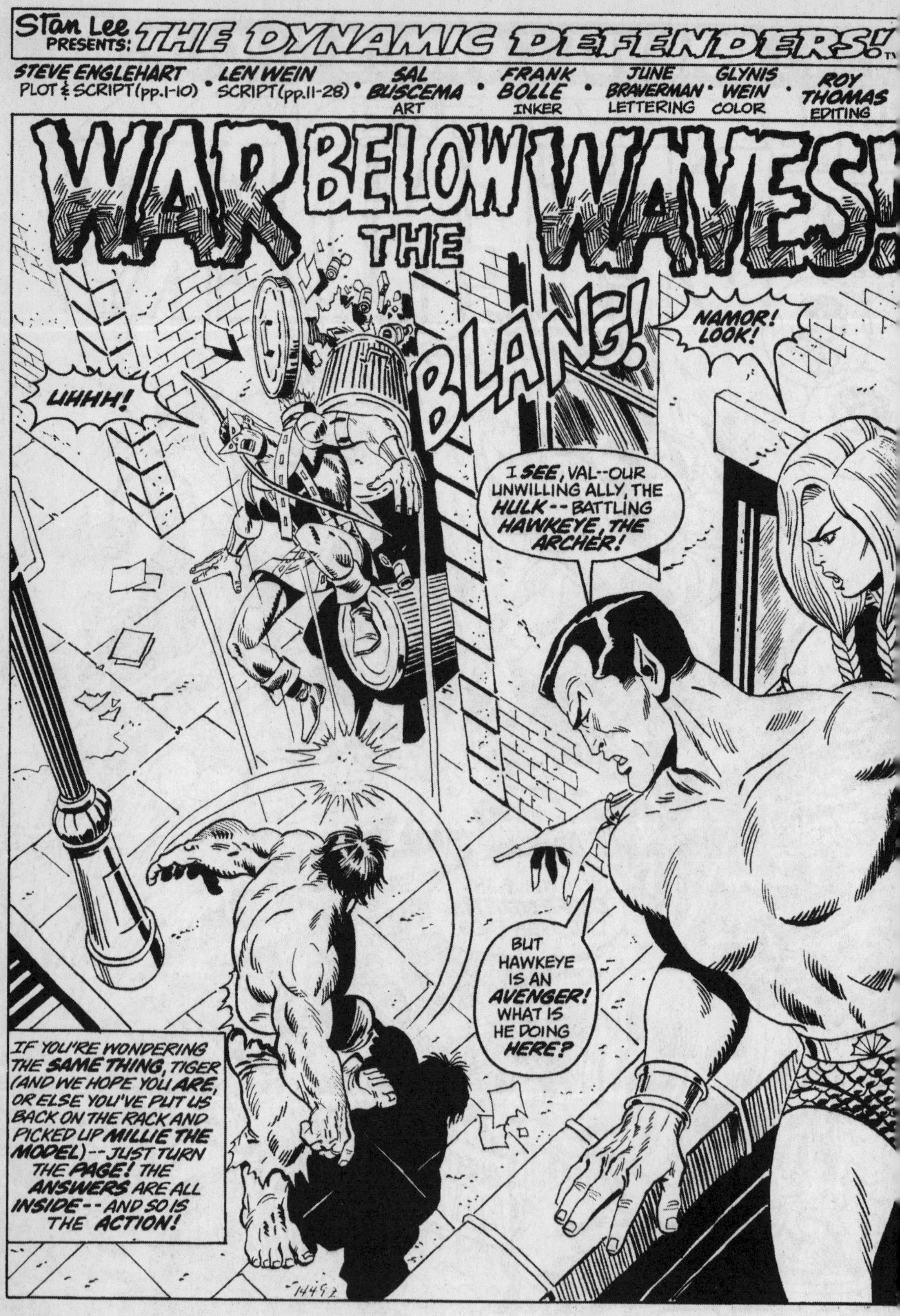
Stan Lee PRESENTS: THE DYNAMIC DEFENDERS!
STEVE ENGLEHART PLOT & SCRIPT (pp.1-10) • LEN WEIN SCRIPT (pp.11-28) • SAL BUSCEMA ART • FRANK BOLLE INKER • JUNE BRAVERMAN LETTERING • GLYNIS WEIN COLOR • ROY THOMAS EDITING
WAR BELOW THE WAVES!
BLANG!
UHHH!
NAMOR! LOOK!
I SEE, VAL--OUR UNWILLING ALLY, THE HULK--BATTLING HAWKEYE, THE ARCHER!
BUT HAWKEYE IS AN AVENGER! WHAT IS HE DOING HERE?
IF YOU'RE WONDERING THE SAME THING, TIGER (AND WE HOPE YOU ARE, OR ELSE YOU'VE PUT US BACK ON THE RACK AND PICKED UP MILLIE THE MODEL)--JUST TURN THE PAGE! THE ANSWERS ARE ALL INSIDE--AND SO IS THE ACTION!

HULK HAS HAD *ENOUGH* OF PUNY PURPLE-MAN *FOLLOWING* HIM! ALL ACROSS *CITY*, HE WON'T LET HULK *ALONE!*

LISTEN TO HULK, PURPLE-MAN--*STAY* WHERE HULK HAS *PUT* YOU!

NOT ON YOUR LAMENTABLE *LIFE*, YOU GREEN-SKINNED *GOOFBALL!*

WHILE WE WERE FIGHTIN' *ZZZAX*,* I HEARD YOU MUMBLE YOU WERE LOOKIN' FOR *DOC STRANGE*--

--AND I WANNA KNOW WHAT A BRAINLESS *BABOON* AND A *SORCERER* HAVE IN *COMMON!*

* IN HULKY'S *OWN* BOOK #166, --STILL ON SALE IF YOU *HURRY*.-- ROY.

I QUIT THE *AVENGERS* TO MAKE A NAME FOR MYSELF, AND THAT *MYSTERY* SOUNDS RIGHT UP MY *ALLEY* -- PARDON THE PUN--

BRAK!

--SO YOU'LL JUST HAVE TO--

--BEAR WITH ME?

ARRRGH!

YOU DON'T *LISTEN* TO HULK! *NO ONE* LISTENS TO HULK!

HULK IS *SICK* OF IT!

ER...UH... *SORRY* ABOUT THAT...SIR...

MAYBE I *WAS* KINDA AN *OVER-ACHIEVER*...

HEY--GET *BACK!* I *APOLOGIZED*, AWREADY!

STUPID *FLYING STICKS* CAN'T HURT HULK!

BUT HULK WILL *SMASH* STICK-MAN!

I'M GONNA MAKE A *NAME* FOR MYSELF, ALL RIGHT--*TOP DRAW* ON THE *OBIT PAGE!*

I'D BETTER BACK-PEDDLE ON *OUTTA* HERE---

HUH?

WHO'S BLOCKIN' MY *RETREAT*--?

THE *VALKYRIE!*

OR--THAT'S WHAT YOU *CALL* YOURSELF, BUT YOU'RE *REALLY* THE *ENCHANTRESS!**

WELL, LADY--*NO-BODY'S* TRAPPIN' BR'ER *HAWKEYE!*

*THAT WAS TRUE *IN* AVENGERS #83 --BUT *NO LONGER.* --R.

RIGHT *ON*, ROY--BECAUSE READERS OF *DEFENDERS* #4 UNDERSTAND THAT *THIS* VALKYRIE IS A GOOD-HEARTED *CREATION* OF THE EVIL *ENCHANTRESS*--AND SHE IS FIERCELY *LOYAL* TO ANY AND ALL *DEFENDERS!*

WAP!

STOP *HOUNDING* THE HULK!

TOO BAD THE WORLD DOESN'T EVEN KNOW THE *DEFENDERS* EXIST!-- INCLUDING HAWKEYE--

PURPLE-MAN WAS FIGHTING *HULK!* NOW HE FIGHTS *OTHER* HUMAN, INSTEAD!

HULK DOESN'T *UNDERSTAND*--

--BUT FOR *ONCE*, HULK THINKS THAT'S *FUNNY!*

LET HUMANS *FIGHT!* HULK WILL *WATCH!*

HA HA HA

NIFTY *SWORD* YOU GOT, VAL-- LOOKS *FAMILIAR*, SOMEHOW--

--BUT I GOTTA *RELIEVE* YA OF IT--

'CAUSE, GIRL OR *NOT*-- *IMMORTAL* OR NOT--

I GOT ME A *SCORE* TO SETTLE WITH YOU, AND I'M MAD ENOUGH TO *DO* IT!

TOUCH THAT GIRL *AGAIN*, ARCHER, AND YOU WILL BE OBLIGED TO ANSWER TO *ME!*

WHAT--? *ANOTHER* ATTACKER?

WELL, I'LL JUST TAKE *YOU* ON, TOO!

CEASE YOUR INANE *BREAST-BEATING*, BOWMAN!

KROW!

THE *SUB-MARINER* HAS HEARD *TOO MUCH* OF IT!

THE SUB---?

WHAT *IS* THIS -- A *CONVENTION* OF SUPER-BADDIES?

WHEN DID THIS *PRIVATE* FIGHT BECOME A COMMUNITY EVENT--

--AND HOW DO I GET THE *POPCORN* CONCESSION?

TALK *FAST*, CLINT -- YOU'RE *WAY* OUTCLASSED!

POPCORN! HE *MOCKS* US, NAMOR, BUT *I'LL* SHOW HIM--

NO, VAL! THAT'S ONLY HIS *MANNER* -- AND HE'S QUIET *NOW!*

WHAT DO YOU *WANT* HERE, HAWKEYE?

WELL... I DON'T KNOW WHY I SHOULD *TELL* YOU...

...BUT I SUPPOSE IT CAN'T *HURT.*

--*ME!*

"I'D BEEN PUTTIN' THE MOVES ON THE *SCARLET WITCH*... BUT SHE THREW ME OVER FOR THE *VISION.* THAT MADE IT TOO *PAINFUL* TO STAY WITH THE AVENGERS, SO I *SPLIT.**

*AVENGERS #109.--ROY.

"TO CLEAR MY *HEAD*, I TOOK A JOB WITH A STUD NAMED *CHAMPION*--

"--BUT MY *TRUST* WAS *MISPLACED!* HE TURNED OUT TO BE JUST ANOTHER WOULD-BE WORLD-BEATER!"

"AFTER THAT, I WAS PRETTY **STRUNG OUT.** I WENT BACK TO MY **FIRST** LADY, THE **BLACK WIDOW**--BUT HER **CURRENT** HEART THROB DIDN'T **GO** FOR THAT IN A BIG WAY.*

"JUST WHEN I WAS THINKIN' THINGS COULDN'T GET ANY **WORSE**--THEY **DID.** THE AVENGERS SHOWED UP TO **RECRUIT** DD AND TASHA AS MY **REPLACEMENTS!**

"THEY CLAIMED THEY WANTED ME BACK, TOO--BUT I WASN'T HAVIN' ANY O' THEIR **SYMPATHY!**

"SO I TRUCKED BACK TO NEW YORK BY MY **LONESOME** -- WHERE I HEARD ABOUT SOME **ELECTRIC MONSTER** RAMPAGIN' AROUND.

"I FIGURED I'D **NAB** IT-- BUT THE **HULK** GOT THERE FIRST."

*AVENGERS #110 & DAREDEVIL #99.--R.

THING **WAS,** GREENIE SAID HE WAS ON HIS MERRY WAY TO **DOC STRANGE'S** DIGS AT THE TIME-- AND I WONDERED **WHY.**

THAT'S **EASY,** HAWK-EYE. STEPHEN STRANGE IS OUR **LEADER** IN THE **DEFENDERS!**

HOLD, VAL!

DEFENDERS?

JUMP TO NO **CONCLUSIONS,** ARCHER--THE **DEFENDERS** IS MERELY A **NAME,** AND NO MORE.

AT TIMES WE **BATTLE** TOGETHER AGAINST A **COMMON** FOE--BUT THE DEFENDERS IS **NOT** AN ALLIANCE...

...THERE IS **NO** LEADER, **NO** RULES, **NO** CHARTER SUCH AS IN **YOUR** AVENGERS.

AT **ANY** RATE, HAWKEYE, WE WERE **ALSO** GOING TO STEPHEN'S SANCTUM. WHY NOT **JOIN** US?

THEY AIN'T "MY" AVENGERS, CHARLIE TUNA.

FOR THE **WALK** ONLY, ARCHER!

TOO MUCH **WORD-PLAY** FOR HULK!

GOOD EVENING, WONG. IS YOUR *MASTER* AT HOME?

NO, PRINCE NAMOR. HE IS *AWAY.* *

PLEASE *ENTER,* HOWEVER-- THOUGH YOU MUST *EXCUSE* MISS CLEA AND MY HUMBLE SELF.

WE MUST *MEDITATE* ...FOR MY *MASTER'S* SAFE *RETURN.*

CERTAINLY, WONG. WE *WON'T* NEED YOU.

* THE *UNDERSTATEMENT* OF THE *CENTURY!* AT THIS VERY MOMENT, THE *MASTER OF THE MYSTIC ARTS* IS TRAPPED IN THE *CRYPTS OF KAA-U,* FACING HIS FINAL BATTLE WITH THE DREAD *SHUMAGORATH* FOR THE VERY LIFE OF THE *COSMOS!* THE FULL STORY IS IN *MARVEL PREMIERE #9* AND 10. --ROY.

WHATTA *SET-UP!* SO *THIS* IS WHERE THE GOOD DOCTOR HANGS HIS CAPE!

KINDA MAKES ME THINK OF *AVENGERS MANSION*--IN A *COCKEYED* WAY--BUT THIS GUY *WONG* SURE AIN'T NO *JARVIS!*

OKAY, WE'RE *HERE*-- BUT THERE IS *STILL* A LOTTA JAZZ I DON'T *GET* ABOUT YOU PEOPLE.

AND *NUMBER ONE* ON MY HIT PARADE IS HOWCUM THE *VALKYRIE'S* GONE THE *SWEETNESS-AND LIGHT* ROUTE?

SO VAL RUNS IT *DOWN* FOR HIM, JUST THE WAY WE RAN IT DOWN FOR *YOU.*

--AND *NOW,* I FIND MYSELF *ORPHANED* ON THIS PLANET-- VERY *MUCH* LIKE AN ABANDONED CHILD.

IF I DIDN'T HAVE THE *DEFENDERS* TO LEAN ON ---

NOK NOK NOK

A VIOLENT *POUNDING* ON THE MAGE'S *FRONT* DOOR!

I'LL *ANSWER* IT FOR WONG!

YES? WHAT DO YOU **WISH?**

MY PRINCE... **LORD VASHTI** HAS SENT ME ...I...

BY **NEPTUNE'S TRIDENT!** THIS MAN IS AN **ATLANTEAN!**

HE'S BEEN **INJURED!**

MY PRINCE... VASHTI'S **SPIES** TELL HIM... **ATTUMA** IS GOING TO ATTACK THE **SURFACE WORLD**... FOR REASONS **UNKNOWN...**

HE WILL STRIKE... IN BUT **HOURS**... AT THE PLACE CALLED **ATLANTIC CITY...**

ATTUMA -- THE ONE FROM THE **MURKY DEPTHS!** HE WHO HAS NO CREED BUT **CONQUEST**, AND--

HE WHO **KEPT** ME FROM SAVING THE LIFE OF **MY LADY DORMA!** *

I LEAVE AT **ONCE!**

* IN THE CLASSIC **SUB-MARINER #37.** --R.

WAIT, NAMOR! WE'LL **ALL** GO!

WHO'S "**WE**," LADY? I JUST **QUIT** A GROUP-- REMEMBER?

BUT THEN... THIS **IS** A GROUP OF **INDIVIDUAL** SUPERSTARS...

...AND **YOU'RE** PRETTY SUPER IN THE **LOOKS** DEPARTMENT...

AH, WHAT THE **HECK!** I'M **IN!**

HULK CARES NOTHING FOR A-TOOM-A...

...BUT IF STUPID **STICK- MAN** CAN GO, HULK WILL GO, **TOO!**

THE BOARDWALK IN ATLANTIC CITY: HERE, EACH SEPTEMBER, A SACCHARINE-SWEET BERT PARKS SINGS THE LILTING PRAISES OF AN EQUALLY SUGARY BEAUTY QUEEN--

--BUT THIS MAY AFTERNOON, THE AIR IS FILLED NOT WITH MUSIC, BUT WITH THE ENTICING FRAGRANCE OF FRESH-BAKED KNISHES--

--THE BRISK SALT SMELL OF THE SEA FOR WHICH THE CITY IS NAMED--

--AND THE MERRY LAUGHTER OF THE FEW YOUNG SOULS DARING ENOUGH TO ASSAULT THE STILL-CHILL WATER...

DUMP SAND DOWN MY TRUNKS, WILL YA?

MARY BETH, WHEN I GET MY HANDS ON YOU--!

FIRST YOU HAVE TO CATCH ME, LEAD-FOOT--

--AND I DON'T THINK YOU HAVE A SNAIL'S CHANCE OF DOING THAT!

OH, YEAH! WE'LL JUST SEE ABOUT THAT, LITTLE LADY--!

--MUST BE SEEING THINGS!

--A HORRIBLE TENTACLE OF SOME KIND--!

RISING FROM THE SEA FLOOR-- BEHIND MARY BETH--

A TENTACLE, INDEED --A SLIMY, SLICKER-CUSHIONED EXTREMITY--

--ATTACHED TO AN EVEN MORE HIDEOUS BEAST!

THE GIANT SQUID-- HAS MARY BETH--!

GOT TO DO SOMETHING TO SAVE HER FROM--!

NO--NOOO! IT CAN'T BE--! IT'S NOT POSSIBLE--!

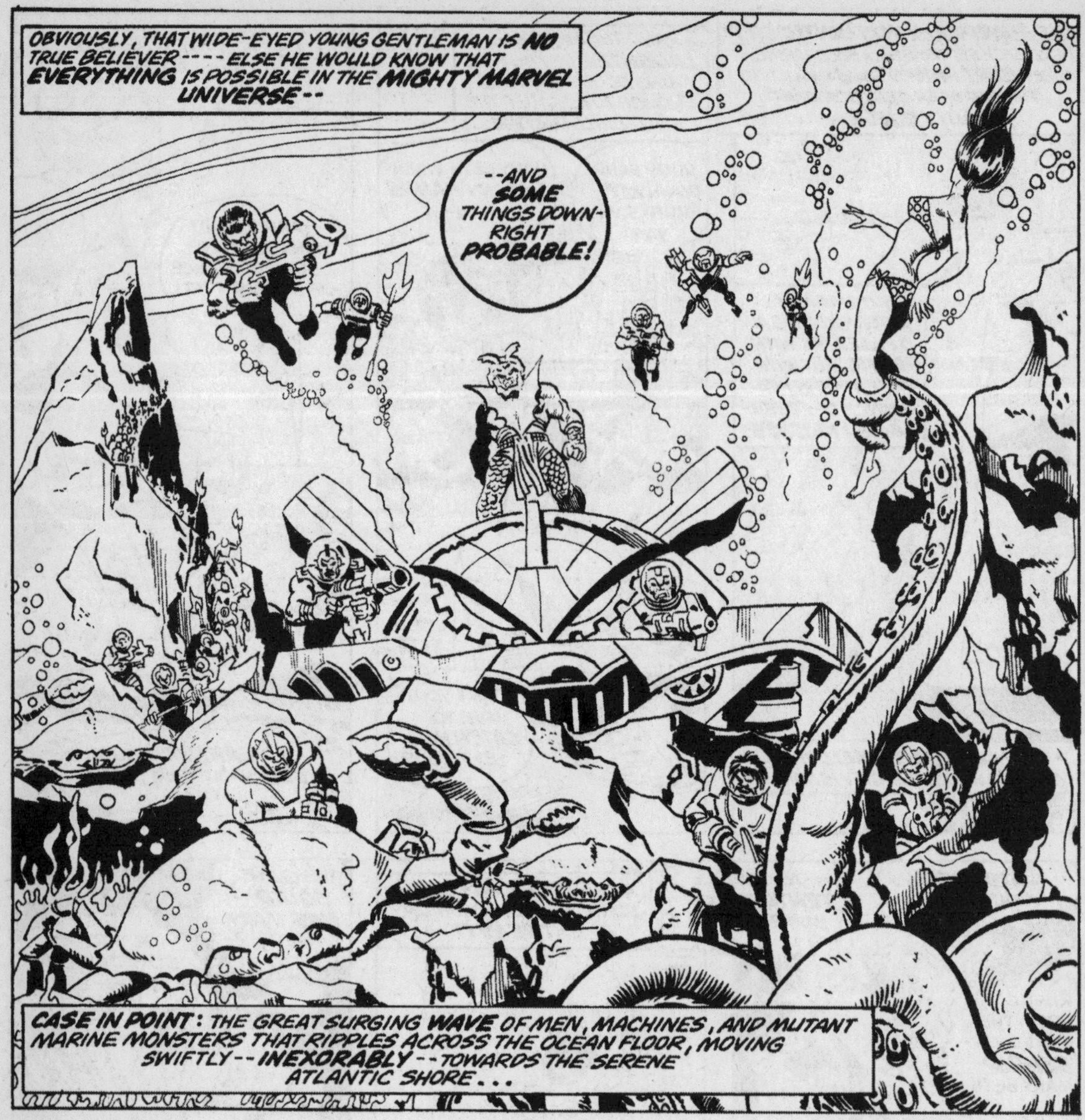
OBVIOUSLY, THAT WIDE-EYED YOUNG GENTLEMAN IS NO TRUE BELIEVER ---- ELSE HE WOULD KNOW THAT EVERYTHING IS POSSIBLE IN THE MIGHTY MARVEL UNIVERSE --
--AND SOME THINGS DOWN-RIGHT PROBABLE!
CASE IN POINT: THE GREAT SURGING WAVE OF MEN, MACHINES, AND MUTANT MARINE MONSTERS THAT RIPPLES ACROSS THE OCEAN FLOOR, MOVING SWIFTLY -- INEXORABLY -- TOWARDS THE SERENE ATLANTIC SHORE . . .

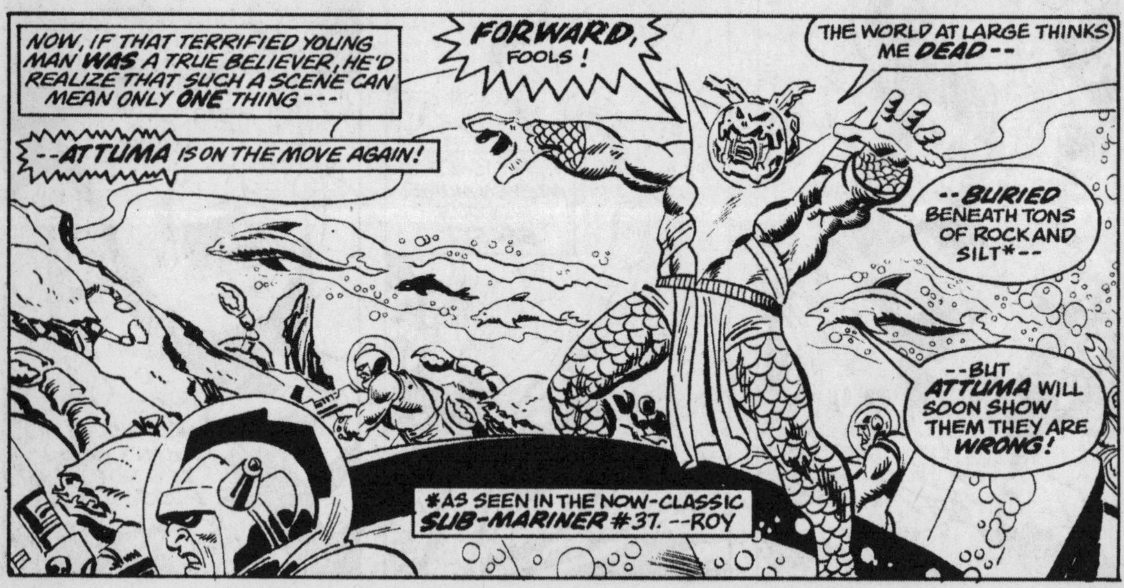
NOW, IF THAT TERRIFIED YOUNG MAN WAS A TRUE BELIEVER, HE'D REALIZE THAT SUCH A SCENE CAN MEAN ONLY ONE THING ---
--ATTUMA IS ON THE MOVE AGAIN!
FORWARD, FOOLS!
THE WORLD AT LARGE THINKS ME DEAD --
--BURIED BENEATH TONS OF ROCK AND SILT* --
--BUT ATTUMA WILL SOON SHOW THEM THEY ARE WRONG!
*AS SEEN IN THE NOW-CLASSIC SUB-MARINER #37. --ROY

AND, MOMENTS LATER, THE MONOTONOUS GRUMBLE OF THE ROLLING SURF IS INTERRUPTED BY...

H-HEY, WHAT'S *WITH* THOSE GUYS?

THEY DON'T EVEN ALLOW *SURFING* AROUND HERE!

WH-WHAT--? THOSE C-CREATURES CAN'T COME UP *HERE!*

THIS IS A *RESTRICTED BEACH!*

BUT 'THO THE *BEACH* MAY BE RESTRICTED -- THE *PANIC* THAT SETS IN ALMOST INSTANTLY IS *FREE* FOR ONE AND ALL --

--AS THE TERRIFIED BATHERS SCRAMBLE SWIFTLY ACROSS THE SANDS, RACING DESPERATELY AWAY FROM *ONE* HORROR --

-- ONLY TO FIND THEMSELVES RUNNING RIGHT SMACK INTO *ANOTHER!*

NO -- NOT *HIM,* TOO?!?

HUH? WHY DO PUNY HUMANS *RUN* FROM HULK *THIS* TIME?

WHAT HAS HULK DONE WRONG *NOW?*

NOT A *THING,* JADE-JAWS.

IN FACT, COMPARED TO *SOME* OF THE MONSTROSITIES PROWLING THE SHORE TODAY, YOU'RE A GREEN-SKINNED *ANGEL.*

HELP! PUT ME *DOWN!*

THIS MONSTER IS -- *CRUSHING* M-ME --!

COWARDLY SURFACE *SCUM!* BE *SILENT* -- AND DIE LIKE A *MAN!*

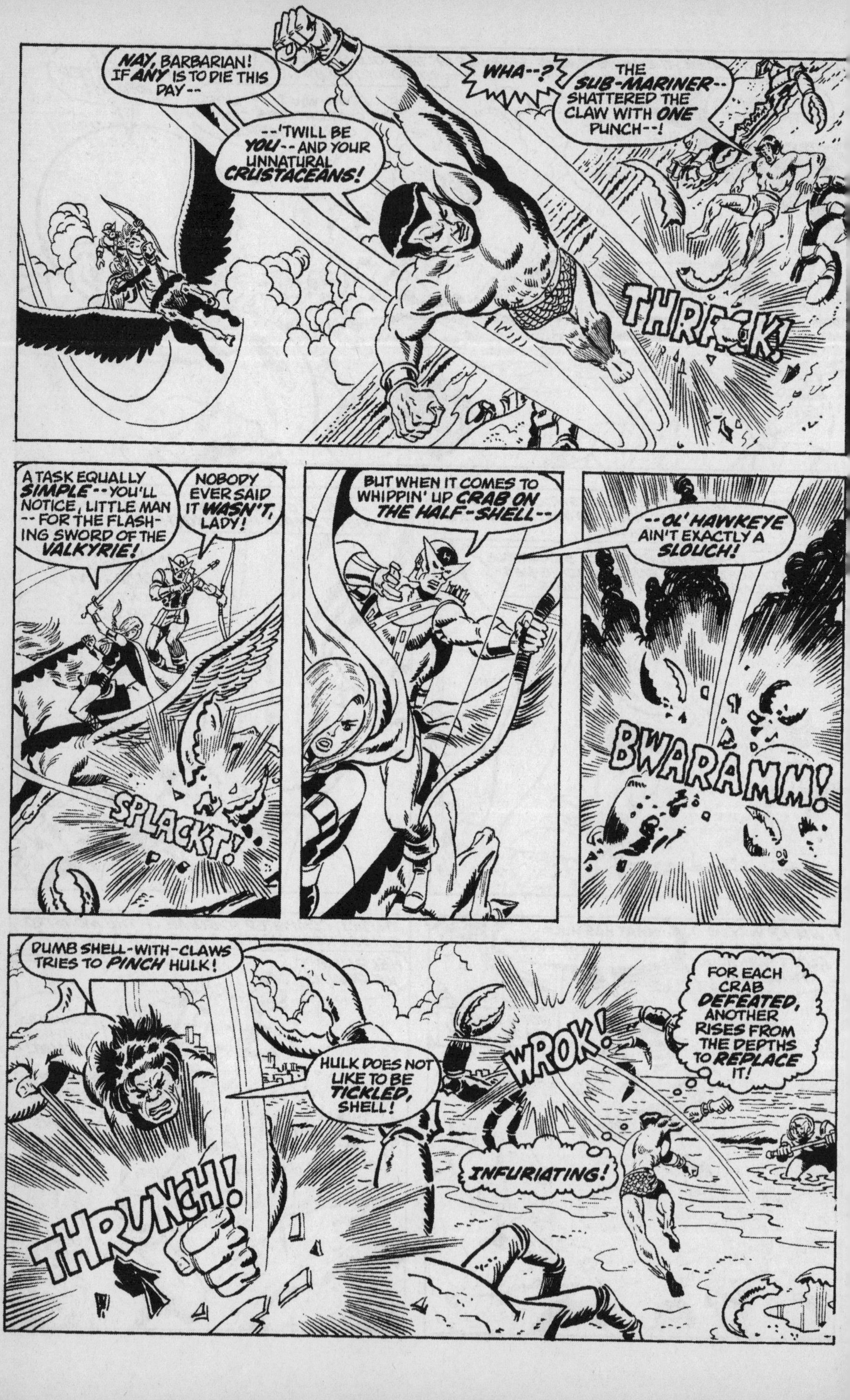

NAY, BARBARIAN! IF ANY IS TO DIE THIS DAY--
--'TWILL BE YOU--AND YOUR UNNATURAL CRUSTACEANS!
WHA--?
THE SUB-MARINER--SHATTERED THE CLAW WITH ONE PUNCH--!
THRACK!
A TASK EQUALLY SIMPLE--YOU'LL NOTICE, LITTLE MAN--FOR THE FLASHING SWORD OF THE VALKYRIE!
NOBODY EVER SAID IT WASN'T, LADY!
SPLACKT!
BUT WHEN IT COMES TO WHIPPIN' UP CRAB ON THE HALF-SHELL--
--OL' HAWKEYE AIN'T EXACTLY A SLOUCH!
BWARAMM!
DUMB SHELL-WITH-CLAWS TRIES TO PINCH HULK!
HULK DOES NOT LIKE TO BE TICKLED, SHELL!
WROK!
FOR EACH CRAB DEFEATED, ANOTHER RISES FROM THE DEPTHS TO REPLACE IT!
INFURIATING!
THRUNCH!

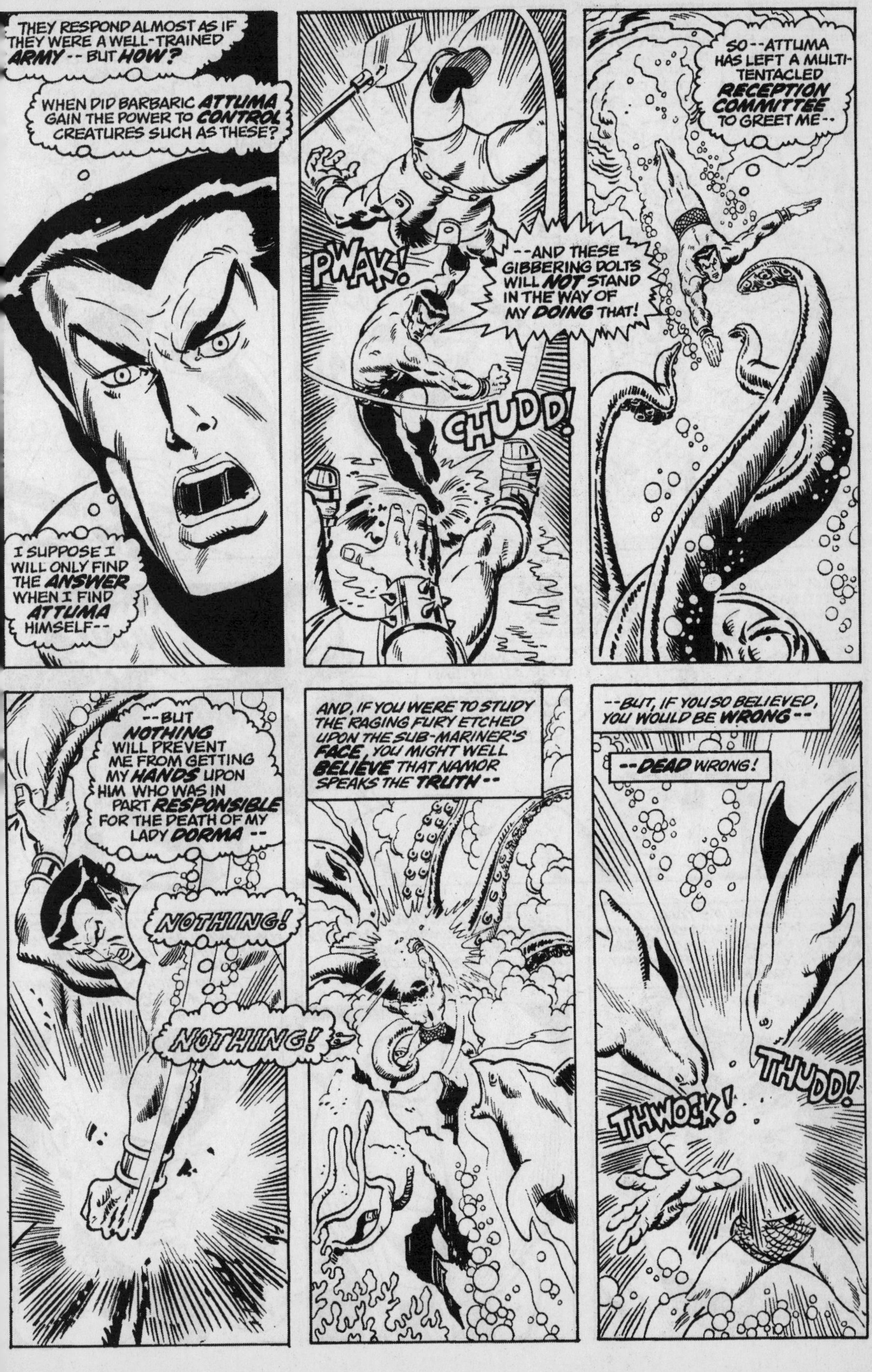

THEY RESPOND ALMOST AS IF THEY WERE A WELL-TRAINED ARMY -- BUT HOW?
WHEN DID BARBARIC ATTUMA GAIN THE POWER TO CONTROL CREATURES SUCH AS THESE?
I SUPPOSE I WILL ONLY FIND THE ANSWER WHEN I FIND ATTUMA HIMSELF--
PWAK!
--AND THESE GIBBERING DOLTS WILL NOT STAND IN THE WAY OF MY DOING THAT!
CHUDD!
SO--ATTUMA HAS LEFT A MULTI-TENTACLED RECEPTION COMMITTEE TO GREET ME--
--BUT NOTHING WILL PREVENT ME FROM GETTING MY HANDS UPON HIM WHO WAS IN PART RESPONSIBLE FOR THE DEATH OF MY LADY DORMA --
NOTHING!
NOTHING!
AND, IF YOU WERE TO STUDY THE RAGING FURY ETCHED UPON THE SUB-MARINER'S FACE, YOU MIGHT WELL BELIEVE THAT NAMOR SPEAKS THE TRUTH--
--BUT, IF YOU SO BELIEVED, YOU WOULD BE WRONG--
--DEAD WRONG!
THUDD!
THWOCK!

SPLENDID! THE PORPOISES STRUCK THE HALFBREED PRECISELY WHERE DIRECTED--

--AT THE EXACT NERVE CENTERS NECESSARY TO RENDER NAMOR TEMPORARILY HARMLESS--

--LONG ENOUGH FOR ME TO IMPRISON HIM IN THESE SPECIALLY-PREPARED SHACKLES--

--DESIGNED TO SAP HIS INFERNAL STRENGTH!

NOW, TO THE SURFACE, YOU SIMPERING LACKEYS --QUICKLY!

OUR WORK IS NOT YET DONE!

HOLD, HUMANS --ATTUMA COMMANDS IT!

YOU HAVE ONE SECOND TO SURRENDER YOURSELVES--

--OR WATCH YOUR ATLANTEAN COMRADE SLAUGHTERED BEFORE YOUR EYES!

HUH!

FOR AN ETERNAL INSTANT, THE GREAT GREEN BEHEMOTH'S MIND REELS, UNABLE TO FULLY COMPREHEND THE SITUATION THAT CONFRONTS HIM--

BLUE MEN--?

--JUST AS A SECOND MIND HESITATES, UNABLE TO FIRMLY DECIDE WHETHER NAMOR WOULD CHOOSE HIS OWN SACRIFICE AS THE BETTER PART OF VALOR--

--BUT, FORTUNATELY, THERE IS ONE MIND AMONG THEM THAT IS USED TO CONSIDERING THE WELFARE OF A TEAMMATE-- ONE MIND WHICH TAKES NO TIME AT ALL IN DECIDING FOR THE REST...

OKAY, CRAB-HEAD-- YOU WIN!

WE--GIVE UP.

MASTER, WE HAVE **CAPTURED** THE HUMAN YOU SOUGHT --**AND** HIS BAB-BLING WOMAN!

WHAT SHALL WE **DO** WITH THEM?

BRING THEM ABOARD **SHIP,** WORTA!

BRING THEM **ALL** ABOARD SHIP -- **NOW!**

VICIOUSLY, THE FRIGHTENED COUPLE IS HUSTLED ABOARD THE SEACRAFT --

-- FOLLOWED INSTANTS LATER BY THE GRIM-FACED DEFENDERS --

WELL, MAYBE NOT **ALL** THE DEFENDERS ...

HULK **KNOWS** THIS THING.

IT IS A **WATER SHIP!**

HULK HAS **BEEN** ON A WATER SHIP!

HULK HAS BEEN **PRISONER** ON A WATER SHIP RUN BY STRANGE LITTLE MAN!*

YES -- HULK HAS **BEEN** ON A WATER SHIP.

*HULK #164-165 -- RT.

DIDN'T **LIKE** IT.

GREAT ONE, THE MONSTER IS **ESCAPING!**

THEN LET HIM **GO,** FOOL!

HE IS TOO **FEEBLE-MINDED** TO BOTHER FOLLOWING US!

NOW **COME** -- LET US BE **GONE!**

WELL HERE'S **ANOTHER** FINE MESS YOU'VE GOTTEN US INTO!

YES, NAMOR -- LET ME **REMOVE** THIS FROM YOUR NECK.

YOU **OKAY,** FIN-FACE?

NAY, VAL -- TO REMOVE THIS **SPECIAL** SHACKLE -- WOULD SURELY **KILL** ME --!

AND SO OUR HEROES SAIL OFF INTO THE BRINY DEEP -- BUT **DON'T** EXPECT A CERTAIN GREEN GOLIATH TO **RESCUE** THEM --

-- FOR THE HULK'S TENUOUS FRIENDSHIP WITH THOSE CALLED THE **DEFENDERS** IS A **FRAGILE** THING AT BEST --

-- WHILE HIS HATRED OF **WATER** IS VERY NEARLY **LEGEND.**

BESIDES, BY NOW HIS SIMPLE MIND HAS PROBABLY **FORGOTTEN** THEM.

WE HAVE **ARRIVED,** SURFACE-SCUM!

COME OUT -- **SLOWLY** -- AND **SHIELD** YOUR EYES --

-- LEST YOU BE **STUNNED** BY THE **BEAUTY** OF ATTUMA'S NEW DOMAIN!

ONE BY ONE, THE COSTUMED **CAPTIVES** CLIMB FROM THE CRAMPED CARGO HOLD -- AND THEY ARE **STUNNED** INDEED.--

-- FOR THE **SPECTACLE** THAT GREETS THEIR SQUINTING EYES SEEMS TORN FROM AN ARCHITECT'S **NIGHTMARE!**

MAGNIFICENT, IS IT NOT, LAND-DOGS? ATTUMA HIMSELF **DESIGNED** IT!

NOW **COME!** THE **GREAT ONE** AWAITS YOU IN THE MAIN HALL!

WELL, I HOPE HE'S AT LEAST SERVING **LUNCH!** I'M **FAMISHED!**

SHORTLY ...

HAIL, OH GREAT ONE! AS ORDERED, I HAVE BROUGHT YOU THE **PRISONERS!**

AYE, -- BUT PRISONERS THROUGH **TREACHERY** ONLY!

WERE IT NOT FOR YOUR PERFIDIOUS **PORPOISES,** ATTUMA, WE'D --!

YES, ATLANTEAN -- MY **PORPOISES!** THEY RESPONDED TO ORDERS QUITE **CAPABLY,** DON'T YOU THINK?

BUT **HOW,** BARBARIAN? WHEN DID **YOU** GAIN SUCH **MASTERY** OVER THE CREATURES OF THE DEEP?

SINCE I GAINED MYSELF A NEW **PARTNER,** HALFBREED--

--ONE WHO IS **EXPERT** AT CON-TROLLING NATURE'S LESSER BEASTS--

-- THE **RED GHOST!** *

BUT A **NEW** RED GHOST, AMPHIBIAN -- ONE WHO HAS **LEARNED** AND **PROFITED** FROM THE MISTAKES OF THE PAST!

*LAST SEEN IN **IRON MAN** #16 FOR ALL YOU COMPLETISTS OUT THERE -- ROY.

NEVER AGAIN WILL I ALLY MYSELF WITH *APES!* THEY ARE TOO *UNPREDICTABLE* -- TOO *DIFFICULT* TO CONTROL --!

BUT *PORPOISES*--! *THEIR* INTELLIGENCE IS ALMOST THE *EQUAL* OF MAN'S --

--AND, WITH THE AID OF DR. JENNINGS, THE WORLD'S FOREMOST *MARINE BIOLOGIST*, AND MY OWN AWESOME *COSMIC RAYS*--

-- I SHALL BEND THEM TO MY *WILL* --

" --AND FORGE FROM THEM AN ALMIGHTY *ARMY*-- SWIFT, DEADLY -- THAT WILL *CONQUER* YOUR NATIVE ATLANTIS WITHOUT ONCE EVER FIRING A *SHOT* --

"--AND, FROM ATLANTIS, IT IS JUST A *SMALL STEP* TO CONQUERING THE *WORLD!* "

NEVER, VILLAIN -- NEVER SHALL PROUD *ATLANTIS* FALL TO SUCH AS *YOU!*

COULD I BUT LAY MY *HANDS* ON YOU --!

YOU *CAN'T*, NAMOR-- AND YOU *WON'T* --

-- BUT *WE* HAVE OTHER -- MORE *INTERESTING*-- PLANS FOR *YOU!*

TIME *PASSES* -- AND WHEN WE REJOIN *TWO* OF OUR CAST...

-- AND THAT'S MY *PLAN*, VALKYRIE. YOU GOT IT *STRAIGHT?*

I *HAVE* IT, ARCHER -- BUT I'M NOT ENTIRELY SURE I *LIKE* IT!

"I'M NOT OVERLY *FOND* OF IT MYSELF, LADY -- BUT IT'S THE *ONLY* PLAN WE GOT!"

"SHHHHH -- THE *GUARD* APPROACHES."

I BRING YOU *FOOD*, LITTLE PRETTY -- BUT IF YOU *WANT* IT, YOU MUST BE *NICE* TO BIG GROKKO!

NICE, BIG GROKKO? HOW DO YOU *MEAN?*

YOU *KNOW*, LITTLE PRETTY-- LIKE PUTTING YOUR SOFT *ARMS* AROUND BIG GROKKO--

--AND *HUGGING* HIM REAL *TI*-- --*IIIEEEKK!*

FILTHY, SEXIST PIG!

HAHAHH!

I THINK YOU LEFT OUT "*MALE CHAUVINIST*" IN THERE SOMEWHERE, VAL--!

JUST GET THE *KEYS*, ARCHER! I CANNOT SUPPORT THIS SCUM *FOREVER!*

THEN *DUMP* 'IM, LADY-- WE'RE *SET!*

WHERE DO WE GO *NOW*, HAWKEYE?

TO FIND YOUR SPOCK-EARED *BUDDY*, VALKYRIE!

WE CAN PLAY IT *OFF THE CLIFF* FROM THERE!

ONCE WE'VE FREED *SUBBY*, WE CAN--!

MAYBE WE *DON'T* HAFTA GO INTO THIS MESS *EMPTY-HANDED!*

THE *JUNK* AROUND HERE GIVES ME AN *IDEA!*

HEY, HOLD *UP* A SEC.

AND MINUTES LATER...

BANNISTER-POST *ARROWS* FLETCHED WITH PILLOW *FEATHERS*-- AND A BROKEN-BED-SLAT *BOW!*

NOT EXACTLY IN THE *ROBIN HOOD* CLASS-- BUT THEY OUGHTA COUNT FOR *SOMETHIN'!*

TWO SETS OF **FOOTSTEPS** ECHO DOWN A MILDEWED CORRIDOR--

--ONE ECHO IS **SOFT, DELICATE**--

--THE OTHER **CRUDE** AND **GRUFF**--

BUT **BOTH** ARE TINGED WITH AN AIR OF **DETERMINATION**--

--DETERMINATION THAT GROWS **STRONGER** AS--

WELL, WILL YA LOOK AT **THAT!?**

PLEASE, HAWKEYE -- WE HAVE NOT YET FOUND **NAMOR!**

"UH-HUH--BUT WHAT WE **HAVE** FOUND IS JUST AS **IMPORTANT**-- MAYBE **MORE** SO!

"DON'T KNOW WHAT THOSE **BUBBLE-HEADS** ARE **FORCIN'** THE DOC TA **DO**--

--BUT WHATEVER IT **WAS** -- IT AIN'T **NO MORE!**

THRASH!

I CAN SEE THERE IS NO **REASONING** WITH YOU, HAWKEYE!

CHOOM!

IF I HOPE TO LOCATE **NAMOR**--

--I MUST FIRST **ELIMINATE** YOUR **PLAYMATES!**

PLAYMATES?

NO WAY!

JUST CAN'T IMAGINE ONE'A **THESE** DUDES WITH A **STAPLE** THRU HIS NAVEL!

BAF!

OKAY--FUNTIME'S **OVER!**

GRAB THE **DOC** -- AN' LET'S GET **OUTTA** HERE!

WITH **PLEASURE!**

NOW WE CAN CONTINUE THE SEARCH FOR **NAMOR!**

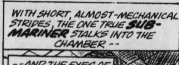

You need search no **FURTHER**, woman --

-- for you have **FOUND** the one you seek!

NAMOR -- **STAND FORTH!**

With short, almost-mechanical strides, the one true **SUB-MARINER** stalks into the chamber --

-- and the eyes of his anxious companions grow **WIDE**, their jaws grow **SLACK** --

-- for the visage Namor presents is by no means one **BEFITTING** the monarch of all **ATLANTIS!**

It is more like the face of -- a **MADMAN!**

You **WANTED** the Sub-Mariner, fools --

-- and now you **HAVE** him!

COME, my mindless Atlantean **SLAVE** --

-- come -- and **DESTROY** them all!!

To be continued **NEXT MONTH!!**

That's right, tiger -- we said **NEXT** month, not **TWO** months from now -- 'cause, as of this moment, those darlin' **DEFENDERS** have gone **MONTHLY!** (hoohah!)

THE DEFENDERS

MARVEL COMICS GROUP™

APPROVED BY THE COMICS CODE AUTHORITY

20¢

8 SEPT

02152

THE DEFENDERS ™

STRIKE, SKY-RIDER!

HAWKEYE AND THE VALKYRIE MUST BE *FREED* BEFORE IT'S *TOO LATE!*

YOU ARE *ALREADY* TOO LATE, FOOLS! YOUR FELLOW DEFENDERS ARE *DOOMED* TO BECOME--

IT HAD TO HAPPEN! DR. STRANGE AND THE SENSATIONAL *SILVER SURFER* BATTLE SIDE BY SIDE!

MIND-SLAVES OF THE *RED GHOST!*

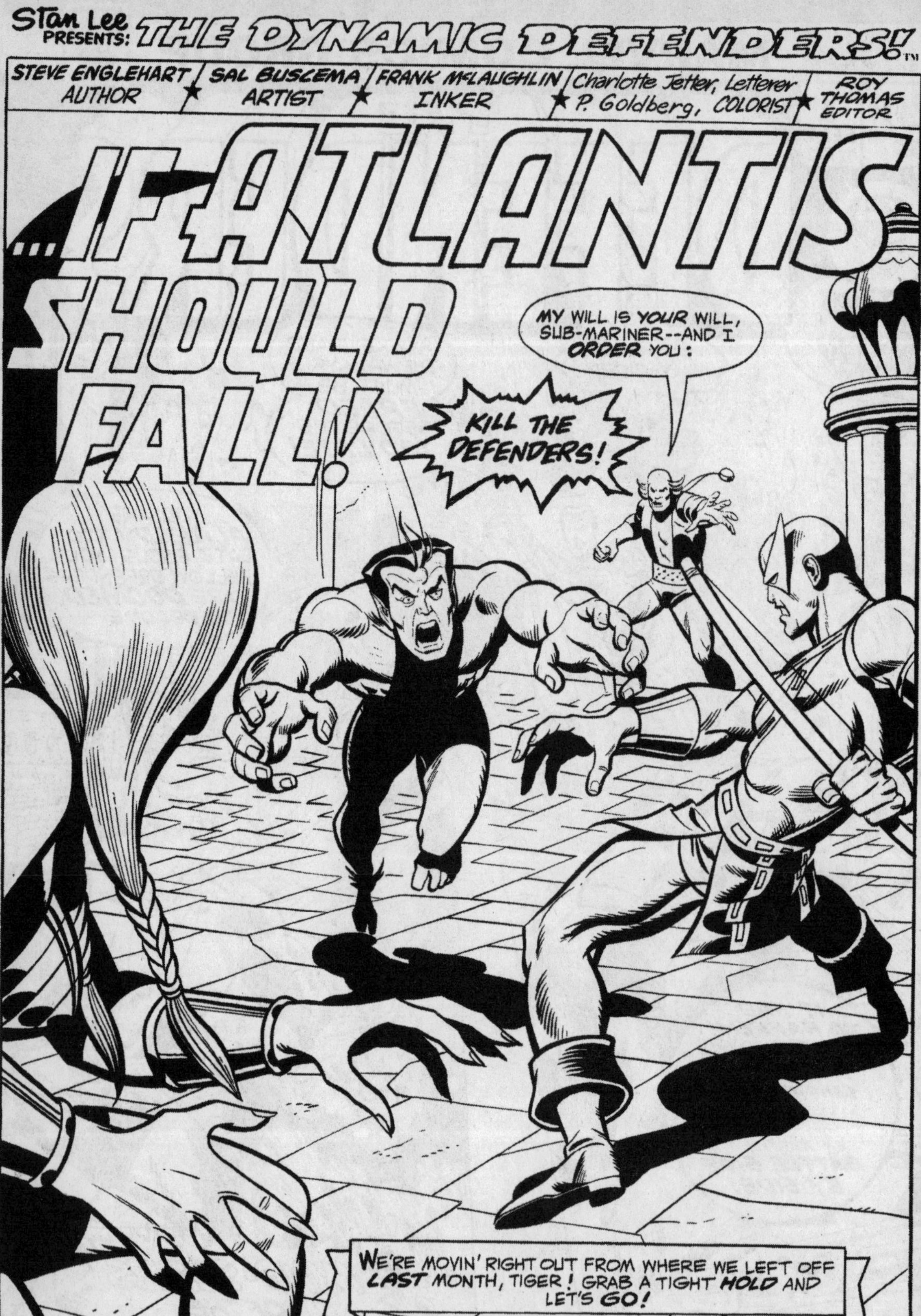
Stan Lee PRESENTS: THE DYNAMIC DEFENDERS!
STEVE ENGLEHART AUTHOR ★ SAL BUSCEMA ARTIST ★ FRANK McLAUGHLIN INKER ★ Charlotte Jetter, Letterer P. Goldberg, COLORIST ★ ROY THOMAS EDITOR
...IF ATLANTIS SHOULD FALL!
MY WILL IS YOUR WILL, SUB-MARINER--AND I ORDER YOU:
KILL THE DEFENDERS!
WE'RE MOVIN' RIGHT OUT FROM WHERE WE LEFT OFF LAST MONTH, TIGER! GRAB A TIGHT HOLD AND LET'S GO!
15137

HAWKEYE HAS NO STRENGTH! HE IS NOT *WORTH* THE WASTING OF MY PRINCELY *POWERS!*

POW

BUT THE *VALKYRIE*-- NOW *THAT* IS ANOTHER MATTER!

STAY *BACK*, NAMOR! DON'T YOU *UNDERSTAND*-- THE RED GHOST HAS USED HIS *COSMIC RAY TREATMENTS* TO CONTROL YOUR *MIND!*

I KNOW *NO* SUCH THING! I KNOW ONLY THAT I MUST *KILL* YOU!

KRAK

HE AIN'T *KIDDIN'!*

HE NEVER EVEN *FELT* MY MAKE-SHIFT SHAFT CONTACT HIS *CRANIUM!*

GHOSTY'S GOT 'IM *GOOD!*

BUT I'VE READ THIS STORY *BEFORE*--

--IF I PUT THE GUY *CONTROLLIN'* SUBBY'S BRAIN *OUT* OF IT, *SUBBY'LL* WAKE UP *SMILIN'!*

THE BAD GUYS CLEANED ME OUTTA *FANCY* ARROWS, AND THESE *HOME-MADE* JOBBIES ARE SO ERRATIC, THEY MIGHT *KILL* 'IM--

--BUT WITH A LITTLE OF THE OLD-TIME HAWKEYE-THE-ARCHER *SKILL*--

BOING!

--I CAN *BOMB* THE BIG STIFF!

CRASH!

DYNAMITE! I KNEW SITTIN' IN FOR THIS ONE GIG WITH THE *DEFENDERS* WAS A GOOD MOVE!

WAIT'LL THE *AVENGERS* GET A LOAD O' *THIS!*

"DUMB OLD HAWKEYE" SAVES THE DAY WITH *BRAIN* POW---

POW!

ON YOUR *FEET,* BOWMAN!

WHAT *FOR,* FISH-FACE? SO I CAN *FALL* FARTHER WHEN YOU PUNCH MY *FOOL HEAD?*

YOU *NEARLY* TURNED OUT THE LIGHTS WITH THAT *LAST* SMASH! I'M TOO *GROGGY* TO EVEN *TRY* TO DEFEND MYSELF!

IF YOU *HAVE* TO HIT ME-- MAKE IT *GOOD!*

THE VALIANT, BUT *REALISTIC,* ARCHER KNOWS HIS OPPONENT CAN GIVE *THOR* AND THE *HULK* A RUN FOR THEIR MONEY. WITHOUT HIS *WEAPONS,* HAWKEYE CAN ONLY *RESIGN* HIMSELF TO HIS *FATE!*

BUT, AS A BLINDING *FLASH* EXPLODES IN HIS TEMPLE, AND GRAY *GAUZE* FALLS OVER HIS EYES, HE SEES ONE LAST *SIGHT*--THE FALLEN *VALKYRIE*-- AND HE ASKS ONE LAST *QUESTION*--

"WHY?"

I HAVE GROWN **WEARY** OF HEARING YOU MUMBLE THAT INSIPID QUESTION DURING YOUR UNCONSCIOUSNESS --

--SO I WILL **GLADLY** PUT YOUR MIND AT **EASE**.... BEFORE I **STEAL** IT FROM YOU!

I, **IVAN KRAGOFF**, AM THE WORLD'S ONE TRUE **AUTHORITY** ON **COSMIC RAYS!**

IN MY STUDIES, I HAVE DISCOVERED THAT BOMBARDING A SUBJECT WITH SMALL BURSTS OF EXTRA RADIATION RENDERS THEM MINE TO **COMMAND** --

--AS YOU WELL **KNOW!**

BUT IT IS NOT MY **BRAIN** WHICH MAINTAINS MY DOMINANCE, BUT RATHER **NATURAL** COSMIC RAYS --

--**RAYS** THAT STRIKE **EVERYWHERE** ON EARTH, **CONTINUOUSLY!**

KNOCKING ME **UNCONSCIOUS** IS NO DEFENSE AGAINST THE **RED GHOST!** THERE **IS** NO DEFENSE!

"I BEGAN MY STUDIES WITH **APES** -- YET I MISTAKENLY GAVE THEM **TOO MUCH** RADIATION AND THEY TURNED **AGAINST** ME! I WAS FORCED TO **FLEE** WITH MY PARTNER, THE **UNICORN!***

* IRON MAN #16. --R.T.

"THE USELESS UNICORN WANTED MY **AID** IN CURING HIM OF A FATAL **MALADY**, BUT **INTERNAL MEDICINE** IS **NOT** MY FIELD. HE SOON **LEFT** ME --*

"--ALLOWING ME TO BEGIN MY **PRESENT** STUDIES ON CREATURES MORE **TRACTABLE** TO MY WILL:

"PORPOISES, SQUID AND **OTHER** UNDERSEA LIFE!

* WE FOLLOWED **UNI'S** LATER LIFE IN I.M. #57-58. --ROY.

"ONCE I ESTABLISHED MY **SUPREMACY** IN THE FIELD, I TOOK A **NEW** ALLY -- WHOSE **HERITAGE** AND LUST FOR **CONQUEST** IDEALLY SUITED MY PLANS!

"YOU HAVE ALREADY **MET** HIM. HIS NAME IS **ATTUMA!**"

OF COURSE, MY TREATMENTS ARE ALLOWED TO AFFECT ONLY THE MIND, AND NOT THE BODY...

...AS HAPPENED WITH THE CURSED *FANTASTIC FOUR* AND MYSELF!*

I HAVE BEEN QUITE *SUCCESSFUL* IN OBTAINING THE RESULTS I DESIRE WITH MY *FINNED* MINIONS--BUT *NOT*, UNFORTUNATELY, WITH *HUMANS*.

*AS TOLD IN *COUNTLESS* ISSUES OF THE *FANTASTIC FOUR*.-- R.T.

OFTEN, INSTEAD OF PRODUCING *MIND-SLAVES* LIKE *NAMOR*-- I *KILL* MY SUBJECTS!

CHERISH THAT THOUGHT AS YOU FACE MY *WILL-DESTROYER!* EITHER WAY, IT WILL BE YOUR *LAST!*

FADE TO BLACK...

...UNTIL OUR NARRATIVE RESUMES *TWO WEEKS* LATER, AT THE GREENWICH VILLAGE SANCTUM OF *DR. STRANGE.*

CLEA! WONG!

I HAVE MET WITH *SUCCESS*-- AT *LAST!*

THE POWERS I GAINED FROM MY DEPARTED *MENTOR* HAVE FINALLY ENABLED ME TO MAKE *PROGRESS* IN MY STRUGGLE TO UNDO THE SPELL WHICH TURNED THE *BLACK KNIGHT* TO *STONE!* *

WONDERFUL, MASTER!

* OBVIOUSLY, THIS TAKES PLACE *AFTER* THE EPOCHAL EVENTS IN *MARVEL PREMIERE* #10.--ROY.

STEPHEN, YOU MUST SUMMON THE *DEFENDERS.* THEY *DESERVE* THE PLEASURE OF THIS KNOWLEDGE!

YOU'RE *RIGHT*, CLEA. I SHALL SEND A *MENTAL SUMMONS* TO *EACH* OF MY ERSTWHILE ALLIES!

DEFENDERS-- HEAR ME--

AND ON A *METEOR* HURTLING JUST ABOVE EARTH'S ATMOSPHERE--

--AS WELL AS IN A GRIMY *BACK ALLEY* OF NEW YORK...

FOLLOW THIS *IMAGE* TO MY *DWELLING.*

...THE MESSAGE IS *RECEIVED.*

HOWEVER.... THERE WAS NO RESPONSE FROM EITHER THE *VALKYRIE* OR *NAMOR!*

I COULD NOT FIND ANY EVIDENCE OF THEIR *CEREBRAL EMANATIONS* ABOVE, BELOW, OR UPON THE ENTIRE PLANET!

THEY LIVE THEIR *OWN LIVES*, DOCTOR!

I IMAGINE IT IS NOTHING TO *WORRY* ABOUT.

HOWEVER...

THEY APPEAR *DEAD* TO ME GHOST. HOW MAY ATTUMA BE *CERTAIN* YOU HAVE NOT *KILLED* THEM?

BECAUSE IT IS *I* WHO *TELLS* YOU THEY LIVE!

YES, YOU ALSO *TOLD* ME THEY WILL FIGHT AT THE *FOREFRONT* OF MY LEGIONS WHEN WE ATTACK *ATLANTIS*--

--PROVIDING NOT ONLY *INSPIRATION*, BUT ALSO SOMETHING MORE WORTHY OF *FOLLOWING* THAN YOUR TRAINED *FISH!*

YET SO *FAR*, WE ARE NO NEARER NAMOR'S REALM THAN ON THE DAY I *MET* YOU!

THEN HEAR ME *WELL*, BARBARIAN: WE HAVE WAITED ONLY UNTIL THE *SCIENTIST* WE CAPTURED* AND I COULD PLACE A SUFFICIENT NUMBER OF CREATURES UNDER MY *CONTROL.*

THAT MOMENT HAS NOW *ARRIVED!*

THESE *SUPER-HEROES*, YOUR SCALED *"SOLDIERS"* --ALL ARE *READY!*

* LAST ISH.--R.

FINALLY! WITH THE *SUB-MARINER* AT MY SIDE--WITH AN ARMY OF MINDLESS *SLAVES*, ABLE TO PENETRATE WHERE MEN *CANNOT*--

--TODAY ATLANTIS *FALLS!*

GROM!

DOCTOR, I WAS NOT WITH THE *REST* OF YOU WHEN THE BLACK KNIGHT WAS *TRANSFORMED*--

--BUT AS A FELLOW *BEING*, I HAVE AN INTEREST IN HIS *FATE*. COULD WE NOT *PROCEED*?

YES... OF *COURSE*, SURFER. WORRY OVER TWO PEOPLE AS STRONG AS *NAMOR* AND *VAL* MUST SURELY BE *GROUNDLESS*.

STILL, I WISH I *KNEW*...

THEN, *UNEXPECTEDLY*--

HULK KNOWS WHERE FISH-MAN AND GIRL ARE.

--HE THINKS.

YOU *KNOW*? THEN *TELL* US, HULK, AND SET OUR MINDS AT *REST*!

BAH! WHY SHOULD HULK DO ANYTHING *DUMB MAGICIAN* WANTS?

HULK SHOULDN'T HAVE *COME* HERE IN *FIRST* PLACE--

--AND HE IS *LEAVING* --NOW!

WAIT, BRUTE!

IF YOU *TRULY* POSSESS THE INFORMATION WE NEED, YOU *MUST* GIVE IT TO US!

I HAVE NO WISH TO *HARM* YOU, BUT I WILL *RESTRAIN* YOU UNTIL YOU *SPEAK*!

SO SWEARS THE *SILVER SURFER*!

SO--ONE WHO HULK *LIKED* TURNS ON HIM LIKE EVERY-ONE ELSE!

LET *GO*, SHINY-FACE, OR HULK WILL--

--HULK WILL...

...WHAT?

ENOUGH, SURFER. YOUR ACTIONS PROVIDED ME WITH THE *TIME* NEEDED TO INDUCE A *TRANCE* IN THE *BEHEMOTH*!

NOW, HULK-- *TELL* US OF THE FISH-MAN AND THE GIRL!

"HULK CAME...TO YOUR *HOUSE*...WITH THEM...AND WITH PUNY PURPLE-MAN CALLED *HAWKEYE*. THEN, *BLUE-MAN* FROM NAMOR'S *HOME* CAME...SAID A-TOOM-A WOULD HURT ATLANTIC CITY."

"HULK DIDN'T *UNDERSTAND*. HULK *NEVER* UNDERSTANDS. BUT HE WENT *WITH* OTHERS..."

"...AND HAD GOOD *FIGHT* WITH BIG, SHELLS WITH CLAWS."

"THEN A-TOOM-A CAPTURED *OTHERS*...MADE THEM GET ON *WATER SHIP*. HULK DIDN'T WANT TO *GO*. HE *LEFT*."

"THAT IS ALL HULK KNOWS."

YET SURELY, THAT IS PLENTY.

HAWKEYE WAS WITH OUR FRIENDS--? AND THEY WERE ALL TAKEN *PRISONER*?

DOCTOR... IF YOU COULD NOT FIND THEIR *MIND-EMANATIONS*?

WHEN, HULK?

HULK DOES NOT UNDERSTAND TIME.

WE HAVE TOO FEW *FACTS* FOR *CONJECTURE* AT THIS TIME, SURFER--AND VISIONS OF *DOOM* WILL ONLY *DISTRACT* US!

I SHALL CAUSE THE HULK TO *SLEEP* UNTIL WE RETURN--

--NOW, LET US SEARCH THE OCEANS OF THE *WORLD* FOR THOSE WHO *NEED* US!

AND PRAY WE ARE NOT *TOO LATE*!

THEY FLASH THROUGH THE MYSTIC'S PROTECTIVE *INVISIBILITY* SCREEN--AND ARE *GONE*!

MEANWHILE, MANY THOUSANDS OF LEAGUES UNDER THE SEA...

SHOK

TO THE DEFENSES! ALERT TAMARA AND THE IMPERIAL GUARD!

WHALES-- BURSTING THROUGH THE VERY WALLS OF ATLANTIS, HERSELF!

AND BEHIND THEM: SQUIDS! PORPOISES!

BY THE SEVEN SECRET SEAS! PRINCE NAMOR SWIMS WITH OUR FOES!

THE SHOCK OF SEEING THEIR NEWLY-RETURNED MONARCH LEADING THE ATTACK SHOULD BE WORTH THREE LEGIONS ALONE, ATTUMA!

TODAY, THE REALM ETERNAL WILL INDEED BE YOURS--

--AND WITH ITS MIGHT AS A BASE, TOMORROW, THE WORLD SHALL BE OURS!

ON LAND, ONLY A HANDFUL OF BEINGS CAN EVEN HOLD THEIR OWN AGAINST THE TRUE SUB-MARINER--

--UNDERWATER, THERE ARE NONE!

FLANKING NAMOR TO THE LEFT, IS HAWKEYE, HIS MIND ALSO DRAINED OF ALL THOUGHTS SAVE THOSE OF BATTLE--

--AND HIS STRONG ARMS LOOSING SPECIAL ARROWS ADAPTED BY THE RED GHOST FROM THE COMMON SPEAR-GUN!

BRINGING UP THE RIGHT, COMES THE VALKYRIE-- TO WHOSE STRENGTH WATER IS NO HARDER TO CLEAVE THAN AIR!

ABRUPTLY, HOWEVER, THE WARRIOR WOMAN STOPS STONILY IN HER DRIFTING TRACKS!

REASON FLICKERS FOR A SECOND IN HER BLUE EYES-- BUT BEFORE IT CAN FLARE, FEAR EXTINGUISHES IT!

AND NOT MERE FEAR, EITHER-- BUT SHEER, STARK TERROR!

AAAA

THE SURFACE-CRAWLING HARRIDAN FALLS TO HER KNEES, GIBBERING INSANELY!

PERHAPS THE PRESSURE HAS AFFECTED HER--

--BUT IT MATTERS NOT! WE STILL HAVE LUCID FOES TO FIGHT!

LEAVE HER ALONE! WE MUST HURRY TO THE GATES!

THEIR WORDS MEAN NOTHING TO THE VALKYRIE--IN FACT, THEY SOUND LIKE THE SAVAGE GROWLS OF MONSTROUS BEASTS!

SHE GROPES HER WAY TOWARD THEM--AND HER MAD EYES PROTRUDE FROM THEIR STRETCHED SOCKETS AS SHE CLEARLY SEES--

--MONSTROUS BEASTS!

WAIT, SURFER! SUDDENLY--I FEEL A MIND--A FAMILIAR MIND!

THE THOUGHTS ARE JUMBLED--NOTHING IS CLEAR--

--BUT I AM SURE IT IS THE VALKYRIE!

THEN GUARD YOURSELF WITH YOUR MAGIC, DOCTOR!

WE SHALL INVESTIGATE!

GUIDE YOUR COSMIC CONVEYANCE TO THE RIGHT! SHE IS THERE!

SLOOSH!

BY THE HEAD OF MY FATHER! THAT MUST BE FABLED ATLANTIS-- UNDER SIEGE!

THEN UNDOUBTEDLY NAMOR IS NEARBY, THOUGH I STILL FIND NO SIGN OF HIS BRAIN!

BUT THERE IS THE PERSON WE SEEK!

VALKYRIE! VAL!

ONCE MORE, SHE TURNS...ONCE MORE, HER THROAT CONSTRICTS AS SHE PREPARES TO SCREAM THAT THROAT RAW...

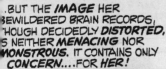

...BUT THE *IMAGE* HER BEWILDERED BRAIN RECORDS, THOUGH DECIDEDLY *DISTORTED,* IS NEITHER *MENACING* NOR *MONSTROUS.* IT CONTAINS ONLY CONCERN....FOR *HER!*

SHE'S BECOME *CALM*--NOW I CAN MAKE OUT WHAT SHE'S *THINKING!*

HER *ORIGINAL* PERSONALITY--THAT OF THE *INSANE* GIRL *BARBARA*--HAS PARTIALLY BROKEN *FREE*--

--BECAUSE SOMEONE CALLED THE *RED GHOST* HAS THWARTED HER *VALKYRIE* PERSONALITY! THE *TWO* WOMEN WITHIN HER ARE TRYING TO *KILL* EACH OTHER!

QUICKLY, SURFER!

HER MIND TELLS ME THAT OUR *OTHER* MISSING ALLIES ARE *ALSO* BELOW--

--AND, MORE *IMPORTANTLY,* THAT THIS *BRAIN-NUMBING* PROCESS DEPENDS UPON THE CONTINUAL FLOW OF *COSMIC RAYS!*

WE MUST *DAM* THAT FLOW!

YOU CANNOT BE *SERIOUS!*

I AM! TRUST ME!

LET US *COMBINE* OUR POWERS--- MINE THE *MYSTIC,* YOURS THE *COSMIC*--

--AND, THOUGH IT WILL TAKE *EVERY* IOTA OF STRENGTH WE TWO *POSSESS*--

"--WE SHALL CAUSE A *BARRIER* TO FORM AROUND THIS SPINNING SPHERE--

"--A BARRIER WHICH SHALL BE A *SHIELD* AGAINST *COSMIC RADIATION* STRIKING *ANYWHERE* ON EARTH!"

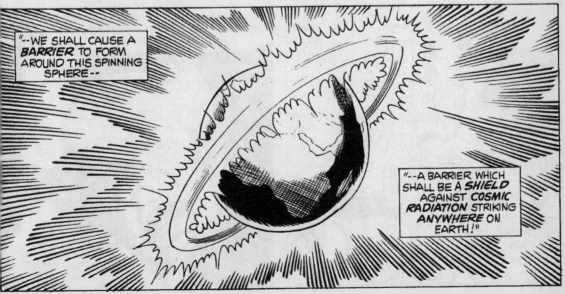

YOUR POWERS *ASTOUND* ME, STRANGE-- AND ONE WHO HAS SEEN THE *STAR SWARMS* OF THE *GALAXY* IS NOT *EASILY* ASTOUNDED!

I MUST *ALSO* ADMIT THAT I AM THE SLIGHTEST BIT *AFRAID!* YOU ARE VERY *DIFFERENT* FROM ANYONE I HAVE EVER ENCOUNTERED!

AFRAID OF...*ME? COME* NOW--I ONLY DO WHAT *ANYONE* COULD, HAD HE MY *BACKGROUND!*

YOU HAVE SEEN SO MUCH THAT ANYTHING YOU DO *NOT* UNDERSTAND SEEMS *UNNATURAL*--

--BUT *I* AM NOT A *HOBGOBLIN!* I AM MERELY A *MAN*--LIKE YOURSELF!

MEANWHILE--

ONWARD, YOU MINDLESS BARBARIAN WARRIORS!

FOLLOW MY *MIST-FORM* THROUGH THE *BREACHED BORDERS* OF *ATLANTIS!* FOLLOW THE *RED GHOST* TO VIC---

--TUUGG...

PLOOG

WHAT *HAPPENED?* MY BODY NO LONGER *SHAPES* ITSELF TO MY *DESIRES*--AND THAT IS *IMPOSSIBLE!*

AS LONG AS THE *COSMIC RAYS* FLOW--*WAIT!* WHAT'S *THAT?*

THE *FISH* I PLACED UNDER MY COMMAND ARE SWIMMING *AWAY*--

--AND THE *VALKYRIE* IS CHARGING *TOWARD* ME!

THIS IS *MADNESS!* SOMETHING IS *TERRIBLY* WRONG WITH THE NATURAL LAWS OF *SCIENCE!*

I DON'T DARE LET THE *GIRL* GET ME! I'VE GOT TO *RUN--FLEE---!*

UGG!

NOT PAST *ME*, NIKITA!

B'RER *HAWKEYE'S* BACK IN THE LAND OF THE LIVING, *TOO!*

THAT STEEL *BOW* SOMEONE EQUIPPED YOU WITH MAKES A GOOD WEAPON EVEN *WITHOUT* ARROWS, HAWKEYE!

TOO GOOD, IF YOU ASK *ME*. I WANTED TO FEED HIM EBONY *AGONY* FOR WHAT HE PUT ME *THROUGH!*

WHOA, LETHAL LADY. *BLOOD* WOULD JUST CLOUD UP THE *WATER!*

WE *GOT* 'IM. LET IT *GO!*

BUT, ALTHOUGH THE WARRIOR WOMAN SILENTLY SHEATHES HER *SWORD*, SHE CANNOT FORGET THE *INSANITY* THAT HAD COME UPON HER--UNTIL THE END OF HER *TRANCE* ALLOWED THE *VALKYRIE* TO ONCE MORE GAIN *CONTROL* IN HER MIND!

AND *SUBBY'S* NONE TOO THRILLED WITH HIS LAST FEW WEEKS, *EITHER!*

WHAT'S WRONG WITH MY *TROOPS*, JENNINGS? THEY FALL BACK IN *CONFUSION!*

ATTUMA-- HE WHO HINDERED ME FROM SAVING MY BELOVED *DORMA* FROM THE SEA-WITCH *LLYRA*.※

IN MY *HASTE*, I DID NOT *DESTROY* HIM THAT DAY--

*SUBBY #37. ---R.

--BUT WHAT SWEET **PLEASURE** IT GIVES ME **NOW** TO ENGAGE HIM AGAIN!

TURN, LORD OF THE MURKY DEPTHS! TURN AND FACE THE LORD OF **ATLANTIS**--

--**NAMOR,** *THE AVENGING SON!*

NO! THIS TIME THE PLAN WAS **PERFECT!** YOU **CANNOT** BE HERE!

READY YOURSELF, BRIGAND--

KLOP!

--THE TRUE **SUB-MARINER** WILL USE BUT **ONE SOUL-FULFILLING BLOW** FOR THE LIKES OF **YOU!**

WHEN A MAN FEELS EVERY **OUNCE** OF POWER AT HIS **COMMAND** RIDING ON HIS FIST--AND THAT **FIST** CONNECTS WITH HIS MORTAL **FOE**--

--THAT IS **VENGEANCE,** AND IT IS **COMPLETE!**

SO, AFTER ROUNDING EVERYBODY UP, THE DEFENDERS, MORE OR LESS--HEAD FOR **ATLANTIC CITY...**

ATLANTIS HAS WEATHERED **ANOTHER** STORM. **COME,** PROFESSOR--WE SHALL **RETURN** YOU TO YOUR VACATION.

...THEN TO THE HOUSE OF **DR. STRANGE,** WHERE NEW **MYSTERY** AND **ADVENTURE** AWAIT!

THEY ALSO AWAIT ON THE **NEXT PAGE,** TIGER--SO DON'T STOP **HERE!**

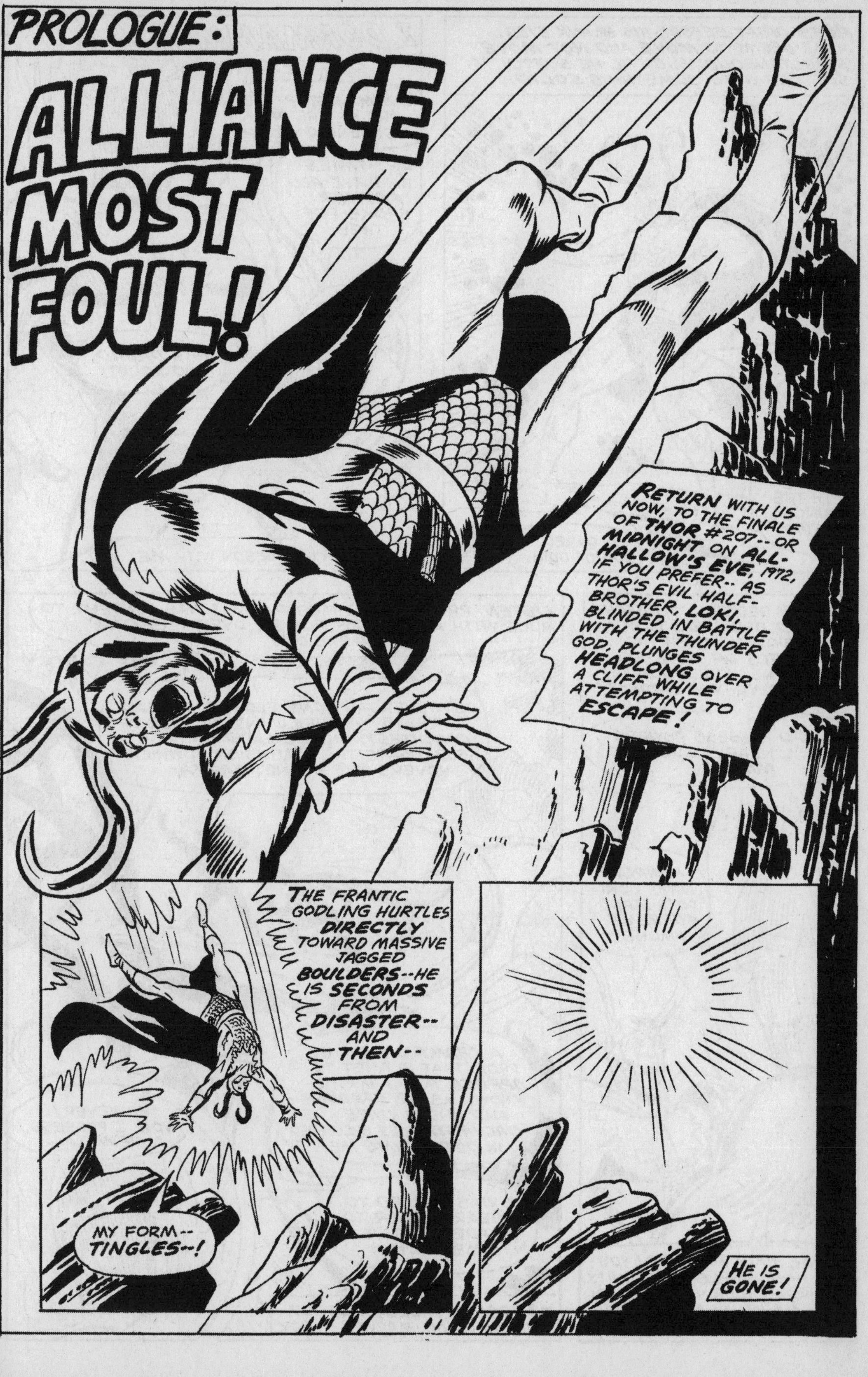

PROLOGUE:
ALLIANCE MOST FOUL!
RETURN WITH US NOW, TO THE FINALE OF THOR #207-- OR MIDNIGHT ON ALL-HALLOW'S EVE, 1972, IF YOU PREFER-- AS THOR'S EVIL HALF-BROTHER, LOKI, BLINDED IN BATTLE WITH THE THUNDER GOD, PLUNGES HEADLONG OVER A CLIFF WHILE ATTEMPTING TO ESCAPE!
THE FRANTIC GODLING HURTLES DIRECTLY TOWARD MASSIVE JAGGED BOULDERS--HE IS SECONDS FROM DISASTER-- AND THEN--
MY FORM-- TINGLES--!
HE IS GONE!

AGES DRIFT BEFORE HIS BLANK EYES... TIME SEEMS TO *MOVE* AND *NOT MOVE* SIMULTANEOUSLY...UNTIL HE SOFTLY SETTLES ONTO SOMETHING *SOLID.*

WHERE *BE* I? WHO HATH DARED TO *TRIFLE* WITH THE PRINCE OF *EVIL?*

I *DARED,* SON OF ODIN--

I, DORMAMMU!

DORMAMMU? THE LORD OF THE *DARK DIMENSION?*

OFT-TIMES HATH THE *ALL-FATHER* SPOKEN OF THEE!

WITH *DREAD,* NO DOUBT!

NAY! IN COMPARISON WITH *ME!*

THEN MY DECISION TO *RESCUE* YOU-- TO BRING YOU TO *MY* DIMENSION THROUGH THE *CHANNELS OF TIME* SO THAT NONE WOULD SUSPECT OUR *MEETING*--WAS *CORRECT!*

YOU *DO* POSSESS POWERS OF EVIL NEARLY EQUAL TO *MINE!*

NEARLY? NAY! LOKI DOTH STAND *SUPREME* AMONG---

CEASE YOUR BOASTING! YOU WILL HAVE *AMPLE* OPPORTUNITY TO PROVE YOUR VALUE IF YOU JOIN ME IN MY GRANDEST *SCHEME!*

LISTEN, PRINCE-- IN TIMES *PAST,* I WAS CONTENT TO RULE WITH *ABSOLUTE POWER* OVER THIS *ONE* DIMENSION!

HOWEVER, AS *EONS* FLOWED, I BEGAN TO CRAVE THE THRILL AND THUNDER OF *CONQUEST,* AND I CREATED PLANS TO SUBJUGATE THE DIMENSION IN WHICH HOVERS THE PLANET *EARTH!*

A *CHAMPION* CAME FROM THAT PLANET TO *OPPOSE* ME-- A MYSTIC KNOWN AS *DR. STRANGE*-- AND UNDER *DIRE CIRCUMSTANCES,* SUCCEEDED IN *DEFEATING* ME!

I WAS FORCED TO SWEAR *NEVER* TO INVADE EARTH'S DIMENSION. *

HOWEVER, *NOW* I POSSESS A *NEW* PLAN.

STRANGE TALES #126-127, FRIENDS OF OL' MARVEL.-- ROY.

"*I* HAVE DISCOVERED THE EXISTENCE OF A DEVICE CALLED THE *EVIL EYE* WITH POWER ENOUGH TO *EXPAND* MY DIMENSION UNTIL IT *SWALLOWS* THAT OF EARTH!"

"*ONCE THAT IS DONE,* THE PLANET SHALL BE *MINE* FOR THE TAKING-- FOR WITH EARTH THEN *INSIDE* MY *DOMINION,* I MAY *CONQUER* IT WITHOUT BREAKING MY *WORD!*"

BUT-- *LEGEND* HATH IT THAT THE *EVIL EYE* WAS *DESTROYED* --EXPLODED BY ITS OWN *LIMITLESS POWER!* *

*LEGEND-- AND *FANTASTIC FOUR #54,* TRUE BELIEVER! --*RASCALLY.*

TRUE-- IT *WAS* SHATTERED INTO ITS *SIX COMPONENT PARTS!* YET *YOUR* MYSTICAL MIGHT, COMBINED WITH *MINE,* CAN *REASSEMBLE* IT!

SINCE *I* MAY NOT GO TO EARTH, AND SINCE *YOU* ARE *BLIND,* WE NEED ONLY TO HAVE SIX *EARTHLINGS* GATHER THOSE SIX PARTS-- AND I HAVE *JUST* THE SIX IN *MIND:*

THE FRIENDS OF THE CURSED *DR. STRANGE-- THE DEFENDERS!*

WILL YOU *AID* ME IN THIS ENDEAVOR, PRINCE OF EVIL?

AYE, DORMAMMU -- I *SHALL!*

THIS TIME, MY HALF-BROTHER'S *BELOVED EARTH* SHALL INDEED *PERISH AWAY!*

*T*IGER, YOU HAVE NOW TAKEN THE *FIRST STEP* ALONG A ROAD WHICH WILL LEAD TO THE MOST *TITANIC* CONFLICT EVER PRESENTED IN COMICS: THE LONG-AWAITED *CLASH* BETWEEN THE MIGHTY *AVENGERS* AND THE DYNAMIC *DEFENDERS!*

*I*N FACT, THIS CONFLICT IS *SO* OVERWHELMING, SO *BREATH-TAKING,* THAT IT CANNOT BE CONTAINED WITHIN MERELY ONE TITLE -- SO IT WILL RUN IN *BOTH* THE *AVENGERS* AND THE *DEFENDERS,* SIMULTANEOUSLY, FOR THE ENTIRE SUMMER!

*T*HERE ARE SIX MORE INSTALLMENTS COMING, AND THE NEXT ONE APPEARS IN *DEFENDERS #8,* ON SALE NOW! DON'T MISS IT-- AND THEN *REJOIN* US FOR *AVENGERS #116* NEXT MONTH!

*H*APPY READING -- FROM *US* TO *YOU!*

AVENGERS #115 (NOW ON SALE) CONTAINED THE *PROLOGUE* TO THE LONG-AWAITED *EPIC* OF THE INEVITABLE CLASH BETWEEN *THEM* AND *US*! MAKE SURE YOU'VE SAVORED *THAT* MINI-GEM BEFORE PERUSING *THIS* ONE:

CHAPTER ONE DECEPTION!!

I HAVE BROUGHT THE *DEFENDERS* HERE-- AND YOU, *TOO*, HAWKEYE --BECAUSE I WISH TO *IMMEDIATELY* PURSUE A DISCOVERY I MADE SCANT *HOURS* AGO--

--THE FIRST *BREAKTHROUGH* IN MY EFFORTS TO *UNDO* THE *SPELL* WHICH TURNED THE *BLACK KNIGHT* TO *STONE!*

HOLY COW! IT *IS* HIM: MY OLD *AVENGIN'* PARTNER!

I *WONDERED* WHY MY *BACK-STABBIN'* BUDDIES DIDN'T RING *HIM* IN AS MY REPLACEMENT!*

*A SIDEWAYS REFERENCE TO *DAREDEVIL #99.*--ROY.

MAGICIAN AND SILVER-FACE MADE HULK *SLEEP* TILL THEY CAME BACK! NOBODY CAN *MAKE* HULK DO ANYTHING AND NOT GET *HURT!*

BLACK KNIGHT *HELPED* HULK ONCE, SO HULK WILL *WAIT* TO SEE IF MAGICIAN CAN *FIX* HIM. BUT *THEN*--!

THE BLACK KNIGHT! I FEEL AN OVERPOWERING, IRRATIONAL *LOVE* FOR HIM--UNDOUBTEDLY BECAUSE *MY* EXISTENCE AND *HIS* PRESENT STATE *BOTH* SPRANG FROM THE ENCHANTRESS'S *PSYCHE!*

BUT IF I'M *CRACKING UP*, I'M MORE THAN *EVER* CONVINCED I DON'T WANT TO LOVE *ANYONE!* IF HE SHOULD BECOME *FLESH AND BLOOD* AGAIN--!

LET *NOW* RISE THE OCCULT *ORB OF AGAMOTTO!*

I HAVE FOUND DANE WHITMAN'S *ESSENCE*-- HIS *SOUL*-- IN THE DARK REALM TO WHICH IT *FLED* WHEN HIS *BODY* BECAME *STONE!*

I PROPOSE TO *CONTACT* IT!

A TENDRIL OF *TURQUOISE* SLIPS FROM ORB TO FOREHEAD--- IT PLAYS ACROSS THE GRAY GRANITE--

AND THEN BURSTS BLINDINGLY *THROUGH*--

UNERRINGLY, THE MYSTIC BOLT BEARING THE THOUGHTS OF THE *MAGICIAN* QUESTS ALONG UNSEEN PATHS, EVER *DEEPER* INTO A COSMOS *UNNAMED* AND *UNNAMABLE*--

INTO THE BEYOND!

--UNTIL IT REACHES ITS LONG-SOUGHT *GOAL:* THE *SHADE* OF HIM WHOM BOTH THE *WORLD* AND THE *NETHERWORLD* CALL--

--THE BLACK KNIGHT!

AS THE MYSTIC BOLT DID ONLY *MINUTES* BEFORE, IT STREAKS DIRECTLY FOR HIS *FOREHEAD*--

--AND WHEN IT *STRIKES,* THE SEPULCHRAL VOICE OF *DR. STRANGE* FILLS THE VOID!

DANE WHITMAN! THIS IS THE *DEFENDERS!* CAN YOU *HEAR* US?

WE ARE WORKING TO *RESCUE* YOU, BUT THE *IMMORTAL SORCERESS'* SPELL IS NEARLY *UNSHAKABLE!*

HAVE YOU LEARNED ANYTHING FROM *YOUR* VANTAGE POINT THAT MAY AID US?

YES, I CAN *HEAR* YOU! I *CAN!*

BUT THERE'S *NOTHING* HERE EXCEPT *EMPTINESS*-- *DESOLATION!* I KNOW *NOTHING!* STILL, *TIME* DOESN'T MOVE HERE, AND I'M NOT *SUFFERING!*

I HAVE HAD *FAITH*--AND NOW I HAVE CERTAIN *HOPE*--THAT YOU WILL *SAVE* ME!

THEN THAT MESSAGE BEGINS THE LONG *RETURN* TO DR. STRANGE!

BUT IN THE INTERDIMENSIONAL GULFS.... LURKS *TROUBLE!*

HOW *LONG* MUST WE WAIT HERE FOR THIS ACCURSED *MESSAGE* THOU DOST EXPECT, DORMAMMU?

LOKI DOTH NOW DWELL IN CONTINUAL *DARKNESS*, AND DOTH NOT *APPRECIATE* CONTINUAL *SILENCE!*

ACCEPT MY *APOLOGIES*, PRINCE OF EVIL! I HAD *FORGOTTEN* THE *BLINDNESS* YOUR HALF-BROTHER BROUGHT UPON YOU!✷

*IN *THOR* #207.--R.

I TRUST THOU HAST *NOT* FORGOTTEN THY PROMISE TO *CURE* ME OF MY AFFLICTION, IN EXCHANGE FOR MY HELPING YOU TRICK THE *DEFENDERS!*

HOW COULD I FORGET *THAT?* IT IS *CENTRAL* TO MY PLAN TO CONQUER *EARTH'S DIMENSION!*

NO, WE ARE *PARTNERS*, YOU AND I--

HOLD! THERE IS THE BLACK KNIGHT'S *REPLY*, HURTLING TOWARD EARTH'S *DIMENSIONAL GATE!*

BUT A SIMPLE *SPELL* SHALL *DIVERT* IT MOMENTARILY!

IT WAS *I* WHO GUIDED STRANGE'S *ORIGINAL* PSYCHIC FEELERS TO THE KNIGHT'S ESSENCE--SO *IMPERCEPTIBLY*, THE MAGE NEVER *KNEW*--

--SOLELY IN ORDER TO *BRING ABOUT* THIS MESSAGE!

--FOR THE *CRUX* OF MY SCHEME IS TO *SUBSTITUTE* THE KNIGHT'S WORDS WITH MY *OWN*--

--AND IT WILL TAKE OUR *COMBINED POWERS* TO DO SO WITHOUT *ALERTING* DR. STRANGE!

THERE! IT IS *DONE*--AND NONE BUT *WE TWO* COULD HAVE EVEN *ATTEMPTED* IT!

TO *COMPREHEND* THE MESSAGE IN AN *INSTANT*--TO ALTER *ONLY* WHAT *NEEDED* TO BE ALTERED--THESE ARE THE PROOFS OF OUR *SUPERIORITY*--!

--AND IT IS *BECAUSE* WE ARE SUPERIOR THAT *EARTH* SHALL SOON BE *OURS!*

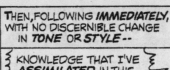

AND SO, MINUTES LATER....

LISTEN! THAT'S THE BLACK KNIGHT'S VOICE!

YES, I CAN HEAR YOU! I CAN!

THEN, FOLLOWING *IMMEDIATELY,* WITH NO DISCERNIBLE CHANGE IN *TONE* OR *STYLE* --

KNOWLEDGE THAT I'VE *ASSIMILATED* IN THIS MYSTIC REALM TELLS ME I CAN BE RESCUED THROUGH THE POWER OF THE *EVIL EYE!* HURRY, *PLEASE!*

I HAVE HAD *FAITH* -- AND NOW I HAVE CERTAIN *HOPE* -- THAT YOU WILL *SAVE* ME!

THAT....WAS A *STRAIN,* EVEN FOR ONE AS *PRACTICED* IN MYSTICISM AS I.

STILL, AT *LAST* WE HAVE AN IDEA OF HOW TO *FREE* THE MAN!

BUT *DOCTOR,* THE EVIL EYE IS *NO MORE!*

REED RICHARDS TOLD ME THAT THE HUMAN TORCH SAW IT EXPLODE INTO *NOTHINGNESS!* ※

MAYBE *SO,* NICKLE-PLATE-- BUT IF SOMEBODY HANGIN' OUT IN A *NAMELESS DIMENSION* SAYS IT'S AROUND, *THIS* EARTH-BOUND BOY AIN'T GONNA *ARGUE!*

※ IN *FANTASTIC FOUR* #54.-- ROY.

I *AGREE!* SOMEHOW, THE EVIL-EYE *MUST* STILL EXIST--

--AND THE DEFENDERS WILL *FIND* IT-- OR *PERISH* IN THE *ATTEMPT!*

THE DEFENDERS-- AND *HAWKEYE!* I'M NOT PLAYIN' A *LONE HAND* IF A GUY WHO NEVER *HASSLED* ME NEEDS HELP!

SO SAY WE *ALL* ARCHER! SO SAY WE ALL!

NEXT MONTH -- THIS EPIC SAGA CONTINUES WITH *FULL-LENGTH* STORIES IN BOTH...

THE AVENGERS AND *THE DEFENDERS!*

DON'T MISS:

AVENGERS #116 FOR CHAPTERS 2 AND 3 AND THEN REJOIN US IN *DEFENDERS* #9 FOR CHAPTERS 4 AND 5!

FACE IT, YOU LUCKY MARVELITE: YOU'VE SEEN BIG ONES, BUT THIS IS-- *THE BIG ONE!!*

AVENGERS
MARVEL COMICS GROUP
APPROVED BY THE COMICS CODE AUTHORITY
20¢
116
OCT
02458
EARTH'S MIGHTIEST HEROES!
AVENGERS
WHERE STRIKES THE SILVER SURFER-- THERE FALLS AN ENEMY TO HIS DOOM!!
VISION! NO! NO!! DON'T FALL!! THE VOLCANO!
IT'S AVENGER VS. DEFENDER-- TO THE DEATH!!

TEN YEARS AGO THIS MONTH, STAN LEE and JACK KIRBY CREATED...
THE MIGHTY AVENGERS!®
TODAY, STEVE ENGLEHART and BOB BROWN CONTINUE THE STANDARD OF EXCELLENCE THAT HAS ALWAYS MARKED MARVEL'S MIGHTIEST, MOST EXCITING GROUP-- IN A NEW CHAPTER OF THEIR CATACLYSMIC CLASH WITH THE DYNAMIC DEFENDERS!
THE SCENE IS THE SANCTUM SANCTORUM OF DR. STRANGE-- AND THE PASSWORD IS ACTION!
CHAPTER 2
BETRAYAL!
READ ON...
MIKE ESPOSITO, inker
JOHN COSTANZA, letterer
PETRA GOLDBERG, colorist
JOHNNY ROMITA, art director
ROY THOMAS, editor

ODIN'S BLOOD! I DID BUT PLACE MY HAND 'PON THE LATCH TO DR. STRANGE'S ABODE--

--AND AN UNSEEN FORCE HURLED US INTO THE SKY!

FOR A ROUGH GUESS, THOR-- I'D SAY HE DOESN'T WANT VISITORS!

I WOULDN'T EITHER, WANDA-- IF I'D TAKEN THE BLACK KNIGHT AWAY FROM HIS CASTLE AND KEPT IT A SECRET FROM HIS TEAMMATES!

I NEVER DID PUT MUCH TRUST IN A MAN WHO CLAIMS TO WORK MAGIC, CAP--

--AND REPULSOR RAYS OR WHATEVER HE'S GOT RIGGED UP IN HIS FRONT DOOR DON'T INSPIRE TRUST!

I WANT SOME ANSWERS FROM HIM!

BLAM! BLAM!

THAT IS THE REASON WE ALL HAVE COME, IRON MAN--

--AND WHAT WE SHAN'T DEPART WITHOUT!

YES? HOW MAY THIS HUMBLE ONE *SERVE* YOU, SIR?

THOU MAYEST INFORM THY *MASTER* THAT THE *AVENGERS* WISH WORDS WITH HIM--AND *QUICKLY!*

I AM MOST *DEEPLY* SORRY, SIR, BUT MY MASTER IS ENGAGED IN VITAL *RESEARCH* AT THE MOMENT, AND HAS REQUESTED THAT HE NOT BE *DISTURBED!*

OUR RECEPTION THUS FAR HATH *SORELY* TRIED OUR PATIENCE!

GOOD DAY, SIR.

BY HOGUN'S MACE!

THE *GOD OF THUNDER* SHALL ENDURE *NO MORE!*

CHOOM!

SO! IF *MYSTICAL WARNINGS* AND *CONVERSATION* WILL NOT STOP YOUR INTRUSION--

--*WONG* SHALL!

MANTIS MAY MAKE LIES OF YOUR BOASTS, SERVANT!

THE NEXT *SPLIT-INSTANT,* THE SUPPLE *MISTRESS* OF THE MARTIAL ARTS SLAMS THE STARTLED *WONG* AGAINST A FAR *DOOR*--

--AS SEVERAL *AVENGERIAL EYES* SNAP *WIDE* AT WHAT THEY SEE *WITHIN* THAT DARKENED CHAMBER--

--AND *THEN*--

--A *NEW SORCEROUS* FORCE ENFOLDS THEM--

--AND--

STRANGE DID IT TO US *AGAIN!*

THAT'S IT! I WASN'T *SURE* BEFORE, BUT THERE'S NO *ROOM* FOR DOUBT *NOW!*

THE BLACK KNIGHT'S *IN* THERE, ALL RIGHT-- TURNED TO *STONE*

AND STRANGE IS *DETERMINED* TO KEEP US *OUT!*

WE KNOW FULL *WELL* THAT WE CANNOT FIGHT THY *SPELLS,* MAGICIAN!*

YET THE *AVENGERS* SHALL NEVER ADMIT *DEFEAT!*

WHEN WE HAVE DETERMINED HOW *BEST* TO *BATTLE* THY MAGIC, WE SHALL *RETURN!*

*SEE LAST ISSUE.--ROY.

UPRAISED *FISTS:* HOW *ODD* THAT, IN AN ENTIRELY *DIFFERENT* DIMENSION, THE SAME GESTURE NOW LAUDS TOTAL *TRIUMPH!*

WE HAVE *DONE* IT, LOKI: DECEIVED *DR. STRANGE* AND THE *DEFENDERS* IN BELIEVING THE *EVIL EYE* CAN BREAK THE SPELL HOLDING THE BLACK KNIGHT A PRISONER IN STONE!*

FINE, DORMAMMU--I BE *PLEASED* THAT *THOU* ART PLEASED!

*DEFENDERS #8.--R.T.

YET IS IT NOT THEN *TIME* TO *CURE* ME OF MY *BLINDNESS,* AS THOU DIDST *PROMISE?*

IN DUE *COURSE,* PRINCE OF EVIL.... IN DUE *COURSE.*

THE DEFENDERS HAVE NOT YET GATHERED THE *PIECES* OF THE EYE.

HE DOTH TREAT ME LIKE A WHINING *CHILD!* CAN IT BE THAT MORE THAN MINE *EYES* HAVE BEEN BLIND...?

BUT *NOW*, BACK TO THAT MYSTERIOUS ROOM IN THE HOME OF *DR. STRANGE* -- OCCUPIED, WE NOW SEE, BY *MORE* THAN JUST A *STATUE* --

-- TO THE TUNE OF FIVE *DEFENDERS*... AND A RECENT *RECRUIT* CALLED *HAWK-EYE!*

WHATEVER THAT *DISTURBANCE* MAY HAVE BEEN, THE MYSTIC *SEAL* I PLACED AROUND US HAS *ENDED* IT.

IT IS WELL. WE HAVE NO *TIME* TO INVESTIGATE ANYTHING BUT THE TASK BEFORE US!

TO *SAVE* THE BLACK KNIGHT, WE SHALL NEED THE *EVIL EYE* -- SO I HAVE CONJURED THE *ORB OF AGAMOTTO* TO UNFOLD ITS RECENT *HISTORY!*

AN *IMAGE* APPEARS! IN *MOMENTS*, WE SHALL ALL HEAR A *TELEPATHIC VOICE!*

BE *SILENT* -- AND *LISTEN!*

EACH HEARS THE VOICE *DIFFERENTLY*... BUT *ESSENTIALLY*, IT SAYS: "THE EVIL EYE BELONGED TO *PRESTER JOHN*, SOLE SURVIVOR OF THE *WIZARD-ISLE* CALLED *AVALON*, WHO WAS AWAKENED FROM HIS *700*-YEAR SLEEP BY THE *HUMAN TORCH* AND *WYATT WINGFOOT*. *

* THE ORACULAR ORB HAS BEEN READING *FANTASTIC FOUR #54* ON THE SLY, METHINKS. --ROY.

"THE TORCH *STOLE* THE WANDERER'S WEAPON WHEN HE PERCEIVED THAT ITS LIMITLESS *POWER* COULD DESTROY THE *GREAT REFUGE* --

"-- BEHIND WHICH HIS *THEN*-LOVE *CRYSTAL*, OF THE LEGENDARY *INHUMANS*, WAS IMPRISONED.

"HOWEVER, *UNKNOWN* TO HIM, THE DEVICE'S ENERGY WAS BUILDING TOWARD A CRITICAL *OVERLOAD* AND *EXPLOSION*.

"PRESTER JOHN AND WYATT WINGFOOT *FOLLOWED* HIM, ATTEMPTING TO *SAVE* HIM, AS HE FLEW ACROSS THE AFRICAN DESERT.

"AT THE LAST *MOMENT,* THE INDIAN WAS FORCED TO RISK *SHOOTING* THE WEAPON FROM THE TORCH'S HAND WITH A *POLARIZER GUN* INVENTED BY THE *BLACK PANTHER.*

"HE DID NOT MISS,

"SECONDS *LATER,* THE DEVICE *DETONATED* WITH THE FORCE OF AN *ATOMIC BOMB.*

"THE EVIL EYE, *INVINCIBLE* AS IT WAS, COULD NOT BE *DESTROYED* BY THE BLAST. HOWEVER, IT BURST INTO *SIX SIMILAR PARTS* THAT WERE DRIVEN *THROUGH* THE PLANET.

"THIS WAS IN ACCORDANCE WITH *INSTRUCTIONS* BUILT INTO IT BY THE MEN OF AVALON, TO INSURE THAT ANYONE WHO *DARED* USE THE WEAPON AT *FULL POWER* COULD NEVER HAVE A *SECOND CHANCE.*

"THE PROGRAMMED PARTS HURTLED *ONWARD* UNTIL THEY ONCE AGAIN FELT *SUNLIGHT,* ENDING THEIR JOURNEYS IN--

"OSAKA, JAPAN.

"FT. WAYNE, UNITED STATES.

"RURUTU, FRENCH POLYNESIA.

"LOS ANGELES, UNITED STATES.

"MONTERREY, MEXICO.

"SUCRE, BOLIVIA."

THE IMAGE HAS *ENDED*... THE VOICE NO LONGER *SPEAKS!*

RETURN TO YOUR *CASK OF CONCEALMENT,* ORB! YOUR *OCCULT POWERS* HAVE SERVED US WELL *AGAIN.*

SIX: THE *SACRED NUMBER* OF HALF-MYTHICAL AVALON!

THAT EXPLAINS WHY THEY CONSTRUCTED THE EVIL EYE IN *SIX SECTIONS.*

AND THERE ARE *SIX* OF *US!*

SAY NO *MORE,* SIX FIEND. WE'LL *CORRAL* THOSE PARTS FOR THE BLACK KNIGHT!

ONLY *THING* IS-- I SEEM TO HAVE LEFT MY *AVENGERS QUINJET* IN MY *OTHER SUIT.* I'LL NEED A LIFT.

RIDE WITH THE *VALKYRIE,* ARCHER! WE'LL TAKE THE *SOUTHERN* LANDS.

THE *SILVER SURFER* AND I SHALL FLY TO THE *FURTHEST SHORES!*

HULK, WE UNDERSTAND YOUR *ANIMOSITY* TOWARD MANY OF US, BUT FOR THE *KNIGHT'S* SAKE, YOU MUST *ALSO* HELP US!

THE KNIGHT'S SOUL MUST BE RESCUED *QUICKLY,* HULK! HE NEEDS *ALL* OF US!

YES... HULK WILL *DO* IT!

THEN LEAP TO *LOS ANGELES,* BEHEMOTH. I SHALL MYSTIC-ALLY GUIDE *ALL* OF YOU TO THE *EXACT LOCATIONS* SHOWN BY THE ORB, WHILE I REMAIN HERE TO GUARD THE *KNIGHT.*

WHEN ONE OF YOU RETURNS, I SHALL *THEN* GO TO THE *CLOSEST* SITE IN *INDIANA.*

NOW--

--BEGONE!

MEANTIME, HOWEVER, *LOKI'S* DIRE SUSPICIONS HAVE SUDDENLY *CRYSTAL-IZED* INTO CERTAIN *KNOWLEDGE!*

WHAT A *FOOL* I HAVE BEEN! WHAT AN *ABYSMALLY STUPID* FOOL!

SHOULD THAT STRUTTING *PEACOCK* GAIN THE POWER TO CONQUER *EARTH'S* DIMENSION--

"-- HE WOULD *LIKEWISE* POSSESS THE POWER TO CONQUER *ASGARD--* AND WOULD USE IT! I HAVE *PREOCCUPIED* MYSELF WITH MY HATRED FOR *ONE* PLANET-- AND NEVER SEEN THE *GRANDER* SCHEME!"

"THOUGH *DRIVEN* FROM THE FABLED REALM MORE TIMES THAN I DO CARE TO *RECALL*, STILL AM I AN *IMMORTAL!*

"NONE BUT I MUST E'ER WREST THE *ODIN-POWER* FROM THE *ALL-FATHER!*"

YET, I BE *BLIND!* I MUST NEEDS SEEK *AID* TO THWART THIS HIDEOUS PLAN I DID HELP *LOOSE!*

ASGARD IS *DENIED* ME, BY ODIN'S *DECREE!* THEN, THOUGH MY *SOUL* DOTH CURDLE AT THE THOUGHT, THERE BE BUT *ONE* TO WHOM I MAY TURN FOR ASSISTANCE--

--THOR!

* IN *THOR* #194.-- ROY.

AND SO IT COMES TO PASS THAT CAPTAIN AMERICA'S THOUGHTS ON THE *DR. STRANGE* PROBLEM ARE QUITE *UNIQUELY* INTERRUPTED!

GOOD LORD! APPEARING FROM *THIN AIR*--

--LOKI!

QUICKLY, WHOEVER THO ART-- I HAVE *DRAINED* MYSELF TO SEND THIS PROJECTION HITHER--

-- THOU MUST *CONDUCT* ME TO MY *HALF-BROTHER* ERE THE STRAIN DOTH PULL ME *HENCE* ONCE MORE, AND I BE UNABLE TO *WARN* YE!

BASE *VARLET!* THY *DECEIT* BE TOO *WELL KNOWN* FOR THY TRICKERY TO FIND *SUCCESS* WITH THE *GOD OF THUNDER!*

NO, THOR! DON'T YOU SEE THAT HE *CAN'T SEE?*

HEAR HIM *OUT!*

THERE IS ACTUALLY A MOMENT, THEN, WHEN LOKI CONSIDERS TELLING THE AVENGERS THE *TRUTH*--

--BUT *THAT* WOULD INVOLVE BLAMING *HIMSELF*-- AND THE PRINCE OF EVIL COULD *NEVER* DO THAT!

AVENGERS, I HAVE DISCOVERED A PLOT MOST *FOUL*, THREATENING OUR ENTIRE *UNIVERSE*--

A PLOT DEVISED BY A GROUP OF EARTH'S MOST FEARSOME *VILLAINS*, WHO NAME THEMSELVES-- FOR UNKNOWN REASONS-- THE *DEFENDERS!*

THEIR *LEADER* IS THE MOST *MYSTERIOUS* MAN OF MIDGARD, HE WHOSE VERY *EXISTENCE* DOTH REMAIN HIDDEN AWAY FROM MOST MORTAL MINDS:

DR. STRANGE!

"AYE," RUMBLES THOR. "WE DO *KNOW* OF HIS PERFIDY!"

THEN KNOW YE THAT HE BE *ALLIED* WITH THE VENGEFUL *VALKYRIE*, WHO HATH RETURNED TO MAKE *EVERYONE* SUFFER FOR HER DEFEAT AT YOUR HANDS MONTHS AGONE! *

* IN ISH #83... BUT *WE* KNOW SHE'S *NOT* THE SAME WARRIOR WOMAN. -- ROY.

IN *ADDITION*, THIS CABAL INCLUDES THE MURDEROUS MONSTER CALLED *HULK*, WHOSE HATE FOR HUMANITY IS AS WELL KNOWN...

... AS THAT OF THE *FOURTH* MEMBER, THE SAVAGE *SUB-MARINER!* HIS WARS AGAINST THE WORLD HAVE RECENTLY BEGUN *ANEW*, I HEAR.

THEN THERE IS THE *SILVER SURFER!* HIS *BITTERNESS* AT BEING HELD PRISONER UPON THIS PLANET HATH DRIVEN HIM TO STRIKE *BACK* AT IT, WITH THESE *OTHER* OUTCASTS!

FINALLY, IN THE FATES' *CRUELEST* JEST, YOUR ERSTWHILE FRIEND AND TEAMMATE, *HAWKEYE*--

HAWKEYE!?!

O BASE *TREACHERY!* WE MUST NEEDS HALT THIS TRAGEDY ERE IT MAY PROCEED ANY *FURTHER!*

TELL US THE *REST* OF IT, LOKI!

So HE *DOES*--IN AN *EDITED* VERSION--AND THEN...

RIGHT! LOKI DOESN'T KNOW *WHICH* DEFENDER WENT *WHERE*, SO WE'LL HAVE TO CHOOSE AT *RANDOM.* *ALL*

I HAVEN'T SEEN JAPAN SINCE THE *WAR.* I'LL TAKE WHOEVER'S THERE!

WANDA AND I SHALL JET TO *RURUTU.*

I'LL GO WITH MANTIS TO *BOLIVIA.* I OWE SOUTH AMERICA A *DEBT!* *

NO, MY LOVE. THIS ONE *WANTS* TO BE AT YOUR SIDE, BUT I SENSE THAT THE *PANTHER* WILL NEED ME *MORE.*

BUT I'M ONLY GOING TO THE *CLOSEST* POINT: *INDIANA*--

* FROM *AVENGERS SPECIAL #1.* --R.

I'VE COME TO *RESPECT* HER HUNCHES, T'CHALLA. YOU SHOULD, TOO.

THEN *MEXICO* AND *CALIFORNIA* REMAIN--AND I CHOOSE THE *LATTER*, FOR IT IS THE MOST *CENTRAL* LOCATION!

AS THE MOST *POWERFUL* AVENGER, I CAN AID YE OTHERS MOST *EASILY* FROM THERE SHOULD THE NEED *ARISE!*

THAT LEAVES THE LAND OF *SUNNY SEÑORITAS* FOR ME--

--WHICH IS *FINE*, SINCE TONY STARK AND I HIT THE WEST COAST JUST A FEW MONTHS *BACK!*

LET'S *DO IT!*

THE DIE IS CAST! TWO SUPER TEAMS--THE WORLD'S *MIGHTIEST HEROES*--ARE NOW *COMMITTED* TO THE BATTLES OF THEIR *LIVES*... AGAINST *EACH OTHER!*

DECEPTION BEGAN THIS...PERHAPS ONLY *DEATH* WILL END IT! READ ON...

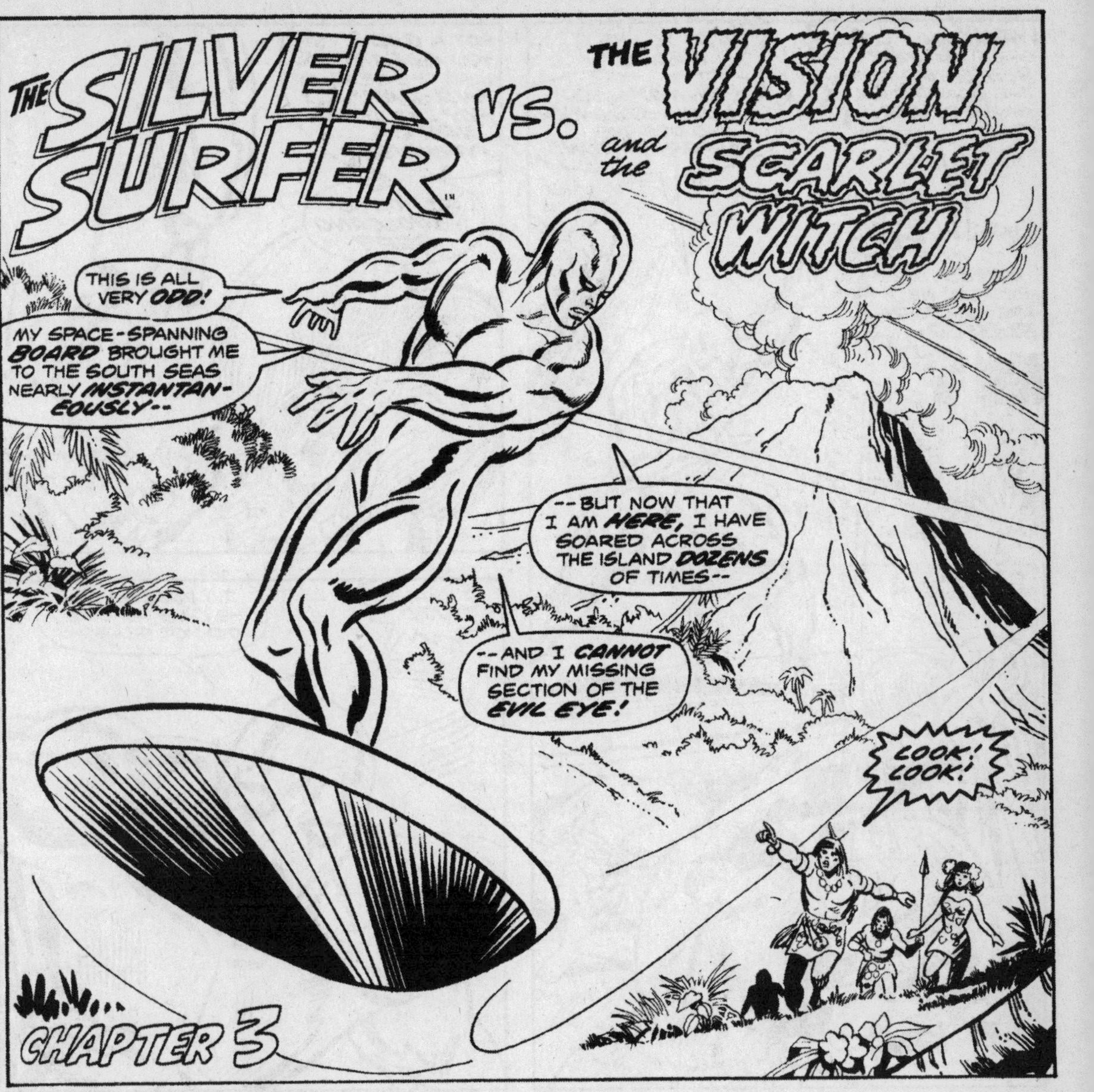
THE SILVER SURFER vs. THE VISION and the SCARLET WITCH
THIS IS ALL VERY ODD!
MY SPACE-SPANNING BOARD BROUGHT ME TO THE SOUTH SEAS NEARLY INSTANTANEOUSLY--
--BUT NOW THAT I AM HERE, I HAVE SOARED ACROSS THE ISLAND DOZENS OF TIMES--
--AND I CANNOT FIND MY MISSING SECTION OF THE EVIL EYE!
LOOK! LOOK!
CHAPTER 3

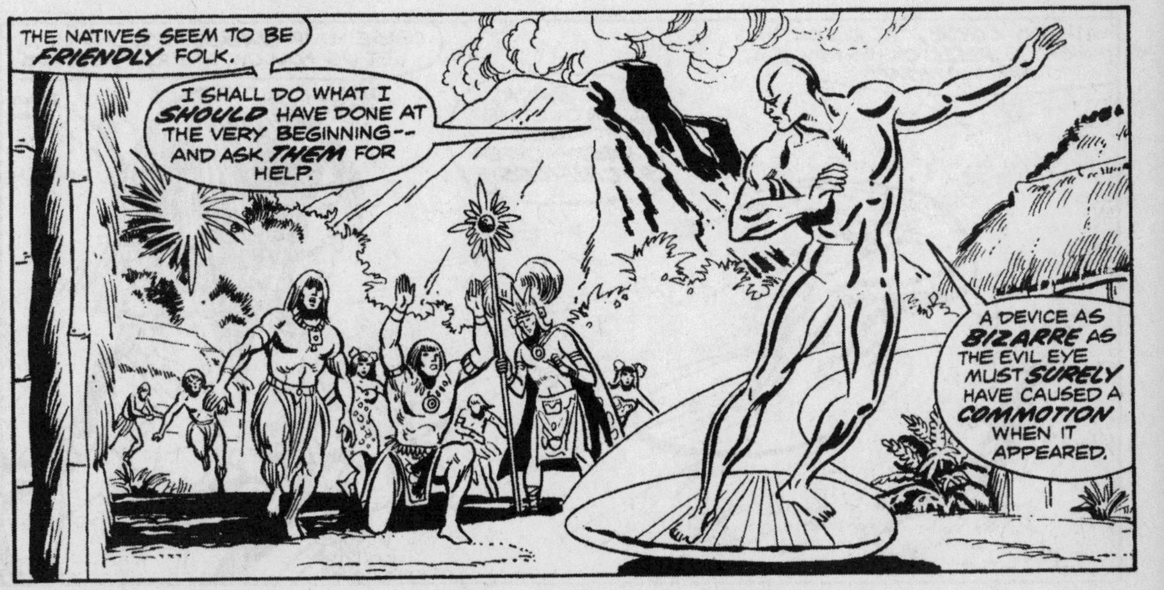
THE NATIVES SEEM TO BE FRIENDLY FOLK.
I SHALL DO WHAT I SHOULD HAVE DONE AT THE VERY BEGINNING--AND ASK THEM FOR HELP.
A DEVICE AS BIZARRE AS THE EVIL EYE MUST SURELY HAVE CAUSED A COMMOTION WHEN IT APPEARED.

HAIL! HAIL TO THE GREAT *SILVER BEING* WHO RIDES THE BOARD OVER WAVES OF *AIR!*

NO! YOU'RE *WRONG!*

I AM *NOT* A GOD! I AM BUT A *STRANGER,* WHO DESIRES *INFORMATION!*

TO YOUR *KNEES,* MY PEOPLE! WE ARE HONORED-- *BLESSED--*

NOT A *GOD?* YET YOU *GLEAM* LIKE THE SEAS AT *MID-DAY!* YOU *FLY* LIKE THE *BIRD OF PARADISE!*

ARE YOU NOT THE *VOLCANO GOD?*

VOLCANO--?

THAT'S *IT!*

THE *VOLCANO--* THE *ONE* PLACE I DID NOT SEARCH!

WITH ANY *LUCK,* THE BLACK KNIGHT IS *WELL* ON HIS WAY TO *SALVATION!*

COME *BACK,* SILVER ONE! WE MUST HAVE A *FEAST--* OFFER *SACRIFICES--*

CEASE YOUR *BABBLING,* OLD MAN! LET US FOLLOW WHERE HE *LEADS!*

THIS VENT IN THE EARTH'S CRUST IS STILL *ACTIVE,* WITH MOLTEN *ROCK* BUBBLING UP FROM THE PLANET'S *CORE*--

--BUT *THAT* WILL NOT AFFECT A FORM WHICH HAS FLOWN INTO THE HEARTS OF *SUNS!*

NOT MORE THAN FORTY SECONDS LATER...

HERE WE *ARE,* VISION. I ONLY HOPE OUR QUIN-JET HAS GOTTEN US HERE IN *TIME!*

YES...BUT I *TELL* YOU, WANDA --*DESPITE* THE EVIDENCE AT THE BLACK KNIGHT'S *CASTLE* AND DR. STRANGE'S *HOUSE*--

--DESPITE THE *PLAUSI-BILITY* OF LOKI'S STORY--

--I FIND CERTAIN... *DOUBTS*...WITHIN MY MIND.

I DON'T WISH TO LAUNCH AN *ATTACK* WITHOUT EXPLORING MORE *PEACEFUL* ALTERNATIVES--

--SO LET ME *SCOUT* AHEAD BEFORE WE *COMMIT* OURSELVES FULLY.

PERHAPS I CAN FIND OUR *ADVERSARY* AND *TALK* WITH HIM.

WHILE BELOW, HIS BODY HIDDEN IN THE HEAVY CLOUDS AT THE CRATER'S LIP AND THE NOISE OF HIS COSMIC BLASTS DROWNED BY THE VOLCANO'S INCESSANT RUMBLING...

"SWIMMING" THROUGH LAVA IS USELESS. I SHALL HAVE TO CLEAR *SMALL AREAS* FOR MY SEARCH.

SOMETIMES I THINK THE VISION IS *TOO* LOGICAL! WE KNOW THE BLACK KNIGHT WAS KIDNAPPED BY DR. STRANGE AND *OTHERS* IN COSTUMES--*

--*THE HULK, SUB-MARINER,* AND *VALKYRIE* HAVE ALL FOUGHT US *BEFORE*--

--THE *SILVER SURFER* HAS *STRUCK OUT* AT MANKIND AS OFTEN AS HE HAS *HELPED* IT--

--AND *HAWKEYE* BELIEVES THE AVENGERS HAVE *WRONGED* HIM.

IT ALL TIES *TOGETHER!*

WAIT! WHAT'S *HAPPENING* DOWN THERE?

* FROM LAST ISH. --R.

BY THE *HEAD* OF MY *FATHER!*

MY *BLASTING* HAS ACCIDENTALLY TRIGGERED AN *ERUPTION!* MY POWER CANNOT *STOP* IT!

I AM HELPLESS!

BRA-TOOM!

AAIIIEEE!

MORTALS, IMMORTALS, ANDROIDS, BEINGS FROM OTHER WORLDS-- ALL HAVE THEIR ABILITIES TO *DESTROY*... BUT *NONE* IS AS PRIMITIVE, AS *VIOLENT*, AS *NATURE* WHEN *AROUSED!*

IN ONE SENSES-SHATTERING SECOND, THE SCARLET WITCH FINDS HERSELF *SMASHED* FROM THE SKY!

WANDA!!!

HER JET'S *SHATTERED*-- *MELTED!*

SHE'S FALLING TO HER *DEATH!*

BUT I BECOME TOO *EMOTIONAL!* COMPUTATION OF *DISTANCE* VERSUS OUR *SPEEDS* SHOWS I CAN *STILL* SAVE HER IF I *ACT* RATHER THAN *TALK*--

--AND I *WILL!*

WHAT'S HAPPENING?

THE BLAST OF HEAT SEARED HER *LUNGS*-- RAISED *SECOND DEGREE* BURNS-- BUT THERE'S NO *PERMANENT*---

WHAT? SOMEONE RISES FROM WITH-IN THE VOLCANO!

THE *SILVER SURFER!!*

"TOO LOGICAL," SAID THE *SCARLET WITCH.*

AN UNWARRANTED *ATTACK*-- WHEN WE CAME IN *PEACE*-- STRUCK FROM *AMBUSH*-- IN THE *DISGUISE* OF A *NATURAL EVENT*-- WITH A FORCE THAT COULD KILL *HUNDREDS*--

"TOO EMOTIONAL," SAID HE.

--AGAINST *ONE* LONE GIRL!

"TOO MUCH IN LOVE!"

TRY YOUR COSMIC POWER ON *ME*, SKYRIDER!

LET'S SEE HOW YOU FARE AGAINST ONE WHO CAN *FIGHT BACK!*

THE VISION! WHAT IN ALL THE GALAXIES ARE YOU DOING HERE?

BUT AMIDST THE VOLCANO'S *INCESSANT ROARING*, NEITHER THE *ANDROID* NOR THE *BEING FROM ANOTHER WORLD* CAN *HEAR* THE OTHER.

CHOPF!

NO, WAIST-DEEP IN MOLTEN LAVA IS NO PLACE FOR A *MEANINGFUL* DIALOGUE *ANYWAY*. IT IS *MUCH* BETTER SUITED FOR *WAR*, BECAUSE *WAR* IS --

--HELL!

I DO NOT *UNDERSTAND* WHY HE *ATTACKS* ME, BUT HIS *STRENGTH* IS NEARLY COMPARABLE TO MY *OWN!*

MUST SUMMON MY *BOARD*--

-- USE MY *THOUGHT-CONTROL* OF IT TO SAVE ME!

PLOW!

I DO NOT *NATURALLY* TAKE TO OFFENSE! I AM MUCH MORE OF A *DEFENDER*!

THIS BLAST SHOULD *IMMERSE* HIS INVULNERABLE BODY IN LAVA UNTIL I CAN *ESCAPE*--

::UNHH!!::

HE MISJUDGED HIS *DISTANCE* FROM THE CRATER WALL IN THE *SMOKE*!

NOW I HAVE HIM!

*H*OWEVER, AT THAT VERY MOMENT--

AIIEEE! THE VOLCANO WILL DESTROY US *ALL*! WE NEED A *SACRIFICE* TO APPEASE THE SILVER GOD!

YES! YES!

PLACE THIS STRANGE *GIRL* IN THE LAVA'S PATH!

WE HEAR AND OBEY, GREAT CHIEF!

IT WILL BE UPON HER IN LESS THAN A *MINUTE,* AND WE SHALL BE *SAVED*!

*Y*ET INSIDE THE HOLOCAUST, THE FIGHT GOES ON-- OR *DOES* IT?

WHAT--?

THE *EVIL EYE*! MY POWER BLAST HAS ACCIDENT- ALLY *DISCLOSED* IT!

IF I CAN ONLY *REACH* IT AND *FLEE*--!

THAT MUST BE THE PIECE OF THE *WEAPON* HE SOUGHT! HE MUST NOT *HAVE* IT!

IS THIS BEING *INSANE?* THE BLACK KNIGHT IS AN AVENGER, *ALSO--* A *TEAM MATE* OF HIS!

WHY DOES HE NOT WANT ME TO HELP *SAVE* HIM?

THERE WILL BE NO *ANSWER* TO THAT FERVENT QUESTION, SURFER-- NOT *TODAY,* AT ANY RATE! FOR THE *EVIL EYE,* LIKE YOUR *COSMIC BOARD,* IS COMMANDED BY *THOUGHT--*

--AND THE THOUGHTS THAT REACH THIS SECTION OF IT *NOW* ARE DECIDEDLY *UNFRIENDLY!*

EVEN WITH ITS CAPABILITIES DIVIDED BY SIX, IT IS STILL *AWESOME* IN ITS CATASTROPHIC POWER! WITH A ROAR LIKE DYING *WORLDS,* IT DETONATES *BOTH* COMBATANTS AND *ITSELF* INTO THE YAWNING SKY!

BUT *NEITHER* LEARNS A THING.

THE *EYE!* THIS IS MY *CHANCE!*

OH *NO,* SURFER! I'M *CLOSER* THAN Y--.

OH NO!

THERE IS NOT A *FRACTION* OF HESITATION!

THE *VISION* SWOOPS TOWARD *WANDA--*

--THE *SURFER* TAKES THE *PRIZE!*

YET WE WON'T ARGUE *SEMANTICS*--

--A PRIZE IS *ONLY* A PRIZE IF IT IS *VALUABLE* TO ITS *POSSESSOR!*

GOODBYE, *VISION!* I SHALL *REMEMBER* THIS!

HE'S *ESCAPING* --AND I CANNOT *CATCH* HIM! OUR JET IS *DEMOLISHED*--AND MY *NATURAL* FLYING SPEED CAN NEVER MATCH *HIS!*

BUT IF THE *QUINJET'S* *RADIO* STILL FUNCTIONS, I CAN WARN THE *OTHER* AVENGERS--

--THE *DEFENDERS* ARE OUT FOR *BLOOD*-- AND MUST BE MET WITH *FULL FORCE!*

I MUST RETURN TO *DR. STRANGE* AT FULL SPEED, SO THAT HE CAN WARN THE *OTHER* DEFENDERS--

THE AVENGERS SEEK THE EVIL EYE FOR THEIR *OWN* ENDS, AND THEY *ATTACK* WITHOUT *CAUSE!*

WE *MUST* BE READY TO FIGHT THEM TO THE *DEATH!*

THIS EPIC CONTINUES IN *DEFENDERS #9* ON SALE THIS MONTH

AND THEN IN *AVENGERS #117* ON SALE NEXT MONTH

MISS THEM NOT, TRUE BELIEVER! WE'VE JUST BEGUN TO SWING!

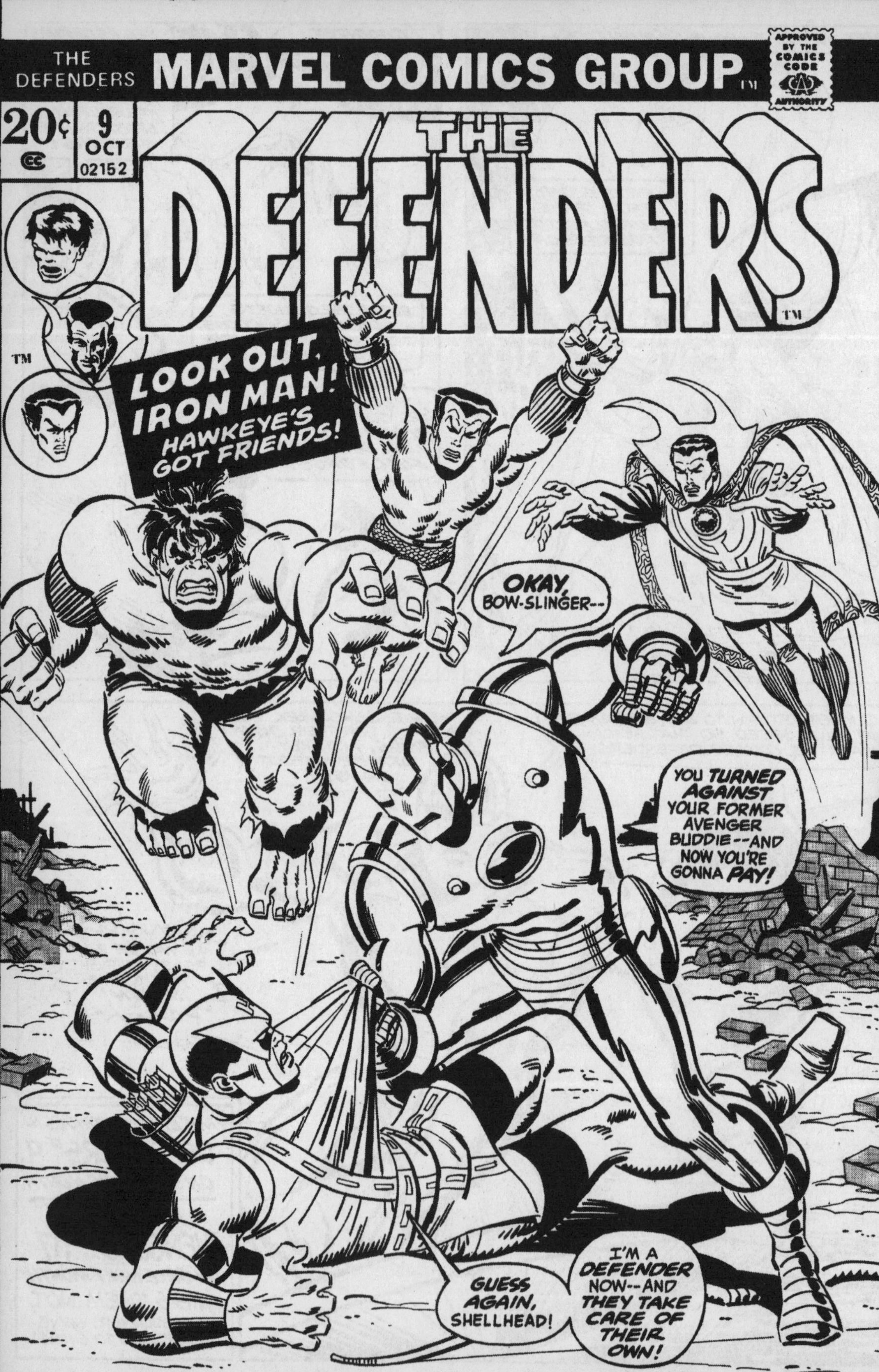
THE DEFENDERS
MARVEL COMICS GROUP
APPROVED BY THE COMICS CODE AUTHORITY
20¢
9 OCT 02152
THE DEFENDERS
LOOK OUT, IRON MAN! HAWKEYE'S GOT FRIENDS!
OKAY, BOW-SLINGER--
YOU TURNED AGAINST YOUR FORMER AVENGER BUDDIE--AND NOW YOU'RE GONNA PAY!
GUESS AGAIN, SHELLHEAD!
I'M A DEFENDER NOW--AND THEY TAKE CARE OF THEIR OWN!

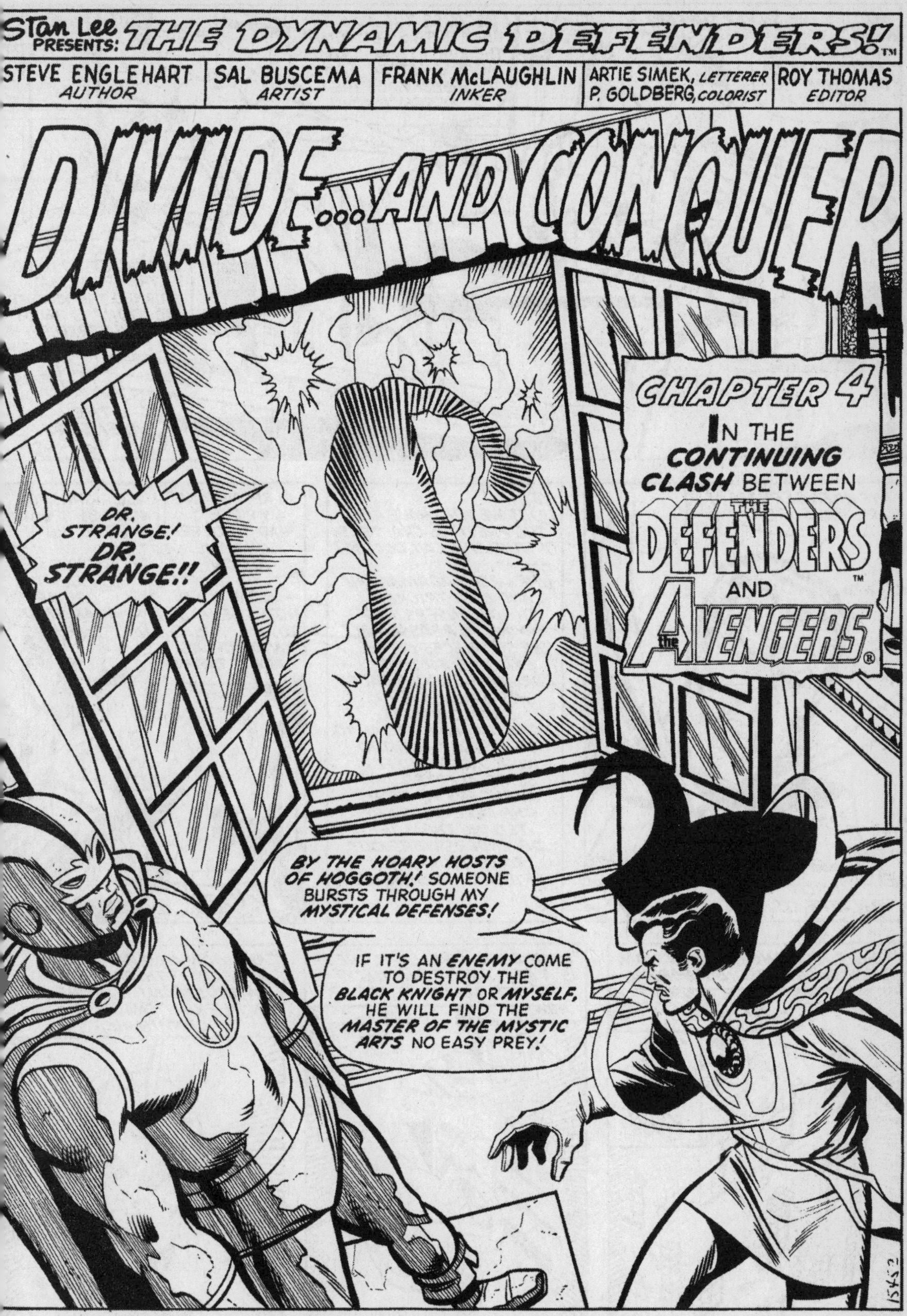

Stan Lee presents: THE DYNAMIC DEFENDERS!™
STEVE ENGLEHART AUTHOR
SAL BUSCEMA ARTIST
FRANK McLAUGHLIN INKER
ARTIE SIMEK, LETTERER P. GOLDBERG, COLORIST
ROY THOMAS EDITOR
DIVIDE...AND CONQUER
CHAPTER 4 IN THE CONTINUING CLASH BETWEEN THE DEFENDERS™ AND THE AVENGERS®
DR. STRANGE! DR. STRANGE!!
BY THE HOARY HOSTS OF HOGGOTH! SOMEONE BURSTS THROUGH MY MYSTICAL DEFENSES!
IF IT'S AN ENEMY COME TO DESTROY THE BLACK KNIGHT OR MYSELF, HE WILL FIND THE MASTER OF THE MYSTIC ARTS NO EASY PREY!

NO! IT'S THE *SILVER SURFER!*

WHY DIDN'T YOU *WAIT* UNTIL I *LET DOWN* THE BARRIER?

BECAUSE THE *POWER* HELD IN THIS SECTION OF THE EVIL EYE ALLOWED ME TO *SHATTER* IT, AND *SPEED* IS OF THE *ESSENCE* NOW!

OUR *QUEST* TO UNDO THE SPELL THAT TURNED THE KNIGHT TO *STONE* IS BEING *COUNTERED* BY--

--THE *AVENGERS!*

THE *AVENGERS?!* ARE YOU *SURE?*

I CANNOT *BELIEVE* IT!

B̲UT WE WHO HAVE READ THE *PREVIOUS* CHAPTERS OF THIS EPIC CAN, DOCTOR!

T̲HE DREAD *DORMAMMU* AND *LOKI* TRICKED THE DEFENDERS INTO TRYING TO *REASSEMBLE* THE SIX PIECES OF THE EVIL EYE, SO THAT DORMAMMU COULD CAUSE *HIS* DIMENSION TO *SWALLOW OURS.* HOWEVER, LOKI BEGAN TO FEAR THAT ASGARD WOULD *ALSO* SUFFER, SO HE ALERTED THE *AVENGERS* TO *STOP* THE DEFENDERS--BY TELLING THEM THE DEFENDERS WERE OUT TO CONQUER THE UNIVERSE *THEMSELVES!*

IN RECOVERING MY PIECE, I HAD TO OVER- COME THE *VISION*--

--AND IF I DID NOT LOSE MY *LIFE* TO HIM, IT WAS *NOT* FOR HIS LACK OF *TRYING!*

ALL RIGHT...YOU *MUST* BE SPEAK- ING THE TRUTH--

--BUT LET ME CONSULT THE *ORB OF AGAMOTTO.*

"THERE IS AVENGERS MANSION. IT SEEMS DESERTED, BUT *NORMAL*--

"--NO, *WAIT!* I SENSE... SOME- THING *AMISS!*

"INSIDE THE DWELLING, THERE IS A FEELING OF *INIQUITY!* THE ORB MAKES IT *CLEAR* NOW!

"LOKI, PRINCE OF EVIL, HAS *HELD SWAY* OVER THE OCCUPANTS!

"AND NOW A *NEW FACE* APPEARS--THAT OF THE *SWORDSMAN!* WHY, HE IS AN *INTERNATIONALLY-KNOWN CRIMINAL...*

"...YET HE HAS BECOME AN *AVENGER!*"

THEN IT'S *TRUE!* THE AVENGERS *ARE* TAINTED WITH EVIL! THEY *HAVE* GONE BAD!

PERHAPS, DOCTOR. WE HAVE NO WAY OF *KNOWING.*

ALL *I* KNOW IS THAT TO RETRIEVE THE EYE'S COMPONENTS, WE SHALL HAVE TO *FIGHT!*

LOKI MUST BE CONTROLLING THEIR *MINDS!*

THAT IS WHY I HAVE SPED *BACK* TO YOU—SO THAT YOU CAN SEND *MENTAL WARNINGS* TO THE *OTHER* DEFENDERS!

NOW I SHALL FLY TO *AID* THEM!

NO, SURFER...

...IF THERE *MUST* BE A STRUGGLE TO SAVE THE BLACK KNIGHT, *DR. STRANGE* WILL DO HIS SHARE!

THE KNIGHT HAS BEEN MY RESPONSIBILITY FROM THE *BEGINNING!*

YOU STAY TO *GUARD* HIM FROM ANY ASSAULT! I SHALL ALERT THE OTHERS AS I FLY TO THE *FRAY!*

Ⓑ*UT MEANWHILE,* ON THE SOUTH SEAS ISLAND OF RURUTU...

—SURFER ATTACKED WANDA UNDER COVER OF AN ERUPTING VOLCANO, WITHOUT *PROVOCATION.*

IT'S AS LOKI TOLD US: THESE "DEFENDERS" WILL GO TO ANY LENGTHS TO OBTAIN THIS *ULTIMATE WEAPON!*

"THEY MUST BE STOPPED BEFORE THEY *SUCCEED!* GUARD YOURSELVES!"

AND AT FIVE POINTS ACROSS THE GLOBE, THE VISION'S GRIM WORDS ARE HEARD—AND BELIEVED—

—BECAUSE HE TRULY BELIEVES THEM.

IT *SCARES* ME, VISION. THE AVENGERS HAVE FACED EVERY *CONCEIVABLE* MENACE— AND *WON*—

—BUT THE DEFENDERS ARE SO *POWERFUL*— SO *RUTHLESS* —AND YET SO LIKE *US!*

I KNOW, WANDA, UNDER *OTHER* CIRCUMSTANCES, THEY COULD HAVE BEEN OUR *FRIENDS,* BUT NOW...

I HOPE THE *OTHERS* FARE BETTER THAN WE DID!

THE INVINCIBLE IRON MAN VS. HAWKEYE THE ARCHER

THERE IT *IS*, VALKYRIE: *MONTERREY, MEXICO!*

SOMEWHERE DOWN THERE IS *MY CHUNK* OF THE EVIL EYE!

STEPHEN STRANGE SAID HE'D HELP US *MYSTICALLY* IN OUR SEARCHES, HAWKEYE. IT SHOULDN'T BE *TOO* DIFFICULT TO UNCOVER THE PIECES.

DOWN, ARAGORN!

CHAPTER 5

¡*CARAMBA!* UN CABALLO CON *ALAS,* Y *DOS PERSONAS FANTÁSTICAS!*

¡*NUNCA* BEBERÉ TEQUILA ANTES DE LA NOCHE *OTRA VEZ!*

I *KNEW* I SHOULD'A TAKEN THAT SECOND YEAR OF SPANISH, BLONDIE.

¿*QUÉ PASA AQUÍ?* ¿*QUÉ* QUIEREN VDS.?

THAT'S *SPANISH?* YES, I SUPPOSE IT *MUST BE.*

BEING CREATED AS AN *ENGLISH-SPEAKING* ENTITY LEAVES ME OUT IN THE *COLD* WHEN IT COMES TO *OTHER* LANGUAGES OR--

WHAT'S *THAT?*

LOOK! UP IN THE *SKY!*

IT'S *DOC!*

HEAR ME, *DEFENDERS*--

--LOKI HAS CORRUPTED THE MINDS OF THE *AVENGERS,* AND THEY ARE TRYING TO *BLOCK* OUR OBTAINING THE EVIL EYE!

THE SURFER HAS *ALREADY* BEEN ATTACKED! REMAIN *ALERT* AND *PREPARED*--

--AND *DO NOT FAIL!*

THE BLACK KNIGHT-- *DANE WHITMAN*-- IS *RELYING* ON US!

AVEN...GERS?

THE AVENGERS?

I'LL *ADMIT* THEY WERE ACTIN' *WEIRD* AN ALL, BUT--

BUT *NOTHING!* IF *STEPHEN* SAYS THEY'RE AFTER US, IT'S *TRUE!*

I *HATE* THE AVENGERS, *ANYWAY!*

YOU'VE NEVER EVEN *MET* 'EM, LADY. THAT'S THE *ENCHANTRESS* SPEAKIN' THROUGH YA!

BUT ANYHOW--TAKE *CARE* O' YOURSELF, HUH?

HA! THE VALKYRIE *CRAVES* ACTION, HAWKEYE!

MAKE IT *"CLINT,"* VAL--

--AND *I* CRAVE ACTION, TOO!

CATCH MY DRIFT?

MALE CHAUVINIST PIG!

WHOA, BLONDIE! THAT'S THE ENCHANTRESS TALKIN', TOO--AN' SHE TALKS IN CLICHES!

BUT I KINDA CATCH *YOUR* DRIFT-- AN' I'M *SORRY!*

YOU *SHOULD* BE, MISTER!

--THOUGH I CAN'T *HONESTLY* SAY IT WAS *COMPLETELY* UNPLEASANT.

GOODBYE...

...I'LL PICK YOU UP ON MY WAY BACK FROM *BOLIVIA!*

NOW THERE'S A *WOMAN*, BOY-- EVEN IF SHE *IS* MIXED-UP!

I SUPPOSE I SHOULD *SWEAR OFF* CHICKS, AFTER *WANDA* AND THE *WIDOW* DUMPED ME...

...BUT *THAT'D* BE LIKE SWEARIN' OFF AIR.

VAL'S A LOT *LIKE* TASHA, I GUESS...ONLY NOT SO *UPTIGHT...*

...KINDA LIKE TASH WAS WHEN I *FIRST* MET 'ER, BACK WHEN WE WERE *CROOKS* TRYIN' TO TAKE ON--

--TO TAKE ON--

..IRON MAN???

NOW LET'S *SEE*...LOKI SAID ONE OF THESE SO-CALLED *"DEFENDERS"* WOULD BE LURKING AROUND SOMEWHERE. I WISH HE'D KNOWN *WHICH ONE*.

LAST MINUTE *SURPRISES* ARE THINGS I TRY TO *AVOID!*

HOWEVER, SINCE THERE'S NO *HELP* FOR THAT LITTLE PROBLEM...

...I'LL JUST HAVE TO CHARGE RIGHT ON *IN* LIKE I DIDN'T HAVE A *CARE* IN THE *WORLD*, AND SEE WHAT *DEVELOPS*.

SO...IT STANDS TO *REASON* THAT IF THE EYE WERE *FOUND* WHEN IT APPEARED HERE, IT WOULD BE TAKEN TO THE *UNIVERSITY* FOR EXAMINATION.

INSTITUTO TECNOLÓGICO, HERE I COME.

UNQUIRIES TAKE BUT MINUTES FOR AN AVENGER, AND SOON INTERNATIONAL BUSINESSMAN TONY STARK IS TRADING FLUENT SPANISH*(THROUGH HIS ALTER EGO'S MOUTH APERTURE) WITH PROFESOR MARTIN FIGUERAS.

YES, SEÑOR, I *HAVE* BEEN STUDYING A DEVICE SUCH AS YOU DESCRIBE.

*WHICH THE BULLPEN LINGUIST DIVISION WILL TRANSLATE FOR FREE.-- ROY.

IT BURST FROM THE GROUND NEAR THE MOUNTAINS SEVERAL YEARS AGO, AND WAS IMMEDIATELY BROUGHT TO ME.

AT A *GUESS,* I WOULD SAY IT WAS PERHAPS *700 YEARS* OLD, BUT ITS *PURPOSE* REMAINS A *TOTAL MYSTERY.*

MAY I TAKE A *LOOK* AT IT, PROFESSOR? WORKING AT *STARK INDUSTRIES* HAS TAUGHT ME A *LITTLE* ABOUT ELECTRONICS AND MECHANICS.

OF COURSE, HOMBRE DE HIERRO.

HMMM...THERE ARE FAINT *GROOVES* ALONG THE SIDES, AS IF IT FITS INSIDE *ANOTHER* PIECE--

--AND IT'S *HOLLOW,* AS IF STILL *ANOTHER* PIECE FITS INSIDE *IT!*

THAT IS *MY* THEORY, SEÑOR. I BELIEVE IT IS BUT *PART* OF A *GREATER--*

CLAK!

WHAT THE DEVIL!

AN ARROW--!

IT STOLE THE DEVICE AS IF IT HAD A MIND OF ITS OWN!

MAYBE IT DOES, PROFESSOR!

I'VE GOT A VERY GOOD IDEA WHO MADE IT!

IT'S TIME FOR ACTION-- IRON MAN STYLE!

HOWDY, SHELLHEAD! LONG TIME NO SEE!

TOO BAD IT COULDN'T'A BEEN LONGER!

I WAS RIGHT! IT IS HAWKEYE--AND HE'S SPOILING FOR A FIGHT!

REMEMBER HOW IT USED TO BE, TIN-FACE?

WELL, THAT WAS JUST ME AGAINST YOU-- BUT NOW IT'S MORE!

NOW IT'S DEFENDER AGAINST AVENGER--

--AND THE DEFENDERS ARE GONNA WIN!

BLAST ARROW! -UHHH!-

ZOOM!

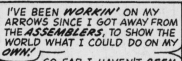

Panel 1:

I'VE BEEN *WORKIN'* ON MY ARROWS SINCE I GOT AWAY FROM THE *ASSEMBLERS*, TO SHOW THE WORLD WHAT I COULD DO ON MY *OWN!*

SO FAR I HAVEN'T *BEEN* A SOLO STAR, BUT AT LEAST I'VE GOT NEW FRIENDS WHO *ARE* FRIENDS, AND A *GOOD CAUSE* TO FIGHT FOR!

SAVING THE BLACK KNIGHT!

RULING THE UNIVERSE!

Panel 2:

ZAK!

YOU DON'T THINK I'LL LET YOU HIT ME A *SECOND* TIME, DO YOU?

YOU'VE HAD *GRANDIOSE* IDEAS ABOUT HOW *INVINCIBLE* YOU ARE SINCE THE DAY WE *MET!**

*IN TALES OF SUSPENSE #57--R.

Panel 3:

FIRST YOU THOUGHT YOU WERE *BETTER* THAN *ME--* THEN, ONCE YOU JOINED THE *AVENGERS*, IT WAS *CAP--*

--THEN THE *WHOLE* TEAM!

Panel 4:

AND *I* PROPOSED YOU FOR MEMBERSHIP! I BELIEVED YOU'D *CHANGED!*

MAYBE YOU *WANTED* TO-- TRIED TO-- FOR YEARS--

--BUT A *LEOPARD* JUST CAN'T CHANGE HIS *SPOTS!*

YOU'RE TALKIN' *CRAZY*, BUT I *EXPECTED* THAT--

Panel 5:

--AND *YOU* SHOULDN'T EXPECT ME TO *FIRE* ALL MY ARROWS!

SHUD!

Panel 6:

THAT'S *ACID* EATIN' AT YOUR *FEVERED* BROW, MR. METAL!

I MAY BE THE *WEAKEST* DEFENDER, AND *YOU* MAY BE THE *SECOND STRONGEST* AVENGER, BUT THE PERSON WHO CARRIES THE *EYE* AWAY IS GONNA BE *ME!*

BURNING-- MELTING MY ARMOR--!

THERE'S NOTHING HERE TO *NEUTRALIZE* IT WITH! THE ACID WILL *DESTROY* ME IN SECONDS!

ONLY ONE *CHANCE*--

--FLY SO FAST THE *AIR FRICTION* WILL *EVAPORATE* IT BEFORE IT DOES ANY MORE HARM!

THAT *DID* IT--BOTH FOR THE *ACID* AND MY *TEMPER!*

HAWKEYE, YOU HAVE MADE ME *MAD!*

IN A *WAY,* YOU ALSO MAKE ME *GLAD*--BECAUSE BURNING MY HELMET GENERATED *HEAT*--

--AND THE *THERMO-COUPLE* BUILT INTO MY ARMOR TURNS *HEAT* INTO *POWER!*

HOLY COW! HE *DISINTEGRATED* THAT SHAFT!

WHAM!

SEE WHAT I *MEAN?*

I WON'T *HURT* YOU, CLINT, BECAUSE YOU WERE A *GOOD MAN* WHEN YOU WERE WITH US IN THE PAST!

YOUR *EGO'S* JUST GOTTEN THE BETTER OF YOU!

BUT MY *REPULSOR RAYS* WILL BACK YOU UP AGAINST THE BUILDING AND *HOLD* YOU THERE--

--SO I CAN LIGHTLY *KNOCK YOU OUT!*

YOU-- BUM--!

I'LL--BEAT--YOU--*YET!*

IF--I CAN--*PRESS BACK*--AGAINST YOUR FORCE--*LONG ENOUGH*--TO--DRAW--ONE MORE--*ARROW!*

STOP *DELUDING* YOURSELF! YOU HAVEN'T A CHANCE OF *AIMING* YOUR BOW!

YOU *SEE!* YOUR ARMS FLIPPED *BACK!* YOU FIRED *STRAIGHT UP!*

RIGHT ON--SHERLOCK--

--BUT WHAT GOES *UP* MUST COME *DOWN*--IN *EXACTLY* THE TRAJECTORY I *PLANNED!*

WHAT--? THE ARROW'S *MAGNETIZED*--YANKING MY ARM AROUND *TOWARD* IT!

*A*ND BEFORE IRON MAN CAN THINK TO *TURN OFF* HIS REPULSOR BLAST--

I'VE CAVED IN THAT *CONSTRUCTION SITE!*

KUMP!

DEBRIS FALLING *EVERYWHERE!*

NO SE *PREOCUPE*, HOMBRE!

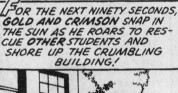

*F*OR THE NEXT NINETY SECONDS, GOLD AND CRIMSON SNAP IN THE SUN AS HE ROARS TO RES-CUE *OTHER* STUDENTS AND SHORE UP THE CRUMBLING BUILDING!

*O*NLY NINETY SECONDS--

--BUT WHEN HE ONCE MORE CAN TURN HIS ATTENTION TO HAWKEYE THE ARCHER--

HE'S GONE!

DISCRETION IS THE BETTER PART OF *VALOR*, AND SO ON, AND *SO* ON!

I'VE *GOT* WHAT I CAME FOR, AND SHELLHEAD'LL *NEVER* FIND ME IN THESE WOODS!

I'VE *WON!*

*A*ND SO *TWO* PARTS OF THE *EVIL EYE* FALL TO THE *DEFENDERS!*

DR. STRANGE ™
MASTER OF THE MYSTIC ARTS
VS. THE BLACK PANTHER ™
AND MANTIS!

INDIANA.

SOMEWHERE IN THIS FIELD OF CORN LIES A PIECE OF THE **EVIL EYE!** I CAN **SENSE** IT!

THIS **SPELL** WILL **REVEAL** IT TO ME!

CHAPTER 6

YES! *THAT* SPOT CONTINUES TO GLOW!

WITH LUCK, I CAN **OBTAIN** THIS COMPONENT AND BE **GONE** BEFORE ANY **AVENGERS** ARRIVE!

HOWEVER, THOUGH DR. STRANGE HAS COME THE **SHORTEST DISTANCE** FROM NEW YORK, HIS LATE **BEGINNING** HAS ALLOWED THE **BLACK PANTHER** AND **MANTIS** TO **BEAT** HIM HERE. ALREADY, THEY HAVE SPENT NEARLY AN **HOUR** IN FRUITLESS SEARCHING...

...AND NOW--

MANTIS! THAT **RADIANCE** ON THE OTHER SIDE OF THE FIELD!

IT MAY BE THE SIGNAL THAT OUR **HUNT** HAS ENDED-- OR THAT OUR **WAR** HAS **BEGUN**, T'CHALLA!

LET US **SEE!**

THE EYE IS *MINE*!

YET, RUNNING THIS *WAY*-- THE *BLACK PANTHER* AND AN UNFAMILIAR *WOMAN*!

MY *LAST HOPE* THAT THE SURFER WAS WRONG *DIES*! STILL, NO BEING SHOULD FIGHT ANOTHER IF THERE IS AN *ALTERNATIVE*!

MY *WISEST* COURSE IS TO SLIP AWAY *UNSEEN*!

THE GLOW HOVERS AT *THIS* LOCATION, PANTHER-- BUT THERE IS NO *DEFENDER* HERE.

HMMMM...

THERE *WAS*! LOOK AT THE WAY THE *CORN STALKS* ARE PUSHED ASIDE!

HE WENT TOWARD THE *ROAD*!

OF COURSE. I *APOLOGIZE* FOR MY LACK OF *SIGHT*.

TRACKING IS *SECOND NATURE* TO ME. I HAVE THE *FEELING*, THOUGH, THAT YOU MEANT *MORE* THAN MERE TRACKING.

YOU HAVE A *DIFFERENT* WAY OF LOOKING AT THE WORLD--NO...*NOT* THE WORLD. *MORE* THAN THAT.

YOU TRY TO LOOK AT *EVERYTHING*.

PLEASE, PANTHER. I AM NOTHING TO SPEAK OF.

THERE ARE *PEOPLE*.

GLORY BE! YOU CAN'T BE--THAT IS, I HEARD THAT OVER TO *CHICAGO* THERE WAS A *CAT* PERSON...BUT *IT* WAS A *SHE*!

I IMAGINE *SPIDER-MAN* HAS THE SAME PROBLEM WITH THE *BLACK WIDOW*.

NO, SIR, I AM THE *BLACK PANTHER*.

HAVE NO *FEAR*. HE IS WITH THE *AVENGERS*.

B-BLACK PANTHER?

WE WISH ONLY TO KNOW THE DIRECTION THE *OTHER* STRANGER CHOSE.

OTHER STRANGER? MA'AM, NOBODY ELSE'S COME BY HERE THE TWENTY MINUTES *I* BEEN WAITIN' FOR THE BUS. YOU MUST'A MADE A *MISTAKE*.

IMPOSSIBLE. I COULD *NOT* HAVE BEEN WRONG.

WAIT, PANTHER! I SENSE...*MAGIC*!

NOW IT'S *GONE!* AS SOON AS I *SPOKE,* IT WAS *SHUT* OFF... BUT I *FELT* VIBRATIONS I HAVE FELT *BEFORE*--

THE VIBRATIONS OF *DR. STRANGE!**

*SEE *AVENGERS #115.*--R.

*W*ITH A CUSHIONED SHRIEK OF *AIR BRAKES* AND A GALE OF HOT *DIESEL FUMES,* THE *BUS* PULLS UP...

...IN *THIRTY SECONDS,* THE PEOPLE WILL BE GONE.

*T*IME TICKS... MANTIS PROBES...

*T*HEN--

STOP!

YOU *SHALL NOT GO!*

MANTIS!

*T*HE OLD LADY CRASHES HARD FROM THE PRECISE BLOW--HER MOMENTUM THROWS HER UNDER THE BUS!

WHAT ARE YOU *DOING?*

GET BACK! THAT IS *DR. STRANGE!*

DR. STRANGE? MANTIS, YOU CAN'T BE *SURE!*

STOP *FIGHTING!*

AGAINST ONE WHO WISHES TO MAKE *SLAVES* OF OTHERS?

I *KNOW* MY FOE, T'CHALLA! I *AM* SURE OF WHAT I *FEEL!*

-AIIEE!- A *MYSTICAL FORCE* STRIKES ME--

--FROM *UNDERNEATH* THE BUS!

THE GIRL *DOES* HAVE A SENSITIVITY FOR THE OCCULT!

I HAD *HOPED* TO SIMPLY DISAPPEAR WITHOUT VIOLENCE, BUT NOW I MAY BE DENIED THE *CHANCE!*

WHY, HE LOOKED JUST LIKE *MIZ CARPENTER!*

HE CAN LOOK LIKE *ANYONE,* I IMAGINE! HE *IS* THE MASTER OF THE MYSTIC ARTS!

EVEN WITH *MANTIS'* POWERS, HOW CAN THE TWO OF *US* DEFEAT A MAN LIKE *HIM?*

BETTER *FIND* A WAY, PRINCE OF THE WAKANDAS! IT *MUST* BE DONE!

THE AVENGERS HAVE *NO ONE* WHO CAN TRULY BATTLE *MAGIC.* I WAS *NEVER* IN ANY *REAL* DANGER--

--BUT THEIR SEEING WHERE I *GO* ALLOWS THEM TO *CHASE* ME IN THEIR JET.

I *COULD* BECOME INVISIBLE, BUT *THAT* WOULD LESSEN MY POWERS FOR CONTROLLING THE *CLOAK OF LEVITATION.*

I HOPE THEY JUST LET ME LEAVE WITHOUT FURTHER *INCIDENT,* FOR *ALL OUR* SAKES.

I SEE NO SIGN OF *PURSUIT.*

YET SUDDENLY, FROM THE LEAFY ROWS OF CORN BELOW, COMES T'CHALLA--WHO LEARNED FROM HIS CHILDHOOD--

--HOW TO RUN *UNSEEN* THROUGH A JUNGLE--

--JUST AS HE LEARNED *OTHER* SECRETS OF THE PANTHER GOD, REGARDING *STRENGTH--*

--AND *COORDINATION--*

--AND A COLD STEEL *NERVE!*

GRUMP!

WHAM!

BY THE VIPERS OF VALTORR!

SURPRISE, MAGICIAN!

I DON'T KNOW WHAT I'M GOING TO *DO* WITH YOU--

--BUT THE *FIRST* THING IS TO KEEP YOU FROM *RECITING* ANY SPELLS OR MAKING ANY *GESTURES!*

YOU CANNOT BLOCK THE *EYE OF AGAMOTTO*, PANTHER!

THAT STIFLED HIS *ATTACK*--

--YET *NOW* HE PLUMMETS LIKE A *STONE!*

I HAVE NO DESIRE TO *KILL* HIM!

I MUST *CATCH* HIM BEFORE HE STRIKES THE EARTH!

SWOOPING SWIFTLY, THE MAN OF MYSTERY REACHES--STRAINS-- AND GRABS! JUST TEN FEET ABOVE THE GROUND, HE YANKS HIS FOE BACK FROM SERIOUS INJURY OR DEATH!

BUT T'CHALLA CANNOT ALLOW HIMSELF GRATITUDE.

TO SAVE THE WORLD FROM THIS SORCERER, HE MUST ALWAYS TAKE THE OFFENSIVE!

POW!

HE BELIEVES.

MEANWHILE, HOWEVER, ALL THIS FURIOUS FIGHTING HAS NOT GONE UNNOTICED!

WHAT'S GOIN' ON IN THE BACK YARD?

TWO MANIACS--TEARIN' UP MY PROPERTY!

BLAST IT! THEY'LL SPOOK THE LIVESTOCK!

WELL, THE FARM'S POSTED WITH "NO TRESPASSING"! THEY WERE WARNED!

NOW THEY CAN TASTE SOME BUCKSHOT!

BLAM!

BUT IN THAT SAME SPLIT-INSTANT--

HAEEE!

THIS ONE WAS IN *TIME!* THE PELLETS DID NOT *STRIKE* YOU!

YET THE FOOL WITH THE *WEAPON* MAY FIRE *AGAIN*--

--AND *AGAIN,* MANTIS MUST *THWART* HIM!

NOW, DR. *STRANGE*--

YES, MANTIS. NOW *WE* MUST FACE EACH OTHER!

THOUGH MAGIC HAS *OFTEN* SPARED ME PHYSICAL COMBAT--

--MY STUDIES IN THE HIMALAYAS *NATURALLY* INCLUDED THE *MARTIAL ARTS!*

YOU AVOIDED THIS ONE'S *THRUST!* ONLY THREE OTHERS HAVE *EVER* DONE SO!

STILL, *CHALLENGE* COMES ALL TOO *RARELY* TO ME!

WIN OR LOSE, I SHALL *ENJOY* THIS!

KEEP HIM *BUSY*, MANTIS! I'LL *OUTFLANK* HIM!

WE'LL TAKE HIM *YET*!

HE MAY BE *CORRECT*! AND IF *THAT* OCCURS... WHAT *THEN*?

THE *EVIL EYE* WILL REMAIN *INCOMPLETE*-- AND THE *BLACK KNIGHT* WILL REMAIN *TRAPPED*!

THAT *MUST* NOT HAPPEN! WITH A MAN'S *SOUL* AT STAKE, I *DARE* NOT TAKE *CHANCES*! THUS--

IN THE EXALTED NAME OF THE ETERNAL *VISHANTI*-- AND OTHER GODS BEYOND AND BELOW-- LET THE STRENGTH AND CUNNING OF *THESE*, MY ENEMIES--

--FROM THEIR MORTAL BODIES FLOW!

THE BATTLE IS *ENDED*-- WITHOUT *UNDO* COMBAT.

I SHOULD FEEL *SATISFACTION*... BUT SOMEHOW, I *CANNOT*. I HAVE *WON*--

--BUT I AM *FILLED* WITH *LOSS*.

WE WERE NO MORE THAN ANTS TO HIM! WHEN HE *FELT* LIKE IT, HE JUST *STEPPED* ON US!

IF THE *OTHER* AVENGERS CAN'T *REVERSE* THIS TREND--WE ARE ALL *DOOMED*!

NEXT: THE BATTLE ROYAL CONTINUES, IN...

AVENGERS #117: SWORDPLAY LIKE YOU'VE NEVER SEEN IN COMICS! *THE VALKYRIE* VS. *THE SWORDSMAN*!

PLUS--FOR THE *FIRST TIME* IN THE MARVEL AGE! *CAPTAIN AMERICA* VS. *THE SUB-MARINER*!

DEFENDERS #10: THE SLAM-BANG *SHOCKER* OF THE CENTURY! *THOR* VS. *HULK*!

PLUS-- SURPRISES, TWISTS, AND OTHER GOODIES WE CAN'T YET *REVEAL*!

BOTH ON SALE *NEXT* MONTH! GET 'EM *QUICK*, 'CAUSE YOU'RE WATCHING *COLLECTORS' ITEMS* IN THE MAKING! WE HAVE *SPOKEN*!

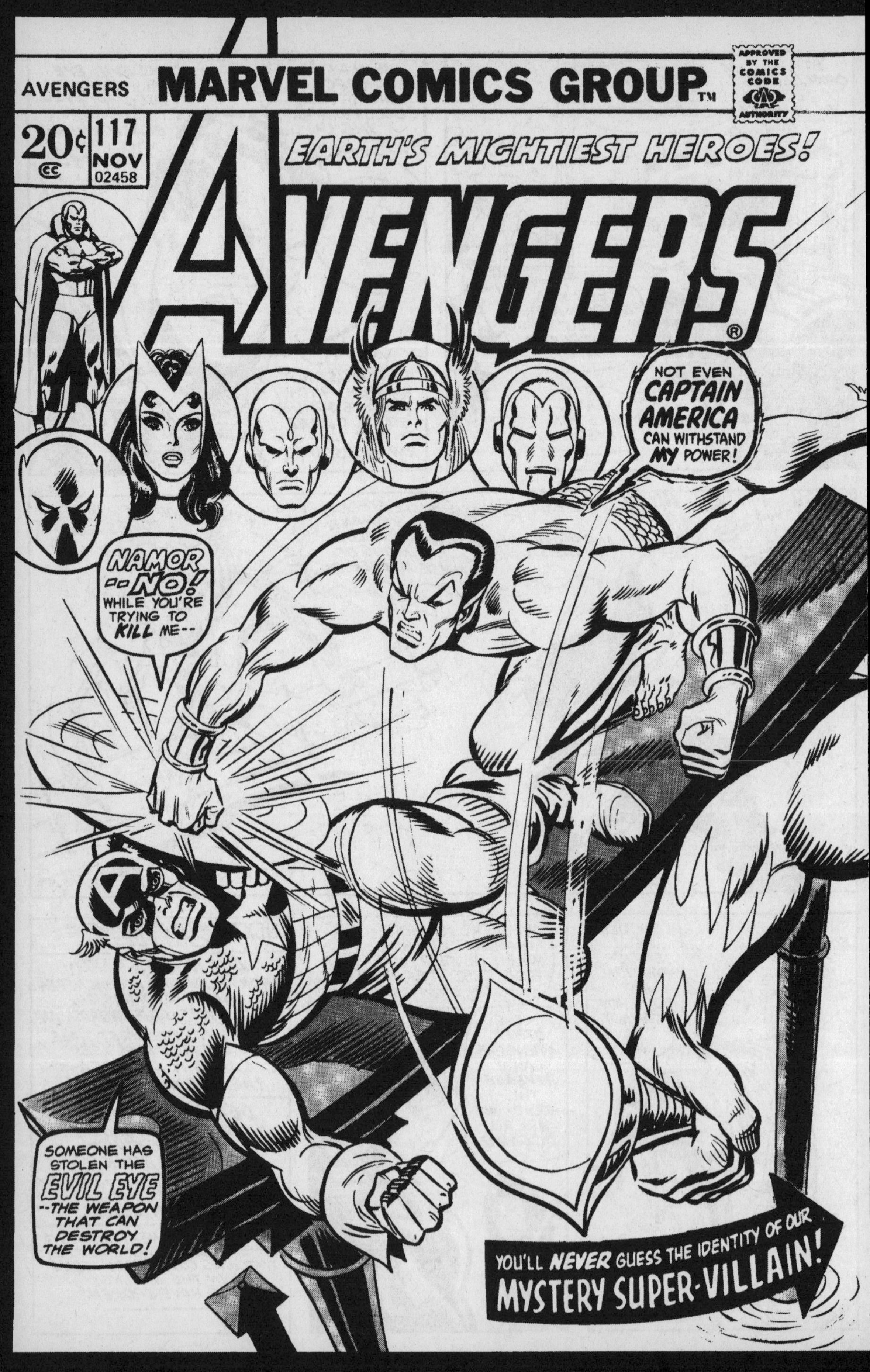

AVENGERS
MARVEL COMICS GROUP™
APPROVED BY THE COMICS CODE AUTHORITY
20¢ 117 NOV 02458
EARTH'S MIGHTIEST HEROES!
AVENGERS®
NOT EVEN CAPTAIN AMERICA CAN WITHSTAND MY POWER!
NAMOR --NO! WHILE YOU'RE TRYING TO KILL ME--
SOMEONE HAS STOLEN THE EVIL EYE --THE WEAPON THAT CAN DESTROY THE WORLD!
YOU'LL NEVER GUESS THE IDENTITY OF OUR MYSTERY SUPER-VILLAIN!

Stan Lee PRESENTS: **THE MIGHTY AVENGERS!**

STEVE ENGLEHART, AUTHOR // BOB BROWN ARTIST // MIKE ESPOSITO INKER // J. BRAVERMAN, LETTERER P. GOLDBERG, COLORIST // ROY THOMAS, EDITOR

HOLOCAUST

WHAT IS **THIS?**

THE AVENGERS FIGHTING THE DEFENDERS?

1642 Z

BY THE UNSPEAKABLE UMAR! MY SCHEME TO *TRICK* THE DEFENDERS INTO GATHERING THE SIX COMPONENTS OF THE *EVIL EYE* SHOULD HAVE BEEN *FOOLPROOF!*

HOW *COULD* THE AVENGERS HAVE FOUND IT OUT?

YOU HAVE NO IDEAS ON THE SUBJECT, DO YOU, LOKI?

I, DORMAMMU? THOU DOST WELL *KNOW* THAT I BE *BLIND!* I BE *POWERLESS* TO ACT WITHOUT THY GUIDANCE!

PRAY *ODIN* THOU DOST *BELIEVE* ME, LORD OF THE DARK DIMENSION -- FOR IN TRUTH, 'TWAS I WHO DID ALERT THINE ENEMIES --

BAH! IT WAS *FOOLISH* TO SUSPECT YOU, PRINCE OF EVIL! IF ONLY I COULD *PERSONALLY* AFFECT THE BATTLE AND *KILL* THE AVENGERS...

...BUT ANY USE OF MY *MAGIC* MIGHT BE *DETECTED* BY DR. STRANGE, AND REVEAL MY *HIDDEN HAND* IN THIS CONFLICT.

--AND I DO NOT WISH TO FACE THY *WRATH* WHILE DEPRIVED OF MY *SIGHT!*

SO I MUST BUT *OBSERVE!* STILL, THE DEFENDERS ARE A SOMEWHAT *UNCONVENTIONAL* GROUP OF SUPER-BEINGS.

PERHAPS THEIR *UNIQUE-NESS* WILL GIVE THEM THE *ADVANTAGE* OVER THE AVENGERS!

THEN--CANST THOU NOT TURN THINE ATTENTION TO RESTORING MY *VISION* NOW?

I CAN DO *NOTHING* FOR YOU UNTIL THESE BATTLES ARE *ENDED,* LOKI! THEY TOTALLY OCCUPY MY MIND AT *THIS* TIME!

NOW BE *SILENT!* A *NEW* SKIRMISH BEGINNING!

AT LAST --
THE JUNGLES
OF *BOLIVIA!*

BUT--THAT LOOKS LIKE
A *GERMAN CASTLE!* WHAT IN THE WORLD
IS *IT* DOING HERE?

SWORDSMAN VS THE VALKRIE

CONTINUING THE
INCREDIBLE 6-PART
AVENGERS-DEFENDERS EPIC!

Chapter 7

AH, WELL... IT WAS *PROBABLY*
BUILT BY SOME FLEEING *NAZI.*
FUNNY HOW THINGS THAT WERE
SO *IMPORTANT* IN THE *PAST*
ONLY LOOK *RIDICULOUS* TODAY!

FOR
INSTANCE,
MY *LIFE.*

UNTIL LAST YEAR,
I WAS ALL CAUGHT
UP IN BEING A
SUPER-VILLAIN--
TELLING MYSELF I
WAS A *SWASHBUCK-LING ROGUE!*

AND NOW THAT I'VE
TURNED THE CORNER TO
BECOME AN *AVENGER,*
THAT ERA SEEMS
LIKE SUCH A SHAM!

ALL I EARNED FROM THOSE
LOST YEARS WAS *HATE* AND
DISGUST--NEVER ENOUGH
MONEY TO BE COMFORTABLE,
AND NEVER THE *RESPECT* OF
ANYONE WHO MATTERED...
UNTIL I MET *MANTIS.*

IN TRUTH, I WAS HARDLY
ANYTHING MORE THAN A
HIRED HAND!

--LIKE WHEN I CAME *HERE*, TO *SOUTH AMERICA*, AND *FOUGHT* THE AVENGERS FOR THE *MANDARIN!**

AND EVEN AFTER *THAT*, THE GROUP *ACCEPTED* ME.

*AVENGERS SPECIAL #1.--ROY.

WELL, ONCE I *LAND* THIS QUINJET OF THEIRS, I'LL *SHOW* THEM THAT THE SWORDSMAN *DESERVES* THEIR ACCEPTANCE!

I'LL FIND WHICHEVER DEFENDER IS TRYING TO GRAB THE *BOLIVIAN* CHUNK OF THE *EVIL-EYE*--AND FORCE HIM AT *SWORDPOINT* TO GIVE IT TO ME! BUT, WAIT-- WHAT'S *THAT*--?

CLA-DAM!

GOOD, ARAGORN! OUR SUDDEN WEIGHT WILL FORCE THE AVENGERS JET *OUT OF CONTROL*--

--*DIVERTING* THE PILOT'S ATTENTION WHILE WE MAKE OUR *MOVE*!

ANYONE AS SKILLFUL AS I'VE HEARD THESE *AVENGERS* ARE SHOULD BE ABLE TO *PULL OUT* OF THAT SPIN.

WHAT--? IT'S THE *VALKYRIE!*

DON'T KNOW HOW SHE *KNOCKED* OUT THE PLANE--

BUT, IF I LET THIS BLASTED MACHINE'S *WING* TOUCH THE GROUND, THE ONLY SIGHT I'LL BE SEEING IS THE INSIDE OF A *PINE BOX!*

MADE IT!

BUT-- THE GIRL IS -- *GONE!*

THE HARD-EYED ADVENTURER SCANS THE SKY *ABOVE*, THE MUD *BELOW*, AND THE WALLS OF JUNGLE *BETWEEN* THEM, MISSING *NOTHING* -- AND SO...

SHE MUST BE *INSIDE* THE CASTLE. THERE'S NO OTHER *OPEN GROUND* TO LAND THAT STALLION ON.

IN ADDITION, I MUST BE CLOSE TO THE EVIL EYE'S *HIDING PLACE*, OR SHE'D NEVER *REVEAL* HERSELF JUST TO *DIVERT* ME. IF SHE'D HAD *MURDER* IN MIND, SHE'D HAVE MADE *CERTAIN* I *CRASHED*.

YES, THE CASTLE'S THE *PRIZE*, ALL RIGHT. AND WITHIN ITS WALLS WAITS MY *PIGEON*!

THE *VALKYRIE* ...! THE AVENGERS -- THE *OTHER* AVENGERS, I MEAN -- KNOW HER FROM THE *PAST*, THEY SAID.

RIGHT NOW, I WISH I *DID* -- SINCE I'LL PROBABLY HAVE TO *GO UP* AGAINST HER.

NOK NOK

YES? WHAT IS IT?

YOU SPEAK *ENGLISH*? GOOD.

I'M THE *SWORDSMAN*, OF THE *AVENGERS*, AND I BELIEVE YOU HAVE AN UNWELCOME *VISITOR*.

WON'T YOU COME IN?

SWORDSMAN, I BELIEVE I CAN *ASSURE* YOU THAT NO ONE OTHER THAN *OURSELVES* IS INSIDE THIS STRUCTURE.

IT WAS BUILT IN 1946 BY AN ESCAPED *NAZI*, AFTER HIS ORIGINAL GERMAN CASTLE -- BUT HE WAS *CAPTURED* IN 1949 AND THE PLACE WENT *UNTENANTED* UNTIL THREE MONTHS AGO, WHEN *I* MOVED HERE FROM *AMERICA*.

I CHERISH *SOLITUDE*, YOU SEE -- AND *FEW* SPOTS ON EARTH ARE MORE DESERTED THAN THIS JUNGLE.

YOU ARE THE *FIRST* HUMAN BEING I'VE SEEN SINCE I'VE *ARRIVED*.

I'LL BE *DARNED*! IT *IS* A NAZI CASTLE! WHAT DO YOU *KNOW*!

WELL, SIR, YOU MAY BE *RIGHT* ABOUT YOUR SOLITUDE, BUT IT'S POSSIBLE SOMEONE'S *BURGLARIZING* YOU WITHOUT YOUR KNOWING --

KREEK

A *SOUND* -- FROM *UPSTAIRS*!

MAYBE YOU'VE GOT *GHOSTS*, OR MAYBE *RATS*, SIR --

-- OR *MAYBE* YOU'VE GOT THAT *VISITOR* I WAS TALKING ABOUT!

SINCE YOU SAY YOU'RE *ALONE*, YOU WON'T MIND MY CHECKING THINGS OUT, NOW *WILL* YOU?

SO!

SO -- WHAT?

SO THIS, LADY: DESPITE THAT HEFTY *SWORD* YOU'RE SPORTING, YOU'RE NOT LEAVING HERE *ALIVE* WITH THE *EVIL EYE!*

THREATS? FROM A MAN WITH A PRETTY *MOUSTACHE?*

FOR YOUR *INFORMATION,* AVENGER, I HAVEN'T *FOUND* THE EYE YET--

--AND WHERE THE *VALKYRIE* WALKS IS SOMETHING YOU HAVE *ABSOLUTELY* NO CONTROL OVER! I'LL LEAVE HERE WHENEVER I *PLEASE!*

BUT *FIRST,* SINCE YOU *ADMIRE* THE BLACK KNIGHT'S SWORD SO MUCH, WE'LL SEE HOW *HIS* BLADE FARES *AGAINST* YOU!

THEN YOU'LL *FEEL* HOW MY BLADE FARES AGAINST YOU!

THE DEFENDERS COULDN'T EVEN STOP AT *BEWITCHING* THE KNIGHT! THEY HAD TO STEAL HIS *EFFECTS,* AS WELL!

YOU HAVE THE BLACK KNIGHT'S SWORD?

AGILITY WON'T HELP YOU, VILLAINESS! NOT WHEN YOU MATCH *STEEL* WITH *THE BEST SWORDSMAN IN THE WORLD!*

HE'S *CRAZED* WITH A LUST FOR BATTLE! MY BEST EFFORTS DON'T EVEN MAKE HIM *BLINK!*

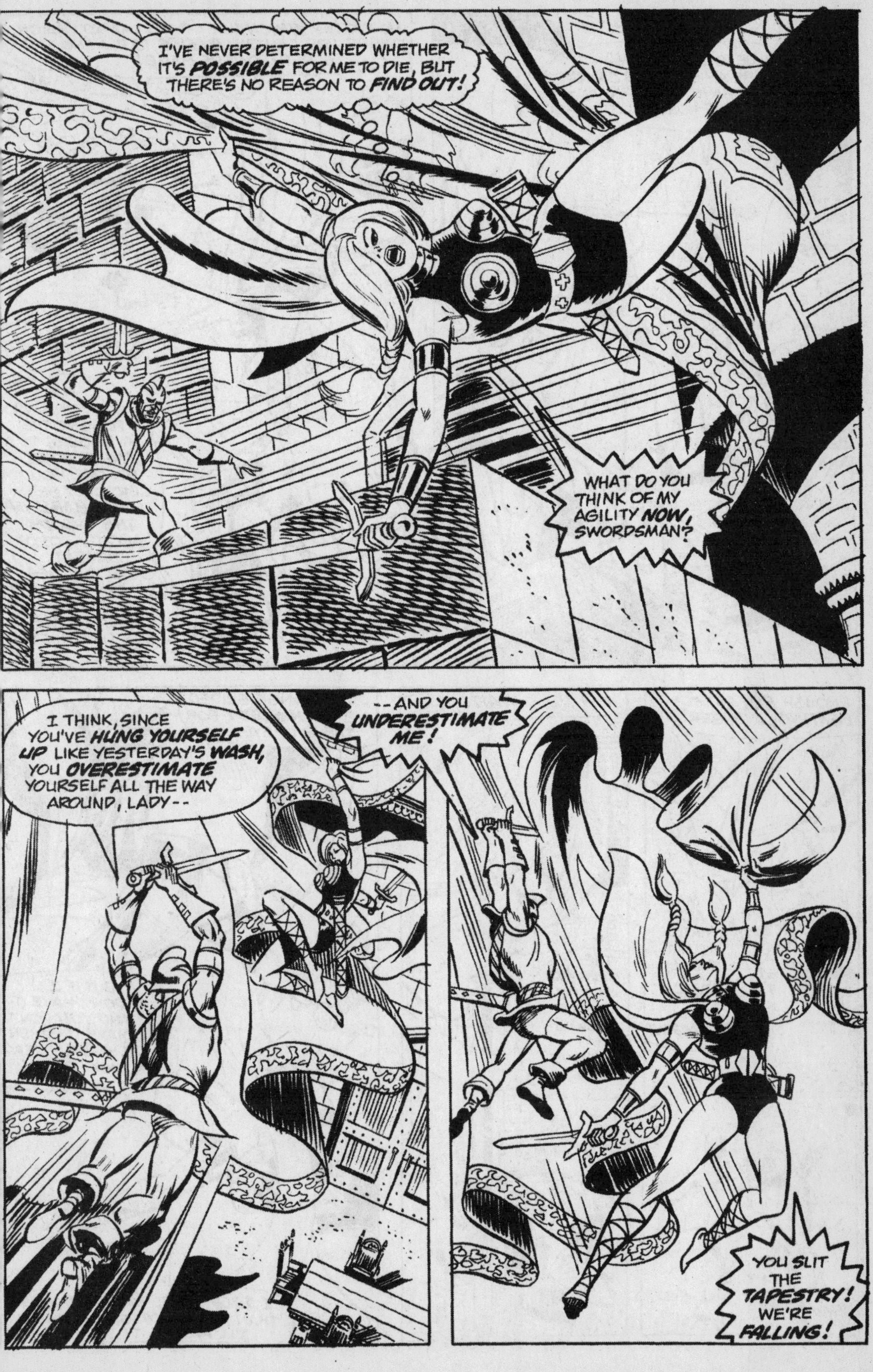

I'VE NEVER DETERMINED WHETHER IT'S POSSIBLE FOR ME TO DIE, BUT THERE'S NO REASON TO FIND OUT!
WHAT DO YOU THINK OF MY AGILITY NOW, SWORDSMAN?
I THINK, SINCE YOU'VE HUNG YOURSELF UP LIKE YESTERDAY'S WASH, YOU OVERESTIMATE YOURSELF ALL THE WAY AROUND, LADY--
--AND YOU UNDERESTIMATE ME!
YOU SLIT THE TAPESTRY! WE'RE FALLING!

BLUE-EYES, IF YOU WANT TO BE A HIGH-CLASS *CROOK*, YOU HAVE TO LEARN TO *TAKE* LONG FALLS!

IT WAS ONE OF THE *FIRST* THINGS *I* PICKED UP!

BLAM!

TUNK!

NO MATTER *WHICH* SIDE OF THE LAW YOU'RE ON, THERE ARE CERTAIN *BASICS* TO PLAYING THE SUPER-POWERS GAME!

FOR SOMEONE WHO FOUGHT THE *AVENGERS* TO A *STAND-STILL* BEFORE, YOU CERTAINLY SEEM LIKE A *BABE-IN-THE-WOODS* ABOUT A LOT OF COMBAT TECHNIQUES!

YOU'D NEVER CATCH *ME* LIKE THIS!

ENOUGH *BREAST-BEATING*, AVENGER!

I MAY *NOT* MATCH YOU AT *SKILL*, BUT I EXCEL YOU IN *STRENGTH!*

NOW I'LL -- *WAIT!*

THE *OWNER* OF THIS CASTLE -- LOCKING THAT MASSIVE *DOOR*...?

DR. STRANGE GUIDED ME TO *THIS* SPOT FOR THE EVIL-EYE!

BUT IF *I* DON'T HAVE IT -- AND *YOU* DON'T HAVE IT -- THEN I HAVE AN IDEA WHO *DOES!*

I *TOLD* YOU I WAS STRONGER THAN YOU, SWORDSMAN, AND NOW I'LL *PROVE* IT!

AS FOR *YOU*, MISTER-- --DON'T BE IN *TOO MUCH* OF A HURRY TO CLOSE THAT DOOR *BEHIND* YOU.

I WANT TO SEE WHAT-- *GOOD LORD!* A TREASURE CHEST OF *JEWELS* -- AND THE *EVIL EYE!*

A TREASURE *I'LL* TAKE CHARGE OF, BLUE EYES. WHEN THERE'S A *BOODLE* TO BE HAD, THE SWORDSMAN DOESN'T LET A LITTLE *LOVE TAP* STOP HIM!

GOT IT! AND NOW FOR THE WELL-KNOWN *"HASTY RETREAT"!*

NOT SO *FAST* HERO'--

--IT WAS *NEVER* MY INTENTION TO LET YOU LEAVE HERE *ALIVE!*

≈ARRGH!≈

QAZ!

I COULDN'T TAKE THE *RISK* THAT YOU'D LEAVE AND *TELL* ANYONE ABOUT MY *TREASURE!*

YOU-- *SHOT* ME--!

I--DON'T CARE *WHY*-- YOU DID IT! BUT YOU'RE *NOT* GETTING AWAY WITH IT!

FUNNY-- TO BE-- *"GENTLEMAN ROGUE"* --AND DIE AT HANDS OF-- SCUM LIKE *HIM.*

NO JUSTICE--*ANY-WHERE*--ANY MORE--

LET ME SEE YOUR WOUND, AVENGER.

YOU UNDERESTIMATE YOURSELF, *AFTER* ALL. IT'S *SERIOUS,* BUT I DOUBT YOU'LL *DIE.*

I'LL MAKE YOU *COMFORTABLE*--THEN GET A *DOCTOR.*

NO... IF YOU GO... YOU'LL TAKE... EYE. AVENGERS... TRUST ME...TO... KEEP. ...

THROATY BUT STILL *CLEAR*, HIS VOICE SIMPLY *STOPS* THERE, AS THE SHOCK OF HIS *INJURY* WASHES OVER HIS MIND. SLOWLY, FEELING ALMOST *SACRILEGIOUS*, THE VALKYRIE PRIES THE *PRIZE* FROM HIS LIMP FINGERS...

THEN THE SPELL IS *BROKEN!*

TROMP
TROMP

FOOT-STEPS! SOMEONE'S COMING!

BUT, *CAPITAN* -- WE WILL FACE GREAT *TROUBLE* FOR ENTERING THE AMERICAN'S CASTLE IF YOUR SUSPICIONS ARE *INCORRECT!*

THE AMERICAN'S *HERMIT-LIKE* BEHAVIOR, THE REPORTS OF A *FLYING HORSE* AND A STRANGE *JET* --

--THERE IS MUCH FOR WHICH I DESIRE AN EX-PLANATION, AND I WILL STIFLE MY DESIRE NO LONGER!

I MUST *LEAVE*, SWORDS-MAN. YOU WILL BE IN *GOOD HANDS.*

YOU ARE AN *ENIGMATIC* MAN -- AND, IN TRYING TO PREVENT ME FROM RECOVERING THIS PIECE OF THE EYE, A *PRESUMPTUOUS* ONE --

--*BUT I SALUTE* YOU AS A *GALLANT FOE.* IF YOU WERE *CONSCIOUS,* I THINK YOU'D LIKE THAT.

THUNDERING BOOTS AROUND THE CORNER *DAMN* WHATEVER ELSE SHE MIGHT WISH TO SAY. ONLY *SECONDS* BEFORE THE POLICE ARRIVE, THE VALKYRIE LEAPS TO *CONCEALMENT* --

-- WHERE SHE *WATCHES* AS THE *DEAD* MAN AND THE *WOUNDED* AVENGER ARE QUICKLY CARRIED AWAY.

IT IS WHEN SHE IS *CERTAIN* THE SWORDS-MAN WILL RECEIVE *PROPER CARE* --

-- THAT SHE SILENTLY *WINGS AWAY.*

AWAY FROM *BATTLE*, FROM *BLOODSHED* -- AND AWAY FROM A STONE *MONUMENT* TO MAN'S RECURRING DREAM OF *ABSOLUTE POWER FRAUDULENT-LY HELD* --

-- AND THE INEVITABLE, FEARFUL COST.

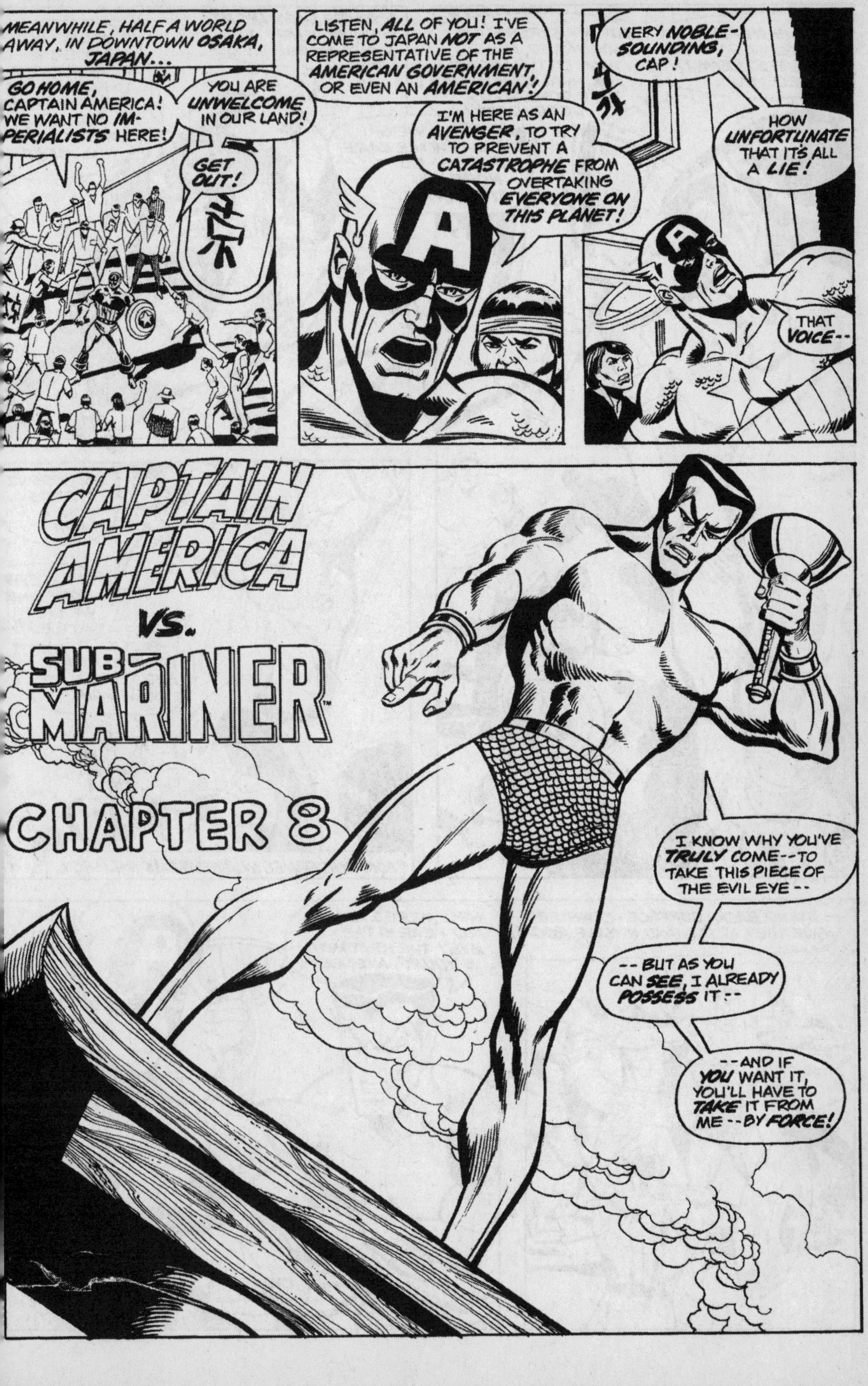
MEANWHILE, HALF A WORLD AWAY, IN DOWNTOWN OSAKA, JAPAN...
GO HOME, CAPTAIN AMERICA! WE WANT NO IMPERIALISTS HERE!
YOU ARE UNWELCOME IN OUR LAND!
GET OUT!
LISTEN, ALL OF YOU! I'VE COME TO JAPAN NOT AS A REPRESENTATIVE OF THE AMERICAN GOVERNMENT, OR EVEN AN AMERICAN!
I'M HERE AS AN AVENGER, TO TRY TO PREVENT A CATASTROPHE FROM OVERTAKING EVERYONE ON THIS PLANET!
VERY NOBLE-SOUNDING, CAP!
HOW UNFORTUNATE THAT IT'S ALL A LIE!
THAT VOICE--
CAPTAIN AMERICA
VS.
SUB-MARINER
CHAPTER 8
I KNOW WHY YOU'VE TRULY COME--TO TAKE THIS PIECE OF THE EVIL EYE--
--BUT AS YOU CAN SEE, I ALREADY POSSESS IT--
--AND IF YOU WANT IT, YOU'LL HAVE TO TAKE IT FROM ME--BY FORCE!

I HAVE *HEARD* THAT YOU GAINED LIMITED *SUPER-STRENGTH* RECENTLY!

BUT *MY* STRENGTH IS *UNLIMITED,* AND I HAVE LITTLE *LIKING* FOR WHAT YOUR *ALLIES* HAVE DONE TO US *DEFENDERS!*

SO WEIGH YOUR CHOICE *CARE-FULLY--* BUT I *HOPE* YOU *ATTEMPT* IT!

YOU'RE DARN *RIGHT* I'LL ATTEMPT IT, SUB-MARINER!

YOU'RE NOT THE FOE I'D HAVE *PICKED* TO FACE, BUT IF THE CHALLENGE IS *THERE,* CAPTAIN AMERICA WILL *MEET* IT!

IMPRESSIVE *WORDS...* FROM A *FOOL!*

IT HAS BEEN *YEARS* SINCE WE LAST BATTLED*--

--BUT I *BEAT* YOU *THEN,* AND I SHALL DO IT *AGAIN!*

*FOR *ONE PANEL* IN *AVENGERS #4.--ROY.*

STAND *BACK,* SURFACE-CRAWLERS! GIVE THE CAPTAIN AND MYSELF *ROOM!*

WELL, HERE I *AM--* AND HERE IS THE *EYE!* THE NEXT MOVE IS *YOURS,* AVENGER!

OKAY, NAMOR...

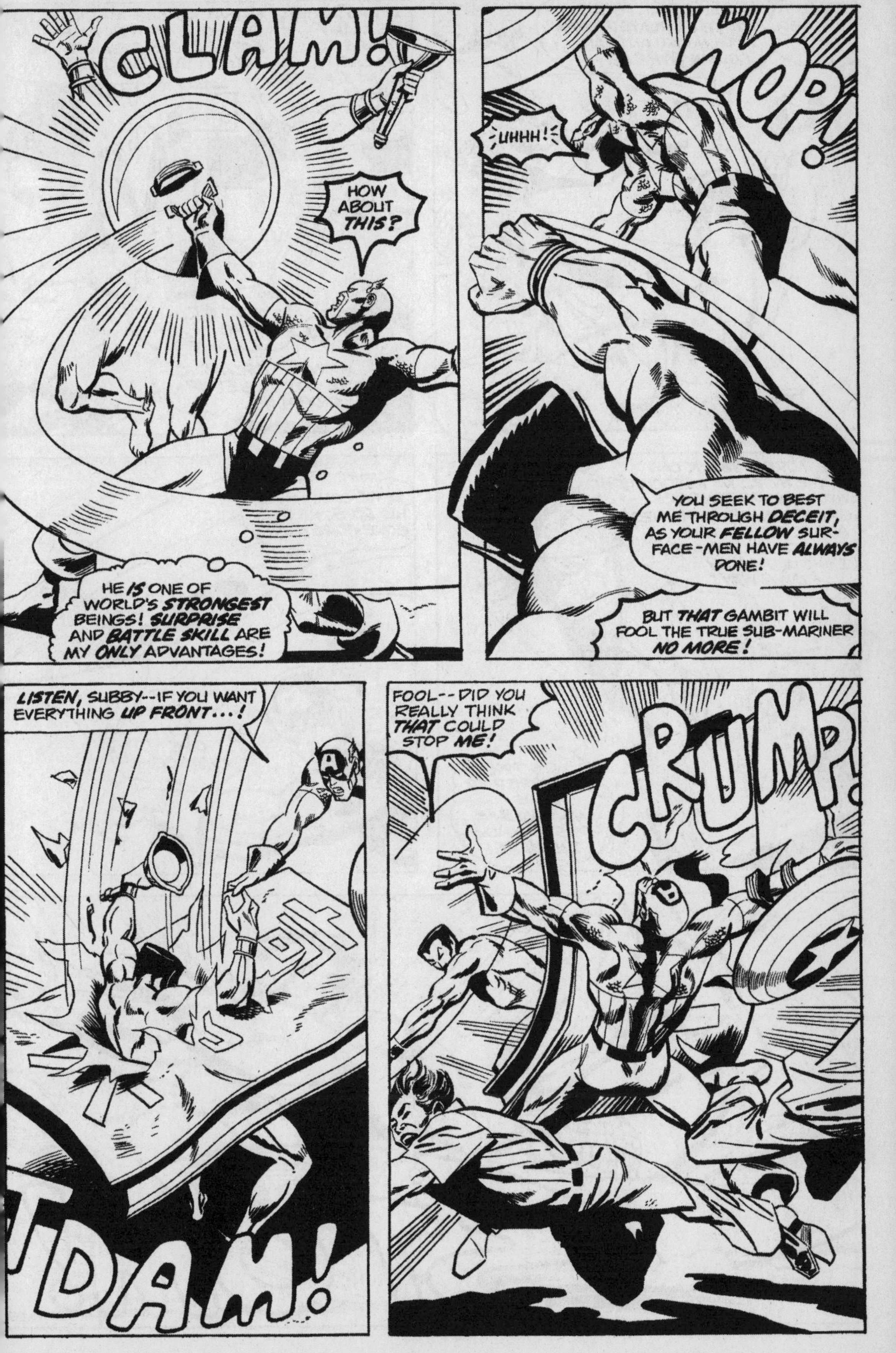
CLAM!
HOW ABOUT THIS?
HE IS ONE OF WORLD'S STRONGEST BEINGS! SURPRISE AND BATTLE SKILL ARE MY ONLY ADVANTAGES!
WOP!
UHHH!
YOU SEEK TO BEST ME THROUGH DECEIT, AS YOUR FELLOW SURFACE-MEN HAVE ALWAYS DONE!
BUT THAT GAMBIT WILL FOOL THE TRUE SUB-MARINER NO MORE!
LISTEN, SUBBY--IF YOU WANT EVERYTHING UP FRONT...!
TDAM!
FOOL--DID YOU REALLY THINK THAT COULD STOP ME!
CRUMP!

THAT DOWNED HIM!

TO THINK THAT, AS A *YOUTH*, I PLAYED "WAR" WITH MY ATLANTEAN COUSIN *BYRRAH*--

--AND I USUALLY CHOSE TO BE THE "AMERICAN"!

IT HAS TAKEN ME *MANY YEARS* TO RELEARN WHAT I ALREADY KNEW IN *WORLD WAR II*--

--THAT *NO SUB-MARINER*, NOT EVEN ONE WITH AN AMERICAN *FATHER*, CAN BE ANYTHING *BUT A SUB-MARINER*!

WHAT'S GOING--?

NAMOR--*ESCAPING*! I'VE GOT TO *GET UP*-- *STOP* HIM!

THE MORE I *THINK* ON IT, THE MORE MY ASSOCIATION WITH THE *DEFENDERS* GRATES MY SENSIBILITIES! AFTER I TAKE THIS PIECE TO DR. STRANGE, I SHOULD GO MY *OWN WAY*!

HE'S *TOO WRAPPED UP* IN HIS *MUSINGS*-- DOESN'T KNOW I'M *HERE*!

IF HE COMPLETES HIS *DIVE*, HE'S GONE *FOREVER*!

THERE'S ONLY *ONE CHANCE*--!

STOM!

SO YOU *PERSIST*, EH? WHAT DOES IT *TAKE* TO TEACH YOU YOUR LESSON?

IF MY LESSON IS THAT *MIGHT MAKES RIGHT*, NAMOR--

--PEOPLE HAVE BEEN TRYING TO *FORCE* MY BELIEF IN *THAT* SINCE THE *WORLD WAR* YOU SPOKE OF--

--AND I'VE FLUNKED THE COURSE *EVERY TIME* -- AS YOU SHOULD WELL *KNOW*!

FROM *NAZIS* TO *NOW*, AGAINST *ANY ODDS*, CAPTAIN AMERICA *NEVER SAYS DIE*!

BY THE SEVEN SECRET SEAS! I'D *LAUGH* AT YOUR NAIVETE, EXCEPT THAT YOU TRULY *BELIEVE* WHAT YOU SAY!

BE *THAT* AS IT MAY -- I LAUGH AT *BOTH* OF YOU!

A BOLT OF *FIRE* -- FROM *ABOVE*! WHO--?

WHO *ELSE* CAN PROTECT THE *LAND OF THE RISING SUN* FROM THOSE WHO INVADE IT, YANKEE?

ONLY I -- *SUNFIRE*!*

*THE JAPANESE MUTANT WAS LAST SEEN IN *SUBBY* #54.-- ROY.

YOU WOULD HAVE BEEN BETTER ADVISED TO *HEED* MY COUNTRYMEN, CAPTAIN AMERICA! WE ARE *ALL* WEARY OF FOREIGNERS THRUSTING THEIR GAME UPON US!

OKAY! *FINE!* BUT GIVE ME THE EYE, *QUICK!*

SUNFIRE, *I* WANT THAT BAUBLE! GIVE IT TO *ME*, OR--

YOU DO NOT FRIGHTEN ME, SUB-MARINER!

ALTHOUGH PRESSED INTO *PARTNERSHIP* WITH YOU DURING OUR PREVIOUS ENCOUNTER, I AM NO *GEISHA* TO SERVE YOUR WHIMS!

YOU TWO *INVADED* MY LAND FOR THIS OBJECT AS IF *ABOVE* SUCH PETTY DETAILS AS *INTERNATIONAL BOUNDARIES* --

--BUT YOU ARE *WRONG*, AND I SHALL *CONVINCE* YOU OF THAT FACT BY TAKING YOUR OBJECT *MYSELF!*

WHY, YOU *NATIONALISTIC MORON!*

I WON'T *STAND* FOR THIS IDIOCY! THE *PRINCE OF ATLANTIS* DOES WHAT HE *PLEASES!*

NOT IF IT'S RETRIEVING THE *EYE*, PRINCE!

WHAT IN THE NAME OF *FATHER NEPTUNE?*

I *AGREE* THAT SUNNY'S MOTIVES ARE PRETTY *REACTIONARY* --

--BUT THEY KEEP THE EYE *AWAY* FROM YOU, AND THAT PUTS HIM ON *MY SIDE!*

KLOP!

THE DEFENDERS WILL *NEVER* GAIN POSSESSION OF THAT WEAPON --

--WHILE THERE'S AN *AVENGER* LEFT *ALIVE!*

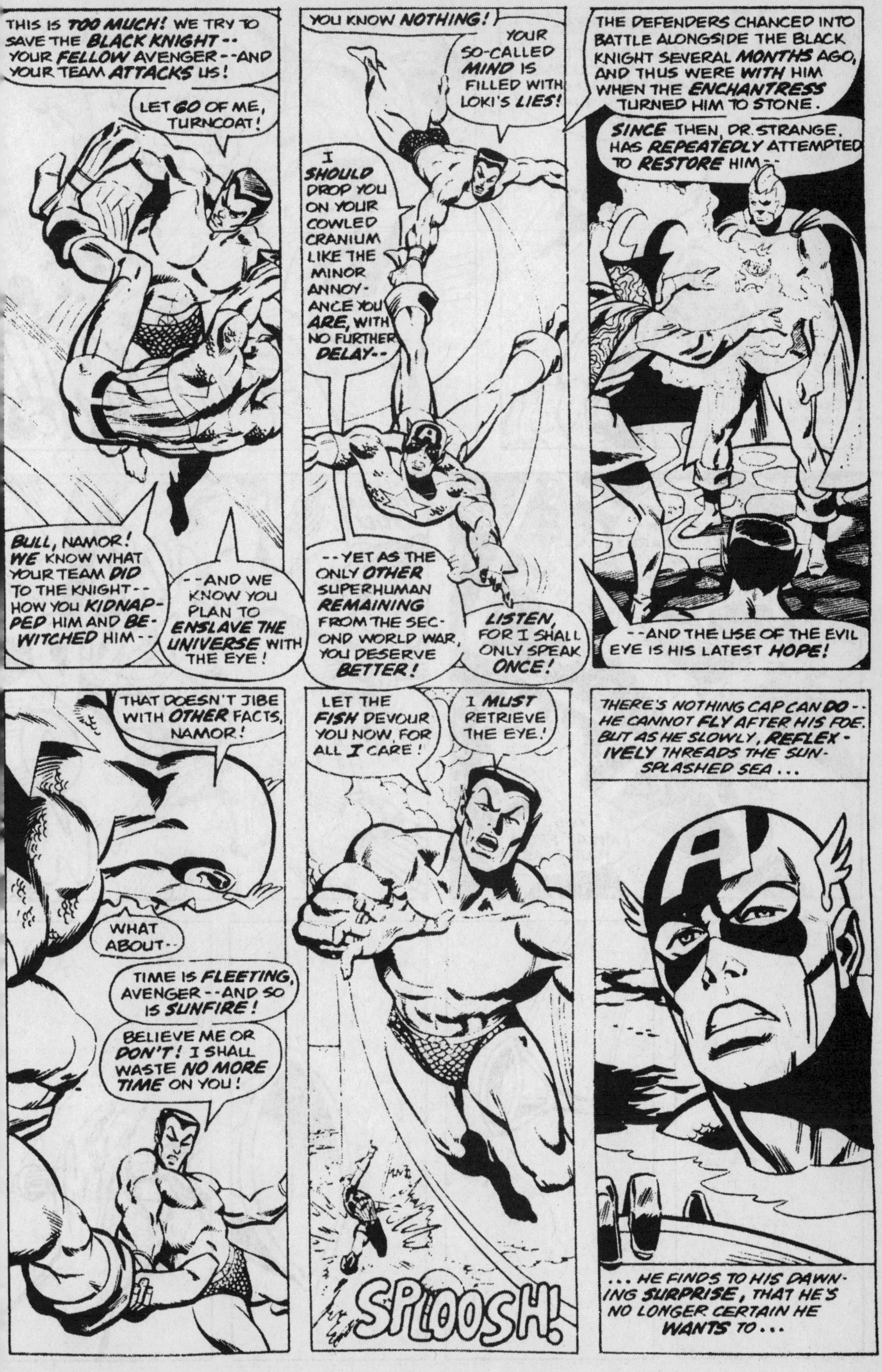
THIS IS TOO MUCH! WE TRY TO SAVE THE BLACK KNIGHT -- YOUR FELLOW AVENGER -- AND YOUR TEAM ATTACKS US!
LET GO OF ME, TURNCOAT!
BULL, NAMOR! WE KNOW WHAT YOUR TEAM DID TO THE KNIGHT -- HOW YOU KIDNAPPED HIM AND BEWITCHED HIM --
-- AND WE KNOW YOU PLAN TO ENSLAVE THE UNIVERSE WITH THE EYE!
YOU KNOW NOTHING!
YOUR SO-CALLED MIND IS FILLED WITH LOKI'S LIES!
I SHOULD DROP YOU ON YOUR COWLED CRANIUM LIKE THE MINOR ANNOYANCE YOU ARE, WITH NO FURTHER DELAY --
-- YET AS THE ONLY OTHER SUPERHUMAN REMAINING FROM THE SECOND WORLD WAR, YOU DESERVE BETTER!
LISTEN, FOR I SHALL ONLY SPEAK ONCE!
THE DEFENDERS CHANCED INTO BATTLE ALONGSIDE THE BLACK KNIGHT SEVERAL MONTHS AGO, AND THUS WERE WITH HIM WHEN THE ENCHANTRESS TURNED HIM TO STONE.
SINCE THEN, DR. STRANGE, HAS REPEATEDLY ATTEMPTED TO RESTORE HIM --
-- AND THE USE OF THE EVIL EYE IS HIS LATEST HOPE!
THAT DOESN'T JIBE WITH OTHER FACTS, NAMOR!
WHAT ABOUT --
TIME IS FLEETING, AVENGER -- AND SO IS SUNFIRE!
BELIEVE ME OR DON'T! I SHALL WASTE NO MORE TIME ON YOU!
LET THE FISH DEVOUR YOU NOW, FOR ALL I CARE!
I MUST RETRIEVE THE EYE!
SPLOOSH!
THERE'S NOTHING CAP CAN DO -- HE CANNOT FLY AFTER HIS FOE. BUT AS HE SLOWLY, REFLEXIVELY THREADS THE SUN-SPLASHED SEA...
... HE FINDS TO HIS DAWNING SURPRISE, THAT HE'S NO LONGER CERTAIN HE WANTS TO...

WHILE, HIGH ABOVE ---

HOLD, SUNFIRE! I CALL UPON YOU ONE LAST TIME TO SURRENDER THAT WEAPON!

AND I TELL YOU NO, NAMOR!

YOU SHALL NOT HAVE ANYTHING THAT BELONGS TO JAPAN!

TOO SLOW, MUTANT!

FOOM!

MY WINGED FEET CAN EASILY CARRY ME AWAY FROM YOUR BLASTS!

YES, AWAY FROM YOUR BLASTS--

--AND TOWARD YOU!

KA-DOW!

SUNFIRE DROPPED THE EYE RIGHT INTO MY *HAND!* LUCK LIKE *THAT* MUST BE TRYING TO *TELL* ME SOMETHING!

IT'S SAYING "DON'T ASK *QUESTIONS*-- JUST DO WHAT YOU *CAME* FOR AND *GET OUT!*"

THAT MAY BE WHAT *LUCK* IS SAYING, CAPTAIN AMERICA--BUT I SAY--

--"*LUCK* CAN BE *BROKEN* -- EXACTLY LIKE *YOU!*"

YOUR *CHOICE*, AVENGER: SHALL I HAVE THE EYE *PEACEFULLY* OR THROUGH FURTHER *VIOLENCE?*

WELL?

ALL RIGHT, NAMOR. I *STILL* DON'T UNDERSTAND -- BUT THAT'S THE *POINT.*

THERE'S *TOO MUCH* THAT DOESN'T MAKE SENSE IN THIS WAR BETWEEN THE AVENGERS AND THE DEFENDERS--

--AND MAYBE *TRUST* IS THE *ONLY THING* THAT CAN *CREATE* SOME SENSE.

IF *YOUR* REASONS FOR FIGHTING AREN'T THE SAME AS *MINE*, IT'S *BEGINNING* TO OCCUR TO ME THAT WE'VE BEEN *MANIPULATED!*

NOW THAT *DOES* MAKE SENSE, CAP!

AND IF WE *HAVE* BEEN TRICKED, I SWEAR THERE'LL BE *HELL* TO PAY!

AT LAST -- A POSSIBLE *BREAK-THROUGH* IN THE NET OF DECEPTION THAT HAS DRAPED ITSELF ACROSS THE MIGHTIEST SUPER-TEAMS ON EARTH!

THE PLOT'S ONLY BEEN *THICKENING* UP UNTIL NOW, TRUE BELIEVER! IN THE *NEXT CHAPTERS*, IT COMES TO A BOIL!

DEFENDERS #10 (ON SALE NOW!) THE *FINAL BATTLE* -- BETWEEN THE MIGHTY THOR AND THE INCREDIBLE HULK! PLUS -- THE UNITING OF THE TEAMS, AS DORMAMMU TIPS HIS HAND!

AVENGERS #118 (ON SALE NEXT MONTH!) SUPER-VILLAINS MEET SUPERHEROES (14 OF 'EM!) IN THE WILDEST, MOST AWE-INSPIRING CLIMAX EVER RECORDED! WE'VE BEEN TELLING YOU ALL ALONG THIS WAS GOING TO BE BIG, BUT YOU'LL HAVE TO *SEE* IT TO BELIEVE IT! BE HERE, BABY!

MARVEL MOVES OUT!

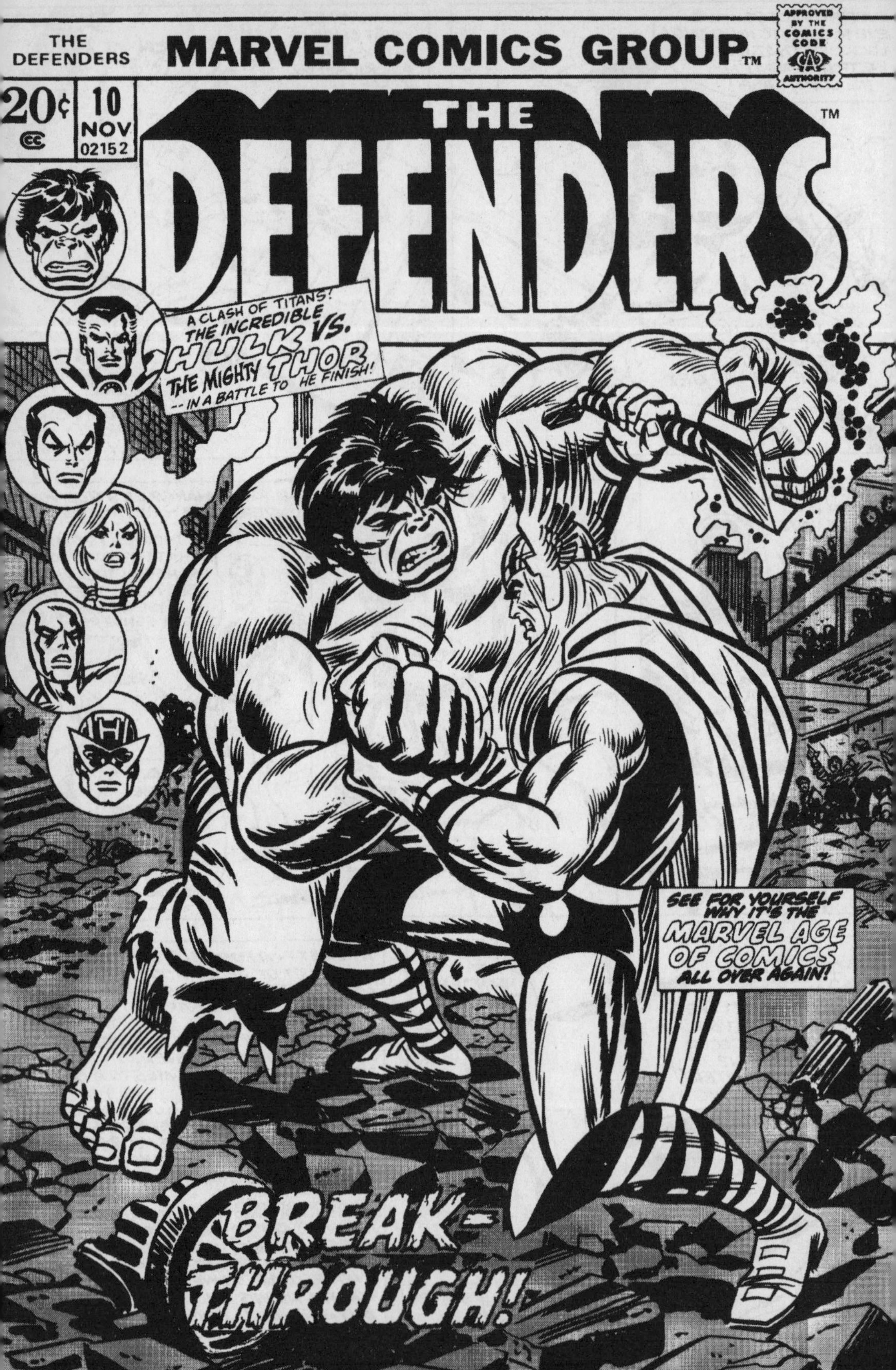
THE DEFENDERS
MARVEL COMICS GROUP™
APPROVED BY THE COMICS CODE AUTHORITY
20¢
10 NOV
02152
THE DEFENDERS™
A CLASH OF TITANS! THE INCREDIBLE HULK VS. THE MIGHTY THOR --IN A BATTLE TO HE FINISH!
SEE FOR YOURSELF WHY IT'S THE MARVEL AGE OF COMICS ALL OVER AGAIN!
BREAK-THROUGH!

Stan Lee presents: THE DYNAMIC DEFENDERS!™

STEVE ENGLEHART * SAL BUSCEMA * FRANK BOLLE * T. ORZ, Letterer * ROY THOMAS
AUTHOR ARTIST INKER P. GOLDBERG, Colorist EDITOR

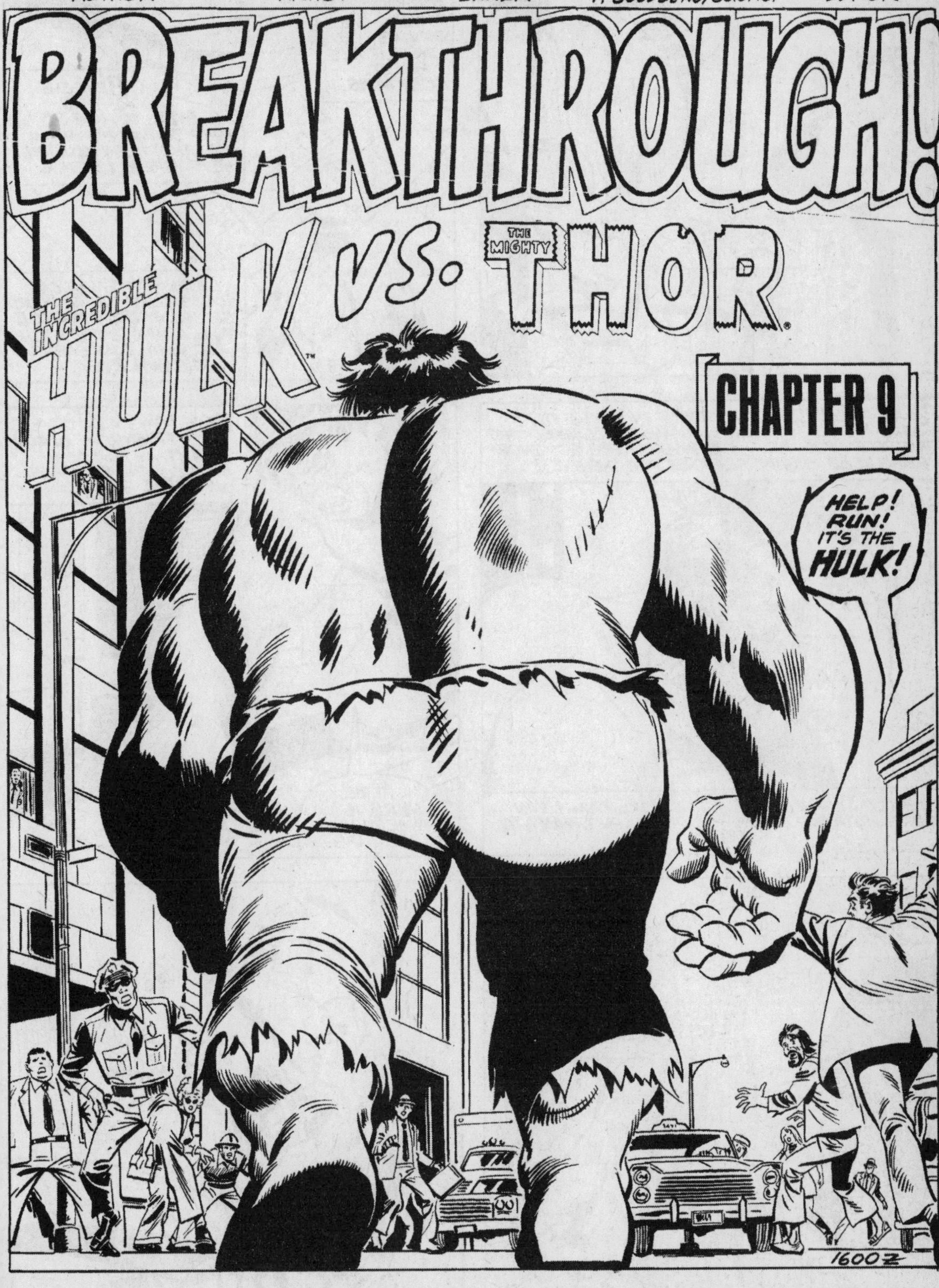
BREAKTHROUGH!
THE INCREDIBLE HULK™ VS. THE MIGHTY THOR®
CHAPTER 9
HELP! RUN! IT'S THE HULK!

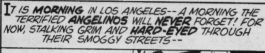

IT IS **MORNING** IN LOS ANGELES -- A MORNING THE TERRIFIED **ANGELINOS** WILL **NEVER** FORGET! FOR NOW, STALKING GRIM AND **HARD-EYED** THROUGH THEIR SMOGGY STREETS --

-- COMES THE WORLD'S **MOST POWERFUL MONSTER!**

LIKE A LIVING **TANK**, THE HULK POUNDS FORWARD, TOWARD ONE OF L.A.'S FINEST HOTEL'S FINEST **FOUNTAINS.**

HE SEEMS, MORE THAN **EVER**, TO HAVE **NO** MIND BEHIND HIS BROW, BUT THAT IS AN **ILLUSION.** HE IS MERELY... LISTENING...

... LISTENING TO MYSTICAL VOICES COMMANDED HOURS BEFORE BY **DR. STRANGE** TO LEAD HIM TO THE SIXTH AND **FINAL** COMPONENT OF THE **EVIL EYE!**

IN THE **PRECEEDING** CHAPTER OF THIS SAGA, THE **SUB-MARINER** AND CAPTAIN AMERICA LEARNED THAT THE DEFENDERS AND THE AVENGERS WERE SOMEHOW BEING **USED** IN THEIR SEARCHES FOR THE EYE...

... BUT THE **HULK**, BEING HALF A WORLD AWAY, CAN KNOW **NOTHING** OF THIS -- AND WOULDN'T **WANT** TO, ANYWAY.

HE IS DOING A FAVOR FOR HIS **FRIEND**, THE **BLACK KNIGHT**, AS FAR AS HE KNOWS... AND IT MAKES HIM **FEEL** GOOD...

HERE... **HERE** IS WHERE HULK MUST DIG.

... AND SO THE STAGE IS SET FOR A **CLASH** OF **TITANS!**

PUNY **HUMANS** WOULD HAVE TO USE **MACHINES** TO GO WHERE HULK IS GOING.

... BUT **HULK** IS **NOT** HUMAN!

RRIP!

HAH! HULK DID NOT HAVE TO DO MUCH AT **ALL**!

THERE IS PIECE OF EVIL EYE!

HOWEVER, AS WE SAID, THIS STAGE IS **NOW** SET FOR A **CLASH** OF TITANS... AND WE HARDLY EVER **LIE**.

COMING IN LOW OVER MAYOR BRADLEY'S BABY AT THIS **VERY** MOMENT IS ASGARD'S MOST POWERFUL GOD...

...THE MIGHTY **THOR**!

WOULD YOU **AGREE** THAT IN THE REALM OF COMICS, **THESE** TWO BEINGS ARE THE BEST THERE **ARE**--

--THE **ONLY** **TRUE** TITANS?

THEN LET THE CLASH **BEGIN**!

HOLD, HULK! I WOULD HAVE **WORDS** WITH THEE!

I WELL **COMPREHEND** THY HATRED FOR A WORLD'S **MISTREATMENT** OF THEE, YET THE **DEFENDERS'** SCHEME TO **CONQUER THE UNIVERSE** IS **WRONG**!

AS ONE **AVENGER** TO **ANOTHER**, I BESEECH THEE--

YES... HULK **WAS** AVENGER ONCE...

...DIDN'T LIKE IT!

HULK DOESN'T LIKE *DEFENDERS*, EITHER. WOULDN'T HELP *THEM* EXCEPT THEY HELP *BLACK KNIGHT*.

WHEN HE GETS BACK TO DUMB *MAGICIAN*, MAYBE HULK WILL SMASH *HIM*, TOO! HULK HAS PUT UP WITH--

WHAM!

=UHH!=

SURELY THOU HAST NOT FORGOTTEN OUR *PREVIOUS* BATTLE, MONSTER?*

HOW CANST THOU *TURN AWAY* WHEN THOU DOST KNOW I BE THY *SUPERIOR?*

*NOBODY *ELSE* WHO READ *JOURNEY INTO MYSTERY* #112 HAS! -- ROY.

SUPERIOR?

YOU SAID... YOU ARE *BETTER* THAN HULK?

AYE, FOR THOUGH *NO ONE* ACTUALLY STRODE FORTH *VICTORIOUS*--

-- I KNOW MY PROWESS DID EXCEED THINE.

THUS, I *AGAIN* CALL UPON THEE--

BOOM

YOU ARE NOT BETTER THAN HULK!

FOOM

NO ONE IS BETTER THAN HULK!

WELL, THAT'S **TWICE** THE GOD OF THUNDER HAS OPENED HIS MOUTH, AND **TWICE** HE'S PUT HIS **FOOT** IN IT. BUT THAT WON'T STOP **OTHER** MOUTHS FROM OPENING...

...IN **FEAR**...

REINFORCEMENTS! YEAH, ON THE **DOUBLE**!

...IN **AWE**...

... OR IN **EXCITEMENT**!

GET DOWN ON 'IM, THOR!

DO IT TO 'IM, GREENSKIN!

IT WILL ONLY STOP THOR FROM TALKING **REASON**!

KA- DOW!

ACTIONS SPEAK LOUDER THAN WORDS!

IF THOU WANT BATTLE, BEHEMOTH, THOR SHALL MEET THEE **BLOW** FOR **BLOW**!

BOM!

THE **GREEN GOLIATH CRASHES** TO THE PAVEMENT, BUT HIS **INDESTRUCTIBLE BODY** IMPATIENTLY **SHRUGS IT OFF!** FURIOUS, HE CLAMPS ONTO THOR'S FLAPPING **CAPE**--

--AND YANKS GOLDILOCKS INTO A SIZZLING *SPIN*--

--*SCREWING* HIM INTO THE *SIDEWALK!*

THOR WAS TOO *SURPRISED* TO SAVE HIMSELF! DOESN'T *THINK* FAST!

DOESN'T THINK AT *ALL*, TO CHALLENGE *HULK!*

HULK BEATS *EVERYBODY!* ANYONE WHO SAYS *DIFFERENT* IS *CRAZY!*

HULK IS *STRONGEST* THERE *IS!*

WAIT! GROUND SHAKES FROM *BELOW!*

BUT-- IT CAN'T BE *THOR!* HE IS NOT--

--AS STRONG AS *THEE*, MONSTER?

NAY! I BE *STRONGER!*

THE HULK LIFTS HIMSELF *FRENZIEDLY* FROM THE RUBBLE, HIS *MOUTH* WORKING BUT HIS *VOCAL CHORDS* CONSTRICTED WITH RAGE!

RRRRR

EMITTING ONLY A DEFIANT *ROAR,* HE SEIZES A TUMBLED *CAR* TO THROW--

--BUT--

KLOW!

HE THROWS *HAMMER*-- BUT IT WILL DO NO GOOD!

HULK THOUGHT OF THROWING SOMETHING *FIRST!*

WELL THOR WILL NOT GET HAMMER *BACK!* HULK WILL CATCH--

CHOOM!

WHAT *HAPPENS?*

HULK CAN DO *ANYTHING,* BUT HE CAN'T PICK UP *HAMMER!*

VERILY, BRUTE-- FOR BY ODIN'S IMPERIAL *DECREE,* NONE BUT HIS *TRUE SON* MAY LIFT SACRED MJOLNIR!

YON *URU MALLET* IS THOR'S *ALONE!*

TDAM!

YOUR STRONGEST HIT DOESN'T HURT *HULK!* BUT NOW *HE* WILL DESTROY *YOU!*

BY MY *TROTH!* HE HATH TURNED *BERSERK!*

NAUGHT BUT MY *DEATH* WILL SATISFY HIM *NOW!*

As IF THAT COLD THOUGHT CLOSES A *PSYCHIC SWITCH,* THE VERY *ATMOSPHERE* IN LOS ANGELES SUDDENLY TURNS *CLAMMY!* FEAR HAS COME TO CLAW AT THE CROWD'S HEARTS--

--FEAR THAT, WITH NO *QUARTER* ABLE TO BE GIVEN, *ONE* OF THESE GREAT BEINGS WILL *PERISH* HERE TODAY!

THEIR EYES SEARCH *THOR'S* TIGHT FACE, READING THE *PURPOSE* AND *COMMITMENT* THERE--

--THEN THEY SCAN THE *HULK'S* TWISTED VISAGE--

--AND *RECOIL!*

EACH PERSON THERE ASSEMBLED SILENTLY MAKES HIS CHOICE FOR THE *WINNER* OF THIS FINAL STRUGGLE -- AND THEN STANDS *TRANSFIXED,* ABLE ONLY TO LOOK ON IN *MUTE HORROR!*

HULK WAITING, THOR.

HERE I *STAND,* HULK!

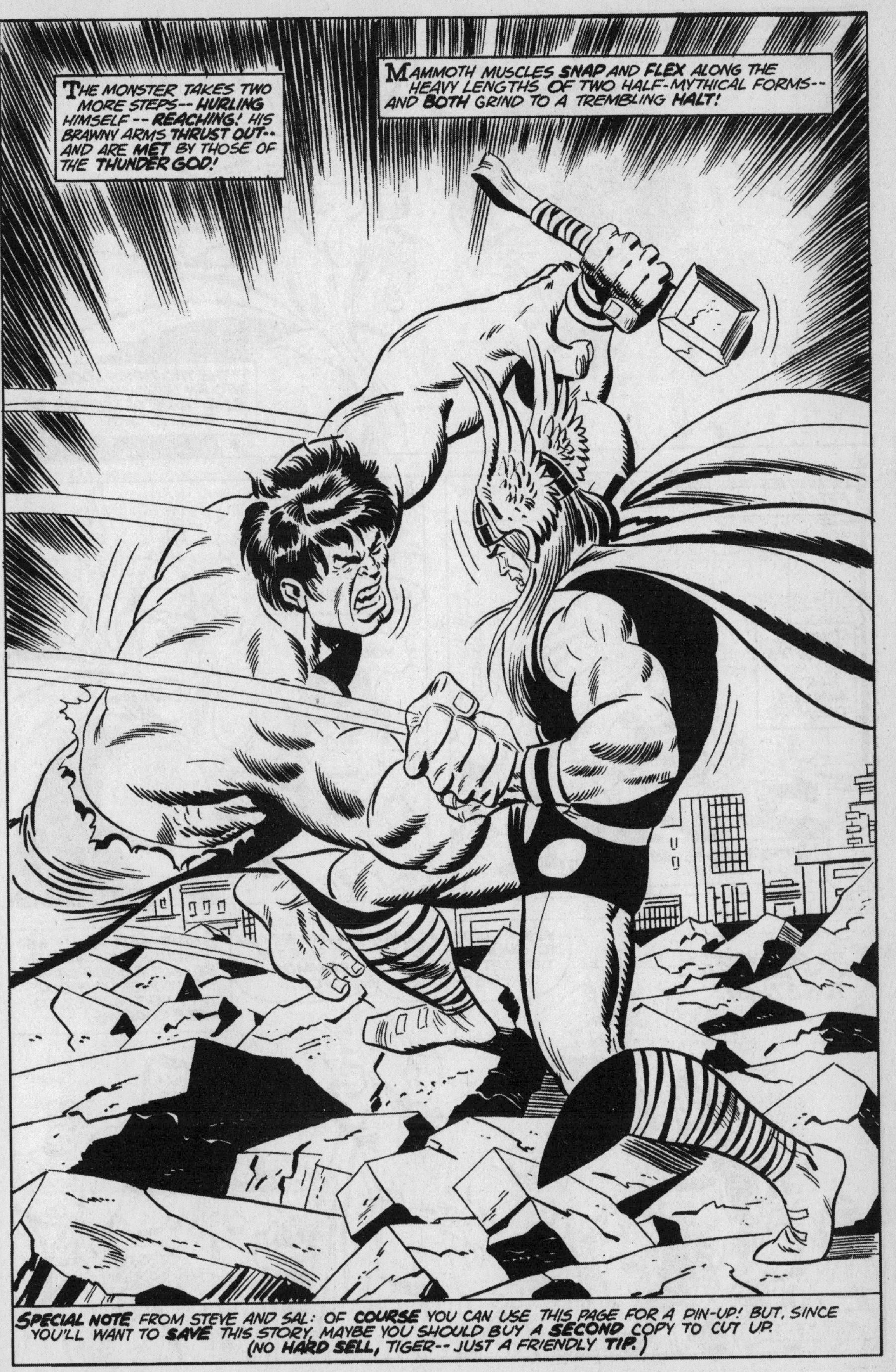
THE MONSTER TAKES TWO MORE STEPS-- HURLING HIMSELF -- REACHING! HIS BRAWNY ARMS THRUST OUT-- AND ARE MET BY THOSE OF THE THUNDER GOD!
MAMMOTH MUSCLES SNAP AND FLEX ALONG THE HEAVY LENGTHS OF TWO HALF-MYTHICAL FORMS-- AND BOTH GRIND TO A TREMBLING HALT!

SPECIAL NOTE FROM STEVE AND SAL: OF **COURSE** YOU CAN USE THIS PAGE FOR A PIN-UP! BUT, SINCE YOU'LL WANT TO **SAVE** THIS STORY, MAYBE YOU SHOULD BUY A **SECOND** COPY TO CUT UP.
(NO **HARD SELL**, TIGER-- JUST A FRIENDLY **TIP**.)

SWEAT-SLICK FACES ONLY *INCHES* FROM EACH OTHER, PANTED *BREATHS* MIXING--

--THE TWO TITANS *LOCK* INTO AN UNMOVING *SCULPTURE* OF SEETHING, BRIDLED FORCE!

TEN MINUTES THEY HOLD THEIR POSE, EACH STRAINING *FUTILELY* TO BREAK THE STATUS QUO!

TWENTY MINUTES THEY HOLD! *THIRTY MINUTES!* ONE *HOUR!*

NEITHER SHOWS *ANY* SIGNS OF TIRING!

AND THEN--

HOLD! THERE IS NO *NEED* FOR SUCH VIOLENCE!

ODIN'S BLOOD! WHO--?

YOU!

THE *DEFENDERS--* AND THE *AVENGERS--* TOGETHER!

YES-- UNITED AT *LAST*, TO *OVERRIDE* THE LIES THAT SET US AT EACH OTHER'S THROATS--

--AND *READY* TO FACE THE *COMMON FOE!*

SURPRISED, FOLK? WE THOUGHT YOU *WOULD* BE. BUT THE *EXPLANATION* COMES UP IN OUR VERY NEXT CHAPTER, SO *KEEP READING!*

UNITED WE STAND!

THE TIME IS *ONE HOUR AGO,* AND THE PLACE, OF COURSE, IS THE *SANCTUM SANCTORUM* OF THE MASTER OF THE MYSTIC ARTS, *DR. STRANGE.*

FOUR PIECES OF THE EVIL EYE!

DESPITE *FORMIDABLE* OPPOSITION FROM THE *AVENGERS,* WE HAVE *WON* OUR BITTERLY-CONTESTED BATTLES THUS FAR--

--AND IF *NAMOR* AND THE *HULK* FARE AS WELL, THE *BLACK KNIGHT* WILL SOON BE A STATUE *NO MORE!*

HOW *STRANGE* THE PIECES ARE, STEPHEN. EACH LOOKS THE *SAME,* EXCEPT THAT THEIR *SIZES* ARE DIFFERENT!

CHAPTER 10

THEY *TELESCOPE--* EACH INSIDE *ANOTHER--* IT SEEMS, VALKYRIE.

AS WE *KNOW,* EACH CONTAINS A *CERTAIN* AMOUNT OF POWER IN AND OF *ITSELF.* ONCE *JOINED,* THE EYE WILL BE *INVINCIBLE.*

SILENCE-- PLEASE!

WHAT *IS* IT, STEPHEN?

I SENSE THE *SUB-MARINER* OUTSIDE THE MYSTIC DEFENSES I PLACED AROUND THIS DWELLING! HE HAS *RETURNED* FROM HIS QUEST!

I SHALL *DISSOLVE* THE BARRIERS FOR A MOMENT, AND ALLOW HIM TO *ENTER!*

WINDS RISE FROM NOWHERE, WITHIN AND *WITHOUT* THE STRUCTURE, DARTING THROUGH BILLOWING SHADOWS AND LICKING ACROSS THE DEFENDERS' NECKS. A VOICELESS *CHILL* TOUCHES THEIR MINDS.

THEN ALL THAT IS *GONE*, AND A *DOOR* SWINGS OPEN TO REVEAL THE ONCE-AND PRESENT *PRINCE OF ATLANTIS!*

GOOD *DAY*, DEFENDERS. I HAVE BROUGHT *GUESTS*...

...THE AVENGERS!

WHAT?!! YOU LET OUR *ENEMIES* INTO OUR *HEADQUARTERS?*

NAMOR, HOW *COULD* YOU?

'CAUSE HE'S A *TRAITOR*, LADY-- A REGULAR *TROJAN FISH!*

THEY MUST'A MADE 'IM A *BETTER* OFFER!

WE *WILL* NOT BE DEFEATED WHEN WE ARE SO CLOSE TO *SUCCESS!*

IF WE *MUST* DEFEND OURSELVES, NAMOR--

BUT THE CRISP *COMMANDING* VOICE OF THE ATLANTEAN MONARCH SLICES *THROUGH* HIS TEAMMATES' OUTRAGED CHORUS.

HEAR ME OUT! I HAVE *VITAL* NEWS!

IN MY BATTLE FOR MY SECTION OF THE EYE, I FACED *CAPTAIN AMERICA*-- UNTIL AN OLD FOE, *SUNFIRE*, STOLE THE PIECE FROM *BOTH* OF US!

YOU SHALL NOT BRING YOUR CONFLICT INTO *MY* LAND! *

*AVENGERS #117-- ROY.

TO COUNTER THE **COMMON** THREAT, CAP AND I WERE FORCED INTO A **TRUCE**-- AND FORCED TO **TALK**.

WHAT WE DISCOVERED FRANKLY **SCARED** ME!

THE AVENGERS WERE TOLD BY **LOKI** THAT WE WANT TO CONQUER THE **UNIVERSE**!

OBVIOUSLY, **ALL** OF US NEED TO TALK ABOUT THIS--

--SO AS CAP AND I FLEW BACK FROM **JAPAN**, WE SWUNG THROUGH THE SOUTH PACIFIC, SOUTH AMERICA AND CENTRAL AMERICA TO GATHER **OTHER** AVENGERS.

IF WE CAN **DEFEND** OURSELVES, DEFENDERS, WE HAD PLENTY OF **OTHER** EVIDENCE BESIDES LOKI'S STORY--

--BUT IF THERE'S A **LOGICAL EXPLANATION**, WE'RE **EAGER** TO **HEAR** IT!

--THE MYSTERIOUS **DISAPPEARANCE** OF THE BLACK KNIGHT, THE MAGICAL **FORCES** THAT KEPT US OUT OF THIS HOUSE, THE **SILVER SURFER'S** ATTACK ON THE VISION AND THE SCARLET WITCH--

FIRST, HOWEVER, SINCE WE DON'T APPEAR TO BE IN ANY **IMMINENT** DANGER FROM **EACH OTHER**, I HAVE A MORE **BASIC** QUESTION TO BE ANSWERED.

IF YOU'RE **NOT** SEEKING REVENGE ON HUMANITY, WHY **HAVE** YOU JOINED TOGETHER?

REVENGE ON HUMANITY? YES, I CAN **SEE** HOW YOU WOULD ACCEPT THAT.

ALL OF US **DO** FOLLOW OUR OWN PATHS, AWAY FROM THE **WELL-TRAVELED** ROUTES OF THE **MASS** OF MANKIND. WE **ARE** OUTSIDERS.

BUT FROM **TIME** TO **TIME**, OUR SEPARATE PATHS LAY **SIDE** BY **SIDE**, OR EVEN **OVERLAP**.

AT THESE TIMES, WE **MAY** CHOOSE TO TRAVEL **TOGETHER**-- OR WE MAY **NOT**. WE RETAIN OUR **FREEDOM**!

AND FAR FROM DESIRING **REVENGE** ON ANYONE, WE ONLY WANT TO **DEFEND**! HUMANITY MEANS A **GREAT DEAL** TO **SOME** OF US, AND **LITTLE** TO OTHERS, BUT IT'S WORTH **DEFENDING** IF NEED BE!

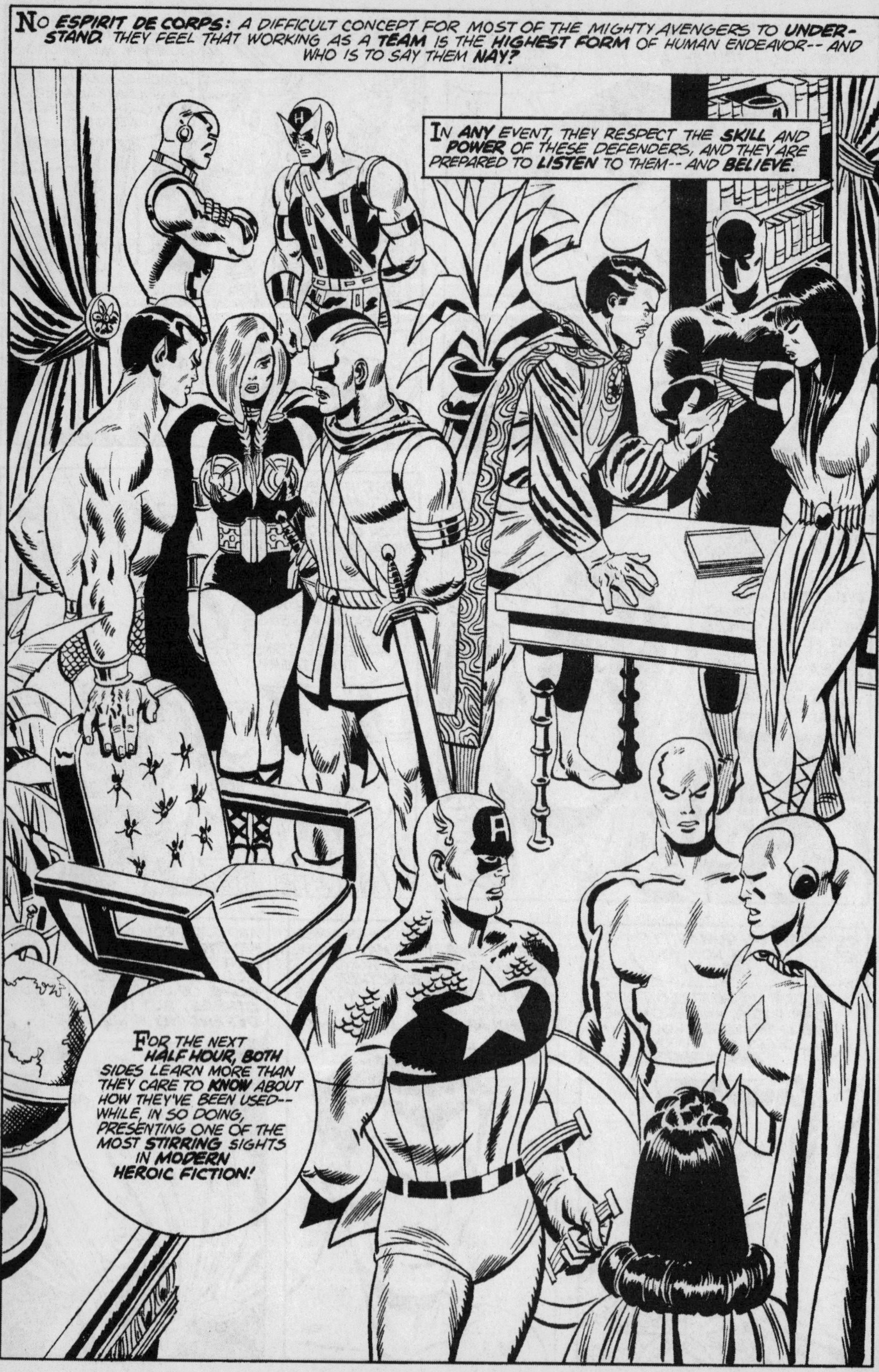
NO ESPIRIT DE CORPS: A DIFFICULT CONCEPT FOR MOST OF THE MIGHTY AVENGERS TO UNDERSTAND. THEY FEEL THAT WORKING AS A TEAM IS THE HIGHEST FORM OF HUMAN ENDEAVOR-- AND WHO IS TO SAY THEM NAY?
IN ANY EVENT, THEY RESPECT THE SKILL AND POWER OF THESE DEFENDERS, AND THEY ARE PREPARED TO LISTEN TO THEM-- AND BELIEVE.
FOR THE NEXT HALF HOUR, BOTH SIDES LEARN MORE THAN THEY CARE TO KNOW ABOUT HOW THEY'VE BEEN USED-- WHILE, IN SO DOING, PRESENTING ONE OF THE MOST STIRRING SIGHTS IN MODERN HEROIC FICTION!

COMING DOWN...

WANDA, I HAD NO IDEA MY ACCIDENTAL TRIGGERING OF THE EYE HAD *INJURED* YOU! I AM MOST ABJECTLY *SORRY!*

APOLOGIES...

THERE'S NO *NEED* TO BE. ALL *THREE* OF US JUMPED TO CONCLUSIONS.

ALL OF US DID, WANDA! *ALL* OF US!

RATIONALIZATIONS...

WELL, AFTER I *CUT OUT* ON THE AVENGERS AND YOU GUYS STARTED *HASSLIN'* ME-- EITHER *ON PURPOSE* OR *NOT*-- WHAT WAS I *SUPPOSED* TO THINK?

HECK, I WAS JUST *GETTIN'* INTO *DIGGIN'* YOU AS THE *BADDIES!*

RECRIMINATIONS...

I SUPPOSE I SHOULDN'T ANTAGONIZE A *HOT-HEAD* LIKE YOU WHILE I'M SO *BANDAGED UP* UNDER THIS TUNIC*--

BUT, CLINT, YOU'RE JUST AS *DUMB* AS *EVER!*

LOOK WHO'S *TALKIN'!* THE *SPARE-TIRE* AVENGER!

*AVENGERS #117-- RT.

IF I HADN'T'A *LEFT*, YOU WOULDN'T'A GOT IN THE *BACK DOOR!*

BOTTLE IT, HAWKEYE! WE'VE DONE *ENOUGH* TALKING! BUT IN OUR RUSH TO *GET* HERE--

--WE LEFT *THOR* ON THE *BATTLEFIELD!*

AND THE *HULK*, TOO!

AS OUR *STRONGEST* MEMBER, HE COULD BE TRUSTED TO *TAKE CARE* OF HIMSELF WHILE WE *INVESTIGATED!* BUT IF HE'S FIGHTING THE *HULK*--!

OUTSIDE-- WHERE I MAY MAKE USE OF THE *SUNLIGHT* TO WEAVE A *SPECIAL SPELL!*

I SHALL TRANSPORT US ALL TO *LOS ANGELES!*

SO, IT IS THAT WE RETURN TO THE CITY OF THE ANGELS, AND A SLIGHTLY *BEMUSED* PAIR OF *TITANS...*

SO *BE* IT! *SOMEONE* HATH PLAYED THE MIGHTIEST MEN AND WOMEN OF EARTH LIKE HUMBLE *PAWNS!*

OUR TASK MUST BE TO *DISCOVER WHO!*

HULK UNDERSTANDS *NONE* OF THIS.

ONE FOE, OF COURSE, IS MY HALF-BROTHER, *LOKI*-- HE WHO SO *HELPFULLY* CONFIRMED OUR DARKEST *SUSPICIONS* WITH THE BASEST OF *LIES!*

YET, WHEN I LAST *SAW* OF HIM-- AS HE DID *ATTACK* ME IN THE HALLOWEEN-DARK FORESTS OF *RUTLAND, VERMONT ★*--

--HE LOST HIS *SIGHT!* HE *CANNOT* HAVE MANAGED THIS PERFIDY *ALONE!*

★ THOR #207-- RASCALLY.

IN *RUTLAND*, YOU SAY? WHY, ONE OF THE *DEFENDERS'* EARLIEST BATTLES *ALSO* TOOK PLACE THERE!

THERE ARE *ARCANE FORCES* LOOSE IN THOSE MOUNTAINS!

AND THE MOST *ARCANE* OF *ALL* IS HIM WHOM WE *FOUGHT,* DOCTOR--

"--THE DREAD *DORMAMMU!*"★

*★REMEMBER THE THRILLING *CLIMAX* OF *MARVEL FEATURE #2?--* RIGHT- ON-ROY.*

DORMAMMU COULD *EASILY* HAVE BEEN IN INVISIBLE *ATTENDANCE* DURING THOR AND LOKI'S COMBAT!

SHOULD *HE* BE THE PRINCE OF EVIL'S PARTNER, WE ARE IN *SERIOUS* TROUBLE!

I BELIEVE WE SHOULD EXAMINE THE *EVIL EYE* MORE CLOSELY. GIVE ME YOUR SECTION, HULK.

HUH?

HULK FOUGHT THUNDER GOD FOR A *LONG TIME* TO KEEP HIS PIECE, AND NOW *STUPID MAGICIAN* SAYS GIVE IT *UP!*

BAH!

FOOM

WHOA!

WHOA!

WHOA!

HE DESTROYED THE *ENTIRE STREET*-- JUST 'CAUSE HE WAS *BUGGED!*

GET *BACK*, ALL OF YOU! WE CAN'T GUARANTEE YOUR *SAFETY* EVEN FROM SOME OF *US*, LET *ALONE* ANYTHING OUR *ENEMIES* MIGHT UNLEASH!

THIS AREA IS *OFF-LIMITS* ON *AVENGERS'* AUTHORITY!

LETTUCE-HEAD'S ALL THE AUTHORITY YOU *NEED*, MY FRIEND!

"*LETTUCE-HEAD*"! WHAT DID PUNY HUMAN *MEAN?*

HERE, MAGICIAN-- TAKE HULK'S SECTION! BUT THIS IS THE *LAST TIME* HE DOES *ANYTHING* YOU ASK!

THANK YOU, HULK.

I BROUGHT THE *OTHER* SECTIONS, DOCTOR.

GOOD! I'LL PUT THEM IN THEIR PROPER *ORDER.*

YES, THEY INCREASE *EVENLY* IN SIZE. THEY WOULD FIT TOGETHER *PERFECTLY*, IT APPEARS.

DO I DARE *ATTEMPT* IT?

HEY! WHAT THE DEVIL IS *THAT* THING?

IT CAME OUT OF *NOWHERE*-- *AND IT'S GOBBLING THE PIECES!*

THE BIZARRE MASK NEVER *FALTERS* AS IT SKIMS THE GROUND AND THEN HURTLES BACK INTO THE *BLUE!*

THAT'S *ASTI,* THE *ALL-SEEING!* A SERVANT OF *DORMAMMU!* *

*AS SEEN IN *STRANGE TALES* #144 -- ROY.

OUR FEARS ARE *AFFIRMED!* WE *DO* FACE DR. STRANGE'S ARCH-FOE!

ASTI MUST NOT ESCAPE!

YET, EVEN AS THE SILVER SURFER *SPEAKS* --

IT *FADED* OUT! IT'S *GONE!*

BACK TO *DORMAMMU'S* DIMENSION, NO DOUBT!

THE LORD OF THE DARK DIMENSION MUST HAVE BEEN *HIDING* THE USE OF HIS POWER FROM ME-- A TASK THAT COSTS *GREAT* POWER IN *ITSELF!*

TO BE WORTH *REVEALING* HIMSELF, THE EVIL EYE MUST BE OF *PARAMOUNT* IMPORTANCE TO HIM! BUT WHY-- *BY THE HOARY HOSTS OF HOGGOTH!*

GREAT T'CHAKA!

"THE *LANDSCAPE-- THE CITY!* IT'S... *CHANGING!* BEFORE OUR VERY EYES!"

"EVERYTHING'S *REFORMING--* BECOMING *ALIEN!* THE PEOPLE ARE *PANICKING!*"

"WAIT! WHAT'S HAPPENING TO *THAT MAN?*"

"HE'S CHANGING, **TOO**! THEY **ALL** ARE! EVERYONE'S TURNING INTO **MONSTERS**!"

SUDDENLY, FLASHING **GARISHLY** INTO THE MULTI-HUED HEAVENS: A **FACE**-- AND **WHAT A FACE**!

HEED ME, EARTH! ONCE I, **DORMAMMU**, SWORE NEVER TO **INVADE** YOUR DIMENSION!

YET **NOW**, WITH THE UNLIMITED MIGHT OF THE **EVIL EYE** AT MY COMMAND, I AM **MERGING** YOUR DIMENSION WITH **MINE**!

YOUR **WORLD** IS BECOMING **MY** WORLD-- AND IN **MY** WORLD, I AM **UNDISPUTED KING**!

IN **ONE EARTHIAN HOUR**, YOU WILL ALL BE MY **SLAVES**!

NO, DORMAMMU! **NEVER**!

YOU HAVE **USED** US UNTIL THIS POINT-- BUT NOW THE **DEFENDERS** AND THE **AVENGERS** WILL **FIGHT BACK**!

WHILE **ANY** OF US STILL **BREATHES**, WE WILL **NEVER** BE SLAVES!

IF YOU WANT **EARTH**, FIEND, YOU WILL HAVE TO **KILL US ALL**!

TO BE CONTINUED!
NEXT MONTH:
AVENGERS #118--
THE **FINAL WAR**--WITH MORE **SURPRISES** THAN YOU'D EVER **GUESS**!

DEFENDERS #11--
THE **FATE** OF THE **BLACK KNIGHT**!

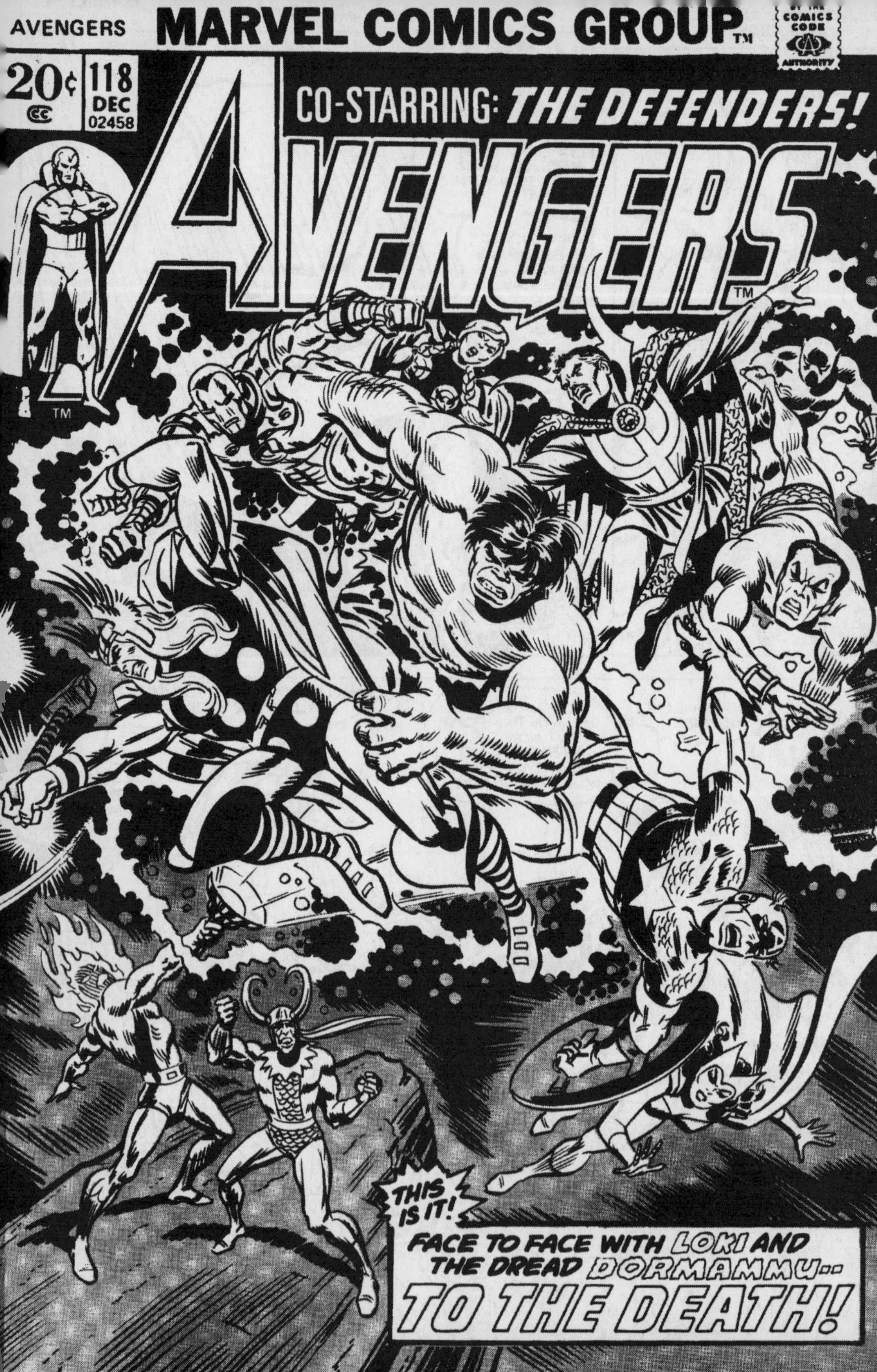

AVENGERS
MARVEL COMICS GROUP™
APPROVED BY THE COMICS CODE AUTHORITY
20¢
118 DEC 02458
CO-STARRING: THE DEFENDERS!
AVENGERS™
THIS IS IT!
FACE TO FACE WITH LOKI AND THE DREAD DORMAMMU--
TO THE DEATH!

Stan Lee PRESENTS: **THE MIGHTY AVENGERS!**

STEVE ENGLEHART, AUTHOR | M. ESPOSITO & F. GIACOIA, INKERS | TOM ORZECHOWSKI, LETTERER GEO. ROUSSOS, COLORIST | ROY THOMAS EDITOR

BE WARNED, DORMAMMU: BEFORE YOU CAN CONQUER THE UNIVERSE, THE AVENGERS AND THE DEFENDERS WILL FIGHT YOU--

TO THE DEATH!

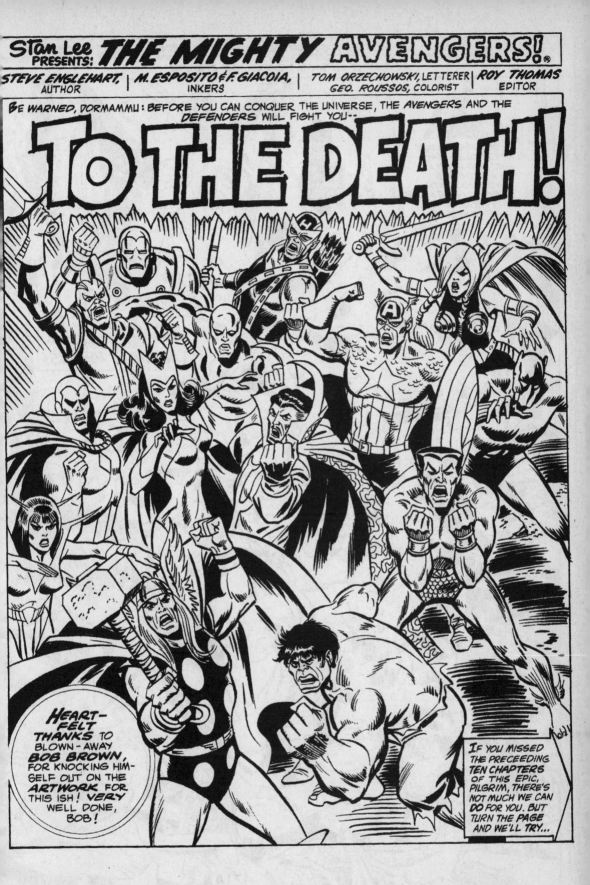

HEART-FELT THANKS TO BLOWN-AWAY BOB BROWN, FOR KNOCKING HIMSELF OUT ON THE ARTWORK FOR THIS ISH! VERY WELL DONE, BOB!

IF YOU MISSED THE PRECEEDING TEN CHAPTERS OF THIS EPIC, PILGRIM, THERE'S NOT MUCH WE CAN DO FOR YOU. BUT TURN THE PAGE AND WE'LL TRY...

As SEEN IN THE PAST THREE MONTHS, THE **FOURTEEN MIGHTIEST BEINGS** ON EARTH WERE **DUPED** BY THE DREAD **DORMAMMU,** LORD OF THE DARK DIMENSION, AND **LOKI,** PRINCE OF EVIL, INTO ASSEMBLING AN ALMOST-MYTHICAL WEAPON, THE **EVIL EYE!**

NOW, DORMAMMU HAS **STOLEN** THE EYE, AND USED IT TO **MERGE HIS DIMENSION** WITH **OURS!** IN ONE HOUR, THE PROCESS WILL BE **COMPLETE--**

--AND ALREADY, AS THE LANDSCAPE SHIFTS AND HUMANS MUTATE, **INSANITY REIGNS!**

HOLD THE CREATURES *BACK*, BUT DON'T *INJURE* THEM! IF WE CAN *STOP* DORMAMMU, THEY'LL BECOME *PEOPLE* AGAIN!

GIVE ME *TIME* TO PROTECT *US*!

DOLEFUL *DEMONS* OF DENAK-- TURN FROM YOUR FEASTS-- SAVE THOSE WHO *STRIVE* WITH ME-- FROM TURNING TO *BEASTS*!

SO SPEAKS-- DR. STRANGE!

I CAN DO *NO MORE*! TO EXPEND THE POWER NECESSARY TO SAVE THESE *OTHERS* WOULD LEAVE ME TOO *WEAKENED* TO *FACE* DORMAMMU!

NOW, *FOLLOW* ME TO HIS DIMENSION!

AS EACH SECOND SLIPS AWAY, OUR SITUATION BECOMES MORE AND MORE *DIRE*! WE MUST ACT *IMMEDIATELY*!

BUT--WE CAN'T SIMPLY *DESERT* EARTH! I GRANT YOU THAT DOR-MAMMU IS THE *CAUSE* OF ALL THIS, BUT THE *EFFECTS* CAN'T BE IGNORED!

RRARR

IF WE *ALL* GO TO ANOTHER DIMENSION, *HUNDREDS* OF PEOPLE WILL DIE *HERE*--

--KILLED WHILE IN THEIR *MONSTER* FORMS!

YOUR SENTIMENTS ARE *WELL TAKEN,* CAPTAIN AMERICA! THE DILEMMA PLEASES ME NO BETTER THAN IT DOES *YOU!* YET YOU *MUST* BOW TO MY *EXPERIENCE* WITH DORMAMMU--

--AND I TELL YOU, *HIS* POWER, COUPLED WITH THE *EVIL EYE,* CANNOT BE *OVERESTIMATED!*

WE *DARE NOT* CONFRONT HIM WITH LESS THAN OUR *FULL STRENGTH!*

THIS IS *HIDEOUS!*

BOTH THE *AVENGERS* AND THE *DEFENDERS* ARE SWORN TO *PROTECT* HUMANITY, AND STILL--

WAIT! WHAT'S *THAT--* SWOOPING IN FROM THE SKY?

IT'S -- *SHIELD!*

FOOM!

KA-WAM!

YES, SHIELD--THE INTERNATIONAL LAW-ENFORCEMENT AGENCY--

--LED BY ITS CHIEF AGENTS: COLONEL *NICK FURY*--

--COUNTESS *VALENTINA ALLEGRO DE FONTAINE*--

--AND *DUM DUM DUGAN!*

FURY! WHAT ARE *YOU* DOING HERE?

FOLLOWIN' YOU INTO *HELL,* LOOKS LIKE! I GOT REPORTS ABOUT YOUR BATTLES ALL OVER THE *WORLD,* AND *THEN* THAT YOU WAS ALL *HERE,* SO I FIGURED I'D SEE WHAT'S UP!

I GUESS I'M *SEEIN'! CRIPES!*

NICK FURY AIN'T WATCHIN' THE *END O' THE WORLD* IN *BED,* MISTER! 'SICK OR WELL, I'M A FIGHTER!

FURY, YOU'RE TOO *BADLY HURT* TO BE HERE!*

*SEE RECENT ISSUES OF CAPTAIN AMERICA AND THE FALCON. --ROY.

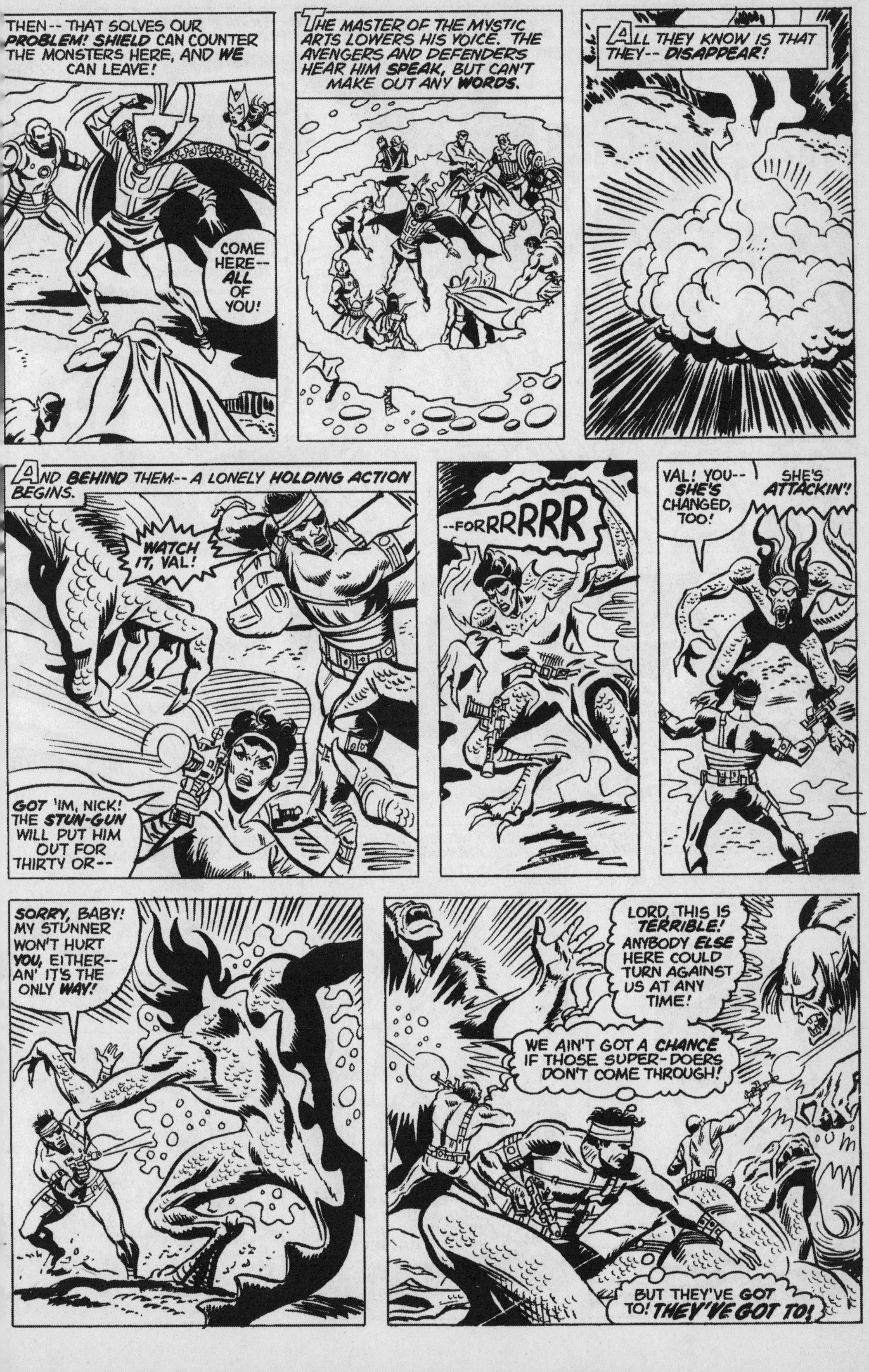

THEN-- THAT SOLVES OUR PROBLEM! SHIELD CAN COUNTER THE MONSTERS HERE, AND WE CAN LEAVE!
COME HERE-- ALL OF YOU!
THE MASTER OF THE MYSTIC ARTS LOWERS HIS VOICE. THE AVENGERS AND DEFENDERS HEAR HIM SPEAK, BUT CAN'T MAKE OUT ANY WORDS.
ALL THEY KNOW IS THAT THEY-- DISAPPEAR!
AND BEHIND THEM-- A LONELY HOLDING ACTION BEGINS.
WATCH IT, VAL!
GOT 'IM, NICK! THE STUN-GUN WILL PUT HIM OUT FOR THIRTY OR--
--FORRRRRR
VAL! YOU-- SHE'S CHANGED, TOO!
SHE'S ATTACKIN'!
SORRY, BABY! MY STÜNNER WON'T HURT YOU, EITHER-- AN' IT'S THE ONLY WAY!
LORD, THIS IS TERRIBLE! ANYBODY ELSE HERE COULD TURN AGAINST US AT ANY TIME!
WE AIN'T GOT A CHANCE IF THOSE SUPER-DOERS DON'T COME THROUGH!
BUT THEY'VE GOT TO! THEY'VE GOT TO!

--AS THEY BEGIN THE *STRANGEST ODYSSEY* EVER UNDERTAKEN!

THIS IS THE *DARK DIMENSION*, DORMAMMU'S LAIR! THERE CAN BE NO *TURNING BACK!*

THAT *GLOW* AT THE END OF OUR *SPACIAL PATH* MARKS OUR *GOAL!*

THEN THOSE OF US WHO POSSESS THE POWER OF *FLIGHT* MUST HASTEN AHEAD!

NO, THOR!

UNDER *NO CIRCUMSTANCES* MUST YOU STRAY FROM THIS TRAIL!

THE LAWS OF REALITY YOU KNOW ARE *ALTERED* OR *NEGATED* HERE! TERRORS YOU CANNOT EVEN *COMPREHEND* LURK IN THE OUTER DARKS!

WE WILL STAY *TOGETHER!*

METHINKS WE DO SOUND *MUCH* LIKE THE *AVENGERS ALONE* IN OUR EARLY YEARS: *ARGUING* AMONGST OURSELVES AT EVERY TURN!

YET, THE MAGICIAN IS *CORRECT!* THE AVENGERS WILL *FOLLOW* HIS LEAD AND ACCEPT HIS *AUTHORITY* ON ALL OCCULT MATTERS!

*R*ESENTMENT FLICKERS MOMENTARILY ON SOME FACES. CAP NODS. HAWKEYE AND THE VALKYRIE *SMILE* TIGHTLY.

*A*ND THEN THEY ARE CHARGING *LUSTILY* TOWARD, QUITE POSSIBLY, THEIR *DOOM!*

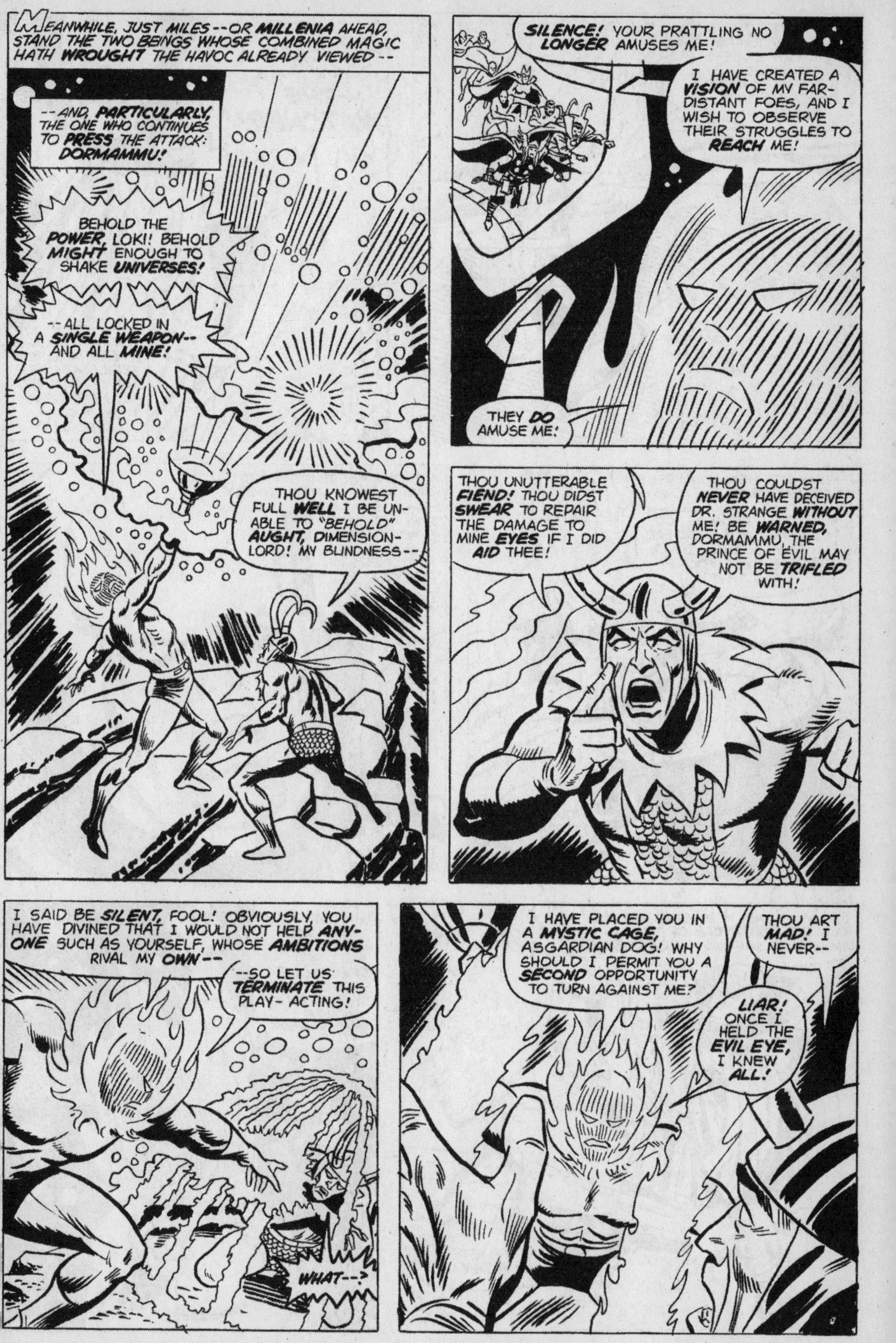

MEANWHILE, JUST MILES--OR MILLENIA AHEAD, STAND THE TWO BEINGS WHOSE COMBINED MAGIC HATH WROUGHT THE HAVOC ALREADY VIEWED--
--AND, PARTICULARLY, THE ONE WHO CONTINUES TO PRESS THE ATTACK: DORMAMMU!
BEHOLD THE POWER, LOKI! BEHOLD MIGHT ENOUGH TO SHAKE UNIVERSES!
--ALL LOCKED IN A SINGLE WEAPON-- AND ALL MINE!
THOU KNOWEST FULL WELL I BE UNABLE TO "BEHOLD" AUGHT, DIMENSION-LORD! MY BLINDNESS--
SILENCE! YOUR PRATTLING NO LONGER AMUSES ME!
I HAVE CREATED A VISION OF MY FAR-DISTANT FOES, AND I WISH TO OBSERVE THEIR STRUGGLES TO REACH ME!
THEY DO AMUSE ME!
THOU UNUTTERABLE FIEND! THOU DIDST SWEAR TO REPAIR THE DAMAGE TO MINE EYES IF I DID AID THEE!
THOU COULDST NEVER HAVE DECEIVED DR. STRANGE WITHOUT ME! BE WARNED, DORMAMMU, THE PRINCE OF EVIL MAY NOT BE TRIFLED WITH!
I SAID BE SILENT, FOOL! OBVIOUSLY, YOU HAVE DIVINED THAT I WOULD NOT HELP ANYONE SUCH AS YOURSELF, WHOSE AMBITIONS RIVAL MY OWN--
--SO LET US TERMINATE THIS PLAY-ACTING!
WHAT--?
I HAVE PLACED YOU IN A MYSTIC CAGE, ASGARDIAN DOG! WHY SHOULD I PERMIT YOU A SECOND OPPORTUNITY TO TURN AGAINST ME?
THOU ART MAD! I NEVER--
LIAR! ONCE I HELD THE EVIL EYE, I KNEW ALL!

YOU ALERTED THE *AVENGERS* TO THE DEFENDERS' QUESTS FOR THIS DEVICE, TO THWART MY *PLANS!* I *PERCEIVE* THAT NOW!

HOLD! A HUGE, MENACING *SHADOW* FALLS OVER ME-- FROM *BEHIND!*

BY MY *SISTER!* IT IS--

--*THE WATCHER!**

*FROM NEARLY *EVERY* MARVEL SERIES AT ONE TIME OR ANOTHER, BUT *LAST* SEEN IN ISH #101,-- RASCALLY.

I KNOW NOT HOW YOU PASSED MY *DEFENCES,* SILENT ONE--

--BUT I PROMISE YOU YOU WILL *NOT* INTERFERE WITH MY SCHEME! I WILL BATTLE EVEN *YOU* IF YOU TRY!

CALM YOURSELF, DORMAMMU.

ALTHOUGH IN TIMES PAST, I HAVE ACTED... *IMPULSIVELY...*

...MY HERITAGE IS YET THAT OF THE RACE OF WATCHERS, PLEDGED SOLELY TO *OBSERVE* AND *RECORD.*

I WILL NOT MOLEST YOU.

I HAVE COME, IN MY OWN WAY, TO VIEW THE *SPECTACLE* OF TWO DIMENSIONS SHIFTING THEIR *ESSENCES.*

THAT IS *ALL* I DESIRE HERE.

I BELIEVE YOU MEAN IT...!

THEN *WATCH,* WATCHER! *TODAY* YOU WILL SEE *SPECTACLE* ENOUGH TO JUSTIFY YOUR *ENTIRE* EXISTENCE!

THOR! THE PATH *ENDS* HERE! WHAT DO WE DO *NOW?*

WOULD THAT. I *KNEW,* WANDA. OUR JOURNEY HATH BROUGHT US QUITE *NEAR* THE GLOW, YET WITHOUT THE *PATH,* WE HAVE GAINED *NAUGHT!*

TIME DOTH LEAVE US *BEHIND,* SO THAT--

ODIN'S BLOOD!

CREATURES APPEAR-- RIDING THEIR *OWN* PATH FROM *NOWHERE!*

WE ARE *ATTACKED!*

VIPERS OF VALTORR! THOSE ARE THE *MINDLESS ONES,* WHO ROAM THE *OUTSKIRTS* OF *DORMAMMU'S* DOMAIN--

--TOTALLY DEVOID OF ANY *THOUGHT* EXCEPT A PRIMITIVE LUST FOR *DESTRUCTION!*

AT *LAST* DUMB MAGICIAN SAYS SOMETHING *GOOD!*

HULK HAS *WANTED* TO HIT SOME- THING--

--AND *NOW* HE KNOWS HE HAS GOOD TARGET!

FOOM

BUT THESE ARE NOT *THE* TARGET WE SEEK!

WE MUST NEEDS REACH *DORMAMMU*-- WE MUST NOT TARRY IN USELESS STRUGGLE WITH HIS *VASSELS!*

PHYSICAL COMBAT CANNOT HALT THE MINDLESS ONES! IT ONLY *EXCITES* THEM!

ONLY *CONCENTRATED FORCE* CAN DRIVE THEM BACK! TO MY SIDE, DEFENDERS AND AVENGERS!

AT MY SIGNAL--

--FIRE!

FOR SEVERAL SECONDS, THE FAR REACHES OF THE *ABYSS* AROUND THEM *SHIMMER* WITH THE CORUSCATING *BRILLIANCE* THERE UNLEASHED--

--THEN, AS IT *FADES...*

THEY HAVE *FLED!*

NOT ONLY OUR *FOES* MAY COMBINE POWERS TO GOOD EFFECT!

STILL, MANTIS *LITERALLY* FEELS EACH *SECOND* BEING RIPPED FROM THE COSMOS AROUND HER BY THE INVISIBLE HANDS OF *TIME!*

THIS ONE SENSES ONLY *TWENTY MINUTES* LEFT TO US NOW!

AND WE HAVE NOT YET EVEN *ENCOUNTERED* DORMAMMU!

I *FEAR* FOR EARTH--AND *ALL* OF OUR DIMENSION!

OUR DIMENSION! NEVER BEFORE IN ITS CHECKERED HISTORY HAS THIS TROUBLED, TEMPESTUOUS COSMOS FACED SUCH A **CRITICAL THREAT** TO ITS VERY **BEING!** BUT THERE **ARE** THOSE IN OUR DIMENSION WHOSE LIVES ARE DEDICATED TO **MEETING** THREATS -- **OTHERS** BESIDES **THE AVENGERS** AND **THE DEFENDERS** -- AND IN THIS AWFUL HOUR OF **CRISIS**, THEY, **TOO**, ARE GIVING THEIR **ALL** TO COUNTER A MENACE **NONE** OF THEM TRULY UNDERSTANDS!

TAKE HIM, BEN!

HOWCUM **I** ALWAYS GET THE DIRTY WORK?

NAUGHTY, NAUGHTY, SWEETUMS! IF YOU KEEP **GROWING**, YOU'LL MAKE ME USE **ALL** MY WEB FLUID ON YOU --

-- AND THEN YOUR **FELLOW FIENDS** WON'T GET **THEIR** FAIR SHARE!

STRIKE, GORGON! **NOW!**

HUSH, KARNAK! IF MY HOOF THUNDERS TOO **SOON**, THE **GREAT REFUGE** WILL SUFFER!

SWEET SISTER! BROADWAY'S GOIN' **PSYCHO** ALL **AROUN'** ME --

-- AN' THIS WAS **'SPOSED** TO BE MY **DAY OFF!**

ZABU -- THE **SWAMP MEN** BECOME MISSHAPEN **MONSTERS** BEFORE OUR EYES!

ATTACK, MY BROTHER!

SATAN'S ONLY HASSLED **ME** UP UNTIL NOW!

THIS **CAN'T** BE **HIS** DOING!

NOT ALL OF THEM ARE HUMAN ...

... OR **HEROES** ...

LATVERIA IS IN **FLAMES!** MY **KINGDOM** IS COLLAPSING!

BUT **NOTHING** SHALL DESTROY **DOCTOR DOOM'S** HOMELAND! I **SWEAR** IT!

... OR EVEN **ALIVE** ...

SHOULD THIS EVIL CONTINUE, EVEN **DRACULA** MIGHT FACE ANNIHILATION!

AND **THAT** MUST NEVER BE!

... BUT ANYWHERE THERE IS **COURAGE** AND **DARING**, ON **EARTH** --

-- OR **COUNTER-EARTH** --

-- OR **SATURN'S** MOON OF **TITAN** --

-- ANYWHERE --

-- THE THREAT IS MET -- AND **HELD!**

YET WHAT GOOD WILL **ANY** OF IT DO-- IF **DORMAMMU** HOLDS THE **EVIL EYE** FOR THE REMAINDER OF THE HOUR?

THE **DIMENSIONAL TRANSFORMATION** RAPIDLY NEARS ITS **CLIMAX**, DOCTOR! YOU CAN **FEEL** IT IN THE VERY **AIR** AROUND YOU!

I **KNOW**, SURFER! DON'T YOU THINK I **KNOW**?!

THERE'S THE **FLAME-VISAGED** DEMON JUST IN **FRONT** OF US, AT LAST--

--BUT **NOW** WE'VE REACHED THE **MYSTIC SHIELD** HE EMPLOYS TO KEEP THE MINDLESS ONES AWAY FROM **HIMSELF**!

I CAN **SUNDER** IT, BUT IT WILL TAKE **TIME**!

TIME-- ALWAYS TIME! THAT IS OUR **REAL** ENEMY!

HOLD! CAN THIS BE **TRUE**--? I SPY THE **WATCHER**!

THEY SEEM **HAPPY** TO SEE YOU HERE, WATCHER!

I BEGIN TO **WONDER** IF YOUR SOLEMN WORDS OF **NEUTRALITY** EARLIER WERE SOLEMN **LIES**?

YOUR **SUSPICIONS** WASTE YOUR **ENERGY,** DORMAMMU.

I BELIEVE **ONLY** IN TRUTH, AND **NON-INTERVENTION.** IT HAS BEEN MY WAY FOR **EONS**!

I TELL YOU IN COMPLETE **CANDOR** THAT MY MIND **CHERISHES** THE VALIANT BEINGS YOU SEEK TO ENSLAVE --

--BUT YOU WILL FIND NOT THE SLIGHTEST **HINT** OF IT IN MY **ACTIONS**!

CALM YOURSELF, WATCHER. I CERTAINLY DID NOT MEAN TO IMPLY--

WHY, THE EARTHLINGS HAVE **BURST** THROUGH MY BARRIER! HOW **DELIGHTFUL**!

LET US BOTH **FORGET** MY ANGER, WATCHER! THIS IS A TIME FOR **LAUGHTER**!

MY HATED ENEMY, DR. STRANGE, HAS HELPED MOUNT A **COMMENDABLE** ATTACK UPON ME --

BUT NOW, WITH THE POWER OF THE **EVIL EYE** BEHIND ME, A SINGLE WAVE OF MY HAND--

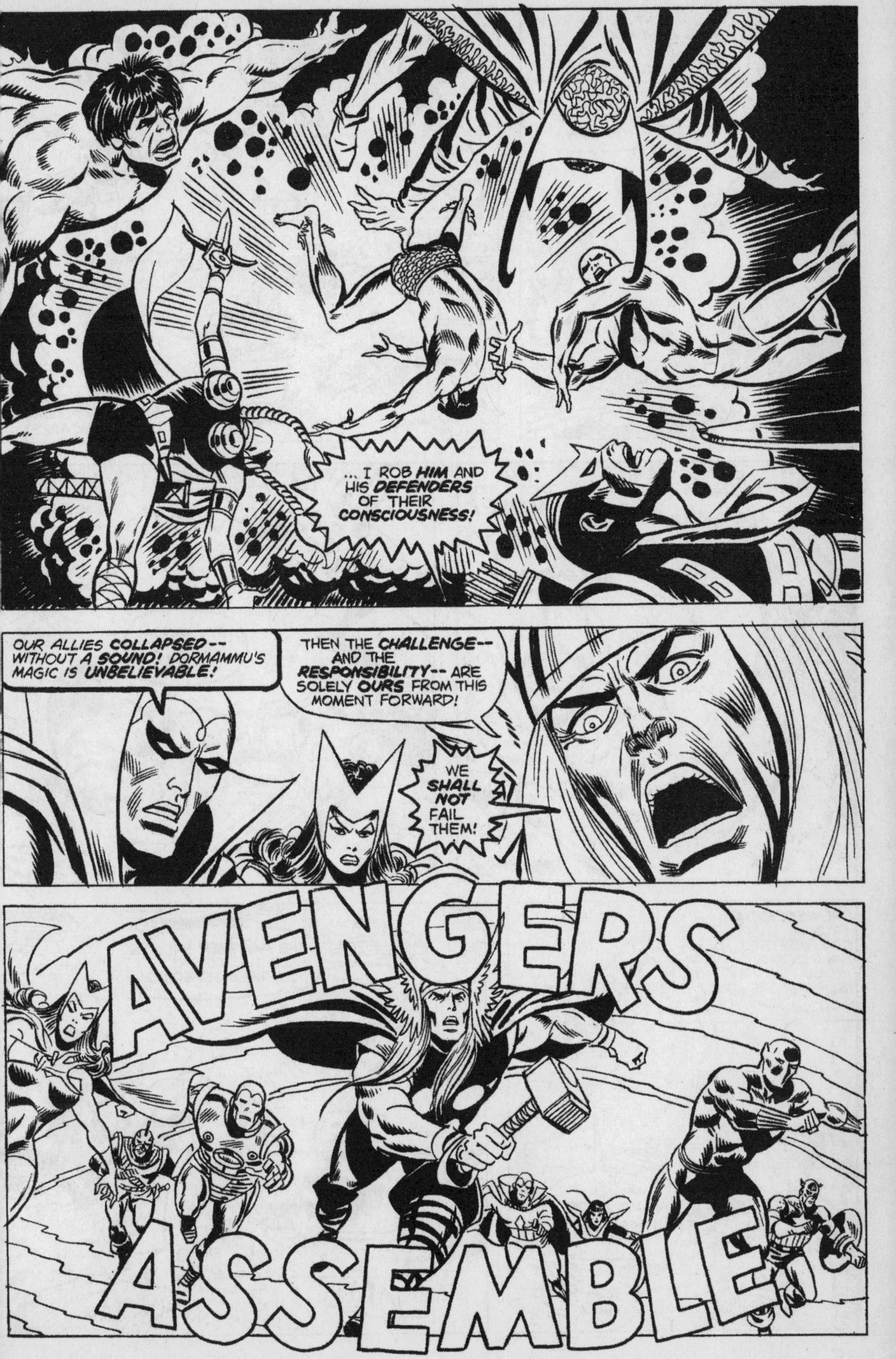
...I ROB HIM AND HIS DEFENDERS OF THEIR CONSCIOUSNESS!
OUR ALLIES COLLAPSED-- WITHOUT A SOUND! DORMAMMU'S MAGIC IS UNBELIEVABLE!
THEN THE CHALLENGE-- AND THE RESPONSIBILITY-- ARE SOLELY OURS FROM THIS MOMENT FORWARD!
WE SHALL NOT FAIL THEM!
AVENGERS ASSEMBLE

LOUD-MOUTHED **BUFFOONS!** YOUR **ASSEMBLY** IS TO PROVIDE ME WITH **SPORT,** AND FOR NO OTHER REASON!

PASS THIS **QUICKSAND BOG** I CREATE -- IF YOU **CAN!**

INSTANTLY, IRON MAN AND THOR **FLY** ABOVE THE SUCKING POOL--

--AND WANDA LOOSES A **HEX SPHERE** TO **BLAST** HERSELF OVER IT--

--BUT THE OTHERS QUICKLY **FLOUNDER** IN THE MIRE!

VISION -- FLY **OUT** OF THERE! TURN **WEIGHTLESS!**

WHY DON'T YOU **MOVE?**

I -- I **CANNOT** --

IRON MAN! I **NEED** YOU!

YOU AND **THOR** HAVE TO PULL THEM **FREE!**

NO, WANDA! DON'T STOP FOR **US!**

THE **HEAT RAYS** FROM MY SWORD CAN **FUSE** THIS SAND INTO SOLID **ISLANDS!**

IF WE CAN **HANG ONTO** THEM, WE'LL BE **ALL RIGHT!**

THE **PANTHER** WILL HELP THE VISION! YOU THREE GET **GOING!**

YOU *HEARD* THE MAN, PEOPLE! WE CAN LICK EACH OTHER'S WOUNDS IN THE *LOCKER* ROOM AFTER THE GAME IS *OVER!*

MIX YOUR METAPHORS SOME *OTHER* TIME, IRON MAN-- AND FOR A MORE *APPRECIATIVE* AUDIENCE!

I'M RIGHT *WITH* YOU!

THEY *ARGUE*-- AT A TIME LIKE *THIS!* THE *HUMANITY* OF THESE "SUPERHEROES" MAKES THEM EVEN *MORE* FUN TO PLAY WITH!

IN FACT, SINCE THEY *ARE* SO HUMAN--

-- LET THEM BECOME SO IN *FLESH* AS WELL AS IN *SPIRIT!*

GOOD LORD! MY *ARMOR'S* DISAPPEARING! AND *THOR'S* CHANGING TO HIS *OTHER* IDENTITY!

THOR! IRON MAN!

THEY NO LONGER *EXIST,* MY DEAR!

BUT-- NEITHER SHOULD *YOU*--

--NOT AS A *COSTUMED WITCH!*

MY *MUTANT ABILITY* WAS MIDWIVED ALONG *WITH* ME, DORMAMMU! YOU *CANNOT* SEPARATE ME FROM MY POWER!

YOU CANNOT *STOP* ME!

*S*HE IS THE ONLY ONE OF THE ORIGINAL *FOURTEEN* LEFT-- THE SOLE *SURVIVOR* OF THE STRONGEST GROUP EVER GATHERED...

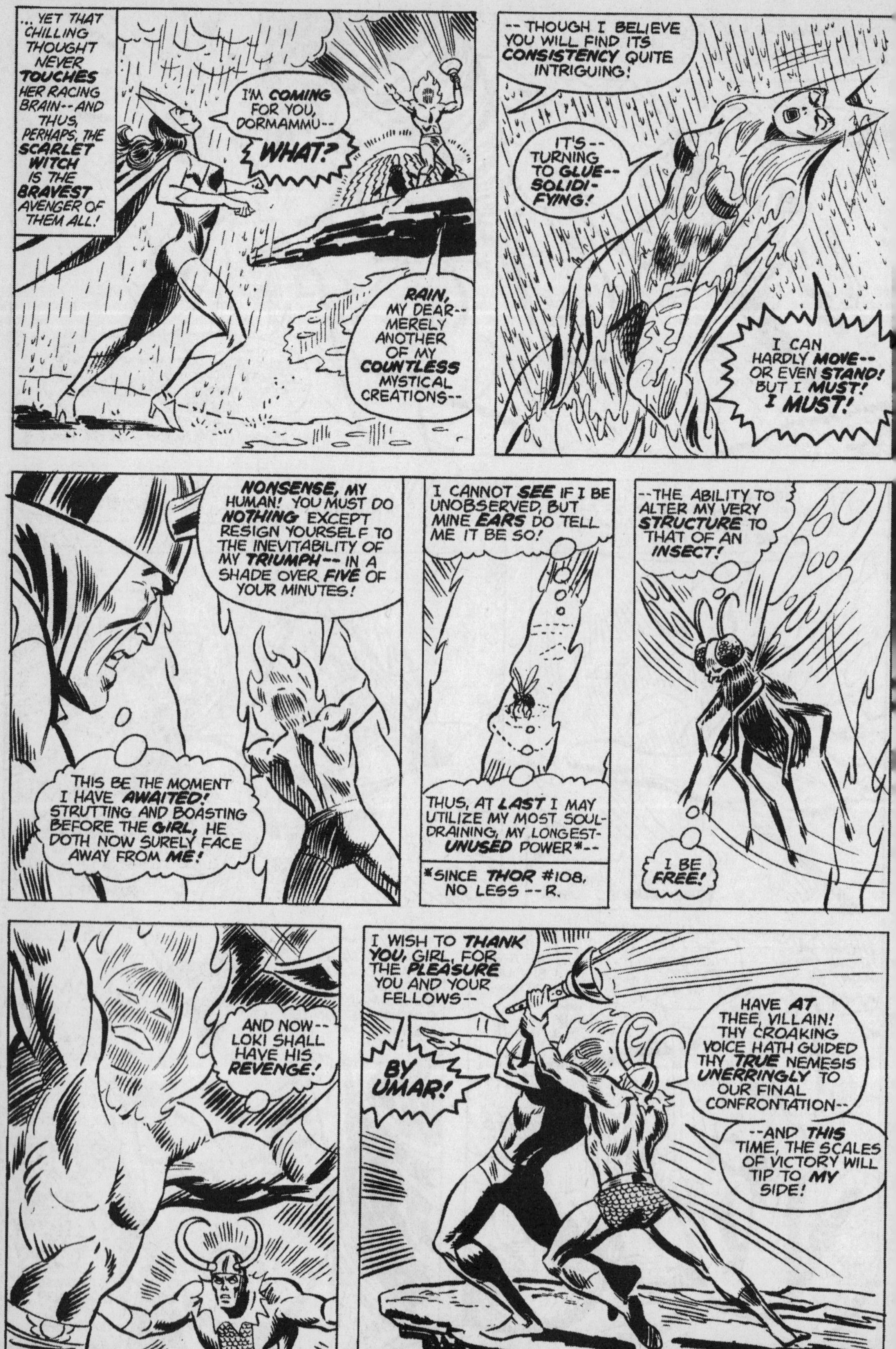
...YET THAT CHILLING THOUGHT NEVER TOUCHES HER RACING BRAIN--AND THUS, PERHAPS, THE SCARLET WITCH IS THE BRAVEST AVENGER OF THEM ALL!
I'M COMING FOR YOU, DORMAMMU--
WHAT?
RAIN, MY DEAR--MERELY ANOTHER OF MY COUNTLESS MYSTICAL CREATIONS--
--THOUGH I BELIEVE YOU WILL FIND ITS CONSISTENCY QUITE INTRIGUING!
IT'S--TURNING TO GLUE--SOLIDIFYING!
I CAN HARDLY MOVE--OR EVEN STAND! BUT I MUST! I MUST!
NONSENSE, MY HUMAN! YOU MUST DO NOTHING EXCEPT RESIGN YOURSELF TO THE INEVITABILITY OF MY TRIUMPH--IN A SHADE OVER FIVE OF YOUR MINUTES!
THIS BE THE MOMENT I HAVE AWAITED! STRUTTING AND BOASTING BEFORE THE GIRL, HE DOTH NOW SURELY FACE AWAY FROM ME!
I CANNOT SEE IF I BE UNOBSERVED, BUT MINE EARS DO TELL ME IT BE SO!
THUS, AT LAST I MAY UTILIZE MY MOST SOUL-DRAINING, MY LONGEST-UNUSED POWER*--
*SINCE THOR #108, NO LESS --R.
--THE ABILITY TO ALTER MY VERY STRUCTURE TO THAT OF AN INSECT!
I BE FREE!
AND NOW--LOKI SHALL HAVE HIS REVENGE!
I WISH TO THANK YOU, GIRL, FOR THE PLEASURE YOU AND YOUR FELLOWS--
BY UMAR!
HAVE AT THEE, VILLAIN! THY CROAKING VOICE HATH GUIDED THY TRUE NEMESIS UNERRINGLY TO OUR FINAL CONFRONTATION--
--AND THIS TIME, THE SCALES OF VICTORY WILL TIP TO MY SIDE!

MOMENTARILY **FORGOTTEN** BY HER TORMENTOR, WANDA KNOWS WITH AN ICY CERTAINTY THAT THIS WILL BE HER **ONLY** MOMENT TO ACT!

WEAKENED FROM HER STRUGGLES AND HER EARLIER HEX SPHERE, DREADFULLY **UNSURE** OF HER CAPACITY TO FORM **ANOTHER** HEX SO SOON AFTER THE FIRST--

--STILL--

-- THE SCARLET WITCH LIFTS HER UNLIFTABLE ARMS AND **LETS IT ALL GO!**

FLASH! THE THOUGHT-CONTROLLED **EVIL EYE** **TRIGGERS** ITSELF--

--SUCKING THE **LIVING POWER** THAT IS DORMAMMU INTO ITS SEETHING INTERIOR--

--AND THEN **BLASTING** THE TOTALITY OF ITS ENERGY **OUT** AGAIN--

--INTO **LOKI'S FACE!**

IN THAT MOMENT OF PROBABILITIES GONE MAD, THE EVIL EYE FULFILLS THE PRINCE OF EVIL'S MOST **FERVENT** HOPE, COMPLETELY **RETURNING** HIS LONG-SOUGHT SIGHT--

--AND SIMULTANEOUSLY DRIVING HIM TOTALLY **INSANE!**

AND IN THAT SAME MOMENT, IN EVERY FAR-FLUNG CORNER OF A BRUISED AND BATTERED DIMENSION WE'VE ALL COME TO KNOW AND LOVE --

BENJY-- MEDUSA-- **LOOK!** THE ALIEN LANDSCAPES ARE **GONE**-- AND THE **PEOPLE** ARE BACK TO **NORMAL!**

YEAH, WEBFACE... I GUESS WE **DID** IT.

-- DORMAMMU'S INSANITY **ENDS!**

WHA'D WE **DO?**

THAT **DAZED** QUERY WILL BE ANSWERED IN JUST A **FEW** HOURS, MR. GRIMM, WHEN THE AVENGERS MAKE A **REPORT** TO A WONDERING WORLD *--

--BUT FOR NOW, YOU AND THEY AND EVERYBODY ELSE WILL **GLADLY** SETTLE FOR A QUIET TIME TO **UNWIND!**

* THOUGH WARLOCK, THE TITANS, THE KREE, THE SKRULLS, THE BADOON, AND OTHER OFF-WORLDERS WILL PROBABLY **NEVER** KNOW. -- STEVE.

GREETINGS, AVENGERS AND DEFENDERS.

I AM SUPREMELY **GRATIFIED** BY WHAT I HAVE WITNESSED THIS DAY. **CONGRATULATIONS** ARE DUE YOU.

YOU'RE WELCOME, WATCHER. BUT--

I **ANTICIPATE** YOUR CONFUSION, BLACK PANTHER, AND SHALL **DISPEL** IT.

DORMAMMU'S EXTRA-DIMENSIONAL FORM IS COMPOSED OF RAW **ENERGY,** CONTINUALLY AFIRE. THAT ENERGY IS **GENERATED** BY LESSER BEINGS' BELIEF IN AND WORSHIP OF HIM, AS WITH **MOST** MYSTICAL ENTITIES.

WHEN THE SCARLET WITCH'S VALIANT SECOND HEX **DISRUPTED** THE FLOW OF EVENTS AROUND THE EVIL EYE, IT DREW THE ENERGY TO **ITSELF** AND **DESTROYED** HIM.

YET, BE WARNED THAT DORMAMMU WILL RISE **AGAIN,** FOR THOSE WHO LOVE SIN WILL CONTINUE TO **CALL** UPON HIM-- AND IN **TIME,** THEIR REVERENCE WILL **RESHAPE** HIM!

IN THE **MEANTIME,** HOWEVER, HIS ENERGY HAS BEEN RAMMED THROUGH **LOKI'S** MIND, AND **NO** BRAIN OF **YOUR** DIMENSION CAN **COPE** WITH SO MUCH SORCEROUS FORCE.

THE ASGARDIAN'S INTELLECT HAS **COLLAPSED** UNDER THE STRAIN, BECOMING **NO MORE** THAN THAT OF AN **INFANT!**

NOW, I HAVE BUT **ONE** QUESTION CONCERNING THIS AFFAIR, DIRECTED TOWARD THE **VISION**.

COULD YOU EXPLAIN, PLEASE, WHY **PANIC** OVERWHELMED YOUR COMPUTER-MIND AT THE INSTANT THE **QUICKSAND** OPENED BEFORE YOU--

--IF SUCH A QUESTION DOES NOT **OFFEND**.

LOGICAL EXPLORATION OF IDEAS **NEVER** OFFENDS ME. BUT I CAN'T PROVIDE A SATISFACTORY EXPLANATION AT THIS TIME.

I DON'T UNDERSTAND IT MYSELF.

WELL, AT LEAST WE'VE RECOVERED THE EVIL EYE, AND DORMAMMU'S PLAN HAS FAILED. WE **NEED** KNOW NO MORE!

AYE... WELL...

LET US RETURN TO **EARTH**-- FOR THE **DEFENDERS** STILL HAVE A COMMITMENT TO USE THIS WEAPON IN RESCUING THE **BLACK KNIGHT**!

TAKE **CHARGE** OF YOUR HALF-BROTHER, THOR-- --WHILST I **MYSTICALLY ERASE** THE KNOWLEDGE OF YOUR CIVILIAN IDENTITY AND IRON MAN'S FROM EACH OTHER'S MINDS--

--TILL THE DAY YOU DEEM TO FREELY **REVEAL** THEM TO EACH OTHER.

AND NOW WE MUST **DEPART!**

FOR LONG, LINGERING MOMENTS, THE AURA OF THEIR PASSING ILLUMINES THE WATCHER'S EMOTIONLESS FACE... AND THEN HE SPEAKS--

THOSE EARTHLINGS MOVE SO **FAST**, SEARCHING **EVER** FOR SOME NEW **STRUGGLE**...

...AND PAUSING **NEVER** TO **SAVOR** WHAT THEY SEE ALONG THE WAY, AS **I** DO.

YET, I MUST NEVER FORGET THAT IT WAS **THEY** WHO SAVED THEIR DIMENSION. ALL **I** SAVE ARE MEMORIES OF THEIR DOING IT.

AND **THAT** IS WHY I **TREASURE** THEM-- WHY THEY ARE **HUMAN**--

--AND WHY **I** AM **ONLY**... THE WATCHER.

FINIS

THE DEFENDERS CONCLUDE THEIR STRUGGLE FOR THE BLACK KNIGHT'S **SOUL** IN **DEFENDERS #11**, NOW ON SALE.

THE AVENGERS BEGIN A **NEW** ADVENTURE NEXT MONTH, AT THE **RUTLAND HALLOWEEN PARADE!** BE HERE TO **SHARE** IT WITH THEM!

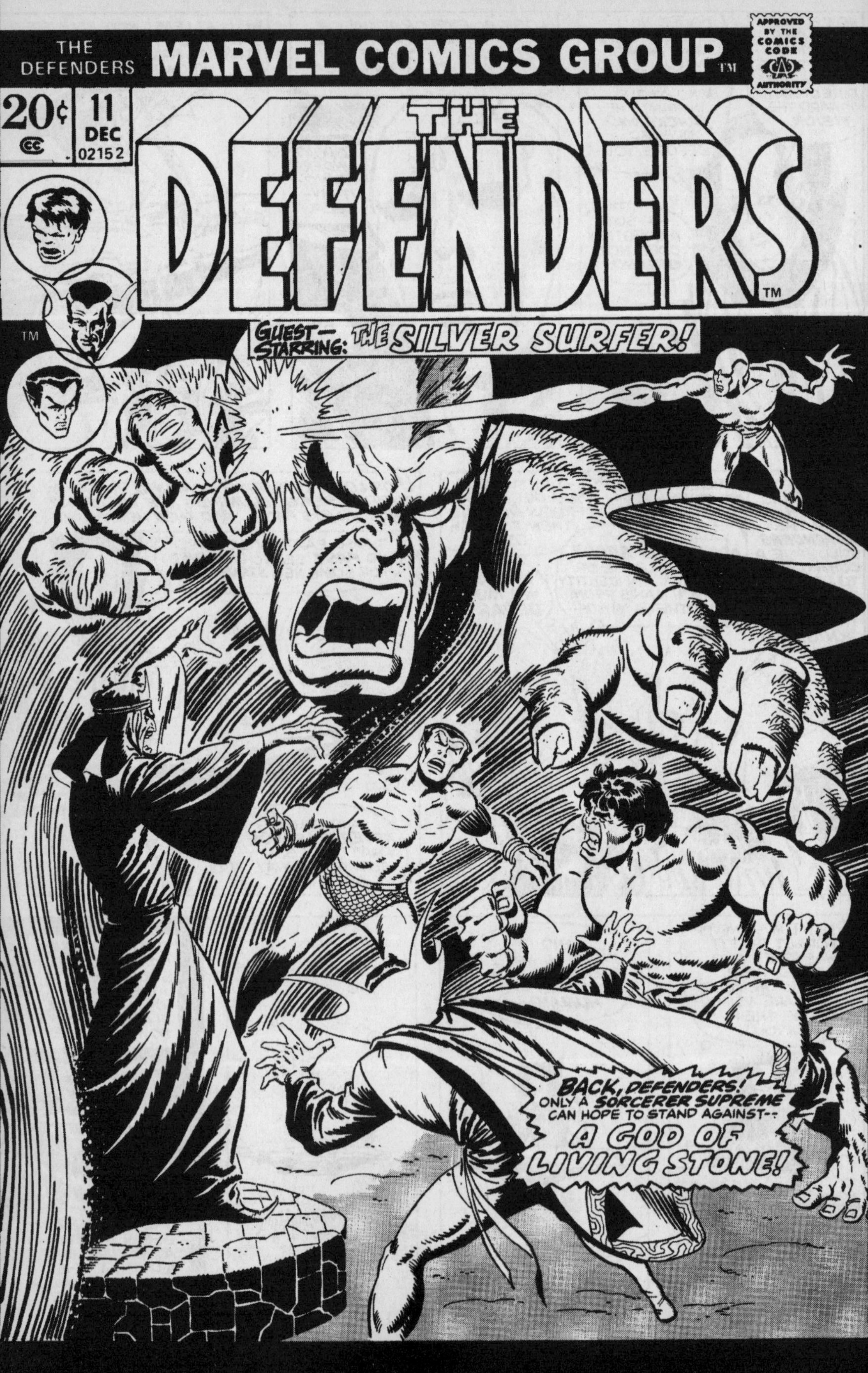
THE DEFENDERS
MARVEL COMICS GROUP
APPROVED BY THE COMICS CODE AUTHORITY
20¢
11
DEC
02152
THE DEFENDERS
GUEST-STARRING: THE SILVER SURFER!
BACK, DEFENDERS! ONLY A SORCERER SUPREME CAN HOPE TO STAND AGAINST--
A GOD OF LIVING STONE!

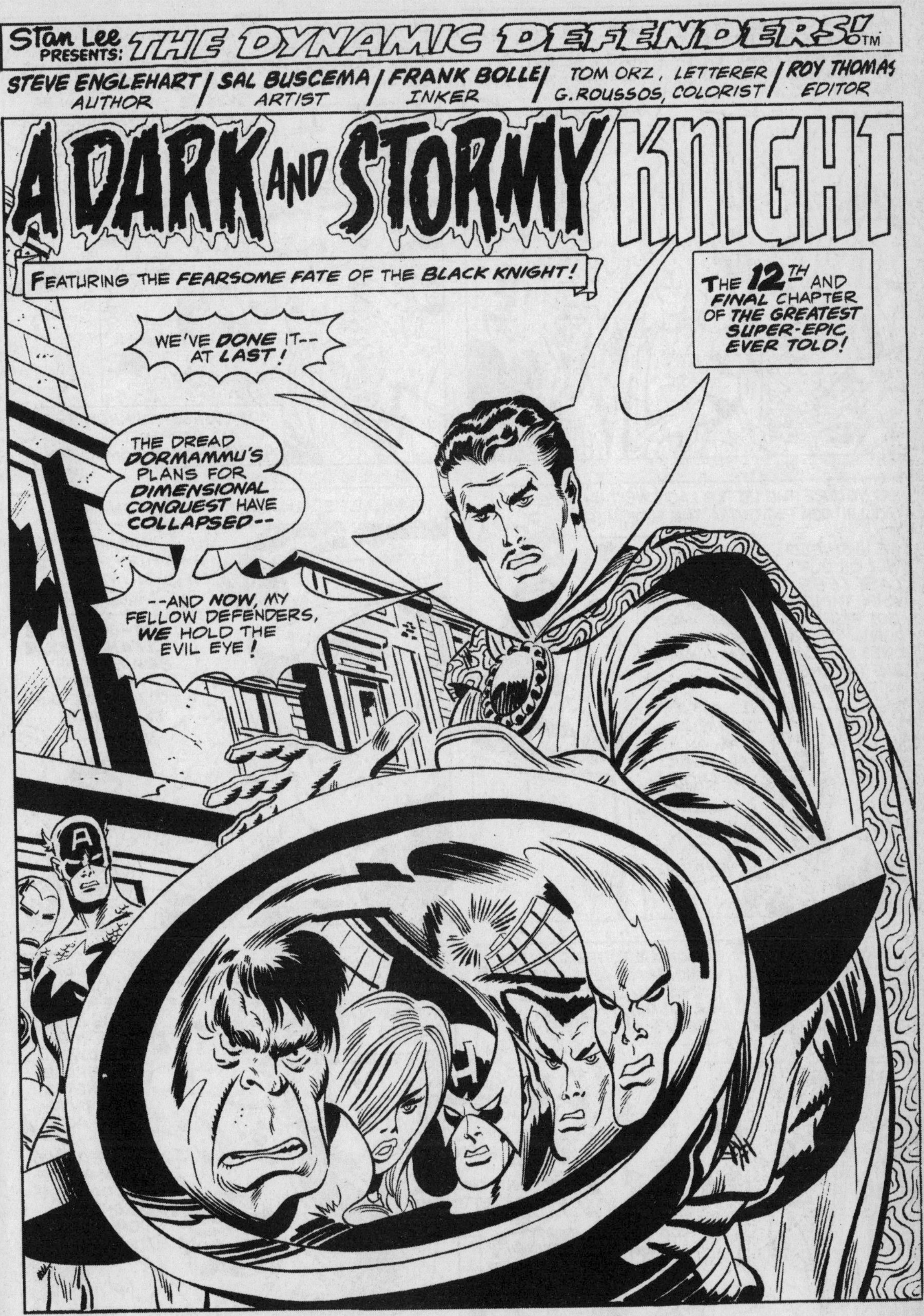
Stan Lee PRESENTS: THE DYNAMIC DEFENDERS!™
STEVE ENGLEHART AUTHOR / SAL BUSCEMA ARTIST / FRANK BOLLE INKER / TOM ORZ, LETTERER G. ROUSSOS, COLORIST / ROY THOMAS EDITOR
A DARK AND STORMY KNIGHT
FEATURING THE FEARSOME FATE OF THE BLACK KNIGHT!
THE 12TH AND FINAL CHAPTER OF THE GREATEST SUPER-EPIC EVER TOLD!
WE'VE DONE IT-- AT LAST!
THE DREAD DORMAMMU'S PLANS FOR DIMENSIONAL CONQUEST HAVE COLLAPSED--
--AND NOW, MY FELLOW DEFENDERS, WE HOLD THE EVIL EYE!

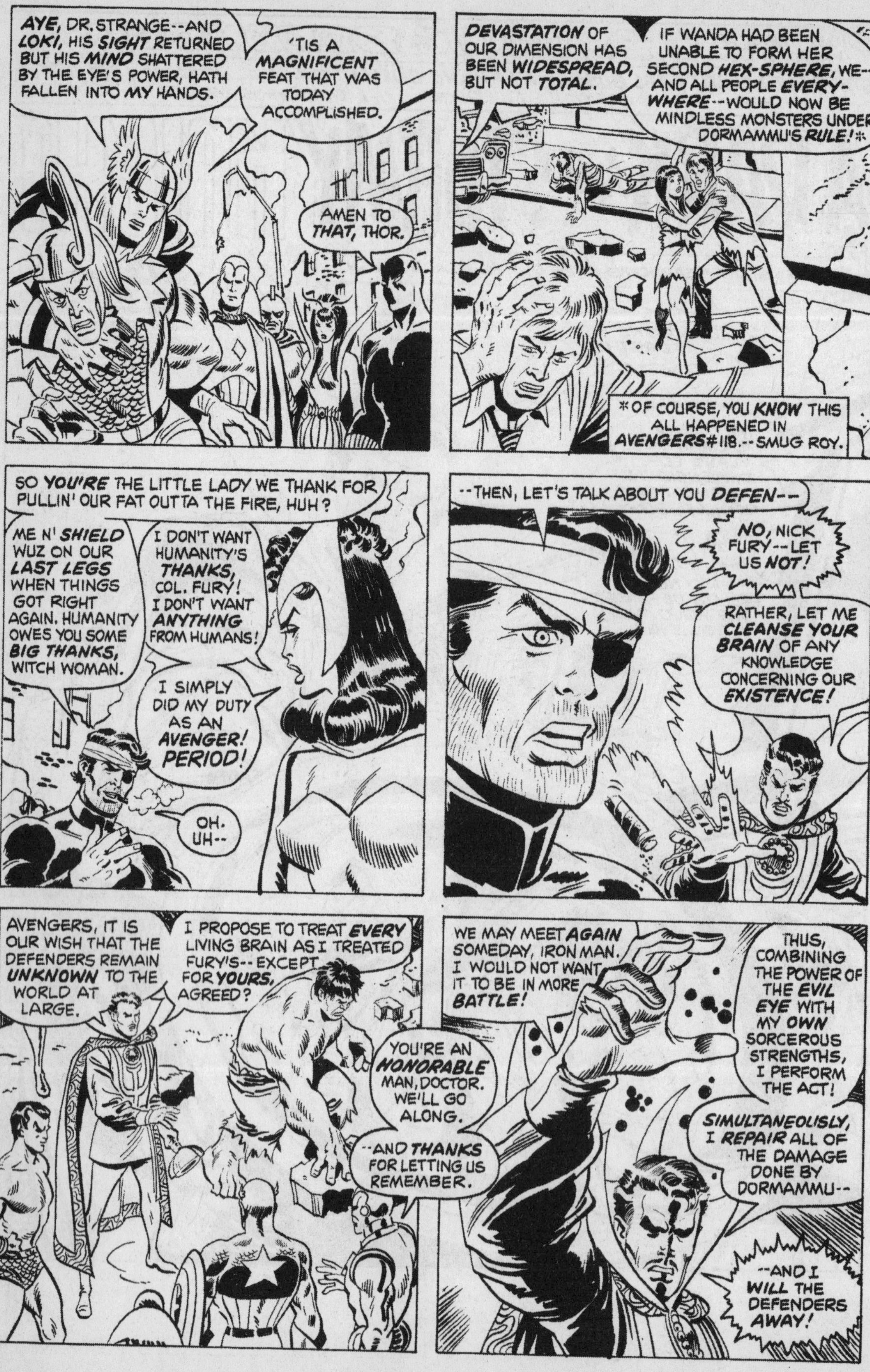
AYE, DR. STRANGE--AND LOKI, HIS SIGHT RETURNED BUT HIS MIND SHATTERED BY THE EYE'S POWER, HATH FALLEN INTO MY HANDS.
'TIS A MAGNIFICENT FEAT THAT WAS TODAY ACCOMPLISHED.
AMEN TO THAT, THOR.
DEVASTATION OF OUR DIMENSION HAS BEEN WIDESPREAD, BUT NOT TOTAL.
IF WANDA HAD BEEN UNABLE TO FORM HER SECOND HEX-SPHERE, WE--AND ALL PEOPLE EVERY-WHERE--WOULD NOW BE MINDLESS MONSTERS UNDER DORMAMMU'S RULE!*
*OF COURSE, YOU KNOW THIS ALL HAPPENED IN AVENGERS #118.--SMUG ROY.
SO YOU'RE THE LITTLE LADY WE THANK FOR PULLIN' OUR FAT OUTTA THE FIRE, HUH?
ME N' SHIELD WUZ ON OUR LAST LEGS WHEN THINGS GOT RIGHT AGAIN. HUMANITY OWES YOU SOME BIG THANKS, WITCH WOMAN.
I DON'T WANT HUMANITY'S THANKS, COL. FURY! I DON'T WANT ANYTHING FROM HUMANS!
I SIMPLY DID MY DUTY AS AN AVENGER! PERIOD!
OH. UH--
--THEN, LET'S TALK ABOUT YOU DEFEN--
NO, NICK FURY--LET US NOT!
RATHER, LET ME CLEANSE YOUR BRAIN OF ANY KNOWLEDGE CONCERNING OUR EXISTENCE!
AVENGERS, IT IS OUR WISH THAT THE DEFENDERS REMAIN UNKNOWN TO THE WORLD AT LARGE.
I PROPOSE TO TREAT EVERY LIVING BRAIN AS I TREATED FURY'S--EXCEPT FOR YOURS. AGREED?
YOU'RE AN HONORABLE MAN, DOCTOR. WE'LL GO ALONG.
--AND THANKS FOR LETTING US REMEMBER.
WE MAY MEET AGAIN SOMEDAY, IRON MAN. I WOULD NOT WANT IT TO BE IN MORE BATTLE!
THUS, COMBINING THE POWER OF THE EVIL EYE WITH MY OWN SORCEROUS STRENGTHS, I PERFORM THE ACT!
SIMULTANEOUSLY, I REPAIR ALL OF THE DAMAGE DONE BY DORMAMMU--
--AND I WILL THE DEFENDERS AWAY!

WHEN THE *MIGHTIEST MAGICIAN* IN THE COSMOS SAYS THINGS LIKE THAT, TRUE BELIEVER, HE'S *NOT* JUST EXERCISING HIS *MOUTH!*

EVEN AS HE SPEAKS, IT COMES TO *PASS!* EARTH AND EVERY *OTHER* PLANET IN THIS REALM RETURN TO THEIR PREVIOUS STATES--AND THESE *SIX* RETURN TO THE MYSTIC MASTER'S *SANCTUM!*

(CONFUSED ABOUT SUBBY'S LACK OF *NEW UNIFORM*, TIGER? REMEMBER THAT THIS CONTINUED SAGA *BEGAN* --AND SO *TAKES PLACE-- BEFORE* HE DONNED IT. -- STEVE & R.T.)

I HOPE YOU OTHERS *CONCUR* WITH MY DECISION BEFORE THE *AVENGERS.*

I *ASSUMED* YOUR FEELINGS ABOUT THE DEFENDERS MATCHED MINE, BUT DIDN'T *CONSULT* WITH YOU BEFORE *ACTING--*

--BECAUSE THE BLACK KNIGHT HAS BEEN *IMPRISONED* AS A STATUE FOR *MANY WEEKS* NOW.

I WANTED TO *GET* TO HIM WITHOUT ANY FURTHER *DELAY!*

YOU ACTED *CORRECTLY,* DOCTOR.

ALL RIGHT, THEN, BEFORE* I COULD ONLY SEND A *MENTAL CONTACT* TO DANE WHITMAN'S LIMBO-LOST-SOUL--

*ISH #8--R.

--BUT *THIS* TIME, EMPLOYING THE POWER OF OUR *PRIZE--*

--I SHALL SEND MYSELF!

BY NEPTUNE'S TRIDENT! HE ALSO BECOMES AS A STATUE!

THE MAGE'S ASTRAL *FORM* HAS SEPARATED FROM HIS *MORTAL* FORM!

NOT UNLIKE A *COMET*, EXCEPT FOR ITS PURPOSIVE *TWISTING* AND *TURNING*, A TURQUOISE STREAK *BURSTS* INTO LIMBO AND SLICES CLEANLY *ACROSS* IT!

YET, IF WE INSPECT THE COMET MORE *CLOSELY*, WE FIND THAT IT IS *ACTUALLY* THE MASTER OF THE MYSTIC ARTS!

HOW *IRONIC* THAT DORMAMMU WAS ATTEMPTING TO *DECEIVE* US WHEN HE TOLD US THE KNIGHT WOULD BE HELPED BY OUR RECOVERING THE EVIL EYE--

--BUT IN THE *END*, THAT IS *EXACTLY* WHAT IS HAPPENING!

NOW, ONCE I REACH THE LOCATION AT WHICH I CONTACTED DANE *EARLIER*, THE EYE'S POWER WILL ALLOW ME TO BRING HIS ESSENCE *BACK* WITH ME.

HE SHOULD BE JUST *AHEAD*--

BUT NO! BY THE MANY MOONS OF MUNNOPOR!

HE IS NOT *HERE!*

HOW CAN THIS *BE?* ONLY A MYSTIC FORCE OF *INCREDIBLE* MAGNITUDE COULD HAVE SPIRITED HIM AWAY!

WHO COULD HAVE *DONE* IT?

MEANWHILE, BACK IN THE REAL WORLD, THE FORMER AVENGER NAMED HAWKEYE IS ALSO BUSY POSING QUESTIONS--

OKAY, BOW-SLINGER--WHEN DO YOU START YOUR JOB ASSISTING *DALE CARNEGIE?*

I MEAN, THE AVENGERS DIDN'T SAY *ANYTHING* NASTY ABOUT YOUR JOINING THE DEFENDERS.

--THEN AGAIN, THEY DIDN'T SEEM TO *MISS* YOU, EITHER.

I DON'T SEE THE **PROBLEM**, HAWKEYE. YOU HAVE A PLACE WITH **US**.

DIG IT, VAL--BUT I **LEFT** MY OLD GROUP BECAUSE I WANTED TO PROVE I COULD GO IT **ALONE**.

WHAT **GOOD** DOES IT DO ME TO JUST MOVE FROM **ONE** ROSTER TO **ANOTHER**?

EVEN THOUGH I **LIKE** YOU FOLKS, I'M NOT DOING WHAT I SET **OUT** TO DO.

AND **AGAIN**, I WAS SO IN **LOVE** WITH THE IDEA OF FIGHTING **SHELLHEAD**, THAT NOW THAT I KNOW I WAS **WRONG**--

--MY WHOLE **DEFENDIN'** SHTICK SEEMS KINDA **SOUR**.

I UNDERSTAND THE ARCHER'S POINT!

BEING IN A **GROUP** IS **NOT** THE WAY ONE DEMONSTRATES HIS TRUE WORTH.

I, **MYSELF**, PLAN TO LEAVE THE **DEFENDERS** AFTER DR. STRANGE AND THE KNIGHT RETURN.

NAMOR, IT'S **YOU** WHO ALWAYS SAYS THERE **ARE** NO DEFENDERS--EH?

DUMB MAGICIAN COMES **BACK**--BUT HE COMES **ALONE**!

HULK **KNEW** HE COULDN'T DO WHAT HE SAID.

THE MAN OF MYSTERY REANIMATES HIS MORTAL SHELL AND STEPS FORWARD--

DEFENDERS, AN **ENIGMA** CONFRONTS US! THE KNIGHT IS **GONE**, AND HE--

--BUT NO MORE CAN HE **SAY**, BEFORE A **NEW** SORCEROUS FORCE ENVELOPES **EVERYONE** IN THE ROOM!

STEPHEN! WHAT'S HAPPENING?

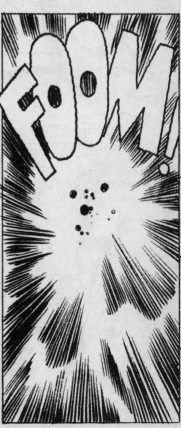

FOOM!

WHAT *TRICK* IS THIS? THIS IS *DESERT*, WHERE ROSS AND HULKBUSTERS LIVE!

YOU WANT THEM TO *CAPTURE* HULK!

NO! THIS ISN'T *AMERICA!* THE *ARCHITECTURE* IS MORE *MIDDLE EASTERN!*

FORGET *WHERE* WE ARE AND CONCENTRATE ON *WHEN* WE ARE!

THAT *CATAPULT*--THE *NON-POLLUTED AIR* I SMELL--

--WE'RE IN THE *PAST!*

AND *LOOK*--

--THERE IS THE *BLACK KNIGHT* --RUNNING AS IF *MEPHISTO HIMSELF* WERE CHASING HIM!

WHAT--? THE *DEFENDERS*-- *HERE?*

I DON'T KNOW WHERE YOU *CAME* FROM, OR *HOW*, BUT YOU'RE THE *BEST* SIGHT FOR SORE EYES I'VE EVER *ENCOUNTERED!*

PREPARE YOURSELVES! THIS IS THE *TWELFTH CENTURY*-- WE'RE IN THE *MIDDLE* OF THE *CRUSADES*--

--AND THE *ARABS* ARE ATTACKING!

KILL THE *INFIDELS! KILL THEM!*

WAIT! THIS IS NOT *OUR* WAR!

I'LL *IMMOBILIZE* THEM WITH A SPELL SO WE CAN GET OUR *BEARINGS* BEFORE WE ARE PRESSED TO VIOLENCE!

ORDERS! MAGICIAN *ALWAYS* GIVES HULK ORDERS!

WELL, HULK WANTS *NO* MORE ORDERS AND *NO* MORE *WAITING!*

HULK WANTS TO *FIGHT!*

PTOW!

WUMP!

MAYBE THE *OTHER* DEFENDERS *DIDN'T* WANT TO FIGHT, MONSTER--

--BUT IT DOESN'T MAKE MUCH DIFFERENCE *NOW*, DOES IT?

AND THEN--

BY THE GODS ABOVE, BELOW, AND BEYOND!

THAT MISSHAPEN *CREATURE*--APPEARS TO BE AN *EARTH SPIRIT*--

--A GNOME!

YET IT LOOMS *MANY TIMES* ITS NORMAL SIZE! IT'S *GIGANTIC!*

YES, INVADER! MEET HIM WHO *GUARDS* ALLAH'S FAITHFUL!

TEMAX!

MY MYSTIC ASSAULT *EVAPORATES* AROUND HIM! HIS ELEMENTAL FORCES MUST BE AT LEAST *QUINTUPLED!*

WE HAVE NEVER FAILED *BEFORE*, DOCTOR.

CAN *NOTHING* HALT HIM?

AND THE *FULL FORCE* OF MY *POWER COSMIC* FARES NO *BETTER!*

WELL-- BRIGHT LIGHTS FROM HANDS AREN'T GOOD FOR *FIGHTING!* DON'T EVEN MAKE *SENSE!*

HULK KNOWS WHAT MAKES SENSE!

HULK'S *FIST!*

BOM!

POW

TRAHH!

HE HANDLES THE HULK WITH *EASE*-- EVEN *DISDAIN!* THE SPIRIT *IS* UNSTOPPABLE!

WE ARE *STILL* BEST SERVED BY AVOIDING COMBAT --NOT FOR OUR *FOES'* SAKE NOW--

--BUT FOR *OURS!* LET US *LEAVE,* FELLOW DEFENDERS.

THOSE WORDS CAME *HARD* TO DR. STRANGE'S LIPS--

--MUCH HARDER THAN TEMAX'S PROPOSED NEXT *WEAPON* COMES TO *HIM*--

--BUT THE SORCER- ER'S ORANGE- GLOVED *HANDS* HAVE BEEN ANYTHING BUT *IDLE* SINCE HE SPOKE--

--AND SO--

TROAH??

I SHARE YOUR ASTONISHMENT, DEMON!

WITHER HAVE THEY *GONE?*

MILES AWAY--

THE ARABS WILL NOT DISCOVER US *NOW*--SO THAT ALLOWS *US* TIME TO DISCOVER THE *STORY* BEHIND OUR PREDICAMENT!

--IF YOU *KNOW* IT, DANE WHITMAN.

I KNOW IT, DR. STRANGE. AT LEAST I CAN HAZARD A *GOOD GUESS.*

JUST GIVE ME A MOMENT. IT'S ALL BEEN SO *SUDDEN!*

THAT'S BETTER. NOW, BRIEFLY: THROUGH A *SPELL* CAST AT THE TIME OF *CAMELOT'S* COLLAPSE BY *MERLIN THE MAGNIFICENT*--

--MY ANCESTOR, THE *ORIGINAL BLACK KNIGHT,* LIVES *AGAIN* IN ME!*

* THERE WERE 22 PAGES OF *DETAILS* IN *MARVEL SUPER-HEROES #17,* ARMOR AFFICIONADO.--R.

OUR SPIRITS ARE *MINGLED* IN A QUEST TO *FIND* AND *FIGHT* THE MAN WHO *MURDERED* MY ANCESTOR-- *MODRED THE EVIL!*

MODRED *ALSO* DIED CENTURIES AGO, BUT HIS ESSENCE *LIVES ON,* AND CAN APPEAR *ANY-WHERE--*

--AT *ANY TIME!*

I SEE.

HE IS *HERE,* THEN?

"YES--SMACK IN THE MIDDLE OF *KING RICHARD THE LION-HEARTED'S* CRUSADES TO RECOVER THE *HOLY LAND* FROM THE *MOHAMMEDANS!*

"EVERYTHING IS IN *CHAOS* BECAUSE OF HIS PRESENCE--

"-- THE KING *HIMSELF* IS AN ARABIAN *PRISONER--*

"--AND RICHARD'S SINISTER *BROTHER,* PRINCE JOHN, HAS TAKEN *COMMAND* OF PLANNING TO *DESERT* THE KING!

"MODRED HAS *ALLIED* HIMSELF WITH JOHN, AND THUS ASSUMED *HUMAN FORM* AGAIN-- WHICH IS WHY *I* AM HERE.

MERLIN'S SPELL BRINGS *OPPOSITION* TO MODRED! IT PLUCKED MY SOUL FROM *LIMBO* TO EXACT MERLIN'S VENGEANCE--

--AND APPARENTLY, *YOU* WERE SWEPT UP BY IT, TOO!

OUR ENEMIES, AS YOU SAW, HAVE *MAGIC* ON THEIR SIDE! THAT *MUST* BE WHY *YOU* WERE CHOSEN!

IT *TAKES* A WHILE FOR ALL THAT TO SINK INTO THE DEFENDERS' HEADS--IN FACT, IT NEVER *DOES* SINK *COMPLETELY* INTO THE *HULK'S* PEA-GREEN PATE--

--BUT LATER THAT SAME *EVENING,* AS DARK DESERT CLOUDS SCUD *OMINOUSLY* ACROSS A PEARL-DROP MOON--

--*SEVEN COWLED FIGURES* PASS SLOWLY AND CONFIDENTLY PAST BORED GUARDS SURROUNDING KING RICHARD'S *PRISON.*

PRIESTS! MAY ALLAH *PRESERVE* US FROM *PRIESTS!*

BUT THAT *RELIGION-WEARY* PROTECTOR OF THIS BLOOD-DRENCHED LAND MEN CALL *HOLY* WOULD BE EVEN *MORE* DISMAYED BY THESE PERSONS, HOWEVER--

--IF HE COULD JOIN *US* IN SEEING THEIR *FACES!*

NOW IS THE TIME.

NAMOR, THE HULK, AND I SHALL SEEK TO DESTROY THE *SORCERY* MOUNTED AGAINST US--

--YET, THOUGH OUR *COMBINED* POWER IS *INCREDIBLE,* WE FACE THE *UNKNOWN,* AND SO MAY FAIL.

DO NOT DELAY IN YOUR ATTEMPT TO FREE THE *KING!*

WE *WON'T,* STEPHEN, *GOOD LUCK!*

CONSIDERING WHAT YOU'VE *TOLD* ME OF YOURSELVES, YOU SEEM RATHER *OVERCONFIDENT,* VALKYRIE.

THE *SILVER SURFER* IS THE *ONLY* ONE OF US WITH ANY *REAL* POWER--

--ALTHOUGH *YOU* CARRY MY ENCHANTED *EBONY BLADE!*

SHE GOT IT *FAIR 'N' SQUARE,* AVENGER! DON'T FORGET, YOUR *REAL* BODY IS STILL A *STATUE!*

THE ARCHER IS *CORRECT,* KNIGHT. MERLIN'S ANCIENT SPELL MAY HAVE CLOTHED YOUR SPIRIT WITH FLESH IN *THIS* TIME, TO COUNTER MODRED'S MENACE--

--BUT IN OUR *OWN* CENTURY, YOU ARE AS MUCH A PRISONER AS *RICHARD.*

--A PRISONER THE DEFENDERS'VE BEEN *TRYIN'* TO *BUST LOOSE* SINCE THE DAY THE ENCHANTRESS *ZAPPED* YOU, MISTER!

VAL'S NOT THE KIND--*HOLD IT!*

WHAT *IS* IT, HAWKEYE?

I *DUNNO.* GUESS I'M JUST GETTIN' *JUMPY!*

THOUGHT I *HEARD* SOMETHIN'--BUT IT'S QUIET NOW.

MEANWHILE-- OF ALL THE *CORRIDORS* WE HAVE DISCOVERED IN THIS FORTRESS, ONLY *THIS ONE'S* FLOOR IS NOT COVERED WITH *SAND*, THOUGH IT IS EQUALLY *FOOT-WORN*.

HUMANS COMING IN FROM THE DESERT WOULD *NATURALLY* SCATTER SAND AS THEY WALKED--BUT AN *EARTH-SPIRIT* WOULD *ABSORB* IT.

SO YOU BELIEVE THE CREATURE WAS *BIRTHED* HERE? A CLEVER *ANALYSIS*, DOCTOR.

BUT HALL ENDS AT *BIG DOOR*, FISH-MAN--

--UNLESS HULK DOESN'T *WANT* IT TO!

KRAK!

GOOD *WORK*, HULK! DESPITE YOUR *ANTIPATHY* TOWARD ME, I AM *PLEASED* THAT YOU HAVE ENTERED INTO THE *SPIRIT* OF OUR ENDEAVOR.

HUH?

HSST! *SILENCE*, BOTH OF YOU!

MEN APPROACH!

YES--NOW *I* HEAR THEM TOO, NAMOR!

MOHAMMEDANS!

NO, BY *SALADIN!* MY CAMEL *DID* OUTRUN YOURS, DOG! THE WAGER FALLS TO ME!

FAH! YOU *CHEATED!*

MY DAUGHTER SAW YOU PLACE *HERBS* IN MY BEAST'S DRINKING WATER THE EVENING BEFORE OUR *RACE!*

I *WARN* YOU, ABDUL, I WANT MY *MONEY* RETURNED!

FOOL! YOU CAUSED ME TO DROP THE *TORCH!*

BESIDES, WHAT WILL THESE *PRIESTS* THINK--

BY ALLAH! YOUR-- YOUR FOOT IS *GREEN!*

WHO *ARE* YOU?

THIS IS A *MONSTER*--BUT NOT *OUR* MONSTER!

ALARM! ALARM!

ALARRRK!

KPOW

HURRY! THEIR CRIES MAY HAVE REACHED ANY *NUMBER* OF *EARS!*

THE TITANIC TRIO RACES *SWIFTLY* AWAY INTO TWISTED CORRIDORS OF BLACK--AND--

--MEANWHILE--

LISTEN! DO YOU HEAR *SHOUTS* --FROM *FAR BELOW?*

YES--BUT THEY ARE *NOT* OUR CONCERN! WE HAVE BUT *ONE MISSION* TO COMPLETE!

HOW ODD! NOW NOW THAT I'VE MET THE *KNIGHT* AGAIN, I KEEP WAITING FOR THE *LOVE* I THOUGHT I HELD FOR HIM--

--BUT *NOTHING* COMES! *NOTHING!*

STILL, IF THE GUARDS HAVE BEEN *ALERTED*---

COME TO *THINK* OF IT, SURFER, WHERE *ARE* THE GUARDS? HOW HAVE WE REACHED *RICHARD'S CELL* AND MET *NO ONE?*

I LIKE IT NO BETTER THAN *YOU,* DANE WHITMAN. I BELIEVE WE SHOULD *PREPARE* OURSELVES FOR *ACTION*--

--FOR ONCE MY *POWER COSMIC* SHATTERS THE BONDS HOLDING THE ENGLISH MONARCH, WE SHALL BE UNABLE TO MASK OUR *PURPOSE* HERE ANY *LONGER!*

FFET!

HIS *SHACKLES* BROKE JUST AS EASILY, KNIGHT-- BUT I FEAR LONG DAYS OF *CAPTIVITY* HAVE *WEAKENED* THIS MAN.

YOU-- THE ONE CALLED THE *BLACK KNIGHT*-- WHO JOINED US FROM *NOWHERE*--IN THE FINAL DAYS-- BEFORE OUR CAPTURE--

YES, SIRE! I AM HERE, WITH MY *FRIENDS!*

YOU ARE *SAFE* NOW!

TRRURRRGH!

I DON'T THINK YOU SHOULD'VE USED A *STRAIGHT LINE* LIKE THAT, B.K.

GOOD LORD! *BEHIND US!*

MORE GIANT GNOMES!

NEVER HAVE I SEEN SUCH CRAGGY FORMS-- NOT IN ALL OF *SPACE!*

THESE CREATURES ARE LIKE *LIVING ROCK*-- YET THEY DO NOT *CRACK* OR *CRUMBLE* BEFORE MY POWER BLASTS!

WE HAVE *TROUBLE,* MY FRIENDS!

THUD!

SURFY'S HAD IT--AND THEY DON'T EVEN *FEEL* ANY OF MY *ARROWS!*

GOODBYE, KIDDIES-- ≶UHHH!≷

HAWKEYE ALWAYS *LAUGHS,* EVEN WITH THE JAWS OF *DEFEAT* SNAPPING SHUT AROUND HIM!

BUT THE *VALKYRIE'S* BEWITCHED BLADE CAN *SLICE* YOU--

MY ARM! I DIDN'T *DREAM* YOU COULD MOVE SO FAST!

UNFORTUNATELY, VAL...

FOOM!

...IT CAN!

NOW, I'M THE ONLY ONE LEFT--WHAT?

TAKE THE EBONY BLADE, KNIGHT. IT BELONGS--TO YOU!

YES--YES! I ONLY HAVE TO HOLD IT AGAIN TO FEEL THE SINGING POWER IT LOCKS DEEP WITHIN ITS POLISHED BLACK METAL!

THIS IS THE WEAPON I WAS BORN TO USE! THIS IS THE COMBAT I WAS BORN TO WAGE!

THIS IS WHY I AM THE BLACK KNIGHT!

ALL RIGHT, BOYS-- YOU HEARD THE LADY!

THIS SWORD CAN COUNTER MAGIC!

HE IS VALIANT, AND SKILLFUL--

--BUT HE IS ONE MAN AGAINST THREE GIANTS, AND EVEN AS HIS BLADE CLEAVES ONE GROTESQUERIE--

--THAT GNOME AND ANOTHER LAND SOLID STONE FISTS ON HIS HEAD!

AN UNFITTING FINALE FOR A FIGHT AFTER THE PRIDE AND THE PASSION DANE WHITMAN EXHIBITED?

AGREED--BUT GNOMES, STRANGE AS IT SOUNDS, HAVE THEIR OWN PRIDE.

THAT'S LIFE-- AND, PERHAPS ...DEATH!

BUT FIRST--

WE'VE GONE AS FAR AS WE CAN GO, AND LOOK!

IN THE CHAMBER BELOW--

PRINCE JOHN, MODRED, AND SOME ARABIAN WIZARD--

--CONJURING MORE GNOMES AS WE WATCH! WE MUST STOP THEM!

I PLACE MY HOPES FOR SUCCESS THIS TIME IN THE EVIL EYE!

ITS POWER, COMBINED WITH MINE HAS NOT FAILED YET!

DEFENDERS, ATTACK!!

MODRED--WHO ARE THESE MONSTROSITIES? I BETRAYED MY BROTHER ON YOUR ASSURANCE THAT YOU AND YOUR ARABIAN MYSTIC WOULD GUARANTEE MY SAFETY!

I KNOW NOT, MY LIEGE!

CHANDU!

I HEAR, MODRED--

--AND I ALREADY ACT!

THE WORDS HE HAS UTTERED ARE ARABIC, OF COURSE-- BUT NOW SOUND WORDS DR. STRANGE UNDERSTANDS, FOR THEY ARE THE NAMES OF FORCES HE HIMSELF CALLS UPON!

HE IS STRUCK WITH MAGIC NEVER DIRECTED AGAINST HIM BEFORE--AND DROPS THE EYE!

CHANDU ATTACKED NOT KNOWING *MY STRENGTH*--

--SO I END HIS *MENACE!*

BUT-- HE MUST KNOW SPELLS ONLY *STRANGE* KNOWS IN *OUR* TIME

--SPELLS BACKED BY ENTITIES WHO WILL NOT *BEFRIEND* DR. STRANGE FOR *800 YEARS!*

BY PROTEUS! THAT GNOME--

--IT *MATERIALIZED* FROM THE SMOKE!

THE SAVAGE *SUB-MARINER* WAS OBVIOUSLY REASONING OUT HIS ALLY'S DEFEAT BECAUSE HE THOUGHT HE FACED NO IMMEDIATE *DANGER!*

BLAM!

IMAGINE HIS *SURPRISE!*

THE MONSTER'S SLAB-LIKE *CHEST* AND UNYIELDING *ARMS* PRESS AGONY INTO NAMOR'S RAW FLESH!

BUT THEN THEY SLAM INTO *WATER*-- WATER FROM THE FORTRESS'S *OASIS*--AND *STRENGTH* FLOWS BACK INTO HIS *HOMO MERMANUS* FORM!

IMAGINE HIS *EXULTATION!*

AND *NOW* IMAGINE THE *FURTHER* THRILL THAT GRIPS HIM--

--AS HE WITNESSES WHAT WATER *DOES* TO AN *ELEMENTAL SPIRIT* OF *THE EARTH!*

IT'S *DISSOLVING!*

THEN-- I KNOW HOW TO *OVERCOME* OUR ENEMIES' SEEMING *INVULNERA-BILITY*--

--THE *SIMPLEST* SOLUTION OF ALL--

--FOR AS I UNDERSTAND SO *WELL*, WATER AND LAND ULTIMATELY *DESTROY* EACH OTHER!

MIGHTY IS THE SUB-MARINER'S BLOW--PERHAPS AS MIGHTY AS HE HAS EVER *STRUCK*--

--AND IT *EMPTIES* THAT OASIS, CATAPULTING LIQUID SALVATION *OVER* AND *INTO* THE ENTIRE FORTIFICATION!

INSIDE, AT GROUND LEVEL, WATER *FLASH-FLOODS* THROUGH THE MYSTIC CHAMBER BEFORE SPILLING BACK OUT--

--LEAVING *NO* GNOMES, *THREE* WATER-CHOKED HUMANS--AND A *VERY* CONFUSED *HULK*.

WHILE, IN THE TOWER, *THREE* GNOMES BITE THE...WATER...

....LEAVING SUDDENLY RETURNED *CONSCIOUSNESS, SHOCK,* AND THEN A DAWNING *COMPREHENSION*.

BELOW, A *MAN* STANDS--A MAN WHO *DISLIKES* SURFACE-DWELLERS.....A MAN WHO *HATES* GROUPS...A MAN WHO SWIMS AND WALKS *UNIQUE* AMONG ALL *OTHER* MEN; WITH BOTH THE *JOYS* AND *SORROWS* THAT ENTAILS...

...A MAN WHO SWELLS WITH *FIERCE* PRIDE AT THE AID HE HAS GIVEN THE DEFENDERS!

THE *THOUGHT* FLICKERS IN HIS BRAIN--THAT, FOR MANY *DAYS*, THE DEFENDERS FOUGHT FOR THE *EVIL EYE*, PINNING THEIR HOPES FOR THE BLACK KNIGHT'S *REVIVIFICATION* ON THAT WONDROUSLY *WIZARDLY* WEAPON.

AND NOW ALL DANGER TO THE BLACK KNIGHT IS *PAST*--

--BUT THE *EVIL EYE* WAS LEFT *UNUSED*.

THEIR *VICTORY* WAS *NOT* GAINED THROUGH *MAGIC*.

BUT *WAIT!* HAVE THE EVIL EYE-- AND *VICTORY*--*TRULY* BECOME HISTORY AS YET?

NO!

BACK, ALL OF YOU! MODRED AND I HAVE DISCOVERED A RATHER *INCREDIBLE* WEAPON--

--AND WE HAVE NOT DISCOVERED OTHER *RECOURSE* FOR US NOW BUT THE COMPLETE AND UTTER *DESTRUCTION* OF ALL WITNESSES TO TONIGHT'S BATTLE!

I AM, *SORRY* RICHARD, BUT I *MUST* BE KING! GOODBYE!

AND THEN, EVEN AS THE EVIL EYE BEGINS TO *GLOW*--

WHAT? SOMEONE *APPEARS!*

I *RECOGNIZE* THE MAN! HE SERVED *RICHARD* FROM TIME TO TIME!

IT IS--*PRESTER JOHN!**

* FIRST, AND LAST SEEN IN F.F. # 54.--ROY.

AYE, KNAVE: *PRESTER JOHN*--

--HE WHO IS *MASTER* OF THE EVIL EYE!

--HE WHO HAS WANDERED *TIME ITSELF* TO RECOVER THE LAST REMAINING REMNANT OF THE FABLED LAND OF *AVALON!*

FWAM!

THEY ARE *UNHARMED*, BUT NOW *FULLY AWARE* OF THE FOLLY OF THEIR DEEDS!

SINCE THE DAY MY *INNER SENSES* TOLD ME THE EVIL EYE HAD BEEN *RESTORED*, I HAVE SOUGHT IT, FOR IT WAS GIVEN INTO MY *CHARGE!*

NOW, AT LAST-- *BEFORE* THE TIME I RECEIVED IT-- I HOLD IT *AGAIN!**

*YEP, IT'S ANOTHER 20¢ TIME *PARADOX!*--ROY.

IT IS ONLY *JUST* THAT I SHOULD *FIND* MY PRIZE IN THE ERA OF MY BIRTH. IT IS THE ERA I *BELONG* IN--

--EVEN AS *YOU*, DANE WHITMAN, WITH YOUR *VALOR*, YOUR SKILL IN *SWORDPLAY*, AND YOUR LOVE FOR THE LIFE *CHIVALRIC* --BELONG *HERE!*

HOW-- *DID* YOU *KNOW*--?

I KNOW WHAT I *NEED* TO KNOW.

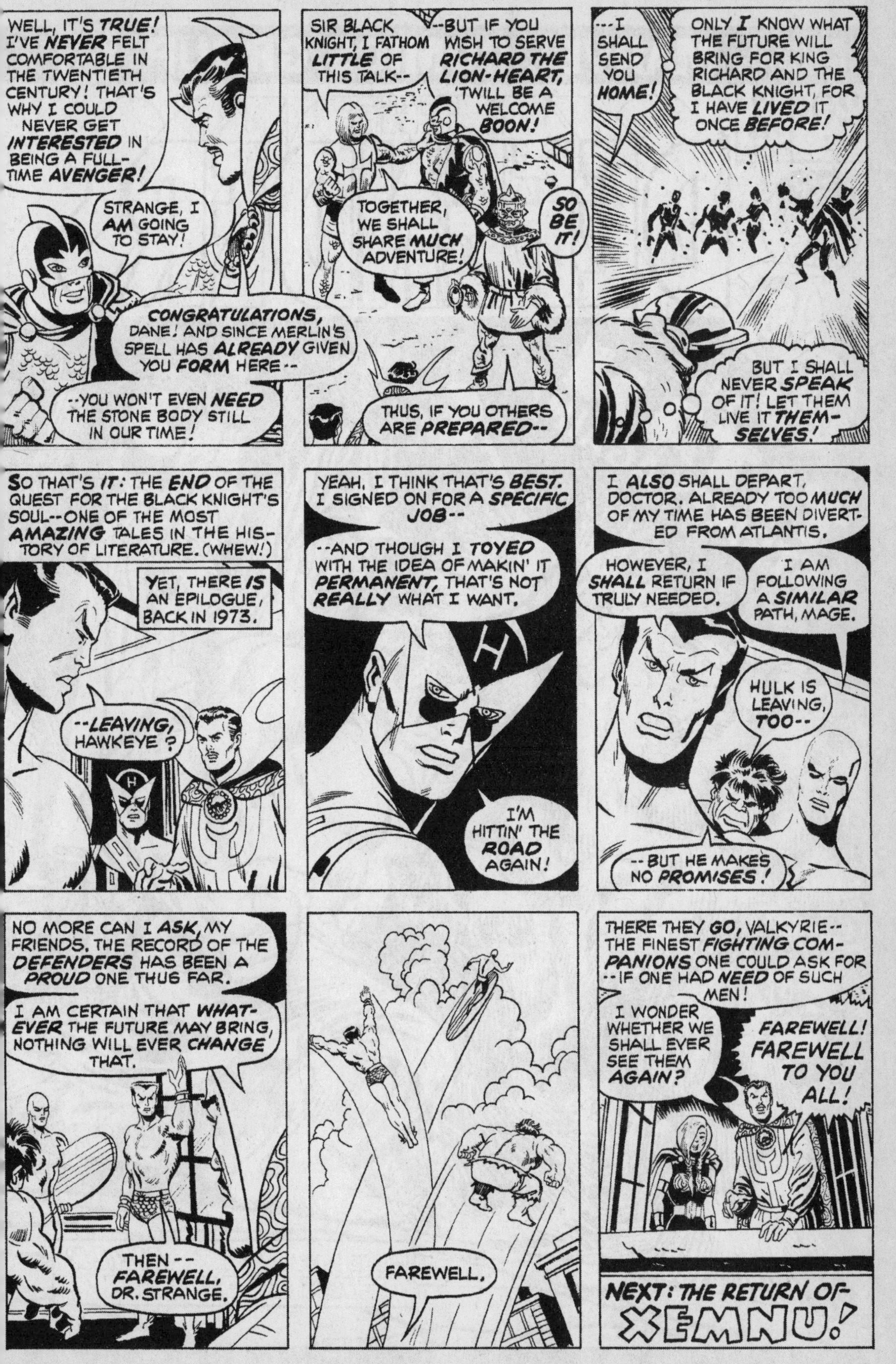
WELL, IT'S TRUE! I'VE NEVER FELT COMFORTABLE IN THE TWENTIETH CENTURY! THAT'S WHY I COULD NEVER GET INTERESTED IN BEING A FULL-TIME AVENGER!
STRANGE, I AM GOING TO STAY!
CONGRATULATIONS, DANE! AND SINCE MERLIN'S SPELL HAS ALREADY GIVEN YOU FORM HERE--
--YOU WON'T EVEN NEED THE STONE BODY STILL IN OUR TIME!
SIR BLACK KNIGHT, I FATHOM LITTLE OF THIS TALK--
--BUT IF YOU WISH TO SERVE RICHARD THE LION-HEART, 'TWILL BE A WELCOME BOON!
TOGETHER, WE SHALL SHARE MUCH ADVENTURE!
SO BE IT!
THUS, IF YOU OTHERS ARE PREPARED--
--I SHALL SEND YOU HOME!
ONLY I KNOW WHAT THE FUTURE WILL BRING FOR KING RICHARD AND THE BLACK KNIGHT, FOR I HAVE LIVED IT ONCE BEFORE!
BUT I SHALL NEVER SPEAK OF IT! LET THEM LIVE IT THEM-SELVES!
SO THAT'S IT: THE END OF THE QUEST FOR THE BLACK KNIGHT'S SOUL--ONE OF THE MOST AMAZING TALES IN THE HISTORY OF LITERATURE. (WHEW!)
YET, THERE IS AN EPILOGUE, BACK IN 1973.
--LEAVING, HAWKEYE?
YEAH, I THINK THAT'S BEST. I SIGNED ON FOR A SPECIFIC JOB--
--AND THOUGH I TOYED WITH THE IDEA OF MAKIN' IT PERMANENT, THAT'S NOT REALLY WHAT I WANT.
I'M HITTIN' THE ROAD AGAIN!
I ALSO SHALL DEPART, DOCTOR. ALREADY TOO MUCH OF MY TIME HAS BEEN DIVERTED FROM ATLANTIS.
HOWEVER, I SHALL RETURN IF TRULY NEEDED.
I AM FOLLOWING A SIMILAR PATH, MAGE.
HULK IS LEAVING, TOO--
--BUT HE MAKES NO PROMISES!
NO MORE CAN I ASK, MY FRIENDS. THE RECORD OF THE DEFENDERS HAS BEEN A PROUD ONE THUS FAR.
I AM CERTAIN THAT WHAT-EVER THE FUTURE MAY BRING, NOTHING WILL EVER CHANGE THAT.
THEN--FAREWELL, DR. STRANGE.
FAREWELL.
THERE THEY GO, VALKYRIE--THE FINEST FIGHTING COMPANIONS ONE COULD ASK FOR--IF ONE HAD NEED OF SUCH MEN!
I WONDER WHETHER WE SHALL EVER SEE THEM AGAIN?
FAREWELL! FAREWELL TO YOU ALL!
NEXT: THE RETURN OF XEMNU!

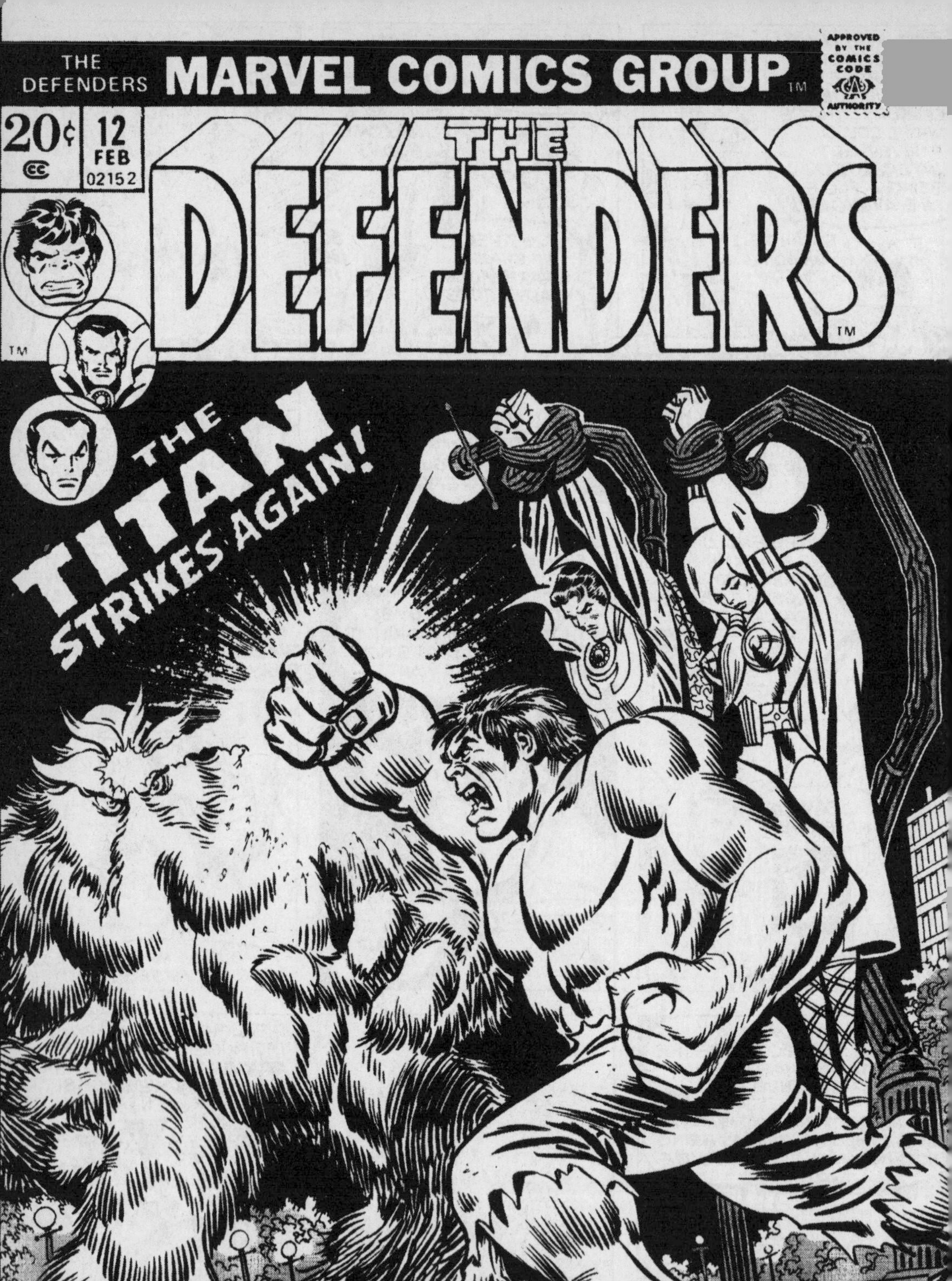
THE DEFENDERS
MARVEL COMICS GROUP
APPROVED BY THE COMICS CODE AUTHORITY
20¢
12
FEB
02152
THE DEFENDERS
THE TITAN STRIKES AGAIN!
..AND NOT EVEN THE HULK CAN STOP HIM!

LEN WEIN WRITER ✳ **SAL BUSCEMA & JACK ABEL** ARTISTS ✳ **P. GOLDBERG,** COLORIST **C. JETTER,** LETTERER ✳ **ROY THOMAS** EDITOR

TO LOOK AT HIM, YOU WOULD NOT THINK THAT THE EMERALD BEHEMOTH WHO LUMBERS THIS DAY THRU THE GREAT AMERICAN HEARTLAND IS REALLY A MOST *GENTLE* SOUL --

--BUT LOOK *CLOSELY*-- SEE THE *TILT* OF HIS *HEAD*--

--HIS FLARING *NOSTRILS* TAKING IN THE *SCENT* OF TURNING LEAVES --

--HIS *RED-RIMMED* *EYES* BATHING IN NATURE'S SIMPLE *BEAUTY.*

YES, HE *LOVES* THE FOREST, THIS GREAT, GREEN *BRUTE* --

--AND PERHAPS IT LOVES *HIM* IN TURN--

--BUT REGARDLESS, IT IS A TRIFLE *MUCH* TO BELIEVE THAT ANY *TREE* COULD LOVE THE *HULK* ENOUGH TO WANT TO RISE UP-- AND *FOLLOW* HIM !

THE TITAN STRIKES BACK!

BUT IS IT *LOVE* THE GNARLED OLD FOREST-DWELLER FEELS --OR *HATE?*

HUH? SOMETHING WRAPS AROUND HULK'S *NECK*-- TRIES TO *STRANGLE* HULK!

EVEN *HERE*-- EVEN IN PEACEFUL *FOREST* --THEY WILL NOT LEAVE HULK *ALONE!*

WHEREVER HULK GOES, ENEMIES *FOLLOW* HIM-- TRY TO *HURT* HIM!

WHY? HULK DOES NOT *KNOW!* ALL HULK *DOES* KNOW IS--

--WHEN ENEMIES *ATTACK*, HULK FIGHTS BACK--AND *SMASHES* --*HUH?*

SKRAKK!

IS NOT *ENEMY*--IS *TREE!* HULK IS ATTACKED BY--*TREE??*

BELIEVE IT, GREENSKIN--AND BY THE WAY--

--THAT TREE IS NOT *ALONE!*

WHA--? NOW *OTHER* TREES ATTACK HULK--AND *ROCKS*--

--*FLYING* ROCKS--!

THROCK!

HULK IS *CONFUSED*-- DOESN'T *UNDERSTAND*--!

HULK *LIKED* TREES. HULK *LIKED* ROCKS.

HULK THOUGHT THEY WERE HIS *FRIENDS*-- HULK'S *ONLY* FRIENDS--

--BUT IF PEACEFUL *FOREST* ATTACKS HULK, TOO--

--THEN HULK *HAS* NO FRIENDS--

BOK!

--AND HULK WILL *CRUSH* ANYTHING THAT GETS IN HULK'S WAY!

DO YOU *HEAR* HULK, ROCKS?

DO YOU *HEAR* HULK, TREES?

LEAVE HULK-- ALONE--

KRAK!

--OR HULK WILL MAKE YOU *REGRET* IT!

BUT THE GREEN GOLIATH'S MADDENED WORDS FALL ON *DEAF* EARS.

IN FACT, THEY FALL ON *NO* EARS, SAVE HIS OWN.

ROCKS AND TREES ARE NOTORIOUSLY *HARD OF HEARING.*

WHUDD!

KRUPP!

BAH! FOR EVERY ROCK OR TREE HULK *SMASHES*--

--MORE ROCKS AND TREES COME TO TAKE THEIR *PLACE!*

BUT WHY? *WHY??*

WHAT HAS HULK DONE TO MAKE FOREST STUFF *HATE* HIM?

YOU IGNORANT *BUFFOON!* THE *FOREST* DOESN'T HATE YOU--

--I *DO!*

HUH? WH-WHO ARE YOU?

YOU DON'T *REMEMBER* ME, HULK?

OF COURSE-- I SHOULD HAVE REALIZED THAT ONE WITH YOUR *LIMITED INTELLIGENCE* WOULD HAVE A *LIMITED MEMORY* AS WELL.

ALLOW ME TO *REINTRODUCE* MYSELF--

I AM *XEMNU THE TITAN*--

--BUT YOU WILL SOON CALL ME-- *MASTER!*

UUNNHH-- FUNNY RAY FROM WHITE THING'S HEAD *HURTS* HULK--

--MAKES HULK FEEL *WEAK*-- SO WEAK--

--BUT HULK *CAN'T* FEEL WEAK. HULK DOESN'T *UNDERSTAND!*

DUMB MAGICIAN! HE WOULD UNDERSTAND!

YES--DUMB *MAGICIAN* WOULD KNOW WHAT IS *WRONG* WITH HULK.

DUMB *MAGICIAN* WOULD MAKE HULK FEEL *BETTER.*

HULK DOESN'T REALLY *LIKE* DUMB MAGICIAN--

-- BUT HULK WISHES HE WAS *HERE!*

HULK WISHES DUMB MAGICIAN WAS *HERE!*

HULK WISHES DUMB MAGICIAN WAS *HERE!*

HULK WISHES--

Panel 1:

YEAH, GREENSKIN, SO DO *WE*--BUT SINCE HE'S *NOT,* WHY DON'T WE GO WHERE HE *IS*--

--IN *OTHER* WORDS, LET'S LOOK IN ON THE GREENWICH VILLAGE TOWNHOUSE OF *DOCTOR STRANGE*--

--AND, PARTICULARLY, THE BATTLE-GARBED *BEAUTY* WHO GAZES PENSIVELY OUT AN UPSTAIRS *WINDOW*--

Panel 2:

--THE *VIKING VIXEN* MEN NOW CALL--

VALKYRIE! SO *THERE* YOU ARE. I--ER--*HAVE* SOMETHING FOR YOU.

SOMETHING--FOR *ME?* WH-WHAT DO *YOU* MEAN?

Panel 3:

A *SWORD*--TO *REPLACE* THE EBONY BLADE YOU RETURNED TO THE *BLACK KNIGHT.**

I RECALLED *THIS* RESTED IN AN ALMOST-FORGOTTEN *NICHE* IN MY STUDY--AND I THOUGHT YOU MIGHT LIKE TO *HAVE* IT.

* IN PITCHED BATTLE AGAINST THE SARACEN HORDES LAST ISH.-- R.T.

Panel 4:

MIGHT I? STEPHEN, IT'S *SPLENDID!*

ITS *HILT* FITS MY HAND AS IF IT WERE CARVED FOR ME.

INDEED IT *WAS* CARVED, VAL--BUT YOU COULD NOT *DREAM* FROM *WHAT.*

Panel 5:

THE SWORD HAS A *NAME,* VAL--*DRAGONFANG*--

--FOR 'TIS SAID THAT CENTURIES AGONE, THE WIZARD, *KAHJI-DA,* SLEW SUCH A BEAST--

--THEN CARVED THIS *ENCHANTED* WEAPON *WHOLE* FROM ONE OF THE CREATURE'S *TUSKS!*

A MOST *FORMIDABLE* WEAPON, VAL--AND ONE YOU *DESERVE* TO WIELD.

Panel 6:

I AM *TOUCHED,* STEPHEN--*HONORED* MORE THAN YOU COULD BEGIN TO KNOW--

--BUT I'M AFRAID I WILL HAVE LITTLE *NEED* OF YOUR GENEROUS *GIFT*--

--FOR *I,* TOO, HAVE DECIDED TO *LEAVE* THE DEFENDERS!

LEAVING-- BUT-- BUT WHY?

IF I'VE SOMEHOW OFFENDED YOU, PERMIT ME AT LEAST TO--

OFFEND ME? NO, STEPHEN-- YOU'VE BEEN KINDER TO ME THAN PERHAPS I DESERVE.

IT'S JUST THAT-- I DON'T KNOW IF THE WOMAN YOU'VE SHOWN SUCH KINDNESS TO IS REAL--

--OR THE FIGMENT OF A WARPED IMAGINATION!

"REMEMBER, STEPHEN-- THE GIRL BARBARA THAT YOU AND THE OTHER DEFENDERS RESCUED FROM THE DREAD DIMENSION OF THE NAMELESS ONE WAS QUITE INSANE--*

* ISH # 3.-- R.T.

"--AND WAS FREED FROM THAT INSANITY PURELY AT THE WHIM OF THE ELDRITCH ENCHANTRESS--

"--FREED TO LOSE HER IDENTITY POSSIBLY FOREVER SO THE VALKYRIE COULD LIVE AGAIN!*

* ISH #4.-- RT. AGAIN.

NOW SOMEWHERE DEEP WITHIN THIS WARRIOR'S FORM IS LOCKED THE SPIRIT OF A WOMAN NAMED BARBARA-- A WOMAN WITH HOPES-- ASPIRATIONS!

I HAVE TO LEAVE-- TRY TO FIND THAT WOMAN-- FIND OUT WHO SHE WAS. I OWE HER THAT MUCH AT LEAST.

YOU DO UNDERSTAND, DON'T YOU, STEPHEN?

STEPHEN...?

THE VALKYRIE'S NEXT WORDS DIE IN HER THROAT-- FOR THE EXPRESSION ON HER NECRO-MANTIC COMPANION'S FACE IS INHUMANLY UNNERVING--

--THE EXPRESSION OF A MAN WHOSE MIND HAS TAKEN FLIGHT FROM HIS BODY-- A MAN WHOSE EYES ARE STUDYING WHAT CAN-NOT BE SEEN--

--AND WHEN THE SHAKEN VAL-KYRIE SHAKES THE MYSTIC MAGE IN TURN--

WHA--? WHERE--? WHERE AM I?

STEPHEN, WHAT'S WRONG? ARE YOU ALL RIGHT?

I-- AM QUITE ALL RIGHT, VALKYRIE--

--IT'S THE HULK WHO IS IN DIRE TROUBLE!

I'VE LONG KNOWN THE GIANT'S BRUTISH BRAIN WAS SOMEHOW STRANGELY *ATTUNED* TO MY MYSTIC VIBRATIONS--

--BUT NOW, FOR THE *FIRST* TIME, THE HULK'S MIND HAS CALLED OUT TO ME-- *NEEDED* ME--

--AND 'TIS A *SUMMONS* THAT MUST QUICKLY BE *ANSWERED!*

BUT HOW WILL WE *FIND* HIM, STEPHEN?

IF MY *INTERRUPTING* YOUR TRANCE HAS COST US A MEANS OF *LOCATING* THE HULK, I'LL--

DON'T *CHASTISE* YOURSELF, VAL--I HAVE THE MEANS.

NOW *QUICKLY*-- WE MUST FLY.

AND WHEN THE *MASTER OF THE MYSTIC ARTS* SAYS "FLY--"

WELL, HE AIN'T JUST WHISTLIN' THRU HIS *TEETH*--

UP! ARAGORN! WE GO TO SAVE A *FRIEND!*

THE STRIDENT CRY SEEMS TO *URGE* THE SLEEK-WINGED STALLION ONWARD--AND NOT TOO LONG AFTER--

THERE, VALKYRIE-- *BELOW* US! THE TRAIL OF MYSTIC EMANATIONS LEFT BY THE HULK'S MENTAL MESSAGE *TERMINATES* IN THE FOREST AHEAD.

AND FROM THE LOOK OF THE LOCAL *TERRAIN,* STEPHEN-- I'D AGREE HE'S DEFINITELY *BEEN* HERE.

THE QUESTION *NOW* IS --WHERE DID HE GO *FROM* HERE?

PERHAPS THE LIGHT OF MY MYSTIC *AMULET* CAN SHOW US THE *WAY!*

THE UNEARTHLY GLOW *SWEEPS* THE AREA AND--

BY THE VAPORS OF VAL-TORR! I HAVE MADE *CONTACT!*

MY ALL-SEEING AMULET HAS DETECTED A FAINT TRAIL OF THE HULK'S OWN PECULIAR *VIBRATIONS* LEADING FROM THIS GLADE!

VALKYRIE, TETHER YOUR *STEED* WHERE HE CAN *GRAZE*--

--AND FOLLOW ME!

FOR A TIME, THE TWO DEFENDERS *PURSUE* THE FADING GLOW--

--UNTIL, AS THEY TOP A VERDANT *RIDGE*--

THE TRAIL ENDS *YONDER*, VALKYRIE --IN THAT MODEST LOOKING *TOWN*!

THERE? BUT THE VILLAGE SEEMS TOO *PEACEFUL*--TOO *SERENE.* EVERYTHING IS STILL--*INTACT.*

THERE'S NOT A SINGLE DEMOLISHED BUILDING TO *PROVE* OUR RAMPAGING FRIEND HAS *PASSED* THIS WAY.

I NOTICED THAT AS WELL, VALKYRIE--BUT NONETHE-LESS, HE IS *THERE* --

--OR *HAS* BEEN!

STILL--WHETHER THE BEHEMOTH IS *IN* THE VICINITY OR *NOT*--

--IT WOULD NOT DO FOR *US* TO ATTRACT UNDUE *ATTENTION* BY ENTERING YON VILLAGE *GARBED* AS WE ARE.

THUS I UTTER A SIMPLE *SPELL OF TRANSFORMATION*--

--AND IT IS AS TWO INOBTRUSIVE *TRAVELERS* THAT WE SHALL BEGIN OUR SEARCH FOR *THE HULK!*

BUT BEGINNING A SEARCH FOR A SEVEN-FOOT, HALF-TON, GREEN-COMPLECTED *GRUESOME* IN TATTERED PURPLE PANTS IS NOT QUITE AS *EASY* AS THE MAN CALLED *STRANGE* MIGHT THINK.

FOR *EXAMPLE*:

AH--ONE OF THE LOCAL *INHABITANTS.* I SHALL *APPROACH* HIM, VALKYRIE--

--AND *INQUIRE* OF THE ONE WE *SEEK.*

EXCUSE ME, SIR--BUT I WAS WONDERING IF PERHAPS YOU'VE *SEEN* A *FRIEND* OF MINE?

FRIEND, MISTER? WHUT'S 'E *LOOK* LIKE?

WELL, HE'S ABOUT-- ER--THAT IS, HIS *SKIN* IS --I MEAN HE'S--

LOOK, MISTER-- I'D REALLY *LIKE* TA HELP YUH--

--BUT IF'N YUH DON'T EVEN KNOW WHUT THIS FRIEND O' YOURN *LOOKS* LIKE--

WELL-- THERE AIN'T MUCH I KIN *DO*--

PLEASE, SIR--WE--

NO, VALKYRIE--THE MAN IS *RIGHT.* 'TWILL BE *DIFFICULT* FOR US TO GAIN *AID* IN OUR SEARCH WITHOUT CAUSING A *PANIC* THAT WOULD--

'SCUSE ME, SON-- BUT *MAYBE I* CAN HELP.

WHO--?

NAME'S *MOSES*--AMOS MOSES. I'M *MAYOR* OF PLUCKETVILLE.

HEAR TELL YOU'RE LOOKIN' FOR A *FRIEND* OF YOURS --BIG *GREEN* FELLA.

WELL, I THINK I *KNOW* WHERE HE *IS*.

IF YOU'LL FOLLOW *ME*...?

WITH *PLEASURE*, MR. MOSES.

GREAT LITTLE TOWN, *PLUCKET-VILLE* IS--GROWIN'--GETTIN' *BIGGER* EVERY DAY.

THAT OVER THERE'S A STATUE OF *COL. BRADLEY PLUCKET*--FOUGHT AT *GETTYSBURG*--

--THEN *FOUNDED* PLUCKETVILLE WHEN HE FINALLY DECIDED TO *SETTLE DOWN*.

YESSIR, WE'VE GROWN A *LOT* SINCE THEN. THAT *THERE* IS OUR NEW *CITY HALL*-- JUST *COMPLETED* IT LAST WEEK--

--BUILT IT *OURSELVES*, WE DID--EVERY *BRICK* OF IT-- AND WE'RE *PROUD* FIT TO *BUST*.

FASCINATING, MR. MAYOR-- YOU HAVE *REASON* TO BE PROUD. BUT ABOUT OUR *FRIEND*--?

OF COURSE. *EXCUSE* ME. COUPL'A *HUNTERS* FOUND HIM LAYIN' IN THE *FOREST* NEARBY--AND LET ME KNOW.

WE *CARRIED* HIM INTO TOWN *OURSELVES*.

SEEIN' AS WHAT HE *LOOKS* LIKE, WE WERE AFRAID HE MIGHT *SCARE* MOST FOLKS IN TOWN--

--SO WE CARRIED HIM HERE IN *SECRET*--BROUGHT HIM TO MIZZ BROPHY'S PLACE TO *TEND* HIM.

MIZZ BROPHY'S IS ABOUT A *BLOCK* OR SO--BUT WE CAN TAKE A *SHORT-CUT* THRU THIS *ALLEY*.

WE DO INDEED *APPRECIATE* YOUR ASSISTANCE, MR. MAYOR--

--BUT MIGHT YOU KNOW WHAT OUR FRIEND'S CONDITION IS *NOW?*

MR. MAYOR?

MR. MAY...?

VALKYRIE-- WE'VE BEEN *DUPED!*

MOSES IS *GONE*-- AND THE ALLEY ENTRANCE IS NOW *BLOCKED*--

--BY A SHEER *BRICK WALL!*

THERE IS *NECROMANCY* AFOOT HERE--*MAGIC* MOST FOUL.

APPARENTLY, OUR DISGUISES HAVE BEEN EASILY *SEEN THRU*--

--SO, IN THE NAME OF THE ALL-SEEING AGAMOTTO, I *DISSOLVE* THEM--

--*NOW!*

BEWARE, VALKYRIE--WE WERE MOST SURELY *LURED* TO THIS DISOLATE ALLEY FOR SOME *SINISTER* PURPOSE AND--

STEPHEN-- *BEHIND* YOU--!

WATER PIPES-- COMING *ALIVE*-- PINIONING OUR *LIMBS*--

--BUT IF OUR UNSEEN FOE THINKS SO EASILY TO *DEFEAT* US--

NO, STEPHEN, I THINK THE PIPES ARE INTENDED ONLY TO *HOLD* US.

I THINK OUR MYSTERIOUS ENEMY INTENDS TO *KILL* US WITH--*THAT!*

"A *STEAM-ROLLER*--CHURNING OUT OF THE DARKNESS--SO *WIDE* IT FAIRLY *FILLS* THE ALLEY BEFORE US--AND POSSESSED, IT SEEMS, OF A MALEVOLENT *LIFE* OF ITS OWN."

THESE *PIPES* -- SO IMPOSSIBLY *STRONG* --

CAN'T *FREE* MYSELF --!

NORMALLY, I COULD DESTROY OUR *STEEL* BONDS WITH A *GESTURE* --

-- BUT MY POWERS ARE SOMEWHAT *CONSTRAINED* WHEN MY *HANDS* ARE THUS TIED.

YET, THE POWER OF *DOCTOR STRANGE* IS NOT ONLY IN HIS *HANDS* --

-- BUT IN HIS *MIND* -- HIS *HEART* -- HIS *SOUL* --

-- AND THE VERY *SKIES* MAY TREMBLE WHEN SPEAKS *THE MASTER OF THE MYSTIC ARTS!*

OH POWERS OF *CELESTIAL WORTH*, THIS FAITHFUL ONE BESEECHES THEE: HURL THY *SKYBORN FIRE* TO EARTH --

SKRUMPP!

-- ~ *THAT MAID* AND I MIGHT YET BE -- *FREE!!*

STAND *BACK*, VALKYRIE -- AND MY MYSTIC MIGHT SHALL *DEAL* WITH YON MECHANIZED *MENACE!*

NO, STEPHEN -- YOU'VE DONE *YOUR* SHARE IN *FREEING* US.

NOW IT IS *YOUR* TURN TO STAND AND BE *WITNESS* --

-- WHILE I SEE IF *THIS* FINELY-HONED *GIFT* OF YOURS IS *WORTHY* OF ALL ITS *LEGENDS.*

KWA-RAAAM

IT'S **WORTHY**.

THEN ALLOW ME TO OPEN A **PASSAGE** IN THIS NEWLY-GROWN BRICK **BARRICADE**--

--AND WE SHALL SEE IF WE CAN LEARN THE **REASON** FOR THIS PERFIDIOUS **AT**--**EH?**

STEPHEN, WHAT-- WHAT'S **HAPPENED** TO THE **PEOPLE?**

THEY'RE **ENTRANCED**, GIRL--COMPLETELY IN MY **POWER**.

WERE I TO **COMMAND** IT, THEY WOULD KILL YOU BOTH WITHOUT **HESITATION**-- TEAR YOU TO STREAMING SCARLET **RIBBONS**--

--AND I **COMMAND** IT **NOW!**

THEN LET YOUR MINDLESS ARMY **COME**, MADMAN! WE SHALL **MEET** IT WITH WAITING **BLADE** AND--

NO, VALKYRIE-- **SHEATH** YOUR WEAPON!

A TRUE **DEFENDER** MAY NEVER RAISE **ARMS** AGAINST THE **INNOCENT**, NO MATTER **HOW** THEY MIGHT THREATEN YOU--

-- ESPECIALLY WHEN THE ONE *RESPONSIBLE* FOR THAT THREAT STANDS IN PLAIN *VIEW*--!

EH? HE'S *PROTECTED* FROM MY SORCERY BY SOME SORT OF *PSYCHIC AURA!*

MUST *CHANGE* MY TACTICS BEFORE--

--IT'S *TOO LATE,* DOCTOR.

UUNNGG!

SPAK
BROK

MUCH TOO LATE--

UUHHH!

THRAK!

--FOR *BOTH* OF YOU.

HA HA HA HA HA HA HA HA HA HA HA

WHILE, BACK AT THE *MYSTIC MAGE'S* SANCTUM SANCTORUM, AN INCIDENT IS ABOUT TO TRANSPIRE THAT WILL SOON HAVE DRAMATIC BEARING ON THE CAREERS OF EARTH'S *DEFENDERS*--

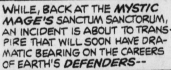

--ASSUMING, OF COURSE, THEY *LIVE* THAT LONG.

IS YOUR *MASTER* AT HOME? I MUST SPEAK TO HIM ON A MATTER OF GREAT *URGENCY.*

I AM *SORRY*-- BUT MY MASTER IS NOT *HERE!*

THEN DO YOU KNOW WHERE I CAN *REACH* HIM? I *MUST* SPEAK TO HIM--*SOON!*

AGAIN I AM *SORRY*-- BUT YOU MUST *WAIT* UNTIL HE *RETURNS.*

I WAIT *THAT* LONG, FRIEND--AND THE GOOD DOCTOR MIGHT HAVE *NOTHING* TO COME HOME TO.

IN FACT, NOBODY WILL HAVE *ANYTHING..* ANYWHERE IN THE WORLD.

AND IN THE BRADBURYAN TOWN OF *PLUCKETVILLE, U.S.A.,* THE GOOD DOCTOR AND HIS ARMOR-CLAD COMPANION TUMBLE OUT OF *DARKNESS* TO FIND THEMSELVES--

--*SHACKLED* AGAIN-- BOUND BY TWISTING *LAMP-POSTS* IN THE *VILLAGE SQUARE*--

--BUT THE *ENCHANTMENT* THAT FREED US *BEFORE* WILL SERVE *AGAIN* TO--

NO, DOCTOR-- NOT *THIS* TIME!

JUST AS I TOOK THE LIBERTY OF *REMOVING* THE VALKYRIE'S BLADE --SO, TOO, HAVE I REMOVED *YOUR* POWERS--

--BY CREATING WITHIN YOU A *MENTAL BLOCK* AGAINST *USING* THEM.

HE'S *RIGHT!* NO MATTER HOW HARD I *STRAIN,* I CAN THINK OF NO *SPELLS* --NO *CONJURATIONS.*

WE'RE *TRAPPED*--TRULY *PRISONERS* OF THIS *MADMAN!*

YOU THINK ME A *MADMAN,* DON'T YOU?

WELL, YOU'RE *WRONG,* DOCTOR STRANGE--*QUITE* WRONG.

I AM NOT IN THE LEAST *MAD*--

--*NOR* AM I TRULY A *MAN!*

XEMNU--THE *TITAN!* BUT HOW--?

HOW DID I SURVIVE OUR *LAST* ENCOUNTER?

I ASSURE YOU, DOCTOR-- IT WAS NOT *EASY!*

"WHEN YOUR HULKING GREEN COMRADE TOOK IT INTO HIS ALMOST-EMPTY HEAD TO PUMMEL ME INTO THE ASPHALT OF THE BASE YOU CALL THE CAPE--*"

*DETAILED IN MARVEL FEATURE #3. --R.T.

"--I TOOK THE ONLY RE-COURSE OPEN TO ME--"

"--ABANDONED MY PHYSICAL FORM AND LET MY MENTAL ESSENCE DRIFT SILENTLY AWAY, OUT OF THE BEHEMOTH'S REACH--"

"--UNTIL I REACHED THE CITY CALLED MIAMI AND HAPPEN-ED UPON THE BODY OF AMOS MOSES, THE MAYOR OF THIS FAIR VILLAGE--"

"--A BODY THAT I QUICKLY POSSESSED--THEN ALLOWED TO CARRY ME HERE!"

AGAIN, TITAN-- WHY?

OF WHAT POSSIBLE ADVANTAGE COULD THE PEOPLE OF THIS SIMPLE LITTLE TOWNSHIP BE TO YOU?

THEY HAVE BEEN OF GREAT ADVANTAGE-- IN BRINGING NEARLY TO COMPLETION MY LIFE'S GREATEST DREAM...

OBSERVE THE NEW TOWN HALL, DOCTOR--

--WATCH IT MOST CLOSELY AS I BATHE IT WITH A MINOR MENTO-BLAST--

--A BLAST WHICH TEARS ASUNDER ITS BRICK-FRONT FACADE TO REVEAL--

A STAR-SHIP, GOOD DOCTOR--

--CAPABLE OF CARRYING COUNTLESS HUMANS THRU THE COSMOS-- TO REPOPULATE MY LONG-DEAD HOMEWORLD...

--SPECIFICALLY, THE ENTIRE POPULATION OF THIS ISO-LATED COMMUNITY--EARTH-LINGS HELD COMPLETELY UNDER MY MENTAL CONTROL!

OBSERVE, DOCTOR, AS I ORDER MY OBEDIENT SLAVES TO ENTER THE SHIP!

LOOK at them, Doctor--helpless to disobey me--as are YOU--

--AS WAS THE HULK once he'd fallen under my SPELL.

"UNDER MY SPELL!" THEN THE HULK IS NOT DEAD--merely held mental CAPTIVE somewhere--

--SOMEWHERE NEAR, I'LL WAGER--SINCE XEMNU COULD NOT HAVE HAD TIME ENOUGH TO REMOVE HIM.

THE HULK'S MIND SOMEHOW REACHED MINE BEFORE--NOW I MUST ATTEMPT TO REVERSE THE PROCESS--

REACH THE BEHEMOTH'S MIND--AND FREE IT FROM XEMNU'S DOMINATION!

HEAR ME, HULK--AND FREE YOURSELF--

--FREE YOURSELF--

FREE YOURSELF--

FREE YOURSELF!

HULK HEARS DUMB MAGICIAN'S VOICE IN HEAD, TELLING HULK TO FREE HIMSELF--

--SO HULK IS FREE!

THRANGG!

BUT YOU'LL NOT REMAIN THAT WAY LONG, BRUTE! WHEN MY GREATEST, MOST POTENT MENTO-BLAST STRIKES YOU, IT WILL--

AGAIN STUPID WHITE THING HITS HULK WITH RAY FROM ITS HEAD--

--STUPID WHITE THING HURTS HULK--

--BUT WHEN HULK IS HURT, HULK IS MAD--

--AND WHEN HULK IS MAD, HULK IS STRONGEST OF ALL!

STRONG BRUTE? PERHAPS--

--BUT IS EVEN THE HULK STRONG ENOUGH TO OVERCOME--

"--THE RAGING WRATH OF A MINDLESS MURDEROUS MOB?"

BAH! IS ONLY PUNY HUMANS-- --NOT WORTH SMASHING--

THOOM!

"--SO HULK WILL KNOCK PUNY HUMANS OUT OF HULK'S WAY--"

--AND SMASH STUPID WHITE THING INSTEAD!

I WARN YOU-- BRUTE-- KEEP AWAY FROM ME--

MY POWERS HAVE *INCREASED* SINCE LAST WE MET, DOLTISH ONE--

-- FOR NOW I MAY MENTALLY *CONTROL* THE *INANIMATE*--BRING TO *LIFE* ROCKS--TREES-- STEAMROLLERS--

--AND *MORE*, HULK, *MUCH* MORE!

FIRE HYDRANTS-- LAMPPOSTS--FLYING THRU AIR AT HULK JUST LIKE *ROCKS* AND *TREES*--!

THEN *YOU* ARE THE ONE WHO MADE FOREST *HATE* HULK--!

CROOM!

WELL, HULK HATES *YOU* BACK--

--AND WHEN HULK *CATCHES* YOU, HULK WILL SMASH YOU INTO *NOTHING* LIKE HE DID *BEFORE!*

AND THE IMBECILIC BRUTE CAN *DO* IT, TOO --FOR MY MENTAL POWER NO LONGER SEEMS TO *AFFECT* HIM.

MUST *ESCAPE* WHILE I *CAN*--

--BUT THE TITAN WILL SOON *RETURN*--

--FOR HIS *GREAT GLEAMING SHIP*--AND THE PEOPLE OF *PLUCKETVILLE!*

COME *BACK*, WHITE THING-- OR HULK WILL--

AND SUDDENLY THE GREEN BEHEMOTH'S DULLISH EYES ESPY...

SHIP.

BIG SHIP.

STUPID WHITE THING SAID IT WOULD COME *BACK* FOR SHIP.

--SO HULK WILL *PICK UP* SHIP--

--AND GIVE IT *BACK* TO WHITE THING--

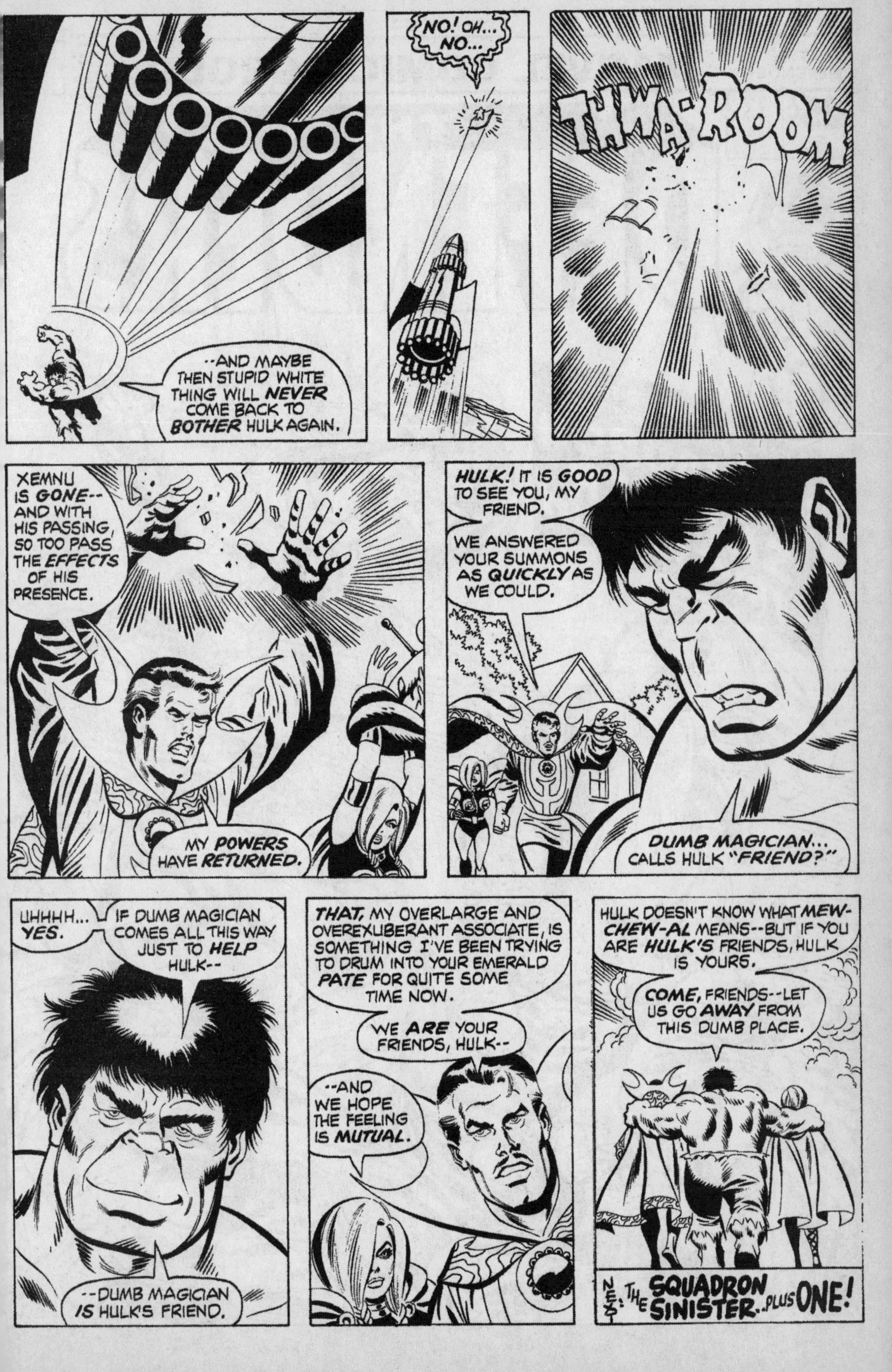

--AND MAYBE THEN STUPID WHITE THING WILL NEVER COME BACK TO BOTHER HULK AGAIN.
NO! OH... NO...
THWA-ROOM
XEMNU IS GONE-- AND WITH HIS PASSING, SO TOO PASS THE EFFECTS OF HIS PRESENCE.
MY POWERS HAVE RETURNED.
HULK! IT IS GOOD TO SEE YOU, MY FRIEND.
WE ANSWERED YOUR SUMMONS AS QUICKLY AS WE COULD.
DUMB MAGICIAN... CALLS HULK "FRIEND?"
UHHHH... YES.
IF DUMB MAGICIAN COMES ALL THIS WAY JUST TO HELP HULK--
--DUMB MAGICIAN IS HULK'S FRIEND.
THAT, MY OVERLARGE AND OVEREXUBERANT ASSOCIATE, IS SOMETHING I'VE BEEN TRYING TO DRUM INTO YOUR EMERALD PATE FOR QUITE SOME TIME NOW.
WE ARE YOUR FRIENDS, HULK--
--AND WE HOPE THE FEELING IS MUTUAL.
HULK DOESN'T KNOW WHAT MEW-CHEW-AL MEANS--BUT IF YOU ARE HULK'S FRIENDS, HULK IS YOURS.
COME, FRIENDS--LET US GO AWAY FROM THIS DUMB PLACE.
NEXT: THE SQUADRON SINISTER...PLUS ONE!

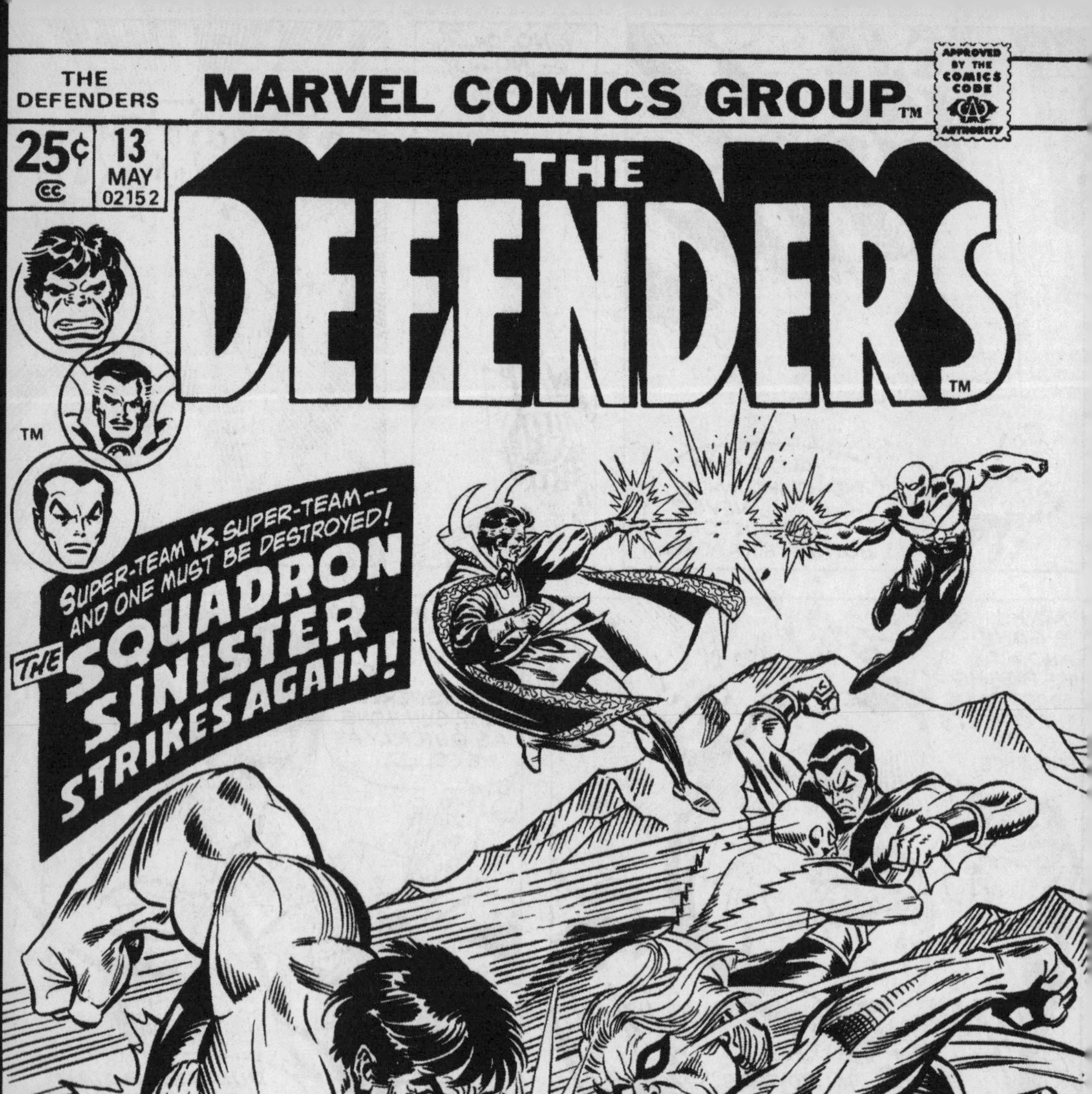
THE DEFENDERS
MARVEL COMICS GROUP™
APPROVED BY THE COMICS CODE AUTHORITY
25¢
13 MAY 02152
THE DEFENDERS™
™
SUPER-TEAM VS. SUPER-TEAM--AND ONE MUST BE DESTROYED!
THE SQUADRON SINISTER STRIKES AGAIN!

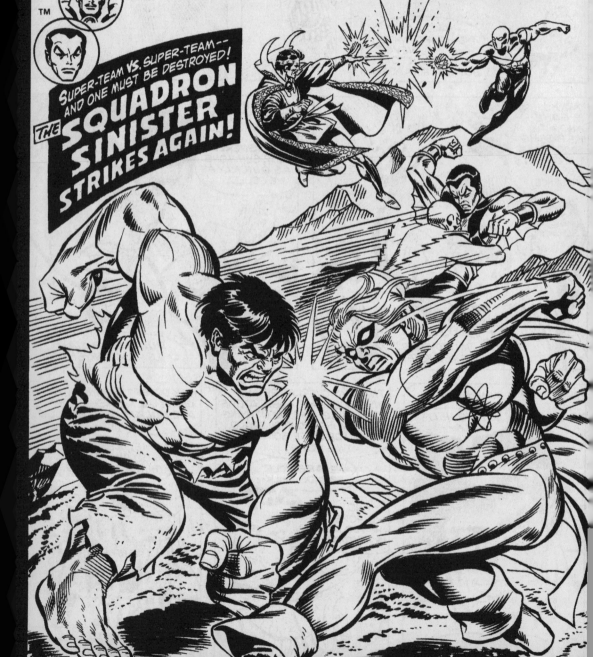

STan Lee PRESENTS: THE DYNAMIC DEFENDERS! ™

LEN WEIN / SAL BUSCEMA / KLAUS JANSON / GLYNIS WEIN, colorist / ROY THOMAS
WRITER   ARTIST   INKER   JOHN COSTANZA, letterer   EDITOR

FOR SALE: ONE PLANET.. SLIGHTLY USED!

GREENWICH VILLAGE: THE NEIGHBORHOOD'S GAINED QUITE A REPUTATION OVER THE YEARS. FIRST, AS THE HOME OF THE FILTHY RICH; THE DELANCYS, THE BREVOORTS, THE BAYARDS--

THEN, AS THE SANCTUARY OF THE ARTIST, THE WRITER; FROM HOMER AND TWAIN TO O'NEILL AND ST. VINCENT MILLAY-- LATELY, AS THE STOMPING GROUND OF THE BOHEMIAN, THE BEATNIK, THE HIPPIE, THE...

OH, LEST WE FORGET, IT IS ALSO THE HOME OF ONE STEPHEN STRANGE, MASTER OF THE MYSTIC ARTS-- AND 'TIS HIS SANCTUM SANCTORUM A MYSTERIOUS HAWK-CLOAKED FIGURE WATCHES SO INTENTLY THIS NIGHT...

A FASCINATING PEOPLE, THE *JIVARO*. 'TIS SAID THEY COULD SHRINK A *HEAD* IN...

BAH-- HULK DOES NOT CARE ABOUT *HEADS*. HULK WANTS TO HEAR YOU RING FUNNY-LOOKING *BELL* AGAIN.

--THE EVER-LOVIN' *HULK* AND THE VIBRANT *VALKYRIE!*

I'M AFRAID THE HULK IS *RIGHT,* STEPHEN. THIS EVENING HAS BEEN-- *INFORMATIVE*--

--BUT A *TRIFLE* ON THE *QUIET* SIDE, IF YOU *UNDERSTAND* MY MEANING.

AND IF THAT ISN'T A PERFECT *CUE,* MARVELITE--

--WE DON'T KNOW *WHAT* IS.

THWOOM!

FORGIVE THE SUDDEN *INTRUSION*--

--BUT I'VE GOT *BUSINESS* WITH YOU PEOPLE THAT JUST WON'T *WAIT* ANY LONGER.

THIS IS *MAGICIAN'S* HOUSE, BIRD-NOSE. YOU DON'T *BELONG* HERE.

GO *AWAY*--

--OR HULK WILL *MAKE* YOU GO AWAY!

YOU'LL HAVE TO *CATCH* ME FIRST, LETTUCE-LIPS--

--AND I DON'T THINK YOU'RE *FAST* ENOUGH TO *DO* THAT!

HUH? WHAT HAPPENED TO *BIRD-NOSE?*

HE WAS RIGHT IN *FRONT* OF HULK--

--AND NOW HE IS *GONE!*

NOT GONE, GREENSKIN-- MERELY RELOCATED.

NOW-- WILL YOU LET ME TALK, OR DO I--

YOU'LL DO WHAT I TELL YOU TO, MISTER--

--ONCE YOU'VE HAD A TASTE OF DRAGONFANG, MY ENCHANTED BLADE!

YOU PEOPLE AREN'T EXACTLY AVID LISTENERS, ARE YOU?

WELL, I HAVE TO TALK--

--AND YOU ARE GONNA LISTEN--

HUH?

"--IF I HAVE TO FLATTEN ALL OF YOU-- THEN SIT ON YOUR CHESTS-- TO MAKE YOU DO IT!"

WHUDD!

FOR A MOMENT, THE VIKING VIXEN IS LOST FROM SIGHT BEHIND THE OVERTURNED COUCH--

--AND IN THAT MOMENT, A GREEN GOLIATH-- MOVES!

IF YOU HURT GIRL, BIRD-NOSE--

--HULK WILL SMASH YOU!

NO, HULK-- WAIT--!

BUT THE LUMBERING BEHEMOTH IS TOO ENRAGED TO HEAR.

GOTTA GIVE YOU CREDIT, GRUESOME--

--YOU'RE PERSISTENT!

STAND STILL, BIRD-NOSE-- AND HULK WILL--

HULK WILL DO *NOTHING,* JADE-JAWS--

--UNLESS YOU THINK YOU HAVE *POWER* ENOUGH TO SUNDER THE *CRIMSON BANDS OF CYTTORAK*--

--AND FRANKLY, HULK--YOU *DON'T!*

FORGIVE THE *SPELL* I CAST, MY FRIEND--BUT I HAD TO PREVENT YOU FROM DOING SOMETHING WE MIGHT *REGRET.*

LET HULK *OUT* OF HERE!

WILL YOU *CALM DOWN* ENOUGH TO HEAR OUR VISITOR OUT?

HULK WILL CALM DOWN--BUT HULK WILL NOT *LIKE* IT!

NO ONE ASKS YOU TO *LIKE* IT, MY FRIEND--JUST *ABIDE* IT.

THUS LET THE CRIMSON BANDS-- *BEGONE!*

MAYBE *THE HULK* HAS CALMED DOWN--

--BUT THE VALKYRIE IS *ENRAGED!*

THEN YOU WILL *QUELL* THAT RAGE, VALKYRIE--AND *QUICKLY!*

WE WILL ALL *LISTEN* TO WHAT OUR MYSTERIOUS VISITOR HAS TO *SAY*--

--AND, HAVING FORCED ME TO STAND AGAINST MY *FRIENDS* AS HE DID--

--WHAT HE HAS TO TELL US HAD BEST BE *GOOD!*

ALL DEPENDS ON YOUR *DEFINITION* OF THE TERM, DOC.

MY NAME IS-- *NIGHTHAWK*--

--AND WHAT I'VE COME TO *WARN* YOU ABOUT IS QUITE POSSIBLY *BEYOND BELIEF!*

"IT STARTED WITH THE *LETTER*--NO RETURN ADDRESS--NO POSTMARK--THAT APPEARED ON MY DESK SIX DAYS AGO--

"--A LETTER WHICH THREATENED TO EXPOSE MY DUAL IDENTITY--UNLESS *NIGHTHAWK* SHOWED UP AT THE *CRAYTON OBSERVATORY* BY TWELVE THAT SAME NIGHT.

"EVEN AS MY HAWK-PLANE'S *VTOL* * JETS LOWERED ME ALMOST SILENTLY TO THE OBSERVATORY'S LAWN, I WONDERED WHAT *AWAITED* ME WITHIN--

"--WHO KNEW ENOUGH ABOUT *NIGHTHAWK'S* BRIEF *CRIMINAL* CAREER ** TO *BLACKMAIL* ME?

*VERTICAL TAKE-OFF AND LANDING.

** AS WITNESSED IN *AVENGERS* #70 & *DAREDEVIL* #62.--RT.

"THE ONLY ONES WHO KNEW ANYTHING *ABOUT* ME WERE THE THREE MEN WHO HAD BEEN MY *PARTNERS*--

"--AND *THEY* WERE ALL *DEAD* OR IN *PRISON* NOW--

"--OR SO I HAD *HOPED!*

I DIDN'T WANT TO *ADMIT* IT--

YOU--!!

--BUT I GUESS THERE WAS NOBODY ELSE IT *COULD* BE!

"THEY SAT AROUND THE TABLE, SMILING *GRIMLY*--

"--AND I GOT THE IMPRESSION THEY REALLY WERE NO HAPPIER TO SEE ME THAN I WAS TO SEE *THEM!*

DON'T STAND THERE *GAWKING,* MAN--*SIT DOWN!*

C'MON, BEAK-FACE-- YOU *HEARD* DR. SPECTRUM. LET'S *MOVE* IT!

THE FOUR OF US HAVE *BUSINESS* TO TAKE CARE OF--

--AS THE *SQUADRON SINISTER!*

BUT, SPECTRUM, WHAT ARE YOU *DOING* HERE--WITH YOUR POWER PRISM *INTACT?*

I READ IT WAS *DESTROYED* WEEKS AGO WHEN YOU BATTLED *IRON MAN* IN DETROIT! *

* A CONFLICT RECOUNTED IN *IRON MAN #63-66.*--OL'RASCALLY.

THEN YOU SHOULD LEARN NOT TO *BELIEVE* ALL YOU READ, NIGHTHAWK.

WHIZZER-- DO YOU NOT *AGREE?*

SURE, DOC. TOO MUCH *READING* IS BAD FOR THE *EYES!*

WHIZZER, YOU'RE A WISE-MOUTH *JACKASS!*

BUT *YOU,* HYPERION--

--*YOU* WERE IMPRISONED IN A SMALL GLASS *GLOBE* ✳ WHEN LAST I SAW YOU! *HOW--*

* COMPLIMENTS OF THE MIGHTY *THOR* IN *AVENGERS #70.*--RT.

HOW DID I *ESCAPE,* NIGHTHAWK? I ESCAPED AS ALL THE *OTHERS* DID!

WE HAD *HELP,* MISTER--HELP LIKE YOU COULDN'T *IMAGINE!*

"SUDDENLY, ALMOST AS IF IN *RESPONSE* TO HYPERION'S *CRYPTIC* COMMENT, A *BLINDING* BURST OF *LIGHT* ERUPTED IN THE ROOM--

"-- AND WHEN THE BRILLIANCE FADED, WE FOUR WERE NO LONGER *ALONE.*

"BEFORE US STOOD A BEING SO *AWESOME,* HE SEEMED NOT SO MUCH *HUMAN* AS HE DID *HEAVEN* IN THE SHAPE OF A *MAN*--

"--AND HE SPOKE IN A VOICE LIKE THE RINGING OF A THOUSAND CRYSTAL *GONGS...*

WHO SUMMONS *NEBULON?*

WHO CALLS *THE CELESTIAL MAN* FROM THE PLACE BEYOND THE SKY?

HEY, WAIT JUST ONE *MINUTE*, CHUMS.

I DON'T KNOW WHAT'S *GOING ON* AROUND HERE--BUT I DON'T *LIKE* IT!

JUST WHO IS THIS *NEBULON* CHARACTER, ANYWAY?

FOOL, IT IS *HE* WHO RESTORED MY *POWER PRISM* TO ME--*MINUS* ITS MOST IRRITATING *PERSONALITY!*

AND HE'S THE ONE WHO RELEASED *ME* FROM MY GLASS PRISON-- THEN GAVE ME BACK MY *SUPER-POWERS!*

WHAT HE *IS*, BEAK-FACE IS A *GODSEND!*

WITH *NEBULON* BESIDE US, THERE IS NOTHING WE CAN'T *ATTEMPT* --NOTHING WE CAN'T *SUCCEED* IN!

SURE -- AND WHAT'S *HIS* CUT OF THE ACTION?

I DON'T CARE IF HE COMES FROM *OUTER SPACE* -- OR *OUTER MONGOLIA* --

NOBODY DOES ALL THAT YOU SAY *HE* DID WITHOUT EXPECTING *SOMETHING* IN RETURN!

DON'T YOU WORRY ABOUT *THAT*, FRIEND --

-- NEBULON HAS ALREADY *GOTTEN* WHAT HE'S ASKED FOR!

YOU SEE, OLD "BUDDY"! IN RETURN FOR NEBULON'S *SERVICES* --

-- I'VE *SOLD* HIM THE PLANET *EARTH!*

HO-KAY, THAT *DOES* IT! WHATEVER YOU GUYS HAVE *PLANNED*, YOU CAN LEAVE ME *OUT* OF IT!

I'M NOT WORKING WITH A BUNCH OF *YO-YOS*!

"BUT AS I TURNED TO GO...

HUMAN, NEBULON WISHES YOU TO *STAY*!

"--AND NEBULON WAS A HARD MAN TO *ARGUE* WITH.

HUH? I CAN'T-- *MOVE*!

AND YOU *WON'T* MOVE-- UNTIL YOU AGREE TO *JOIN* US.

WE MAY NOT *LIKE* YOU, BEAK-FACE-- BUT WE *NEED* YOU.

WELL, NIGHTHAWK-- WHAT DO YOU *SAY*?

WHAT *CAN* I SAY? I'LL *STAY*.

THEN YOU MAY *MOVE*!

OKAY, NOW THAT I'M *INVOLVED* IN THIS *MESS*-- EXACTLY WHAT *SORT* OF MESS IS IT?

WHAT DO YOU NEED *NIGHT-HAWK* FOR THAT THE THREE OF YOU CAN'T DO WITH YOUR *SUPER-POWERS*?

BASICALLY, IT'S VERY *SIMPLE*...

"OH, IT WAS *SIMPLE*, AL'RIGHT. IT WAS ALSO THE MOST *COLD-BLOODED* PLAN I'D EVER HEARD..."

I LISTENED *INTENTLY* AS HYPERION EXPLAINED, BUT EVEN THEN--

--I KNEW I COULD NOT GO *THRU* WITH IT!

I HAD TO GET *OUT*-- TO *WARN* SOMEONE-- BUT I WAS NEEDED TO HELP *CONSTRUCT* THE SQUADRON'S *WEAPON*--

--UNTIL *TONIGHT!*

"*SLIPPING* OUT OF THE OBSERVATORY ON SOME *PRETEXT,* I HEADED FOR THE ONE PLACE I FIGURED TO FIND *HELP*--

--AVENGERS' *MANSION*--

--"BUT MY '*PARTNERS*' HAD BEEN THINKING ONE JUMP *AHEAD* OF ME.

"*FEARING* THE ASSEMBLERS MIGHT *INTERFERE* BEFORE THEY COULD ACTIVATE THEIR PLAN, THE SQUAD HAD ARRANGED-- VIA *NEBULON*--TO BECOME *INVISIBLE* AND IN- *TANGIBLE* IF THE AVENGERS CAME TOO *NEAR*--

"--SO, DESPERATELY 'THOUGH I *TRIED,* I COULDN'T *IN-TERRUPT* CAPTAIN AMERICA'S CONVERSATION--

--AND MAYBE THAT'S JUST AS *WELL*-- 'CAUSE CAP WAS TALKING ABOUT *YOU*--

--ABOUT HOW THE *DEFENDERS* HAD HELPED SAVE THE WORLD FROM *LOKI* AND *DORMAMMU**--

IN CASE YOU HAVEN'T *GUESSED* BY NOW-- THAT'S WHY I CAME *HERE!*

* AS ACCOUNTED IN MORE ISSUES OF *AVENGERS* AND *DEFENDERS* THAN WE WANT TO *THINK* ABOUT.
      --EXHAUSTED ROY.

WHY? SO YOU COULD USE SOME *TRICK* EXPLOSIVE TO BLOW DOWN STEPHEN'S *FRONT DOOR?*

I *TRIED* SEEING YOU A FEW HOURS EARLIER, IN *DISGUISE*-- BUT YOU WEREN'T *HERE.* *

THIS TIME I HAD TO BE *SURE* YOU'D HEAR ME OUT!

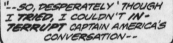

AND SO WE *HAVE,* NIGHTHAWK-- BUT STILL WE DO NOT KNOW THE MOST *IMPORTANT* POINT--

EXACTLY WHAT *IS* THE SQUADRON SINISTER'S *PLAN?*

IT'S PART OF THEIR *DEAL* WITH THE CELESTIAL MAN. HAVING *SOLD* HIM THE *EARTH,* THEY'VE PROMISED TO DELIVER IT PRECISELY THE WAY HE *WANTS* IT--

--AND HE WANTS IT-- *UNDERWATER!*

* OKAY, FAITHFUL ONE-- IF YOU GUESSED THAT WAS *NIGHTHAWK* IN THE TRENCH COAT LAST ISH, TAKE A *GIANT STEP* FORWARD. -- RT.

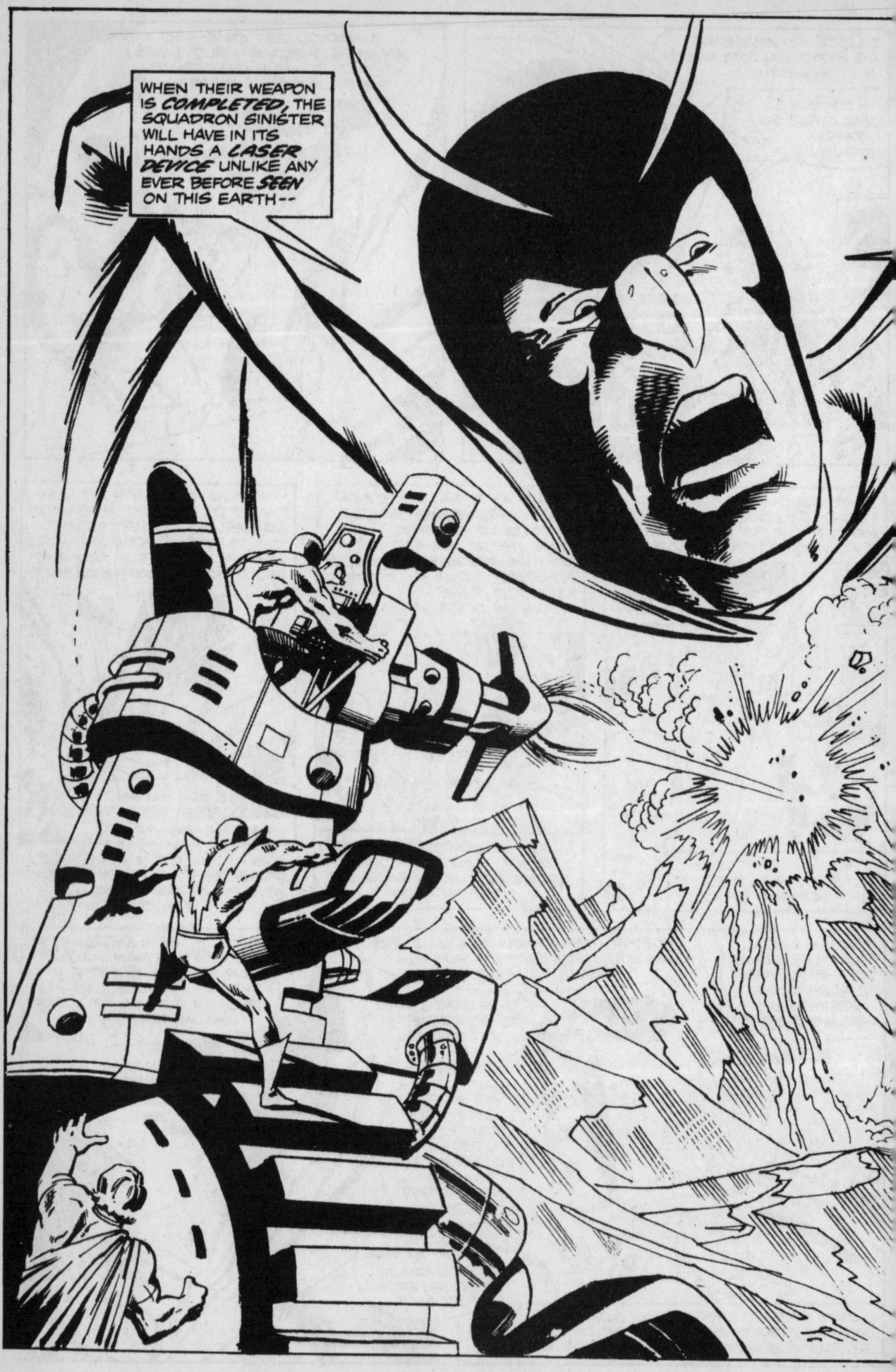
WHEN THEIR WEAPON IS COMPLETED, THE SQUADRON SINISTER WILL HAVE IN ITS HANDS A LASER DEVICE UNLIKE ANY EVER BEFORE SEEN ON THIS EARTH--

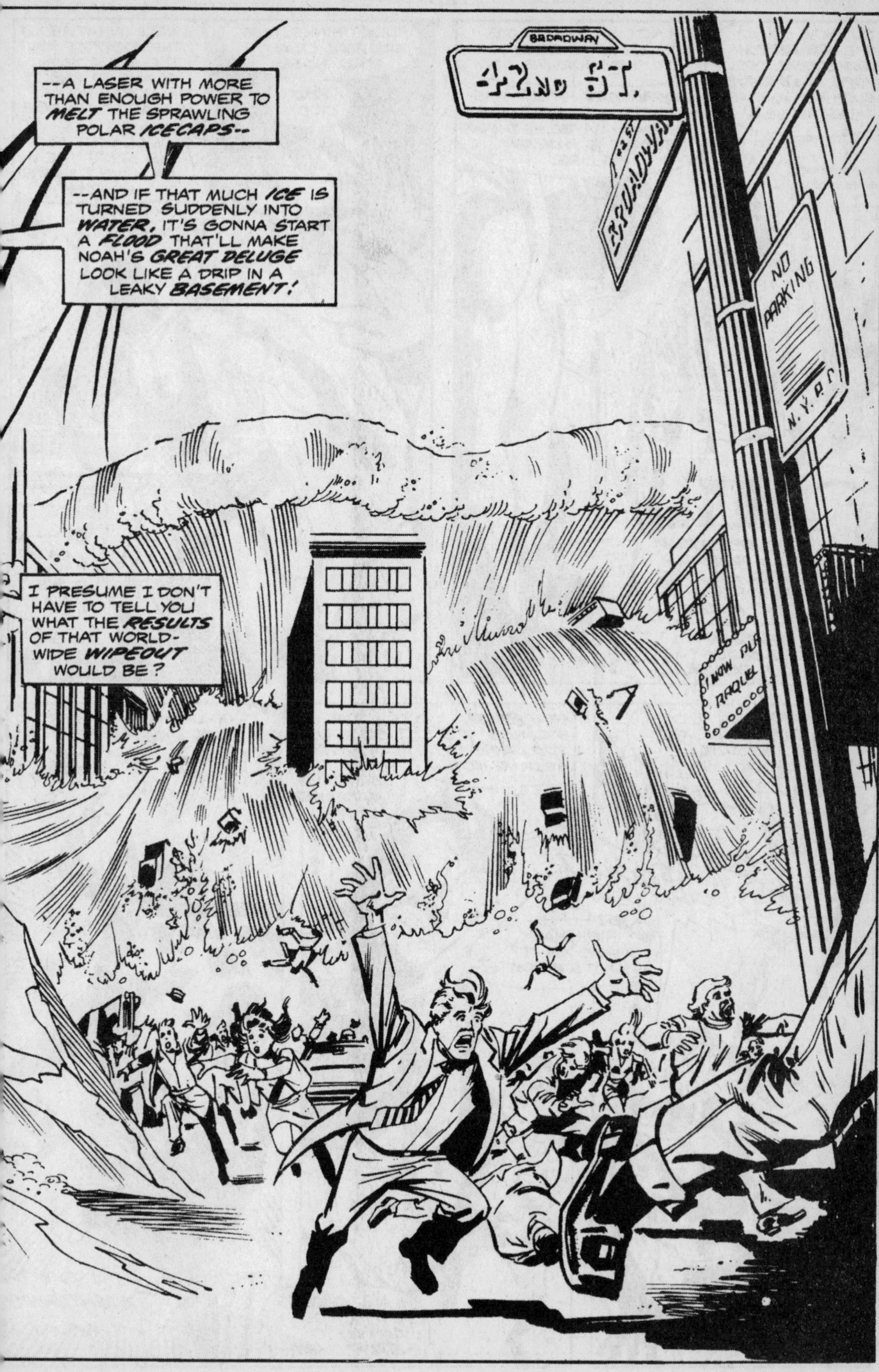
--A LASER WITH MORE THAN ENOUGH POWER TO MELT THE SPRAWLING POLAR ICECAPS--
--AND IF THAT MUCH ICE IS TURNED SUDDENLY INTO WATER, IT'S GONNA START A FLOOD THAT'LL MAKE NOAH'S GREAT DELUGE LOOK LIKE A DRIP IN A LEAKY BASEMENT!
I PRESUME I DON'T HAVE TO TELL YOU WHAT THE RESULTS OF THAT WORLD-WIDE WIPEOUT WOULD BE?
BROADWAY
42ND ST.
NO PARKING
N.Y.P.D.

BUT HOW COULD THE *SQUADRON SINISTER* ITSELF HOPE TO *SURVIVE* SUCH A PLANETARY CATASTROPHE?

I'M NOT ALL THAT SURE THEY *CARE* WHETHER OR NOT THEY SURVIVE, DOC. *HYPERION* HATES THIS WORLD FOR DESTROYING HIS OWN. MAYBE HE THINKS REVENGE IS *WORTH* HIS LIFE.

DOC SPECTRUM WOULD PROBABLY PREFER *KILLING* THE EARTH IF HE CAN'T *RULE* IT.

AND *WHIZZER*-- I THINK HE'S JUST FLAT-OUT *CRAZY!*

HULK THINKS THEY ARE *ALL* CRAZY, BIRD-NOSE. *YOU* TOO.

WELL, WHAT ABOUT THE *REST* OF YOU? THE SQUADRON PLANS TO *MELT* THE NORTH POLAR ICECAP AT *SUNRISE.*

WILL YOU HELP ME *STOP* THEM-- OR HAVE I WASTED MY *TIME?*

AND THIS PLANET'S *LIFE!*

OF *COURSE* WE'LL JOIN YOU, NIGHTHAWK-- BUT THERE ARE *STILL* THINGS WE MUST--

AARRGGH!

NIGHTHAWK, WHAT *IS* IT? WHAT'S *WRONG*..?

STAY *BACK*, STRANGE! IT'S *TOO LATE* TO HELP ME NOW--!

THE SQUADRON'S *FOUND* ME--! THEY KNOW I'VE *BETRAYED* THEM--

-- AND THERE'S NOTHING YOU CAN DO TO *STOP* THEM--

-- FROM HAVING THEIR *REVENGEEEEEEE!!*

NIGHTHAWK!!

STEPHEN, HE--HE'S GONE!

AYE, VALKYRIE-- HE SACRIFICED HIMSELF THAT EARTH MIGHT LIVE.

HE TRUSTED US--

--AND 'TIS A TRUST WE MUST NOT BETRAY!

THEN COME, STEPHEN! PERHAPS WE CAN REACH THE POLAR ICECAP BEFORE THE SQUADRON SINISTER.

IN A MOMENT, VALKYRIE.

A MENACE OF SUCH MAGNITUDE CALLS FOR NO LESS THAN A FULL COMPANY OF DEFENDERS--

--THUS, WITH THE AID OF THE ETERNAL VISHANTI, I SEND MY MIND CASTING OUTWARD--

"--TO SUMMON THE ONE WE REQUIRE!"

INSTANTANEOUSLY, THE SUPREME SORCERER'S MENTAL IMAGE SKITTERS AROUND THE EARTH--

--TO APPEAR IN MID-ATLANTIC, ABOVE THE FLOATING FORTRESS CALLED HYDRO-BASE--

--AND BEFORE A MOST IMPATIENT AVENGING SON--

I CARE NOT WHY YOU NEED ME, STRANGE--

--FOR I WILL NOT COME!

THE FATE OF THIS VERY PLANET DOES NOT CONCERN YOU, NAMOR?

MY CONCERN IS HERE-- WITH THE AMPHIBIANS WHO'VE COME TO DEPEND UPON ME!

I CARE NOT AT ALL WHAT HAPPENS TO THOSE SELF-SERVING MANIACS WHO DWELL UPON THE SURFACE!

I TRULY AM SORRY YOU FEEL THAT WAY, SUB-MARINER-- FOR I DO CARE-- DEEPLY--

--AND IT SEEMS YOU LEAVE ME NO OTHER CHOICE BUT-- THIS!

WHAT--? SOME MYSTIC FORCE IMPRISONS ME--!

STRANGE, RELEASE ME! I DEMAND YOU--

POOF!

--RELEASE--

--ME--?

WELCOME, NAMOR.

FORGIVE MY MANNER OF *BRINGING* YOU HERE-- BUT I FEAR YOUR *ATTITUDE* MADE IT *NECESSARY.*

YOU *KIDNAPPED* ME-- AGAINST MY OWN *WILL*?

SORCERER, I'LL MAKE YOU *RUE* THE DAY YOU FIRST HEARD MY *NAME!*

SEA PRINCE, I'VE NO WISH TO *FIGHT* YOU--BUT IF I *MUST*-- EH?

NAMOR, PLEASE-- *WAIT!* HEAR ME OUT BEFORE YOU *STRIKE!*

THE VALKYRIE'S WORDS ARE SLOW, DELIBERATE, AS SHE RETELLS THE NIGHTHAWK'S GRIM *TALE* -- AND WHEN, AT LAST, SHE IS *FINISHED*--

NOW DO YOU UNDERSTAND WHY WE *BROUGHT* YOU HERE, NAMOR?

IF THE SQUADRON SINISTER IS PERMITTED TO *COMPLETE* ITS OPERATION, ALL *LIFE* ON EARTH-- *ATLANTEAN* INCLUDED-- IS CERTAIN TO *PERISH!*

I SEE YOUR *POINT,* VAL--

--AND, THOUGH IT *PAINS* ME TO DO SO, I'M FORCED TO *AGREE.*

THUS, THOUGH I OWE THE SURFACE WORLD NOTHING BUT *LOATH-ING*--

--NAMOR THE FIRST WILL STAND AT YOUR SIDE *AGAINST* THE SQUADRON SINISTER!

GOOD, HULK WOULD NOT HAVE LIKED *SMASHING* FISH-MAN--

--EVEN IF FISH-MAN *DOES* WEAR FUNNY NEW CLOTHES.

YES, NAMOR, ABOUT YOUR NEW *OUTFIT*--?

IT IS A LONG, *UNPLEASANT* STORY, VAL-- ONE I WOULD RATHER *NOT* GO INTO HERE.

NOW *COME!* WE HAVE A *JOB* TO DO *ELSEWHERE!*

DAWN IN THE ARCTIC: WHITE UPON WHITE, STREAKED WITH BANNERS OF GOLD AND VERMILION--

--AND, THIS MORNING, DOTTED WITH A HANDFUL OF HUMANOID SHAPES-- THE DYNAMIC *DEFENDERS!*

VIGILANTLY, ACROSS THE VAST EXPANSE OF *IVORY,* THEY SOAR--

--UNTIL THE SUB-MARINER'S SEA-SHARP EYES *ESPY*--

SOMETHING *MOVING* ON THE GLACIER BELOW US--!

NOT JUST *"SOMETHING",* NAMOR-- SPECIFICALLY, THE SQUADRON SINISTER!

C'MON, SPECTRUM-- CAN'T YOU MOVE ANY *FASTER?*

YOU EXPECT TO HOLD THIS BLASTED *LASER* UP ALL DAY?

PATIENCE, HYPERION. MY *POWER PRISM* CAN ONLY DO SO MUCH AT *ONE* TIME.

YOU'LL *ALL* BE DOING TIME, *"PARTNERS"*-- --ONCE I BREAK OUT OF THIS ROTTEN *FORCE-GLOBE* AND GET MY *HANDS* ON YOU!

G'WAN, CHUMP-- TALK AS *BIG* AS YOU WANT-- --'CAUSE YOU AIN'T GOT A *SNOWBALL'S CHANCE* OF BREAKING NEBULON'S *GLOBE--* AN' YOU *KNOW* IT!

AN' EVEN IF YOU *DID* BREAK FREE, WE GOT YOU SO FAR *OUT-NUMBERED,* IT'S--

UH-OH,

HEADS UP, SQUAD! WE GOT *COMPANY!*

THERE THEY *ARE,* DEFENDERS!

CHOOSE YOUR *OPPONENTS--* AND *STRIKE!*

STOP *TALKING,* MAGICIAN-- AND PUT HULK *DOWN!*

HULK WANTS TO *SMASH!*

PUT DOWN *MACHINE*, MASKED MAN-- AND *FIGHT*-- --OR HULK WILL *SQUASH* YOU WHERE YOU STAND!

UH-UH, UGLY! IF THERE'S ANY *SQUASHING* TO DO AROUND HERE--

--*HYPERION* IS GONNA BE THE ONE TO *DO* IT!

AARRRGH!

MASKED MAN IS *STRONG*-- ALMOST AS STRONG AS HULK!

WHADDAYA MEAN-- "*ALMOST*"? ANYONE WHO CAN WITH-STAND THE HAMMER OF *THOR* LIKE I CAN HAS TO BE THE *STRONGEST* MAN THERE IS!

NO-- HULK IS *STRONGER!*

HULK IS STRONGER THAN *ANY-ONE*-- THAN *ANYTHING*--

THEN YOU'RE JUST *ASKING* FOR THIS, UGLY!

--AND HULK WILL *PROVE* IT!

THEY MEET WITH AN IMPACT THAT RADIATES STAGGERING *SHOCK WAVES*-- THAT CAUSES THE GROUND BENEATH THEM TO *SHUDDER* VIOLENTLY--

--AND COUNT-LESS MILES AWAY, GEOLOGISTS LOOK TO THEIR *SEISMOGRAPHS* --THEN SHAKE THEIR HEADS IN *DISBELIEF.*

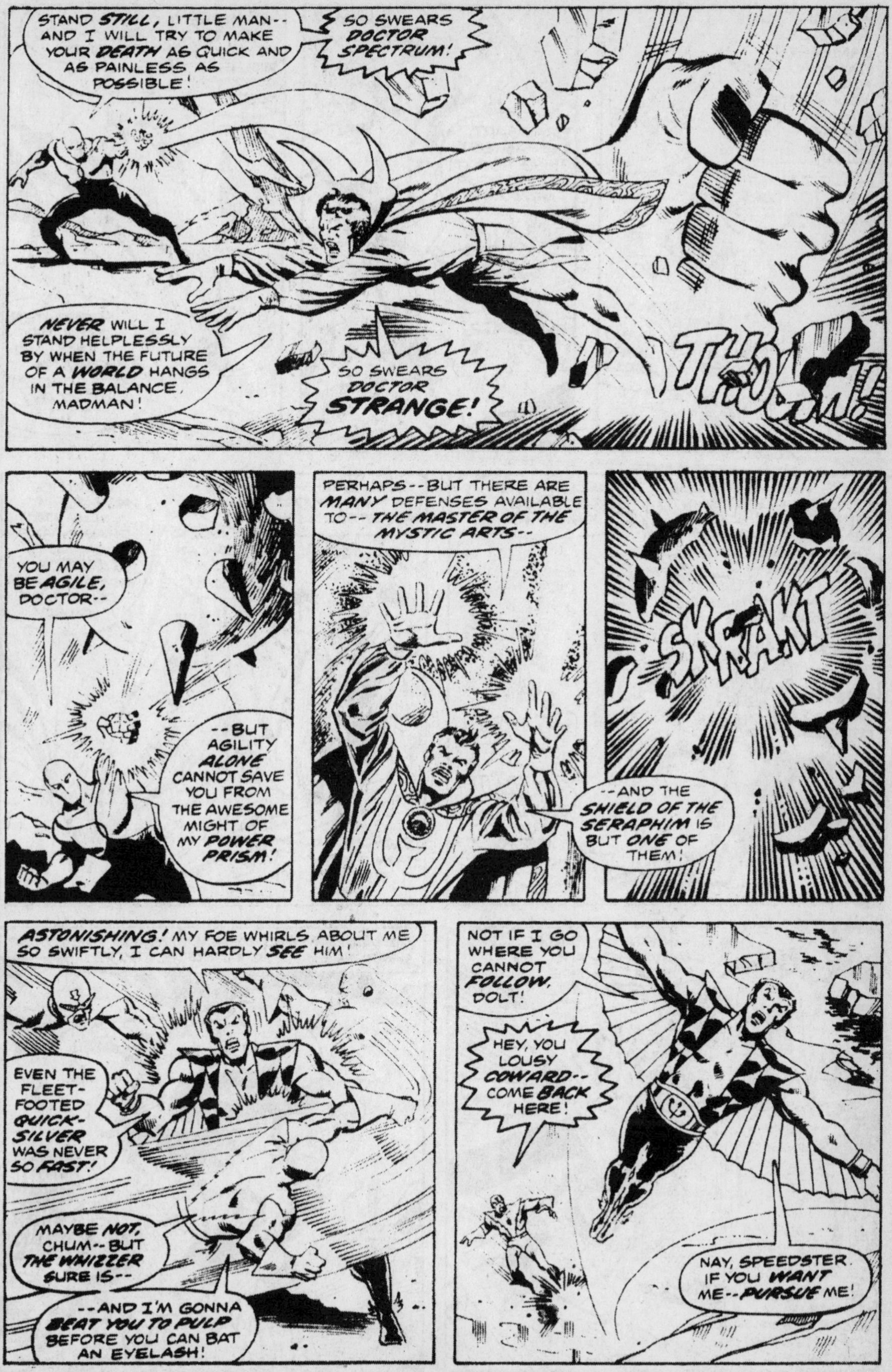
STAND STILL, LITTLE MAN-- AND I WILL TRY TO MAKE YOUR DEATH AS QUICK AND AS PAINLESS AS POSSIBLE!
SO SWEARS DOCTOR SPECTRUM!
NEVER WILL I STAND HELPLESSLY BY WHEN THE FUTURE OF A WORLD HANGS IN THE BALANCE, MADMAN!
SO SWEARS DOCTOR STRANGE!
THOOM!
YOU MAY BE AGILE, DOCTOR--
--BUT AGILITY ALONE CANNOT SAVE YOU FROM THE AWESOME MIGHT OF MY POWER PRISM!
PERHAPS--BUT THERE ARE MANY DEFENSES AVAILABLE TO-- THE MASTER OF THE MYSTIC ARTS--
--AND THE SHIELD OF THE SERAPHIM IS BUT ONE OF THEM!
SKRAKT
ASTONISHING! MY FOE WHIRLS ABOUT ME SO SWIFTLY, I CAN HARDLY SEE HIM!
EVEN THE FLEET-FOOTED QUICK-SILVER WAS NEVER SO FAST!
MAYBE NOT, CHUM--BUT THE WHIZZER SURE IS--
--AND I'M GONNA BEAT YOU TO PULP BEFORE YOU CAN BAT AN EYELASH!
NOT IF I GO WHERE YOU CANNOT FOLLOW, DOLT!
HEY, YOU LOUSY COWARD-- COME BACK HERE!
NAY, SPEEDSTER. IF YOU WANT ME--PURSUE ME!

PURSUE YOU? FIN-FACE, I CAN PASS YOU--SO FAST YOU'D THINK YOU WERE STANDING STILL--

--BUT I DON'T WANT TO PASS YOU, I WANT TO CATCH YOU--

--AND WHEN I DO--

WHA--?

BRAGGART, THE FASTEST THING ABOUT YOU IS YOUR MOUTH!

YOU WERE HIDING BEHIND THE RIDGE-- WAITING FOR ME!

IT WAS ALL A TRICK--! IT'S NOT FAIR!

SPEEDSTER, I'D HAVE THOUGHT "FAIR" TO BE A CONCEPT QUITE ALIEN TO YOU.

EH? THE SPEEDSTER TWISTS HIS BODY IN MID-AIR--REGAINING HIS FOOTING--NEGATING THE FORCE OF MY THROW--

--AND NOW HE RUSHES TOWARDS ME AT BLINDING SPEED--!

AND WHEN I REACH YOU, FISH-MAN--

--YOU'RE NOT GONNA HAVE TIME TO REGRET IT!

C'MON, LADY--VALKYRIE-- GET ME OUTTA THIS BLASTED GLOWBALL!

YOUR PALS CAN USE MY HELP!

THERE IS NOTHING MY ENCHANTED DRAGONFANG CANNOT CLEAVE! A MOMENT--AND YOU WILL BE FREE!

DON'T SAY IT, SWEETHEART-- DO IT!

THAN STAND BACK, CHAUVINIST--AND LET THE VALKYRIE STRIKE!

THRANG!

GOOD SHOT, SISTER-- EXCEPT THAT IT'S NOT DOING ANYTHING!

THE REMAINING DEFENDERS, ON THE OTHER HAND, SEEM TO BE DOING PLENTY...

PUNY MASKED MAN, HULK TOLD YOU HE WAS THE STRONGEST ONE OF ALL!

TH--OOM!

ONE AFTER ANOTHER, TO RISE NO MORE, THESE SINISTER SQUADSMEN *FALL*--

--BEFORE BRUTE FORCE-- SORCEROUS INCANTATION--

BY THE *VAPORS* OF *VALTOR*, I COMMAND YOU-- *SLEEP!*

--AND THE FURY OF RIGHTEOUS *ANGER*--

I'VE HEARD *ENOUGH* FROM YOU, *SPEEDSTER!* *AWAY* FROM ME, I SAY-- *NOW!*

--BUT 'TIS A *VICTORY* NOT LONG RETAINED-- FOR *SUDDENLY*--

BY *NEPTUNE'S TRIDENT!*

HULK IS *TRAPPED* IN FUNNY GLOBE-- WITH FISH-MAN, GIRL, AND MAGICIAN-- BUT *HOW*--?

'TIS AN *ENERGY-GLOBE*, MY EMERALD FRIEND-- SUCH AS THAT WHICH SURROUNDS THE *NIGHT-HAWK!*

IT SEEMS WE'VE *ALL* BECOME PRISONERS OF--

SILENCE, HUMANS--AND NEBULON WILL BE *LENIENT* WITH YOU!

I HAVE NO WISH TO *HARM* YOU--UNLESS I AM *FORCED* TO!

THEN LET HULK OUT OF FUNNY *BALL*, GOLD-FACE-- AND HULK WILL *SMASH* YOU!

TO PROTECT OUR *PLANET*, ALIEN--SO SAY WE *ALL!*

THEN YOU LEAVE ME NO OTHER *CHOICE*, YOU FOOLISH HUMANS--

--EXCEPT TO *DESTROY* YOU ALL!

NEXT: "...AND *WHO* SHALL INHERIT THE EARTH?"

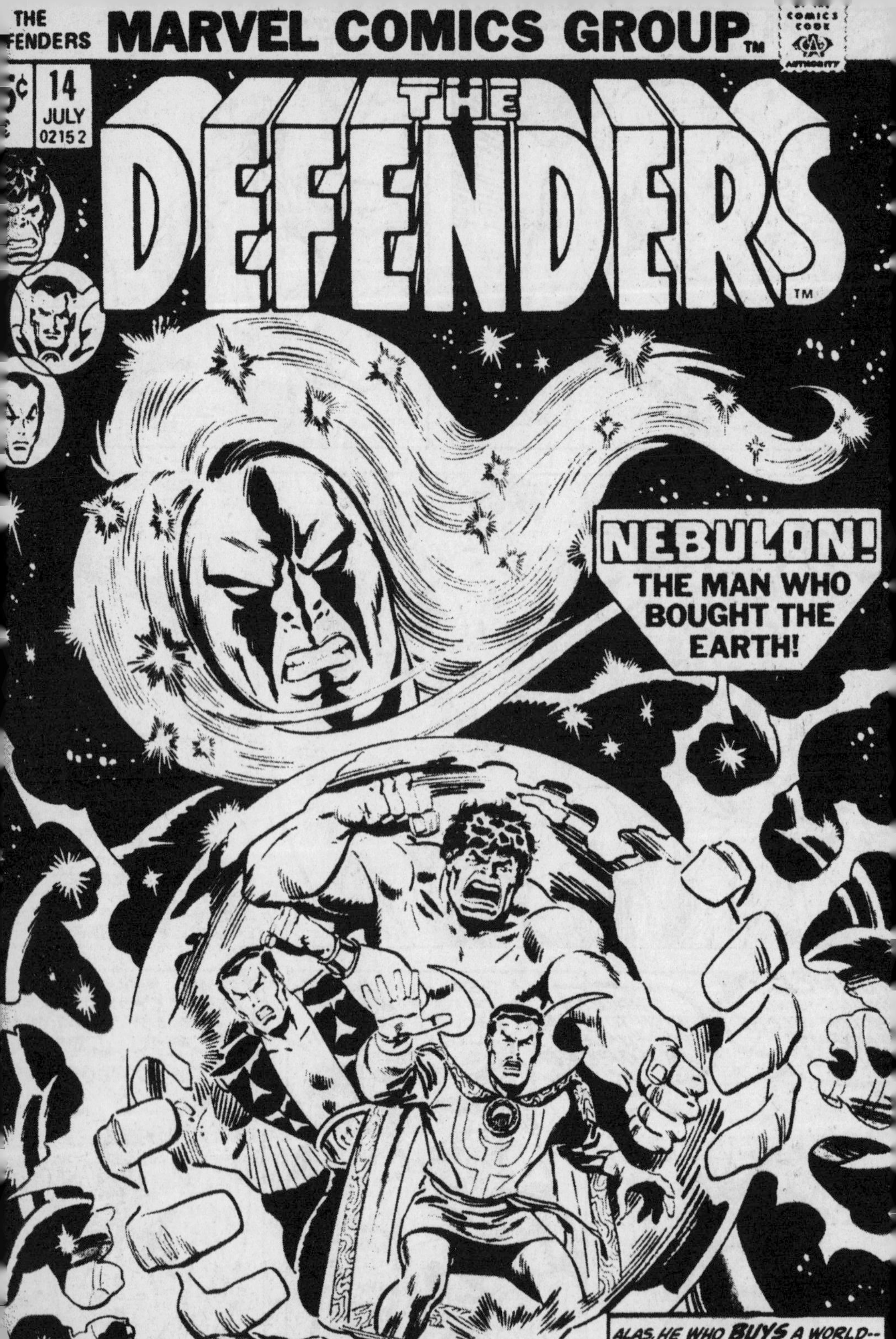
THE DEFENDERS
MARVEL COMICS GROUP
COMICS CODE AUTHORITY
14
JULY
02152
THE DEFENDERS
NEBULON!
THE MAN WHO BOUGHT THE EARTH!
ALAS, HE WHO BUYS A WORLD-- MAY ALSO DESTROY IT!!

STAN LEE PRESENTS: **THE DYNAMIC DEFENDERS!**™

LEN WEIN * SAL BUSCEMA & DAN GREEN * GLYNIS WEIN, COLORIST * ROY THOMAS * IRVING FORBUSH
WRITER — ARTISTS — ARTIE SIMEK, LETTERER — EDITOR — KIBITZER

AND WHO? SHALL INHERIT THE EARTH?

ATTENTION! THE PLANET SOL-III (CALLED EARTH), HAVING BEEN DULY PURCHASED BY ONE NEBULON (CALLED THE CELESTIAL MAN), FROM ITS PREVIOUS OWNERS HYPERION, DOCTOR SPECTRUM AND THE WHIZZER (CALLED THE SQUADRON SINISTER), MUST BE EVACUATED IMMEDIATELY! WOULD ALL 3½ BILLION PREVIOUS TENANTS PLEASE COLLECT ANY NECESSARY BELONGINGS AND REPORT TO THE CORNER OF MADISON AVENUE AND 57TH STREET FOR REMOVAL TO NEW QUARTERS! THIS HAS BEEN A PUBLIC SERVICE ANNOUNCEMENT.

NEBULON, I DEMAND YOU RELEASE US-- OR SUFFER THE CONSEQUENCES!

WELL, MARVELITE, IT APPEARS THE SQUADRON SINISTER HAS PULLED OFF THE GREATEST SWINDLE SINCE SOMEBODY SOLD THE BROOKLYN BRIDGE TO A BAND OF DESERT NOMADS--

--UNLESS, OF COURSE, THE FOUR STALWART DEFENDERS IMPRISONED IN THE ENERGY GLOBE ABOVE CAN DO SOMETHING TO STOP THEM!

BUT JUST TO BE ON THE SAFE SIDE, TIGER--YOU'D BETTER START PACKING, ANYWAY!

RELEASE YOU, HUMAN? WHY SHOULD I PERMIT YOU TO CAUSE ME *FURTHER* INCONVENIENCE?

ALREADY YOU'VE *DISABLED* THOSE WHO SOUGHT TO *HASTEN* MY *POSSESSION* OF THIS *MISERABLE* WORLD*--

*IN A BATTLE ROYAL LAST ISH. --ROY.

--SO I SEE NO REASON WHY I SHOULD NOT *HASTEN* YOUR *ELIMINATION* IN TURN--!

NO, NEBULON-- *WAIT!*

WHAT--?

SO, HYPERION-- AT LAST YOU *AWAKEN!*

BUT WHY DO YOU SEEK TO *DELAY* THESE HUMANS' *DESTRUCTION?*

BECAUSE THE *TIMING* ISN'T RIGHT, NEBULON-- NOT *RIGHT* AT ALL!

KILL THEM *NOW* AND ALL WE HAVE ARE FOUR IGNORANT *CORPSES* WHO'LL NEVER KNOW *WHY* THEY WASTED THEIR LIVES--

AND WHAT DIFFERENCE IS THAT TO *US?*

YEAH, MUSCLES-- DOC SPECTRUM IS *RIGHT.* JUST KNOCK 'EM OFF AND BE *DONE* WITH IT!

NO, WHIZZER-- THEY MUST KNOW *WHY* THEY DIE-- AND WHAT THEIR *FAILURE* MEANS TO THE *FUTURE* OF YOUR WORLD!

YES, FOOLS, I SAID *YOUR* WORLD...NOT *MINE!*

"*MY* WORLD WAS AN *ATOM*...TOO SMALL FOR MAN TO *SEE*...

"...BUT *NOT* SMALL ENOUGH TO ESCAPE BEING THE *FIRST* ATOM SPLIT BY A MAN-MADE *CYCLOTRON!*

"SOMEHOW, I *SURVIVED*...DRIFTED UNCONSCIOUS IN THE *ATOMIC VOID*, TILL ONE DAY I WAS *AWAKENED*...*ENLARGED*...BY THE GAMES-PLAYING *GRAND-MASTER*...

"...ENLARGED TO BATTLE THE AVENGER CALLED *THOR* IN A CONTEST TO DETERMINE THE *FATE* OF YOUR WORLD!

"AT FIRST, MY ATOMIC POWERS PLAYED *HAVOC* WITH THE ASGARDIAN...

"...BUT, AT LAST, HIS MYSTIC HAMMER *MJOLNIR* WAS BROUGHT INTO PLAY...

"...WHIRLING AROUND ME AT SUPER-SPEED...CREATING AN ELECTRICALLY-CHARGED *VORTEX*...

"...A VORTEX THAT SOMEHOW *REVERSED* MY ATOMIC ENLARGEMENT...AND IMPRISONED ME INSTEAD IN A BUBBLE OF GLAZED *SAND!*

* THE PRECEDING SEQUENCE COURTESY OF *AVENGERS* #70. --RASCALLY ROY.

"THERE I REMAINED UNTIL THE GRAND-MASTER *DEPARTED* YOUR EARTH...

"...AND THE SUPER-POWERFUL *BACKWASH* OF HIS PASSING SOMEHOW SUCKED ME INTO THE BLACK VOID OF *SPACE!*

"FOR MONTHS, I DRIFTED THRU THAT INTERSTELLAR EMPTINESS, HELPLESS TO *FREE* MYSELF..."

"...HOPING FOR SOME-THING--EVEN THE FINALITY OF *DEATH*--TO *RELEASE* ME FROM MY PRIVATE HELL..."

"...BUT MY HOPES WERE *ANSWERED* IN A FAR LESS *DRASTIC* FASHION..."

WHAT IN--? AN ALIEN STARCRAFT--PASSING NEARBY--!

MUST DO SOMETHING TO ATTRACT ITS ATTENTION OR...

"BUT, APPARENTLY, IT HAD ALREADY *DETECTED* ME... FOR *SUDDENLY*..."

A GRAPPLE-BEAM OF SOME SORT--PULLING ME INTO THE SHIP--!

"AND ONCE I WAS SAFELY *INSIDE*..."

THAT SHADOW--MUST BE THE ONE WHO RESCUED ME--!

HELLO? IS SOMEBODY HERE? IF SO, I ASK YOU TO SHOW YOURSELF--!

THEN HAVE A MOMENT'S PATIENCE, ALIEN!

"AND A MOMENT LATER, A SHIMMERING *CURTAIN* WAS DRAWN ASIDE TO REVEAL..."

ALLOW ME TO RELEASE YOU FROM YOUR STRANGE CONVEYANCE, ALIEN--AND THEN LET US TALK!

"WITH THE GLOBE'S DESTRUC-TION, I INSTANTLY *REGAINED* MY FULL SIZE...THEN, FOR HOURS, NEBULON AND I *TALKED*..."

"...AND WHAT I DIS-COVERED IN THE COURSE OF THAT CONVERSATION PROVED MOST *INTERESTING*, INDEED..."

I AM OF A RACE OF INTER-STELLAR *GEOLOGISTS,* SURVEYING THE COSMOS FOR VARIOUS MATERIALS NEEDED TO INSURE MY HOME WORLD'S CONTINUED EXISTENCE--

--BUT UNLIKE MY *FELLOW* PROSPECTORS, I HAVE BEEN *SINGU-LARLY UNSUCCESSFUL* IN MY ENDEAVORS!

IF I DO NOT DISCOVER A MINERAL-RICH PLANET WITHIN THIRTY GALACTIC UNITS, I SHALL SURELY FALL FROM *GRACE--*

NEBULON-- *WAIT!* YOU SAY YOU NEED A *PLANET?*

--AND AT THIS POINT IN TIME, *SUCCESS* DOES NOT SEEM LIKELY TO...

WELL, I JUST HAPPEN TO *OWN* A BEAUTY!

"I SHOWED HIM *EARTH* THEN... EXTOLED ITS *VIRTUES*... AND AT LENGTH WE STRUCK A *BARGAIN*..."

"...THE MINERAL-RICH *PLANET* NEBULON WANTED...IN EXCHANGE FOR THE *VENGEANCE* I SO DEEPLY CRAVED..."

YOU'RE *MAD,* HYPERION! DESTROY THE EARTH AND YOU SURELY DESTROY *YOURSELVES!*

NOT *SO,* STRANGE-- THERE ARE COUNTLESS OTHER DIMEN-SIONAL WORLDS THAT NEBULON MAY *TRANSPORT* US TO!

WHY DON'T YOU HAVE HIM TRANSPORT YOU UNDER A *ROCK,* UGLY? THAT'S WHERE ALL OF YOU *BELONG!*

AND, IF I WEREN'T *TRAPPED* IN THIS *CURSED GLOBE,* I'D...

ENOUGH, NIGHTHAWK!

SINCE YOU SEEM TO *SHARE* THE VIEWPOINT OF THOSE CALLED THE *DEFENDERS--*

--IT IS ONLY FITTING THAT YOU SHARE THEIR *FATE* AS WELL!

WHAT IN--? I'VE SWITCHED GLOBES!

OKAY, BIG BUDDY--YOU'VE FINISHED *TALKIN'*--SO LET'S GET DOWN TO THE *KILLIN'* ALREADY!

I WANNA SEE THOSE DO-GOODERS *BLEED!*

NO, WHIZZER-- THERE'LL BE *NO* BLOODSHED.

WHADDAYOU-- *KIDDING?* I DIDN'T GET MY *BUTT* KICKED IN FOR *NOTHIN'!*

I SAY WE *WASTE* 'EM!

AND...I...SAY...

NO!

SMAK!

DEATH IS TOO *SWIFT* A PUNISHMENT FOR THESE SO-CALLED *DEFENDERS!* THEY MUST BE MADE TO *SUFFER* AS *I* HAVE SUFFERED--

--MADE TO DRIFT HELPLESSLY THRU SPACE AS *I* DID-- WITHOUT HOPE OF *SALVATION!*

IT IS *DONE,* HYPERION--

--AND I *REMIND* YOU--*TIME* IS GROWING *SHORT!*

THEN LET US GET BACK TO *WORK,* SQUADSMEN --AND *QUICKLY!*

WE STILL HAVE AN ENTIRE *POLAR ICECAP* TO MELT BEFORE NIGHTFALL!

BUT BEFORE YOU FORGET THE NAME OF THIS MAG, MARVELITE--FOLLOW US TO THE VERY EDGE OF SPACE--

--AND WITNESS THE PLIGHT OF THE DEFENDERS...

BAH! HULK IS STRONGEST ONE OF ALL--

--BUT HULK CANNOT BURST BUBBLE!

YOU ARE NOT ALONE, FRIEND. MY POWER IS USELESS AS WELL.

PERHAPS THAT'S BECAUSE YOU'RE GOING ABOUT THIS ALL WRONG, DOCTOR.

WHY DON'T YOU ALL COMBINE YOUR EFFORTS--FOCUS EVERYTHING YOU'VE GOT ON ONE SPOT?

OF COURSE! I'VE BEEN A FOOL!

NO, STRANGE-- YOU'VE MERELY BEEN HUMAN--

--AND THAT IS QUITE ENOUGH.

NO MORE TALK, FISH-MAN! HULK WANTS TO HIT SOMETHING!

THEN, MY FELLOW DEFENDERS, LET US STRIKE--

"NOW!

BWOOM!

STAY CALM, VALKYRIE-- I HAVE YOU.

AND I HAVE ALL THE REST, NAMOR.

STOP SQUIRMING, BIRD-NOSE-- OR HULK WILL DROP YOU.

WE'RE BREATHING-- IN THE ALMOST-AIR-LESS STRATOSPHERE-- BUT HOW--?

A MYSTIC AURA I'VE CONJURED WILL PROVIDE US ALL WITH OXYGEN, NIGHTHAWK-- UNTIL WE RETURN TO EARTH--

--AND THE BATTLE!

THUS, SHORTLY... THE *LASER-CANNON* THAT NIGHTHAWK HELPED DESIGN WORKS *SPLENDIDLY.*

ALMOST A *SHAME* HE ISN'T HERE TO *SEE* IT.

AHH--HE GOT WHAT HE *DESERVED,* SPECTRUM!

WE GAVE HIM HIS CHANCE TO BE ON THE *WINNING* TEAM, BUT HE *BLEW* IT--AND HE *PAID* FOR--*EH?*

THAT *WHOOSHING* NOISE--IT SOUNDS LIKE--

AYE, BLOWHARD-- *THE DEFENDERS ARE BACK!*

AND THIS TIME WE WILL *SMASH* YOU ALL!

AGAIN THOSE ANNOYING DEFENDERS--BUT TIME HAS GROWN TOO *SHORT* TO ALLOW YOU TO DALLY WITH THEM!

TEND TO YOUR *CANNON,* HYPERION, AND I SHALL DEAL WITH THEM ONCE AND FOR ALL!

I DON'T *LIKE* IT, NEBULON-- BUT *YOU'RE* THE BOSS!

TURN BACK, GREEN ONE --OR PERISH!

HAH! GOLD-FACE! CAN'T KILL *HULK!* GOLD-FACE CAN'T EVEN *SHOOT* STRAIGHT!

"BUT STRIKING *YOU* WAS NOT MY PURPOSE, DULL-WITTED ONE!"

HUH? GOLD-FACE'S *RAY*-- TURNING ICE INTO-- *MAN?*

NOT "MAN", HULK--*MONSTER*--WITH A CAPITAL 'M'!

POW!

SPRAK!

THIS *MISSHAPEN* CREATURE MAY TAKE THE *HULK* UNAWARES--

--BUT THE ONE TRUE *SUB-MARINER* IS *ANOTHER* CASE ENTIRELY!

AND SO IS *NIGHTHAWK*, BUDDY!

*B*UT THE HAWK-GARBED ACROBAT DOES *NOT* HAVE A CHANCE TO *PROVE* HIS CLAIM--FOR WRITHING IN SEEMING *AGONY*, THE FROSTY GIANT LASHES OUT--

THOK!

--WITH A *VENGEANCE*!

COME, GIANT--LET'S SEE HOW WELL YOU ATTACK THOSE *SMALLER* THAN YOURSELF WHILE LACKING AN *ARM*!

THRAK!

WHAT--? THE GIANT CAN *REGENERATE* ITSELF!

IN MERE *SECONDS*, IT HAS GROWN *ANOTHER* ARM!

*A*ND THE ICY BEHEMOTH WASTES NO TIME IN PUTTING SAID LIMB TO *USE*!

THRUNCH!

VALKYRIE LANDED **UNHARMED**, THANK THE ALL-KNOWING--

--AND THIS LITTLE **DIVERSION** SHOULD GIVE HER TIME ENOUGH TO FIND **SAFETY!**

BUT WHILE **ONE** DEFENDER MOVES OUT OF HARM'S WAY, ANOTHER **GREEN-HUED** DEFENDER HAS COME BACK FOR **SECOND HELPINGS**...

FROZEN MAN **PUNCHED** HULK--**ATTACKED** HULK FOR NO REASON--

--AND, FROZEN MAN, THAT MAKES HULK **MAD!**

CHOOM!

HULK DOES NOT **LIKE** BEING MAD, FROZEN MAN--

--AND SINCE **YOU** ARE THE ONE WHO **MADE** HULK MAD--

--HULK DOES NOT LIKE **YOU**, FROZEN MAN--

--NOT AT **ALL!**

IS IT **COINCIDENCE** THAT THE EMERALD DEFENDER HURLS HIS FRIGID FOE DIRECTLY INTO THE LASER BEAM'S SEARING PATH...OR IS IT **DESIGN?**

SKAK!

NO REAL **MATTER**...FOR THE RESULT IS STILL THE **SAME!**

SO--THIS MAY REQUIRE A BIT MORE *EFFORT* THAN FIRST I BELIEVED!

THEN GIVE *US* ANOTHER CHANCE AT THEM, NEBULON! WE'LL *FINISH* THEM FOR...

NO, HYPERION--REMAIN AT YOUR POSTS!

NO LONGER WILL I EMPLOY ANY SORT OF *AGENT* AGAINST THESE SELF-STYLED *DEFENDERS*--

--WHEN I POSSESS *WITHIN* ME POWER ENOUGH TO *DESTROY* THEM IN ONE *BROAD STROKE!*

POWER? YOU SPEAK OF *POWER* WHEN HULK IS THE *STRONGEST* ONE THERE IS?

SHOW HULK YOUR POWER, GOLD-FACE-- AND HULK WILL SHOW YOU *HIS!*

VERY WELL, *DOLTISH ONE*-- YOU HAVE ELECTED *YOURSELF* THE FIRST TO *DIE!*

BAH! IS *THAT* ALL THE POWER GOLD-FACE HAS? THEN HULK *LAUGHS* AT YOUR *PUNY* POWER!

REMARKABLE! THE GREEN ONE DOES NOT *FALTER*--

--BUT EVEN *HE* MAY NOT LAUGH AT POWER SUCH AS--*THIS!*

UUNNFF!

ZUNT!

YOU MAY HAVE *FLATTENED* HIM, SPACEMAN--BUT *KILLING* THE HULK IS ALTOGETHER SOMETHING *ELSE*--

--AS IS KILLING THE *REST* OF US, I MIGHT ADD!

THEN YOU HAVE *NOT* LEARNED YOUR *LESSON* FROM THE EXAMPLE OF YOUR GREEN-HUED *FRIEND?*

THE *DEFENDERS* TAKE A GREAT DEAL OF *TEACHING*, ALIEN!

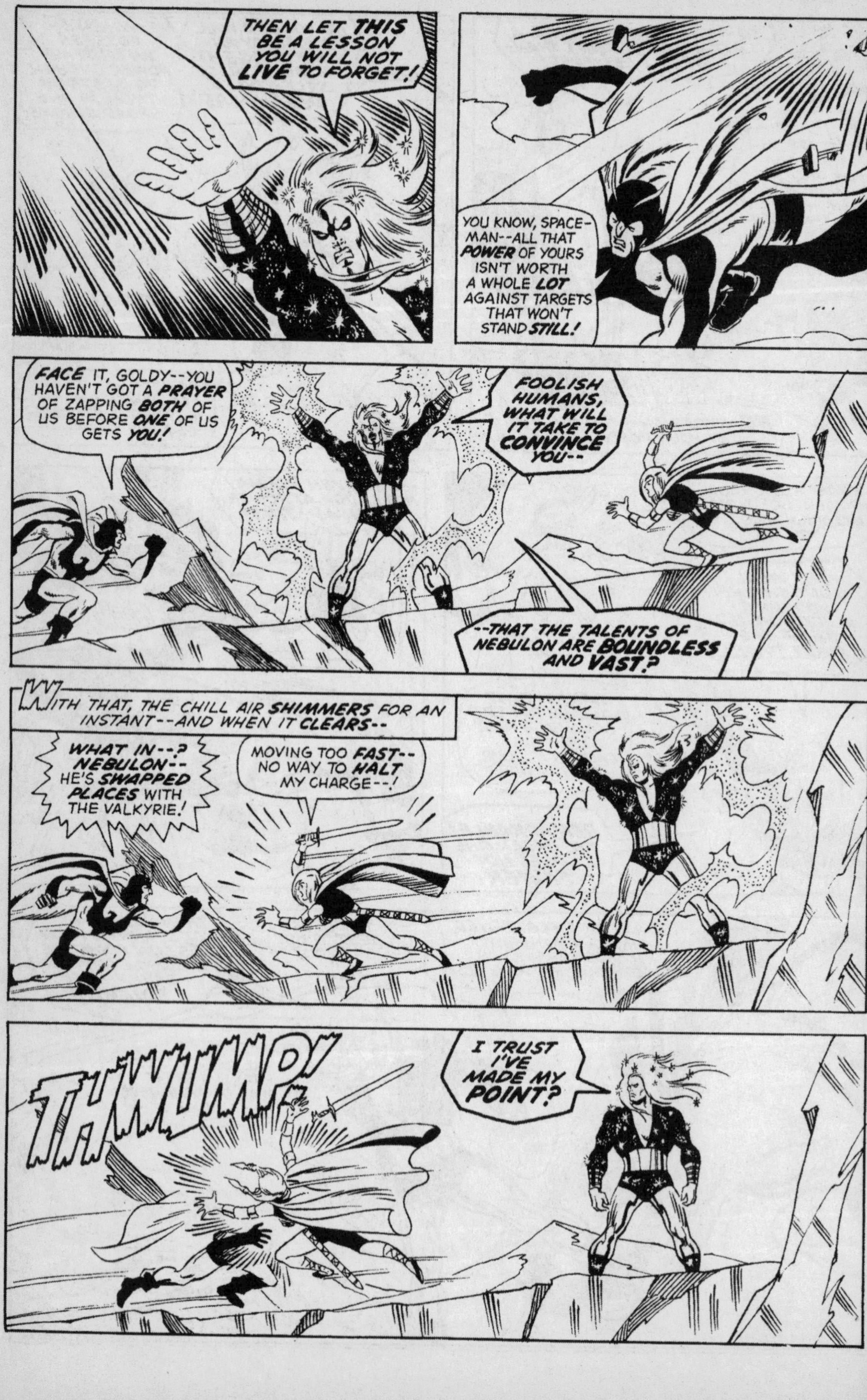
THEN LET THIS BE A LESSON YOU WILL NOT LIVE TO FORGET!
YOU KNOW, SPACE-MAN--ALL THAT POWER OF YOURS ISN'T WORTH A WHOLE LOT AGAINST TARGETS THAT WON'T STAND STILL!
FACE IT, GOLDY--YOU HAVEN'T GOT A PRAYER OF ZAPPING BOTH OF US BEFORE ONE OF US GETS YOU!
FOOLISH HUMANS, WHAT WILL IT TAKE TO CONVINCE YOU--
--THAT THE TALENTS OF NEBULON ARE BOUNDLESS AND VAST?
WITH THAT, THE CHILL AIR SHIMMERS FOR AN INSTANT--AND WHEN IT CLEARS--
WHAT IN--? NEBULON--HE'S SWAPPED PLACES WITH THE VALKYRIE!
MOVING TOO FAST--NO WAY TO HALT MY CHARGE--!
THWUMP!
I TRUST I'VE MADE MY POINT?

BUT, EVEN AS THE CELESTIAL MAN *SPEAKS,* THE FELLED DEFENDERS SCRAMBLE TO THEIR FEET, AND...

A FRONTAL ASSAULT IS *USELESS,* DEFENDERS! NEBULON MUST BE ATTACKED FROM *ALL* SIDES AT ONCE-- FORCED TO *DIVIDE* HIS ATTENTIONS-- AND THEN PERHAPS--

--AND *THEN* PERHAPS--YOU WILL *FAIL* AGAIN--AND *AGAIN*--

--AND *CONTINUE* TO *FAIL* UNTIL NEBULON HAS *WIPED* YOU FROM--

UNNGH!

HAH! MAGICIAN HIT GOLD-FACE A *GOOD* ONE!

BUT *ONE* GOOD BLOW DOES NOT DECIDE A *BATTLE,* BEHEMOTH-- --AND *THIS* BATTLE IS *FAR* FROM *OVER!*

THEN WE WILL DO WHAT WE CAN TO *SHORTEN* IT, ALIEN--

SPRAK!

--AND I ASSURE YOU WE SHALL SHORTEN IT *GREATLY!*

REELING FROM THE SUB-MARINER'S BLOW, NEBULON *STUMBLES*-- THEN SINKS TO HIS *KNEES* BENEATH THE RENEWED ASSAULT OF THE MASTER OF THE MYSTIC ARTS--

SPACE-BORN ONE, EVEN *YOU* CANNOT LONG STAND AGAINST THE *BOLTS OF BEDEVILMENT!*

POWER...TOO MUCH POWER... CAN'T CONCENTRATE...

Panel 1 (top left):

--AND, WRITHING AS IF IN UTTER TORMENT, THE CELESTIAL MAN SPRAWLS FORWARD INTO THE ICE, HIS GOD-LIKE FORM SEEMING SUDDENLY TO SHIMMER--THEN TO BLUR--

--THEN, IN A VOICE LIKE FROZEN THUNDER, NEBULON SCREAMS--

NO--NOT NOW --NOT WHEN I'M SO CLOSE--THIS CAN'T HAPPEN NOW--!

YOUR STRATEGY PROVED MOST SUCCESSFUL, DOCTOR. THE ALIEN IS HELPLESS.

Panel 2 (top right):

HELPLESS, NAMOR? HAVE YOU FORGOTTEN THE SQUADRON SINISTER?

QUICKLY-- BEFORE THE DEFENDERS TURN THEIR ATTENTION BACK TO US WE MUST DO WHAT WE CAN TO AID NEBULON!

WHAT IN BLAZES FOR? AIN'T OUR FAULT HE BLEW HIS CHANCE!

WHIZZER, FOR YOUR OWN SAKE-- I SUGGEST YOU SHUT UP!

Panel 3 (bottom left):

BUT WHEN THE TERRIBLE TRIO GAIN THEIR ALIEN COMPANION'S SIDE...

GET BACK--GET AWAY-- YOU MUSTN'T--MUSTN'T SEE ME LIKE THIS--!

SEE YOU LIKE WHAT?

ALL I CAN SEE IS A SOLID-GOLD BLUR!

Panel 4 (bottom right):

BUT THE WILD-EYED WHIZZER'S NEXT RETORT DIES IN HIS THROAT--AS THE FLICKERING FIGURE OF NEBULON EMITS ONE FINAL BURST OF BRILLIANCE--

--THEN COALESCES-- INTO A FORM THAT HOLDS THE COSTUMED ASSEMBLAGE SPEECHLESS--

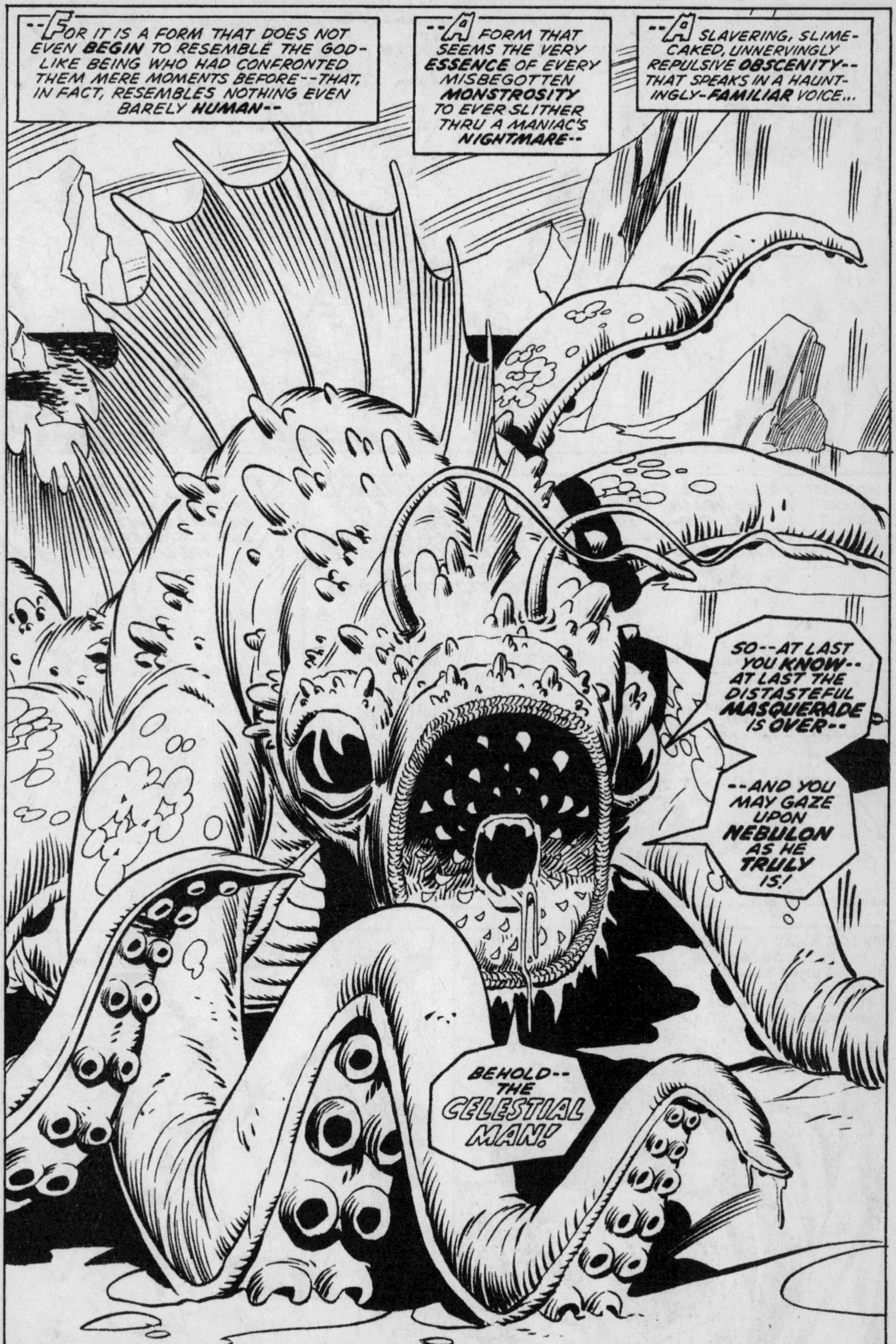
--FOR IT IS A FORM THAT DOES NOT EVEN BEGIN TO RESEMBLE THE GOD-LIKE BEING WHO HAD CONFRONTED THEM MERE MOMENTS BEFORE--THAT, IN FACT, RESEMBLES NOTHING EVEN BARELY HUMAN--
--A FORM THAT SEEMS THE VERY ESSENCE OF EVERY MISBEGOTTEN MONSTROSITY TO EVER SLITHER THRU A MANIAC'S NIGHTMARE--
--A SLAVERING, SLIME-CAKED, UNNERVINGLY REPULSIVE OBSCENITY--THAT SPEAKS IN A HAUNTINGLY-FAMILIAR VOICE...
SO--AT LAST YOU KNOW--AT LAST THE DISTASTEFUL MASQUERADE IS OVER--
--AND YOU MAY GAZE UPON NEBULON AS HE TRULY IS!
BEHOLD--THE CELESTIAL MAN!

IT--IT'S A *TRICK*--AN *ILLUSION*--!

NO, HYPERION-- THE *NEBULON* YOU *PREVIOUSLY BEHELD* WAS THE *ILLUSION*--

--AN *ILLUSION* I CREATED HOPING TO BE MORE EASILY *ACCEPTED* BY YOU AND YOUR RACE!

MY OWN RACE IS *AQUATIC* BY NATURE--THE REASON THIS WORLD HAD TO BE COMPLETELY *INUNDATED* BEFORE I COULD LAY *CLAIM* TO IT!

STILL, IN MY *HUMANOID* GUISE, I MAY EXIST FOR *EXTENDED PERIODS* OUT OF WATER--AND SINCE I CAN *CONCENTRATE* ONCE MORE--

--I WILL *REASSUME* THAT FORM--SO THAT WE MAY *CONTINUE* OUR BUSINESS WHERE WE LEFT OFF!

FROM WHAT I'VE SEEN, THERE ISN'T A *CHANCE* OF THE DEFENDERS DEFEATING NEBULON AND THE SQUADERS BEFORE THEY WREAK *HAVOC* WITH THAT *LASER-CANNON!*

3½ *BILLION* PEOPLE WILL *DROWN* IN THE *FLOODS* RESULTING FROM MELTING THE POLAR ICECAPS--

--UNLESS SOMEBODY DOES SOMETHING TO *STOP* THEM--

--AND DOES IT *NOW!*

GOT TO KEEP THEM *AWAY* FROM THIS CANNON--

--EVEN IF IT MEANS GIVING IT BACK TO THEM *WRONG* END FIRST!

WONDER HOW SOMEONE AS STRONG AS *NEBULON* WILL STAND AGAINST POWER GREAT ENOUGH TO PUNCH *HOLES* THRU DIAMOND MOUNTAINS?

*T*HE ANSWER IS: *NOT WELL!* STRUCK BY THE LASER BLAST, NEBULON'S CONCENTRATION IS AGAIN *BROKEN,* THWARTING HIS ATTEMPT TO *REGAIN* HUMAN FORM--

SKREEE!

--*A*ND THE MUCUS-DRIPPING ALIEN *RETALIATES* IN KIND--

DON'T SEEM TO HAVE *HURT* HIM--! HE'S FIRING *BACK--!*

POWER-- SO MUCH POWER-- ALMOST *MORE* THAN I CAN *ABSORB* IN ONE STROKE--

*Y*ET STILL THE LASER BEAM WHINES ON--POWER FEEDING POWER--BUILDING IN INTENSITY-- UNTIL THE CREATURE CALLED *NEBULON* BEGINS TO PULSE AS WELL--

NO--THE POWER IS *TOO GREAT*--IT FILLS ME--SATIATES ME--*DROWNS* ME--

TAKE IT AWAY-- *AWAY*--

*F*OR AN INSTANT, THE SQUADRON SINISTER STANDS ITS GROUND, UNSURE OF WHAT TO *DO*--THEN, AS ONE, REALIZING THEIR ALIEN COMPANION IS FAR *BEYOND* THEIR HELP--

--THEY TURN TO *RUN*--

*B*UT THEIR SUDDEN REALIZATION HAS COME JUST THE BAREST FRACTION OF AN INSTANT *TOO LATE*--

--*F*OR THE FRIGID GROUND BENEATH THE AFFLICTED CELESTIAL MAN IS ABRUPTLY BATHED IN UNNATURAL *LIGHT*--

--*A*S THE BARREN PATCH OF LAND HEAVES *UPWARD,* SPEWING GREAT CHUNKS OF ICE INTO THE BRITTLE SKY--

--SPROOM!

--AND WHEN THOSE GLEAMING SHARDS SETTLE BACK TO *EARTH* ONCE MORE--

SONUVAGUN! I *DID* IT!

THE LASER POWER WAS *TOO MUCH* FOR NEBULON TO *BEAR.* HE IMPLODED--

--AND TOOK THE *SQUADRON SINISTER* WITH HIM!

NIGHTHAWK, STOP *CONGRATULATING*--AND *JUMP!*

SOMETHING'S GONE *WRONG* WITH THE LASER-CANNON! IT'S...

...GOING *HAYWIRE,* AL'RIGHT. NEBULON'S RAY BLAST MUST HAVE *SHORTED OUT* THE CANNON'S WIRING.

GOT TO PUT *DISTANCE* BETWEEN ME AND THIS MACHINE BEFORE IT'S...

...TOO LATE!

B'KAROOM

EXPLOSIONS ECHO IN THIS DESOLATE WASTE, WHERE JUTTING TOWERS OF SOULLESS ICE DO LITTLE TO ABSORB THE SOUND--

EXPLOSIONS ECHO--AND SO DO ANGUISHED VOICES--

STEPHEN-- IS HE--?

I DON'T *KNOW,* VALKYRIE. HE CAUGHT THE FULL *BRUNT* OF THE EXPLOSION BUT...

BUT *NOTHING,* DOCTOR. THE MAN IS NOT *MOVING.*

STEPHEN, PLEASE... TELL ME HE'S NOT...

...DEAD, VAL? NO...NOT YET...

...BUT HE SOON WILL BE.

THERE IS NOTHING I CAN DO TO HELP HIM...

...UNLESS...

DEFENDERS, WE SURELY OWE THIS MAN OUR LIVES. WOULD IT NOT BE FITTING TO SACRIFICE A SMALL PART OF THOSE LIVES TO SAVE HIS?

WHAT I AM ABOUT TO PROPOSE IS DANGEROUS AT THE LEAST...BUT TO ONE TO WHOM WE OWE SO MUCH...

...CAN WE OFFER ANYTHING LESS?

DOCTOR STRANGE EXPLAINS THEN, IN SLOW CAREFUL PHRASES, IN SIMPLE TERMS EVEN THE SLOW-WITTED HULK CAN UNDERSTAND--

--AND WHEN HE IS FINISHED, HE HOLDS OUT HIS HANDS-- AND SMILES INWARDLY AS HE FEELS THEM FIRMLY CLASPED.

CONCENTRATE, MY FRIENDS! LET PART OF YOU FLOW INTO ME--

--AND THUS FLOW INTO HIM!

IT IS DIFFICULT FOR THE HULK-- BUT HE DOES HIS BEST TO EMULATE HIS FRIENDS--

AND THE GLOW FROM THE MYSTIC EYE OF AGAMOTTO BATHES THE BROKEN AND BLEEDING NIGHTHAWK IN A LIGHT THAT IS NOT A LIGHT--

--BUT RATHER THE COLLECTED ENERGIES OF FOUR DETER-MINED PEOPLE'S SOULS--AND THIS GATHERED LIFE-FORCE SPILLING ACROSS THE NIGHT-HAWK'S PAIN-WRACKED FACE CLEANSES HIM--

--HEALS HIM--AND FILLS HIM WITH THE FIRES OF LIFE ONCE MORE!

WH-WHERE AM I? WHAT HAPPENED?

AND WHEN THE MYSTIC MAGE HAS **EXPLAINED**... --THEN MY LIFE IS SUSTAINED BY YOUR **COLLECTIVE** LIFE-FORCES?

WHEW-- IT'S GONNA TAKE A LITTLE **WHILE** FOR THAT TO **SINK IN**.

IT WAS THE **LEAST** WE COULD DO TO **REPAY** YOU.

YOU KNOW, THERE **IS** SOMETHING **ELSE** YOU COULD DO... GRANTED, I STARTED OUT IN THIS BUSINESS AS PART OF THE **SQUADRON SINISTER**-- BUT IF YOU THINK AN OLD LEOPARD LIKE ME CAN CHANGE HIS **SPOTS**...

WELL, I'D BE **HONORED** IF YOU'D LET ME **JOIN** YOU.

AND WE'D BE HONORED TO **HAVE** YOU-- IF THE DEFENDERS WERE TRULY A GROUP ONE COULD **JOIN**-- --AND **NOT** A LOOSELY-KNIT BAND OF INDEPENDENT **ADVENTURERS** WHO...

A MOMENT, DOCTOR.

I WOULD ADVISE YOU TO **LET** THE NIGHTHAWK JOIN YOUR DEFENDERS-- FOR YOU MAY HAVE **NEED** OF HIM IN DAYS TO COME--

--AS A REPLACEMENT FOR **ME**!

REMEMBER, STRANGE-- I DID NOT **WISH** TO PARTAKE IN THIS BATTLE JUST PAST-- YOU BROUGHT ME HERE AGAINST MY **WILL**--

--AND **NO** MAN CONTROLS THE ACTIONS OF **PRINCE NAMOR THE FIRST**!

DO NOT SEEK TO **SUMMON** ME AGAIN, STRANGE-- FOR IF I COME-- --IT WILL **NOT** BE AS AN **ALLY**!

HUH? FISH-MAN GOES AWAY **ANGRY**--

--BUT **HULK** DOES NOT CARE.

BIRD-NOSE WILL BE HULK'S **NEW** FRIEND.

HULK SPEAKS FOR US ALL, NIGHTHAWK-- IF YOUR REQUEST STILL **STANDS**?

IT **DOES**, DOCTOR. BECOMING A **DEFENDER** IS VERY **IMPORTANT** TO ME.

I ONLY HOPE I NEVER GIVE THE REST OF YOU ANY CAUSE TO **REGRET** IT!

NEXT: **PROFESSOR X**--AND THE **BROTHERHOOD OF EVIL MUTANTS!**

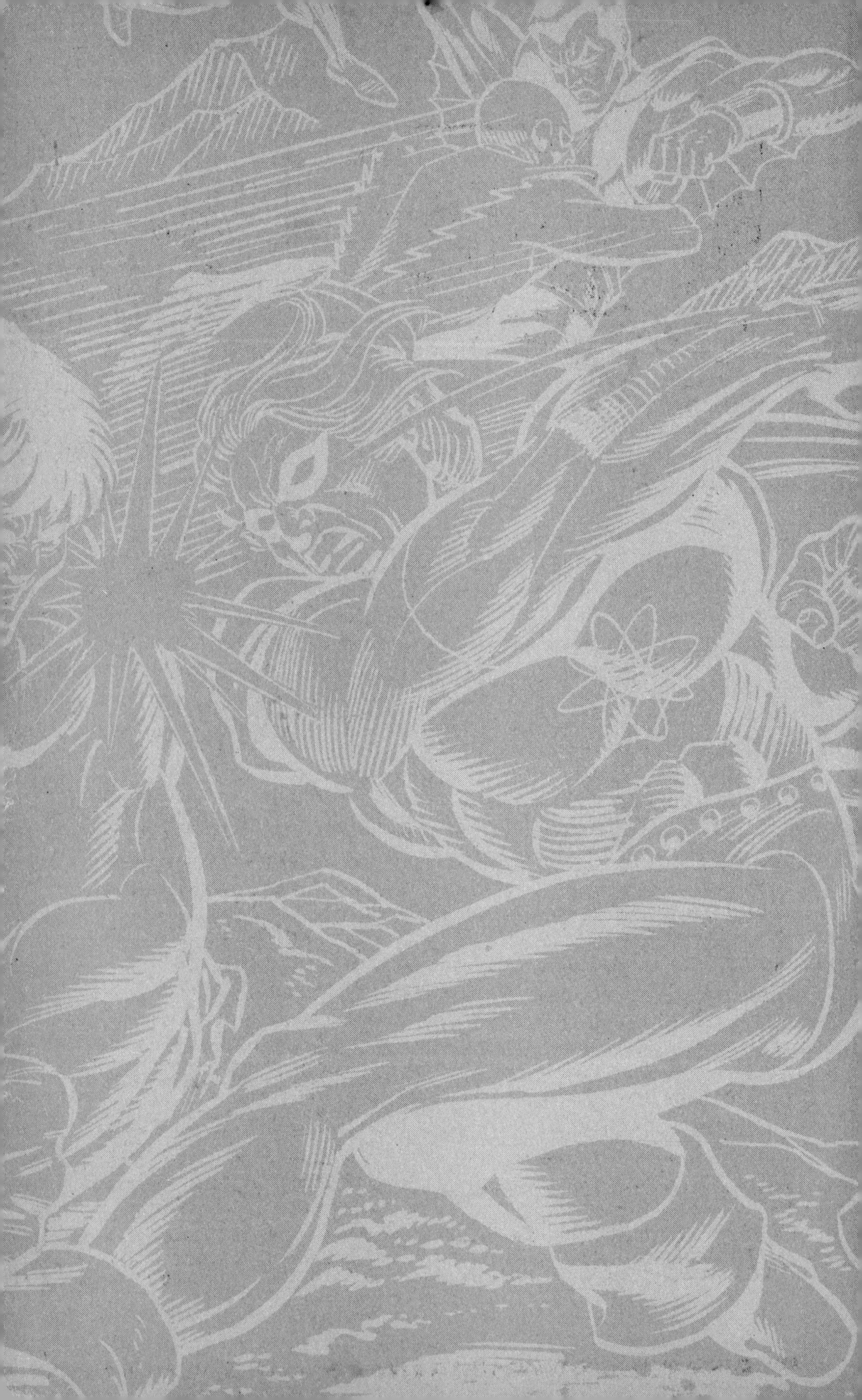